lonely planet

Alaska

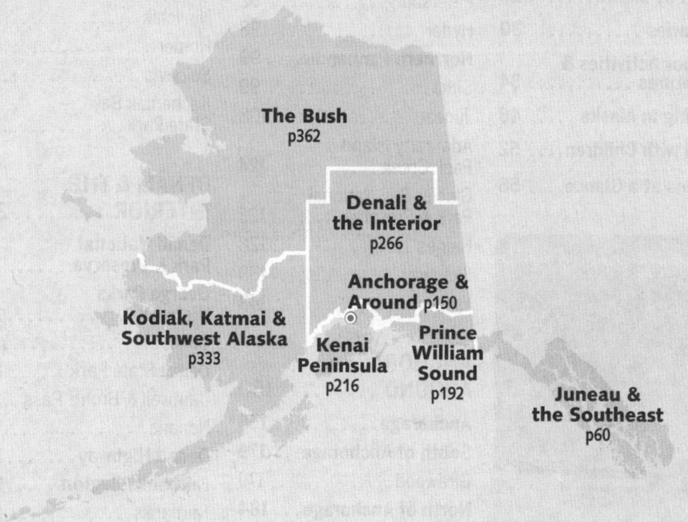

The Bush
p362

Denali &
the Interior
p266

Anchorage &
Around p150

Kodiak, Katmai &
Southwest Alaska
p333

Kenai
Peninsula
p216

Prince
William
Sound
p192

Juneau &
the Southeast
p60

Brendan Sainsbury, Catherine Bodry,
Alexander Howard, Adam Karlin

PLAN YOUR TRIP

PI-LENS KEYWORDS/SHUTTERSTOCK ©
NORTHERN LIGHTS P302

MR.RUJ_THAILAND/SHUTTERSTOCK ©
ROAD TO DENALI NATIONAL PARK & PRESERVE P272

ON THE ROAD

Contents

JAYL/SHUTTERSTOCK ©

GLACIER BAY NATIONAL PARK & PRESERVE P125

COVID-19

We have re-checked every business in this book before publication to ensure that it is still open after the COVID-19 outbreak. However, the economic and social impacts of COVID-19 will continue to be felt long after the outbreak has been contained, and many businesses, services and events referenced in this guide may experience ongoing restrictions. Some businesses may be temporarily closed, have changed their opening hours and services, or require bookings; some unfortunately could have closed permanently. We suggest you check with venues before visiting for the latest information.

UNDERSTAND

SURVIVAL GUIDE

SPECIAL FEATURES

Right: Northern lights near Fairbanks (p298)

PIRIYA PHOTOGRAPHY/GETTY IMAGES ©

WELCOME TO Alaska

Like many travelers, I am drawn to roads less traveled, isolated frontier regions where spontaneity and excitement rule over certainty and home comforts. Alaska fits all of these requirements. Challenging, unpolished and, on occasions, a hard nut to crack, it is, in many ways, the antithesis of the country where I grew up (the UK). Like a stranger in a strange land, I never fail to be astonished by the state's extremes and gaping lack of people. And though travel here isn't always easy, it's a constant education.

By Brendan Sainsbury, writer
@sainsburyb
For more about our writers, see p448.

Alaska

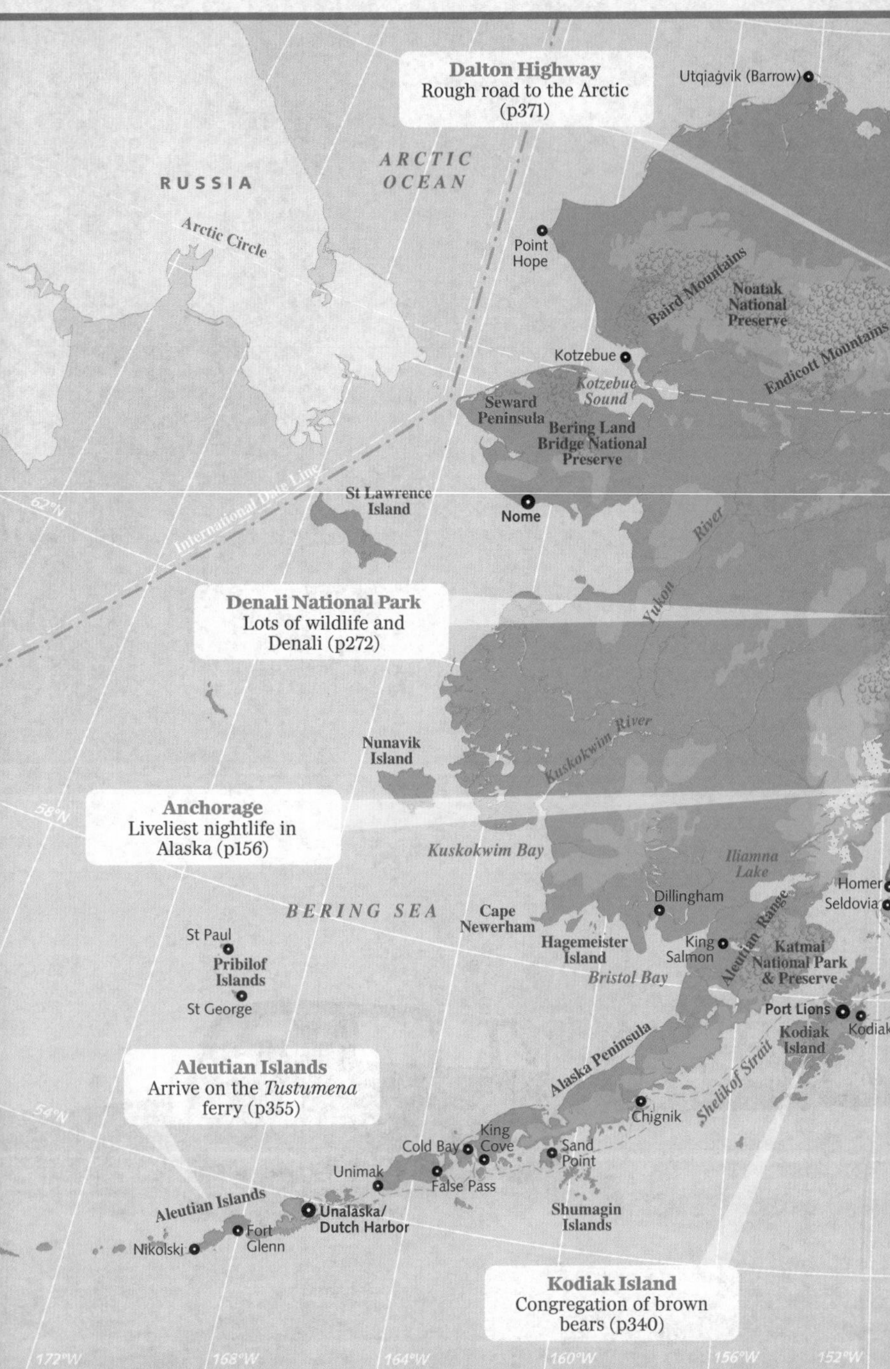

Dalton Highway
Rough road to the Arctic
(p371)
Utqiaġvik (Barrow)
RUSSIA
ARCTIC OCEAN
Arctic Circle
Point Hope
Baird Mountains
Noatak National Preserve
Endicott Mountains
Kotzebue
Kotzebue Sound
Seward Peninsula
Bering Land Bridge National Preserve
International Date Line
62°N
St Lawrence Island
Nome
Yukon River
Denali National Park
Lots of wildlife and
Denali (p272)
Kuskokwim River
Nunavik Island
Anchorage
Liveliest nightlife in
Alaska (p156)
58°N
Kuskokwim Bay
Iliamna Lake
Homer
Seldovia
Dillingham
BERING SEA
Cape Newerham
St Paul
Pribilof Islands
St George
Hagemeister Island
King Salmon
Aleutian Range
Katmai National Park & Preserve
Bristol Bay
Port Lions
Kodiak
Kodiak Island
Alaska Peninsula
Shelikof Strait
Aleutian Islands
Arrive on the *Tustumena*
ferry (p355)
54°N
Chignik
King Cove
Cold Bay
Sand Point
Unimak
False Pass
Aleutian Islands
Unalaska/ Dutch Harbor
Fort Glenn
Nikolski
Shumagin Islands
Kodiak Island
Congregation of brown
bears (p340)
172°W
168°W
164°W
160°W
156°W
152°W

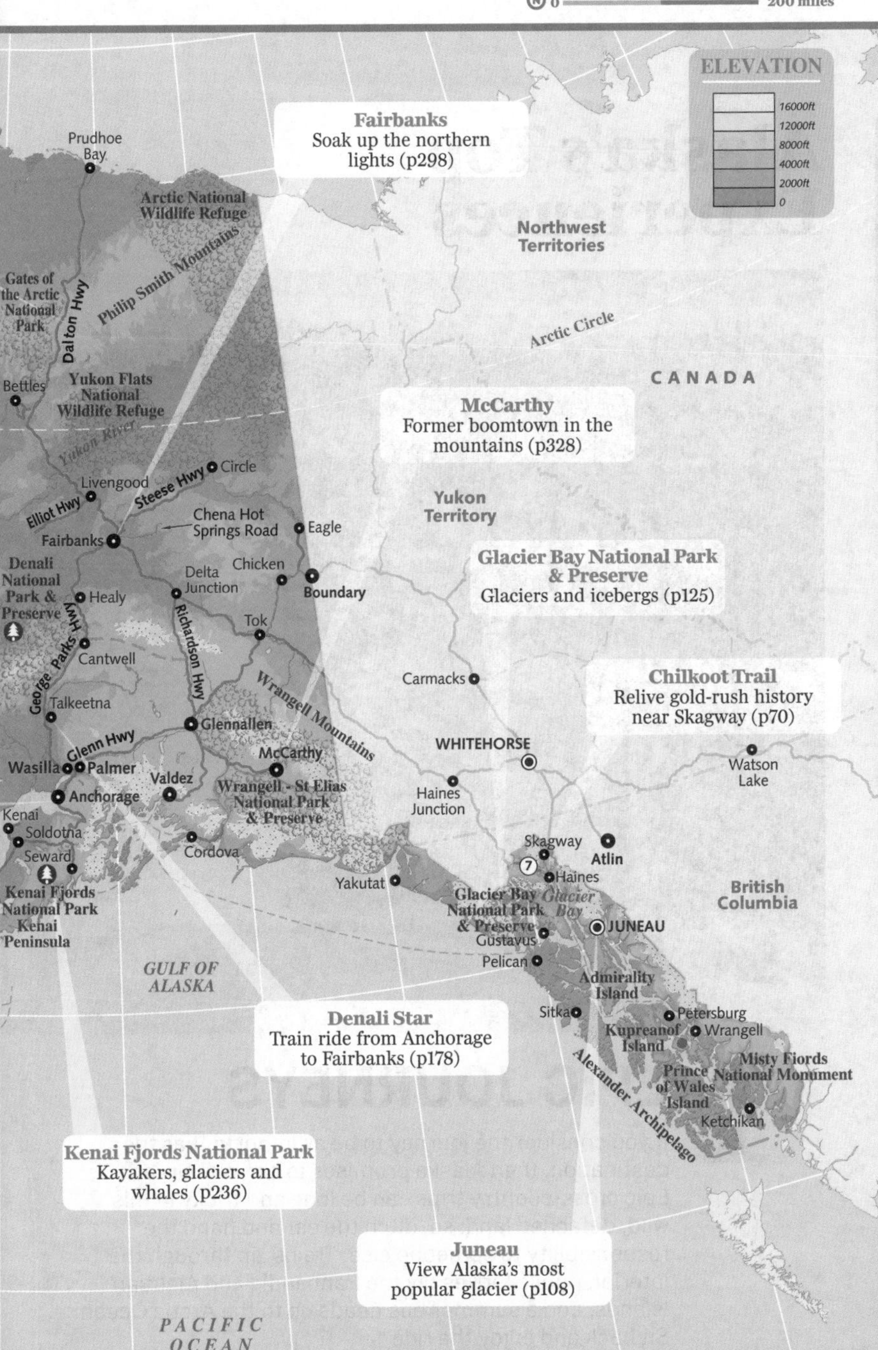

0 400 km
0 200 miles
ELEVATION
16000ft
12000ft
8000ft
4000ft
2000ft
0
Fairbanks
Soak up the northern lights (p298)
McCarthy
Former boomtown in the mountains (p328)
Glacier Bay National Park & Preserve
Glaciers and icebergs (p125)
Chilkoot Trail
Relive gold-rush history near Skagway (p70)
Denali Star
Train ride from Anchorage to Fairbanks (p178)
Kenai Fjords National Park
Kayakers, glaciers and whales (p236)
Juneau
View Alaska's most popular glacier (p108)
Prudhoe Bay
Arctic National Wildlife Refuge
Philip Smith Mountains
Gates of the Arctic National Park
Dalton Hwy
Bettles
Yukon Flats National Wildlife Refuge
Yukon River
Northwest Territories
Arctic Circle
CANADA
Yukon Territory
Circle
Livengood
Steese Hwy
Elliot Hwy
Chena Hot Springs Road
Fairbanks
Eagle
Denali National Park & Preserve
Healy
Delta Junction
Chicken
Boundary
Richardson Hwy
Tok
George Parks Hwy
Cantwell
Talkeetna
Wrangell Mountains
Carmacks
Glennallen
Glenn Hwy
McCarthy
WHITEHORSE
Watson Lake
Wasilla
Palmer
Valdez
Anchorage
Wrangell - St Elias National Park & Preserve
Haines Junction
Kenai
Soldotna
Seward
Cordova
Skagway
Atlin
Haines
Yakutat
Kenai Fjords National Park
Kenai Peninsula
Glacier Bay National Park & Preserve
Glacier Bay
Gustavus
JUNEAU
British Columbia
Pelican
GULF OF ALASKA
Admiralty Island
Sitka
Petersburg
Kupreanof Island
Wrangell
Misty Fiords National Monument
Prince of Wales Island
Alexander Archipelago
Ketchikan
PACIFIC OCEAN
148°W
144°W
140°W
136°W
132°W

Alaska's Top Experiences

1 EPIC JOURNEYS

If you consider the journey to be as important as the destination, then Alaska promises to be your nirvana. Epic cross-country trips can be long and tricky in this wild, detached land; so, ditch the car and hand the responsibility to someone else. Trains zip through the interior, public ferries ply the Panhandle and Aleutian Islands, and a summer bus heads up to the Arctic Ocean. Sit back and enjoy the ride.

Denali Star Train

The northernmost railway line in the US was one of the great triumphs of Gilded-Age engineering when was inaugurated in 1923. A century later, the railway continues to work its steely magic on the *Denali Star* (right), a luxury train that plies a spectacular route between Anchorage and Fairbanks. p178

Ferry to the Aleutians

A few imaginative leaps from your standard Alaskan cruise, the state's public ferries glide from the remote communities of the Panhandle to as far west as Dutch Harbor in the Aleutian Islands. p356

Dalton Highway Bus

Book a ticket with the Dalton Highway Express, stick some Springsteen on your headphones and get prepared for the ride of your life. The 500-mile trawl up the Dalton from Fairbanks to the Arctic Ocean won't be the smoothest bus ride you'll ever take, but it might be the most legendary. p372

Pictured above: Shuttle bus on the Dalton Highway

On facing page: Dalton Highway

2 HITTING THE TRAILS

Hiking in Alaska is an exciting undertaking. They do things differently up here. For the purists, there's unsullied backcountry, a yawning frontier upon a frontier with no trails, no signposts and no official campgrounds: just you and whatever else is lurking in the food chain. For the more cautious, there are less hair-raising paths located closer to cities – although big fauna is never far away.

DR_YU/SHUTTERSTOCK ©

SAM DCRUZ/SHUTTERSTOCK ©

KENWIEDEMANN/GETTY IMAGES ©

Harding Ice Field Trail

A tough but non-technical trail alongside Alaska's Exit Glacier, which climbs through alder forest and colorful meadows to a viewpoint overlooking the colossal Harding Ice Field. p236

Above left: Exit Glacier seen from Harding Ice Field Trail

Chilkoot Trail

They went in search of gold but, in the end, the *journey* was the gold. The ghosts of the 1897–98 Klondike gold rush loom large on the legendary Chilkoot Trail, a 33-mile path surrounded by brawny landscapes that stretches from Dyea near Skagway to Canada. p70

Top: Chilkoot Trail near Skagway

Mount Roberts

Mt Roberts is the craggy sentinel that watches over Juneau. Most people ascend on a cable car to just above the timberline, but it's more fulfilling to hike the incessant 5 miles through forest and meadows to alpine tundra and a narrow windy ridge walk. p114

Above: Views from Mt Roberts

3 THE BEAUTY OF BEARS

Bears are one of the great symbols of Alaska, a haunting reminder of the beauty of the delicate ecosystems that grace this feral state. The ursine beasts come in every shape, size and color: belligerent polar bears, fish-snapping brown bears, mountain-prowling grizzlies and forest-dwelling black bears. If you don't see at least one of these majestic animals during your visit (from a safe distance, of course), count yourself unlucky.

Katmai National Park

Brooks Falls (pictured below) in Katmai National Park is front-cover material for any Alaskan tourist brochure. Giant brown bears, anchored firmly in the white water, catch whole salmon between their teeth as the hapless fish jump instinctively up river. p352

NATURESMOMENTSUK/SHUTTERSTOCK ©

DAVIDHOFFMANN PHOTOGRAPHY/SHUTTERSTOCK ©

MARK KOSTICH/GETTY IMAGES ©

Kodiak Island

The US's second largest island is also home to its largest bears, a subspecies of the brown bear weighing up to 1500lbs. The best way to see them is via floatplane. Granted, it isn't cheap but, as 99% of previous Kodiak visitors will testify, it's worth every cent. p340

Above left: A white bear known as a 'spirit bear', Kodiak Island

Denali National Park

Alaska's most famous and accessible national park offers an endless conveyor belt of big fauna (bears included) as you traverse the 92-mile Park Road on a bus. p272

Above right: Grizzly bear, Denali National Park

4 PERFECT PLACES TO PADDLE

The elongated Alaskan panhandle – with its deep-cut fjords and temperate climate – is made for kayaking. Alaska Natives have been paddling these peaceful shores for millennia, navigating around puzzles of islands and exploring meandering rivers. Further north, the seas get more turbulent as glaciers eject their ice into the ocean and inclement weather whips up white-capped waves. Head inland here and hit a quiet lake, or paddle and portage through a network of canoe trails.

Misty Fiords

A patchwork of misty cliffs, plunging waterfalls and primaeval forests, the trippy landscapes of this revered national monument offer what is, arguably, Alaska's finest multi-day kayaking adventure. p83

Below: Misty Fiords National Monument

JAMES + COURTNEY FORTE/GETTY IMAGES ©

Kenai Fjords National Park

Navigate your way around icebergs, paddle past curious sea lions, and watch the blow of distant whales (preferably with a guide); Kenai Fjords (above) is the ultimate in Alaskan sea kayaking. p236

Swan Lake Canoe Route

This great combo of lakes and streams (right) in the northern lowlands of the Kenai peninsula makes a good multi-day trip for inexperienced kayakers, thanks to calm water and short portages. p220

5 SMALL TOWNS

JOHN ELK/GETTY IMAGES ©

BRIBAR/GETTY IMAGES ©

DESIGN PICS INC/ALAMY STOCK PHOTO ©

Eccentric, esoteric and eclectic, Alaska's small towns revel in their insularity. Local peculiarities abound. Some towns are shaped by their pioneer past: tales of gold rushes and mining booms, settlements created by immigrants and destroyed by earthquakes. Others wear the mark of one or more of Alaska's 11 native cultures, defined by their geography and colored by a history retold through centuries of oral tradition.

Petersburg

Alaska's fleeting nod to Norwegian culture, this independently minded fishing settlement in the southern panhandle is a hub for displaced Vikings and adventurous kayakers. p92

Above: Hammer Slough, Petersburg

Cordova

Surrounded by the impenetrable mountains and glaciers of Prince William Sound, Cordova is a tiny fishing town that the cruise ships forgot to put on their schedule. Accessible only by plane or ferry, it rewards hikers, bird-watchers and lovers of ice worms. p202

Haines

An enterprising town with an abundance of micro-businesses, a museum dedicated to hammers, and a recently revived Tlingit cultural center nearby. p128

6 PROSPECTOR RELICS

They came, they suffered, and some of them found gold. Alaska's early prospectors were a hardy bunch. They had to be: the land they craved to explore was a savage, unforgiving place in the days before motor cars and supermarkets. The imprints they made on the landscape remain; some languish in ruins, others have been revived or rebuilt and stand as tough testaments to a bolder age.

Skagway

The Klondike gold rush's erstwhile launching pad was a wild and debauched place in the 1890s. Today, a town-size national historical park has reconstituted the drama of yore. p139

Nome

Klondike's even rougher sequel played out on the bleak shores of the Bering Sea. In Nome, gold rush remnants include dredges, ghost towns and a cluster of rusting locomotives. p364

Above left: Nome

McCarthy

Not a million miles from a Wild West film set, this former red-light district is now a handsome historic relic cocooned inside the lonely Wrangell–St Elias National Park. p328

Above: Kennecott, McCarthy's mining outpost (p330)

7 NATIVE ALASKA

BARRY WINIKER/GETTY IMAGES ©

TONYMPIX/SHUTTERSTOCK ©

INTENTIONALTRAVELER/SHUTTERSTOCK ©

Juneau

At the vanguard of a recent Alaska Native renaissance, the Sealaska Heritage center in Juneau (left) exhibits a replica clan house and an impressive collection of ceremonial masks. p109

Ketchikan

Home to southeast Alaska's three main indigenous groups – the Tlingit, Haida and Tsimshian – Ketchikan (left) is awash with totem parks, clan houses and heritage centers. p73

Sitka

The site of a crucial 1804 battle between the Tlingit and Russians has been turned into a historical park where towering totems appear serendipitously out of the misty rainforest. p99

Western influences may have brought shopping malls and franchise hotels to Alaska, but the essence of traditional culture lives on in settlements across the state. Most are just a bush-plane flight away, but the best way to begin your understanding is to visit an urban cultural center run by Alaska Natives. Learn about the history and culture of the Tlingit in Haines, the Alutiiq in Kodiak, the Iñupiat in Utqiaġvik, and many others.

8 POWERFUL GLACIERS

Alaska does glaciers like the rest of the US does rivers. Fed by city-size icefields, the frosty behemoths scrape huge chunks out of the landscape on their way down mountainsides, grinding and groaning as they go. Some form moraines, others eject colossal icebergs into the ocean. For those not comfortable in crampons, a select few glaciers are situated close enough to population centers to ensure safe and easy viewing.

Mendenhall

At the Mendenhall Glacier (below), even the most erudite travelers sometimes resort to weak-kneed prose. Take a hike around this immense frozen river that tumbles out of the mountains and choose your own superlatives. p110

GALYNA ANDRUSHKO/SHUTTERSTOCK ©

Kennicott

A humongous ice river buried under a moraine of dirt and rubble that graces one of the few inhabited corners of Wrangell–St Elias National Park (above). You can walk and climb on it with a guide. p330

Exit

Alaska's barometer on climate change inches back a little every year, but Exit Glacier (right) remains refreshingly accessible, 12 miles from the town of Seward. p237

9 REMOTE PLACES

In a state where going off the grid is like popping out for a cup of coffee, the concept of remoteness takes on a whole new meaning. Encased in wilderness, the 49th state is full of tough people living out tough lives in isolated locales, from the subsistence hunters of the North Slope to the lonesome fishers of the Alaska Peninsula. Visiting them offers a lucid insight into what life on the frontier is all about.

Utqiaġvik

The US's most northerly town is a scruffy, perennially chilly outpost patrolled by polar bears and whipped by cutting winds. Brave visitors arrive to dip their toe in the Arctic Ocean. p379

Chicken

A pinprick 'town' (above) on the Taylor Hwy that epitomizes the ruggedness and eccentricities of the Alaskan Bush. Drop by for gold-panning and surprisingly good cinnamon buns. p315

Gates of the Arctic

A national park the size of Ireland, with no roads, no trails and no accommodation save for the tent on your back. If you're diligently self-sufficient and hate crowds, you've come to the right place. p378

Need to Know

For more information, see Survival Guide (p419)

Currency
US dollars ($)

Language
English

Visas
Most international visitors need a visa and should have a multiple-entry one if coming from the lower 48 through Canada.

Money
Prices quoted are in US dollars unless otherwise stated. Keep in mind that the Canadian system is also dollars and cents but is a separate currency.

Cell Phones
Coverage is surprisingly good, even in remote areas. Prepaid SIM cards can be used in some international cell (mobile) phones for local calls and voice mail.

Time
Alaska Time (GMT/UTC minus nine hours)

When to Go

High Season
(Jun–Aug)

- Solstice festivals and 20-hour days are enjoyed in June.
- Salmon runs peak in July and August.
- Mountain trails and passes are snow-free in August.
- Room demand and prices peak in July.

Shoulder
(May & Sep)

- Car-rental rates are 30% lower than in June.
- Southeast Alaska is sunny during May, but rainy in September and October.
- The northern lights begin to appear in late September.

Low Season
(Oct–Apr)

- Brrrrr! Bundle up, it's cold.
- Longer days and warmer temps make late February the best time for winter sports.
- Most tour and activity companies close for winter, especially in cruise-oriented towns.

Useful Websites

Travel Alaska (www.travelalaska.com) Alaska's official tourism site.

Alaska Public Lands Information Centers (www.alaskacenters.gov) Info on parks and activities.

National Park Service (www.nps.gov/alaska) Information on Alaska's national parks, preserves, monuments and historical sites.

Alaska Marine Highway System (www.ferryalaska.com) For booking state ferries.

Lonely Planet (www.lonelyplanet.com/usa/alaska) Destination information, hotel reviews and more.

Important Numbers

Alaska shares a statewide area code of ☎907, except Hyder, which uses ☎250.

Country code	☎1
International dialing	☎011
Emergency	☎911
Road conditions	☎511 or ☎866-282-7577
Alaska Marine Highway	☎800-642-0066

Exchange Rates

Australia	A$1	$0.76
Canada	C$1	$0.79
Euro Zone	€1	$1.18
Japan	¥100	$0.89
New Zealand	NZ$1	$0.69
UK	£1	$1.34

For current exchange rates, see www.xe.com.

Daily Costs

Budget: Less than $120

- Hostel bed or campground: $10–40
- Cheap restaurant meal: $8–12
- Anchorage–Glennallen bus: $75

Midrange: $120–250

- Double room in a midrange motel: $150
- Restaurant mid-afternoon special: $10–15
- Light coffee-shop breakfast: $5–8

Top end: More than $250

- Double room in an upscale hotel: $200-plus
- Dinner main at a top restaurant: $25–30
- Car rental per day: $60–85

Opening Hours

Banks 9am–4pm/5pm Monday to Friday; 9am–1pm Saturday (main branches)

Bars and clubs City bars until 2am or later, especially on weekends; clubs to 2am or beyond

Post offices 9am–5pm Monday to Friday; noon–3pm Saturday (main branches open longer)

Restaurants and cafes Breakfast at cafes/coffee shops from 7am or earlier; some restaurants open only for lunch (noon–3pm) or dinner (4–10pm, later in cities); Asian restaurants often have split hours: 11am–2pm and from 4pm.

Shops 10am–8pm/6pm (larger/smaller stores) Monday to Friday; 9am–5pm Saturday; 10am–5pm Sunday (larger stores)

Arriving in Alaska

Ted Stevens Anchorage International Airport There's a people-mover bus to downtown ($2) hourly from the south terminal; the 20-minute taxi ride to the city costs $25.

Alaska Marine Highway terminals Shuttle vans, public buses or taxis greet ferries in the Southeast, except in Juneau.

Fairbanks International Airport Seven MACS buses run daily to the downtown transit station ($1.50); the 15-minute taxi ride to the city is $18.

Getting Around

Most people in Alaska get around in cars, but public transportation is surprisingly abundant if you know where to look.

Train Geared toward tourists, but provide a scenic if pricey way of traveling between Seward and Fairbanks.

Ferry The standard mode of transportation in the largely roadless southeastern panhandle.

Bus Small shuttles service most of Alaska's interior highways with connections to Canada.

Car The modus operandi for most Americans. Useful for traveling at your own pace. Drive on the right.

Air The only way to get to many off-the-grid communities.

For much more on **getting around**, see p430

First Time Alaska

For more information, see Survival Guide (p419)

Checklist

➡ Organize a fishing license if you intend to go fishing

➡ Prebook rental cars

➡ Study shuttle-bus and ferry timetables

➡ Book a ferry cabin on the Alaska Marine Highway

➡ Prebook campgrounds and hotels, especially in and around national parks

➡ Non-Americans should check entry requirements and, if necessary, purchase travel authorization online through the Electronic System for Travel Authorization (ESTA)

What to Pack

➡ Mosquito repellent

➡ Sun cream and hat

➡ Compass and GPS if hiking

➡ Blindfold for the light summer nights

➡ Binoculars for wildlife-viewing

➡ Water filter if camping

➡ Hand sanitizer

➡ Driver's license if renting a car

Top Tips for Your Trip

➡ Alaska is expensive, but some excursions (bear-watching, flightseeing over Denali) are true once-in-a-lifetime experiences and are worth the investment.

➡ Alaska is highly seasonal. Many businesses close in the off-season (October to April). Check ahead to avoid disappointment.

➡ Acquire enough basic physical fitness before setting out to enjoy a day or two in the wilderness.

➡ The Alaskan wilderness is an amazing place, but it doesn't suffer fools. If you intend to travel off the beaten path, do your homework and take all the necessary precautions.

What to Wear

Dress in layers. Alaskan weather can be unpredictable and varies greatly with altitude. Make sure you pack a warm fleece and waterproof jacket even in the summer. Take a hat and gloves year-round in the Far North.

Leave the tux at home. Alaskans dress informally when going out.

Sleeping

From luxury lodges to bare-bones camping to oil-worker barracks, Alaska's accommodations are as unique as the 49th state. Book well ahead in summer, when rooms fill *fast*.

Campgrounds From rustic, primitive sites to posh 'glamping' (glamorous camping) outposts, campgrounds here occupy some of the nation's most stunning scenery.

Wilderness lodges Well-appointed lodges often must be booked in advance, and many require air transportation to reach.

Cabins Across Alaska you'll find individual cabin rentals and multicabin complexes that occupy an inevitable expanse of gorgeous outdoor space. 'Dry' cabins are cheap, but lack running water and electricity.

Sourdoughs

During the Klondike and Nome gold rushes, experienced gold prospectors often carried a pouch containing a sourdough bread starter around their necks. The starter was used to make unleavened bread, a key source of nutrition during the tough Arctic winters. Before long, the pouch and its valuable contents became a symbol of a savvy Alaskan old-hand who knew how to live in the wilderness, and the word 'sourdough' entered local parlance to denote someone who had survived an Arctic winter (as opposed to a novice cheechako who hadn't). Although it's unlikely you'll encounter anyone carrying a sourdough pouch these days, the word 'sourdough' is still used to describe a rough-and-ready Alaskan old-timer – an important definition in a state where over 50% of the population was born somewhere else.

Bargaining

Alaska, like the rest of the US, doesn't really have much of a bargaining culture, except perhaps in small markets or at some indigenous craft stalls.

Tipping

Alaska is part of the US, thus tipping is expected in most service industries including restaurants, taxis and hotels. It is also customary to tip guides and bus drivers. In general, 15% is the baseline tip, but 20% is usually more appropriate, and 25% if you enjoyed the service.

Hiker in Chugach State Park (p152)

Etiquette

Although it's part of the US, Alaska is a little more laid-back and less rule-bound than other states.

Socializing Informality holds sway. Alaskans are more likely to dress down than up when going out, and high-five greetings are as common as handshakes.

Politics Alaska is one of the US's more conservative states. You're less likely to encounter the liberal consensus prevalent in San Francisco or New York up here.

Go prepared Alaskans love the great outdoors, but they're not always overly sympathetic to outsiders who arrive unprepared and fail to treat it with the respect it deserves.

Eating

Many travelers are surprised that food prices in a Fairbanks or Anchorage supermarket are not that much higher than what they're paying at home. Then they visit their first restaurant and a glance at the menu sends them into a two-day fast. Alaskan restaurants are more expensive than most other places in the country because of the short tourist season and the high labor costs for waiters and chefs.

What's New

The economic challenges of the COVID-19 pandemic hit Alaska hard though the state did its best to keep calm and carry on with innovation and humor. 'Social distancing: it's what we've been doing since 1867' was a popular mantra during the lockdowns of 2020–21. With vaccines delivered and cruise ships returning, things are looking more hopeful.

Alaska's First Ironman Triathlon

Finally, real adventurers can test their mettle on the Last Frontier. Alaska hosted its first Ironman triathlon in Juneau in 2022, with a 2.4-mile swim in Auke Lake, a 112-mile cycle along the Glacier Highway, and a 26.2-mile run through the forests of the Mendenhall Valley (www.ironman.com/im-alaska).

Glamping

The glamorous camping (aka glamping) trend, now popular all over the US, has gained a foothold in Alaska with a growing selection of deluxe tents (p323), fibreglass igloos and even a luxury cabin built atop a nunatak 10 miles from the summit of Denali.

Micro-Booze

Already home to a microbrewery and a micro-distillery, the small town of Haines (p128), population 1700, continues in its quest to be the USA's best small town for micro-booze with the opening of **Three Northmen** (facebook.com/ThreeNorthmen), a meadery plying home-brewed mead (fermented honey water), cider and hard sodas.

Gateway Hotel, Seward

Alaskan-owned boat tour company Major Marine Tours (p230) opened a new hotel in Seward in May 2021. The Gateway is situated close to the small-boat harbor and acts as a convenient base-camp for visitors looking to explore Kenai Fjords National Park.

LOCAL KNOWLEDGE

WHAT'S HAPPENING IN ALASKA

Brendan Sainsbury, Lonely Planet writer

Thanks, in part, to its small, spread out population, Alaska weathered the COVID-19 storm better than most, at least from an epidemiological perspective: only five US states had recorded lower death rates as of early 2022.

Economically, it's been a different story. Relying heavily on seasonal cruise ships, the last two summers have been disastrous for the 49th state. In 2020 Alaska welcomed a grand total of zero cruise passengers to its normally busy ports, compared to 1.36 million the previous year. Not surprisingly, the economy has struggled, especially in the southeast, where empty docks and a historically poor salmon run led to the loss of 6000 jobs.

In 2021 early hopes of a return to normal were quickly dashed when Canada slapped a blanket ban on international cruise ships. A watered down cruise season ultimately kicked off in mid-July with a paltry 80 ships heading north, compared to 577 in 2019. Things can only get better – see Cruising in Alaska (p46) for more on cruising's comeback.

Denali Road Upgrades

Denali National Park's arterial road closed throughout 2022 to fix a longstanding structural problem – the so-called Pretty Rocks landslide. Facilities beyond the mile 43 marker, including the Eielson Visitor Center (p274) and the Igloo Creek (p283) and Wonder Lake (p282) campgrounds, will be inaccessible until 2023.

Anchorage Gets an Aloft

The latest new hotel to grace Anchorage's Midtown neighborhood is from the stable of hi-tech, contemporary design brand Aloft, run by Marriott. Open in April 2022, Aloft Anchorage on W 36th Avenue will have a bar, lounge, gym, pool and spa.

Free Vaccines

In the battle to stymie the COVID-19 pandemic and get back to normal as quickly as possible, Alaska now offers free vaccines (Janssen, Moderna and Pfizer) to travelers at three of its international airports: Anchorage, Fairbanks and Juneau. Walk-ins are accepted.

Northern Pacific Airways

New Alaska-based airline Northern Pacific Airways planned to become the first low-cost trans-Pacific operator in 2022, offering flights between the US and Asia through its Anchorage hub. The aim is to make Alaska a midway one-to-two-day layover between Asia and the Lower 48.

Cruise Comeback

After two terrible seasons, big cruise liners are planning a comeback in 2022 with a full timetable of vessels and itineraries, but several new rules to consider as well, including mandatory vaccinations and mask wearing for indoor areas.

Moose Loop

The Moose Loop (https://anchoragepark foundation.org/moose-loop-trail) is a new public health initiative promoted by the Anchorage Park Foundation. It combines four popular Anchorage trails into a 32-mile cycling loop that when looked at on a map appears (with a little creative thinking) to form the shape of a moose's head.

LISTEN, WATCH & FOLLOW

For inspiration, visit lonelyplanet.com/usa/alaska#latest-stories

Travel Alaska (www.travelalaska.com) Alaska's official tourism site.

Alaska Public Lands Information Centers (www.alaskacenters.gov) Info on parks and activities.

National Park Service (www.nps.gov/alaska) Information on Alaska's national parks, preserves, monuments and historical sites.

Alaska Marine Highway System (www.ferryalaska.com) For booking state ferries.

Brooks Falls Bearcam (www.nps.gov/katm/learn/photosmultimedia/brown-bear-salmon-cam-brooks-falls.htm) The iconic spot to see bears in Alaska.

Edible Alaska (twitter.com/ediblealaska) Magazine dedicated to Alaska's local food movement.

Alaska.org (www.alaska.org) Expert advice and insider tips from park rangers, wildlife biologists, bush pilots, naturalists and photographers, among others. Includes off-the-beaten-track destinations.

FAST FACTS

Pop 733,000

Percentage Alaska Native 14.8%

Highest point Denali (20,237ft)

Number of Rhode Islands that could fit into Alaska 425

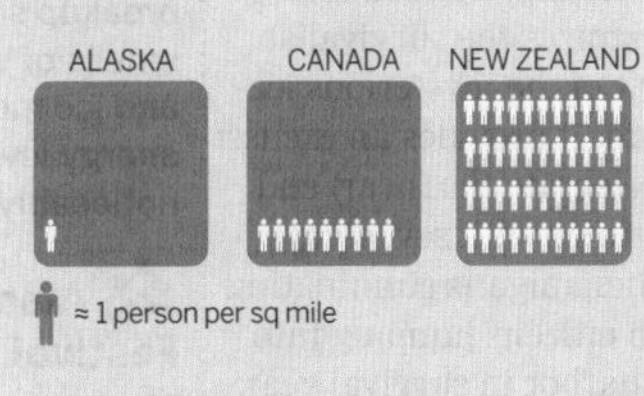

Month by Month

TOP EVENTS

Alaska State Fair, August–September

Midnight Sun Festival, June

Gold Rush Days, July–August

Alaska Bald Eagle Festival, November

February

Only the brave venture into Alaska in the winter when temperatures struggle to travel north of 0°F (-17.8°C) in the Interior. But days are getting longer by February.

Cordova Iceworm Festival

Arguably Alaska's weirdest festival, this celebration recognizes the survivalist spirit of the mysterious iceworm. It provides an excuse to celebrate the (near) end of winter with seven days of shenanigans culminating with citizens jumping into the harbor in survival gear. (p206)

Yukon Quest

The toughest dogsled race in the world (www.yukonquest.com) has resurrected a gold-rush-era mail route between Fairbanks and Whitehorse (Canada) covering over 1000 snow-encrusted miles. It starts in odd-numbered years in Whitehorse and in even-numbered years in Fairbanks.

March

As the sun emerges from hibernation, so do Alaskans. Though the temperatures are still quite low, the sun gives off a welcome hint of warmth and brightness.

April

What most people call spring is 'breakup' in Alaska, and April is full-on breakup season. The air smells of water as snow and ice melt, and the energy level of Alaskans noticeably increases.

Alaska Folk Festival

Musicians from across Alaska and the Yukon descend on Juneau for a week of music and dancing at this folk festival. Who cares if it rains every day? Get wet and dance away. (p117)

May

May is shoulder season and a great month to visit, with discounts on tickets, tours and accommodations. The weather's cool and trails are usually snow-covered, but the days are long and the crowds are thin.

Copper River Delta Shorebird Festival

At this festival birders invade Cordova for four days of workshops, lectures, dinners and exhibitions, all in celebration of some of the greatest migrations in Alaska across one of North America's largest continual wetlands. (p210)

Kachemak Bay Shorebird Festival

If the birders aren't gathering in Cordova, then they're nesting in Homer, enjoying the workshops, field trips and birding presentations by keynote speakers at this festival. It wouldn't be Homer without an arts and crafts fair too. (p252)

Little Norway Festival

Be a Viking for a day in Petersburg and feast on seafood at night at one of

Southeast Alaska's oldest festivals. There are parades and pageants, and the entire town appears to be dressed in Norwegian folk costumes. (p95)

Kodiak Crab Festival

Celebrated since 1958, this festival includes survival-suit races and seafood cook-offs. Grab a plate and dig in to as much of everyone's favorite shellfish as you can fit in your belly. (p348)

June

June marks the height of tourist season in Alaska. The longest day of the year is celebrated in solstice festivities across the state, and salmon begin their runs from sea to spawning grounds.

Spenard Jazz Fest

Alaska is a lightly populated country with a lot of good musicians. Come and see the latest talent improvise with jazz riffs at this rapidly growing festival in Anchorage. (p165)

Midnight Sun Festival

Celebrate summer solstice in Fairbanks with music from 40 bands on three stages, the Yukon 800 Power Boat Races and a baseball game that starts at midnight but doesn't need any lights. The festival is held on the Sunday before the solstice. (p304)

Moose Pass Summer Solstice Festival

At this midsummer festival join in some small-town fun and games, not to mention a short parade and major boogying, down on the Kenai Peninsula in tiny Moose Pass. (p231)

Sitka Summer Music Festival

Since 1972 this festival has been a most civilized gathering, with chamber music, concerts and lots of culture by the sea in beautiful Sitka. You'll need to book tickets in advance. (p104)

Nalukataq (Whaling Festival)

Join Utqiaġvik (Barrow) residents in late June for Nalukataq as they celebrate

Midnight Sun Festival, Fairbanks (p304)

and give thanks for another successful whaling season with dancing and blanket tosses. You'll even get to taste your first *muktuk* (whale blubber). (p382)

July

The days are still long, the mountains are green, salmon streams are full and everyone is in good spirits. Not surprisingly, this month is the busiest for festivals.

Girdwood Forest Fair

Girdwood's magical arts fair is held in the rainforest over the Fourth of July weekend. Come twirl Hula-Hoops to live music, shop for local art and relax in a rainy beer garden by a glacial stream. (p182)

Mt Marathon Race

Take in the exhausting Fourth of July 3.1-mile run up Seward's 3022ft-high peak, which started in 1915. Join the fans as they crane their necks at the racers, many of whom make it up and back in well under an hour. (p230)

Southeast Alaska State Fair

Held in late July in Haines, this unique fair hosts a lively fiddler competition as well as the Ugliest Dog Contest – but make sure you don't miss the pig races. (p133)

Top: Alaska State Fair, Palmer (p190)

Bottom: Bald eagle (p133)

World Eskimo-Indian Olympics

You have to wait four years in between the modern Olympic Games, but the indigenous people of the north congregate in Fairbanks annually for these Olympics to display their sporting prowess in esoteric events such as the blanket toss, the ear pull and the two-foot high kick. (p303)

Gold Rush Days

A five-day festival of bed races, canoe races, dances, fish feeds and floozy costumes in Valdez, plus a boat race for dinghies made of cardboard and duct tape. Oh, and a little gold-rush history too. (p199)

August

Summer is in full swing at the beginning of August, but night and chillier temperatures return at the end. Berries are ripe, produce is ready for harvest and you might even spot the northern lights.

Blueberry Arts Festival

Blue tongues aren't the only thing you'll see at this Ketchikan festival (www.visit-ketchikan.com): slug races, pie-eating contests, a parade and even a poetry slam are all events held at this celebration of everyone's favorite berry.

Alaska State Fair

Palmer's showcase for 100lb cabbages and the best Spam recipes in the state, plus live music, logging shows and deep-fried Twinkies; the Alaska State Fair runs from late August through the first weekend in September. (p190)

September

September is another shoulder month for tourism, with discounted prices and fewer crowds. Night is full-on here, but the hiking is still good and you have a good chance of seeing the northern lights.

Seward Music & Arts Festival

This family-friendly festival incorporates artists and more than 20 musical acts and theatrical companies, including circus lessons for the kiddos. Every year the townsfolk get together and paint a mural; come help them. (p231)

October

In most of Alaska, winter is on. Winds blow the last of the leaves from trees and snow caps the mountains. That doesn't keep Alaskans from having a good time, though.

Alaska Day Festival

Sitka (www.sitka.org) dresses the part in celebrating the actual transfer ceremony when the United States purchased Alaska from Russia in 1867. You'll find community dances, a kayak race and an afternoon tea for kids to learn about life in 1867.

Great Alaska Beer Train

All aboard! The *Microbrew Express* is a special run of the Alaska Railroad (www.alaskarailroad.com) from Anchorage to Portage; it's loaded with happy passengers sipping the best beer made in Alaska and taking in some of Alaska's finest scenery.

November

Bundle up and put on your bunny boots. You won't find many tourists here this time of year, but the nightlife is vibrant in larger towns and cities and there's a palpable sense of community.

WhaleFest!

It's whales galore in Sitka's WhaleFest! – so many you don't even need a boat to view them. This scientific gathering will teach you everything you need to know about these amazing marine mammals. (p104)

Alaska Bald Eagle Festival

This is the largest gathering of bald eagles in the world. There are more birds in Haines than tourists at this festival, when 3000-plus eagles gather along the Chilkat River. Simply spectacular. (p133)

Itineraries

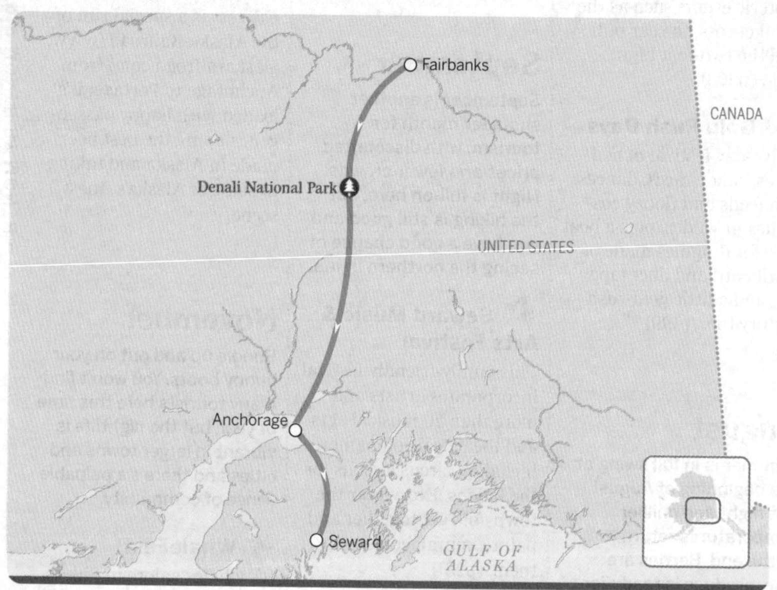

5 DAYS Fairbanks to Seward by Train

This land-based itinerary takes advantage of the beautifully maintained Alaska Railroad.

Start out in **Fairbanks**, the railroad's northernmost terminus, where you can spend a day exploring the museums and a night appreciating that the sun barely sets. Hop on the train to **Denali National Park**, and enjoy a good day hike on the Triple Lakes Trail. The next morning, take the extraordinary eight-hour ride to **Anchorage**. Along this stretch the tracks leave the road and probe into asphalt-free wilderness, paralleling rivers instead of the highway, with the icy mass of Denali in view if you're lucky.

Spend two nights and one full day in Anchorage, taking advantage of its surprisingly sophisticated shopping and dining scene. Check out the world-class Anchorage Museum, or rev up for a salmon bake with a bike ride along the Coastal Trail. Then hop aboard for another spectacular journey to **Seward**. Again, the train deviates from the road and takes you 10 miles into the Chugach Mountains. Seward is the southern terminus of the railroad, ending in gorgeous Resurrection Bay. Be sure to take a tour of Kenai Fjords National Park to spot sea lions, sea otters and whales.

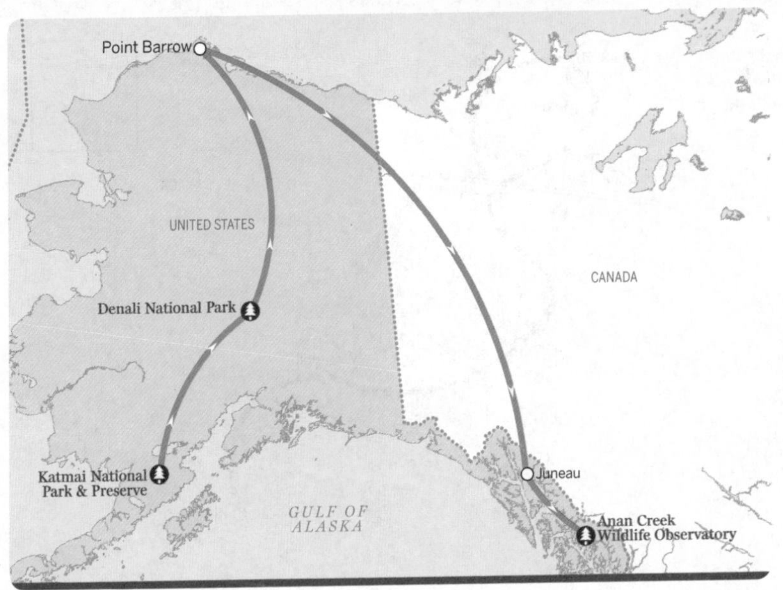

Katmai National Park to Anan Creek

One of the fastest-growing activities in Alaska is bear watching. There's no shortage of bears here, nor tourists wanting to see one – preferably catching and devouring a salmon. Make it to at least one of the following destinations and you're likely to spot one.

One of the most famous bear-viewing sites is Brooks Falls in **Katmai National Park & Preserve**. Here is where you'll catch the ultimate Alaskan photo: a dozen grizzlies perched on the edge of a waterfall, snapping salmon out of the air as they leap upstream. There are so many bears here in July, in fact, that the moment you step out of your floatplane at Brooks Camp you are ushered into the national parks office for a mandatory bear orientation, likely passing a grizzly or two ambling up the shore of Naknek Lake on your way.

A bit more accessible than Katmai National Park & Preserve is **Denali National Park**, which sits on the road system. Here you can jump onto a park shuttle bus and press your face against the glass as you scour the sweeping landscape for both brown and black bears. Not only are you likely to spot one of these legendary beasts, you'll also probably catch sight of caribou and moose.

You"ll need a airplane to get to Utqiaġvik and **Point Barrow** for a chance to spot a polar bear at the top of the world. Photographing one of these massive white creatures is an experience few will ever have. A guided tour will take you out of town where you might also catch sight of a walrus.

For a more urban experience, fly to **Juneau**. The most affordable bear-watching is found here, since you don't have to travel far from the city to catch black bears feasting on salmon at the capital city's Steep Creek near Mendenhall Glacier. Alternatively, you can make a short hop in a seaplane to Pack Creek on Admiralty Island.

Finish off in the southern panhandle at the **Anan Creek Wildlife Observatory** 30 miles southeast of Wrangell, one of the only places in Alaska where black and brown bears coexist.

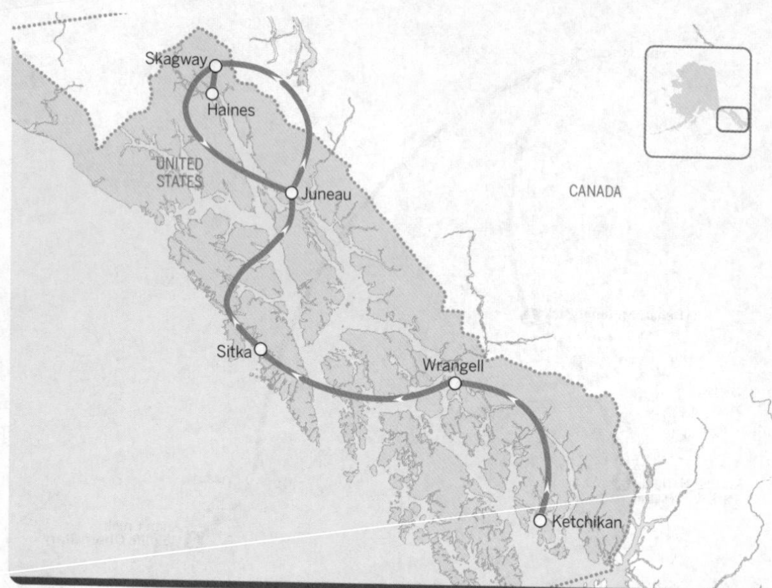

2 WEEKS Cruising Southeast Alaska

One of the most exciting trips is taking the Alaska Marine Highway from Bellingham, WA, to Skagway. It's an easy-to-plan journey through a scenic region of Alaska, although you should reserve space on the Alaska Marine Highway ferry if you want a cabin.

Board the ferry in Bellingham and enjoy the coastal scenery of Canada – including staffed lighthouses – for a couple of days before disembarking for two days at **Ketchikan**. If it's not raining, spend a day climbing Deer Mountain and enjoy lunch on the peak with panoramic views of the Inside Passage. Head out to Totem Bight State Park to see totems and a colorful community house. If it *is* raining, book a flightseeing tour of Misty Fiords National Monument, an almost-mystical landscape of steep fjords and waterfalls running off foggy green mountains.

Catch the ferry to **Wrangell** and take a wild jet-boat tour up the Stikine River, North America's fastest navigable river. Be sure to visit Petroglyph Beach, where ancient rock carvings of faces and spirals emerge at low tide. Continue to **Sitka** on the ferry for an afternoon at Sitka National Historical Park and another on a whale-watching cruise.

Head to **Juneau** and sign up for a walk across the beautiful ice of Mendenhall Glacier. Top that off the next day by climbing Mt Roberts and then having a beer (or two) before taking the Mt Roberts tramway back to the city. In the evening enjoy one of the city's salmon bakes and indulge in the tourist trap that is the Red Dog Saloon.

Climb aboard high-speed catamaran MV *Fairweather* for two days in **Skagway**, the historic start of the Klondike gold rush. Board the White Pass & Yukon Route Railroad for a day trip to Lake Bennett and in the evening catch the rollicking *Days of '98 Show*. If you can eke out another day, take the fast ferry to **Haines**, a quiet, local-loving Alaskan town with some fine hikes and a great brewery. After returning to Skagway, you'll need to backtrack to Juneau if you want to fly home – or you can jump back on the state ferry in Auke Bay.

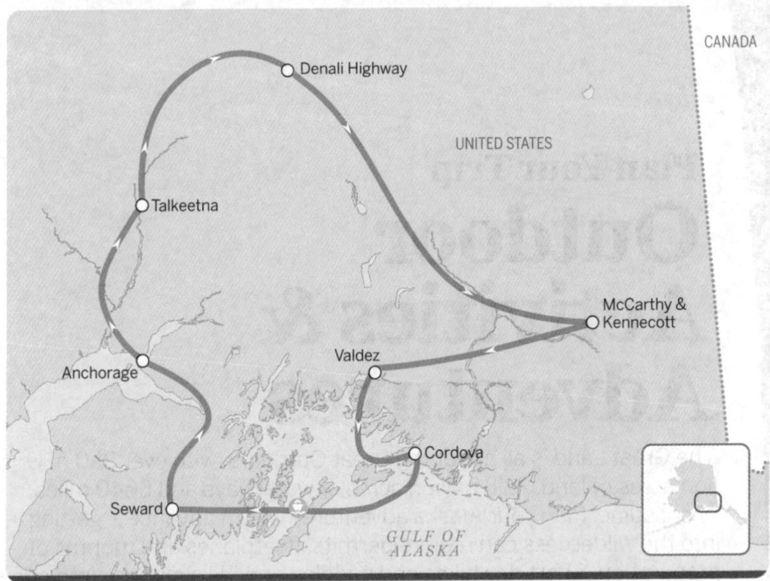

Road-Tripping

Driving the very open roads in such a dramatic land is what road-tripping is all about. Get yourself a rental vehicle and stick on some Springsteen: you're in for an amazing ride.

Fly into **Anchorage** and pick up your car (make sure you book well in advance). Stop at one of the city's large supermarkets, stock up with road-trip goodies and some liquid refreshment and then beat it out of town.

Head north and take the George Parks Hwy through Wasilla. Turn at the Talkeetna Spur Rd and hang out in **Talkeetna**, a laid-back climbers' town. Spend the day on the last flag-stop train in the US, the *Hurricane Turn*. In the evening, be sure to check out the antics at the historic Fairview Inn's bar.

Head back to the Parks Hwy and continue north to the **Denali Highway**. Open only in summer, this 134-mile dirt road traverses the foothills of the Alaska Range. Take your time; the road is rough and the scenery stunning. Pitch a tent along the road wherever it feels right – preferably next to a rushing stream – and then continue heading east in the morning until you hit the Richardson Hwy.

Travel south and then follow the McCarthy Rd east to the Kennicott River, 127 miles from Glennallen. Spend the next day exploring the quaint village of **McCarthy** and the amazing mining ruins at **Kennecott**. Return to the Richardson Hwy and head south and then west.

Continue into **Valdez** and stay an extra day to splurge on a Columbia Glacier cruise. Drive onto the Alaska Marine Highway ferry (reserve this in advance) and sail across Prince William Sound to **Cordova**. Spend 24 hours dissecting the Sound's most attractive town and its free-thinking locals, incorporating a hike around the Copper River Delta with its many bird species. From Cordova take a ferry to Whittier. On the same day drive 90 miles to **Seward**, passing through scenic Turnagain Pass. Stay two days in Seward; book a boat tour or kayak in Resurrection Bay, but on the afternoon of the second day hightail it back to Anchorage (127 miles) to turn in your car before the dealer closes.

Plan Your Trip

Outdoor Activities & Adventures

The Great Land is all about the Great Outdoors, with over 350 million acres of land, 28.8 million acres of waterways and 6640 miles of coastline. Plan your Alaska adventures well in advance – getting into the wilderness can require permits, floatplanes and months of preparation. Short day hikes and paddles provide a glimpse into one of the world's last great frontiers.

Alaska's Best Campgrounds

Starrigavan Recreation Area (p104) Stunning coastal scenery just outside of Sitka.

Fort Abercrombie State Historical Park Campground (p344) Near Kodiak; wooded sites, interesting WWII artifacts and intriguing tidal pools to explore.

Mendenhall Lake Campground (p117) Near Juneau, a beautiful United States Forest Service (USFS) campground with glacial views from some of the sites.

Wonder Lake Campground (p282) Excellent views of North America's largest mountain within Denali National Park.

Exit Glacier Campground (p238) Camp in the shadow of majesty at the only formal campground in Kenai Fjords National Park.

Hiking & Paddling in Alaska

Much of Alaska's wilderness is hard to reach for visitors with limited time or small budgets. The lack of specialized equipment, the complicated logistics of reaching remote areas and lack of backcountry knowledge keeps many out of the state's great wilderness tracts such as the Arctic National Wildlife Refuge (ANWR). To experience such a remote and pristine place, you may need to shell out a premium amount of dollars to a guiding company.

But that doesn't mean you can't sneak off on your own for a trek into the mountains or a paddle down an icy fjord. There are so many possible adventures in Alaska that even the most budget-conscious traveler can take time to explore what lies beyond the pavement. Do it yourself and save.

The best way to enter the state's wilderness is to begin with a day hike the minute you step off the ferry or depart from the Alcan (Alaska-Canada) Hwy. After an initial taste of the woods, many travelers forgo the cities and spend the rest of their trip on multiday adventures into the backcountry to enjoy Alaska's immense surroundings.

There is also a range of paddling opportunities, from calm rivers and chains of lakes for novice canoeists to remote fjords and coastlines whose rugged shorelines and tidal fluctuations are an attraction for more experienced open-water paddlers. Alaska is an icy paradise for kayakers. Double-bladed paddlers can easily escape into a watery wilderness, away from motorboats and cruise ships, and enjoy the unusual experience of gazing at glaciers or watching seal pups snuggle on icebergs from sea level.

Hikes in Denali National Park (p272) are some of the best in Alaska, but they are largely trail-less (with no multiday hikes on trails).

Great Hiking Near Alaska's Cities

Even if you don't have any desire to hoist a hefty backpack, don't pass up an opportunity to spend a day hiking one of the hundreds of well-maintained and easy-to-follow trails scattered across the state. How good is the day hiking in Juneau? The trailhead for the Mt Roberts Trail is only five blocks from the state capitol, while the United States Forest Service maintains 29 other trails accessible from the Juneau road system. Anchorage is also blessed with numerous close-to-home trails. A 15-minute drive from downtown and you can be at a treeline trailhead in Chugach State Park, where a path quickly leads into the alpine. Skagway, Girdwood, Seward and Sitka also have numerous trails close to main streets.

For the state's best close-to-town day hikes, hit the trail on one of the following:

Mt Roberts Trail (p114) Great views, plenty of switchbacks, and extensive wildlife-watching, and it's all accessible from downtown Juneau.

Deer Mountain Trail (p76) Just arrived in Alaska? This 2.5-mile trail from downtown Ketchikan to the top of Deer Mountain will whet your appetite to tie up your hiking boots at every stop.

Perseverance Trail (p114) Head out from Basin Rd in Juneau on this 3-mile hike, which takes in local history and spectacular scenery.

Turnagain Arm Trail (p181) An excellent hike through the Chugach National Forest that's only a few miles from Anchorage.

Mt Marathon Trail (p229) There are several ways to climb 3022ft-high Mt Marathon, which overlooks downtown Seward, but all end at a heavenly alpine bowl just behind the peak.

Tours

If you lack the expertise to head outdoors on your own – or the logistics of visiting remote wilderness, such as the Alaska National Wildlife Refuge, are too daunting – guiding companies will help you get there. Whether you want to climb Denali, kayak Glacier Bay or pedal from Anchorage to Fairbanks, there's an outfitter willing to put an itinerary together, supply the equipment and lead the way.

Useful Websites

Alaska Hike Search (www.alaskahikesearch.com) Includes details on trails around Anchorage and Southcentral Alaska.

Alaska Department of Natural Resources (www.dnr.state.ak.us/parks/aktrails) Has details on trails in every corner of the state.

Alaska Department of Fish & Game (www.adfg.alaska.gov/index.cfm?adfg=educators.notebookseries) The excellent *Wildlife Notebook* covers all the state's major species of animals and birds that you may encounter on the trail or while paddling.

Knik Canoers & Kayakers (www.kck.org) With its tips, safety advice and contacts, this website is a great start for anybody thinking about a paddling adventure in Alaska.

SEAtrails (www.seatrails.org) SEAtrails provides brief descriptions and downloadable maps for more than 80 trails in 19 communities in Southeast Alaska.

Sitka Trail Works, Inc (www.sitkatrailworks.org) Detailed-coverage maps on almost 20 trails around Sitka.

Trail Mix, Inc (www.trailmixinc.org) Trail information in and around Juneau.

JAY YUAN/SHUTTERSTOCK ©

Top: Haines (p128)

Left: Sheep Mountain Lodge (p322), Glenn Highway

Backpacking

There are a number of trails throughout the state that serve as excellent avenues into the wilderness for unguided, multiday treks.

- Denali National Park (p272)
- Chilkoot Trail (p70)
- Petersburg Lake Trail (p94)
- Iditarod National Historic Trail (p229)
- Resurrection Pass Trail (p219)
- Chena Dome Trail (p269)

Cabins

Every agency overseeing public land in Alaska – from the Bureau of Land Management (BLM) and the National Park Service (NPS) to the Alaska Division of Parks – maintains rustic cabins in remote areas. The cabins are not expensive ($25 to $50 per night), but they are not easy to reach either. Most of them are accessed via a floatplane charter. Others can be reached on foot, by boat or by paddling.

Most cabins need to be reserved six months in advance – some are so popular that a lottery system has been implemented – while others are available on a first-come, first-served basis. Depending on the cabin, you'll likely need to bring everything you would on an overnight trek (save the tent).

Tongass National Forest (907-586-8800; www.fs.usda.gov/tongass) has more than 100 cabins available throughout the Southeast.

Chugach National Forest (907-743-9500; www.fs.usda.gov/chugach), covering eastern Kenai, the Copper River Delta and Prince William Sound, is a 5.4-million-acre wilderness with more than 40 cabins.

Alaska Division of Parks (907-269-8400; http://dnr.alaska.gov/parks) has 66 cabins and eight ice huts scattered from Point Bridget State Park (p114), near Juneau, to **Chena River State Recreation Area** (Chena Hot Springs Rd; cabins $35-60; P), east of Fairbanks.

Bureau of Land Management (BLM; 907-271-5960; www.blm.gov) manages 14 cabins in the **White Mountain National Recreation Area** (800-437-7021, 877-444-6777; www.recreation.gov; GPS: N 65°25.650', W 147°14.602'; per night $25; P), north of Fairbanks, and four cabins along the Iditarod National Historic Trail (p229).

Alaska Department of Fish & Game (licensing 907-465-2376, main office 907-465-4100; www.adfg.alaska.gov) has cabins on remote fishing lakes in the Interior.

US Fish & Wildlife Service (USFWS; 907-271-6198; www.fws.gov) has seven cabins on Kodiak Island in the Kodiak National Wildlife Refuge (p344) and 16 cabins in Kenai.

National Park Service (907-983-2921; www.nps.gov/state/ak) maintains three cabins in Kenai Fjords National Park (p236), which are reached by floatplane or water taxi.

Camping

Camping is your cheapest lodging solution. It is so popular that many communities have set up facilities on the edge of town, and there are non-official camping areas throughout. Many highway pull-offs are utilized as both official camping-access points and unofficial car-camping areas.

The best camping is away from towns at the public campgrounds operated by the Alaska Division of Parks, the US Forest Service (USFS) or the Bureau of Land Management BLM in northern Alaska. The state-park system maintains dozens of rustic campgrounds throughout Alaska, with fees ranging from free to $45 a night in the more popular ones. The majority do not take reservations; some have RV hookups, running water and bathrooms; others are simply cleared patches of ground.

Paddling

The paddle is a way of life in Alaska, and every region has either canoeing or kayaking opportunities or both. Both the Southeast and Prince William Sound offer spectacular kayaking opportunities, while Fairbanks and Arctic Alaska are home to some of the best wilderness canoe adventures in the country.

Blue-Water Paddling

In Alaska, 'blue water' refers to the coastal areas of the state, which are characterized by extreme tidal fluctuations, cold water and the possibility of high winds and waves. Throughout Southeast and Southcentral Alaska, the open canoe is replaced with the kayak, and blue-water paddling is the means of escape into coastal areas such as Muir Inlet in Glacier Bay National Park or Tracy Arm-Fords Terror, south of Juneau.

BACKPACKING GEAR

Double-check your equipment before leaving home. Most towns in Alaska will have at least one store with a wall full of camping supplies, but prices will be high and by mid- to late summer certain items will be out of stock.

Absolutely Essential Equipment

- Backpack
- Lightweight tent with rain fly and bug netting
- Three-season sleeping bag with temperature range of -10°F to 40°F (-23°C to 4°C)
- Sturdy hiking boots that are already broken in
- Water filter
- Compass or GPS unit
- Topo map for your route
- Multi-tool and knife
- Lighter/waterproof matches
- Emergency blanket and first-aid kit
- Headlamp/torch (it still might get dark, depending on the time of year and latitude)
- Bug spray (100% DEET)

In Your Clothing Bag

- Warm gloves
- Winter hat, sun hat and sunscreen
- Fleece pullover (it can get cold at night, even in July)
- Rain gear – both pants and parka (because it will definitely rain)
- Extra wool socks

Equipment to Consider Packing

- Self-inflating sleeping pad
- Reliable backpacker's stove
- Small cooking kit
- Sports sandals for a change of footwear at night or for fording rivers and streams
- Bear spray
- Duct tape
- Extra day's worth of food

If you do not know how to do a wet entry to a kayak (or know what a wet entry is), it's recommended that you travel with a guide. They know the tides, the wildlife and how to keep you safe.

Tidal fluctuations are the main concern in blue-water areas. Paddlers should always pull their boats above the high-tide mark and keep a tide book in the same pouch as their topographic map. Cold coastal water, rarely above 45°F (7°C) in the summer, makes capsizing worse than unpleasant. With a life jacket, survival time in the water is less than two hours; without one there is no time. If your kayak flips, stay with the boat and attempt to right it and crawl back in. Trying to swim to shore in arctic water is risky at best.

Framed backpacks are useless in kayaks; gear is best stowed in dry bags or small daypacks. Carry a large supply of assorted plastic bags, including several garbage bags. All gear, especially sleeping bags and clothing, should be stowed in plastic bags (or a dry bag if you have one), as water tends to seep in even when you

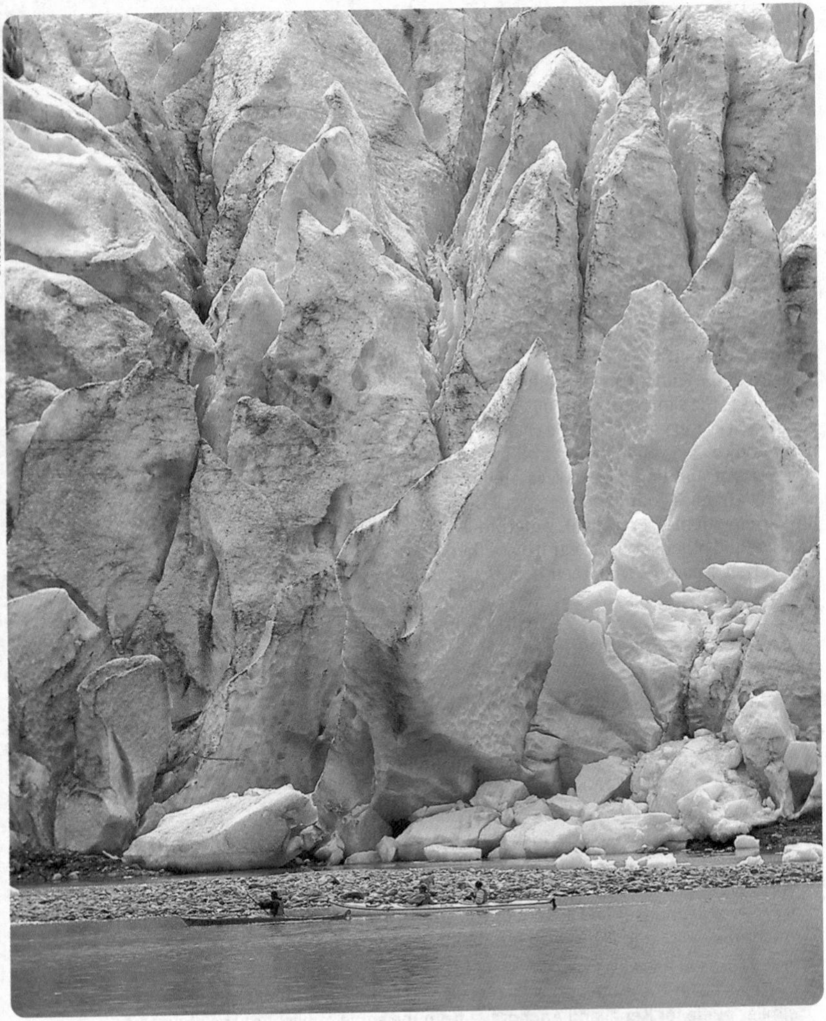

DAVIDHOFFMANN PHOTOGRAPHY/SHUTTERSTOCK ©

RUBEN M RAMOS/SHUTTERSTOCK ©

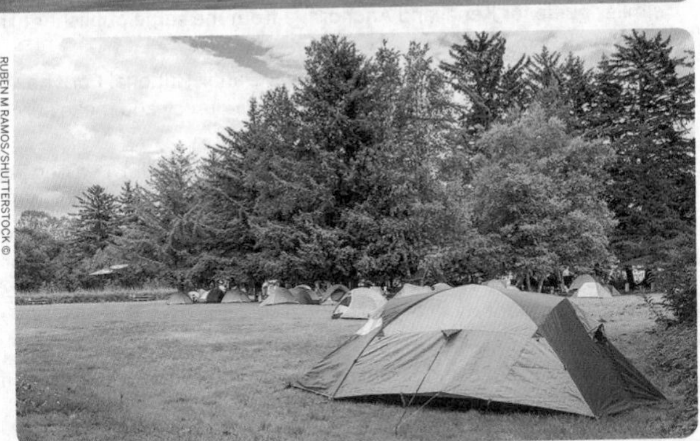

Top: Holgate Glacier, Kenai Fjords National Park (p236)

Right: Camping, Haines (p128)

seal yourself in with a cockpit skirt. Over-the-calf rubber boots are the best footwear for getting in and out of kayaks.

White-Water Paddling

Alaska's rivers vary, but they share characteristics not found on many rivers in the lower 48: water levels tend to change rapidly, while many rivers are heavily braided and boulder-strewn. Take care in picking out the right channel to avoid spending most of the day pulling your boat off gravel. You can survive flipping your canoe in an Alaskan river, but you'll definitely want a plan of action if you do.

Much of the equipment for white-water canoeists is the same as it is for blue-water paddlers. Tie everything into the canoe; you never know when you might hit a whirlpool or a series of standing waves. Wear a life jacket at all times. Many paddlers stock their life jacket with insect repellent, waterproof matches and other survival gear in case they flip and get separated from their boat.

Cycling

With its long days, cool temperatures, lack of interstate highways and growing number of paved paths around cities such as Anchorage, Juneau and Fairbanks, Alaska can be a land of opportunity for road cyclists.

Some roads do not have much of a shoulder – and many are quite rough even when paved – so cyclists should utilize the sunlight hours to pedal when traffic is light in such areas. It is not necessary to carry a lot of food, as you can easily restock on all major roads.

Good sources for cycling maps and news on events are Alaska's major bike clubs:

Arctic Bicycle Club (907-566-0177; www.arcticbike.org)

Bike Anchorage (907-891-8906; www.bikeanchorage.org)

Fairbanks Cycle Club (www.fairbankscycleclub.org)

Juneau Rides (https://juneaurides.org)

RECOMMENDED HIKING & PADDLING READS

- *Denali National Park Guide to Hiking, Photography & Camping* (2010) – Longtime Alaskan Ike Waits has produced the most comprehensive guide to Alaska's best-known national park.
- *Klondike Trail: the Complete Hiking and Paddling Guide* (2001) – From the legendary Chilkoot Trail to a paddle down the Yukon River, this book by Jennifer Voss will lead you on an adventure of a lifetime.
- *55 Ways to the Wilderness in Southcentral Alaska* (2002) – Check out this book by Helen Nienhueser and John Wolfe for trails around the Kenai Peninsula, the Anchorage area and from Palmer to Valdez.
- *50 Hikes in Alaska's Chugach State Park* (2001) – Shane Shepherd and Owen Wozniak cover the state park's best trails and routes near Anchorage. There's a similar guide for Kenai and Anchorage from the same publisher (The Mountaineers Books).
- *Hiking with Grizzlies* (2006) – Former Denali National Park bear observer Tim Rubbert tells you how to travel into grizzly country and make sure you come back out.
- *Hiking Alaska's Wrangell-St Elias National Park* (2008) – Greg Fensterman will keep you from getting lost on 50 hikes and backpacking treks in this book, which includes GPS waypoints.
- *The Alaska River Guide* (2008) – Karen Jettmar provides the complete river guide for Alaska, covering 100 trips, from the Chilkat in the Southeast to Colville on the arctic slope.
- *The Kenai Canoe Trails* (1995) – Daniel L Quick's guide to Kenai National Wildlife Refuge's Swan Lake and Swanson River canoe routes, with maps, fishing information and photos.

Mountain biking in Alaska

Mountain Biking

With a mountain bike you can explore an almost-endless number of dirt roads, miner's two-tracks and even hiking trails that you would never consider with a road bike.

Always pack a lightweight, wind-and-water-resistant jacket and an insulating layer because the weather changes quickly in Alaska and so can the terrain. Even when renting a bike, make sure you can repair a flat with the proper spare tube and tools. Water, best carried in a hydration pack, is a must, as is energy food.

There is much mountain-bike activity around Anchorage, which has several places to rent bikes. Within the city, mountain bikers head to Kincaid Park (p159) and Far North Bicentennial Park (p159) for their fill of rugged singletrack. In surrounding Chugach State Park, the Powerline Pass Trail is an 11-mile round-trip adventure into the mountains, while the popular 13.5-mile Lakeside Trail (p186) is a leisurely ride that skirts Eklutna Lake.

The Resurrection Pass, Russian River and Johnson Pass Trails in the Chugach National Forest (p37) are popular among off-road cyclists in the Kenai Peninsula.

North of Anchorage, Hatcher Pass (p154) is a haven of mountain-biking activity, with riders following Archangel Rd (also known as the Archangel Valley), Craggie Creek Trail and Gold Mint Trail to glaciers and old mines in the Talkeetna Mountains.

The most popular area for riders near Fairbanks is the Chena River State Recreation Area, while in Juneau mountain bikers head to Perseverance Trail (p114) near downtown, and Montana Creek Trail near the Mendenhall Glacier.

From Valdez, head out on Mineral Creek Rd for excellent views.

If you are able to travel with equipment on your bike (sleeping bag, food and tent), you can partake in a variety of overnight trips or longer bicycle journeys. The 92-mile Denali Park Rd is off-limits to vehicles, but you can explore it on a mountain bike. Another excellent dirt road for such an adventure is the 135-mile Denali Hwy from Paxson to Cantwell.

Want the ultimate cycling adventure? Prep your legs and your butt for the gritty, unrelenting 414-mile pedaling trip up the Dalton Hwy, through taiga, across the Brooks Range.

SEEING ALASKA FROM ABOVE

Most flightseeing is done in small planes, holding three to five passengers, with the tours lasting, on average, one to two hours. A much smaller number are taken by helicopter due to the high costs of operating the aircraft. With the rising price of fuel, expect to pay anywhere from $270 to $400 per person for a one-hour flight.

The following are some of Alaska's most spectacular flights:

Glacier Bay National Park (p125) From Haines; glaciers, Fairweather Mountains, maybe a whale or two.

Misty Fiords National Monument (p83) Two-hour flights that include a rainforest walk in this wilderness near Ketchikan.

Denali (p272) The bush pilots who fly climbers to the mountain will also take visitors around it for Alaska's most spectacular flightseeing tour.

Valdez Heli-Ski (p198) Take the fun way up (and down) with a helicopter to the top of some of the world's gnarliest ski terrain.

Wrangell-St Elias National Park (p327) From McCarthy you can view the stunning peaks and glaciers in the USA's largest national park.

Fishing

Alaska has a fish-every-cast reputation, but serious anglers visiting the state carefully research the areas they plan to fish and arrive equipped with the right gear and tackle. They often pay for guides or book a room at remote camps or lodges where rivers are not fished out by every passing motorist.

Those planning wilderness trips should pack a backpacking rod that breaks down into four or five sections and is equipped with a light reel. In the Southeast and Southcentral backcountry, anglers can target cutthroat trout, rainbow trout and Dolly Varden. Further north, especially around Fairbanks, they can catch grayling, with its sail-like dorsal fin, and arctic char. In August salmon seem to be everywhere.

An open-face spinning reel with light line – something in the 4lb to 6lb range – and a small selection of spinners and spoons will allow you to fish a wide range of waters, from streams and rivers to lakes. For fly-fishing, a 6-weight rod with a matching floating line or sinking tip is well suited for Dolly Vardens, rainbows and grayling. For salmon, a 7-weight or 8-weight rod and line are better choices. You can purchase the locally used lures and flies after you arrive.

You will also need a fishing license. A nonresident's fishing license costs $145 a year, but you can purchase a one-/three-/seven-/14-day license for $25/45/70/105. Every bait shop in the state sells them; you can also purchase one online through the Alaska Department of Fish & Game (p37).

Many visiting anglers invest in a fishing charter. Joining a captain on a boat can be pricey, given the cost of fuel (expect at least $200 per person for a four- to six-hour trip, and those are rates for someone in a group). Still, local knowledge is the best investment you can make to put a fish on your line. Communities with large fleets of charter captains include Homer, Seward, Petersburg, Kodiak and Ketchikan, with halibut most in demand among visitors. Head to Soldotna to land a 50lb king salmon in the Kenai River.

If money is no object, fly-in fishing adventures are available from cities such as Anchorage and Fairbanks. These outings use small charter planes to reach wilderness lakes and rivers for a day of salmon and steelhead fishing. It's an expensive day trip – usually at least $500 per person – but the fishing is legendary, sometimes even a catch per cast.

Glacier Trekking & Ice Climbing

The glaciers may be melting, but glacier trekking is still a popular activity in Alaska. Most first-time glacier trekkers envision a slick and slippery surface, but in reality the ice is very rough and embedded with gravel and rocks that provide surprisingly good traction. There are several roadside-accessible glaciers, the Matanuska Glacier (p322) being the best known.

Glaciers are dangerous areas. Not only do they have ice-bridges and crevasses, they also move, meaning the surface changes from time to time. Dry glaciers have no snow on top, and are OK for limited travel without technical equipment. Wet glaciers may have snowbridges. Don't venture beyond the edge without a rope, ice axe and basic knowledge of glacier travel.

Your best bet is to hook up with a guiding company that offers glacier treks. On such outings you'll be outfitted with a helmet, crampons and an ice axe, and roped up for several miles of walking on the frozen surface.

Glaciers are also the main destination in Alaska for ice climbers in the summer. Icefalls and ice faces, where the glacier makes its biggest vertical descents out of the mountains, are where climbers strap on crampons and helmets and load themselves with ropes, ice screws and anchors. Inexperienced climbers should sign up for a one-day ice-climbing lesson, in which guides lead you to an ice fall and then teach you about cramponing, front pointing and the use of ice tools.

Outfitters that offer glacier trekking or ice-climbing excursions:

Above & Beyond Alaska (p117) of Juneau leads an eight-hour glacier trek and climb on Mendenhall Glacier (p110).

St Elias Alpine Guides (p328) is based in tiny McCarthy and offers half- and full-day treks on Root Glacier (p331) as well as ice climbing.

MICA Guides (p323) of Sutton has fun walks on the Matanuska Glacier (p322).

Ascending Path (p180) of Girdwood offers Midnight Sun Glacier Hikes that start at 8pm and uses Byron Glacier for its ice-climbing outings.

Exit Glacier Guides (p230) is a top operation, based in Seward, for exploring Kenai Fjords National Park's Exit Glacier.

Rafting

Both white-water and expedition rafting are extremely popular in Alaska. The Nenana River just outside of Denali National Park is a mecca for white-water thrillseekers, with companies like the Denali Outdoor Center (p275) offering daily raft trips in the summer through Class IV rapids. The season climaxes on the second

PLANNING FOR A FORTUNE

There's still gold in them hills. Geologists estimate that only 5% of what the state contains has been recovered. And even short-term visitors can strike it rich.

Alaska has more than 150 public prospecting sites where you can recreationally pan for gold without staking a claim. The best options are in the Interior. They include: on Taylor Hwy, American Creek at Mile 151; the Petersville State Recreation Mining Area on Petersville Rd off the George Parks Hwy at Trapper Creek; the beach at Nome; and on Glenn Hwy, Caribou Creek at Mile 106.8.

When panning for gold, you must have one essential piece of equipment: a gravity-trap pan, which can be purchased at most hardware stores. Those who have panned for a while also show up with rubber boots and gloves to protect feet and hands from icy waters; a garden trowel to dig up loose rock; a pair of tweezers to pick up gold flakes; and a small bottle to hold their find. If you really want to go pro, try wearing a floppy hat and growing a beard to your stomach. Kidding!

Panning techniques are based on the notion that gold is heavier than the gravel it lies in. Fill your pan with loose material from cracks and crevices in streams, where gold might have washed down and become lodged. Add water to the pan, then rinse and discard larger rocks, keeping the rinsing in the pan. Continue to shake the contents toward the bottom by swirling the pan in a circular motion, and wash off the excess sand and gravel by dipping the front into the stream. You should be left with heavy black mud, sand and, if you're lucky, a few flakes of gold. Use tweezers or your fingernails to transfer the flakes into a bottle filled with water.

JARED CARLSON/500PX ©

Ice climbing, Mendenhall Glacier (p110)

weekend after the Fourth of July holiday with the Nenana River Wildwater Festival, two days of river races and a wild-water rodeo. Other rivers that attract white-water enthusiasts include the Lowe River near Valdez, Sixmile Creek with its Class V rapids near Hope, the Matanuska River east of Palmer, and Kennicott River near Kennecott.

Expedition rafting tours are multiday floats through wilderness areas. While some white water may be encountered, the raft is mainly used as transportation. Thanks partly to publicity created by the oil-drilling controversy, the Arctic National Wildlife Refuge (ANWR) is very popular for people seeking this type of remote experience. But it's not cheap. **Arctic Treks** (☎907-455-6502; www.arctictreksadventures.com; $4100-5300), for example, offers a 10-day float through the ANWR on the Hulahula River costing $5200 per person. The Tatshenshini–Alsek River system is also a highly regarded wilderness raft trip that begins in the Yukon Territory and ends in Glacier Bay National Park.

Rock Climbing & Mountaineering

Denali and the other high peaks in Alaska draw the attention of mountain climbers from around the world. There's a mountain for every taste, from short alpine-style ascents to longer expedition climbs.

Rock climbing has also been growing in popularity in recent years. On almost any summer weekend, you can watch climbers working bolt-protected sport routes just above Seward Hwy along Turnagain Arm. Canyons in nearby Portage are also capturing the attention of rock climbers. Off Byron Glacier, several routes grace a slab of black rock polished smooth by the glacier. Not far from Portage Lake, a short hike leads to the magnificent slate walls of Middle Canyon.

Fairbanks climbers head north of town to the limestone formations known as Grapefruit Rocks, or else pack a tent and sleeping bag for the Granite Tors Trail Loop (p311) off the Chena Hot Springs Rd. A 7-mile hike from the trailhead leads to the tors, a series of 100ft granite spires in a wilderness setting.

For climbing equipment there's Alaska Mountaineering & Hiking (p177) in Anchorage or **Big Ray's** (☎907-452-3458; www.bigrays.com; 507 2nd Ave; ⏲8am-8pm Mon-Fri, 9am-7pm Sat, 10am-6pm Sun) in Fairbanks.

Information

➡ For more information, visit www.alaskaiceclimbing.com and www.mountainproject.com.

➡ For information on scaling the state's loftiest peaks, start with the Mountaineering Club of Alaska. On its website is the excellent *An Introduction to Alaskan Peaks* (www.mtnclubak.org/index.cfm/peaks).

➡ The best climbing guidebooks to the state are *Alaska: A Climbing Guide* by Michael Wood and Colby Coombs, and *Alaska Rock Climbing Guide* by Kelsey Gray.

➡ A great website for climbing tips and inspiration is William Finley's Akmountain.com (www.akmountain.com).

➡ The Walter Harper Talkeetna Ranger Station (p294) in Talkeetna is a useful source of information about climbing Denali (and any climbing in the Interior region).

BACKCOUNTRY CONDUCT

- Check in with the nearest United States Forest Service (USFS) office or National Park Service (NPS) headquarters before entering the backcountry.
- Take time to check out the area before unpacking your gear. Avoid animal trails (whether the tracks be moose or bear), areas with bear scat, and berry patches with ripe fruit.
- Throughout much of Alaska, river bars and old glacier outwashes are the best places to pitch a tent. If you come along the coast stay well above the high-tide line – the last ridge of seaweed and debris on the shore – to avoid waking up with salt-water flooding your tent.
- Do not harass wildlife. Avoid startling an animal, as it will most likely flee, leaving you with a short and forgettable encounter. Never attempt to feed wildlife; it is not healthy for you or the animal.
- Use biodegradable soap and do all washing away from water sources.
- Finally, be thoughtful when in the wilderness. It is a delicate environment. Carry in your supplies and carry out your trash. Never litter or leave garbage smoldering in a fire pit. In short, leave no evidence of your stay. Only then can an area remain a true wilderness.

Guides

Alaska Mountain Guides & Climbing School (p130) runs a climbing school in Haines and leads high-altitude climbing expeditions to Denali, Mt Fairweather and other peaks.

Alaska Mountaineering School (p291) of Talkeetna specializes in Denali.

St Elias Alpine Guides (p328) tackles Mt Blackburn and other peaks in Wrangell-St Elias National Park.

Surfing

Alaska has more coastline than any other state in the USA, but the last thing most people associate with the frozen north is surfing. Until now. Following a *Surfer* magazine cover story on surfing in Alaska, the state's first surf shop, Icy Waves Surf Shop (p149), opened in Yakutat. That caught the attention of CBS News, which sent a camera crew to the remote town for three days. Yakutat's 20-minute segment on the news show *Sunday Morning* with Charles Osgood propelled it into the limelight and transformed the small town into 'Surf City Alaska.'

Due to its big waves and uncrowded beaches, Yakutat was named one of the five best surf towns in the USA by *Outside* magazine. Surfers from all over the world now visit the surf capital of Alaska every summer to join 20 or so locals for 'surfing under St Elias,' the 18,000ft peak that overshadows the town. The best waves occur from mid-April to mid-June and from mid-August through September, and – to the surprise of non-Alaskan surfers – the water isn't all that cold. The Japanese current pushes summer water temperatures into the mid-60s (around 18°C), while the rest of the surfing season they range from the mid-40s to the mid-50s (around 7°C to 13°C).

Surfers have also hit the beaches of Sitka and Kodiak. Alaska's 'Big Island' has an almost-endless number of places to surf, but the majority of surfers head to the beaches clustered around Pasagshak Point, 40 miles south of town.

An Alaskan-style surfin' safari means packing a wet suit with hood, booties and gloves, and often wearing a helmet. You'll also need to watch for brown bears, who often roam the beaches in search of washed-up crabs, salmon and other meals. Surfers have been known to encounter gray whales, sea otters, and even chunks of ice if they hit the waves too soon after the spring breakup.

Plan Your Trip

Cruising in Alaska

With a tightly packed jumble of islands, and landscape-molding glaciers sliding down mountainsides to kiss the ocean, Alaska's waterways hold an obvious allure. Add in the fact that many of Alaska's ports and cities aren't accessible by road, and you've got another reason to eschew terra firma and take to the high seas.

Pandemic-Era Cruising

COVID-19 restrictions decimated the cruise industry in 2020–21 (see p24). As of early 2022, the CDC was still posting a level-four travel-health notice for cruises, recommending all people, regardless of vaccination status, avoid traveling on ships.

However, these advisories are likely to change. Anticipating a relaxation, most major cruise lines are posting relatively normal schedules. Returning favorites include international giants Princess and Holland America Line, as well as smaller companies such as Lindblad Expeditions and UnCruise Adventures.

Cruising post-pandemic promises to be a little different than before, at least in the short term. Cruise companies were only accepting bookings from fully vaccinated passengers in 2022; international visitors also need proof of a negative COVID-19 test taken within 24 hours of departure (the CDC recommends US passengers also get tested).

Once on board, masks will be mandatory in communal indoor areas and plated meals will be served instead of buffets. Guests can also expect random temperature checks, health questionnaires, and further testing if or when the need arises.

Why Cruise?

Alaskan cruises allow people who might not otherwise have the opportunity (or inclination) to glimpse into a vast natural wilderness once only accessible to hard-nosed adventurers and explorers with piles of money and equipment. On top of this, it enables ordinary people to do it with a high degree of comfort and convenience. Trips that once took intrepid explorers and 19th-century gold-rush pioneers months, if not years, can now be shoehorned into a manageable two- to three-week itinerary taking in hundreds of miles of coastline.

On standard cruises, you'll disembark at a port most days for anywhere from four to eight hours, where you can bop around town, take in a hike or an excursion, or even a longer trip inland to places such as Denali National Park, Talkeetna or Eagle. You can also sit on deck and spot bald eagles hunting, humpback whales breaching and glaciers calving: not a bad sightseeing experience. On the smaller cruise lines, there will be more wildlife excursions and more stops.

Cruises aren't for everyone. If you hate all-inclusive resorts, rigidly organized tours or other carefully manufactured forms of travel, this type of vacation is probably not for you.

PORTS LESS VISITED

Petersburg Few large ships can navigate the Wrangell Narrows, and fewer still can dock in Petersburg's shallow harbor, meaning this wonderful Norwegian-flavored town only welcomes about two small ships a week in season.

Wrangell Rough-and-ready Wrangell is the antithesis of a cruise port. Good job too as it only gets about one cruise ship docking a week – and a small one at that.

Nome Although it's now included on the pioneering Northwest Passage cruises, this erstwhile gold-rush outpost still only gets a half-dozen cruise ships stopping in any given year.

Dutch Harbor The treeless outpost of the Aleutian Islands, with its Russian church and half-forgotten WWII history, gets a dozen small cruises ships stopping a year, plus twice-a-month visits from the MV *Tustumena* ferry.

Yakutat This tiny fishing town in the Gulf of Alaska gets just one cruise-boat call a year, the equally tiny *Silver Discoverer*, which briefly disgorges its 120 passengers.

There *is* an alternative. Backpackers, independent travelers and spendthrifts on shoestring budgets can hop on the Alaska Marine Highway ferry, which plies an almost-identical route up the Inside Passage. On board, you'll see the same sights as most cruisers, but you won't get a casino, heated pool, hot tub, all-you-can-eat buffet and you won't have to wear a name-badge.

When to Go

Cruises run from the beginning of May to late September. You will have the best weather in July and August, but for a bit less traffic and cheaper tickets consider taking a cruise in the shoulder seasons of early May and late September.

It's always colder than you expect. While you may get a few shorts-worthy days, it's worthwhile bringing several warm sweaters, a wool cap and a good waterproof jacket.

Picking Your Ship

Cruises in Alaska aren't just the preserve of retirees playing bingo on crowded sundecks. Sure, you can meet Mickey Mouse on a Disney cruise or stroll the deck with 3000 others on the *Emerald Princess*, but, for every aquatic skyscraper there's a smaller, cozier option. Some of the state's best and most adventurous cruises take place on boats carrying barely a dozen passengers that sail between little-visited ports, stopping off in wilderness areas in between.

Cruise Ships

Some of the world's largest cruise-line companies ply the waters of Alaska, including Princess, Norwegian and Holland America. Most of the bigger ships are pretty luxurious. However, these so-called resorts on the sea do have limitations. You won't be able to stop at as many places as you can on a smaller ship, and you'll be sharing your Alaska wilderness experience with up to 3000 other vacationers.

Most large cruises stop only in the major ports of call, and generally start from Vancouver or Seattle. Excursions range from heli-seeing trips and zipline tours to guided hikes, kayaks and day trips to inland attractions such as Denali National Park. Costs for Alaskan cruises average around $120 a night (per person), but that does not include your flight to the port of embarkation. You can save good money (sometimes as much as 50%) by hopping on a 'repositioning' cruise, which takes the boat back to its home port.

Check the small print about what's included in the price before you commit. Unless you're on a luxury cruise, you'll likely be paying extra for alcoholic beverages, shore excursions and tips. Then there's the spa, casino, gift shop and so on.

Here's how the big cruise companies break down:

Carnival (☎800-764-7419; www.carnival.com) Young people rule on these ships that aren't known for their environmental stewardship. The bonus: they're one of the cheapest options.

SUSTAINABLE CRUISING

While all travel causes certain environmental and cultural impacts, by their very size, cruise ships leave a heavy wake.

The Impact

Pollution A large cruise liner like the *Queen Mary* emits 1lb (0.45kg) of carbon dioxide per mile, while a long-haul flight releases about 0.6lb (0.27kg). In Alaska, an 11-day cruise from Seattle to Juneau on a small boat with around 100 guests will burn about 71 gallons of fuel per passenger, releasing some 0.77 tons of carbon into the air per passenger. The flight from Seattle to Juneau releases 0.17 tons of carbon per passenger. Cruise ships also release around 17% of total worldwide nitrogen-oxide emissions, and create around 50 tons of garbage on a one-week voyage. In 2013, the US Environmental Protection Agency estimated that cruise ships produce about 1 billion gallons of sewage a year.

Cultural impact While cruise lines generate much-needed money and jobs for their ports of call, thousands of people arriving at once can change the character of a town in a second. Big cruise ports such as Juneau and Ketchikan see six or seven cruise ships a day – that's around 15,000 people, or close to one million visitors in a five-month season. And with such short stays, there is little of that cultural interchange that makes travel an enriching endeavor for both tourist and 'townie.'

What You Can Do

The cruise industry notes it complies with international regulations, and adapts to stricter laws in places such as Alaska and the US west coast. As consumer pressure grows, more and more ships are being equipped with new wastewater treatment facilities, LED lighting and solar panels. In several Alaska ports (as well as San Francisco, Vancouver and Seattle) 'cold-ironing' allows ships to plug into local power supplies and avoid leaving the engine running while in port. Knowing that customers care about these things has an effect on cruise-ship operations. There are also organizations that review the environmental records of cruise lines and ships. These include the following:

Friends of the Earth (www.foe.org/cruisereportcard) Gives out grades for environmental impact.

US Centers for Disease Control & Prevention (www.cdc.gov) Follow the travel links to the well-regarded sanitation ratings for ships calling into US ports.

World Travel Awards (www.worldtravelawards.com) Annual awards for the 'World's Leading Green Cruise Line.'

Celebrity (☎877-202-4345; www.celebritycruises.com; 👪) Family-friendly and laid-back cruises on large 2000-plus-passenger ships.

Disney (☎800-951-3532; www.disneycruise.disney.go.com; 👪) Plenty of family fun and activities on a ship with good environmental credentials. Slightly pricier than other big-name favorites.

Holland America (☎877-932-4259; www.hollandamerica.com) One of the world's largest cruise companies and considered a classy option. It runs seven ships carrying 1500 to 2000 passengers in Alaska and owns the local Westmark Hotel chain.

Norwegian (☎866-234-7350; www.ncl.com) Many modern details make this a top pick for young couples.

Princess (☎800-774-6237; www.princess.com) The largest ship visiting Alaska is the 3082-capacity *Emerald Princess*, one of seven used by the company in the region. It also owns five plush hotels.

Regent Seven Seas Cruises (☎844-437-4368; www.rssc.com) Lauded as one of the most luxurious lines. Its two Alaska ships are smaller than average, carrying between 500 and 700 passengers.

Royal Caribbean (☎866-562-7625; www.royalcaribbean.com) Despite the name, it offers voyages to Alaska each summer on the ship *Radiance of the Seas*.

FON THACHAKUL/SHUTTERSTOCK ©

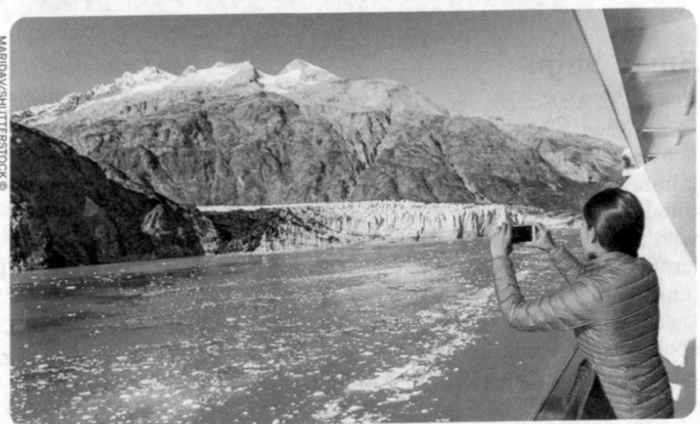

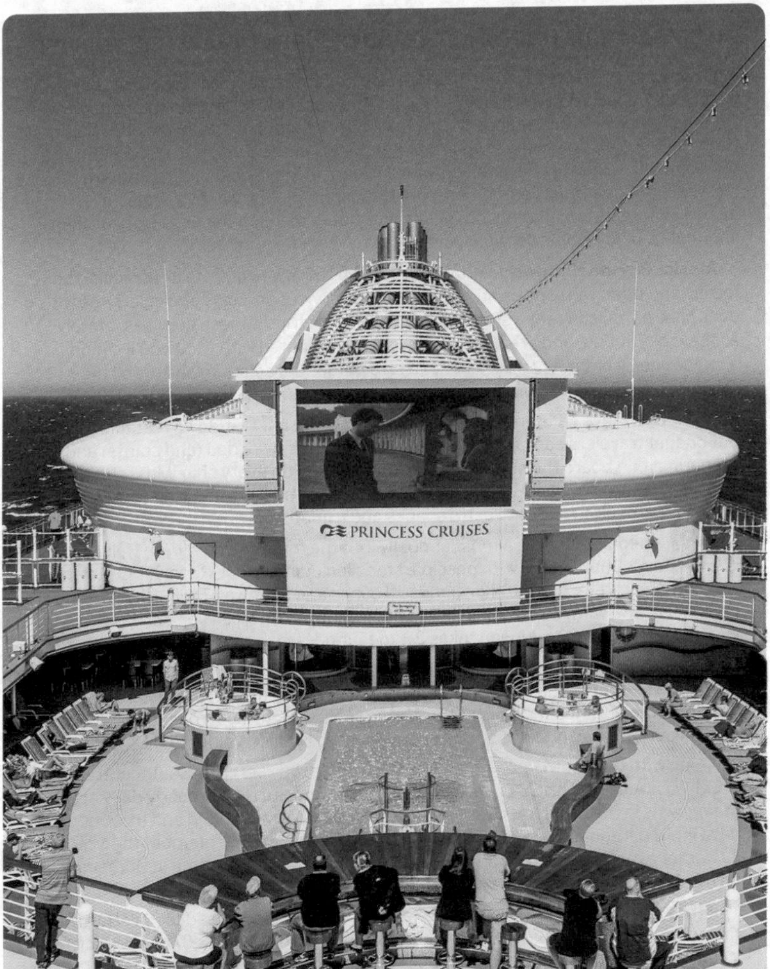

MARIDAV/SHUTTERSTOCK ©

Top: Princess cruise ship

Bottom: Cruising Glacier Bay (p125)

ALASKA MARINE HIGHWAY: THE INDEPENDENT TRAVELER'S CRUISE

Alaska's extensive ferry system has many potential descriptions: 'long-distance water bus,' 'poor-person's cruise liner,' and 'the world's most spectacular public-transportation network' among them. Taking passengers up the Inside Passage from Bellingham, WA, in the lower 48 to Ketchikan and beyond, the unsophisticated but comfortable ferries never stray far from land, meaning you are treated to a real life *National Geographic* documentary of tumbling glaciers, weeping waterfalls, misty rainforests and crenelated mountains, not to mention the possibility of sighting whales, bald eagles, sea lions and, if you're very lucky, bears.

Alaska Marine Highway (AMHS; ☎800-642-0066; www.dot.state.ak.us/amhs) runs ferries equipped with observation decks, food services, lounges and solariums with deck chairs. You can rent a stateroom for overnight trips – these aren't as 'stately' as they may sound, and are downright spartan compared with what you'll get on a cruise liner – but many travelers head straight for the solarium and unroll their sleeping bags on deck chairs, camping out in the covered, open-air rear deck.

The ferries have cafeterias or snack bars and a few have sit-down restaurants, but budget travelers can save money by bringing their own food (and spirits) and preparing it on board the ship. There are microwaves on every ship. Most ships have onboard naturalists who give a running commentary on the trip. Bring your headphones, warm clothes, some extra snacks and a good book.

Ferry schedules change almost annually, but the routes stretch from Bellingham, WA, to the Aleutian Chain, with possible stops including Prince Rupert, BC, Ketchikan, Wrangell, Petersburg, Sitka, Juneau, Haines and Skagway. From Haines you can drive north and within a couple of hours pick up the Alcan (Alaska-Canada) Hwy. A trip from Bellingham to Juneau takes 2½ to four days, depending on the route.

Nine ships ply the waters of Southeast Alaska and twice a month the MV *Kennicott* makes a special run from Southeast Alaska across the Gulf of Alaska to Whittier. This links the Southeast routes of the Alaska Marine Highway ferries to the Southcentral portion that includes such ports as Homer, Kodiak, Valdez and Cordova.

Along with the Southeast, the Alaska Marine Highway services Southcentral and Southwest Alaska, with 35 ports in the system. There are ferries nearly daily at the main towns in the Southeast, while routes in Prince William Sound and the Aleutians have limited frequency. Twice a month from May through to September the MV *Tustumena* makes a special run along the Alaska Peninsula, starting in Homer and terminating in Dutch Harbor on the Aleutian Islands.

If the Alaska Marine Highway ferries are full in Bellingham, head to Port Hardy at the north end of Vancouver Island, where **BC Ferries** (☎888-223-3779; www.bcferries.com) leave for Prince Rupert, BC. From this Canadian city you can transfer to the Alaska Marine Highway and continue to Southeast Alaska on ferries not as heavily in demand as those in Bellingham.

Small Ships

Just 3% of Alaska cruisers take a small-ship voyage. While you'll have tighter quarters, bumpier seas and fewer entertainment options than on the big boys, these vessels offer better chances of seeing wildlife. There will also be more land and kayak excursions, onboard naturalists (most of the time), good food, a more casual atmosphere (you can leave that blue sports coat at the office where it belongs) and a more intimate portrait of Alaska.

These boats sleep anywhere from 12 to 100 and are more likely to depart from within Alaska. While this is probably your best bet if you are looking to match comfort with quality and authentic experience, it does come with a steeper price tag: anywhere from $400 to $1200 a night.

Each small cruise ship is different. Here's a breakdown of some of our favorites:

Adventure Life Voyages (☎800-344-6118; www.adventure-life.com; per person 9-day cruise $3555-4965) Specializes in top-end trips up the Inside Passage. Carries 42 to 74 passengers, with some unique activities including snorkeling and paddleboarding.

AdventureSmith Explorations (☎877-620-2875; www.adventuresmithexplorations.com; per person $1595-10,900) This company offsets its carbon emissions and focuses on learning and adventure cruises in Southeast Alaska aboard its fleet of small boats (accommodating from 40 to 50 people). The boats have kayaks and small skiffs for numerous excursions that include everything from kayaking in Glacier Bay National Park to wildlife-watching near Tracy Arm, the ABC Islands, Icy Straight, Misty Fiords and Frederick Sound. Most trips depart from Juneau.

Discovery Voyages (☎800-324-7602; www.discoveryvoyages.com; per person $2500-7150) Small 12-berth yacht that specializes in wildlife and photography tours of Prince William Sound – including stops in quiet ports like Cordova – an area few cruise ships visit. The yacht's small size enables it to negotiate narrow fjords and land in wilderness areas for hiking and kayaking. It has a good environmental record.

Lindblad National Geographic Expeditions (☎800-397-3348; www.expeditions.com; per person from $8990) Backed by *National Geographic*, Lindblad offers kayaking, wilderness walks, onboard naturalists and Zodiac excursions during eight-day cruises in the Southeast. Many trips include the airfare from Seattle and take visitors from Juneau through the Inside Passage. Plus you get the unique opportunity of pretending to be a *National Geographic* explorer for the week.

Un-Cruise Adventures (☎888-862-8881; www.un-cruise.com; per person $2995-8095) Offers themed seven- to 21-day cruises, carrying 22 to 86 passengers, that focus on whale-watching, Glacier Bay, wildlife-watching or adventure travel. The small boats (the company calls them yachts) have modern, elegant staterooms, and a naturalist is on board to teach you the ways of the Alaska wilderness. Most trips depart from Juneau, but one leaves from Seattle.

Picking Your Route

Inside Passage

This is the classic route, sailing from Seattle or Vancouver. The 'Great Land' coastal views don't start until Prince Rupert Island. Most trips stop in Ketchikan – with about as many bars as people and some fine totem poles – then continue to Juneau, home to a great glacier and heli-seeing tours; Skagway, a gold-rush port with good hiking close to town; and the granddaddy attraction of Alaska cruises, Glacier Bay, where you'll see 11 tidewater glaciers spilling their icy wares into the sea. The pros: this is classic Alaska and the coast is rarely (if ever) out of sight. The cons: busy ports and ships following a more well-trammeled path sometimes kill the wilderness feel.

Gulf of Alaska

This trip includes the Inside Passage but then continues to the Gulf of Alaska, with stops in Seward, the Hubbard Glacier and Whittier in Prince William Sound. While you get a broader picture of coastal Alaska on this one-way cruise and reap the benefit of pulling into some quieter ports, it also comes at a price, as you'll generally need to arrange flights from separate start and end points.

Bering Sea & Northwest Passage

These trips are more expensive and generally focus on natural and cultural history. People that enjoy learning on their vacations will like this trip, with stops in the Pribilof Islands, Nome and, on the really expensive cruises, King Island.

Since the mid-2010s some ships have started to ply the Northwest Passage (now partly ice-free in August and early September), sailing all the way to Greenland or, in some cases, New York. In 2016 the first luxury cruise liner, the *Crystal Serenity*, began offering a 32-day Anchorage–New York cruise with stops in Kodiak, Dutch Harbor and Nome en route. Prices start at $22,000. European cruise companies such as Ponant and Hapag-Lloyd send smaller boats on Northwest Passage tours, stopping in Nome and Utqiaġvik (Barrow).

'Cruisetours'

These trips give you the chance to get off the boat for about half of your journey. Most begin with the Inside Passage cruise, then head out on a tour bus or (even better) the Alaska Railroad, with stops in Talkeetna, Denali National Park, Fairbanks, Eagle or the Copper River. Big cruise companies such as Princess and Holland America have all-inclusive hotels in these destinations (basically cruise ships without the rocking).

Plan Your Trip

Travel with Children

Everybody is a kid in Alaska. Whether it's a sitting by a stream full of bright red salmon or watching a bald eagle winging its way across an open sky, encounters with nature's wonders will captivate five-year-olds just as much as their parents.

Best Regions for Kids

Anchorage & Around

Packed with parks, urban salmon streams, bike paths and plenty of artificial amusements. Head south to ride the Alyeska Tram or take the whistle-stop train out to Spencer Glacier for unique ways into the backcountry.

Kenai Peninsula

Ice-blue rivers for floating and fishing, boat tours that cruise right up to calving glaciers and sea-lion rookeries, and wilderness cabins for roughing it – but not too much.

Denali & the Interior

A combination of intensely wild lands and the distractions of 'Glitter Gulch' or Fairbanks, the Interior entertains with big animals, huge mountains, hot springs and even an amusement park. Plus there's pizza readily available.

Southeast

Gold mines and glaciers, whales and salmon, hiking trails and boat tours: the Southeast has a little bit of everything but on an Alaskan-sized scale.

Alaska for Kids

The best that Alaska has to offer cannot be found in stuffy museums or amusement parks filled with heart-pounding rides. It's outdoor adventure, wildlife and scenery on a grand scale, attractions and activities that will intrigue the entire family – whether you're a kid or a parent.

Outdoor Activities

If your family enjoys the outdoors, Alaska can be a relatively affordable place once you've arrived. A campsite is cheap compared to a motel room, and hiking, backpacking and wildlife-watching are free. Even fishing is free for children, since anglers under 16 don't need a fishing license in Alaska.

The key to any Alaskan hike is to match it to your child's ability and level of endurance. It's equally important to select one that has an interesting aspect to it – a glacier, ruined gold mine, waterfalls or a remote cabin to stop for lunch.

Paddling with children involves a greater risk than hiking due to the frigid temperature of most water in Alaska. You simply don't want to tip at any cost. Flat, calm water should be the rule. Needless to say, all rentals should come with paddles and life jackets that fit your child. If in doubt, hire a guide to go along with you.

Children marvel at watching wildlife in its natural habitat but may not always have the patience for a long wait before something pops out of the woods. In July and August, however, you can count on seeing a lot of fish in a salmon stream, a wide variety of marine life in tidal pools, and bald eagles where the birds are known to congregate. Marine wildlife boat tours work out better than many park shuttles because, let's face it, a boat trip is a lot more fun than a bus ride. Nature tours that are done in vans are also ideal for children as they stop often and usually include short walks.

Eating Out

Like elsewhere in the USA, most Alaskan restaurants welcome families and tend to cater to children, with high chairs, kids' menus of smaller sizes and reduced prices, and waiters quick with a rag when somebody spills their drink. Upscale restaurants where an infant would be frowned upon are limited to a handful of places in Anchorage. Salmon bakes are a fun, casual and colorful way to introduce Alaska's seafood, especially since they often come with corn and potatoes – familiar items at any barbecue.

Children's Highlights

Hiking Trails

Flattop Mountain Trail (p153) Anchorage's most popular family day hike.

Mt Dewey Trail (p88) Short grunt up steps and over boardwalks to the top of a wooded hill above Wrangell.

Perseverance Trail (p76) A path into the heart of Juneau's mining history.

Park Entrance Area (p278) Around the entrance to Denali National Park lies an assortment of short, safe trails, including the Horseshoe Lake Trail leading to an oxbow lake where moose are often seen.

For a Rainy Day

Anchorage Museum (p156) Tons of stuff for kids, including an Imaginarium Discovery Center and planetarium.

Alaska Sealife Center (p227) Diving seabirds, swimming sea lions and a tide-pool touch tank are found in Seward's marine research center.

Dimond Park Aquatic Center (☎907-586-2782; www.juneau.org/parkrec; 3045 Riverside Dr; adult/child $8/3; ⏰6am-10:30am Mon, 6am-8pm

NATIONAL PARKS FOR KIDS

America's national park system offers numerous activities specifically geared toward children, and many of them are enshrined in the 'Junior Ranger Program.' This program, designed for kids between the ages of five and 12, provides activity books on parks, which children complete to receive a sew-on patch and certificate.

Parks with active Junior Ranger Programs in Alaska include the following:

- Denali National Park & Preserve (p272)
- Wrangell-St Elias National Park (p327)
- Glacier Bay National Park & Preserve (p125)
- Sitka National Historical Park (p99)
- Klondike Gold Rush National Historical Park (p139)

Of all Alaska's parks, Denali is probably the best set up for kids. The Murie Science & Learning Center (p280) has a number of hands-on exhibits suitable for children, and a few of the 'Denali-ology' day courses are specifically designed for families with younger children. Denali Education Center (p281) also has day and multiday youth programs ranging from 'bug camps' (for budding entomologists) to extended backpacking trips. Look out for free 'Discovery Packs,' available at the visitor center, which include a binder filled with scientific activities and also the tools needed to carry out experiments. Among other fun things, kids can test the water quality of nearby streams and make plaster casts of animal tracks. Other kid-friendly Denali attractions are sled-dog demonstrations, nightly campground talks and a daily ranger-led hike to Horseshoe Lake.

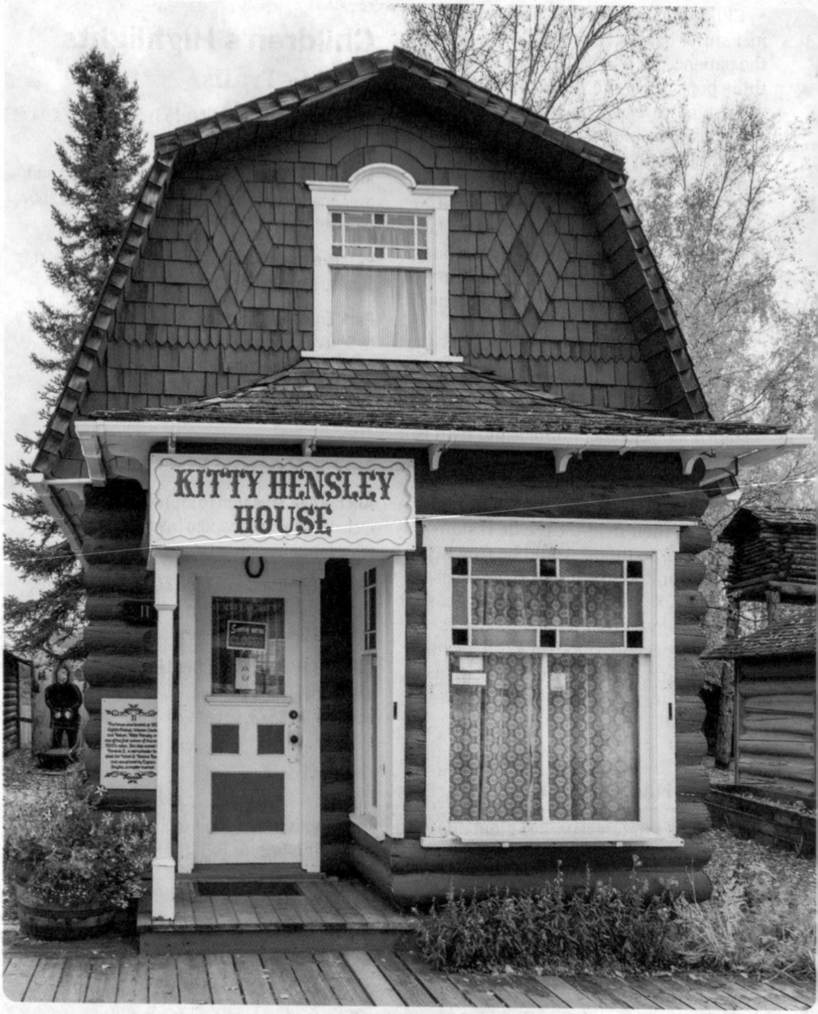

PHOTORADNC/SHUTTERSTOCK ©

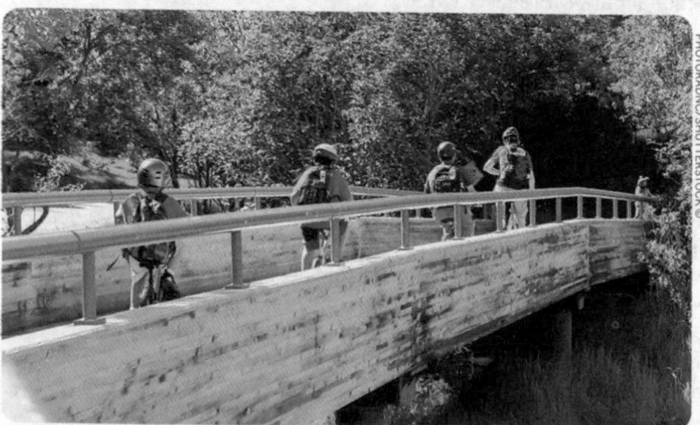

Top: Historic building in Pioneer Park (p301), Fairbanks

Bottom: Cyclists on the Tony Knowles Coastal Trail (p160), Anchorage

Tue-Fri, 9am-6pm Sat, noon-6pm Sun;) Flume slides, bubble benches, tumble buckets and interactive water sprays in Juneau.

Sitka Sound Science Center (p101) Five aquariums, three touch tanks and a working hatchery.

Outdoor Fun

Pioneer Park (p301) Train rides, salmon bakes and genuine pioneer history entertain the offspring in Fairbanks.

Mendenhall Glacier (p110) Fascinating and easily accessible natural feature that's capable of dropping the jaws of any age group.

Sitka Sound (p104) Sheltered waters, plenty of wooded islands and a good local guiding company make this one of Alaska's best family sea-kayaking spots.

Petroglyph Beach (p87) Search for ancient rock carvings and sea life at low tide in Wrangell.

Planning

When to Go

Summer is by far the best time to visit: the odds of spotting wildlife are good, salmon are swimming upstream, hiking trails are free of snow and the weather is as good as it's going to get. Crowds and lines are rarely a problem, unless everyone is stopped and staring at the same large mammal, so traveling during high season doesn't pose too much of a problem crowd-wise. Festivals abound during the summer, and most are family friendly.

A lot of Alaska's tourist-oriented businesses close down between October and April.

Note that between May and September you're going to have to deal with bugs. A lot of them.

Accommodations

Many independently owned accommodations and lodges in small towns won't offer amenities such as rollaway beds or cribs, but chain motels will. If you absolutely need a crib at night, either check in advance or bring your own travel crib.

Sleeping under the stars – or Alaska's midnight sun – can be a memorable experience and is easy on the budget. Numerous campgrounds are connected to the road system, which means you won't have to lug heavy backpacks around. For toddlers and children younger than five years, the best way to escape into the wilderness is to rent a wilderness cabin. Many are reached by floatplane, an exciting start to any adventure for a child. The rustic cabins offer secure lodging in a remote place where children often have a good chance of seeing wildlife or catching fish. Cabins usually sleep between four and eight.

Transportation

Many national car companies have safety seats for toddlers and young children for about $10 extra per day. Unfortunately, the smaller, independent agencies away from the airports, which generally offer better rental rates, often do not have car seats.

One of the best ways to see Alaska with toddlers or young children is on a cruise ship. The larger the ship, the more family amenities and activities it will offer. Disney (p48) cruises serve Alaska. Smaller cruise ships, those that hold fewer than 200 people, do not work as well as they are usually geared more toward adventurous couples. But the Alaska Marine Highway (p50) System is well suited to families. Children have the space to move around, and large ferries such as the MV *Columbia*, MV *Kennicott,* MV *Malaspina* and MV *Matanuska* feature both current movies and ranger programs on marine life, birds and glaciers.

On the **Alaska Railroad** (800-544-0552; www.alaskarailroad.com) children can walk between passenger carriages and spend time taking in the scenery from special domed viewing cars.

For all-round information and advice, check out Lonely Planet's *Travel with Children*.

What to Pack

You'll be able to find almost anything that you forgot to pack in the larger towns. The most important thing to remember is layers – you simply can't pack warm enough. High-quality outerwear, especially rain gear, is important on any hike or camping trip. Don't forget a hat. Finally, sunscreen and insect repellent are indispensable.

Regions at a Glance

The regions you visit in Alaska will depend on your budget and time. The bulk of travelers stick to the few areas that roads reach, as getting off the road can be pricey and plenty of excellent sites are within range of road and ferry, not to mention tourist infrastructure.

The majority of tourists visit Southeast Alaska on a cruise or the Alaska Marine Highway Ferry, fly into Anchorage and explore the Kenai Peninsula or head up to visit Denali National Park. A smaller number fly to remote streams and lodges for salmon fishing, bear-watching or simply an epic river float.

Juneau & the Southeast

Wildlife
Glaciers
Hiking

Marine Life

The sea is the lifeblood of Southeast Alaska, and it teems with life. You'll rarely get a better chance to spot whales, seals, Dall's porpoises, sea otters and more.

Rivers of Ice

The massive Mendenhall Glacier outside Juneau is the most visited in Alaska, and for good reason: easily accessible, the half-mile face stretches in a glowing line across an iceberg-studded lake. Further north, Glacier Bay National Park & Preserve is the best place to witness calving tidewater glaciers.

Rainforest Walks

Hiking through the Tongass National Forest or up Mt Roberts, behind Juneau, in the green, sweet-smelling trees can be a divine experience, if a soggy one. Excellent trails meander out of almost every town, offering glimpses into an amazing rainforest ecosystem.

p60

Anchorage & Around

Hiking
Urban culture
Cycling

The Front Range

Anchorage is backed by the Chugach Mountains, a backyard playground for the state's largest city. Flattop Mountain is the most popular climb, but you can delve into the backcountry or simply take a boardwalk stroll at Potter Marsh.

Bistros & Boutiques

No longer a frontier tent city, Anchorage now serves up fancy cocktails and designer duds, and is home to a world-class museum. Hit the trails, then hit the shower and enjoy an evening on the town.

Rolling Around

With over 120 miles of paved trails, most of them in urban greenbelts, Anchorage is a great place to explore by bike. If you fancy mountain biking, head to Girdwood, where you'll find an excellent mountain-bike course.

p150

Prince William Sound

Kayaking
Bird-watching
Glaciers

Sea Adventures in the Sound

A 15,000-mile cirque with only three small towns to its name, Prince William Sound is packed with quiet coves, rainy islands, tidewater glaciers and remote wilderness cabins. Kayaking trips from Valdez, Cordova and Whittier are all worthwhile.

Delta Day Trips

The flat, reedy Copper River Delta is heaven for migratory birds and equally celestial for budding ornithologists, who can roam with their binoculars along more than a half-dozen hiking trails originating from the Copper River Hwy. There's even an annual bird festival.

Massive Calves

Outside Valdez, the giant Columbia Glacier emits huge chunks of ice, some that release under water and pop to the surface without warning. Outside Cordova, the colossal Childs Glacier rumbles louder than thunder as it releases pieces of ice the size of small houses.

p192

Kenai Peninsula

Paddling
Angling
Road-tripping

Glacial Fjords

Kenai Fjords National Park, outside Seward, and Kachemak Bay, outside Homer, are two excellent kayaking spots, with opportunities for seeing marine life, access to remote hiking trails and cabins, and accessible tidewater glaciers.

Combat Fishing

The Kenai Peninsula is where 'combat fishing' is at its fiercest; here hundreds of anglers lined shoulder to shoulder pull fat, meaty salmon out of icy blue water. The Russian and Kenai Rivers are the most popular, but are by no means the only places to hook a salmon.

Highways & Byways

Two main roads splinter across the peninsula, which is larger than Maryland. Running almost the entire length of both is winding, two-lane scenery overload, with mountains, glaciers and rivers rolling by outside your window.

p216

Denali & the Interior

Mountains
Rivers
Northern lights

Floating & Fishing

Giant mountains have giant glaciers, which in turn create giant rivers, filled with salmon, or perfect for bobbing down in a raft. You can choose between a seemingly endless number of these waterways. The most popular are near Talkeetna and Denali National Park.

Rainbows in the Sky

It doesn't really get dark around Fairbanks during the summer, but when it does you're in for a laser show à la Mama Nature. The northern lights are actually out over 300 days a year here. Head to Chena Hot Springs for an awesome soak and a show.

The Big One(s)

This is the home of North America's tallest mountain: the incomparable Denali. But Foraker and Hunter mountains, perennial bridesmaids to Denali, are stunners too, as is Mt St Elias to the southeast.

p266

Kodiak, Katmai & Southwest Alaska

Bears
Wilderness
History

World's Biggest Bruins

Kodiak is home to the world's largest bear, the Kodiak brown bear. It also has the highest concentration of these mighty creatures. In Katmai National Park & Preserve, grizzlies snap salmon as the fish jump up a waterfall, mere feet from where you stand.

Wide Open Spaces

The National Park Service's least visited outpost (Aniakchak) is found here, as well as the astounding Valley of Ten Thousand Smokes. There are very few developed trails and getting to these spots requires pricey flights, but the scenery and satisfaction are worth every dollar.

Alaska Natives & WWII

Head out to the Aleutian Chain for forgotten history: you'll see bunkers, pillboxes, Quonset huts and more, all remnants of WWII. Equally intriguing is the Alaska Native history, which is particularly accessible in Unalaska.

p333

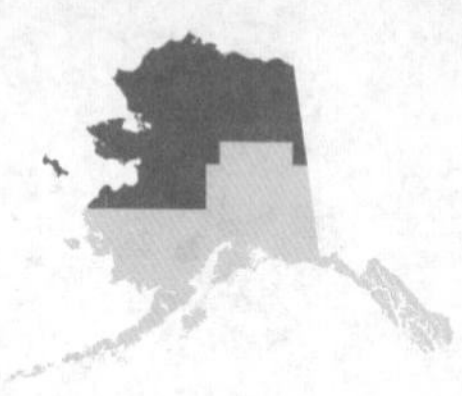

The Bush

Wilderness
Culture
Wildlife

Untrodden Tundra

Here, places like Gates of the Arctic National Park & Preserve don't have trails or even visitor facilities. The Dalton Hwy scrapes through the Brooks Range and on to the North Slope, through mind-boggling space.

Small Towns & Villages

Small Alaska Native villages dot the Bush, some connected by the Yukon River; Kotzebue serves as a hub for many of these. Nome emits a Wild West vibe: a gold-rush town and the end of the Iditarod Trail that sits like an exclamation mark at the end of America.

Musk Ox & Caribou

The herd of porcupine caribou, whose calving grounds are in the Arctic National Wildlife Refuge, is a stunning sight to behold. Other arctic animals in the region are musk ox, outside Nome, and polar bears, near Utqiaġvik (Barrow).

p362

On the Road

Juneau & the Southeast

Includes ➡

Best Places to Eat

- Ludvig's Bistro (p106)
- Rookery (p119)
- Salty Pantry (p96)
- Saffron (p119)

Best Places to Sleep

- Gustavus Inn (p128)
- Alaska's Capital Inn (p118)
- Inn at Creek Street – New York Hotel (p79)
- Silverbow Inn (p118)
- Stikine Inn (p91)

Why Go?

Southeast Alaska is so *un-Alaska*. While much of the state is a treeless expanse of land with a layer of permafrost, the Panhandle is a slender, long rainforest that stretches 540 miles from Icy Bay, near Yakutat, south to Portland Canal and is filled with ice-blue glaciers, rugged snowcapped mountains, towering Sitka spruce and a thousand islands known as the Alexander Archipelago.

Before WWII, the Southeast was Alaska's heart and soul, and Juneau was not only the capital but the state's largest city. Today the region is characterized by big trees and small towns. Each community here has its own history and character: from Norwegian-influenced Petersburg to Russian-tinted Sitka. You can feel the gold fever in Skagway and see a dozen glaciers near Juneau. Each town is unique and none of them is connected to another by road. Jump on the state ferry or book a cruise and discover the idiosyncrasies.

When to Go

Juneau

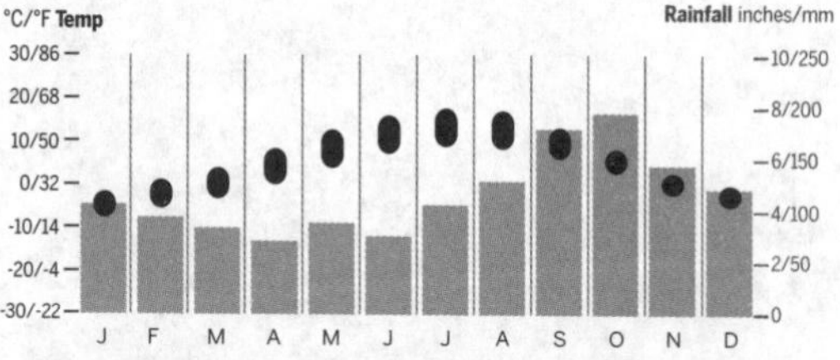

May The sunniest month in this rainy region, with better prices than the following month.

Aug Alpine trails are snow-free; bears are at salmon streams everywhere.

Sep A bit rainy, but the crowds and high prices are gone.

Mendenhall Glacier (p110)

Juneau & the Southeast Highlights

❶ **Misty Fiords National Monument** (p83) Gliding quietly in a kayak through the steep-sided fjords of this majestic wilderness area.

❷ **Chilkoot Trail** (p70) Following this historic trail across two countries, spectacular landscapes and scattered remnants of the Klondike gold rush.

❸ **Glacier Bay National Park** (p125) Watching out for whales, bears and floating icebergs the size of houses in the Southeast's largest national park.

❹ **Haines** (p128) Enjoying a craft beer or whiskey after a day of hiking in one of Alaska's most authentic small towns.

❺ **Sitka National Historical Park** (p99) Going back to where Alaska's colonial history began in Russian- and Tlingit-flavored Sitka.

❻ **Mendenhall Glacier** (p110) Hiking near, paddling up to, walking on, or flying over this immense ice floe not a dozen miles outside Juneau.

❼ **Ketchikan** (p73) Appreciating the iconic totem poles and rich Alaska Native culture in the museums and parks around Alaska's 'first city'.

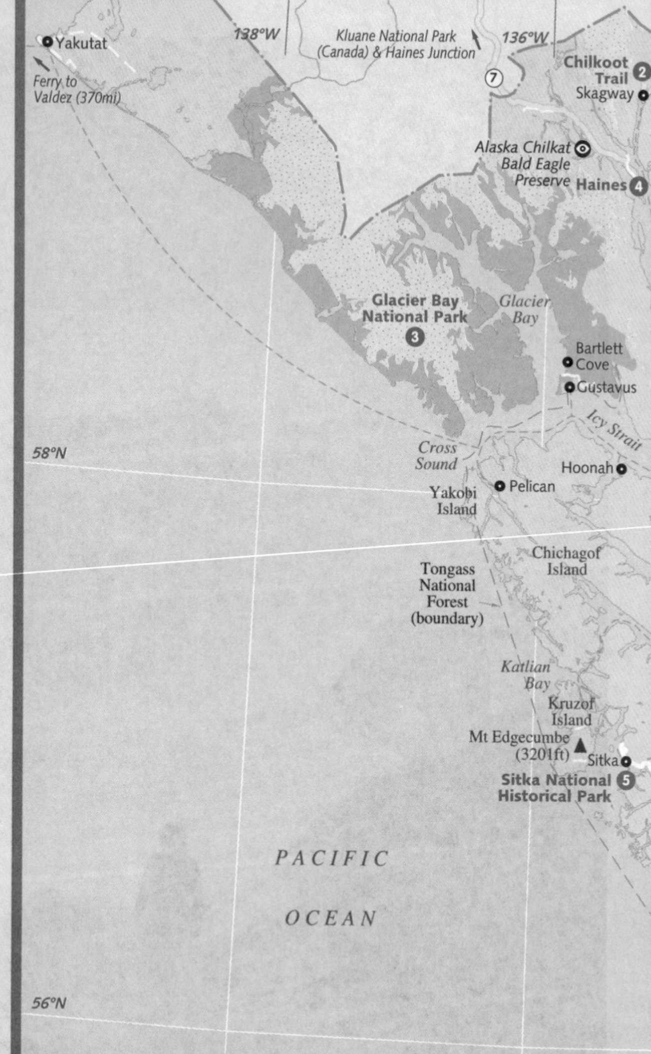

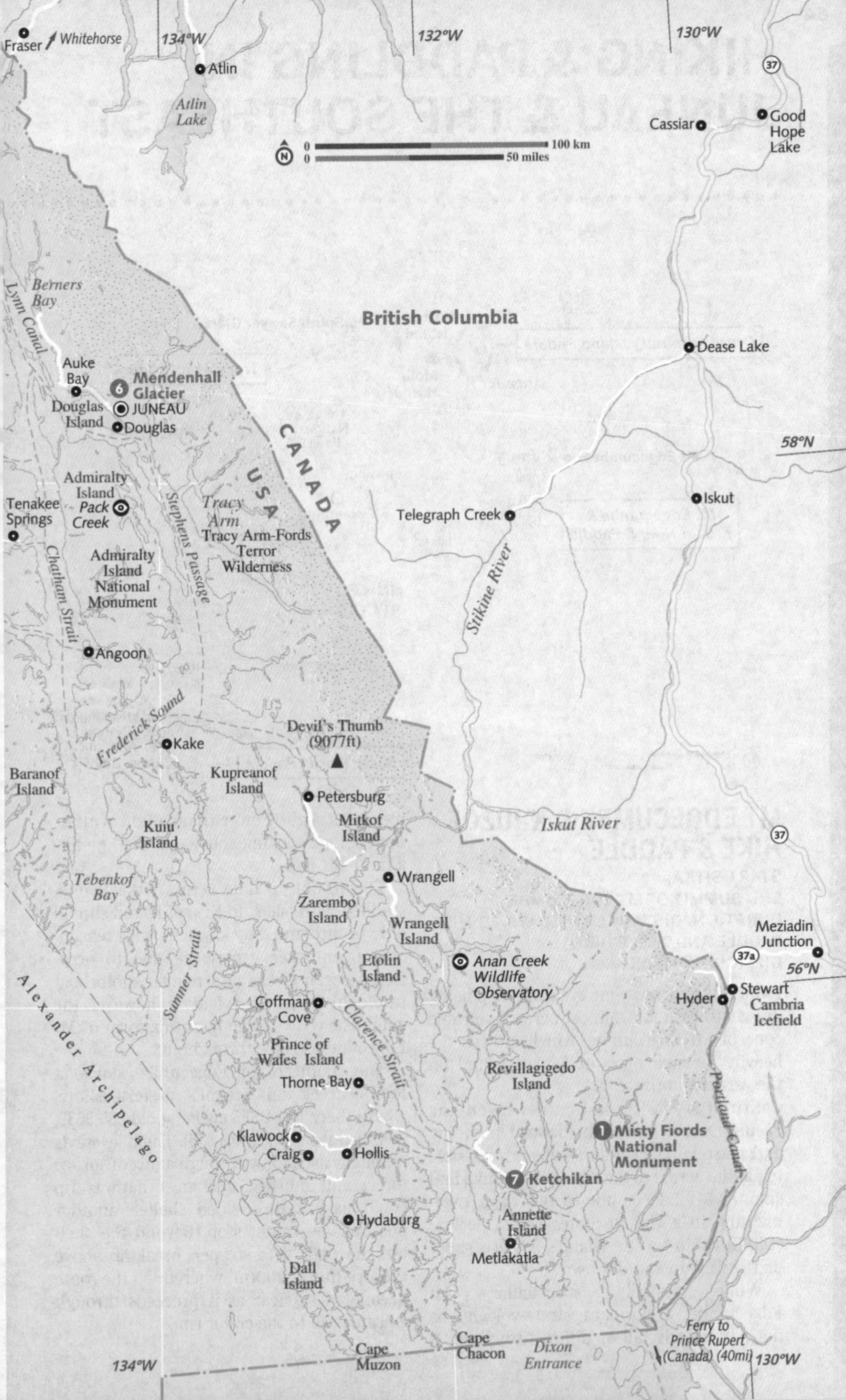

Fraser
Whitehorse
134°W
132°W
130°W
Atlin
Atlin Lake
37
Cassiar
Good Hope Lake
0 100 km
0 50 miles
British Columbia
Dease Lake
Berners Bay
Lynn Canal
Auke Bay
6 Mendenhall Glacier
JUNEAU
Douglas Island
Douglas
CANADA
USA
58°N
Admiralty Island
Pack Creek
Tenakee Springs
Stephens Passage
Tracy Arm
Tracy Arm-Fords Terror Wilderness
Telegraph Creek
Iskut
Admiralty Island National Monument
Chatham Strait
Stikine River
Angoon
Frederick Sound
Devil's Thumb (9077ft)
Kake
Baranof Island
Kupreanof Island
Petersburg
Mitkof Island
Iskut River
37
Kuiu Island
Tebenkof Bay
Wrangell
Zarembo Island
Wrangell Island
Etolin Island
Anan Creek Wildlife Observatory
Meziadin Junction
37a
56°N
Stewart
Hyder
Cambria Icefield
Summer Strait
Alexander Archipelago
Coffman Cove
Clarence Strait
Prince of Wales Island
Thorne Bay
Revillagigedo Island
Portland Canal
1 Misty Fiords National Monument
Klawock
Craig
Hollis
7 Ketchikan
Hydaburg
Annette Island
Metlakatla
Dall Island
Cape Muzon
Cape Chacon
Dixon Entrance
Ferry to Prince Rupert (Canada) (40mi)
134°W
130°W

HIKING & PADDLING IN JUNEAU & THE SOUTHEAST

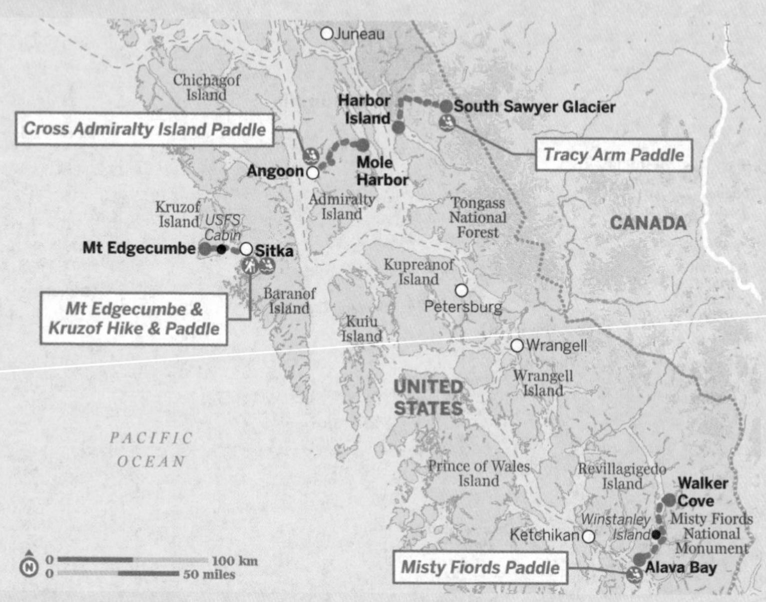

MT EDGECUMBE & KRUZOF HIKE & PADDLE

START SITKA
END SUMMIT OF MT EDGECUMBE
DURATION/DISTANCE TWO DAYS/10-MILE PADDLE AND 7-MILE HIKE
DIFFICULTY MEDIUM

From Sitka harbor your eye can't help being drawn toward the almost-perfect volcanic cone of Mt Edgecumbe, which crowns the heavily forested mass of Kruzof Island on the western horizon.

Kruzof is Alaska's last barrier before the Pacific Ocean, and with forward planning and reasonable kayaking skills, it's possible to paddle across to the island from Sitka and summit Mt Edgecumbe in two days, overnighting in a United States Forest Service (USFS) cabin on the island's eastern shore on the way up and/or down.

While suitably spectacular, Mt Edgecumbe, a dormant strata-volcano, is not particularly tall or difficult to climb. It measures slightly more than 3000ft with its upper slopes poking above the tree line like a mini–Mt Fuji.

The 10-mile paddle across Sitka Sound, studded with islets, to Kruzof Island should only be attempted by kayakers with reasonable open-water experience due to occasional ocean swells and regular motorboat traffic. In terms of navigation, however, the going is easy with the haunting form of Mt Edgecumbe visible throughout.

The trailhead for Edgecumbe starts at Fred's Creek on Kruzof's eastern shore, where there is a **USFS cabin** (☎518-885-3639; www.recreation.gov; cabins $55). The hike starts gradually ascending through a mix of spruce forest and muskeg. Just over halfway up you'll pass a three-sided shelter, another potential overnight stop. Beyond the shelter, the path gets steeper, breaking above the tree line at 2000ft, whereupon the route becomes less clear as it proceeds through volcanic ash to the crater rim.

There's no better place in North America for a wild and adventurous combination of hiking and kayaking than the thickly forested Alexander Archipelago.

MISTY FIORDS PADDLE

START ALAVA BAY
END WALKER COVE
DURATION/DISTANCE THREE TO FOUR DAYS/40 MILES
DIFFICULTY MEDIUM, OPEN WATER

The Misty Fiords National Monument encompasses 3594 sq miles of wilderness and lies between two impressive fjords – Behm Canal (117 miles long) and Portland Canal (72 miles long). The two natural canals give the preserve its extraordinarily deep and long fjords with sheer granite walls that rise thousands of feet out of the water. Misty Fiords is well named – annual rainfall is 14ft.

The destinations for many kayakers are the smaller but impressive fjords of Walker Cove and Punchbowl Cove in Rudyerd Bay, off Behm Canal. Dense spruce-hemlock rainforest is the most common vegetation type throughout the monument, and sea lions, harbor seals, brown and black bears, mountain goats and bald eagles can all be seen.

Misty Fiords has 15 USFS cabins, but only two – Alava Bay and **Winstanley Island** (☎ 515-885-3639; www.recreation.gov; cabins $55), both in Behm Canal – are directly on the water, meaning kayakers should also be prepared for some wilderness camping.

An alternative option is to use the Winstanley Island cabin as a central base and make short day forays out into the surrounding waters.

You can't do this trip without good rain gear and a backpacker's stove – wood in the monument is often too wet for campfires. Be prepared for extended rain periods and make sure all your gear is sealed in plastic bags.

Experienced kayakers can paddle straight out of Ketchikan to Alava Bay at the entrance to Misty Fiords (23 miles/seven to 12 hours) but most paddlers arrange to be dropped off either at Alava Bay at the mouth of the fjord, or at Winstanley Island, halfway in. Southeast Exposure (p77) in Ketchikan rents kayaks from $45 per day and has a water-taxi service costing $300 per hour (for up to eight people). Alava Bay is a two-hour transfer, Winstanley is three hours.

A reasonable intermediate trip would be to paddle from Alava Bay to Walker Cove with stops at Winstanley Island and Punchbowl Cove, a journey of around 40 miles, excluding side trips.

TRACY ARM PADDLE

START SOUTH SAWYER GLACIER
END HARBOR ISLAND
DURATION/DISTANCE TWO TO THREE DAYS/30 MILES
DIFFICULTY EASY, OPEN WATER

Tracy Arm is a 30-mile-long fjord in the Tracy Arm-Fords Terror Wilderness, a 653,000-acre preserve fed by two calving glaciers and guarded by imposing granite walls.

The 'Arm' makes a rugged two- to three-day (30-mile) paddle for people with reasonable kayaking experience. Calm water is the norm due to the protection of the steep granite walls. Camping is limited, however; the best spot deep inside the fjord is on tiny Sawyer Island (note: there's no fresh water source here) at the point where the North and South Sawyer Glaciers branch off. As you paddle west out of the fjord, the cliffs and icy surrounds diminish meaning viable campsites become more common. Note, unlike Misty Fiords further south, there are no USFS cabins in Tracy Arm.

The magnificence of the fjord has one notable downside – the area attracts copious cruise ships, tour boats and flightseeing planes, which can detract somewhat from the wilderness experience, though by late afternoon, most have gone home.

Most kayakers arrange for a deep-water drop-off at the head of the fjord close to the calving South Sawyer Glacier. From here it's possible to make a quick side trip to the North Sawyer Glacier where more deep-blue chunks of ice are sent crashing into the water.

Sawyer Island is a good place to camp on the first night with a second night spent further west. There's a good mossy campsite next to a creek at the point where the Arm swings south (sometimes known as 'Elbow Camp'). An ideal pickup point at the end of day three is Harbor Island in Holkham Bay at the mouth of Tracy Arm.

The departure point for Tracy Arm is Juneau, where drop-offs and pickups can be arranged to make the trip considerably easier. Kayaks can be rented from Adventure Bound Alaska (p117), which also offers a water-taxi service for drop-off and pickup services deep inside Tracy Arm for around $190 per person.

CROSS ADMIRALTY ISLAND PADDLE

START ANGOON
END MOLE HARBOR
DURATION/DISTANCE THREE TO FOUR DAYS/31.7 MILES
DIFFICULTY MEDIUM; MOSTLY CLASS 1 WATER

Admiralty Island National Monument, 50 miles southwest of Juneau, is the site of one of the most interesting canoe routes in

CRITTERBIZ/SHUTTERSTOCK ©

Humpback whales near Juneau

ROBERT SZYMANSKI/SHUTTERSTOCK ©

Remote cabin, Alaska Marine Highway (p430)

Alaska. This preserve is a fortress of dense coastal forest and ragged peaks, where brown bears outnumber anything else on the island, including humans. The Cross Admiralty Canoe Route is a 31.7-mile paddle and portage (where you'll have to carry your canoe) that spans the center of the island from the village of Angoon to Mole Harbor.

The majority of the route consists of calm lakes connected by streams, but there are a half-dozen portages on undulating trails, the longest of them around 3 miles long.

The initial 10-mile paddle from Angoon to Mitchell Bay is subject to strong tides that must be carefully timed. Avoid Kootznahoo Inlet as its tidal currents are extremely difficult to negotiate; instead, paddle through the maze of islands south of it. Leave Angoon at low tide, just before slack tide so that the water will push you into Mitchell Bay.

The traditional route is to continue on to Mole Harbor via Davidson Lake, Lake Guerin, Hasselborg Lake, Beaver Lake and Lake Alexander, all connected by portages. Because of the logistics and cost of being picked up at Mole Harbor with a canoe, most paddlers stop in the heart of the chain and after a day or two of fishing backtrack to Angoon to utilize the Alaska Marine Highway for a return to Juneau.

There are good camping spots at Tidal Falls on the eastern end of Salt Lake, on the islands at the south end of Hasselborg Lake and on the portage between Davidson Lake and Distin Lake. Complementing these are several USFS cabins along the route, including those on Hasselborg Lake, Lake Alexander and Distin Lake. Book in advance.

This adventure begins with a ferry trip to the village of Angoon aboard the Alaska Marine Highway (p125). The one-way fare from Juneau to Angoon is $51, plus another $26 for a canoe.

You can rent a canoe in Juneau from Alaska Boat & Kayak Shop (p115), which is conveniently located near the ferry terminal in Auke Bay. Canoes are $55 a day, with discounts for rentals of three days or more.

DAY TRIPS FROM JUNEAU

MENDENHALL GLACIER

Not many cities have a slow-moving glacier located a mere 12 miles from their downtown, so, when in Juneau, don't pass up on the opportunity to venture out to the Mendenhall Valley to see this icy tributary of the Juneau Icefield. How you view it depends on your taste (and budget): on a hike, in a kayak, from a helicopter or beneath some crampons on a eerie glacial walk.

☆ Best Things to See/Do/Eat

Mendenhall Glacier Visitor Center Watch the film, listen to the ranger talks and peruse the exhibits at this informative center with panoramic windows looking out toward the glacier. (p111)

Kayaking on Mendenhall Lake Escape the tourist hordes queuing for glacier selfies by going on a guided or self-guided paddle on placid Mendenhall Lake, where you can obtain a close-up, nonimpinged view of the impressive ice floe. Alaska Boat & Kayak Center can help organize. (p115)

Heritage Coffee Co & Café There are no food outlets at the glacier, so pick up some baked goods at Juneau's best cafe before you set out. (p122)

☆ How to Get There

Bus Bus 3 from downtown Juneau stops 1.5 miles from the visitor center.

Car You can hire a car at the cruise terminal in downtown Juneau

Tours The 'blue bus' from M & M Tours offers narrated transport to the glacier from the cruise dock ($35).

MOUNT ROBERTS

Juneau's rugged mountain sentinel has been rendered slightly less rugged in recent years by the installation of a tramway that climbs steeply from the cruise dock up to the timberline. While hiking purists might consider it 'cheating,' the cable car gives instant access to alpine flower meadows for people who wouldn't otherwise have that opportunity.

☆ Best Things to See/Do/Eat

Mt Roberts Tramway Take the steep (nigh-on vertical!) tram up to the timberline, where you can eat food, drink in views and watch a free film on Tlingit culture 1750ft above the cruise dock below. (p109)

Hiking Numerous trails lead on up the mountain and they quickly break into flower-covered meadows. The interpretive 0.7-mile Alpine Loop Trail is the easiest. The more ambitious can press on 2 miles to Mt Gastineau (3666ft) or 3 miles to 3818ft Mt Roberts. (p114)

Timberline Bar & Grill The top station of the tramway has a bona fide restaurant. Menu highlights include crab nachos and pelmeni (Russian dumplings). (p120)

☆ How to Get There

Cable car The tram leaves every five minutes from the cruise dock just south of downtown Juneau.

Hike You can hike up to the upper station of the tram from a trailhead on Basin Rd, 20 minutes' walk from the cruise dock. The trail is 2 miles long.

DOUGLAS ISLAND

Juneau is a two-part city. The smaller western half resides on Douglas Island, accessible from downtown by a bridge and scattered with gold-mining-era remains and thickly forested mountain slopes ideal for hiking, biking and ziplining.

☆ Best Things to See/Do/Eat

Treadwell Mine Site Juneau was built on gold and there was no more profitable mine than the Treadwell, a bustling minicity in its day, whose mossy ruins have since surrendered to the forest. Follow a historical trail around the atmospheric remains. (p110)

Alaska Zipline Adventures It just so happens that one of the most exhilarating activities in Juneau is bivouacked on Douglas Island. Nine ziplines hang high over the forest canopy at the Eaglecrest ski area and are the next best thing to flying. (p116)

Island Pub Locals go out of their way to visit this wooden waterside restaurant and bar, which they'll tell you serves the best pizza in town complemented by an Alaskan Brewing Company beer. (p121)

☆ How to Get There

Bus Routes 1 and 11 serve Douglas Island as far as the Treadwell Mine Site and Island Pub.

Boat Alaska Zipline Adventures offers transport over to Douglas Island from the cruise dock in a boat and/or bus.

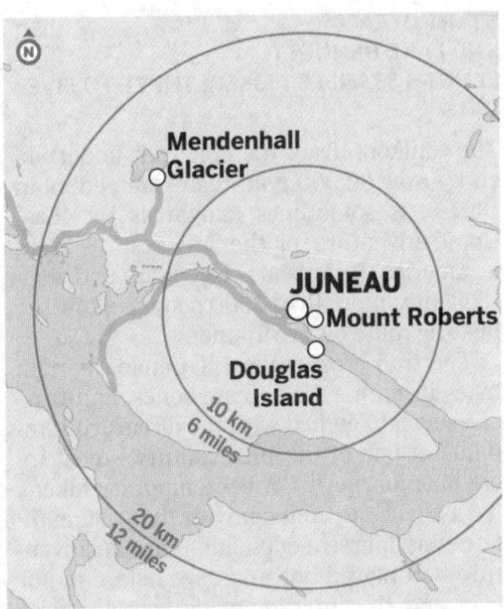

Alaska's busiest cruise port is not your average state capital. Steep mountain slopes rise abruptly behind the Capitol building, bears regularly stroll through quiet residential streets, and a giant glacier resides 15 minutes' drive to the north. The call of the wild has never been more accessible.

HIKING THE CHILKOOT TRAIL

START DYEA
END LAKE BENNETT
LENGTH 33 MILES (53KM); THREE TO FIVE DAYS

The Chilkoot Trail, the epic trek undertaken by over 30,000 gold-rush stampeders in 1897–8, is sometimes known as the 'Last Great Adventure' or the 'Meanest 33 Miles in America'. Its appeal is legendary and, consequently, more than 3000 people follow the historic route every summer.

The trail crosses the US–Canada border, takes in numerous climate zones, and traverses terrain etched with the discarded remnants of one of the 19th century's most incredible journeys. For contemporary hikers, it's a chance to connect with the past, emulate erstwhile struggles, and relive an adventure that played out in an age before motor cars and the internet made everything so damned easy.

The trailhead is at **Dyea**, 9 miles northwest of Skagway, site of a once-rambunctious gold-rush town that came and went in the space of just six years (1897–1903). The first part of the trail is largely flat and parallels the Taiya River. Boardwalks aid passage through the swampy Beaver Pond area. The first campsite is **Finnegan's Point** (5 miles) followed by **Canyon City** (8.4 miles). In 1898 Canyon City was a burgeoning village of over 1500 people built up around a tramway powerhouse, but it was short lived. A narrow 0.7-mile trail branches off to the ruins of an old boiler.

The main trail, still in the trees, gains around 700ft between Canyon City and the next stop at **Pleasant Camp**. It gains another 250ft before **Sheep Camp** (13 miles) a large congregation point during the gold rush and still popular with overnighting hikers. From here the going gets a lot tougher.

Soon after Sheep Camp the path emerges above the tree line at the top of what is called Long Hill. The next landmark is **the Scales** (15.8 miles), where packers had to reweigh their supplies before the push to the summit: Canadian customs required everyone to bring one tonne of supplies into the Yukon – enough to survive a Northern winter.

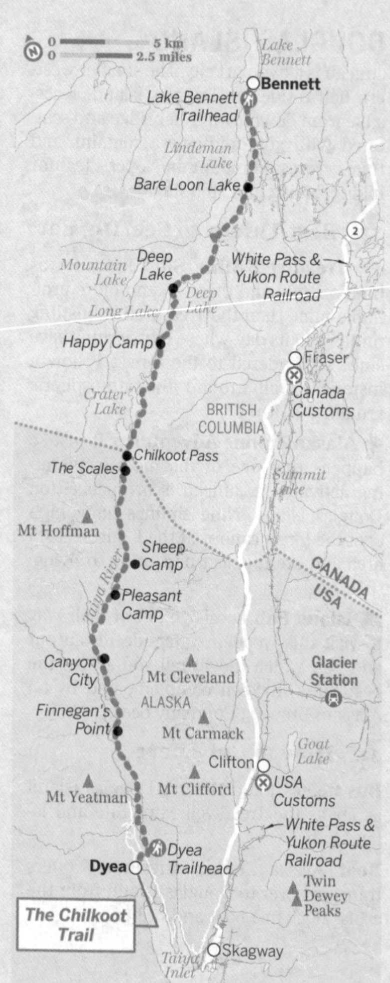

From the Scales the now-rough trail climbs a 45-degree, 1000ft-high slope to 3525ft **Chilkoot Pass**. Although well-marked with orange-tagged poles, the climb is up a scree-slope of massive boulders, meaning you'll be using your hands a lot.

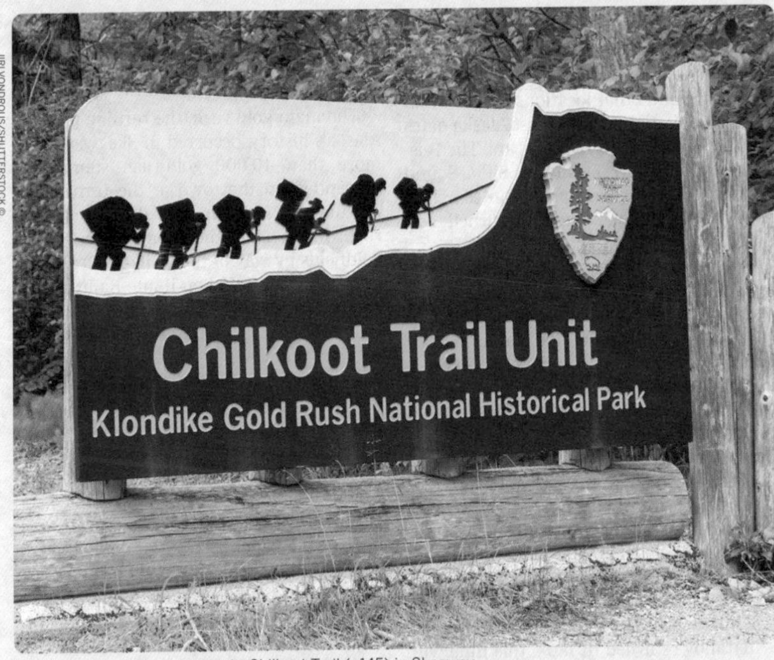

JIRI VONDROUS/SHUTTERSTOCK ©

Welcome sign at the entrance to Chilkoot Trail (p145) in Skagway

The top of the pass is often misty, windy and snow-covered. There's a warming hut if you need rest and a shelter.

Entering British Columbia the trail descends to Cascade Lake and then skirts through high alpine terrain past several more lakes to **Happy Camp** (20.5 miles), another popular overnighter.

You'll duck under the tree line again soon after **Deep Lake** and then proceed atop the north side of a deep gorge that carries an angry white river down to placid Lindeman Lake (26 miles).

Lindeman has one of the trail's busiest campgrounds and a Parks Canada ranger station. From here, it's 3 miles on an undulating trail through scrubby trees to **Bare Loon Lake** and another 4 miles to the finish point on the shores of **Lake Bennett**. Here the Chilkoot and White Pass Trails once converged in a tent city of 10,000 people. In May 1898, 700 homemade wooden boats set sail for Dawson City from the southern shore.

Bennett has a good campground, a railway station and an unusual wooden church dating from 1898. A special 'hiker's train' using the historic White Pass & Yukon Route Railroad (p144) leaves from Lake Bennett for Skagway four times a week (3:15pm on Tuesday, Wednesday and Thursday, and 2:15pm on Saturday). Experiencing the Chilkoot and returning on the train is probably the ultimate Alaska trek, combining great scenery, a historical site and an incredible sense of adventure.

It is possible to 'run' the Chilkoot Trail in a day if you are very fit. Bear in mind that you'll need to start early (4am-ish) if you want to catch the 3.15pm train out of Lake Bennett. Before starting the trail, all hikers must call in at the Trail Center (p148) in Skagway to obtain backpacking permits (adult/child $55/27.45), check out trail conditions and watch a bear-safety video.

Parks Canada allows only 50 hikers per day on the trail and holds only eight permits to be handed out each day at the trail center. It is definitely wise to reserve your permits ($11.70 per reservation) in advance through Parks Canada if you intend walking mid-July to mid-August. Don't forget your passport.

For transport to the Dyea trailhead call the reliable Ann Moore at Chilkoot Trail Dyea Transport (p148). Also see p70 for more on the trail and its history.

History

The Tlingits & the Russians

Petroglyphs along the shoreline in Wrangell, Petersburg and other locations indicate that human habitation in Southeast Alaska dates back at least 8000 to 10,000 years. The Russians arrived in 1741, entered Sitka Sound and sent two longboats ashore in search of fresh water. The boats never returned, and the Russians wisely departed.

What the unfortunate shore party encountered were members of Tlingit tribes, who over time had developed the most advanced culture – in terms of food gathering, art and the construction of large clan houses – of any Alaska Native group. The Tlingits were still there in 1799 when the Russians returned and established the Southeast's first nonindigenous settlement. Aleksandr Baranov built a Russian fort near the present ferry terminal to continue the rich sea-otter fur trade. He was in Kodiak three years later when Tlingits, armed with guns from British and American traders, overwhelmed the fort, burned it to the ground and killed most of its inhabitants.

Baranov returned in 1804, this time with an imperial Russian warship and, after destroying the Tlingit fort, established the headquarters of the Russian-American Company at the present site of Sitka. Originally called New Archangel, Sitka flourished both economically and culturally on the strength of the fur trade and in its golden era was known as the 'Paris of the Pacific.'

In an effort to strengthen their grip on the region and protect their fur-trading interests, the Russians built a stockade near the mouth of the Stikine River in 1834, but in 1840 the political winds shifted and the Russians leased the entire Southeast coastline to the British. After purchasing Alaska from the Russians, the Americans formally took control of the territory in Sitka in 1867.

Gold Fever & Canned Salmon

In 1880, at the insistence of a Tlingit chief, Joe Juneau and Dick Harris went to Gastineau Channel to try their luck and prospect for gold. They hacked their way through the thick forest to the head of Gold Creek, and there they found, in the words of Harris, 'little lumps as large as peas and beans.' The news spurred the state's first major gold strike, and within a year a small town named Juneau appeared, the first to be founded after Alaska's purchase from the Russians. After the decline in the whaling and fur trades reduced Sitka's importance, the Alaskan capital was moved to Juneau in 1906.

The main gold rush, the turning point in Alaska's history, occurred in Skagway when more than 40,000 gold-rush stampeders descended on the town at the turn of the century as part of the fabled Klondike gold rush. Most made their way to the Yukon goldfields by way of the Chilkoot Trail until the White Pass & Yukon Route Railroad was completed in 1900.

In 1887 the population of Skagway was two. Ten years later, it was 20,000 – the gold-rush town was Alaska's largest. A center for saloons, hotels and brothels, Skagway became infamous for its lawlessness. For a time, the town was held under the tight control of crime boss Jefferson Randolph 'Soapy' Smith and his gang, who conned and swindled naive newcomers out of their money and stampeders out of their gold dust. In a gunfight between Smith and city engineer Frank Reid, both men died, ending Smith's reign as the 'uncrowned prince of Skagway' after only nine months.

At the time, Wrangell was also booming as the supply point for prospectors heading up the Stikine River to the Cassiar Gold District of British Columbia in 1861 and 1874, and then using the river again to reach the Klondike fields in 1897. Wrangell was as ruthless and lawless as Skagway. With miners holding their own court, it was said that a man could be tried, found guilty of murder and hanged all in the same day.

Just as gold fever was dying out, the salmon industry was taking hold. One of the first canneries in Alaska was built in Klawock on Prince of Wales Island in 1878. Ketchikan was begun in 1885 as a cannery, and in 1897 Peter Buschmann arrived from Norway and established Petersburg as a cannery site because of the fine harbor and a ready supply of ice from nearby LeConte Glacier.

Capital Question

After WWII, with the construction of the Alcan (Alaska Hwy) and large military bases around Anchorage and Fairbanks, Alaska's sphere of influence shifted from the Southeast to the mainland further north. In 1974 Alaskans voted to move the state capital again, this time to the small town of Willow, an hour's drive from Anchorage. The so-called 'capital move' issue hung over Juneau like a dark cloud, threatening to turn the place into a ghost town. The issue became a political tug-of-war between Anchorage and the Southeast, until voters, faced with a billion-dollar price tag to construct a new capital, defeated the funding in 1982.

Today Juneau is still the capital and the Panhandle a roadless, lightly populated area where residents make a living fishing and catering to tourists and cruise ships.

SOUTHERN PANHANDLE

Residents like to call this region of Alaska 'rainforest islands': lush, green, watery, remote and roadless to the outside world. This is the heart of Southeast Alaska's fishing industry, and the region's best wilderness fishing lodges are scattered in the small coves of these emerald isles. Cruise ships pass through but they only inundate Ketchikan; the other communities receive few if any vessels. Two ferry systems, the Alaska State Marine Highway and the Inter-Island Ferry Authority, serve the area, so island-hopping, even in this remote rainforest, is easy.

Ketchikan

907 / POP 13,750

Close to Alaska's southern tip, where the Panhandle plunges deep into British Columbia, lies rainy Ketchikan, the state's fourth-largest city, squeezed onto a narrow strip of coast on Revillagigedo Island abutting the Tongass Narrows. Ketchikan is known for its commercial salmon fishing and indigenous Haida and Tlingit heritage – there is no better place in the US to see totem poles in all their craning, colorful glory. Every year between May and September, Ketchikan kowtows to around one million cruise-ship passengers, a deluge that turns the town into something of a tourist circus. Some cruisers stay in town, ferrying between souvenir shops and Ketchikan's emblematic totems. Others jump on boats or seaplanes bound for the Gothic majesty of Misty Fiords National Monument, a nearby wilderness area.

Despite the seasonal frenzy, Ketchikan retains a notable heritage exemplified by the jumbled clapboard facades of Creek Street, perched on stilts above a river.

Sights

City Center

★Totem Heritage Center MUSEUM

(907-225-5900; 601 Deermount St; adult/child $5/free; 8am-5pm May-Sep, 1-5pm Mon-Fri Oct-Apr) For a crash course in Southeast Alaska's impressive totem art look no further than the Totem Heritage Center, where old poles brought from deserted Tlingit and Haida communities are kept to prevent further deterioration. Inside the center over a dozen poles, some more than 100 years old, are on display in an almost-spiritual setting that accentuates the reverence Alaska Natives attach to them. More are erected outside, and the entire center is shrouded in pines and serenaded by the gurgling Ketchikan Creek.

Creek Street HISTORIC SITE

Departing from Stedman St is Creek St (a boardwalk built over Ketchikan Creek on pilings), a history book of misshapen wood-paneled houses painted in bright colors to deflect the heaviness of the oft-sodden climate. This was Ketchikan's famed red-light district until prostitution became illegal in 1954. During Creek St's heyday, it supported up to 30 brothels and became known as the only place in Alaska where 'the fishermen and the fish went upstream to spawn.'

Southeast Alaska Discovery Center MUSEUM

(www.alaskacenters.gov; 50 Main St; adult/child $5/free; 8am-4pm;) Three large totems greet you in the lobby of this center run by the National Park Service (NPS), while a school of silver salmon suspended from the ceiling leads you toward a slice of re-created temperate rainforest. Upstairs, the exhibit hall features sections on Southeast Alaska's ecosystems and Alaska Native traditions.

You can even view wildlife here: there's a spotting scope trained on Deer Mountain for mountain goats, while underwater cameras in Ketchikan Creek let you watch thousands of salmon struggling upstream to spawn.

Waterfront Promenade STREET

Ketchikan's newest boardwalk is the Waterfront Promenade, which begins near Berth 4, passes Harbor View Park (a city park that is composed entirely of decking and pilings), follows the cruise-ship docks and then wraps around Thomas Basin Harbor. Along

Ketchikan

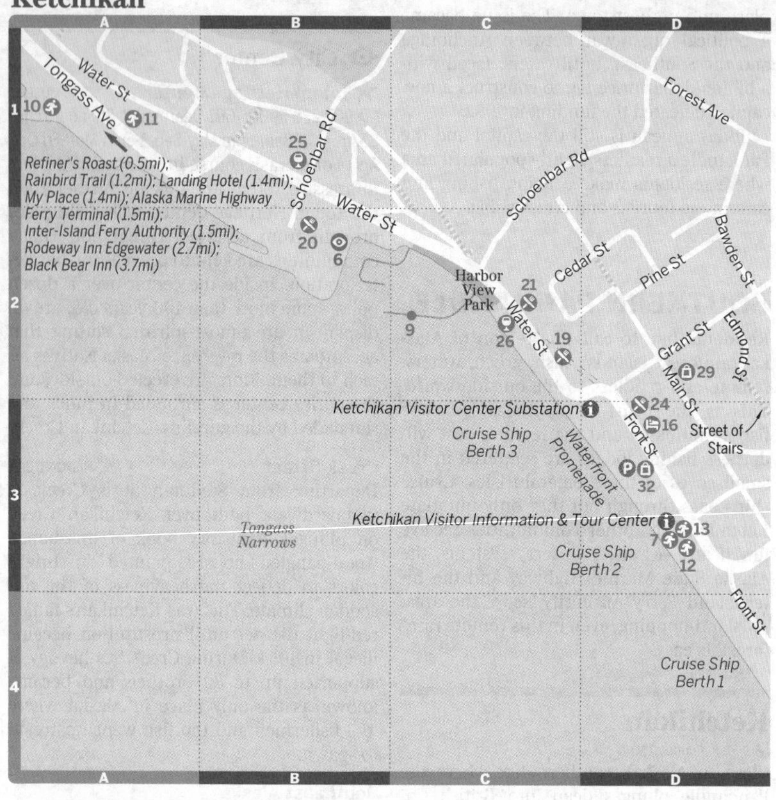

Ketchikan

Sights

1 Creek Street F3
2 Dolly's House F3
3 Southeast Alaska Discovery Center E3
4 Thomas Basin F4
5 Tongass Historical Museum E3
6 Waterfront Promenade B2

Activities, Courses & Tours

7 Alaska Seaplane Tours D3
8 Allen Marine Tours E4
9 Bering Sea Crab Fishermen's Tour C2
10 Family Air Tours A1
11 Ketchikan Town Bike Rental A1
12 Seawind Aviation D3
13 Southeast Aviation D3
14 Southeast Sea Kayaks E4

Sleeping

15 Cape Fox Lodge F2
16 Gilmore Hotel D3
17 Inn at Creek Street - New York Hotel F3

Eating

18 Alaska Fish House E4
19 Alava's Fish n Chowder C2
Annabelle's .... (see 16)
20 Bar Harbor Restaurant B2
21 Burger Queen C2
22 Diaz Café F4
Heen Kahidi Restaurant .... (see 15)
New York Cafe .... (see 17)
23 Pioneer Café E3
24 Sweet Mermaids D3

Drinking & Nightlife

25 49'er Bar B1
26 Arctic Bar C2
27 Potlatch Bar F4

Shopping

28 Crazy Wolf Studio E3
29 Main Street Gallery D2
30 Parnassus Books E3
31 Soho Coho E3
32 Tongass Trading Company D3

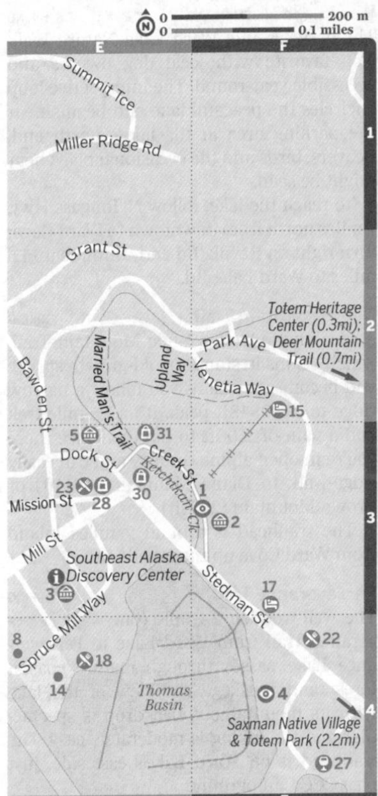

the way there are plenty of whale-tail and halibut benches where you can take a break and admire the maritime scenery.

Dolly's House MUSEUM

(24 Creek St; adult/child $10/free; when cruise ships are in) Dolly's house, in Creek St (p73), looks like a dollhouse from the outside, but it once operated as a bastion of the world's oldest profession (read: prostitution). These days it's a slightly over-theatrical museum dedicated to a notorious era when the whole of Creek St served as a giant den of iniquity.

The house is the erstwhile parlor of the city's most famous madam, Dolly Arthur. Tours include a look at the brothel, including its bar, which was placed over a trapdoor to the creek for quick disposal of bootleg whiskey.

Thomas Basin HARBOR

Thomas Basin is home to Ketchikan's fishing fleet and is the city's most picturesque harbor. When the boats come in, you can photograph them unloading their catch and then follow the crews to the colorful **Potlatch Bar** (907-225-4855; 126 Thomas St; 10am-10pm Tue-Thu, to midnight Fri, 11am-1am Sat) nearby, a classic fishers' pub.

Tongass Historical Museum MUSEUM

(907-225-5600; 629 Dock St; adult/child $3/free; 8am-5pm) Houses a collection of local historical and Alaska Native artifacts, many dealing with Ketchikan's fishing industry. More interesting is the impressive **Raven Stealing the Sun totem** just outside and an observation platform overlooking the Ketchikan Creek falls.

North of Ketchikan

Totem Bight State Park HISTORIC SITE

(907-247-8574; 9883 North Tongass Hwy) FREE Ten miles north of downtown Ketchikan is this seaside park that contains 14 restored totem poles, a colorful community house and a viewing deck overlooking Tongass Narrows. There are various interpretive boards explaining the importance of this attractive site, which was one of the earliest attempts to revive the dying art of totem carving in the 1930s. A park ranger is usually on-site.

Potlatch Park HISTORIC SITE

(907-225-4445; 9809 Totem Bight Rd; 7:30am-4pm) FREE Potlatch Park is right next door to Totem Bight State Park. It's less manicured, but still home to a dozen totems, one of which is 42ft high. There are also five beautiful tribal houses and an on-site carver who is usually working on a totem in the carving shed. One of the structures houses a large collection of antique firearms.

South of Ketchikan

★**Saxman Native Village & Totem Park** HISTORIC SITE

(907-225-4421; www.capefoxtours.com; $5; 8am-5pm) On South Tongass Hwy, 2.5 miles south of Ketchikan, is this incorporated Tlingit village of 475 residents. It's best known for Saxman Totem Park, which holds 24 totem poles from abandoned villages around the Southeast, restored or recarved in the 1930s. Among them is a replica of the Lincoln Pole (the original is in the Alaska State Museum in Juneau), which was carved in 1883, using a picture of Abraham Lincoln as a reference, to commemorate the first sighting of white people.

You can wander around the Totem Park on your own or, by prior appointment (and an extra $32), join an Alaska Native–led two-hour village tour. Tours, which usually include a traditional drum-and-dance performance, a narrated tour of the totems and a visit to the carving shed, are heavily tailored to cruise-ship groups and can be hit and miss. There are several a day in peak season

Alaska Rainforest Sanctuary WILDLIFE RESERVE

(www.alaskarainforest.com; South Tongass Hwy; tours adult/child $89/59) A 40-acre wildlife reserve at Herring Cove, 8 miles south of Ketchikan, where you can go on a naturalist-led walk (with the chance of spotting bears), visit a raptor center and old sawmill, and see a working Alaska Native totem-carving house. It's particularly popular with cruise-ship passengers, who are whisked here straight off the ships.

Activities

Cycling

Ketchikan Town Bike Rental CYCLING

(☎907-225-8829; www.southeastexposure.com; 1224 Tongass Ave; 4hr/full-day rentals $20/30) The folks at Southeast Exposure have a downtown bike-rental outlet open in the summer only (May to September). You can rent Trek hybrids here to use on the lightly trafficked Tongass Hwy.

Hiking

Most Ketchikan area trails – with the notable exception of Deer Mountain – are either out of town or must be reached by boat. The numerous trails around Ward Lake are accessible by bus.

Deer Mountain Trail HIKING

Within walking distance of downtown, Ketchikan's most popular hike is a well-maintained 2.5-mile climb to the 3000ft summit of Deer Mountain. Along the way overlooks provide panoramic views – the first only a mile up the trail. To reach the trail, take the Bus' Green Line to the corner of Deermount and Fair Sts and then head south on Ketchikan Lakes Rd.

Toward the top of the mountain are more trails that extend into the alpine region and a free-use shelter. But keep in mind this is a steady climb and a more challenging hike beyond the shelter.

Ward Lake Nature Walk HIKING

The easy 1.5-mile Ward Lake Nature Walk is a favorite with local dog owners and accessible year-round. The interpretive loop encircles the peaceful lake and begins near the parking area at the lake's north end. Beavers, birds and the occasional black bear might be seen.

To reach the lake, follow N Tongass Hwy, 7 miles north from downtown to Ward Cove; turn right on Revilla Rd and continue up 1.5 miles to Ward Lake Rd.

Dude Mountain Trail HIKING

A nice alpine trek is Dude Mountain Trail, which begins in stands of old-growth spruce and becomes a trail as you follow a narrow ridge to the 2848ft peak. It's a 1.5-mile trek and a gain of 1500ft to the top. Once there you're in open alpine country and can easily ridge-walk to Diana Mountain (3014ft) or Brown Mountain (2978ft).

The trailhead is around 9 miles inland from Ward Cove up the Revilla Rd.

Perseverance Trail HIKING

The well-trodden 2.4-mile (one-way) Perseverance Trail from Ward Lake to Perseverance Lake passes through mature coastal forest and muskeg. The view of the lake with its mountainous backdrop is spectacular and the hiking is moderately easy. The trailhead is on Ward Lake's east side, just past CCC Campground.

Rainbird Trail HIKING

Dedicated in 2010, this 1.3-mile trail is within town, stretching from the University of Alaska-Southeast campus off 7th Ave to a trailhead off Third Ave Bypass. You can ride the Bus to UAS and follow this delightful trail as it winds through a rainforest along a bluff before giving way to striking views of the city and Tongass Narrows below.

Paddling

Ketchikan serves as the base for some of the best kayaking in the Southeast. Possibilities include anything from an easy paddle around the waterfront to a weeklong trip in Misty Fiords National Monument. Pick up charts and topographic maps from the Southeast Alaska Discovery Center (p73), and outdoor supplies from Tongass Trading Company (p82).

Your options: bring your own kayak, rent one in town, or go on a guided day or multi-day trip with a local operator.

LOCAL KNOWLEDGE

TOTEM POLES: A BEGINNER'S GUIDE

There is no finer manifestation of coastal Alaska's indigenous culture than its intricately carved totem poles adorned with ravens, killer whales and carved countenances from native mythology.

Totem poles are peculiar to the Pacific Northwest region, in particular coastal British Columbia and Southeastern Alaska, where they have been sculpted for centuries by the Haida, Tlingit and Tsimshian people. Although the presence of totems predates the arrival of European explorers, the poles became grander and more artistically accomplished when native people gained access to iron tools in the late 18th century.

Usually fashioned out of mature cedars found deep in the forest, totems have a natural lifespan of around 75 years before the sodden Pacific Northwest climate takes its toll. Traditionally poles are rarely touched up. Progressive deterioration is seen as a part of the natural life cycle. Ideally, they are left to rot and return to the earth.

Totems were never intended as objects of worship. Instead, they serve several non-religious functions. 'Welcome poles' are designed to greet visitors to houses and communities, 'memorial poles' honor the dead, 'mortuary poles' contain the remains of deceased ancestors and 'house poles' have a structural function, while 'shame poles' ridicule public figures accused of a transgression.

Totem poles reached their artistic zenith in the mid-19th century. However, by the beginning of the 20th century, their presence had nearly died out. Carving was first rediscovered during the Great Depression when the Civilian Conservation Corps (CCC) were tasked with carrying out work relief programs in Alaska's national forests. The practice was revived more enthusiastically in the 1960s amid a renewed appreciation of America's indigenous culture, primarily as a means of artistic expression.

Ketchikan, Wrangell, Haines and Prince of Wales Island are the best places to immerse yourself in totem art.

Southeast Exposure — KAYAKING

(☎907-225-8829; www.southeastexposure.com; 37 Potter Rd) Outdoor-adventure company and outfitter based in the Clover Pass area that can organize ziplining in nearby Knudson Cove (from $125) and sea kayaking to offshore Eagle Island. It also rents kayaks from $35 per day and offers a water-taxi service to transport them to more distant waters.

Naha Bay — KAYAKING

An 8-mile paddle from Settler's Cove State Park is Naha Bay, the destination of an exciting three- or four-day adventure. At the bay's head is a floating dock; leave your kayak and head down the 5.4-mile Naha River National Recreation Trail. The scenic trail follows the river up to Jordan and Heckman Lakes; both have United States Forest Service (USFS) cabins.

The fishing here is good and black bears are plentiful – in August you might see them catching salmon at a small waterfall 2 miles up the trail from Roosevelt Lagoon.

A narrow outlet connects Naha Bay with Roosevelt Lagoon. You don't have to enter the lagoon to access the trail. Kayakers wishing to paddle into the lagoon must either portage around the outlet or enter it at high slack tide, as the narrow pass becomes a frothy, roaring chute when the tide is moving in or out.

George & Carroll Inlets — KAYAKING

From Hole in the Wall Bar & Marina (p81), 7.5 miles southeast of Ketchikan down the South Tongass Hwy, you can start an easy one- to four-day paddle north into George or Carroll Inlets or both. Each inlet is protected from the area's prevailing southwesterlies, so the water is usually calm (although north winds occasionally whip down George Inlet).

From Hole in the Wall to the top of George Inlet is a 26-mile paddle.

Betton Island — KAYAKING

West of Settler's Cove State Park at the north end (Mile 18.2) of N Tongass Hwy is this island and several smaller islands nearby, making it an excellent day paddle if you're staying at the Settler's Cove campground (p79). Although Clover Pass is a highly trafficked area, the back side of Betton Island offers a more genuine wilderness setting.

You can turn this into an overnight excursion by camping on the great beaches of the **Tatoosh Islands** on the west side of Betton Island.

Snorkeling

Snorkel Alaska SNORKELING
(☎907-247-7782; www.snorkelalaska.com; 4031 South Tongass Hwy; per person $112) It might not be the world's first choice of snorkeling destination, but Alaska offers surreal aquatic scenery for those brave enough to dip their toes in the 45°F (7°C) water. This company hands you a wet suit, complete with hood, gloves and boots, and then leads you into the water at Mountain Point for a fascinating underwater wildlife tour.

Wildlife includes starfish, urchins, sea cucumbers and more. The three-hour tour includes transportation from the downtown area. Book online.

Ziplining

Ketchikan has the two main requirements to be the zipline capital of Alaska: lush rainforests and elevation. There are three zipline operations now; more are bound to come.

Alaska Canopy Adventures ADVENTURE SPORTS
(☎907-225-5503; www.alaskacanopy.com; 116 Wood Rd; per person $189;) Operating two of Ketchikan's ziplines is Alaska Canopy Adventures. The sites are both at Herring Cove, 8 miles south of Ketchikan via the South Tongass Hwy: **Bear Creek** has seven lines, a skybridge above a waterfall, a 250ft slide and a 4WD vehicle to transport you up the mountain. It is more suitable for beginners and appropriate for kids.

The **Rainforest Canopy** at Eagle Creek is more advanced and enables you to view wildlife, including salmon runs in Herring Creek and bears that feast on them.

The company maintains a desk in the downtown visitor bureau (p82) or you can book online.

Tours

Ketchikan, with its cruise-ship economy, is well set up for guided tours, especially day trips. The Ketchikan Visitor Information & Tour Center (p82) building on City Dock has a whole wing devoted to a gauntlet of 20 tour providers touting their services. Flightseeing, wildlife-watching, kayaking, and boat tours to Misty Fiords are all well represented.

★Bering Sea Crab Fishermen's Tour BOATING
(☎907-247-2721; www.56degreesnorth.com; Berth 3; tours adult/child $179/115) This fantastically popular and highly original tour employs a veteran crabbing boat, the F/V *Aleutian Ballad* (that once featured in the Discovery Channel's *Deadliest Catch* series) to take people out on an authentic Alaskan crab-fishing trip. Watch the masters at work as they haul in crustaceans and listen to their incredible stories from the tempestuous waters of the Bering Sea.

The trip lasts three hours and the boat has a 100-seat heated amphitheater for on-deck viewing. Wildlife-watching is an added bonus, as are the complimentary hot drinks and snacks.

Southeast Sea Kayaks KAYAKING
(☎907-225-1258; www.kayakketchikan.com; 3 Salmon Landing;) Kid-friendly kayak specialists located downtown right on the harborside. Offers tours, including a 2½-hour paddle of Ketchikan's waterfront (adult/child $89/59). A much better paddling experience is its Orcas Cove trip (adult/child $169/139), a four-hour adventure that begins with a boat ride across the Tongass Narrows and then paddling among protected islands looking for sea lions, orcas and seals.

Ketchikan Kayak Company KAYAKING
(☎907-225-1272; www.ketchikankayakco.com; 407 Knudson Cove Rd; 4hr tours $129) Offers four-hour guided tours of Sea Star Alley (guess what you'll see there?) and other points close to Ketchikan. The company will arrange pickups from your hotel/cruise ship.

Allen Marine Tours TOUR
(☎907-225-8100; www.allenmarinetours.com; 5 Salmon Landing, Suite 215; adult/child $200/127) The fastest and most comfortable way to see Misty Fiords National Monument is with this experienced Alaska operator (which has additional offices in Juneau and Sitka). The 4½-hour fjords tour on an 80ft catamaran includes narration, snacks and use of binoculars to look at wildlife. It's understandably popular with the cruising set. Book online.

Sleeping

Ketchikan's accommodations were once pretty scant, but a couple of midrange openings have widened the field. There's a 14%

tax on lodging comprised of city and bed taxes.

The closest public campground is at Ward Lake Recreation Area, 7 miles from the town center.

Some 29 USFS cabins (p121) dot the Ketchikan area. Some can be reached by boat, some you fly to.

Settler's Cove State Recreation Area CAMPGROUND $
(tent & RV sites $15) Tongass Hwy ends 18 miles north of Ketchikan at a pretty coastal recreation area, with a lush rainforest bordering a gravel beach and rocky coastline. Its campground has 13 sites, a cabin ($50) and a quarter-mile trail to a waterfall and observation deck, and is rarely overflowing.

Last Chance Campground CAMPGROUND $
(Ward Lake Rd; tent & RV sites $10) In a beautiful area north of Ketchikan, a couple of miles beyond Ward Lake, with four scenic lakes, 19 drive-in sites and three trails that run through the lush rainforest.

★Inn at Creek Street - New York Hotel BOUTIQUE HOTEL $$
(☎907-225-0246; www.thenewyorkhotel.com; 207 Stedman St; r $89-149, ste $119-289;) A historic boutique hotel that walks a delicate balance between old-world ambience and modern comfort. The eight rooms have a 1920s period feel without seeming 'olde', with soft quilts, flat-screen TVs, refrigerators and private baths.

The hotel also has seven suites a short walk away, five of them on Creek St, which feature comfortable living rooms, small kitchen areas and sleeping for four.

Landing Hotel HOTEL $$
(☎907-225-5166; www.landinghotel.com; 3434 North Tongass Ave; r $230; P) The aptly named Landing, directly opposite the Alaska Marine Highway ferry dock, is, arguably, Ketchikan's best all-round hotel, equipped with an on-site restaurant, a popular pub and over 100 businesslike rooms. The spacious common areas are endowed with nature-themed murals and cozy corners to relax in and the service is famously friendly.

It's run by the Best Western chain.

My Place HOTEL $$
(☎907-220-9201; www.myplacehotels.com; 3612 Tongass Ave; ste from $200; P) Yours for a reasonable price is My Place, part of a small franchise but locally run. It is equipped with 64 pet-friendly rooms (some with kitchenettes), a 24-hour convenience store and on-site laundry facilities. My Place's niche is extended stayers, but there are also nightly rates. It's all new, clean and comfortable, if a little beige.

Gilmore Hotel HISTORIC HOTEL $$
(☎907-225-9423; www.gilmorehotel.com; 326 Front St; d from $169;) Built in 1927 as a hotel and renovated several times since, the Gilmore has 34 small, sometimes-dark rooms that don't really emulate the grand downstairs bar. Notwithstanding, some of the rooms have recently been done up and equipped with cable TV, coffeemakers and hair dryers.

Rodeway Inn Edgewater MOTEL $$
(☎907-247-2600; 4871 North Tongass Hwy; r from $185; P) A mile north of the airport ferry on the waterfront, the Edgewater is a posher-than-average motel with a good aspect overlooking the Tongass Narrows. The 44 standard rooms are well kept and very clean – you pay extra for an ocean-view courtesy of the little balconies. The inn also includes a bar, a restaurant and a marina where fishing charters can be booked.

Black Bear Inn B&B $$$
(☎907-225-4343; www.stayinalaska.com; 5528 North Tongass Hwy; r $215-265; P) This incredible B&B offers a range of waterfront accommodations 2.5 miles north of the ferry terminal and near a bus stop. There are four bedrooms in the home and a small apartment on the 2nd floor with a private entrance. Outside is a logger's bunkhouse that was floated to Ketchikan and renovated into a charming honeymooners' cabin.

Among the many amenities is a covered hot tub where you can soak while watching eagles soar and whales swim in the Tongass Narrows.

Cape Fox Lodge HOTEL $$$
(☎907-225-8001; www.capefoxlodge.com; 800 Venetia Way; r $238-283; P) This is Ketchikan's splashiest lodging. Perched atop the hill behind Creek St, it offers the best views in town and can be reached by a high-tech funicular tram from the Creek St boardwalk. The opulent lodge has 72 amenity-filled rooms and suites and the acclaimed Heen Kahidi restaurant overlooking the city.

There is so much Alaska Native art in the lobby it's like walking through a gallery. Also

SEASONAL CLOSURES

The towns of Southeast Alaska are strongly geared toward the cruise ships that arrive between early May and late September. Outside of these times, many of the region's tourist-orientated agencies, trips and excursions don't operate at all or, at best, have limited hours. This is particularly relevant in towns with a lot of summer cruise-ship traffic, notably Ketchikan, Juneau and Skagway.

Independent travelers heading to Alaska outside these months should check ahead if they are planning to partake in any organized activities, many of which are dependent on the weather anyway. A selection of popular restaurants, hotels and shops also close down during these times.

For tranquility and a highly local experience, an off-season trip to Southeast Alaska can be highly rewarding, especially in the shoulder months of April and October when the weather is less frigid.

on-site is a coffee shop and gift store, and staff can arrange tours.

Eating

If Ketchikan's your first stop in Alaska, you'll quickly discover that it makes sense to become a temporary pescatarian here. Fish rules in these parts, especially salmon and halibut, whether it comes in tacos, with chips or in a chowder.

Ketchikan doesn't do much in the way of gourmet cuisine. That said, it has one of the Panhandle's widest selection of restaurants outside Juneau.

Sweet Mermaids CAFE $

(907-225-3277; 340 Front St; lunch $8-11; 7am-4pm) Marketing itself as a *shoppe* as opposed to a shop (think home-baked cakes and staff in flowery aprons) Ketchikan's prime source of sugar replenishment plies the best sweet morsels in town, if the frosted banana and Nutella cake is anything to go by. Also on offer are giant deli sandwiches, smoothies and coffee.

Alava's Fish n Chowder SEAFOOD $

(907-617-5328; 420 Water St; mains $12-15; 11am-5pm) The size of a small trailer, this seafood shack close to the Water St tunnel does a good rendition of fish and chips: everything down to the tartar sauce is homemade. As the sign says, they don't do breakfast 'because we're out catching your lunch.'

Burger Queen BURGERS $

(518 Water St; burgers $7-10; 11am-7pm Tue-Sat, to 3pm Sun & Mon) Ketchikan's favorite burger joint is definitely not a chain. Ten varieties, including one with a Polish sausage *and* a hamburger patty, plus 30 flavors of milkshake are served out of a small space just north of the road tunnel. It's something of a local legend.

Alaska Fish House FISH & CHIPS $$

(907-225-4055; 3 Salmon Landing; mains $13-23; 10am-9pm) Take your pick of fish – cod, salmon or halibut – and then your coating – in batter or a bun. The chips are default. And all this before the menu gets down to the crab: whole or just the legs. For those lacking seafood taste buds there are burgers.

Seating is casual and the place (which overlooks the harbor) gets packed out, especially after the lumberjack show.

Pioneer Café CAFE $$

(619 Mission St; mains breakfast $8-14, lunch $9-14, dinner $11-20; 6am-10pm Sun-Thu, 24hr Fri & Sat) Substantial portions of no-frills, filling food served in a plain but traditional diner with fast service, automatic coffee refills and a plain-speaking cross section of the local populace. Generous opening hours.

Diaz Café ASIAN $$

(907-225-2257; 335 Stedman St; mains $8-18; 11:30am-2pm & 4-7pm Tue-Sat, noon-7:30pm Sun) Located on the south side of Ketchikan Creek, this longtime cafe dates back to the 1920s, when Filipinos and Japanese weren't allowed to live north of the creek. Today the eatery is a favorite among locals who relish the novelty (if not the taste explosion) of hybrid dishes such as burgers with fried rice.

★ **Bar Harbor Restaurant** MODERN AMERICAN $$$

(907-225-2813; 55 Schoenbar Ct, Berth 4; mains $22-42; 11am-2pm & 5-8pm Tue-Fri, 9am-2pm & 5-8pm Sat, 9am-2pm Sun) This slightly pricey fish-biased restaurant, usually touted among locals as the best in town, reopened a few years ago in a new cruise-dock location on Berth 4. Expect larger than normal crowds descending on its modern ocean-themed interior to feast on creative seafood and chowder renditions.

For a taster, draw lots between the impressive fish tacos, coconut prawns, ahi (yellowfin tuna), and crab and pesto gnocchi.

New York Cafe BREAKFAST $$$
(207 Stedman St, New York Hotel; breakfast $8-12, dinner mains $28-35; ⌚7:30am-8:30pm Tue-Thu & Sun, to 9pm Fri & Sat) Beneath the historic New York Hotel (p79) is this wood-paneled cafe which doesn't seem to have changed much decor-wise since its Roaring 1920s opening – if you don't count the food, which has doffed its hat to modern trends (ceviche and falafel included). The breakfast eggs are good, while the lunch and dinner menus are anchored by seafood including crab's legs.

Heen Kahidi Restaurant AMERICAN $$$
(800 Venetia Way; mains $19-42; ⌚7am-9pm) The hilltop dining in Cape Fox Lodge (p79) is about as posh as Ketchikan gets and certainly worth the short climb to get here. Food is split between surf and turf, with the former being slightly better in terms of style and sauce. Choose the pecan-crusted halibut or the blackened rockfish in a mango and pineapple salsa. The views are good and the onsite hotel is replete with Alaska Native art.

Annabelle's SEAFOOD $$$
(☎907-225-6009; 326 Front St; mains $15-32; ⌚10am-10pm) At the Gilmore Hotel (p79), this keg and chowder house has a seafood-heavy menu, a wonderful bar and 1920s decor. The three kinds of homemade chowder are good, and the keg half of the restaurant even better, with its long polished bar, brass footrest and antique slot machine. Where are the spittoons?

Drinking & Nightlife

Hole in the Wall Bar & Marina PUB
(7500 S Tongass Hwy; ⌚noon-2am) A funky little hangout that feels light years away from the tourist madness of Ketchikan in summer. There's not much inside other than a handful of stools, a woodstove, a pool table and a lot of friendly conversation, usually centered on fishing. But the bar is in a beautiful location, perched above a small marina in a narrow cove 7.5 miles south of Ketchikan.

49'er Bar BAR
(1010 Water St; ⌚9am-2am) A Jurassic bar preserving over 100 years of cigarette smoke in a wood-paneled, Wild West–flavored building just north of the main cruise-ship terminal. Beer, darts and hot dogs satisfy old-fashioned appetites.

Green Coffee Bean Company COFFEE
(☎907-247-5621; www.tgcbc.com; 7206 North Tongass Hwy; ⌚6am-5pm Mon-Sat, 9am-4pm Sun) Set in an unlikely location in out-of-town Ward Cove, hidden behind a gas station, this cafe offers the Ketchikan area's best coffee, supplemented by some creative cookies. Bag them up and take a couple out on one of the nearby hikes.

Arctic Bar BAR
(509 Water St; ⌚8am-2am) Just past the tunnel on downtown's northwest side, this local favorite has managed to survive 70 years by poking fun at itself and tourists. On the back deck overlooking the Tongass Narrows is a pair of fornicating bears. And hanging below the wooden bruins, in full view of every cruise ship that ties up in front of the bar, is the sign 'Please Don't Feed the Bears.'

Shopping

Ketchikan has a rich artists' community, meaning you're better off bypassing the predictable trinket shops in search of the real thing. The city is home to Ray Troll, whose distinctive and instantly recognizable work you'll see all over Southeast Alaska. His home gallery, called Soho Coho, is in Creek St.

★Soho Coho ARTS & CRAFTS
(www.trollart.com; 5 Creek St; ⌚9am-5:30pm Mon-Sat, to 4pm Sun) The not-to-be-missed home gallery of one of Alaska's most noted contemporary artists, Ray Troll, whose salmon- and fish-inspired work is seen all around town, including on the sides of buses. Treat yourself to a Star Wars–inspired 'Return of the Sockeye' screen-printed T-shirt.

Crazy Wolf Studio ARTS & CRAFTS
(☎907-225-9653; 633 Mission St; ⌚8am-6pm) In a town full of cruise-ship-oriented trinket shops, the locally run Crazy Wolf provides an authentic alternative. It is owned by a Tsimshian artist and stocks mainly interesting crafts including drums, baskets, jewelry and screen prints.

Main Street Gallery ARTS & CRAFTS
(www.ketchikanarts.org; 330 Main St; ⌚9am-5pm Mon-Fri, 11am-3pm Sat) Operated by the Ketchikan Area Arts & Humanities Council, this small but wonderful gallery stages a reception on the first Friday of every month, unveiling the work of a selected local or

OFF THE BEATEN TRACK

METLAKATLA

Founded in 1887 when Anglican missionary William Duncan arrived at Annette Island with 823 Tsimshians (the smallest of Alaska's three main Southeast coastal tribes) from British Columbia, Metlakatla became a federally recognized Indian Reservation four years later and today is the only one in Alaska. The 20-mile-long island, located due south of Ketchikan and close to the Canadian border, is reserved for the Metlakatla Alaska Natives, whose village (population 1624) is the antithesis of Ketchikan, where much is made for cruise ships. Known for its totems, artists' village and native dancers, Metlakatla is an authentic slice of Native Alaska.

The heart of Metlakatla is Annette Island Packing Company, perched on stilts overlooking a beautiful harbor dotted with small islands. Alaska Marine Highway (p430) runs the MV *Lituya* from Ketchikan to Annette Bay ($52, 45 minutes) twice a day from Thursday to Monday, leaving at 10:45am and 4:15pm. There are three ferries in the opposite direction, the last one, at 5:30pm, giving you plenty of time to explore. The Annette Bay ferry terminal is 15 miles north of Metlakatla. Personally narrated tours can be arranged through **MIC Tourism** (907-886-8687; www.metlakatla.com; per person $40).

Taquan Air has two daily flights between Ketchikan and Metlakatla for around $65.

regional artist. It's an evening of refreshments and presentations by the artist, and of extended hours by other galleries downtown, too.

Parnassus Books BOOKS
(105 Stedman St; 8am-6pm Mon-Fri, 10am-5pm Sat & Sun) This unexpectedly encyclopedic bookstore is a delightful place to spend a rainy afternoon (and there will be many!) browsing Alaskan books, cards and local art.

Tongass Trading Company SPORTS & OUTDOORS
(907-225-5101; 201 Dock St; 9am-6pm Mon-Sat, to 5pm Sun) Large downtown outfitter that can fix you up with most of your outdoor supply needs.

Information

MEDICAL SERVICES

Creekside Family Health Clinic (907-220-9982; www.creeksidehealth.com; 320 Bawden St, Suite 313; 8am-6pm Mon-Fri) A walk-in clinic downtown.

PeaceHealth Ketchikan Medical Center (907-225-5171; 3100 Tongass Ave) Near the ferry terminal.

MONEY

First Bank (907-228-4474; 331 Dock St; 9am-5:30pm Mon-Fri) Has a 24-hour ATM.

Wells Fargo (409 Dock St; 9am-5pm Mon-Fri) One of a handful of banks mixed in with the gift shops downtown.

TOURIST INFORMATION

Ketchikan Visitor Information & Tour Center (907-225-6166; www.visit-ketchikan.com; 131 Front St, City Dock; 7am-6pm) Vast modern building on the cruise-ship dock with brochures, free maps, courtesy phones and toilets. Adjoining it is a huge tour center complete with up to 20 booths where various activity companies set up desks in the summer to catch the cruise-ship trade. Reservations for most activities can be made here.

Ketchikan Visitor Center Substation (Berth 3; 8am-5pm May-Sep) Smaller overflow visitor center near the road tunnel; only opens in the spring/summer.

Southeast Alaska Discovery Center (907-228-6220; www.fs.fed.us/r10/tongass/districts/discoverycenter; 50 Main St; 8:30am-4pm) You don't need to pay the admission fee to get recreation information at this Alaska Public Lands Information Center. Park passes are also sold here.

Getting There & Away

AIR

Flights to Ketchikan from Seattle (two hours), Anchorage (4½ hours) and major Southeast communities including Juneau, Petersburg, Wrangell and Sitka are all possible with Alaska Airlines (p429).

Taquan Air (907-225-8800; www.taquanair.com; 4085 Tongass Ave) offers scheduled floatplane flights between Ketchikan and Prince of Wales Island, including Hollis, Craig/Klawock and Thorne Bay.

CRUISE SHIP

Ketchikan's waterfront is the main cruise-ship port and can accommodate up to four large ships at once. Passengers can simply step off the ship and walk straight into downtown.

FERRY

Ketchikan's **Alaska Marine Highway Ferry Terminal** (☎907-225-6182; www.dot.state.ak.us/amhs; 3501 Tongass Ave) is 2 miles north of the city center.

Northbound ferries leave almost daily in summer, heading for Wrangell ($53, six hours), Petersburg ($72, 9½ hours), Sitka ($109, 25 hours), Juneau ($126, 24 hours) and Haines ($155, 26 hours). Heading south, there's at least one departure a week for Bellingham, WA ($310, 40 hours) and also Prince Rupert in Canada ($63, 7½ hours).

Inter-Island Ferry Authority (☎907-225-4838; www.interislandferry.com) vessels are capable of holding vehicles and depart Ketchikan's ferry terminal at 3:30pm daily, bound for Hollis on Prince of Wales Island (one way adult/child $49/22.50, three hours). Rates for the ferry vary and are based on your vehicle's length; a subcompact one way costs $50.

Getting Around

BICYCLE

Ketchikan has an expanding system of bike paths that head north and south of downtown along Tongass Ave. Rent Trek hybrids at Southeast Exposure (p76), which has a summer rental near the cruise-ship docks.

BUS

Ketchikan's excellent public bus system is called **the Bus** (☎907-225-8726; one way $1).There are two main lines: the Green Line runs from downtown and then north past the airport ferry. The Silver Line heads south past Saxman Village to Rotary Beach and north all the way past Totem Bight State Park.

There's also a free downtown loop. You can't miss the bus: famed artist Ray Troll painted spawning salmon all over it. The 20-minute loop goes from Berth 4 of the cruise-ship dock to the Totem Heritage Center.

CAR

For two to four people, renting a car is a good way to spend a day seeing sights out of town. There's unlimited mileage with either of the following but a 16.5% tax.

Alaska Car Rental (☎800-662-0007; www.akcarrental.com; 2828 Tongass Ave; from $75) Two locations: one at the airport and one on the town side of the water.

First City Car Rental (☎907-225-7368; www.firstcitycarrental.com; 1417 Tongass Ave; midsize per day $70; ⊙7:30am-8:30pm) Will pickup and drop off at major transport areas and many hotels and B&Bs.

TAXI

Cab companies in town include **Sourdough Cab** (☎907-225-5544) and **Yellow Taxi** (☎907-225-5555). The fare from the ferry terminal or the airport ferry dock to downtown is $11 to $15.

Misty Fiords National Monument

This spectacular, 3570-sq-mile national monument, just 22 miles east of Ketchikan, is a natural mosaic of sea cliffs, steep fjords and rock walls jutting 3000ft straight out of the ocean. Brown and black bears, mountain goats, Sitka deer, bald eagles and a multitude of marine mammals inhabit this drizzly realm.

The monument receives 150in of rainfall annually, and many people think Misty Fiords is at its most beautiful when the granite walls and tumbling waterfalls are veiled in fog and mist. Walker Cove, Rudyerd Bay and Punchbowl Cove – the preserve's most picturesque areas – are reached via Behm Canal, the long inlet separating Revillagigedo Island from the mainland.

Well off the road network, the monument is best accessed via floatplane or boat, neither of which are cheap. Close to a dozen rustic USFS cabins attract adventurous overnighters.

Activities

For those with time and an adventurous spirit, kayaking is *the* best way to experience the preserve. Ketchikan's Southeast Exposure (p77) offers a six-day guided paddle ($1150), with transportation by boat to the fjords and back. It also rents kayaks and provides transport for boats and paddlers.

Tours

The most practical way to view the Misty Fiords is on a sightseeing flight or day cruise. Flightseeing may be the only option if you're in a hurry – most tours operate out of Ketchikan and last 90 minutes including a landing on a lake. Keep in mind that this is a big seller on the cruise ships and when the weather is nice it is an endless stream of floatplanes flying to the same area: Rudyerd Bay and Walker Cove. Throw in the tour boats and one local likened such days to 'the Allied invasion of Omaha Beach.'

Getting There & Away

AIR

There isn't an air charter in Ketchikan that doesn't do Misty Fiords. The standard offering is a 1½-hour flight with a lake landing for $219 to $249, and it's easily booked at the **visitor center** (p82). The following air charters offer tours and cabin drop-offs:

Family Air Tours (907-247-1305; www.familyairtours.com; 1285 Tongass Ave, Ketchikan)

Seawind Aviation (907-225-1206; www.seawindaviation.com; Front St, Berth 2, Ketchikan)

Southeast Aviation (907-225-2900; www.southeastaviation.com)

BOAT

Cruises on a speedy catamaran are a viable non-flying option for Misty Fiords–bound travelers. Allen Marine Tours (p78) is the main operator, offering four-hour tours on an 80ft catamaran through the monument that include narration, snacks and use of binoculars to look at wildlife.

Prince of Wales Island

907 / POP 3360

For some tourists, the Alaska they come looking for is only a three-hour ferry ride away from the crowds of cruise-ship tourists they encounter in Ketchikan. At 140 miles long and covering more than 2230 sq miles, Prince of Wales Island (POW) is the USA's third-largest island, after Alaska's Kodiak and Hawaii's Big Island.

This vast, rugged place is a destination for the adventurous at heart, loaded with hiking trails and canoe routes, USFS cabins and fishing opportunities. The 990-mile coastline meanders around numerous bays, coves, saltwater straits and protective islands, making it a kayaker's delight. And, for anyone carrying a mountain bike through Alaska, a week on the island is worth all the trouble of bringing the two-wheeler north. The island has the most extensive road system in the Southeast: 1300 miles of paved or gravel roads that lead to small villages, or shot-rock logging roads heading who-knows-where.

Sights

Totem Historic District – Kasaan HISTORIC SITE

(907-542-2230; New Kasaan) This is one of the great Haida cultural centers in Alaska. It's in Kasaan, one of only two Haida villages in the state, and, since 2002, has been listed on the National Register of Historic Places. The historic district benefited from an extensive renovation in 2016. Things to see include a forested trail meandering past numerous totem poles (both Haida and Tlingit), the Totem Trail Cafe and – the centerpiece – the Chief Son-i-Hat Whale House.

The Whale House, with its exquisite house poles, dates from 1880 and was moved to its present site from Old Kasaan in 1904. The Civilian Conservation Corps (CCC) were the first to restore it in 1938, along with other totem poles brought from Old Kassan. The complex also contains a couple of native cemeteries, the more southerly of which guards the remains of Chief Son-i-Hat (1829–1912). Guided tours are available.

Kasaan is 66 miles south of Coffman Cove by road.

Klawock Totem Park PARK

(Bayview Blvd) FREE Of the three totem parks on POW, the Klawock Totem Park is by far the most impressive and obviously a great source of community pride. Situated on a hill overlooking the town's cannery and harbor, Klawock's 21 totems comprise the largest collection in Alaska and make for a dramatic setting. Some totems are originals from the former village of Tukekan, the rest are replicas.

El Capitan Cave CAVE

(Forest Rd 15; May-Sep) FREE The longest cave in Alaska is a 94-mile drive from Hollis and 11 miles west of Whale Pass. There's a free, two-hour, ranger-led cave tour in summer at 9am, noon and 2:30pm, Thursday through Saturday. Tours are limited to six people and involve a 370-step stairway trail. Contact the Thorne Bay USFS Ranger Station (p86) for reservations (at least two days in advance; no children under seven).

Dog Salmon Fish Pass VIEWPOINT

This is one of best places to see black bears on POW Island as salmon attempt to negotiate a couple of fish ladders during the summer spawning season (late July–early September).

Look out also for river otters and bald eagles from the viewing platforms. Dog Salmon is on the island's southern half, close to Pink Inlet, and accessible by dirt road.

Activities

Hiking

The USFS maintains more than 20 hiking trails on POW, the majority of them being short walks to rental cabins, rivers or lakes. In the south, a good hike can be made to **One Duck Shelter** from a trailhead on the road to Hydaburg, 2 miles south of Hollis Hwy junction. The trail is steep, climbing 1400ft in 1.2 miles, but it ends at a three-sided free-use shelter that sleeps four. To spend the night in the open alpine area with panoramic views of the Klawock Mountains is worth the knee-bending climb. To the north the **Balls Lake Trail** begins in the Balls Lake Picnic Area just east of **Eagle's Nest Campground** (www.recreation.gov; tent & RV sites $8) and winds 2.2 miles around the lake.

Cycling

Mountain bikers have even more opportunities than hikers; unfortunately there are currently no rental facilities so you'll need to bring your own. You can cycle on any road to explore the island. One of the most scenic roads to bike is South Beach Rd (also known as Forest Rd 30) from Coffman Cove to Thorne Bay. It's a 37-mile ride along the narrow, winding dirt road that is skirts Clarence Strait. Along the way is Sandy Beach Picnic Area, an excellent place to see humpback whales, orcas and harbor seals offshore or examine intriguing tidal pools at low tides.

Paddling

Opportunities for paddlers are almost as limitless as they are for mountain bikers. At the north end of POW off Forest Rd 20 is the **Sarkar Lakes Canoe Route**, a 15-mile loop of five major lakes and portages along with a USFS cabin and excellent fishing. For a day of kayaking, depart from Klawock and paddle into **Big Salt Lake**, where the water is calm and the birding is excellent (but be mindful of the inlets at midtide, as they can hold treacherous white-water conditions). **Hollis Adventure Rentals** (907-530-7040; www.hollisadventurerentals.com; 222 Hollis Rd) rents single kayaks as well as canoes (one day/extra day $55/35).

Sleeping

As with many places in off-the-grid Alaska, most of POW's accommodations are geared toward visitors on all-inclusive hunting and fishing tours. However, there are 20 USFS cabins and two campgrounds on the island, plus two lovely designated campsites at **Sandy Beach Picnic Area** (Mile 6, Sandy Beach Rd). Three of the cabins are accessible by road and four can be reached by rowing across a lake, thus eliminating the floatplane expense required with many others.

Red Bay Lake Cabin CABIN $

(www.recreation.gov; cabins $55) Red Bay Lake Cabin is at the north end of the POW, off Forest Rd 20, and reached with a half-mile hike to a boat and then a 1.5-mile row across the lake.

Log Cabin Resort & RV Park CABIN $

(907-755-2205; www.logcabinresortandrvpark.com; Big Salt Lake Rd, Klawock; tent/RV sites $15/30, cabins $95-170, ste $180) Located a half-mile up Big Salt Rd in Klawock, this park offers suites, three rustic beachfront cabins and a grassy spot for tents, plus showers and a community kitchen. It also rents canoes for use on Big Salt Lake or Klawock Lake.

Blue Heron Inn INN $$

(907-826-3608; www.craigblueheron.com; 406 9th St, Craig; r $79-135, ste $155; P) This self-contained inn has a great waterfront location overlooking South Cove Boat Harbor and is only a five-minute walk to shops and restaurants in Craig. There are three cozy, earthy rooms plus an apartment with its own modern kitchen. Best of all is the wonderful covered deck overlooking the harbor.

The owners also rent a fully equipped arts-and-crafts house that sleeps nine from $350 per night.

Dreamcatcher B&B B&B $$

(907-826-2238; www.dreamcatcherbedandbreakfast.com; 1405 Hamilton Dr, Craig; s/d $125/135; P) Three guest rooms in a beautiful seaside home. Big picture windows and a wraparound deck give way to a wonderful view of water, islands, mountains and, of course, clear-cuts. Kayaks and a skiff are available for guests, and you can warm up with a view either in the hot tub or around the fire pit.

Shelter Cove Lodge HOTEL $$

(907-826-2939; www.sheltercovefishinglodge.com; 703 Hamilton Dr, Craig; r $139-149;) Six of the 10 clean and comfortable rooms here overlook the water; you might never want to leave your room. Most guests are part of a fishing package tour, but the lodge does take independent travelers if there's space; it's worth the inquiry.

Eating

Dockside Restaurant BREAKFAST $

(Front St, Craig; mains breakfast $9-14, lunch $10-14; 5:30am-8pm) This wonderful cafe serves the best breakfast on POW, but it's the pies that make it legendary among locals. There's usually a half-dozen different kinds in the cooler, and a $5 slice is money well spent.

Bread Box BAKERY $

(Westwood Shopping Plaza, Craig; 8am-4pm Mon, 7am-6pm Tue-Fri, 8am-6pm Sat) Part bakery, part natural-foods store. There's gourmet coffee and pastries, and you can grab some organic veggies to add to your loaf of fresh bread for a picnic.

Zat's Pizza PIZZA $$

(420 Port Bagial Bvld, Craig; pizza $20-26; 11:30am-8pm Tue-Sat;) A Craig favorite; excellent pizzas in a bustling atmosphere. Vegetarian options include the Popeye: garlic, olive oil, spinach, feta, tomatoes and more.

Information

MEDICAL SERVICES

Alicia Roberts Medical Center (907-755-4800; Hollis–Klawock Hwy, Klawock; walk-ins 9am-4pm Mon-Fri) The main medical facility on the island is in Klawock.

TOURIST INFORMATION

Prince of Wales Chamber of Commerce (907-755-2626; www.princeofwalescoc.org; 6488 Klawock-Hollis Hwy, Klawock; 10am-3pm Mon-Fri;) Operates a visitor center in Klawock.

USFS Office Head to the office in either **Craig** (907-826-3271; 900 Main St, Craig; 8am-5pm Mon-Fri) or the **Thorne Bay Ranger Station** (907-828-3304; 1312 Federal Way, Thorne Bay; 8am-5pm Mon-Fri) for information on trails, cabins and paddling adventures.

Getting There & Away

AIR

Taquan Air (p83) Runs scheduled flights from Ketchikan to 11 destinations on Prince of Wales Island, including daily (except Sunday) services to Craig/Klawock (one way $115), Hollis ($95) and Thorne Bay ($95).

FERRY

Inter-Island Ferry (Hollis Terminal 866-308-4800, Ketchikan Terminal 907-530-4848; www.interislandferry.com) Operates a pair of vessels that depart from Hollis at 8am and from Ketchikan at 3:30pm daily (adult/child $49/22.50, three hours).

Getting Around

POW now has 150 miles of paved roads that connect the main 'towns' of Thorne Bay (population 487), Klawock (population 777), Craig (population 1250) and Coffman Cove (population 183).

There are a couple of car-rental companies on POW; the best is Hollis Adventure Rentals (p85). You'll be met in Hollis with a car packed with a cooler and some essentials. If staying more than a few days, consider renting a car in Ketchikan and driving it onto the ferry.

Island Ride (907-401-1414) connects with ferries in Hollis, but you have to call them in advance to reserve a seat. The one-way fare to Craig is $35 per person.

Wrangell

907 / POP 2400

Wrangell is Southeast Alaska's rough, gruff coastal outpost, a small boom-bust fishing community colored by centuries of native Tlingit settlement and more recent incursions by the Russians and British.

Posh it isn't. Lacking the fishing affluence of Petersburg or the cruise-ship-oriented economy of Ketchikan, the town nurtures a tough outback spirit more familiar to Alaska's frigid north than its drizzly Panhandle. A collapse in the lumber industry in the 1990s hit the town hard, a blow from which it has only recently recovered.

If people stop in Wrangell at all, it's normally as a launchpad for excursions to the Anan bear-watching observatory and the incredible Stikine River delta nearby.

However, the countryside around town, a mishmash of boggy muskeg and tree-covered mountains, offers fine hiking, a fact not lost on Scottish American naturalist John Muir, who decamped here in 1879 on the first of four Alaska visits.

Sights

★**Wrangell Museum** MUSEUM

(907-874-3770; 296 Campbell Dr; adult/child/family $5/2/12; 10am-5pm Mon-Sat late Apr–mid-Sep, 1-5pm Tue-Sat mid-Sep–late Apr) This impressive museum is what the colorful history and characters of Wrangell deserve.

As you stroll through the many rooms, an audio narration automatically comes on and explains each chapter of Wrangell's history, from Tlingit culture and the gold-rush era to the time Hollywood arrived in 1972 to film the movie *Timber Tramps*.

Wrangell

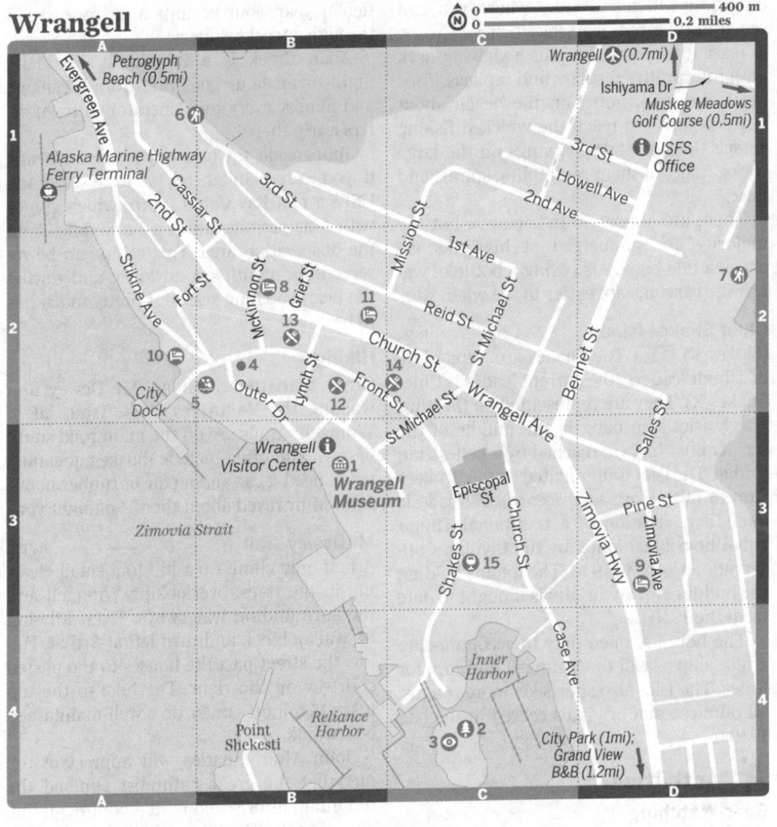

Wrangell

Top Sights
1 Wrangell Museum....B3

Sights
2 Chief Shakes Island....C4
3 Shakes Community House....C4

Activities, Courses & Tours
4 Alaska Charters & Adventures....B2
5 Alaska Vistas....B2
Breakaway Adventures....(see 5)
6 Mt Dewey Trail....A1
7 Volunteer Park Trail....D2

Sleeping
8 Rooney's Roost....B2
9 Squawking Raven B&B....D3
10 Stikine Inn....A2
11 Wrangell Hostel....B2

Eating
12 Diamond C Café....B2
13 J&W's Fast Food....B2
Stikine Inn Restaurant....(see 10)
14 Zak's Cafe....C2

Drinking & Nightlife
15 Rayme's Bar....C3
Stik Cafe....(see 10)

You can marvel at a collection of Alaskan art that includes a Sidney Laurence painting or be amused that this rugged little town has had two presidential visits.

Petroglyph Beach ARCHAEOLOGICAL SITE
(Evergreen Ave;) FREE Thought Alaska's history started with the Klondike gold rush? Not so. Historians and anthropologists should home in on this state historic park

on Wrangell's north side, where you can see primitive rock carvings believed to be at least 1000 years old, plus a viewing deck with interpretive displays and replicas. Turn right and walk north on the beach about 50yd. Before you reach the wrecked fishing vessels, look for faint carvings on the large rocks, many of them resembling spirals and faces.

There are almost 50 in the area, but the majority are submerged at high tide so check a tide book. Also bring a bottle of water; the carvings are easier to see when wet.

Chief Shakes Island PARK

(Shakes St) FREE The Shakes are a long line of Tlingit leaders (the current leader is Chief Shakes X). They are represented on this tiny, grassy islet slap bang in the middle of the scruffy boat harbor, reached by a pedestrian bridge. The islet is dominated by the **Shakes Community House** (when cruise ships are in town), a re-creation of a traditional Tlingit tribal house fashioned by the Civilian Conservation Corps in 1940. The totems holding the building up are originals thought to date from the 1840s.

The house is open only to accommodate cruise ships – call the Wrangell Museum for times. The islet also sports six more totems, all duplicates of originals carved in the late 1930s.

Activities

Bear-Watching

Wrangell is base camp for some of the best bear-viewing in the state and – by definition – the US. Thirty miles southeast of town on the mainland, Anan Creek is the site of one of the largest pink-salmon runs in Southeast Alaska. From the platforms at **Anan Creek Wildlife Observatory** (1-800-877-444-6777; www.fs.usda.gov/recarea/tongass/recreation/natureviewing; permits $10), you can watch eagles, harbor seals, black bears and a few brown bears chowing down gluttonously on the spawning humpies. This is one of the few places in Alaska where black and brown bears coexist – or at least put up with each other – at the same run. Permits are required from early July through August, or basically when the bears are there, and are reserved online or by calling the USFS Office in Wrangell (p92). Almost half of the daily permits go to local tour operators. The rest are available from February 1 for that particular year. Four permits a day are issued through a weekly lottery.

Anan Creek is a 20-minute floatplane flight or an hour boat ride from Wrangell, and almost every tour operator in town offers a trip there.

Tours aside, the best way to see the bears, if you can plan ahead, is to reserve the USFS Anan Bay Cabin (p90), which comes with four permits and is a 1-mile hike from the observation area. This cabin can be reserved six months in advance, and during the bear-watching season it pretty much has to be.

Hiking

Other than the climb up Mt Dewey and walking the **Volunteer Park Trail**, all of Wrangell's trails are off the main road south of town and often include muskeg, meaning you'll need a car and a pair of rubber boots. John Muir raved about them. So might you.

Mt Dewey Trail HIKING

A half-mile climb up a hill to a small clearing in the trees, overlooking Wrangell and the surrounding waterways. From Mission St, walk a block and turn left at 3rd St. Follow the street past the houses to the posted stairway on the right. The hike to the top takes 15 minutes or so, on a well-maintained boardwalk.

John Muir fanatics will appreciate the fact that the great naturalist climbed the mountain in 1879 and built a bonfire on top, alarming the Tlingit people living in the village below. Ironically, the only signs on top now say 'No Campfires.'

Thoms Lake Trail HIKING

A 1.4-mile path to the lake, Thoms Lake Trail is reached by following Zimovia Hwy to its paved end and then turning east on Forest Rd 6267. About halfway across the island, just before crossing Upper Salamander Creek, turn right on Forest Rd 6290 and follow it for 4 miles to the trailhead. There is a cabin half a mile from the end of the trail.

Rainbow Falls Trail HIKING

Well-signposted 4.7 miles south of the ferry terminal on the Zimovia Hwy is this popular trail across from Shoemaker Bay Recreation Area (p90). It's 0.7 miles to the waterfalls, although the best viewing point is at the 0.6-mile mark. Most of the uphill path is on a narrow wooden walkway fitted with wire mesh for better grip.

Institute Creek Trail HIKING

Begins toward the end of Rainbow Falls Trail, which you'll need to hike first, and climbs 1500ft in 2.7 miles on a wooden walkway to the Shoemaker Bay Overlook Shelter with views over the water. Total round-trip distance is 5.6 miles.

North Wrangell Trail HIKING

To access the North Wrangell Trail, you first have to climb the Rainbow Falls Trail and part of the Institute Creek Trail before branching off. From the junction with the Institute Creek Trail, the North Wrangell Trail leads 1.3 miles to High Country Shelter and, in 2.3 miles, to Pond Shelter. The trail descends then to the Spur Rd Extension, on the east side of Wrangell Island, 4 miles from town.

The entire hike from the west side of the island to the east is 6.5 miles (add on another 9 miles if you're hiking to and from Wrangell town), passing three-sided shelters along the way for overnight adventures.

Paddling

One look at a nautical chart of Wrangell will have kayakers drooling and dreaming. Islands and protected waterways abound, though many are across the vast Stikine River flats, where experience is a prerequisite due to strong tides and currents. Novices can enjoy paddling around the harbor, over to Petroglyph Beach or to Dead Man's Island.

Alaska Vistas KAYAKING

(907-874-3006; www.alaskavistas.com; 106 Front St) Inside the Java Junkies espresso shed, a wi-fi hot spot at City Dock, Alaska Vistas rents kayaks (per day single/double $50/65). The company also runs guided kayak tours, a jet boat down the Stikine River ($220) and a LeConte glacier tour ($270).

Tours

★ Breakaway Adventures TOUR

(907-874-2488; www.breakawayadventures.com; Front St) The oldest and probably most comprehensive of Wrangell's tour operators, Breakaway Adventures offers the best options on exploring the Stikine River, from a four hour high-speed tour ($160) to a two- to four-day journey upriver as far as Canada ($1400 to $2000). It also has a handy water-taxi service to various USFS cabins and rents kayaks (single/double $40/60 per day).

Alaska Charters & Adventures TOUR

(907-874-4157; www.alaskaupclose.com; 5 Front St) With an office in the rather artsy Watercolors of Pacific Northwest Gallery, this outfit offers glacier, birding and whale-watching tours as well as an eight-hour boat trip to the Anan Observatory for bear-watching ($338).

> DON'T MISS
>
> **WILDERNESS GOLF**
>
> Completed in 1998 atop sawdust and wood chips from local sawmill operations, Wrangell's nine-hole **Muskeg Meadows Golf Course** (907-874-4653; www.wrangellalaskagolf.com; Ishiyama Dr; per 18 holes $33), a half-mile east of Bennet St, is the first certified course in the Southeast. Surrounded by wilderness, it's uniquely Alaskan – members are rarely alarmed when a bear comes bounding across a fairway.
>
> Then there is the club's Raven Rule: if a raven steals your ball you may replace it with no penalty provided you have a witness. Finally, the course's narrow fairways and tangled roughs of spruce and muskeg have resulted in this warning posted in the clubhouse: 'You got to have a lot of balls to play Muskeg Meadows.'

Festivals & Events

Stikine River Birding Festival NATURE

(late Apr) Celebrating the arrival of spring migrant birds (including large numbers of bald eagles) in the river delta, the festival hosts art and photo contests, guest speakers and special bird tours.

Sleeping

Wrangell levies a 13% sales and bed tax on all lodging. There's one decent hotel, several campgrounds, a hostel and a trio of B&Bs.

Middle Ridge Cabin CABIN $

(877-444-6777; www.recreation.gov; cabins $45) In 2010 the USFS opened Middle Ridge Cabin, the first road-accessible cabin of the 22 in the Wrangell District of Tongass National Forest (until recently all of them were reached via floatplanes, boats or on foot). It's still an adventurous retreat. The cabin is 20 miles south of Wrangell along Forest Rd 50050, which is recommended for high-clearance vehicles. A rowboat is available for use.

Anan Bay Cabin CABIN $
(☎877-444-6777; www.recreation.gov; cabins $55) The best way to see the bears at Anan Creek (p88), if you can plan ahead, is to reserve the two-bunk USFS Anan Bay Cabin, which comes with four permits and is a 1-mile hike from the observation area. This cabin can be reserved six months in advance, and during the bear-watching season it pretty much has to be.

Nemo Point CAMPGROUND $
(☎907-874-2323; Forest Rd 6267; tent & RV sites free) This offers the best camping on Wrangell Island, but unfortunately it is 14 miles from town. Each of the six free wheelchair-accessible sites has a picnic table, an outhouse and a stunning view of Zimovia Strait. Take Zimovia Hwy/Forest Hwy 16 south to Forest Rd 6267. The sites stretch along 4 miles of Forest Rd 6267 and are good for tents or recreational vehicles (RVs), although there are no hookups.

Shoemaker Bay Recreation Area CAMPGROUND $
(☎907-874-2444; Mile 4.5, Zimovia Hwy; tent sites free, RV sites $20-30;) This waterfront campsite is across from the Rainbow Falls (p89) trailhead in a wooded area near a creek. There are 25 sites, 15 with hookups for RVers, and a tent-camping area for everybody sleeping in ripstop nylon. Bonus: there's a pool/gym/shower facility next door which can be used for no extra charge.

Wrangell Hostel HOSTEL $
(☎907-874-3534; 220 Church St; dm $20; ⊙Jun-Sep) The First Presbyterian Church doubles up as a basic hostel, with single-sex dorm rooms with inflatable mattresses, showers and a large kitchen and dining room. It has no curfew and will graciously let you hang out here during an all-day rain. There's no sign, just knock or push on the church door.

★**Stikine Inn** HOTEL $$
(☎907-874-3388; www.stikineinn.com; 107 Stikine Ave; r $167-195, ste $200-214; P) Wrangell's best and largest hotel is also the favorite local urban hangout. Herein lies the town's best restaurant, best coffee bar, and a friendly chamber of commerce dispensing information on local sights and activities. Bag a water-facing room upstairs and you won't have much to complain about, with wildlife and waves to serenade you day and night.

Squawking Raven B&B B&B $$
(☎907-305-0117; www.squawkingravenbnb.com; 612 Zimovia Hwy; r from $130; P) A deluxe B&B hides inside this gabled wooden house

THE MILK RUN

Travelers forging a passage between Southeast Alaska's main settlements – most of them cut off from the main road system by a mixture of water and wilderness – are left with two transportation options: ferry or airplane.

The ferry has its advantages (wild watery vistas), but flying, as well as being faster, is just as much fun, especially if you get to partake in the so-called 'milk run', a daily Alaska Airlines flight between Seattle and Anchorage that stops at Ketchikan, Wrangell, Petersburg and Juneau en route (another milk-run plane serves Juneau, Yakutat and Cordova).

What the milk run lacks in directness, it makes up for in unscripted flightseeing opportunities. Since many of the Panhandle's airports are located in close proximity to one another, airplanes don't have time to gain much height, meaning (weather permitting) you can look down with silent awe on the arboreal beauty of the Tongass National Forest spread out like a satellite map beneath you. The route's shortest hop, between Wrangell and Petersburg, registers only a brief 9½ minutes and is purportedly the shortest jet flight in the world. Grab a window seat for close-up views of the braided Stikine River Delta and the frigid LeConte Glacier.

One of the other joys of the milk run is that it gives crowd-weary travelers the opportunity to experience the calm of Alaska's small, laid-back airports, where check-in agents double up as baggage handlers and the coffee bar is often just a giant flask with an honesty box. The tiny terminal at Petersburg is about as big as the toilets at New York's JFK, while Ketchikan's wind-lashed runway is located on a separate island to the rest of the city, necessitating a short ferry ride into the center.

with panoramic windows overlooking Wrangell harbor. The light-filled supermodern lounge-kitchen is complemented by two bedrooms with lovely private bathrooms. Breakfasts are substantial.

Grand View B&B B&B **$$**
(907-874-3225; www.grandviewbnb.com; Mile 1.9, Zimovia Hwy; s/d/tr $150/165/185;) Just south of City Park, this oceanfront B&B does have the grandest view in town. From the living room a row of picture windows frame Zimovia Strait and the mountains that surround it. The main floor is devoted to guests and includes three rooms, private baths, a large kitchen and an impressive collection of Alaska art and artifacts.

Eating

Wrangell is one of Alaska's more gastronomically challenged towns. The food here is probably better described as 'grub' than 'cuisine' – capable of filling you up after a long hike, but unlikely to extravagantly excite your taste buds.

J&W's Fast Food FAST FOOD **$**
(907-874-2120; 120 Front St; mains $7-9; 8am-7pm) One of Wrangell's best eating joints, a friendly if rudimentary sales window set up in the main street which juggles cheap American staples (burgers, quesadillas and tacos) with simple renditions of locally caught fish (snapper and prawns star).

There are four crumby tables in a covered cafe if you need comfort. Otherwise, hold onto your hat and head for the harborside.

Zak's Cafe CAFE **$**
(316 Front St; breakfast $6-10, lunch $6-12; 11am-2:30pm & 4:40-7pm Mon-Sat, 10am-1pm Sun) Dyed-in-the-wool Wrangell local that looks like it hasn't had a decor rethink since 1978. On offer are diner basics: omelets, pancakes, BLTs, salads and soups. Come for big portions, stick around for town gossip.

★**Stikine Inn Restaurant** AMERICAN **$$**
(107 Stikine Ave; mains lunch $14-18, dinner $16-30; 11am-8pm) It's not hard being the best restaurant in Wrangell, but the Stikine goes above and beyond the call of duty with dishes like rockfish tacos, and a lobster po'boy that manages to be decadent without a decadent price. Everything's made a little more hunky dory by the view (water and fishing boats) and service (small-town Alaska friendly).

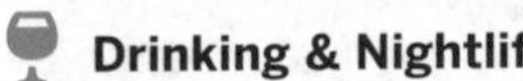

Drinking & Nightlife

Stik Cafe CAFE
(107 Stikine Ave; 6am-5:30pm;) A welcome sight inside the Stikine Inn, the Stik serves the best coffee in the Southern Panhandle along with decent breakfasts and fresh bready snacks. You can enjoy it all in the hotel bar overlooking the water, alternating boat-watching with internet browsing.

Rayme's Bar BAR
(907-874-3442; 532 Front St; 11:30am-11pm) If you're on a tour of gritty Alaskan bars that smell of spilt beer and old carpets, pop into Rayme's, where inhaling deeply is usually enough to make you feel light-headed.

Information

INTERNET ACCESS

Irene Ingle Public Library (907-874-3535; 124 2nd St; 10am-noon & 1-5pm Mon & Fri, 1-5pm & 7-9pm Tue-Thu, 9am-5pm Sat;) A wonderful facility for such a small town; has free wi-fi and a paperback exchange, plus a few terminals.

MEDICAL SERVICES

Wrangell Medical Center (907-874-7000; 310 Bennet St) For anything from aspirin to Zoloft.

MONEY

First Bank (224 Brueger St; 9am-5pm Mon-Fri) Across from IGA Supermarket, it maintains a 24-hour ATM on Front St.

TOURIST INFOMATION

USFS Office (907-874-2323; 525 Bennet St; 8am-4:30pm Mon-Fri) Located 0.75 miles north of town; has information on regional USFS cabins, trails and campgrounds.

Wrangell Visitor Center (907-874-3901; www.wrangell.com; 293 Campbell Dr; 10am-5pm Mon-Sat) In the plush Nolan Center, it stocks the free *Wrangell Guide* and shows a 10-minute film on the area in a small theater.

Getting There & Away

AIR

Daily northbound and southbound flights are available with Alaska Airlines (p429) on the so-called 'Milk Run' serving Seattle, Ketchikan, Petersburg, Juneau and Anchorage. Many claim the flight north to Petersburg is the world's shortest jet flight – around nine minutes on a good day with fabulous views to boot.

The **airport** (907-874-3107) is just over a mile from the town center; an easy walk with light luggage.

FERRY

The Alaska Marine Highway Ferry Terminal (www.dot.state.ak.us/amhs) is a half-mile north of the town center and easily walkable.

Ferry services run almost daily both northbound and southbound from Wrangell in summer. To the north is Petersburg ($40, three hours) via the winding Wrangell Narrows; to the south, Ketchikan ($53, six hours).

Getting Around

Practical Rent-A-Car (907-874-3975), at the airport, rents compacts for $65 per day plus a 17% rental tax.

Chief Shakes Island (p88), Petroglyph Beach (p88) and Mt Dewey (p88) are all walkable from the town center. There's an asphalt walking/cycling path stretching 4.5 miles south of Wrangell town as far as Shoemaker Bay.

Petersburg

907 / POP 2925

The surprise package of Southeast Alaska is the quietly prosperous town of Petersburg, where Norwegian flags fly alongside the stars and stripes, and wide, unhurried streets emit a distinctly Scandinavian sense of tidiness and order.

Petersburg was founded by Norwegian immigrant Peter Buschmann in 1897 and, after a rocky start, quickly found its mojo. Its enduring prosperity is largely a result of a steely independence built around a self-contained fishing industry and aided and abetted by several canneries that abut the busy harbor. The shallow port is inappropriate for large cruise ships, a factor that has worked subtly in Petersburg's favor – there is no summer invasion of tourists here. Hence Petersburg attracts a more intrepid cross section of travelers to a town where fishing trawlers outnumber pleasure craft and, if you leave your bike unlocked outside the post office, it'll probably still be there when you return three hours later.

Sights

North Boat Harbor HARBOR

(Excel St, at Harbor Way) The North Boat Harbor is the best one for wandering the docks, talking to crews and possibly scoring some fresh fish. Begin at the Harbormaster Office; a wooden deck provides a picturesque overview of the commercial fleet and has a series of interpretive panels that will teach you the difference between purse seine and a long-liner.

Continue north to **Petersburg Fisheries** (Dolphin St, at Nordic Dr), the original outfit founded by Peter Buschmann in 1900; today it's a subsidiary of Seattle's Icicle Seafoods.

Sing Lee Alley HISTORIC SITE

If it's historic in Petersburg, you'll find it in Sing Lee Alley, an ensemble of geriatric wooden buildings dating from the 1910s. Much of the street is built on pilings over Hammer Slough, including the **Sons of Norway Hall**, a large white building with colorful rosemaling built in 1912 and the center for Petersburg's Norwegian culture. Come on down and play bingo at 7pm on Friday.

Bojet Wikan Fishermen's Memorial Park PARK

At the southern end of Sing Lee Alley is Bojet Wikan Fishermen's Memorial Park. This deck-of-a-park is built on pilings over Hammer Slough and features an impressive statue of a fisher that honors all his fellow crew members lost at sea. Also on display is the *Valhalla*, a replica of a Viking ship that was built in 1976 and purchased by Petersburg two years later.

Clausen Memorial Museum MUSEUM

(203 Fram St; adult/child $5/free; 10am-5pm Mon-Sat) This museum holds an interesting collection of artifacts and relics, mostly related to local fishing history. Exhibits include the largest king salmon ever caught (126lbs), a giant lens from the old Cape Decision lighthouse, a Tlingit dugout canoe and the 30-minute film *Petersburg: The Town Fish Built*. Outside is *Fisk*, the intriguing fish sculpture that was commissioned in 1967 to honor the Alaska Centennial.

Activities

Hiking

City Creek Trail HIKING

This beautiful little trail leads east along the coast from Sandy Beach Park. It's only 1 mile (one way), but what a mile! The coastal forest here is an enchanted mass of moss-draped branches and misshapen trees and there are regular glimpses of Frederick Sound (and the occasional whale) to your left.

The path ends at City Creek, where you can walk back along the dirt road.

Petersburg Lake Trail HIKING

Petersburg Lake Trail is a 10.5-mile trail in the Petersburg Creek-Duncan Salt Chuck Wilderness on Kupreanof Island; it leads to

Petersburg

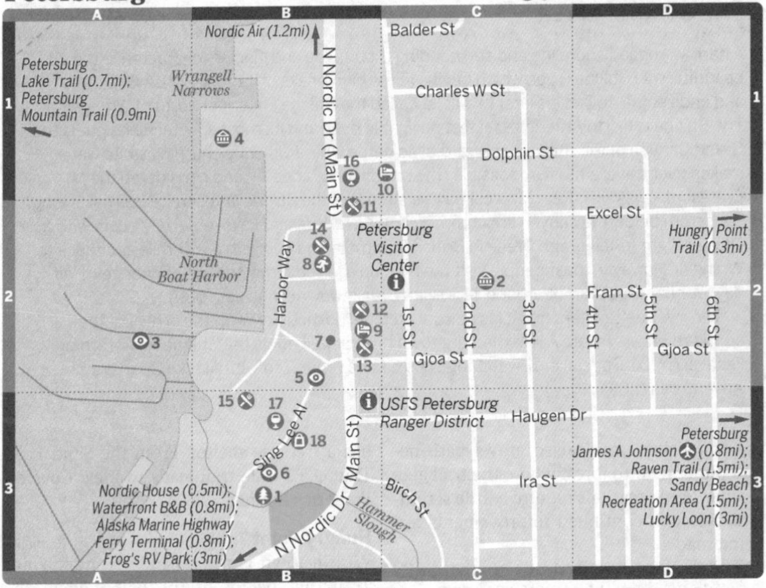

Petersburg

Sights

1 Bojet Wikan Fishermen's Memorial Park B3
2 Clausen Memorial Museum C2
3 North Boat Harbor A2
4 Petersburg Fisheries B1
5 Sing Lee Alley B2
6 Sons of Norway Hall B3

Activities, Courses & Tours

7 Viking Travel B2
8 Whale Song Cruises B2

Sleeping

9 Scandia House B2
10 Tides Inn C1

Eating

11 Coastal Cold Storage B2
12 El Rincón de Carmen B2
13 Inga's Galley B2
14 Pappa Bear's Pizza B2
15 Salty Pantry B3

Drinking & Nightlife

16 Harbor Bar B1
Java Hus .... (see 9)
17 Kito's Kave B3

Shopping

18 Sing Lee Alley Books B3

the USFS **Petersburg Lake cabin** (☎515-885-3639; www.recreation.gov; cabins $45). Due to lack of funds, the trail has suffered from poor maintenance in recent years, but it is still passable with care.

The trek begins at the Kupreanof Island public dock. From the dock a partial boardwalk heads south for a mile past a handful of cabins and then turns northwest up the tidewater arm of the creek, almost directly across Wrangell Narrows from the ferry terminal. A planked trail goes from the saltwater arm and continues along the freshwater creek to the USFS Petersburg Lake cabin.

Plan on reserving the Petersburg Lake cabin at least two months in advance. For transportation across Wrangell Narrows to the public dock on Kupreanof Island, contact Tongass Kayak Adventures.

Raven Trail HIKING

Four-mile Raven Trail is in very good condition, particularly on its lower sections. It starts near the junction of Sandy Beach Rd and Haugen Dr. The first mile takes you

WORTH A TRIP

THE STIKINE RIVER

A narrow, rugged shoreline and surrounding mountains and glaciers characterize the beautiful, wild Stikine River, which begins in the high peaks of interior British Columbia and ends some 400 miles later in a delta called the Stikine Flats, just north of Wrangell. The Stikine is North America's fastest navigable river, and its most spectacular sight is the Grand Canyon of the Stikine, a steep-walled gorge where violently churning white water makes river travel almost impossible (the rapids are graded V+ and considered the Mt Everest of kayaking). John Muir called this stretch of the Stikine 'a Yosemite 100 miles long.' Trips from below the canyon are common among rafters and kayakers. They begin with a charter flight to Telegraph Creek in British Columbia and end with a 160-mile float back to Wrangell. However, most people visit the river on a jet-boat day trip out of Wrangell. Half-day jet-boat trips start at around $160 with Breakaway Adventures (p89).

The river delta offers first-class bird-watching, particularly with the arrival of the spring migrants in late April when the town of Wrangell holds the Stikine River Birding Festival (p90). Special bird-watching trips can be organized with Alaska Charters & Adventures (p89).

across muskeg on a raised gravel path before plunging into forest where the trail gets steeper. Some sections require a little scrambling, though continued improvements are being made.

The trail eventually leads to the USFS **Raven's Roost Cabin** (☎515-885-3639; www.recreation.gov; cabins $40). The cabin is above the tree line, providing easy access to good alpine hiking and spectacular views of Petersburg, Frederick Sound and Wrangell Narrows.

Petersburg Mountain Trail HIKING

On Kupreanof Island, this 3.5-mile trail climbs to the top of Petersburg Mountain (2750ft), which offers views of Petersburg, the Coast Mountains, glaciers and Wrangell Narrows.

To get across the channel, go to the skiff float at the North Boat Harbor and hitch a ride with somebody who lives on Kupreanof Island (warning: it can be tough to find a ride back). Tongass Kayak Adventures also runs hikers across the channel for $25 per trip. On the Kupreanof side, head right on the overgrown road toward Sasby Island. Plan on five hours for the round-trip.

Three Lakes Loop Trails HIKING

Along Three Lakes Rd, a USFS road heading east off Mitkof Hwy at Mile 13.6 and returning at Mile 23.8, are Three Lakes Loop Trails, a series of four short trails that total 4.5 miles.

At Mile 14.2 is a 3-mile loop with boardwalks leading to Sand, Crane and Hill Lakes, all known for good trout fishing. Sand Lake has a free-use shelter. From the Sand Lake Trail, a 1.5-mile trail leads to Ideal Cove on Frederick Sound.

Hungry Point Trail HIKING

Within town is the 0.7-mile Hungry Point Trail that begins at the ball field at the end of Excel St and cuts across muskeg. The gravel path keeps your feet dry, and surrounding you are stunted trees so short you have a clear view of Petersburg's mountainous skyline. The trail ends at Sandy Beach Rd.

Head right a quarter-mile to reach Outlook Park, a marine wildlife observatory with free binoculars to search Frederick Sound for humpbacks, orcas and sea lions.

Paddling

Petersburg has interesting possibilities for kayakers, LeConte Glacier and Tebenkof Bay Wilderness among them, but many of the trips require a week or more. Closer to town, you can paddle up sheltered Petersburg Creek in a half-day trip. Kayak rentals (and anything else you might need, including sleeping bags) are available from Tongass Kayak Adventures.

★ **Tongass Kayak Adventures** KAYAKING

(☎907-772-4600; www.tongasskayak.com; single/double kayaks $55/65) Offers rentals and drop-off transportation, as well as several guided paddles, including a day-long paddle ($365) at LeConte Glacier. Also offers humpback-whale-watching trips in Fredrick Sound ($300). Very friendly and flexible. There's no office; book by phone or online.

★LeConte Glacier KAYAKING

The most spectacular paddle in the region is to LeConte Glacier, 25 miles east of Petersburg. It's North America's southernmost tidewater glacier and often the site of spectacular falling ice and breaching whales. From town, it takes one to two days to reach the frozen monument, including crossing Frederick Sound north of Coney Island. The crossing should be done at slack tide, as winds and tides can cause choppy conditions.

If the tides are judged right, and the ice is not too thick, it's possible to paddle far enough into LeConte Bay to camp within view of the glacier.

Tongass Kayak Adventures offers an easier outing: its 10-hour tour ($365 per person) begins with a cruise to the glacier, then paddling among the icebergs. There's also a shorter version: six hours (two paddling) for $285.

Thomas Bay KAYAKING

Impressive Thomas Bay is 20 miles from Petersburg and north of LeConte Bay on Frederick Sound's east side. The bay has a pair of glaciers, including Baird Glacier, where many paddlers go for day hikes. The mountain scenery around the bay is spectacular. Paddlers should allow four to seven days for the round-trip out of Petersburg.

The area has three USFS cabins: **Swan Lake Cabin** (www.recreation.gov; cabins $50), **Spurt Cove Cabin** (www.recreation.gov; cabins $40) and **Cascade Creek Cabin** (www.recreation.gov; per night $45). All require reservations and a floatplane transfer.

Petersburg Creek KAYAKING

This outstanding steelhead and sockeye stream is across from Petersburg on Kupreanof Island and makes for an easy day paddle, beginning from the South Harbor (beware of strong currents when crossing the Wrangell Narrows). During high tide you can paddle more than 4 miles up the creek and reach a trailhead for the Petersburg Lake Trail.

Tongass Kayak Adventures offers a guided four-hour paddle up the creek ($95 per person).

Whale-Watching

Petersburg offers some of the best whale-watching in Southeast Alaska. From mid-May to mid-September humpback whales migrate through, and feed in, Frederick Sound, 45 miles northwest of Petersburg. Other wildlife that can be spotted includes Steller's sea lions, orcas and seals.

Whale Song Cruises WHALE WATCHING

(☎907-772-9393; www.whalesongcruises.com; 207 N Nordic Dr; per person $371) Has a two-person minimum and is equipped with a hydrophone so you can listen to the whales – orcas and humpbacks – as well as see them.

Tours

For a large selection of area tours, head to the professionally friendly **Viking Travel** (☎907-772-3818; www.alaskaferry.com; 101 N Nordic Dr), which acts as a clearinghouse for just about every tour in town. Possibilities include a four-hour boat tour to LeConte Glacier ($212), or an eight-hour whale-watching tour ($300).

Most of the charter operators that do whale-watching also have sightseeing trips to view LeConte Glacier. **Nordic Air** (☎907-772-3535; www.nordicairflying.com; 409 Sandy Beach Rd) offers flightseeing trips to the glacier starting at $200 per person.

Festivals & Events

Little Norway Festival CULTURAL

(May) Held on the third full weekend in May. The festival celebrates Norwegian Constitution Day (May 17). The locals dress in traditional costumes, there's a foot race in the morning and Nordic Dr is filled with a string of craft booths and beer tents. But best of all are the fish and shrimp evening feeds, all-you-can-possibly-manage-to-eat affairs.

Sleeping

Petersburg town itself is lacking budget accommodations (apart from the campground); your options are limited to one good hotel, a motel and several B&Bs. The city adds 10% sales and bed tax on accommodations.

Frog's RV Park CAMPGROUND $

(☎360-482-8589; 126 Scow Bay Loop Rd; tent/RV sites $10/30; Wi-Fi) Petersburg's only waterfront campground is 2.5 miles past the ferry terminal. It's not much more than a gravel parking lot with seven RV sites and two tent sites, but the views make up for it.

★Scandia House HOTEL $$

(☎907-772-4281; www.scandiahousehotel.com; 110 Nordic Dr; s/d/ste $120/130/200; P Wi-Fi) The most impressive accommodations in town, this hotel has 33 bright and modern rooms, some with kitchenettes, and a subtle sprinkling of Norwegian trim. Rates include courtesy shuttle service from the airport/ferry and muffins and coffee in the morning.

★Lucky Loon GUESTHOUSE $$
(☎907-772-2345; www.theluckyloon.com; 181 Frederick Dr; d $170; P 📶) If you've had it with the cruise-ship crowds, this is your escape: a beautiful home in its own wooded retreat, 3 miles from downtown Petersburg. From the deck, kitchen and living room you enjoy a spectacular view of Frederick Sound, watching an assortment of wildlife pass by every day – from bald eagles and sea lions to humpback whales.

For what you would pay for a room in town, you get the entire home (for two people; $50 per extra person). The only drawback is a five-night minimum, but what a way to spend five days. There is another two-bed apartment, 'the boathouse', next door.

Nordic House B&B $$
(☎907-772-3620; www.nordichouse.net; 806 S Nordic Dr; d with shared/private bath $107/120, apt $164; P 📶) One of the more Norwegian-looking of Petersburg's houses, this stunner is raised on stilts above the water and has Nordic trim painted onto its attractive window shutters. There are several rooms (some with a shared bathroom), a cozy shared 'gathering room,' a kitchen, access to a barbecue and a courtesy shuttle for airport/ferry transfers.

Suffice to say it has a good location halfway between the ferry terminal and the town center.

Waterfront B&B B&B $$
(☎907-772-9300; www.waterfrontbedandbreakfast.com; 1004 S Nordic Dr; r $110-145; 📶) The closest place to the ferry terminal – it's practically next door. It has an outdoor hot tub where you can soak while watching the ferry depart. Five bright and comfortable rooms have private bath and share a living room that overlooks the Petersburg Shipwrights.

For many guests, watching a boat being repaired on dry dock is far more interesting than whatever is on the idiot box.

Tides Inn MOTEL $$
(☎907-772-4288; www.tidesinnalaska.com; 307 1st St; s/d from $175/188; 📶) This basic wood-paneled motel doesn't look particularly handsome from the outside, but friendly service, high levels of cleanliness and waffle breakfasts make up for the lack of good looks. Rooms were recently remodeled.

Eating

★Salty Pantry CAFE, SANDWICHES $
(☎907-772-2665; 14 Harbor Way; sandwiches & snacks from $8; ⏲6:30am-2pm Mon-Fri, to 4pm Sat) Looking like it was flown in ready-made from Seattle's trendy Capitol Hill neighborhood, this wonderful cafe/deli opened in 2017 to much local incredulity. Set on the harborside, it serves wonderful salad medleys, quality coffee, home-baked cakes and creative sandwiches in a glassy, light-filled interior. Join the queue.

Inga's Galley SEAFOOD $
(104 N Nordic Dr; sandwiches $10, dinner mains $8-14; ⏲7am-8pm Mon-Sat, to 7pm Sun May-Aug) From this (surprisingly charming) parking-lot shack comes Petersburg's most creative food. Inga's Mitkof sandwich is seasoned and seared halibut topped with pesto, prosciutto and melted provolone. The fish and chips is fresh rockfish rolled in panko (Japanese breadcrumbs).

There are also nonseafood items on the menu and a large tent with heaters where you can mingle with locals while staying dry and warm.

El Zarape MEXICAN $
(☎907-518-0177; 114 N Nordic Dr; mains $11-14; ⏲11am-7pm Mon-Sat) Little more than a food truck with an awning glued on the side, this Mexican-run spot satisfies Petersburg's small contingent of Latino cannery workers and many more besides. In a town of lean food choices, it can quite easily spice up your day with fish tacos, rice, beans and a scoop of guacamole.

Coastal Cold Storage SEAFOOD $$
(306 N Nordic Dr; breakfast $5-7, lunch $11-18; ⏲7am-2pm Tue-Sat; 📶) You're in Petersburg – indulge in what they catch. Stop at this processor/seafood store/restaurant for a shrimp burger, salmon-halibut chowder or the local specialty, halibut beer bits. Or purchase whatever is swimming in the tanks: steamer clams, oysters or Dungeness crab. In the coolers you find just-made salmon sandwiches, shrimp salads, halibut cheeks

and even squid bait. Need a beer with those? The staff will deliver your order next door to the Harbor Bar.

Pappa Bear's Pizza PIZZA $$
(219 N Nordic Dr; pizzas $14-25; 11am-7pm Mon-Sat) Arrive early at Papa Bear's: the place does a roaring takeaway trade, meaning you may end up waiting an hour or more for your pie. The place specializes in American-style pizza, whole or by the slice, along with subs and burger baskets. It's pretty basic – grab your own cutlery and sit down at a bench – but it hits the spot on a cold and rainy Alaskan evening.

Drinking & Nightlife

Harbor Bar BAR
(310 N Nordic Dr; 10am-2am;) A classic domain of deckhands and cannery workers, with pool tables, free popcorn and a diverse beer selection.

Kito's Kave BAR
(Sing Lee Alley; 10am-2am;) Legendary dive that's been around for eons. Jon Krakauer mentions it in his book *Eiger Dreams;* apparently he was asked to leave for playing morbid music on the jukebox. You have been warned.

Shopping

Sing Lee Alley Books BOOKS
(11 Sing Lee Alley; 9:30am-5:30pm Mon-Sat, 10am-4pm Sun) In a former 1929 boardinghouse, this bookstore is as delightful as it is unexpected in tiny Petersburg, with five rooms of jumbled books and a well-read proprietor.

Information

INTERNET ACCESS

Petersburg Public Library (cnr Haugen Dr & 2nd St; noon-9pm Mon-Thu, 10am-5pm Fri & Sat;) A beauty with works of art adorning the walls and a fire casting a glow over enticing easy chairs.

MEDICAL SERVICES

Petersburg Medical Center (907-772-4299; 103 Fram St) Has a 24-hour emergency room, and on Saturday operates as a drop-in health clinic.

MONEY

First Bank (103 N Nordic Dr; 9am-5pm Mon-Fri)

TOURIST INFORMATION

Petersburg Visitor Center (907-772-4636; www.petersburg.org; cnr Fram & 1st Sts; 9am-5pm Mon-Sat, noon-4pm Sun) Mega-friendly, even by Alaskan standards.

USFS Petersburg Ranger District (907-772-3871; 12 N Nordic Dr; 8am-4:30pm Mon-Fri) For information about hiking trails, paddling, camping or reserving cabins. Worth visiting for the huge map of the Tongass National Forest that adorns one of the walls.

Getting There & Away

AIR

There are daily northbound and southbound flights with Alaska Airlines AS65 on the so-called 'Milk Run' between Seattle and Anchorage.

The **airport** (Haugen Dr) is a quarter-mile east of the post office and walkable from town.

DEVIL'S THUMB

On clear days, the sharp, glacier-encrusted peaks of the Alaska Coast Range are clearly visible from Petersburg on the opposite side of Frederick Sound. Of the rocky behemoths, none is more disquieting than 9077ft Devil's Thumb, an imposing mass of granite that thrusts skywards like a grey meat cleaver over the wild border between Alaska and British Columbia. Although far from being the state's highest mountain, the 'Thumb' is arguably one of its most dangerous. The frighteningly massive northwest face – an intimidating 6700ft-high wall of sheer rock – has never been successfully climbed, though several experienced alpinists have died trying. Instead, the mountain is usually tackled via its east ridge, a route pioneered by legendary US climber Fred Beckey in 1946.

Writer Jon Krakauer famously chronicled his solo attempt on Devil's Thumb in the book *Into the Wild*, using it as an allegory for how youthful hubris can sometimes lead to naive folly. After several abortive attempts on the northwest face, Krakauer, battling the Thumb's notoriously fickle weather conditions, finally summited the mountain via the east ridge, an impressive achievement, nonetheless, for a 23-year-old with little backup or experience.

FERRY

The **Alaska Marine Highway Ferry Terminal** (☎907-772-3855; www.ferryalaska.com) is 0.75 miles south of downtown; in the summer there is a ferry passing through in one direction or the other almost daily.

Boats south go to Wrangell ($40; three hours) with connections on to Ketchikan and Bellingham, WA. Boats north go to Juneau ($78; eight hours) with connections on to Skagway. Another route runs to Kake ($46; four hours) on Kupreanof Island before heading on to Sitka ($70; 14 hours).

Getting Around

Scandia House (p96) rents midsize cars for $70 a day.

At the time of writing there was no bike rental.

Hyder

☎250 / POP 87

On the eastern fringe of Misty Fiords National Monument, at the head of Portland Canal, is Hyder, a misplaced town if there ever was one. It was founded in 1896 when Captain DD Gailland explored Portland Canal for the US Army Corps of Engineers and built four stone storehouses, the first masonry buildings erected in Alaska, which still stand today. Hyder and its British Columbian neighbor Stewart boomed after major gold and silver mines were opened in 1919, and Hyder became the supply center for more than 10,000 residents. It's been going downhill ever since, the reason it calls itself 'the friendliest ghost town in Alaska.'

Because of Hyder's isolation from the rest of the state, it's almost totally dependent on larger Stewart (population 500), just across the Canadian border. Hyder's residents use Canadian money, set their watches to Pacific time (not Alaska time), use Stewart's area code and send their children to Canadian schools.

Sights

Salmon Glacier GLACIER

Twenty miles north of Hyder and back inside Canada lies the fifth-largest glacier in Canada (and the largest in the world accessible by road). The old mine road to the glacier is rough and nerve-racking if you're not used to backcountry driving. However, the sight when you get there is simply incredible. The final overlook has interpretive signs and a toilet block, but no guardrails. Pick up the self-guided 'auto tour' leaflet at the Stewart Visitor Centre before setting out.

Activities

★Fish Creek Wildlife Observation Site WILDLIFE WATCHING

($5; ⏰6am-10pm Jul-Sep) The best reason to descend on the 'ghost town' of Hyder is for bear-viewing: it's one of the least inundated places in Alaska to do this and – ironically – the only one accessible by road. From late July to September, you can head 3 miles north of town to Fish Creek Bridge and watch brown and black bears feed on chum salmon runs; you might even see a wolf.

The **USFS** (☎250-636-2367) has constructed an office in a small cabin and a viewing platform here; interpreters are on-site during summer. The cabin has a regularly updated message board about bear and other wildlife activity in the area. The entry fee is charged whether or not bears are present.

Sleeping

Bear River RV Park CAMPGROUND $

(☎250-636-9205; www.bearriverrvpark.com; 2200 Davis St, Stewart; tent/RV sites C$22/45; P 📶) Sixty-eight sites along the Bear River a mile from Stewart, in BC, Canada. There are washrooms and pay showers.

Ripley Creek Inn INN $$

(☎250-636-2344; www.ripleycreekinn.com; 306 5th Ave, Stewart; r C$115-155; P 📶 🐾) Fantastic array of rooms spread around nine different buildings in Stewart, BC, all of them historic, from an old prospector's house to a former brothel. While the historical essence is heavy, there's no lack of modern comforts.

Drinking & Nightlife

Glacier Inn BAR

(☎250-636-9092; Hyder Ave; ⏰10am-10pm) The most famous thing to do in Hyder is have a (very) stiff drink at one of its 'friendly saloons.' The historic Glacier Inn, where you're encouraged to 'get hyderized' (down a shot of 95% alcohol by volume Everclear liquor), is the best known and features an interior papered in signed bills, creating the '$20,000 Walls' of Hyder. Good luck staggering out afterwards.

Information

Stewart Visitor Centre (☎250-636-9224; 222 5th Ave, Stewart) Contact for information on Stewart or Hyder.

Getting There & Away

A floatplane from Ketchikan or a long drive through BC, Canada, are the only options for getting here.

NORTHERN PANHANDLE

Southeast Alaska gets serious when you enter the northern half of the Panhandle. The mountains get higher, the glaciers are more numerous, fjords seem steeper and there's more snow in the winter that lingers on the mountains longer into the summer. You have the current capital and a former one. You have Alaska's most famous gold rush and two roads that actually go somewhere else. Most of all, the dramatic scenery you witness in the Northern Panhandle leads to great wilderness adventures, whether it's canoeing across Admiralty Island, kayaking in Glacier Bay or hiking on Mendenhall Glacier.

Sitka

☎907 / POP 8800

It's not always easy to uncover reminders of Alaska's 135-year-long dalliance with the Russian Empire – until you dock in Sitka. This sparkling gem of a city, which kisses the Pacific Ocean on Baranof Island's west shore, is one of the oldest non-native settlements in the state and the former capital of Russian Alaska (when it was known as New Archangel).

The bonus for visitors is that Sitka mixes wonderfully preserved history with outstanding natural beauty. Looming on the horizon, across Sitka Sound, is impressive Mt Edgecumbe, an extinct volcano with a graceful cone similar to Japan's Mt Fuji. Closer in, myriad small, forested islands turn into beautiful ragged silhouettes at sunset, competing for attention with the snowcapped mountains and sharp granite peaks flanking Sitka to the east. And in town picturesque remnants of Sitka's Russian heritage are tucked around every corner. It's like Skagway but with less tourists.

Sights

Town Center

★Sitka National Historical Park HISTORIC SITE

(www.nps.gov; Lincoln St; ⌚6am-10pm) FREE This mystical juxtaposition of tall trees and totems is Alaska's smallest national park and the site where the Tlingits were finally defeated by the Russians in 1804.

The mile-long **Totem Trail** winds it way past 18 totems first displayed at the 1904 Louisiana Exposition in St Louis and then moved to the park. These intriguing totems, standing in a thick rainforest setting by the sea and often enveloped in mist, have become synonymous with the national park and, by definition, the city itself.

Eventually you arrive at the site of the Tlingit fort near Indian River with its outline still clearly visible. You can either explore the trail as a self-guided tour or join a ranger-led 'Battle Walk.'

Back in 1804, the Tlingits defended their wooden fort for a week.The Russians' cannons did little damage to the walls of the fort and, when the Russian soldiers stormed the structure with the help of Aleuts, they were repulsed in a bloody battle. It was only when the Tlingits ran out of gunpowder and flint, and slipped away at night, that the Russians were able to enter the deserted fort.

The **visitors center** (8am to 5pm) displays Russian and indigenous artifacts, and a 12-minute video in the theater provides an overview of the Tlingit–Russian battle. There's also a workshop where you can observe and talk to native wood-carvers.

★Russian Bishop's House HISTORIC BUILDING

(☎907-747-0135; Lincoln St; ⌚9am-5pm) FREE East of downtown along Lincoln St, the Russian Bishop's House is the oldest intact Russian building in Sitka. Built in 1843 by Finnish carpenters out of Sitka spruce, the two-story log house is one of only four surviving examples of Russian colonial architecture in North America. The National Park Service (NPS) has restored the building to its 1853 condition, when it served as a school and residence for the Russian bishop, Innocent (Ivan Veniaminov).

Sitka

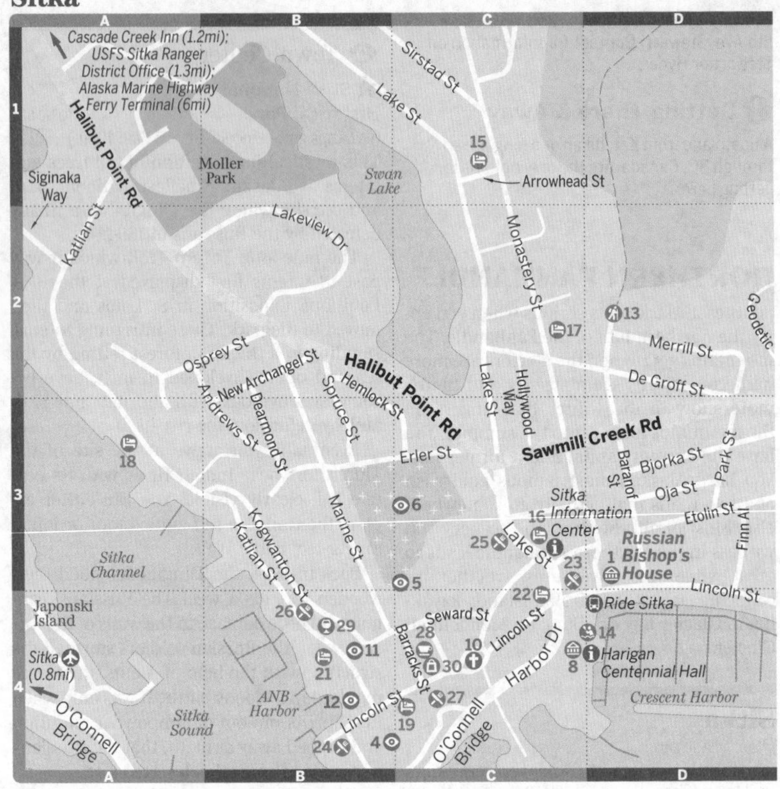

You can wander the ground-floor museum, with its rescued exhibits and short film, at will. Access to the top floor, home to re-created living quarters and the private chapel of Bishop Innocent, is by guide only. Free tours leave on the half-hour.

St Michael's Cathedral CHURCH
(240 Lincoln St; adult/child $5/free; ⌚9am-4pm Mon-Fri or by appt) Built between 1844 and 1848, this church stood for more than 100 years as Alaska's finest Russian Orthodox cathedral. When a fire destroyed it in 1966, the church had been the oldest religious structure from the Russian era in Alaska. Luckily the priceless treasures and icons inside were saved by Sitka's residents, who immediately built a replica of their beloved church.

The interior is rich in detail and iconography. Of particular note is the depiction of *Our Lady of Sitka* rendered by Vladimir Borovikovsky in the 1820s.

Russian Cemetery CEMETERY
(⌚6am-10pm) Old headstones and Russian Orthodox crosses lurk in the overgrown and quintessentially creepy Russian Cemetery (located at the north end of Observatory St), where the drippy verdure seems poised to swallow up the decaying graves. Rarely will you find a more atmospheric graveyard.

Sheldon Jackson Museum MUSEUM
(104 College Dr; adult/child $5/free; ⌚9am-4:30pm) East along Lincoln St on the former campus of Sheldon Jackson College is Sheldon Jackson Museum. The college may be gone, but this fine museum, housed in Alaska's oldest concrete building (1895), survives. The unusual building is home to a small but excellent collection of artifacts from all of Alaska's indigenous groups gathered by Dr Sheldon Jackson, a federal education agent, in Alaska in the 1890s.

Among the artifacts is a raven helmet worn by a Tlingit warrior named Katlian in

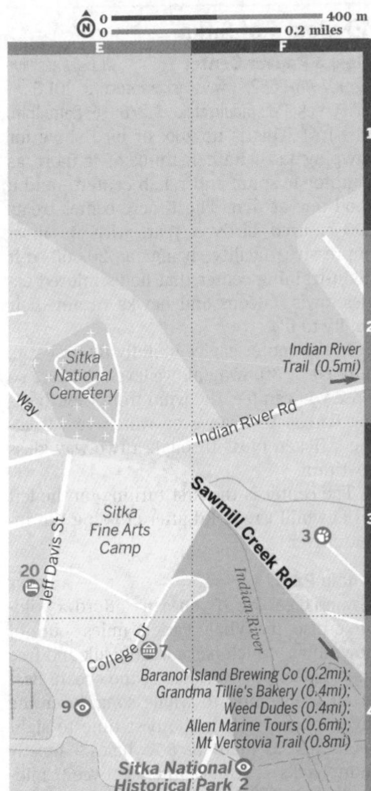

Sitka

Top Sights
1 Russian Bishop's House D3
2 Sitka National Historical Park F4

Sights
3 Alaska Raptor Center F3
4 Castle Hill B4
5 Princess Maksoutoff's Grave C3
6 Russian Cemetery C3
7 Sheldon Jackson Museum E4
8 Sitka Historical Museum C4
9 Sitka Sound Science Center E4
10 St Michael's Cathedral C4
11 Tlingit Clan House B4
12 Totem Square B4

Activities, Courses & Tours
13 Gavan Hill Trail D2
14 Sitka Sound Ocean Adventures D4

Sleeping
15 Ann's Gavan Hill B&B C1
16 Aspen Suites Hotel C3
17 Hannah's B&B C2
18 Longliner Lodge A3
19 Sitka Hotel C4
20 Sitka International Hostel E3
21 Totem Square Inn B4
22 Westmark Sitka Hotel C4

Eating
23 Bayview Pub C3
24 Beak Restaurant B4
25 Highliner Coffee C3
26 Ludvig's Bistro B4
27 Mean Queen C4
Sitka Hotel Bar & Restaurant .... (see 19)

Drinking & Nightlife
28 Back Door Café C4
Ludvig's Wine Bar and Gallery .. (see 26)
29 Pioneer Bar B4

Entertainment
New Archangel Russian Dancers .... (see 8)
Sheet'ka Kwaan Naa Kahidi Dancers .... (see 11)

Shopping
30 Old Harbor Books C4

the 1804 Battle of Sitka, along with rescued totem poles dating from between the 1820s and the 1880s.

Sitka Sound Science Center AQUARIUM
(www.sitkascience.org; 801 Lincoln St; $5; 9am-4pm;) Sitka's best children's attraction is this hatchery and science center. Outside, the facade is being restored to its original appearance. Inside the science center are five aquariums, including the impressive 800-gallon 'Wall of Water' and three touch tanks where kids can get their hands wet handling anemones, sea cucumbers and starfish.

Watch feedings on Tuesday and Friday at 2pm. Outside is a working hatchery where tanks are filled with 60,000 salmon fryling.

Castle Hill HISTORIC SITE
Walk west on Lincoln St for the walkway to Castle Hill. Kiksadi clan houses once covered the hilltop site, but in 1836 the Russians built 'Baranov's Castle' atop the hill to house the governor of Russian America. It was here, on October 18, 1867, that the official transfer of Alaska from Russia to the USA took place. The castle burned down in 1894. A US administrative building briefly took its place, but was demolished in 1955.

Today the lookout is guarded by old Russian cannons and embellished by informative historical boards.

Sitka Historical Museum MUSEUM
(www.sitkahistory.org; 330 Harbor Dr; 9am-5pm) Within Sitka's recently rebuilt Harigan Centennial Hall is the town history museum. It features plenty of relics from Russian Alaska.

Totem Square SQUARE
An exposed grassy plaza close to the O'Connell Bridge and ANB Harbor, anchored by the famous Baranov totem topped by a carved image of Alexander Baranov (1790–1818), the founder of both old and modern Sitka.

Lower down, a two-headed Russian eagle has also been carved on to the pole. The totem was commissioned in 1942 and fully restored in 2011.

Princess Maksoutoff's Grave HISTORIC SITE
At the top of Princess Way lies Princess Maksoutoff's Grave, marking the spot where the wife of Alaska's last Russian governor is buried.

A strategically placed chain-link fence and a bright and shiny sign proclaim this tiny three-grave site as the Lutheran Cemetery.

Cynics might postulate that the princess probably lost her status as a bona fide Lutheran when she married the Russian Orthodox governor, but now that she's a bona fide tourist attraction the Lutherans want her back.

North of Sitka

Old Sitka State Historical Park HISTORIC SITE
(Halibut Point Rd) There are no physical remains of Old Sitka (known historically as the Redoubt), the original Russian settlement in the area, although archaeological digs have unearthed some small treasures.

Redoubt, anchored by a wooden fort, stood on this site for three years between 1799 and 1802 before it was destroyed by angry Tlingit warriors.

A small historical trail with a half-dozen panels tells its short but intriguing story.

The park is accessible on the Ride Sitka (p109) red bus. It's a quarter-mile walk from the last stop (ferry terminal).

South of Sitka

Alaska Raptor Center WILDLIFE RESERVE
(907-747-8662; www.alaskaraptor.org; 101 Sawmill Creek Rd; adult/child $12/6; 8am-4pm; P) This is no zoo, or bird show for gawping kids. Rather, think of it more as a raptor hospital and rehab center – and a good one at that. The 17-acre center treats 200 injured birds a year, with its most impressive facility being a 20,000-sq-ft flight-training center that helps injured eagles, owls, falcons and hawks regain their ability to fly.

In the center eagles literally fly past you, only 2ft or 3ft away, at eye level; they are so close you can feel the wind from their beating wings. You can even watch vets treating stricken birds through a two-way glass partition.

The center is the first turning on the left off Sawmill Creek Rd after crossing the Indian River.

Whale Park PARK
(Sawmill Creek Rd) If you can't afford a wildlife cruise, try Whale Park, 4 miles south of downtown, which has a boardwalk and free spotting scopes overlooking the ocean. Best of all is listening to whale songs over the 'hydrophone.' Fall is the best time to sight cetaceans; as many as 80 whales – mostly humpbacks – can gather between mid-September and year's end.

Fortress of the Bear ANIMAL SANCTUARY
(907-747-3550; www.fortressofthebear.com; adult/child $10/5) If you haven't seen a bear in the wild – or don't want to – this rescue facility offers an opportunity to observe brown bears that were abandoned as cubs. The walls of the 'fortress' are actually wastewater treatment pools left over after the lumber mill near the end of Sawmill Creek Rd closed in 1993.

The setting is a little strange and these are captive bears, but they are incredibly active – swimming, wrestling and just being bears. It's 5.5 miles south of Sitka. Ride Sitka blue-line buses stop outside every hour.

Activities

Hiking

Sitka offers superb hiking in the beautiful and tangled forest surrounding the city. A complete hiking guide is available from the USFS Sitka Ranger District office (p108).

Scared of bears, or lacking a walking companion? Sitka Trail Works (www.sitkatrailworks.org), a nonprofit group that raises money for trail improvements, has additional trail information on its website and arranges guided hikes on weekends throughout the summer.

Harbor Mountain Trail HIKING

This trail ascends in a series of switchbacks to alpine meadows, knobs and ridges with spectacular views. It follows the tundra ridge to the free-use shelter between Harbor Mountain and Gavan Hill, where you can pick up Gavan Hill Trail. Plan on spending two to four hours if you are just scrambling through the alpine area above Harbor Mountain Rd.

The trail is reached from Harbor Mountain Rd, one of the few roads in the Southeast providing access to a subalpine area. Head 4 miles northwest from Sitka on Halibut Point Rd to the junction with Harbor Mountain Rd. A parking area and picnic shelter are 4.5 miles up the rough dirt road. Another half-mile further is the parking lot at road's end, where an unmarked trail begins on the lot's east side.

Gavan Hill Trail HIKING

Close to town, this popular mountain climb ascends 2500ft over 1.6 miles mainly by the use of wooden staircases. The trail, which breaks into alpine terrain higher up, offers excellent views of Sitka and the surrounding area. From the summit, the adventurous can continue to the peaks of the Three Sisters Mountains.

Gavan Hill is linked to Harbor Mountain Trail. Halfway across the alpine ridge is a free-use emergency shelter available on a first-come, first-served basis; it's 3 miles from the Gavan Hill trailhead, a hike of three to four hours.

The trailhead and a small parking area are just before the cemetery gate at the end of Baranof St. Camping is good in the trail's alpine regions, but bring drinking water as it is unavailable above the tree line.

Mosquito Cove Trail HIKING

At the northwest end of Halibut Point Rd, 0.7 miles past the ferry terminal, Starrigavan Recreation Area (p105) offers a number of short but sweet trails. One of them, Mosquito Cove Trail, is an easy 1.5-mile loop over gravel and boardwalk, with a little beach-walking as well.

Beaver Lake–Herring Cove Loop HIKING

(👪) Dedicated in 2010, the Herring Cove Trail is a 1.3-mile route that extends north to Beaver Lake Trail, which loops around the lake from Sawmill Creek Campground. Together the two trails make for a 3.6-mile hike from the Herring Cove Trailhead, featuring three waterfalls, outstanding views of the surrounding mountains, and boardwalks that wind through an interesting muskeg.

It begins at the eastern end of Sawmill Creek Rd, and is a popular trail for families.

Mt Verstovia Trail HIKING

This 2.5-mile (one-way) trail is a challenging climb of 2550ft to the 'shoulder,' a compact summit that is the final destination for most hikers, although it is possible to continue climbing to the peak of Mt Verstovia, also called Mt Arrowhead (3349ft). The panorama from the shoulder on clear days is spectacular, undoubtedly the area's best.

The trailhead is 2 miles east of Sitka along Sawmill Creek Rd and is posted across from Jamestown Bay. The Russian charcoal pits (signposted) are reached within a quarter-mile, and shortly after that the trail begins a series of switchbacks. It's a four-hour round-trip to the shoulder, from where a ridgeline leads north to the peak (another hour each way).

Indian River Trail HIKING

This easy trail is a 4.5-mile walk along a clear salmon stream to Indian River Falls, an 80ft cascade at the base of the Three Sisters Mountains. The hike takes you through typical Southeast rainforest and offers the opportunity to view deer, bald eagles and brown bears (hopefully from a safe distance). Plan on four to five hours round-trip to the falls.

The trailhead is a short walk from the town center, off Sawmill Creek Rd, just east of Sitka National Cemetery. Turn onto Indian River Rd, and go a short way to the end, where you'll find the parking lot and trailhead.

Paddling

The mini-archipelago of tiny islets that crowd Sitka's harbor, coupled with the fact that big ferries and cruise ships dock several miles to the north, make the town's waters ideal for safe kayaking. Just be sure to keep an eye out for motorized fishing and pleasure boats entering and exiting the harbor.

Sitka also serves as the departure point for more adventurous blue-water trips along the protected shorelines of Sitka Sound, Baranof and Chichagof Islands, some of which require water-taxi transfers.

★ Sitka Sound Ocean Adventures KAYAKING
(☎907-752-0660; www.kayaksitka.com) Rents kayaks (single/double $75/95 per day) and runs guided trips; its office is a blue bus outside the Harigan Centennial Hall (p108). The great value 2½-hour 'Harbor & Islands' paddle (adult/child $79/54) takes you on a voyage through the mini-archipelago that decorates Sitka's harbor.

Shelikof Bay KAYAKING
You can combine a 10-mile paddle from Sitka to Kruzof Island with a 7-mile hike across the island from Mud Bay to Shelikof Bay along Iris Meadows Road Trail (an old logging road). Once on the Pacific Ocean side, you'll find a beautiful sandy beach for beachcombing and the USFS **Shelikof Cabin** (☎518-885-3639; www.recreation.gov; cabins $50).

On the northern side of Shelikof Bay, 2 miles due north of the Shelikof Cabin, is the **North Beach Cabin** (cabins $50).

West Chichagof KAYAKING
Chichagof Island's western shoreline is one of Southeast Alaska's best blue-water destinations for experienced kayakers. Slocum Arm marks the southern end of a series of straits, coves and protected waterways that shield paddlers from the ocean's swells and extend over 30 miles north to Lisianski Strait. With all its hidden coves and inlets, the trip is a good two-week paddle.

Unfortunately, the trip often requires other transportation, because few paddlers have the experience necessary to paddle the open ocean around Khaz Peninsula (which forms a barrier between Kruzof Island's north end and Slocum Arm, the south end of the West Chichagof-Yakobi Wilderness). For most paddlers that means a water-taxi service to take you there.

Travelers with more time and a sense of adventure could continue another 25 miles through Lisianski Strait to the fishing village of **Pelican**, where the ferry stops twice a month in summer. Such an expedition would require at least two to three weeks.

Whale-Watching
Many companies in Sitka offer boat tours to view whales and other marine wildlife, and most of them swing past **St Lazaria Island National Wildlife Refuge**, home to 1500 pairs of breeding tufted puffins.

You can often spot whales from shore at Whale Park (p102). The town also has a whale festival in November.

Allen Marine Tours CRUISE
(☎907-747-8100; www.allenmarinetours.com; 1512 Sawmill Creek Rd; adult/child $130/84) Experienced operator with offices in Ketchikan, Juneau and Sitka offering wildlife-focused boat cruises. On the three-hour 'Sea Otter & Wildlife Quest' it promises a $100 refund if you don't see a whale, sea otter or bear!

Tours

Sitka Tours BUS
(☎907-747-5800; www.sitkatoursalaska.com) If you're only in Sitka for as long as the ferry stopover, don't despair: Sitka Tours runs one-hour express bus tours and 3½-hour historic tours just for you. The tour bus picks passengers up from and returns them to the ferry terminal, making brief visits to Sitka National Historical Park (p99) and St Michael's Cathedral (p100).

Time is allotted for the obligatory T-shirt shopping.

Festivals & Events

Sitka Summer Music Festival MUSIC
(☎907-747-6774; www.sitkamusicfestival.org; ⌚Jun) This three-week event in June extends Sitka's reputation as the Southeast's cultural center, bringing together professional musicians for chamber-music concerts and workshops.

WhaleFest! CULTURAL
(☎907-747-7964; www.sitkawhalefest.org; ⌚early Nov) The city stages WhaleFest! during the first weekend of November to celebrate the large fall gathering of humpbacks with whale-watching cruises, lectures, craft shows and more.

Sleeping

Sitka levies a 12% city and bed tax on all lodging. Two USFS campgrounds are in the area, but neither is close to town. There are three or four comfortable, if bland, chain hotels.

Starrigavan Recreation Area CAMPGROUND $
(☎518-885-3639, reservations 877-444-6777; www.recreation.gov; Mile 7.8, Halibut Point Rd; tent & RV sites $12-16) Sitka's finest campground has 35 sites for three types of campers: RVers, car-

and-tenters and backpackers/cyclists. You're 7 miles north of town, but the coastal scenery is beautiful and nearby is Old Sitka State Historical Park (p102). There are bird- and salmon-viewing decks, several hiking trails and (for mountain bikers) Nelson Logging Rd. Sites can be reserved in advance.

On-site is also an attractive spruce-wood USFS cabin ($70).

Sitka International Hostel HOSTEL $

(☎907-747-8661; www.sitkahostel.org; 109 Jeff Davis St; dm/d $24/65; 📶) Sitka's typically bohemian hostel is downtown in the historic Tillie Paul Manor, which once served as the town's hospital. The charismatic building crammed with all sorts of information and mementos features a men's room with its own kitchen and several women's rooms, along with a family room, another small kitchen and a lovely sun porch with a mountain view.

Beds are comfortable and are made up with soft flannel sheets. The hostel is locked from 10am to 6pm, but hostel managers are good about greeting late-night arrivals who call ahead.

Sitka Hotel HOTEL $$

(☎907-747-3288; www.sitkahotel.com; 118 Lincoln St; d $195-220) After an upgrade in recent years, this handsome wood-paneled structure in the center of town looks like a gold-rush-era building given a style make-over and a few extra coats of paint. Rooms are large if nonfancy (this is Alaska!) and a little beige, the owners are keen to please and there's the town's second-best bar and restaurant (p106) out front.

Enter via the back door.

Westmark Sitka Hotel HOTEL $$

(☎907-747-6241; www.westmarkhotels.com; 330 Seward St; r $224-245; P @ 📶) The business traveler's favorite has 106 rooms and suites, a central location, a fine restaurant and bar with views of the harbor and room service.

This is one of six Westmark hotels run by the Holland America cruise line in Alaska.

Cascade Creek Inn INN $$

(☎907-747-6804; www.cascadecreekinnandcharters.com; 2035 Halibut Point Rd; r $130-160; 📶) Perched right above the shoreline, all 10 rooms in this handsome wooden inn face the ocean and have a private balcony overlooking it. There are four top-floor rooms with kitchenettes. Sure, you're 2.5 miles north of town, but the inn's oceanfront deck is worth the ride on the downtown bus.

The inn runs fishing charters and is heavily popular with the fishing set.

Ann's Gavan Hill B&B B&B $$

(☎907-747-8023; www.annsgavanhill.com; 415 Arrowhead St; s/d $80/100; @ 📶) An easy walk (or two-minute bus ride) from downtown is this Alaskan home, with a wraparound deck that includes two hot tubs. There are six bedrooms with shared baths that are comfortable and equipped with TV and DVD. The proprietor is delightfully informative, and serves up a full breakfast.

Hannah's B&B B&B $$

(☎907-747-8309; www.hannahsbandb.com; 504 Monastery St; s/d $125/135) The longtime B&B proprietor here believes that if you're coming to Alaska you're trying to escape, so there are no phones, no TVs and no computers. What she does have is two beautiful rooms with private baths, microwaves, mini-refrigerators and private entrances. There's a small continental breakfast.

Aspen Suites Hotel HOTEL $$$

(www.aspenhotelsak.com/sitka; 210 Lake St; ste $259-269; P @ 📶) This chain has infiltrated several Alaskan cities in the last couple of years, Juneau and Haines among them. The Sitka offering opened in 2017 with Aspen's characteristic selection of businesslike suites complete with kitchenettes, sofas and large bathrooms. There's also an on-site gym and a surgical level of cleanliness throughout.

Totem Square Inn HOTEL $$$

(☎907-747-3693; www.totemsquarehotel.com; 201 Katlian St; r/ste $229/279; P @ 📶) This is one of Sitka's larger hotels, with 68 comfortable rooms featuring the traditional (Alaska Native art and prints on the walls) and the modern (flat-screen TVs, hair dryers and wi-fi). There's a work-out facility, laundry, business center and free airport shuttle. The rooms overlook either the historic square or a harbor bustling with boats bringing in the day's catch.

Longliner Lodge BOUTIQUE HOTEL $$$

(☎907-747-7910; www.longlinersitka.com; 485 Katlian St; r/ste $230/300; P 📶) In the middle of Katlian's bustling harbors and canneries sits this renamed and rebranded lodge with 10 rooms featuring refrigerators, wet bars, microwaves, cable TV and coffeepots. There are also four suites with kitchenettes, a restaurant (serving guests a full breakfast), a small bar and a seaplane dock.

The place is particularly popular with fishers on chartered trips.

Eating

Highliner Coffee CAFE $
(www.highlinercoffee.com; 327 Seward St, Seward Sq Mall; light fare under $5; ⏲6am-5pm Mon-Sat, 7am-4pm Sun; 📶) At the Highliner they like their coffee black and their salmon wild, which explains why the walls are covered with photos of local fishing boats and political stickers like 'Invest in Wild Salmon's Future: Eat One!'. The baked goods are highly edible too.

Sitka Hotel Bar & Restaurant INTERNATIONAL $$
(☎907-747-3288; 118 Lincoln St; mains $15-29; ⏲11am-9pm Mon-Sat, 9am-9pm Sun) Wood decor covers the interior of this remodeled gathering spot, although, with its open kitchen and charismatic bar, the atmosphere's far from wooden. Welcome to Sitka's second-best restaurant – nowhere can yet challenge Ludvig's – where a casual atmosphere meets the kind of creative food you once had to jump on a plane to Seattle to enjoy. No more!

Mean Queen PIZZA $$
(☎907-747-0616; www.meanqueensitka.com; 205 Harbor Dr; pizzas $18-22; ⏲11am-2pm) A pizza joint trying hard to be hip in a bright moddish space on an upstairs floor close to Castle Hill. There's a pleasant rectangular bar, several booths and plenty of young punters. The thin-crust pizzas come in large shareable sizes.

Beak Restaurant BISTRO $$
(2 Lincoln St; small plates $8-12, mains $20-23; ⏲9am-9pm Mon-Sat, 10am-2pm Sun) In the back of the Raven Radio Building is this hip bistro. It's a great place for a post-kayaking or hiking snack such as salmon chowder and lemony hummus with pita, or alternatively, for those needing dinner, there's reindeer sausage. Note: there's a no-tipping policy.

Bayview Pub PUB FOOD $$
(www.sitkabayviewpub.com; 407 Lincoln St; sandwiches $12-16; ⏲11am-late) Head upstairs in the MacDonald Bayview Trading Company Building for the best view from any restaurant in town. The large multifarious interior has numerous nooks set aside for sofa-crashing, playing pool, propping up the bar or eating from a rather mediocre menu of cholesterol-heavy pub-grub favorites. The drinks menu is more promising.

★Ludvig's Bistro MEDITERRANEAN $$$
(☎907-966-3663; www.ludvigsbistro.com; 256 Katlian St; mains $28-40; ⏲4:30-9:30pm Mon-Sat) Sophistication in the wilderness! Sitka's boldest restaurant has only seven tables, and a few stools at its brass-and-blue-tile bar. Described as 'rustic Mediterranean fare,' almost every dish is local, even the sea salt. If seafood paella is on the menu, order it. The traditional Spanish rice dish comes loaded with whatever fresh seafood the local boats have netted that day.

There's an equally salubrious wine bar upstairs. Reservations necessary.

Drinking & Nightlife

★Baranof Island Brewing Co BREWERY
(www.baranofislandbrewing.com; 1209 Sawmill Creek Rd; ⏲2-8pm; 👪) Encased in a handsome new taproom since July 2017, the Baranof is a local legend providing microbrews for every pub and bar in town. For the real deal, however, the taproom's the place. Line up four to six tasters and make sure you include a Halibut Point Hefeweisen and a Redoubt Red Ale.

Families, fear not: it also makes microbrew root beer and serves pizza by the slice.

Back Door Café COFFEE
(104 Barracks St; snacks $1-5; ⏲6:30am-5pm Mon-Fri, to 2pm Sat) Enter this small coffeehouse through either Old Harbor Books on Lincoln St or via the…you guessed it…which is off Barracks St. The cafe is as local as it gets with strong, potent joe and fantastic home-baked snacks including pies.

Ludvig's Wine Bar and Gallery WINE BAR
(www.ludvigsbistro.com; 256 Katlian St; ⏲5-9pm Mon-Sat) Follow the stairs next to Ludvig's Bistro up to a parquet-floored art gallery furnished with tall bar tables. You'll find excellent tapas, homemade ice cream and a diverse wine list. Enjoy live music three times per week and occasional salsa dancing. It's a great place to have dessert after dinner downstairs or appetizers while you're waiting for a table.

Pioneer Bar BAR
(212 Katlian St; ⏲8am-2am) The 'P-Bar' is Alaska's classic maritime watering hole. The

walls are covered with photos of fishing boats and their crews, big fish and a blackboard with messages like 'Experienced deckhand looking for seine job.' Don't ring the ship's bell over the bar unless you're ready to buy every crew member a drink. There are booths, a long bar and billiard tables.

Entertainment

Sheet'ka Kwaan Naa Kahidi Dancers DANCE
(☎907-747-7137; 204 Katlian St; adult/child $10/5) Tlingit dancers perform in the **Tlingit Clan House**, next to the Pioneers Home, with half-hour performances oriented around the cruise-ship crowd. The place has excellent acoustics and a beautifully decorated house screen.

New Archangel Russian Dancers DANCE
(☎907-747-5516; www.newarchangeldancers.com; adult/child $10/5) Whenever a cruise ship is in port, this troupe of more than 30 dancers in Russian costume materializes onstage at the Harigan Centennial Hall (p108) for a half-hour show. A schedule is posted in the hall.

Shopping

Old Harbor Books BOOKS
(201 Lincoln St; ⏲10am-6pm Mon-Fri, to 5pm Sat) One of the loveliest bookstores in the Southeast, with a large Alaska section, featured local authors, and the pie-selling Back Door Café adjoining. Browsing heaven.

Weed Dudes DISPENSARY
(☎907-623-0605; 1321 Sawmill Creek Rd; ⏲10am-8pm) Two thousand and seventeen proved to be a happy new year for Sitka's 'cannassuers' when the town opened its first recreational pot shop. Located discreetly in an out-of-town strip mall, the dudes at this dispensary sell prerolls, edibles and various cannabis strains.

Information

INTERNET ACCESS

Using a head tax on cruise-ship passengers, the city of Sitka has set up free wi-fi throughout the downtown area. It can be picked up in most cafes, stores, bars and hotels along Lincoln St and Harbor Dr.

Kettleson Memorial Library (320 Harbor Dr; ⏲10am-9pm Mon-Fri, 1-9pm Sat; wi-fi) Next door to Harigan Centennial Hall, this waterfront building has one of the best library views in Alaska. There are 10 computers for internet access, free wi-fi and tables overlooking the harbor.

MEDICAL SERVICES

Sitka Community Hospital (☎907-747-3241; 209 Moller Dr) By the intersection of Halibut Point Rd and Brady St.

MONEY

First National Bank of Anchorage (318 Lincoln St; ⏲9:30am-5:30pm Mon-Fri, 10am-2pm Sat) Downtown, with a 24-hour ATM.

TOURIST INFORMATION

Sitka Information Center (☎907-747-5940; www.sitka.org; 104 Lake St; ⏲9am-4:30pm Mon-Fri) Ultra-helpful office opposite the Westmark hotel downtown. Also staffs a desk at the **Harigan Centennial Hall** (☎907-747-8604; 330 Harbor Dr; ⏲9am-5pm) when there's a cruise ship in town.

USFS Sitka Ranger District Office (☎907-747-6671, recorded information 907-747-6685; 2108 Halibut Point Rd; ⏲8am-4:30pm Mon-Fri) Has information about local trails, camping and USFS cabins. It's 2 miles north of town. More central is the visitor center at Sitka National Historical Park (p99).

Getting There & Away

AIR

Sitka Airport (SIT; ☎907-966-2960) On Japonski Island, 1.5 miles, or a 20-minute walk, west of downtown. The Ride Sitka green line bus runs to the island but stops short of the airport.

Alaska Airlines (p429) Flights to/from Juneau (45 minutes) and Ketchikan (one hour).

Harris Aircraft Services (☎907-966-3050; www.harrisair.com; Airport Rd) Floatplane air-taxi service to small communities and USFS cabins as well as larger Southeast towns such as Juneau.

CRUISE SHIP

Large cruise ships dock at **Halibut Point Marine** (Halibut Point Rd), 6 miles north of town. Special cruise-company buses run passengers into town.

Smaller ships dock offshore in Sitka Sound and take passengers into Crescent Harbor in water taxis.

FERRY

The **Alaska Marine Highway Ferry Terminal** (☎907-747-8737; www.dot.state.ak.us/amhs) is 7 miles northwest of town; ferries depart in both directions twice a week to Juneau ($65, nine hours), and once a week to Petersburg ($70, 11 hours).

OFF THE BEATEN TRACK

TRACY ARM-FORDS TERROR WILDERNESS

Some call it Glacier Bay National Park without the extortionate price tag. Tracy Arm, Endicott Arm and Fords Terror are three long, deep fjords that form part of the Tracy Arm-Fords Terror Wilderness, a 653,000-acre preserve where you can spend weeks paddling to a backdrop of glaciers, icebergs and 2000ft granite walls. Tracy Arm is easily visited on a boat trip from Juneau, and outings are around half the price of similar Glacier Bay excursions without any significant drop in the awe-rating.

Sculpted by millennia of ice movement, the fjords are notable for their tidal glaciers. Tracy Arm is fed by the twin Sawyer glaciers. Endicott Arm is backed by the powerful iceberg-dispensing Dawes Glacier. Fords Terror, which branches off the Endicott, is glacier-free, though the steep narrow chasm displays the classic gouging effects of a glacial past.

Equally impressive are the fjords' granite cliffs. So sheer are they in Tracy Arm that finding a patch of shoreline flat enough to pitch a tent on can be difficult. John Muir compared the cliffs to Yosemite. Some modern visitors suggest that, with their weeping waterfalls and coppery coloration, they are even more impressive.

Kayaking in Tracy Arm (p65) is sublime if you're up for some rough camping and can put up with the regular influx of cruise ships. Experienced kayakers could consider Endicott Arm, a 30-mile fjord created by Dawes and North Dawes Glaciers. Fords Terror is named after a US sailor who found himself battling whirlpools and grinding icebergs when he tried to row out against the incoming tide in 1899. Unless you're a serious white-water expert, it's best to leave this aptly named fjord alone.

The once-a-week MV *Fairweather* ferry cuts travel time to Juneau to 4½ hours.

Getting Around

BICYCLE

Yellow Jersey Cycle Shop (☎907-747-6317; www.yellowjerseycycles.com; 329 Harbor Dr; per 2hr/day $20/25), across the street from the library, rents quality mountain bikes for economical prices.

There's a paved bike path as far south as Fortress of the Bear on Sawmill Creek Rd. The road north to the ferry terminal has wide verges and is perfectly safe for cycling.

BOAT

For water-taxi service to USFS cabins or kayaking destinations, contact **Esther G Sea Taxi** (☎907-738-6481, 907-747-6481; www.puffinsandwhales.com; 215 Shotgun Alley) or Sitka Sound Ocean Adventures (p104).

BUS

➡ Sitka's public bus system, **Ride Sitka** (☎907-747-7103; www.ridesitka.com; adult/child $2/1; ⏲6:30am-7:30pm Mon-Fri), runs on three lines and serves practically everywhere of interest to visitors. The only downsides: it doesn't stop at the airport (the last stop is about 0.75 miles short) and it doesn't run on weekends.

➡ The green line does a loop around town. The blue line heads south via Whale Park to the Fortress of the Bear. The red line heads north to the cruise dock and the ferry terminal. Crescent Harbor serves as the terminus for all three lines.

Juneau

☎907 / POP 33,850

Juneau is a capital of contrasts and conflicts. It borders a waterway that never freezes but lies beneath an ice field that never melts.

It was the first community in the Southeast to slap a head tax on cruise-ship passengers but still draws more than a million a year.

It's the state capital but since the 1980s Alaskans have been trying to move it.

It doesn't have any roads that go anywhere, but half its residents and its mayor opposed a plan to build one that would.

Welcome to the USA's strangest state capital. In the winter it's a beehive of legislators, their loyal aides and lobbyists locked in political struggles. In summer it's a launchpad for copious outdoor adventures.

Superb hiking starts barely 10 minutes from downtown, a massive glacier calves into a lake 12 miles up the road, and boats and seaplanes take off from the waterfront bound for nearby bear-viewing, ziplining and whale-watching.

Sights

City Center

Mt Roberts Tramway CABLE CAR

(www.mountrobertstramway.com; 490 S Franklin St; adult/child $33/16; 11am-9pm Mon, 8am-9pm Tue-Sun;) As far as cable cars go, this tramway is rather expensive for a five-minute ride. But from a marketing point of view its location couldn't be better. It whisks you right from the cruise-ship dock up 1750ft to the timberline of Mt Roberts, where you'll find a restaurant, gift shops, a small raptor center and a theater with a film on Tlingit culture.

Or skip all that and just use the tram to access the stunning Mt Roberts alpine area, marked with trails and wildflowers.

In a far better deal, you can hike up the Mt Roberts Trail, spend $10 in the restaurant and then take the tram down for free.

Alaska State Museum MUSEUM

(Map p110; 907-465-2901; www.museums.state.ak.us; 395 Whittier St; adult/child $12/free; 9am-5pm;) Demolished and rebuilt in a snazzy new $140-million complex in 2016, the result is impressive. Sometimes called SLAM (State Library, Archives and Museum), the museum shares digs with the state archives along with a gift store, the Raven Cafe, an auditorium, a research room and a historical library. The beautifully curated displays catalogue the full historical and geographic breadth of the state, from native canoes to the oil industry.

A smaller suite of rooms hosts revolving art exhibitions.

Last Chance Mining Museum MUSEUM

(907-586-5338; 1001 Basin Rd; adult/child $5/free; 9:30am-12:30pm & 3:30-6:30pm) Amble out to the end of Basin Rd, a beautiful 1-mile walk from the north end of Gastineau Ave, to the former Alaska-Juneau Gold Mining Company complex. It's now a museum where you can view remains of the compressor house and examine tools of what was once the world's largest hard-rock gold mine.

There is also a re-created mining tunnel and a 3-D glass map of shafts that shows just how large it was. Nearby is the Perseverance Trail (p114), and combining the museum with a hike to more mining ruins is a great way to spend an afternoon.

Sealaska Heritage CULTURAL CENTRE

(Map p110; 907-463-4844; www.sealaskaheritage.org; 105 S Seward St; $5; 9am-8pm) The Sealaska Heritage Institute, founded in 1980 to promote Alaska Native culture, opened this hugely impressive facility in 2015 in the downtown Walter Soboleff building. The whole place is a work of art with much of the detail completed by Tsimshian artist David Boxley. As well as serving as an HQ for the institute, the center contains a full-scale replica of a clan house and a unique exhibit on native masks.

Juneau-Douglas City Museum MUSEUM

(Map p110; www.juneau.org; 114 W 4th St; adult/child $6/free; 9am-6pm Mon-Fri, 10am-4:30pm Sat & Sun;) This museum focuses on gold, with interesting mining displays including 3-D photo viewers, timelines, interactive exhibits and the video *Juneau: City Built On Gold*. If you love to hike in the mountains, the museum's 7ft-long relief map is the best overview of the area's rugged terrain.

St Nicholas Russian Orthodox Church CHURCH

(Map p110; 907-586-1023; 326 5th St; admission by donation; noon-5pm Mon-Fri, to 4pm Sat & Sun) Of 1893 vintage and etched against the backdrop of Mt Juneau, this diminutive onion-domed church is the oldest Russian Orthodox church in Alaska. Through a small gift shop filled with *matryoshkas* (nestling dolls) and other handcrafted items from Russia, you enter the church where, among the original vestments and religious relics, a row of painted saints stare down at you. Playing softly in the background are the chants from a service. It's a small but spiritual place.

Wickersham State Historical Site HISTORIC SITE

(Map p110; 213 7th St; 10am-5pm Sun-Thu) FREE Overlooking downtown Juneau, this site preserves the 1898 home of pioneer judge and statesman James Wickersham. It's a steep climb, but the house has some interesting ephemera and fine views.

Governor's Mansion NOTABLE BUILDING

(Map p110; 716 Calhoun Ave) This pillared Governor's Mansion is Juneau's most attractive building. Built and furnished in 1912 at a cost of $44,000, the mansion is not open to the public.

Juneau

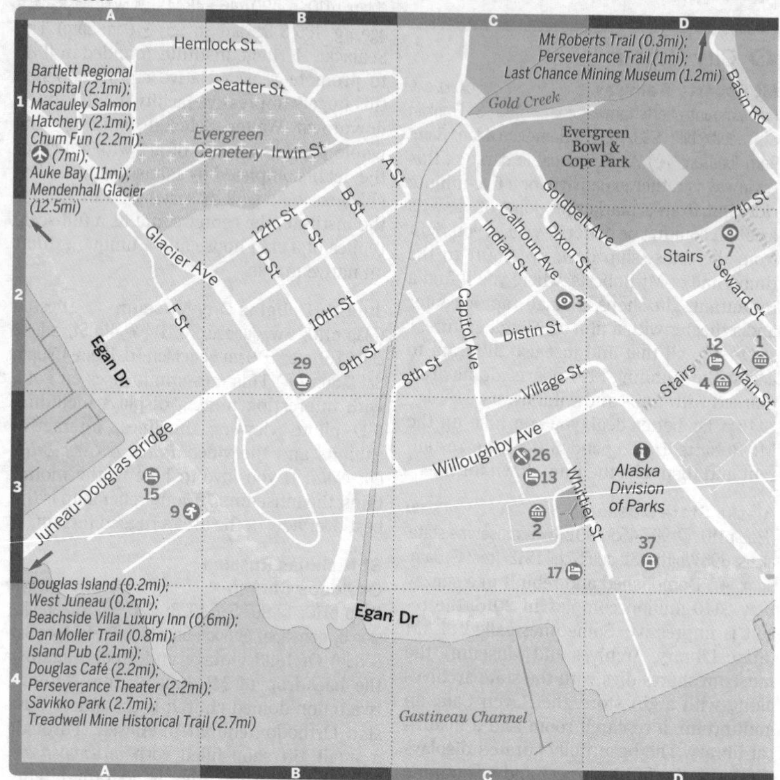

Alaska State Capitol HISTORIC BUILDING

(Map p110; 120 4th St; ⏲8:30am-5pm Mon-Fri, 9:30am-4pm Sat & Sun) One of the US' more prosaic state capitols, this boxy building went up between 1929 and 1931 and looks more like an overgrown high school than a historic bastion of democracy. Stuffed inside are legislative chambers, the governor's office, and offices for the hundreds of staff members who arrive in Juneau for the winter legislative session. A self-guided tour pamphlet of the lobby is available.

◉ Douglas Island

Treadwell Mine Historical Trail HISTORIC SITE

(Map p112) It's hard to envisage today, but the Treadwell mine on Douglas Island was once the largest gold mine in the world, set up like a minitown with its own baseball diamond, stores, dormitories and blacksmith. Reaching its zenith in the 1880s, the mine was subsequently abandoned after part of it slid into the sea in 1917. Today, spooky reminders of Juneau's affluent mining past poke through the forest on this well-signposted historical trail with interpretive boards.

Of note is the concrete 'New Office Building', the 1917 slide site, a 'glory hole' and a restored pump house that stands like a beached tower a few meters offshore.

Treadwell is 3 miles south of the Douglas Bridge adjacent to **Savikko Park** (Map p112; P 👪 🐾). Buses 1 or 11 from downtown will get you there.

◉ North of Juneau

★Mendenhall Glacier GLACIER

(Map p112) Going to Juneau and not seeing the Mendenhall is like visiting Rome and skipping the Colosseum. The most famous

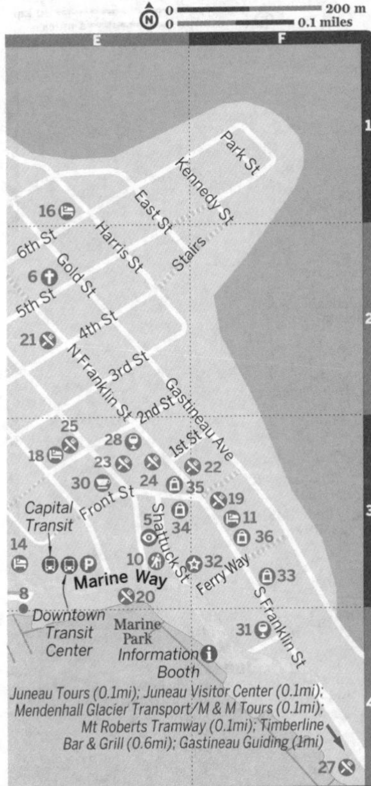

of Juneau's ice floes, and the city's most popular attraction, flows 13 miles from its source, the Juneau Icefield, and has a half-mile-wide face. It ends at **Mendenhall Lake** (Map p112), the reason for all the icebergs.

Naturalists estimate that within a few years it will retreat onto land, and within 25 years retreat out of view entirely from the observation area and visitor center.

On a sunny day it's beautiful, with blue skies and snowcapped mountains in the background. On a cloudy and drizzly afternoon it can be even more impressive, as the ice turns shades of deep blue.

The river of ice is at the end of Glacier Spur Rd. From Egan Dr at Mile 9 turn right onto Mendenhall Loop Rd, staying on Glacier Spur Rd when the loop curves back toward Auke Bay.

Near the face of the glacier is the **Mendenhall Glacier Visitor Center** (Map p112; 6000 Glacier Spur Rd; 8am-7:30pm) FREE,

Juneau

Sights

1 Alaska State Capitol ... D2
2 Alaska State Museum ... C3
3 Governor's Mansion ... C2
4 Juneau-Douglas City Museum ... D2
5 Sealaska Heritage ... E3
6 St Nicholas Russian Orthodox Church ... E2
7 Wickersham State Historical Site ... D2

Activities, Courses & Tours

8 Adventure Bound Alaska ... E3
9 Cycle Alaska ... A3
10 Juneau Parks & Recreation ... E3

Sleeping

11 Alaskan Hotel ... F3
12 Alaska's Capital Inn ... D2
13 Driftwood Hotel ... C3
14 Four Points by Sheraton ... E3
15 Juneau Hotel ... A3
16 Juneau International Hostel ... E1
17 Prospector Hotel ... C3
18 Silverbow Inn ... E3

Eating

19 El Sombrero ... F3
Hangar on the Wharf ... (see 20)
In Bocca Al Lupo ... (see 18)
20 Pel'Meni ... E3
21 Rainbow Foods ... E2
22 Rockwell ... F3
23 Rookery ... E3
24 Saffron ... E3
25 Salt ... E3
26 Sandpiper ... C3
27 Tracy's King Crab Shack ... F4

Drinking & Nightlife

28 Amalga Distillery ... E3
29 Coppa ... B2
30 Heritage Coffee Co & Café ... E3
McGivney's Sports Bar & Grill ... (see 14)
31 Red Dog Saloon ... F4

Entertainment

32 Gold Town Nickelodeon ... F3

Shopping

33 Alaskan Brewing Co Depot ... F3
34 Fireweed Factory ... E3
Foggy Mountain Shop ... (see 28)
35 Hearthside Books ... E3
36 Juneau Artists Gallery ... F3
37 Juneau Arts and Culture Center ... D3

Around Juneau

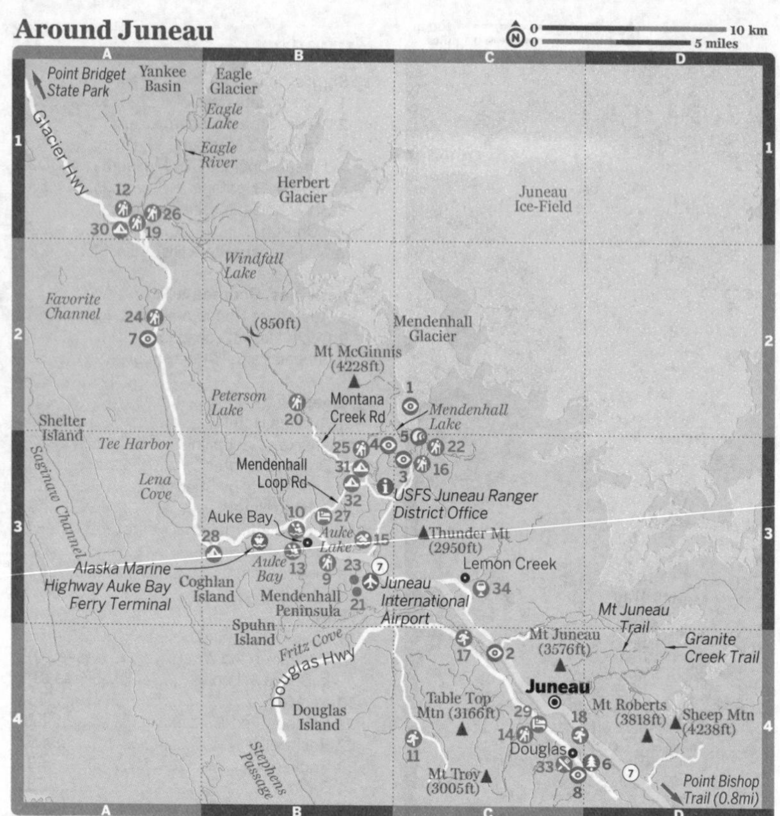

which houses various glaciology exhibits, including a fabricated ice face of the glacier along with a large relief map of the ice field; spotting scopes that let you look for mountain goats; and a theater that shows the 11-minute film *Landscape of Change*.

Outside you'll find several hiking trails. The most popular are the 0.3-mile **Photo-Overlook Trail** and the **Nugget Falls Trail**; the latter leads a half-mile to a huge belting **waterfall** (Map p112) that empties into the lake near the face of the glacier. For many the most interesting path is **Steep Creek Trail**, a 0.3-mile boardwalk that winds past viewing platforms along the stream. From July through September you'll not only see sockeye and coho salmon spawning from the platforms but also brown and black bears feasting on them. This is Southeast Alaska's most affordable bear-viewing site (though it can be partially closed due to heavy bear traffic in summer).

The cheapest way to see the glacier is to hop on a Capital Transit bus ($2). The bus, somewhat bizarrely, drops you 1.5 miles short of the visitor center. Follow the paved path north along the Glacier Spur Rd. More expensive, but easier, is the 'blue bus' operated by **Mendenhall Glacier Transport/M & M Tours** (907-789-5460; www.mightygreattrips.com; per person $35), which picks up from the cruise-ship docks downtown for the glacier, making a run every 30 minutes. The last bus of the day depends on the cruise-ship schedule.

One of the most unusual outdoor activities in Juneau is **glacier trekking**: stepping into crampons, grabbing an ice axe and roping up to walk on ice 1000 years old or older. The scenery and the adventure is like nothing you've experienced before as a hiker. The most affordable outing is offered by Above & Beyond Alaska (p117). Utilizing a trail to access Mendenhall Glacier, it avoids

Around Juneau

expensive helicopter fees on its guided seven-hour outing. The cost is $219 per person and includes all mountaineering equipment and transportation.

Shrine of St Thérèse SHRINE

(Map p112; www.shrineofsainttherese.org; Mile 23.3, Glacier Hwy; ⏲8:30am-10pm) FREE Get ready for some spiritual enlightenment. The Shrine of St Thérèse is a natural stone chapel on a beautifully wooded island connected to the shore by a stone causeway. The Catholic church was commissioned by a Jesuit priest in the late 1930s, and the first Mass was held in 1941. It's a wonderfully tranquil spot.

As well as being the site of numerous weddings, the island lies along the Breadline, a well-known salmon-fishing area in Juneau. It is perhaps the best place to shore fish for salmon.

Point Bridget State Park STATE PARK

(Mile 39, Glacier Hwy; P) Juneau's only state park overlooks Berners Bay and Lynn Canal; salmon fishing is excellent off the Berners Bay beaches and in Cowee Creek. Hiking trails wander through rainforest, along the 2850-acre park's rugged shoreline and past three rental cabins.

The most popular hike is Point Bridget Trail, a 3.5-mile, one-way walk from the trailhead on Glacier Hwy to Blue Mussel Cabin at the point. Here, you can often spot sea lions and seals playing in the surf. Plan on six to seven hours for the round-trip with lunch at the cabin.

Activities

Cycling

There are better cities for cycling than Juneau. For road-cyclists, there's an on-off bike path between Auke Bay, Mendenhall Glacier and downtown.

Because most of Juneau's trails are steep, mountain biking is limited, but the **Windfall Lake** (Map p112), Perseverance and Peterson Lake trails are popular with off-road cyclists.

Pick up a local bike map at the Cycle Alaska store.

Cycle Alaska CYCLING

(Map p110; ☎907-780-2253; www.cycleak.com; 1107 W 8th St; per 4hr/day $37/70; ⏲10am-6pm Mon-Sat, 9am-5pm Sun; 👪) Rents quality road and mountain bikes along with children's bikes and tandems. The company highlight is the Bike & Brew (adult/child $99/75), a four-hour bicycle tour that includes Auke Bay and Mendenhall Glacier, and finishes off at an old seaplane hangar for some beer tasting.

Fishing

Chum Fun

FISHING

(Map p112; ☎907-398-2486; www.chumfun.com; 3100 Channel Dr; $125; 👪) A salmon-fishing charter catering to families with an emphasis on fun, Chum Fun offers three-hour shore-fishing tours from the docks at **Macauley Salmon Hatchery** (Map p112; ☎907-463-4810; www.dipac.net; 2697 Channel Dr; adult/child $5/3; ⊙10am-6pm Mon-Fri, to 5pm Sat & Sun; 👪) – free tour included. Transportation and all gear are provided, and though they'll take care of your fishing license for you, the $25 fee is not included.

Hiking

Few cities in Alaska have such a diversity of hiking trails as Juneau. A handful of these trails start near the city center, the rest are 'out the road' (north of Auke Bay). All USFS cabins (p121) – there are 11 in the Juneau area – should be booked in advance.

Juneau Parks & Recreation (Map p110; ☎907-586-0428; www.juneau.org/parksrec; 155 South Seward St) offers volunteer-led hikes every Wednesday (adults) and Saturday (kids OK) in 'rain, shine or snow.' Call or check the website for a schedule and the trails. Gastineau Guiding (p116) does guided hikes for small groups that include snacks, ponchos if needed and transportation.

★Perseverance Trail

HIKING

The Perseverance Trail, off Basin Rd, is Juneau's most popular. The trail is a path into Juneau's mining history and also provides access to two other popular treks: Mt Juneau Trail and Granite Creek Trail. Together the routes can be combined into a rugged 10-hour walk for hardy hikers, or an overnight excursion into the mountains surrounding Alaska's capital city.

To reach Perseverance Trail, head north out of town on Basin Rd, a dirt road that curves away from the city into the mountains as it follows Gold Creek. The trailhead is at the road's end, at the parking lot for Last Chance Mining Museum (p109). The trail leads into Silverbow Basin, an old mining area that still has many hidden and unmarked adits and mine shafts; be safe and stay on the trail.

From the Perseverance Trail, you can pick up Granite Creek Trail and follow it to the creek's headwaters basin, a beautiful spot to spend the night. From there, you can reach Mt Juneau by climbing the ridge and staying left of Mt Olds, the huge rocky mountain. Once atop Mt Juneau, you can complete the loop by descending along the Mt Juneau Trail, which joins Perseverance Trail a mile from its beginning. The hike to the 3576ft peak of Mt Juneau along the ridge from Granite Creek is an easier but longer trek than the ascent from the Mt Juneau Trail. The alpine sections of the ridge are serene, and on a clear summer day you'll have outstanding views. From the trailhead for the Perseverance Trail to the upper basin of Granite Creek is 3.3 miles one way. Then it's another 3 miles along the ridge to reach Mt Juneau.

West Glacier Trail

HIKING

(Map p112) This 3.4-mile trail begins off Montana Creek Rd past Mendenhall Lake Campground (p118) and hugs the mountainside along the glacier, providing exceptional views of glacial features before ending at a rocky outcropping. As it's away from the visitor center, the trail is less trafficked, though you'll hear persistent helicopter noise overhead in the summer.

The last part of the trail, unmaintained and marked by cairns, heads for the face of the glacier. It involves more scrambling over rocks but is as popular as the main trail.

Mt Roberts Trail

HIKING

The 5-mile climb up Mt Roberts starts a short way up Basin Rd on the edge of town and offers various options for hikers. Some just ascend fairly steeply through the trees for 2 miles to the top of the tramway with its restaurant and nature center, but it's worth pressing on to experience the flower-bedizened alpine meadows immediately above.

The next landmark, a half-mile beyond the tramway, is a wooden cross with good views of Juneau and Douglas. Above the cross you enter high alpine terrain and sometimes encounter snow as the path narrows, traversing a ridge that connects to Mt Gastineau (3666ft). Beyond Gastineau, the path drops into a saddle before ascending again to Mt Roberts (3818ft). Beware, the ridge can be a bit of a scramble in the snow and mist.

You can 'cheat' on the way down by riding the last segment on the Mt Roberts Tramway to S Franklin St for only $10. And, if you purchase $10 worth of food or drink (such as that well-deserved beer) at the visitor center on top, the ride down is free.

East Glacier Loop HIKING

(Map p112) One of many trails near Mendenhall Glacier (p110), this one is a 2.8-mile round-trip providing good views of the glacier from a lookout at the halfway point, where you can also look down on Nugget Falls (p112). Pick up the loop along the **Trail of Time**, a half-mile nature walk that starts at the Mendenhall Glacier Visitor Center (p111).

Amalga Trail HIKING

(Eagle Glacier Trail; Map p112) A level route that winds 7.5 miles to the lake formed by Eagle Glacier. Less than a mile from the glacier's face, Eagle Glacier Cabin offers views that make it well worth reserving in advance. The trailhead is at Eagle Beach State Recreation Area (p121), beyond the Glacier Hwy bridge, 0.4 miles past the trailhead for the Herbert Glacier Trail.

Plan on a round-trip of seven to eight hours (15 miles) to reach the impressive Eagle Glacier and return to the trailhead. Note that the trail is sometimes called the Eagle Glacier Trail.

Nugget Creek Trail HIKING

(Map p112) Just beyond the East Glacier Loop's halfway point lookout, the 2.5-mile Nugget Creek Trail climbs 500ft to Vista Creek Shelter, a free-use shelter that doesn't require reservations. The round-trip to the shelter from the Mendenhall Glacier Visitor Center (p111) is an 8-mile trek.

Hikers who plan to spend the night can continue toward Nugget Glacier, though the route can be hard to follow.

Peterson Lake Trail HIKING

(Map p112) This 4.3-mile route along Peterson Creek to its namesake lake is a favorite among hike-in anglers for the good Dolly Varden fishing. The trailhead is 20ft before the Mile 24 marker on Glacier Hwy, north of the Shrine of St Térèse. Wear rubber boots; it can be muddy. The Peterson Lake Cabin turns this trail into a delightful overnight adventure.

Herbert Glacier Trail HIKING

(Map p112) The Herbert Glacier Trail extends 4.9 miles along the Herbert River to Herbert Glacier, a round-trip of four to five hours. The first 3.5 miles of the trail are wide and easy with little climbing (good for mountain biking), though wet in places. It begins just past the bridge over Herbert River at Mile 28 of Glacier Hwy, north of Juneau.

Point Bishop Trail HIKING

At the end of Thane Rd, 7½ miles southeast of Juneau, this 8-mile trail leads to Point Bishop, an attractive spot overlooking the junction of Stephens Passage and Taku Inlet. The trail is flat and can be wet, making waterproof boots the preferred footwear. The hike makes for an ideal overnight trip; there is good camping at Point Bishop.

Dan Moller Trail HIKING

(Map p112) Dan Moller is a 3-mile trail leading to an alpine bowl at the crest of Douglas Island that traverses muskeg and flower fields. At the turnaround is the Dan Moller Cabin (1800ft), popular in winter with cross-country skiers.

Just across the channel in West Juneau, the public bus conveniently stops at Cordova St and from there, you turn left onto Pioneer Ave and follow it to the end of the pavement to the trailhead. Plan on six hours for the round-trip.

Paddling

Day trips and extended paddles are possible out of the Juneau area in sea kayaks. Alternatively, you can freshwater kayak on Mendenhall Lake (p112).

Alaska Boat & Kayak Center KAYAKING

(Map p112; ☎907-364-2333; www.juneaukayak.com; 11521 Glacier Hwy; single/double kayaks $55/75; ⏲9am-5pm) Based in Auke Bay Harbor, this places offers kayak rental, transportation services and multiday discounts. The company has self-guided ($125) and guided paddles ($169) on Mendenhall Lake. The former includes kayaks, transportation and a waterproof map that leads you on a route among the icebergs. It also shows you where to land for a short hike for close-up glacier views.

Berners Bay KAYAKING

At the top end of Glacier Hwy, 40 miles north of Juneau, is Echo Cove, where kayakers can paddle into Berners Bay's protected waters. The bay, which extends 12 miles north to the outlets of the Antler, Lace and Berners Rivers, is ideal for an overnight trip or longer excursions up Berners River.

The delightful USFS **Berners Bay Cabin** (www.recreation.gov; cabins $45) is an 8-mile paddle from Echo Cove. Contact Alaska Boat & Kayak Center for transporting kayaks to Echo Cove.

WORTH A TRIP

TAKU GLACIER LODGE

The most popular tours in Juneau are flightseeing, glacier-viewing and salmon-bakes, and a trip to the historic off-the-grid **Taku Glacier Lodge** (907-586-6275; www.wingsairways.com; adult/child $315/270) combines all three. **Wings Airways** (907-586-6275; www.wingsairways.com; 2 Marine Way, Suite 175), a local floatplane company, has a monopoly on access. Its trips include flying across a half-dozen glaciers to the lodge where an incredible meal of wild salmon awaits.

The trip is a popular cruise-ship excursion, so don't expect to have this particular slice of wilderness to yourself. Sign up at the Wings Airways office behind Merchant's Wharf on Juneau's waterfront.

Auke Bay KAYAKING
(Map p112) The easiest sea paddle around Juneau is out to and around the islands of Auke Bay. You can even camp on the islands to turn the adventure into an overnight trip. Alaska Boat & Kayak Center rents kayaks from Auke Bay Harbor.

Taku Inlet KAYAKING
This waterway is an excellent four- to five-day trip, with close views of Taku Glacier. Total paddling distance is 30 to 40 miles, depending on how far you travel up the inlet. It does not require any major crossing, though rounding Point Bishop can be rough at times.

You can camp at Point Bishop and along the grassy area southwest of the glacier, where brown bears are occasionally seen.

Whale-Watching

A Juneau tour de force! The whale-watching in nearby Stephens Passage is so good that some tour operators will refund your money if you don't see at least one whale. The boats depart from Auke Bay, and most tours last three to four hours. Some operators offer courtesy transportation from downtown.

Harv & Marv's WHALE WATCHING
(907-209-7288; www.harvandmarvs.com; per person $160) Small, personalized tours with no more than six passengers in the boat. They pick up from the cruise dock and transfer to the boat in Auke Bay.

Gastineau Guiding WHALE WATCHING
(Map p112; 907-586-8231; www.stepintoalaska.com; 1330 Eastaugh Way; adult/child $230/185) Gastineau caters to small groups and specializes in whale-watching, often including a little hiking on the side. Its five-hour 'whale-watching and glacier rainforest trail' tour includes a guided hike near the Mendenhall Glacier (p110).

Ziplining

Juneau has a two zipline courses where you can harness up and fly through 100ft trees like an eagle – or a low-flying floatplane.

★ Alaska Zipline Adventures ADVENTURE SPORTS
(Map p112; 907-321-0947; www.alaskazip.com; adult/child $149/99) Possibly Alaska's most adrenaline-laced zip, these nine lines and two sky bridges are located at beautiful Eaglecrest Ski Area on Douglas Island, from where they zigzag across Fish Creek Valley. Transportation (usually a boat) from the cruise-ship dock is included.

Tours

The easiest way to book a tour in Juneau is to head to the cruise-ship terminal, near the Mt Roberts Tramway, where most of the operators will be hawking their wares from a line of outdoor booths, like sideshow barkers at a carnival.

More adventurous tours include helicopter rides over the Juneau Icefield and excursions to Tracy Arm, a steep-sided fjord 45 miles southeast of Juneau, that has a pair of tidewater glaciers and a gallery of icebergs floating down its length.

Pack Creek Bear Tours TOURS
(Map p112; 907-789-3331; www.packcreekbeartours.com; 1873 Shell Simmons Dr; 9am-7pm) Holds permits and offers a guided 6½-hour, fly-in tour ($789) with naturalist guide for groups of no more than five people. Book online early. Despite the price, it's megapopular.

Era Helicopters SCENIC FLIGHTS
(Map p112; 800-843-1947; www.eraflightseeing.com; 6910 N Douglas Hwy) The Mendenhall Glacier is only a tiny part of the humongous Juneau Icefield and you can see a great deal more of this sprawling white carpet on an expensive but spectacular helicopter tour

($750), which includes a couple of stops on terra firma.

The company also runs shorter but cheaper flights ($350) over the advancing Taku Glacier south of town.

NorthStar Trekking HIKING
(Map p112; ☎907-790-4530; www.northstartrekking.com; 1910 Renshaw Way) NorthStar offers several full-on glacier treks of varying levels that helicopter you directly out to the Juneau Icefield. The two-hour glacier trek ($399) crosses 2 miles of frozen landscape riddled with crevasses for a hike that is as stunning as it is pricey. The three-hour trek ($499) utilizes technical climbing skills and ice-wall descents. Trips include all equipment and training.

Juneau Food Tours FOOD & DRINK
(☎800-656-0713; www.juneaufoodtours.com; tours $95-129) It would have been inconceivable a decade ago, but Juneau is a culinary city on the rise with a microbrewery, a microdistillery and a food culture steeped in crab, salmon and halibut. This locally run outfit dangles three different tours that take you through the taste notes. Book online.

Adventure Bound Alaska BOATING
(Map p110; ☎907-463-2509; www.adventureboundalaska.com; 76 Egan Dr; adult/child $160/95) This longtime tour operator uses a pair of boats that leave daily from the Juneau waterfront to explore Tracy Arm, a 30-mile-long fjord 45 miles south of Juneau that protects the tidewater Sawyer Glacier.

Reserve a seat in advance if you can – the full-day tour is popular with cruise ships – and pack a lunch (you can bring beer or wine!) along with your binoculars.

Juneau Tours TOURS
(☎907-523-6095; www.juneautours.com) Pro company that specializes in quick, economical tours for cruise passengers with limited time. The quickest and cheapest is the 45-minute trolley tour that departs from the Mt Roberts Tram Station and loops around the city's main sights ($30). Other trips include three hours of whale-watching ($115) and a shuttle to the Mendenhall Glacier (round-trip $30).

The company picks up from the cruise-ship dock.

Above & Beyond Alaska HIKING
(Map p112; ☎907-364-2333; www.beyondak.com; 2767 Sherwood Lane; per person $219; ⏲8am-4pm) Utilizing the West Glacier Trail to access Mendenhall Glacier, Above & Beyond Alaska avoids expensive helicopter fees on its guided eight-hour outing, with one hour on the glacier itself.

Festivals & Events

★Celebration CULTURAL
(⏲Jun) In June of even-numbered years, Southeast Alaska's three main tribal groups, the Tlingit, Haida and Tsimshian, gather for the aptly named 'Celebration,' the largest native cultural event in Alaska. The festival's sentiment is as simple as its name: to celebrate and revitalize ancient traditions in native dance, music and art which, by the early 20th century, were in danger of extinction.

Alaska Folk Festival MUSIC
(www.alaskafolkfestival.org; ⏲mid-Apr) Attracts musicians from around the state for a week of performances, workshops and dances at Centennial Hall.

Sleeping

Typically for a state capital, Juneau's hotels are more businesslike than boutique. There's a modest hostel and several out-of-town campgrounds.

The city tacks on 12% in bed and sales taxes to the price of lodging.

★Mendenhall Lake Campground CAMPGROUND $
(Map p112; ☎518-885-3639, reservations 877-444-6777; www.recreation.gov; Montana Creek Rd; tent/RV sites $10/28) One of Alaska's most beautiful USFS campgrounds. The 69-site area (17 sites with hookups) is on Montana Creek Rd, off Mendenhall Loop Rd, and has a separate seven-site walk-in area. The campsites are alongside Mendenhall Lake, and many have spectacular views of the icebergs or even the glacier that discharges them.

All the sites are well spread out in the woods, and 20 can be reserved in advance.

Juneau International Hostel HOSTEL $
(Map p110; ☎907-586-9559; www.juneauhostel.net; 614 Harris St; dm adult/child $12/5; @📶) Welcome to a *real* old-fashioned hostel, the type where the rates are low as long as you perform a daily chore (dish washing anyone?). The chore policy obviously works – the place is kept spotlessly clean with the communal areas avoiding the overflowing clutter of some hostels. In total there are

eight bunk rooms, and amenities include laundry, storage and free internet access.

In the lounge area, the overstuffed sofas are strategically placed around a large bay window with a view of snowy peaks and Douglas Island. The one downside is the strict 9am to 5pm lock-out policy, but for this price, who cares?

Alaskan Hotel HOTEL **$**
(Map p110; ☎907-586-1000; www.thealaskanhotel.com; 167 S Franklin St; r with/without bath $90/80; 📶) Welcome to a quintessential gold-boom hotel, with heavily patterned wallpaper clashing with the heavily patterned carpet, lots of wood paneling and walls that would probably relate some lewd erstwhile antics could they talk (it's the oldest operating hotel in Alaska, dating from 1913).

Bedrooms are smallish, some have shared bathrooms and there's a rowdy bar downstairs, but, if you like to immerse yourself in the ghosts of gold rushes past, this place could stimulate some lucid historical hallucinations. It's cheap, too.

Auke Village Campground CAMPGROUND **$**
(Map p112; www.recreation.gov; Glacier Hwy; tent & RV sites $10) Fancy camping on the site of an old Tlingit village? Then head 2 miles west of the ferry terminal on Glacier Hwy to this first-come, first-served USFS campground with 11 sites in a beautiful wooded location overlooking Auke Bay.

Spruce Meadow RV Park CAMPGROUND **$**
(Map p112; ☎907-789-1990; www.juneaurv.com; 10200 Mendenhall Loop Rd; tent sites $22-29, RV sites $34-38; 📶) Practically next door to Mendenhall Lake Campground (p118), but not nearly as nice, is this full-service campground with laundromat, cable TV and tent sites as well as full hookups. It's right on the city bus route.

Juneau Hotel HOTEL **$$**
(Map p110; ☎907-586-5666; www.juneauhotels.net; 1200 W 9th St; ste $184; 📶) Located within easy walking distance of downtown attractions, this handsome all-suites hotel is Juneau's best deal in midrange accommodations. The 73 suites have full kitchens, sitting areas, two TVs each and even washers and dryers. It's right next to the Douglas Bridge.

Prospector Hotel HOTEL **$$**
(Map p110; ☎907-586-1204; www.prospectorhotel.com; 375 Whittier St; r from $149; P @ 📶) The Prospector is a typical middle-of-the-road Juneau option: unexciting, but perfectly comfortable and in a good location. There's an onsite bar/restaurant, self-service laundry and an efficient reception desk. Rooms are large with plenty of storage, should you arrive with bags full of fishing gear. It's next door to the revamped Alaska State Museum (p109).

Driftwood Hotel MOTEL **$$**
(Map p110; ☎907-586-2280; www.driftwoodalaska.com; 435 Willoughby Ave; r/ste $125/175; P 📶) The woody, slightly scruffy exterior doesn't really do the 63-room Driftwood justice. Sure, it looks like a journeyman motel, but inside the rooms are clean and updated regularly. Two extra bonuses: it's next door to the excellent Sandpiper (p121) brunch spot and it's the only place in town offering 24-hour courtesy transportation to the airport and ferry.

Auke Lake B&B B&B **$$**
(Map p112; ☎907-790-3253; www.aukelakebb.com; 11595 Mendenhall Loop Rd; r $140-190; 📶) Located 10 minutes from Mendenhall Glacier, this valley B&B has five luxurious rooms with phone, TV, refrigerator and coffeemaker. In the living room is a stuffed giant brown bear, while outside is a beautiful deck and hot tub overlooking Auke Lake. A kayak, a canoe, and a BBQ in a gazebo are available. The only pickle is location if you're carless.

★ **Alaska's Capital Inn** B&B **$$$**
(Map p110; ☎907-586-6507; www.alaskacapitalinn.com; 113 W 5th St; r incl breakfast $265-355; P @ 📶) Taking Alaskan B&Bs to a new level is the Capital Inn (suitably situated across the street from the state capitol), where period details mingle with modern comfort. Housed in the gorgeously restored 1906 home of a wealthy gold-rush-era miner, the inn has seven rooms with hardwood floors covered by colorful Persian rugs.

One of many highlights is the family-style breakfast served in the formal dining room – a true feast. For ravenous appetites there's a bottomless cookie jar available all day. The backyard has multiple decks, gardens and a secluded hot tub that even the governor can't spy on.

★ **Silverbow Inn** BOUTIQUE HOTEL **$$$**
(Map p110; ☎907-586-4146; www.silverbowinn.com; 120 2nd St; r $199-244; @ 📶) A swanky (for Alaska) boutique inn with 11 rooms. The 100-year-old building emanates a retro-versus-modern feel with antiques and rooms with private baths, king and queen beds and flat-screen TVs. A 2nd-floor deck features

a hot tub with a view of Douglas Island's mountains. Breakfast is served in the morning and there's a cocoa and cookies 'happy hour' in the afternoon.

Beachside Villa Luxury Inn B&B **$$$**
(Map p112; ☎907-463-5531; www.beachsidevilla.com; 3120 Douglas Hwy; r $229-329;) Luxury is an accurate assessment of this B&B with five rooms and amenities that range from balconies and private entrances to fireplaces and in-room Jacuzzis. Best of all is its Douglas Island location and views. Perched on the Gastineau Channel, its porches and neatly landscaped backyard overlook downtown Juneau, Mt Roberts and the parade of floatplanes and vessels entering the harbor.

Four Points by Sheraton HOTEL **$$$**
(Map p110; ☎907-586-6900; www.fourpointsjuneau.com; 51 Egan Dr; r $175-275; P@) The former Goldbelt hotel – one of Juneau's tallest buildings – has come under the ownership of Sheraton, which has given the place a full refurbishment. Rooms are large with deluxe beds and fittings along with some sharp color accents. The ones facing the water on the higher floors are, not surprisingly, the best. Rear rooms can be a little dark.

Downstairs off the lobby there is a fitness room, coffee on-tap, and access to McGivney's Sports Bar & Grill (p121). Prices fluctuate; check online for the best deals.

Eating

Once a culinary desert in a rainforest setting, Juneau is finally beginning to serve up a restaurant scene worthy of a state capital. Several new bistros and bars are catering to an increasingly savvy crowd who want more than fried fish for dinner.

★Pel'Meni DUMPLINGS **$**
(Map p110; Merchant's Wharf, Marine Way; dumplings $7; 11:30am-1:30am Sun-Thu, to 3:30am Fri & Sat) Juneau was never part of Russia's Alaskan empire, but that hasn't stopped the city succumbing to a silent invasion of pelmeni (homemade Russian dumplings), filled with either potato or beef, spiced with hot sauce, curry and cilantro, and tempered with a little optional sour cream and rye bread on the side.

They're served in what is a cross between a disheveled greasy spoon and a crumby student canteen, where tipsy undergrads mix with grizzled bearded guys over a backing track of scratchy vinyl (shelves of dog-eared LPs fill one wall). There's no menu, no price differential and no credit-card machine; just good vibes, funny late-night antics and even better dumplings. Legend!

Rainbow Foods HEALTH FOOD **$**
(Map p110; ☎907-586-6476; www.rainbow-foods.org; 224 4th St; snacks $8; 9am-7pm Mon-Fri, 10am-6pm Sat & Sun) Ironically juxtaposed right next door to the dig-and-drill politicians in the state capitol is this natural-food store, a hangout for liberals and environmentalists. Along with a large selection of fresh produce and bulk goods, the store has a hot-and-cold food bar for lunch, espresso and fresh baked goods, and a bulletin board with the latest cultural happenings.

Hot Bite BURGERS **$**
(Map p112; ☎907-790-2483; 11465 Auke Bay Harbor Dr; hamburgers $10-14; 11am-7pm) The best milkshakes and burgers in Juneau are in Auke Bay Harbor. Hot Bite is housed in the one-time ticket office of Pan American Airways and has seating outside in nice weather.

It offers almost 40 flavors of milkshake and, as if three scoops of ice cream weren't enough, its cheesecake shake also has cream cheese and graham-cracker crumbs mixed in.

★Rookery CAFE **$$**
(Map p110; ☎907-463-3013; www.therookerycafe.com; 111 Seward St; lunch $9-14, dinner mains $15-24; 7am-9pm Mon-Fri, 9am-9pm Sat) A brilliant combo of laid-back coffee shop by day and hip bistro by night, the Rookery serves Portland, OR's Stumptown coffee and original breakfasts, lunches and dinners. Buttermilk corn cakes, sandwiches on homemade focaccia, and breakfast rice bowls are just some of the daytime offerings. At 4pm, the wi-fi is extinguished and a daily changing menu that includes charcuterie and salads emerges.

The walls are adorned with beautiful Alaska photo art that can be reproduced should you spot one you like.

★Saffron INDIAN **$$**
(Map p110; ☎907-586-1036; www.saffronalaska.com; 112 N Franklin St; mains $8-19; 11:30am-9pm Mon-Fri, 5-9pm Sat & Sun;) Juneau flirts with *nuevo* Indian food at Saffron and the results are commendable. There are plenty of delicate breads to go with the aromatic

curries with a strong bias toward vegetarian dishes (including a good spinach paneer). For lunch it offers *thalis* (small taster-sized plates). Everything is made from scratch and the exotic cooking smells lure you in from the street.

Tracy's King Crab Shack SEAFOOD **$$**
(Map p110; www.kingcrabshack.com; 406 S Franklin St; crab $13-45; ⊙10am-8pm) The best of the food shacks along the cruise-ship berths is Tracy's. On a boardwalk surrounded by a beer shack and a gift shop, she serves up outstanding crab bisque, mini crab cakes and 3lb buckets of king-crab pieces ($110). Grab a friend or six and share.

In Bocca Al Lupo ITALIAN **$$**
(Map p110; ☎907-586-1409; 120 2nd St; pizza & pasta $14-17; ⊙5-9pm Mon-Sat) Another step on Juneau's stairway to culinary heaven is this hip Italian place whose dark (surely temporary) facade hides a beautiful streamlined woody interior where you can sit at the bar and watch the chefs tuck pizzas into a glowing wood-fire oven. It attracts cultured locals and the odd cruiser for its interesting antipasto plates, eclectic wine list and thin-crust pizzas.

Island Pub PIZZA **$$**
(Map p112; www.theislandpub.com; 1102 2nd St; large pizzas $13-20; ⊙11:30am-10pm) This local fave about which they rave is across the channel from Juneau proper. It's a relaxing, unhurried place with a wooden Wild West facade that serves firebrick-oven focaccia and the best pizza in town, with a side of channel and mountain views. Before the pie arrives you can enjoy a drink from an impressive list of cocktails. Don't worry about a Red Dog Saloon (p122) mob scene – you're on Douglas Island.

El Sombrero MEXICAN **$$**
(Map p110; www.elsombrerojuneau.com; 157 S Franklin St; mains $13-21; ⊙11am-9pm Mon-Thu, to 10pm Fri & Sat) Sombrero is practically the only city-center joint that's not packed out when there are five cruise ships in town. But shhh, this is a dearly beloved local stronghold knocking out piquant enchiladas, burritos and fish tacos in a state not renowned for its Latino restaurants.

Snack on the complimentary nachos and salsa, listen to the chatter, and have a day off from halibut and chips.

Rockwell AMERICAN **$$**
(Map p110; www.rockwelljuneau.com; 109 S Franklin St; sandwiches $9-14, dinner mains $13-18; ⊙11am-11pm) Rather dingy looking from the outside, but surprisingly hip within, Rockwell pulls in all sorts for (late) breakfast, lunch and dinner. The menu appears meat-heavy at first with hand-cut steaks and excellent burgers, but the kitchen also makes fine European-style standard salads. Better still is the long bar that serves all the local microbrews and microspirits.

Sandpiper BREAKFAST **$$**
(Map p110; 429 Willoughby Ave; mains breakfast $10-17, lunch $11-14; ⊙6am-2pm) If you conducted a local opinion poll, the Sandpiper could well register as Juneau's best breakfast. Skip the eggs and try one of the Belgian waffles, blueberry buttermilk pancakes or specialty French toasts such as mandarin and mascarpone cheese.

Douglas Café CAFE **$$**
(Map p112; 916 3rd St, Douglas; breakfast mains $11-13, dinner mains $19-24; ⊙11am-8:30pm Tue-Fri, 8:30am-8:30pm Sat, 9am-12:30pm Sun) This casual eatery (one of two restaurants on Douglas Island) serves up 15 different types of burgers, including a Boring Burger. But if it's dinner, skip the bun and go for one of its tempting mains, which range from tarragon-lime chicken to Cajun prawn fettuccine. Serves brunch on weekends.

Timberline Bar & Grill INTERNATIONAL **$$$**
(☎907-463-1338; mains $17-45; ⊙11am-8pm) The top station of the Mt Roberts Tramway (p109) supports this large restaurant which, not surprisingly, sports the best views in town. Highlights include the shareable crab nachos and pelmeni, both of which taste much better if you've hiked up.

Salt AMERICAN **$$$**
(Map p110; ☎907-780-2221; www.saltalaska.com; 200 Seward St; mains $20-36; ⊙4-11pm Mon-Sat, to 10pm Sun) Salt is run by Tracy of Tracy's King Crab Shack and the dedication is evident as soon as you walk in. High-quality, creative Alaskan cuisine is the highlight, accompanied by a long wine list and fresh desserts, as well as attention to locals with unconventional renderings of Alaskan seafood. It's swanky (but still Juneau), with candlelit tables and muted colors. Reservations recommended.

As well as expensive mains, it offers smaller shared plates from 4pm – great with an aperitif.

Hangar on the Wharf SEAFOOD $$$
(Map p110; www.hangaronthewharf.com; 2 Marine Way; mains $13-35; ⏲11am-midnight) Housed in Merchant's Wharf (also called Fisherman's Wharf), a renovated floatplane hangar that sits on pilings above Juneau's waterfront, the Hangar is usually a bit of a bun fight when there's more than one cruise ship in town. Seafood rules and, while it's not cheap, the beer's good, as is the unobstructed channel view, a landing strip for buzzing seaplanes.

Drinking & Nightlife

Nightlife centers on S Franklin and Front Sts, a historic, quaint (but not quiet) main drag, attracting locals and tourists alike.

There's an out-of-town microbrewery and an in-town microdistillery.

Alaskan Brewing Company BREWERY
(Map p112; www.alaskanbeer.com; 5429 Shaune Dr; ⏲11am-6pm) Established in 1986 (ancient history in craft-brewing years), Alaska's largest brewery has always been a pioneer. Its amber ale (along with many other concoctions) is ubiquitous across the state and rightly so. Note: this is not a brewpub but a tasting room with tours. It isn't located downtown either, but 5 miles to the northwest in Lemon Creek.

The brewery runs hourly guided tasting tours ($20) around its small facility, which include samples of up to six lagers and ales. You can arrive by public bus or taxi, but the best way to get here is on a special shuttle (free if you take the tour) that runs from its downtown retail store, Alaskan Brewing Co Depot.

Coppa COFFEE
(Map p110; ☎907-586-3500; 917 Glacier Ave; ⏲6:30am-5pm Mon-Thu, to 9pm Fri, 8am-6pm Sat) A little more than just a coffee shop (though it does serve locally roasted Sentinel Coffee), Coppa serves fresh-baked pastries, loose-leaf teas and housemade gelato – if you can't handle the caramelized-onion flavor, try local favorite rhubarb. Located near the Douglas Bridge.

McGivney's Sports Bar & Grill PUB
(Map p110; 51 Egan Dr; ⏲11am-10pm) This is Juneau's upmarket sports bar with two branches (the other one is out at Auke Bay). There are more than a dozen beers on tap (including local microbrews from Juneau and Sitka), fancy-time cocktails

JUNEAU'S WILDERNESS CABINS

Numerous United States Forest Service cabins are accessible from Juneau, but all are heavily used, requiring advance reservations. If you're just passing through, check with the USFS Juneau Ranger District Office (p123) for a list of what's available. The following cabins are within 30 minutes' flying time of Juneau; air charters will cost around $500 to $600 round-trip from Juneau, split among a planeload of up to five passengers. Alaska Seaplane Service (p124) can provide flights on short notice.

Turner Lake West Cabin (www.recreation.gov; cabins $45) is one of the most scenic, and by far the most popular, cabins in the Juneau area. It's 18 miles east of Juneau on the west end of Turner Lake, where the fishing is good for trout, Dolly Varden and salmon. A skiff is provided.

Admiralty Island's north end has three popular cabins, all $35 a night. **Admiralty Cove Cabin** is on a scenic bay and has access to Young Lake along a rough 4.5-mile trail. Brown bears frequent the area. The two **Young Lake Cabins** have skiffs to access a lake with good fishing for cutthroat trout and landlocked salmon. A lakeshore trail connects the two cabins.

There are also three rental cabins in Point Bridget State Park (p114) that rent for $45 a night. **Cowee Meadow Cabin** is a 2.5-mile hike into the park, **Blue Mussel Cabin** is a 3.4-mile walk and **Camping Cove Cabin** a 4-mile trek. Both Blue Mussel and Camping Cove overlook the shoreline and make great destinations for kayakers.

There are three cabins available at **Eagle Beach State Recreation Area campground** (Map p112; ☎907-586-2506; Mile 28, Glacier Hwy; tent & RV sites $15). Check availability through the Alaska Division of Parks (p123).

and 15 TVs perennially tuned to NFL, NBA or the like.

Happy hour for appetizers is 3pm to 5pm and the food is verging on gourmet.

Amalga Distillery DISTILLERY
(Map p110; ☎907-209-2015; www.amalgadistillery.com; 134 N Franklin St; ⏲1-8pm) First Haines, now Juneau: microdistilling has definitely arrived in Southeast Alaska.

Their potent Juneauper gin is best appreciated with homemade tonic, ice and a slice. The clean-cut family-friendly tasting room, complete with Kentucky-made 'still', inhabits an old Alaska Electric Light & Power building downtown.

Red Dog Saloon BAR
(Map p110; www.reddogsaloon.com; 278 S Franklin St; ⏲11am-10pm) A sign at the door says it all – 'Booze, Antiques, Sawdust Floor, Community Singing' – and the cruise-ship passengers love it! Most don't realize, much less care, that this Red Dog is but a replica of the original, a gold-mining-era Alaskan drinking hole that was across the street until 1987. Now *that* was a bar.

The duplicate is, well...a duplicate, and once you're in, there's only one way out – through the gift shop.

Heritage Coffee Co & Café COFFEE
(Map p110; ☎907-586-1087; www.heritagecoffee.com; 130 Front St; ⏲6am-7:30pm; 📶) Owners of seven perennially busy Juneau cafes, Heritage was an early starter in the coffee boom. It's been roasting beans for over 35 years in an old Starbucks roaster. Of the magnificent seven cafes, this downtown favorite with huge muffins is where you'll most likely end up.

☆ Entertainment

Gold Town Nickelodeon CINEMA
(Map p110; ☎907-586-2875; www.goldtownnick.com; 171 Shattuck St; adult/child $9/5) In among the thick cluster of jewelry shops that plays to the cruise crowd is this delightful art-house theater, which presents small-budget foreign films and documentaries. Seating arrangements include velour couches.

Perseverance Theater THEATER
(Map p112; ☎907-364-2421; www.perseverancetheatre.org; 914 3rd St, Douglas) Founded in 1979, this is Alaska's only genuine full-time professional theater company. Sadly the theater season begins in September and ends in May, though it does host events throughout the summer – check the website for info. The small theater is over the water from downtown in Douglas

Shopping

Juneau Arts and Culture Center ARTS & CRAFTS
(JACC; Map p110; www.jahc.org; 350 Whittier St; ⏲9am-6pm) The impressive JACC gallery features the work of a local artist every month, while the adjacent Lobby Shop is a place for Southeast Alaskans to sell their artworks, including jewelry, paintings and books.

The website is an excellent resource for Juneau happenings.

Juneau Artists Gallery ARTS & CRAFTS
(Map p110; www.juneauartistsgallery.com; 175 S Franklin St, Senate Bldg; ⏲9am-9pm) A co-op of 27 local artists have filled this downtown store with paintings, etchings, glasswork, jewelry and pottery. The person behind the counter ready to help you is that day's 'Artist On Duty.'

Hearthside Books BOOKS
(Map p110; www.hearthsidebooks.com; 254 Front St; ⏲10am-8pm Mon-Fri, to 6pm Sat, noon-5pm Sun; 👪) Juneau has fabulous bookstores for a town of its size. This well-loved nook has good travel and kids sections and helpful staff.

Fireweed Factory DISPENSARY
(Map p110; ☎907-957-2670; 237 Front St; ⏲noon-6pm Mon-Wed, Fri & Sat) Following the legalization of marijuana in Alaska in November 2014, in March 2017 this became the second recreational pot shop to open in Juneau. It's a tiny abode (about the width of an average arm-span), but popular – with cruisers as much as locals. It sells a half-dozen different strains. Photo ID is required for entry.

Alaskan Brewing Co Depot GIFTS & SOUVENIRS
(Map p110; 219 S Franklin St; ⏲9am-6pm Mon-Sat, 10am-6pm Sun) The Alaska Brewing Co's gift store downtown also runs a van out to the brewery for tasting sessions every hour for $20 per person, round-trip.

Foggy Mountain Shop SPORTS & OUTDOORS
(Map p110; www.foggymountainshop.com; 134 N Franklin St; ⏲9:30am-5:30pm Mon-Sat) For packs, outdoor-wear, United States Geological Survey (USGS) topo maps and anything else you need for backcountry trips, stop at Foggy Mountain Shop. This is the only

outdoor shop in town with top-of-the-line equipment, and the prices reflect that.

Information

MEDICAL SERVICES

Bartlett Regional Hospital (907-796-631; 3260 Hospital Dr) Southeast Alaska's largest hospital is off Glacier Hwy between downtown and Lemon Creek.

Juneau Urgent Care (907-790-4111; 8505 Old Dairy Rd; 8am-7pm Mon-Fri, 9am-5pm Sat & Sun) A walk-in medical clinic near Nugget Mall in the Valley.

MONEY

There's no shortage of banks in Juneau. Most have ATMs and branches both downtown and in the Valley.

First Bank (605 W Willoughby Ave; 8am-5:30pm Mon-Fri)

Wells Fargo (123 Seward St; 9:30am-5pm Mon-Fri, 10am-2pm Sat)

TOURIST INFORMATION

Alaska Division of Parks (Map p110; 907-465-4563; www.dnr.state.ak.us/parks; 400 Willoughby Ave; 8am-4:30pm Mon-Fri) Head to the 5th floor of the Natural Resources Building for state-park information, including cabin rentals.

Juneau Visitor Center (907-586-2201; www.traveljuneau.com; 470 S Franklin St; 8am-5pm) The visitor center is on the cruise-ship terminal right next to the Mt Roberts Tramway and has all the information you need to explore Juneau, find a trail or book a room. The center also maintains smaller booths at the airport, at the marine ferry terminal and **downtown** (Map p110; Marine Way; hours vary) near the library.

USFS Juneau Ranger District Office (Map p112; 907-586-8800; 8510 Mendenhall Loop Rd; 8am-4:30pm Mon-Fri) This impressive office is in Mendenhall Valley and is the place for questions about cabins, trails, kayaking and Pack Creek bear-watching permits. It also serves as the USFS office for Admiralty Island National Monument.

Getting There & Away

AIR

Juneau International Airport (Map p112) is located 9 miles northwest of downtown. There is a bus link.

Alaska Airlines (p429) offers scheduled jet service to Seattle (two hours), all major South-east cities, Glacier Bay (30 minutes), Anchor-age (two hours) and Cordova (2½ hours) daily in summer.

Alaska Seaplanes (907-789-3331; www.flyalaskaseaplanes.com) flies daily floatplanes from Juneau to Angoon ($144), Gustavus ($115), Pelican ($180) and Tenakee Springs ($144).

CRUISE SHIP

Cruise ships get a far better deal than the state ferry, pulling into a line of docks that starts just south of the downtown core, next to the Mt Roberts Tramway base station. As many as six ships can dock at once, meaning if you're last in the queue, you'll have further to walk. Free shuttles provide wheels for those who would rather not.

FERRY

Ferries dock at the **Alaska Marine Highway Auke Bay Ferry Terminal** (Map p112; 800-642-0066; www.ferryalaska.com), 14 miles northwest of downtown. In summer, the main-line ferries traversing the Inside Passage depart southbound weekly for Sitka ($65, nine hours), and three times a week for Petersburg ($78, eight hours) and Ketchikan ($126, 19 hours).

You can shorten the sailing times on the high-speed MV *Fairweather*, which connects Juneau to Petersburg and Sitka once a week. Several shorter routes also operate in summer. The smaller MV *LeConte* regularly connects Juneau to the secondary ports of Hoonah ($42, seven hours), Tenakee Springs ($46, eight hours) and Angoon ($51, seven hours). Two times a month, the MV *Kennicott* departs Juneau for a trip to Yakutat ($110, 17 hours) then across the Gulf of Alaska to Whittier ($252, 39 hours); reservations are strongly suggested.

Getting Around

TO/FROM THE AIRPORT

A **taxi** (907-796-2300) to/from the airport costs around $25.

The city bus express route runs to the airport, but only from 7:30am to 5:30pm Monday to Friday. On weekends and in the evening, if you want a bus you'll need to walk 10 minutes to the nearest 'regular route' stop behind Nugget Mall. The regular route headed downtown stops here regularly from 7:15am until 10:45pm Monday to Saturday, and from 9:15am until 5:45pm Sunday. The fare on either route is $2/1 per adult/child.

BUS

Juneau's sadistic and seemingly illogical public bus system, **Capital Transit** (Map p110; 907-789-6901; www.juneau.org/capitaltransit), stops way short of the ferry terminal and 1.5-miles short of the Mendenhall Glacier Visitor Center (p111).

Even getting to/from the airport can be prob-lematic: only the 'express' route goes right to the terminal, and it only runs during business hours on weekdays. At other times, you'll have to carry your bag(s) between the airport and the 'regular' route's stop at Nugget Mall, a 10-minute walk. The 'regular' route buses start around 7am and stop before midnight, running every half-hour after 8am and before 6:30pm.

The most useful routes are buses 3 and 4, which head from downtown to the Mendenhall Valley via Auke Bay Boat Harbor, and buses 1 and 11, which shuttle between downtown and Douglas Island.

Fares are $2/1 each way per adult/child, and exact change is required. All buses stop at the **Downtown Transit Center** (Map p110; Egan Dr, cnr Main St).

CAR

Juneau has many car-rental places, and renting a car is a great way for two or three people to see the sights out of the city or to reach a trailhead.

Decent offers come from **Juneau Car Rental** (☎907-789-0951, 907-957-7530; www.juneaucarrentals.com), which is a mile from the airport but provides pickups and has a designated airport parking spot for when you drop the car off.

You can also rent a car at the airport, but will have to stomach a 26% tax as opposed to a 15% tax elsewhere.

Admiralty Island & Pack Creek

Just 15 miles south of Juneau is Admiralty Island National Monument, a 1493-sq-mile preserve, of which 90% is designated wilderness. The monument has a wide variety of wildlife – from Sitka black-tailed deer and nesting bald eagles to harbor seals, sea lions and humpback whales – but more than anything else, Admiralty Island is known for bears.

The 96-mile-long island has one of the highest populations of bears in Alaska, with an estimated 1500 brown bears, more than all the lower 48 states combined. It's the reason the Tlingit called Admiralty Kootznoowoo, 'the Fortress of Bears.'

The monument's main attraction for visitors is Pack Creek, one of Southeast Alaska's chief bear-viewing sites.

Sights

Angoon VILLAGE

Angoon (pop 450) is the only community on Admiralty Island and serves as the departure point for many kayak and canoe trips into the heart of the monument, including the Cross Admiralty canoe route (p66). The town has long been home to the Kootznoowoo-Tlingit clan, who historically favored the area for its sunnier-than-normal climate. The town is isolated and small. It is popular with summer fishers and kayakers and connected to Juneau via daily floatplanes and twice-weekly ferries.

Activities

Bear-Viewing

Pack Creek on Admiralty Island is one of the top five places to view bears in Alaska. However, because it's so near Juneau, the 24 daily permits get booked up well in advance.

★Pack Creek WILDLIFE WATCHING

(permits adult $25-50, child $10-25) The monument's main attraction for visitors is Pack Creek, which flows from 4000ft mountains before spilling into Seymour Canal on the island's east side. The extensive tide flats at the mouth of the creek draw a large number of bears in July and August to feed on salmon. This, and its proximity to Juneau, make it a favorite spot for observing and photographing the animals.

Bear-viewing at Pack Creek takes place at **Stan Price State Wildlife Sanctuary**, named for an Alaskan woodsman who lived on a float-house here for almost 40 years. The vast majority of visitors to the sanctuary are day-trippers who arrive and depart on floatplanes. Upon arrival, all visitors are met by a ranger who explains the rules and then each party hikes to an observation tower – reached by a mile-long trail – that overlooks the creek.

Pack Creek has become so popular that the area buzzes with planes and boats every morning from early July to late August. Anticipating this daily rush hour, most resident bears escape into the forest, but a few bears hang around to feed on salmon, having long since been habituated to the human visitors. Seeing five or six bears would be a good viewing day at Pack Creek. You might see big boars during the mating season from May to mid-June; otherwise it's sows and cubs the rest of the summer.

From June to mid-September, the USFS and Alaska Department of Fish and Game operate a permit system for Pack Creek and only 24 people are allowed per day from July to the end of August. Guiding and tour companies receive half the permits, leaving 12 for individuals who want to visit Pack Creek on their own. **National Recreation Reservation Service** (☎518-885-3639; www.recreation.gov), the people who handle USFS cabin reservations, also handle Pack Creek permits.

Paddling

Kayaking is a major highlight of Admiralty Island. The main pickle is that nowhere on the island rents kayaks. However, you *can* rent kayaks from Alaska Boat & Kayak Center (p116) at Auke Bay near Juneau and then place them on an Alaska State Ferry.

Alternatively, you can partake in an organized trip. Juneau-based Above & Beyond Alaska (p117) offers a one-day kayaking and bear-viewing trip in and around Pack Creek for $749. A more adventurous three-day trip costs $1299. All trips include flights, kayak rental, food and permits.

Independent kayakers often fly in to paddle the Cross Admiralty Island canoe route (p66), a 31.7-mile paddle that spans the center of the island from the village of Angoon to Mole Harbor. Although the majority of the route consists of calm lakes connected by streams and portages, the 10-mile paddle from Angoon on Admiralty Island's west coast to Mitchell Bay is subject to strong tides that challenge even experienced paddlers.

Sleeping

Most accommodations around Angoon are all-inclusive fishing lodges, the exception being one very pleasant B&B run by the Salvation Army. Services are limited as tourism seems to be tolerated only because the village is a port of call for the ferry. There are 14 USFS cabins; see www.recreation.gov for details.

Eagle's Wing Inn B&B $$
(☎907-788-3234; 922 Killisnoo Rd, Angoon; r $125;) A great place to stay, this large, rambling log home 2 miles from the ferry terminal is run by the Salvation Army. Three of the five rooms have views of the bay, and all come with a hearty breakfast that includes fresh-baked goods.

There's a dinner option for an extra $25, or you can bring your own food to prepare in the kitchen. Book well ahead in summer.

Eating

Angoon has only one rudimentary grocery store and no cafes or restaurants. Come prepared with sufficient supplies.

Eagle's Wing Inn does breakfast and dinners (on request) for guests.

Getting There & Away

AIR

Admiralty Air Service (☎907-796-2000; www.admiraltyairservice.com) offers charter flights to Pack Creek and elsewhere for $450 an hour (up to four people).

Alaska Seaplanes (☎907-789-3331; www.flyalaskaseaplanes.com) has three daily flights from Juneau to Angoon ($144, 35 minutes).

FERRY

Alaska Marine Highway (☎800-642-0066; www.ferryalaska.com) ferries run twice a week between Angoon and Juneau ($51, 6.5 hours). The ferry terminal is 1½ miles south of town.

Glacier Bay National Park & Preserve

Glacier Bay is the crowning jewel of the cruise-ship industry and a dreamy destination for anybody who has ever paddled a kayak. Seven tidewater glaciers spill out of the mountains and fill the sea with icebergs of all shapes, sizes and shades of blue, making Glacier Bay National Park and Preserve an icy wilderness renowned worldwide.

Apart from its high concentration of tidewater glaciers, Glacier Bay is a dynamic habitat for humpback whales. Other wildlife seen at Glacier Bay includes porpoises, sea otters, brown and black bears, wolves, moose and mountain goats.

The park is an expensive side trip, even by Alaskan standards. Plan on spending at least $400 for a trip from Juneau. Of the 500,000 annual visitors, more than 95% arrive aboard a ship and never leave it. The rest are a mixture of tour-group members, who head straight for the lodge, and backpackers, who gravitate toward the free campground.

Sights

Gustavus TOWN
(www.gustavusak.com) About 9 miles from Bartlett Cove is the small settlement of Gustavus, an interesting backcountry

community. The town's 400 citizens include a mix of professional people – doctors, lawyers, former government workers and artists – who decided to drop out of the rat race and live on their own in the middle of the woods. Electricity only arrived in the early 1980s and in some homes you must pump water at the sink or build a fire before you can have a hot shower.

Gustavus has no downtown: it's little more than an airstrip left over from WWII and a road to Bartlett Cove, known to most locals as 'the Road.' Along the Road there is little to see, as most cabins and homes are tucked away behind a shield of trees.

The state ferry docks at Gustavus and Alaska Airlines jets land at the small airport nearby.

Activities

Hiking

Glacier Bay has few trails and in the backcountry foot travel is done along riverbanks, on ridges or across ice remnants of glaciers. The only developed trails are in Bartlett Cove.

Point Gustavus Beach Walk HIKING

The Point Gustavus Beach Walk, along the shoreline south of Bartlett Cove to Point Gustavus and Gustavus, provides the only overnight trek from the park headquarters. The total distance is 12 miles, and the walk to Point Gustavus, an excellent spot to camp, is 6 miles.

Plan on hiking the stretch from Point Gustavus to Gustavus at low tide, which will allow you to ford the Salmon River, as opposed to swimming across it. Point Gustavus is an ideal place to sight orcas and whales in Icy Strait.

Bartlett River Trail HIKING

A 2-mile trail begins near Bartlett Cove, a short way along the Gustavus road, where there is a posted trailhead. It ends at the Bartlett River estuary. On the way, it meanders along a tidal lagoon and passes through quite a few muddy spots. Plan on two to four hours for the 4-mile round-trip.

Nagoonberry Loop HIKING

The Nagoonberry Loop is an accessible 2.2-mile trail that begins and ends at the terminus of Glen's Ditch Rd. Along the way you'll pass through all stages of a forest, from meadow to old growth, and on to a beach. There are benches, two viewing areas and more wildflowers than you can take photos of.

Forest Loop Trail HIKING

The mile-long Forest Loop Trail is a nature walk that begins and ends near the Bartlett Cove dock and winds through the pond-studded spruce and hemlock forest near the campground. Rangers lead walks on this trail daily in summer; inquire at the Glacier Bay National Park Visitor Center (p128).

Paddling

Glacier Bay offers an excellent opportunity for people who have some experience on the water but not necessarily as kayakers, because the *Fairweather Express*, run by Glacier Bay Lodge & Tours, drops off and picks up paddlers at two spots, usually at the entrance of the Muir Inlet (East Arm) and inside the West Arm.

By using the tour boat, you can skip the long and open paddle up the bay and enjoy only the well-protected arms and inlets where the glaciers are located.

The most dramatic glaciers are in the West Arm, but either one will require at least four days to paddle to glaciers if you are dropped off *and* picked up.

With only a drop-off, you need a week to 10 days to paddle from either arm back to Bartlett Cove.

Paddlers who want to avoid the tour-boat fares but still long for a kayak adventure should try the **Beardslee Islands**. While there are no glaciers to view, the islands are a day's paddle from Bartlett Cove and offer calm water, protected channels and pleasant beach camping. Wildlife includes black bears, seals and bald eagles, and the tidal pools burst with activity at low tide.

Alaska Mountain Guides & Climbing School (p130) runs several guided kayak trips into Glacier Bay. A seven-day paddle to the West Arm, which includes tour transportation as well as all equipment and food, is $2450 per person, and an eight-day paddle up the East Arm that begins from Bartlett Cove is $2650.

Spirit Walker Expeditions KAYAKING

(☎907-697-2266; www.seakayakalaska.com; 1 Grandpa's Farm Rd) Kayaking specialist Spirit Walker runs paddling trips to Point Adolphus where humpback whales congregate during the summer. Trips begin with a short boat ride pulling the kayaks across Icy Strait to Point Adolphus and run $439 for a day paddle ($379 per person for four or more) and $1099 for a three-day paddle.

Tours

★ Glacier Bay Lodge & Tours BOATING

(888-229-8687; www.visitglacierbay.com) The *Fairweather Express*, operated by Glacier Bay Lodge & Tours, is a high-speed catamaran that departs at 7:30am for an eight-hour tour (adult/child $205/102.50) into the West Arm taking in two gigantic calving glaciers. It returns by 3:30pm. The tour includes lunch and narration by an onboard park naturalist. For $645, you get the tour for two plus one night at the lodge.

The lodge also rents kayaks, leads guided trips to the Beardslee Islands (half-/full day $95/150) and offers a water-taxi service.

Cross Sound Express WHALE WATCHING

(888-698-2726; www.taz.gustavus.com; tours adult/child $120/60) The 50ft MV *Taz* carries up to 23 passengers and departs the Gustavus dock daily during the summer at 8:30am and 12:30pm for a 3½-hour whale-watching tour.

The company also offers a water-taxi service for kayakers.

Sleeping

Most of the accommodations are in Gustavus, which adds a 7% bed-and-sales tax. The Glacier Bay Lodge is 8 miles out of town at Bartlett Cove.

Seaside Campground CAMPGROUND $

(907-697-2214; State Dock Rd; tent sites $20) On the edge of the Fairweather golf course, this basic campground is in a grassy field and has room for a few tents and RVs. Shower and restroom access is across the road.

Bartlett Cove Campground CAMPGROUND $

(free) This NPS facility a quarter-mile south of Glacier Bay Lodge is set in a lush forest just off the shoreline, and camping is free. There's no need for reservations; there always seems to be space. It's a walk-in campground, so no RVs.

The facility provides a bear cache and warming shelter. Coin-operated showers are available in the park. The closest groceries are in Gustavus, 8 miles away.

Glacier Bay Lodge LODGE $$

(888-229-8687; www.visitglacierbay.com; 199 Bartlett Cove Rd; r $219-249; May-Sep) This is essentially a national-park lodge and the only accommodations in the park itself. Located at Bartlett Cove, 8 miles northwest of Gustavus, the self-contained lodge has 55 rooms, a crackling fire in a huge stone fireplace and a dining room that usually hums in the evening with an interesting mixture of park employees, backpackers and locals from Gustavus.

Nightly slide presentations, ranger talks and movies held upstairs cover the park's natural history.

Packages with bed, breakfast and an eight-hour park boat tour go for around $645 for two people.

Blue Heron B&B B&B $$

(907-697-2293; www.blueheronbnb.net; State Dock Rd; s/d/cottages $125/154/190; P) This B&B is nestled amid 10 acres of wildflowers and surround-sound views of the Fairweather Mountains. The two rooms and two cottages (with kitchenettes) are modern, bright and clean, and each has a TV/VCR and private bath. In the morning everybody meets in the sunroom for a full breakfast ranging from organic rolled oats with blueberries to omelets.

The wonderful proprietor Deb has everything you need to enjoy Gustavus – rubber boots, rain pants, bikes and transportation. Check out the giant eagle's nest outside.

Annie Mae Lodge LODGE $$

(907-697-2346; www.anniemae.com; Grandpa's Farm Rd; s $160-220, d $170-230; P) This large, rambling lodge has wraparound porches and 11 rooms, most with private bath. On the 2nd level all seven rooms have a private entrance off the porch. Continental breakfast is served in a large dining room and common area; lunches, dinners and hot breakfast items are available for an additional charge. Your stay includes ground transfers and free bicycles.

Aimee's Guest House GUESTHOUSE $$

(907-697-2330; www.glacierbayalaska.net; Shooting Star Lane; ste $110-175; P) A former smokehouse on the Salmon River (hence the colorful fish mural outside) has been converted into three bright, airy and comfortable vacation rentals featuring one or two bedrooms, full kitchens and everything you could need for a few days in Gustavus. The upper-level deck, with its hammock, wicker furniture and bed outside, is classic Alaska.

★**Gustavus Inn** INN $$$
(☎907-697-2254; www.gustavusinn.com; Mile 1, Gustavus Rd; r per person all-incl $250; P 📶) This longtime Gustavus favorite is a charming family homestead lodge mentioned in every travel book on Alaska, with good reason.

It's thoroughly modern and comfortable, without being sterile or losing its folksy touch. The all-inclusive inn is well known for its gourmet dinners, which feature homegrown vegetables and fresh local seafood served family-style.

Guests have free use of bicycles, and courtesy transportation to/from Bartlett Cove and the airport is cheerfully provided. Packages with Glacier Bay tours and kayaking trips are available. Even if you can't afford to stay at the inn, book a seat at its dinner table one night. This restaurant was for sale at the time of research.

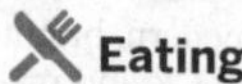

Eating

There is a sprinkling of glorified cafes in the town of Gustavus. Otherwise, you'll probably end up eating at your hotel or B&B.

Sunnyside Market CAFE $
(☎907-697-3060; 3 State Dock Rd; sandwiches $7-10; ⊙9am-6pm;) This bright market and cafe is your one-stop choice for organic sundries, deli sandwiches and breakfast burritos. There are two tables inside and plenty outside under a sunny overhang. On Saturday there's an artsy market.

Drinking & Nightlife

Fireweed Gallery, Coffee & Tea House COFFEE
(www.fireweedcoffee.com; 4 Corners, Gustavus Rd; pastries $3-6; ⊙6am-8pm Mon-Sat, 8am-5pm Sun) You're here for the best coffee in Gustavus (and a whole lot of the Southeast), and freshly baked goods and crepes too. There's an attached gallery selling local, mainly native, art.

Information

Glacier Bay National Park Visitor Center (☎907-697-2661; www.nps.gov/glba; ⊙11am-8pm) On the 2nd floor of Glacier Bay Lodge (p127), this center has exhibits, a bookstore and an information desk. There are also daily guided walks from the lodge, park films and slide presentations.

Gustavus Visitors Association (☎907-697-2454; www.gustavusak.com) Has loads of information on its website.

Visitor Information Station (☎907-697-2627; ⊙7am-8pm May-Sep) Campers, kayakers and boaters can stop at the park's Visitor Information Station at the foot of the public dock in Bartlett Cove for backcountry and boating permits, logistical information and a 20-minute orientation video.

Getting There & Around

AIR

Alaska Airlines (p429) Offers the only jet service, with a daily 25-minute trip from Juneau to Gustavus.

Alaska Seaplanes (☎907-789-3331; www.flyalaskaseaplanes.com) Has up to five flights per day between Gustavus and Juneau for $115 one way.

FERRY

The cheapest way to reach Gustavus is via the **Alaska Marine Highway** (☎800-642-0066; www.ferryalaska.com). Several times a week the MV *LeConte* makes the round-trip run from Juneau to Gustavus (one way $44, 4½ hours) along a route that often features whale sightings. **TLC Taxi** (☎907-697-2239) meets most ferry arrivals and also charges $15 per person for a trip to Bartlett Cove.

Haines

☎907 / POP 1700

The first thing you notice about Haines is that it *isn't* Skagway, the tourist showpiece situated 33 nautical miles to the north. Instead, this is a quiet, independent, unprepossessing town of native artists, outdoor-adventure lovers and 100% Alaskans hooked on the tranquil life.

People come here to see bald eagles in the wild, dissect one thousand years of Chilkat-Tlingit culture, ponder the remains of an old military barracks and enjoy the best drinking scene in a US town of this size.

After logging fell on hard times in the 1970s, Haines swung its economy toward tourism; not so much cruise ships (Haines receives a mere 40,000 cruisers per season), but more independent travelers.

Haines is particularly popular with RVers in summer and heli-skiers in winter. As a result, the businesses here are uniquely Hainesian, and most likely the person behind the counter is the one who owns the store.

Sights

★Jilkaat Kwaan Cultural Heritage & Bald Eagle Preserve Visitor Center

CULTURAL CENTRE

(907-767-5485; www.jilkaatkwaanheritagecenter.org; Mile 22, Haines Hwy; $15; 10am-4pm Mon-Fri, noon-3pm Sat, closed Oct-Apr) Part of a welcome renaissance in Tlingit art and culture in Alaska, this heritage center is located in the ancient native village of Klukwan, 22 miles north of Haines. The center includes some of the most prized heirlooms of Alaska Native culture, namely four elaborate house posts and a rain screen (the legendary 'whale house collection') carved by a Tlingit Michelangelo over 200 years ago and only recently made available for public viewing.

The center includes a museum (containing said artifacts), clan house, carving studio, salmon-drying room and shop. There are also regular dance performances (which usually coincide with cruise-ship visits) and even art classes.

American Bald Eagle Foundation

MUSEUM

(www.baldeagles.org; 113 Haines Hwy; adult/child $10/5; 9am-5pm Mon-Fri, 11am-3pm Sat;) This relatively new museum is a little pricey for what's inside, but the fee *does* go toward a good cause (the museum is currently working on an extension).

There are two live American bald eagles, and a couple of other raptors with handlers giving regular demonstrations. Elsewhere, the museum focuses on Alaskan wildlife with numerous taxidermic exhibits.

Hammer Museum

MUSEUM

(www.hammermuseum.org; 108 Main St; adult/child $5/free; 10am-5pm Mon-Fri, to 2pm Sat) This extravagantly esoteric museum is an exercise in how to make hammers look interesting. And – get this – it largely succeeds.

Plucked from the extensive collection of local tool restorer Dave Pahl, the small, well-utilized space displays more than 2000 hammers, from a stone hammer used to build the pyramids at Giza to the heavy-duty tools of erstwhile dentists, shoemakers and blacksmiths.

There are even five mannequins donated by the Smithsonian Institute and a giant hammer sculpture outside fashioned by Pahl himself.

Sheldon Museum

MUSEUM

(www.sheldonmuseum.org; 11 Main St; adult/child $7/free; 10am-5pm Mon, Tue, Thu & Fri, 9am-5pm Wed, 1-4pm Sat & Sun) The Sheldon Museum is known for its collection of indigenous artifacts, including a particularly interesting display on rare Chilkat blankets. The rest of the museum is devoted to Haines' pioneer and gold-rush days, including such treasures as the sawed-off shotgun that trailblazer Jack Dalton used to convince travelers to pay his toll. There's a small gift shop in the entrance.

Fort Seward

HISTORIC SITE

Alaska's first permanent military post is reached by heading uphill (east) at the Front St–Haines Hwy junction. Built in 1903 and decommissioned after WWII, the fort is now a National Historic Landmark, with a handful of restaurants, lodges and art galleries in the original buildings. A walking-tour map of the fort is available at the visitor center, or you can just wander around and read the historical panels that have been erected there.

Alaska Indian Arts Center

ARTS CENTER

(www.alaskaindianarts.com; 24 Fort Seward Dr; 9am-5pm Mon-Fri) Indigenous culture can be seen in Fort Seward in the former military-post hospital, home of the Alaska Indian Arts Center. During the week you can watch artists carve totems, weave Chilkat blankets or produce other works of art. It's a friendly, congenial place. Check out the totems inlaid with glass pieces inspired by Seattle-based glass artist Dale Chihuly.

Inquire within about Tlingit wood-carving workshops.

Dalton City

FILM LOCATION

(296 Fair Dr) FREE Entering Dalton City, Haines' state fairground, you might feel as if you're walking onto a film set: you are. The gold-rush-era houses were constructed to replicate Dawson City for the movie *White Fang*, starring Ethan Hawke, in 1991 and were moved here from their original location by some enterprising locals. Most of the houses host small businesses, including a bar, a massage parlor and an art studio. It's 1 mile outside town, off the Haines Hwy.

The fairground hosts the Great Alaskan Craftbeer & Home Brew Festival (p133) in May and the Southeast Alaska State Fair (p133) in July.

Haines

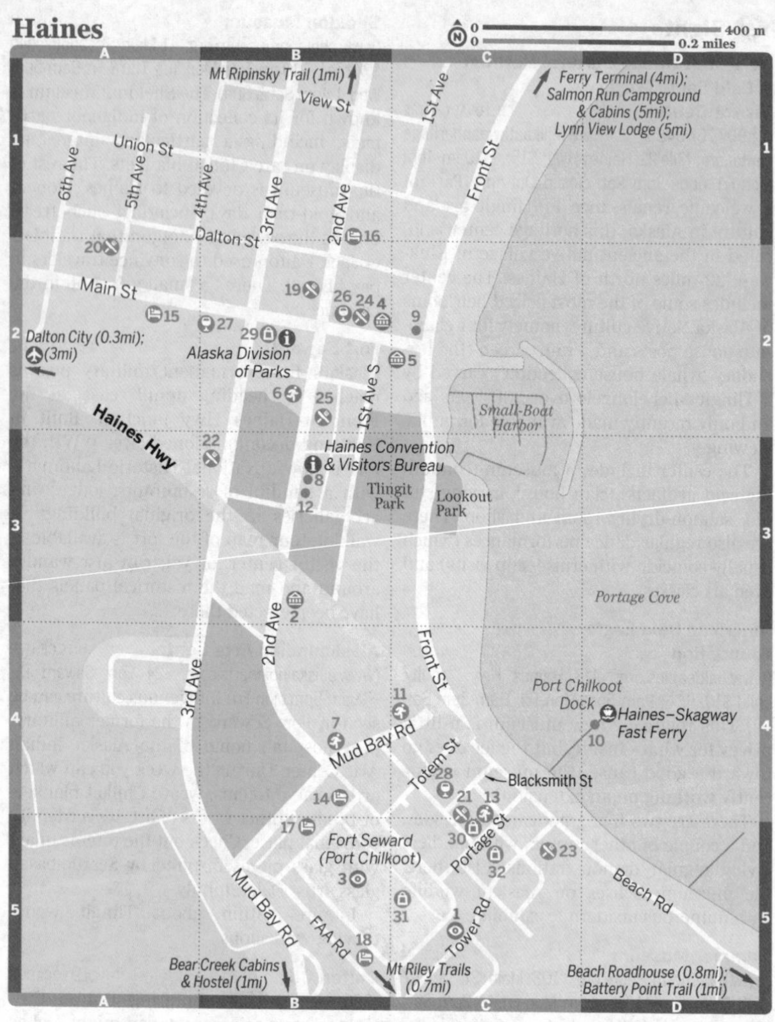

Activities

Alaska Mountain Guides & Climbing School CLIMBING
(☎800-766-3396; www.alaskamountainguides.com; 57 Mud Bay Rd) For white-knuckle indie adventure, these guys should be your first port of call. Multiday trips range from rock climbing, to ice climbing, to heli-skiing, to white-water rafting.

One trip that jumps out is the 'Klondike Route' ($3770), four days trekking along the Chilkoot Trail followed by 11 days kayaking down the Yukon River to Dawson City. In other words, 1898 revisited.

Alaska Backcountry Outfitter OUTDOORS
(☎907-766-2876; www.alaskanaturetours.net; 111 2nd Ave; ⏲10am-5pm) Haines' go-to outdoor-equipment store (well-stocked with the essential bear spray), this experienced supplier is also the umbrella for Alaska Nature Tours (p133).

Cycling

You can discover some great road trips or what little singletrack mountain biking there is in Haines by visiting one of two local bike shops, both of which rent bicycles at good day rates. The most popular

Haines

Sights

1 Alaska Indian Arts Center C5
2 American Bald Eagle Foundation B3
3 Fort Seward B5
4 Hammer Museum B2
5 Sheldon Museum C2

Activities, Courses & Tours

6 Alaska Backcountry Outfitter B2
7 Alaska Mountain Guides & Climbing School B4
8 Alaska Nature Tours B3
9 Fjord Express C2
10 Haines–Skagway Fast Ferry D4
11 Mike's Bikes & Boards C4
12 Mountain Flying Service B3
13 Sockeye Cycle C4

Sleeping

14 Alaska Guardhouse Lodging B4
15 Aspen Suites Hotel A2
16 Captain's Choice Motel B1
17 Hotel Halsingland B5
18 House No 1 B&B B5

Eating

19 Bamboo Room B2
20 Chilkat Bakery & Restaurant A2
Commander's Room ..... (see 17)
21 Fireweed Restaurant C4
22 Mountain Market & Cafe B3
23 Pilot Light C5
24 Rusty Compass Coffeehouse B2
25 Sarah J's B2

Drinking & Nightlife

26 Fogcutter Bar B2
27 Haines Brewing Company B2
28 Port Chilkoot Distillery C4

Shopping

29 Babbling Book B2
30 Dejon Delights C5
31 Sea Wolf Art Studio C5
32 Wild Iris C5

road trip is the 22-mile ride out to Chilkoot Lake.

Sockeye Cycle — CYCLING

(☎907-766-2869; www.cyclealaska.com; 24 Portage St; ⏲9am-5:30pm Mon-Fri, to 4pm Sat) These guys have two stores – the other is in Skagway (p143) – and a good reputation for organizing both day and multiday tours, including the surprisingly synergistic bike-hike-brew tour ($175) which ends up at Haines Brewing Company (p138).

They also rent bikes to DIYers for $45 per day.

Mike's Bikes & Boards — CYCLING

(☎907-766-3232; cnr Mud Bay & Beach Rds; ⏲9am-6pm Mon, Tue & Thu-Sun, 8am-6pm Wed) Rents reliable mountain bikes (four/eight hours $20/30).

Hiking

Two major trail systems are within walking distance of Haines. South of town are the Chilkat Peninsula trails, including Battery Point and the climb to Mt Riley. North of Haines is the path to the summit of Mt Ripinsky. Stop at the visitors bureau (p139) and pick up the brochure *Haines Is for Hikers,* which describes the trails in more detail. For outdoor gear or a guided hike, stop by Alaska Backcountry Outfitter (p131).

Mt Riley Trails — HIKING

This gutsy grunt to a 1760ft summit provides good views in all directions, including vistas of Rainbow and Davidson Glaciers. One trail up the mountain begins at a junction about a mile up the Battery Point Trail out of Portage Cove Recreation Site. From here, you hike 3 miles over Half Dome and up Mt Riley.

Another route, closer to town, begins at the end of FAA Rd, which runs behind Officers' Row in Fort Seward. About a half-mile down the road, turn left onto the Lily Lake access road. After around 2 miles, a short spur branches off to the right and connects with the trail from Mud Bay Rd. The hike is 3.9 miles one way and eliminates the need to find a ride out to the third trailhead to Mt Riley, three miles out on Mud Bay Rd. The trailhead off Mud Bay Rd is posted, and this 2.8-mile route is the steepest but easiest to follow and the most direct to the summit. Plan on a five- to six-hour round-trip.

Seduction Point Trail — HIKING

The seduction begins at Chilkat State Park Campground (p136) and is a 6.8-mile (one-way) hike to the point separating Chilkoot and Chilkat Inlets. The sometimes-swampy and definitely rooty trail swings between forest and beaches, and provides blue-chip views of Davidson Glacier.

If you have the equipment, this trail can be turned into a fruitful overnight hike by setting up camp at the cove east of Seduction Point. Carry in water and check the tides before departing, as the final stretch along the beach after David's Cove should be walked at low tide or midtide. The entire round-trip takes nine to 10 hours.

Mt Ripinsky Trail HIKING

The trudge to Mt Ripinsky's summit gifts a sweeping view of Lynn Canal and the land from Juneau to Skagway. The route, which includes South Summit (3573ft), Peak 3920 and a descent from 7 Mile Saddle to Haines Hwy, is either a strenuous 10-hour journey for experienced hikers or an overnight trip.

The most easily accessed trailhead is less than a mile from the town center. Follow 2nd Ave north, branch into Young Rd and head up the hill. Signs will direct you to the old pipeline road, where parking and the trail are clearly posted.

You can camp in the alpine area between Mt Ripinsky and the South Summit and then continue the next day west along the ridge to Peak 3920. From here you can descend to 7 Mile Saddle and then to the Haines Hwy, putting you 7 miles northwest of town. In recent years the trail has been greatly improved, but this is still a challenging overnight hike with spectacular views. For a 3-mile day hike, trek to the AT&T tower on Ridge Trail, a spur off the east end of the main trail.

Battery Point Trail HIKING

This 2-mile trail is a pleasant, flat walk along the shore to Kelgaya Point; cut across to a pebble beach and follow it to Battery Point for excellent views of Lynn Canal. The trail begins a mile beyond Portage Cove Recreation Site at the end of Beach Rd and has been extensively updated. Not surprisingly, it's a local favorite.

Rafting

Haines is a departure point for numerous raft trips. **Chilkat Guides** (907-766-2491; www.raftalaska.com; floats $133) offers a four-hour float daily down the Chilkat River through the bald-eagle preserve, with opportunities to view eagles and possibly brown bears; there is little or no white water.

On a much grander scale of adventure is the exciting nine- to 10-day raft trip down the Tatshenshini-Alsek River system, from Yukon Territory to the coast of Glacier Bay. This river trip is unmatched for its mix of rugged mountain ranges and dozens of glaciers. Chilkat Guides and **Alaska Discovery/Mt Sobek** (888-687-6235; www.mtsobek.com) both run the trip, which costs roughly $4000 per person.

Tours

Chilkat River Adventures WILDLIFE

(907-766-2050; www.jetboatalaska.com; Haines Hwy) Uses jet boats for its Eagle Preserve River Adventure. The tour includes bus transportation 24 miles up the river to the jet boats and then a 1½-hour boat ride to look for eagles and other wildlife including moose and bears. The price is $100 per person.

Alaska Nature Tours OUTDOORS

(907-766-2876; www.alaskanaturetours.net; 109 2nd Ave;) Offers environmentally focused tours with knowledgeable guides for activities that range from birding and bear-watching to easy hikes to Battery Point. Its Twilight Wildlife Watch is a 2½-hour tour (adult/child $78/60) that departs at 6pm and heads up the Chilkat River, stopping along the way to look for eagles, mountain goats and brown bears who emerge at dusk.

Mountain Flying Service SCENIC FLIGHTS

(907-766-3007; www.mountainflyingservice.com; 132 2nd Ave) Offers an hour-long tour of the Glacier Bay's East Arm for $170 per person and an 80-minute tour of the more dramatic West Arm for $199. The two-hour outer-coast flight lands on beach; it costs $299. On a clear day, it's money well spent.

Fjord Express BOATING

(800-320-0146; www.alaskafjordlines.com; Small-Boat Harbor; adult/child $169/139) Don't have time to make it to Juneau? The Fjord Express zips you down Lynn Canal in a catamaran (will stop for whales, sea lions and other marine wildlife), and then rumbles around Juneau's top sights in a bus before dropping you back in Haines. A light breakfast and dinner are included. It departs Haines at 8:30am and returns at 7:30pm.

Haines–Skagway Fast Ferry BOATING

(907-766-2100; www.hainesskagwayfastferry.com; Beach Rd) If you don't have time to overnight in Skagway, the Fast Ferry has a Rail & Sail Tour (adult/child $179/90) that includes round-trip ferry transportation to Skagway (the Klondike city) and the Summit Excursion on the White Pass & Yukon Railroad.

Festivals & Events

Great Alaskan Craftbeer & Home Brew Festival BEER
(May) In the third week of May, most of the state's microbrews compete for the honor of being named top suds.

Southeast Alaska State Fair FAIR
(www.seakfair.org; 196 Fair Dr; Jul) Staged at the end of July, the fair is five days of live music, an Ugliest Dog Contest, logging and livestock shows and the famous pig races that draw participants from all Southeast communities. It's staged at its own State Fair Grounds, which also incorporate Dalton City (p131), just outside town.

Alaska Bald Eagle Festival WILDLIFE
(www.baldeagles.org/festival; mid-Nov) This five-day event in the second week of November attracts hundreds of visitors from around the country to Haines for speakers and presentations at the Sheldon Museum (p130) and the American Bald Eagle Foundation Center (p129).

The basis of the festival is trooping out to the Chilkat River on 'expedition buses' with naturalists onboard and encountering numbers of eagles that you cannot see anywhere else in the country at any other time of the year.

Sleeping

Haines acquired a slick new hotel a few years ago, making a grand total of three in town. Otherwise, it's B&Bs or campgrounds. There are no hostels.

Haines tacks 9.5% tax onto the price of lodging.

Bear Creek Cabins & Hostel HOSTEL $
(907-766-2259; www.bearcreekcabinsalaska.com; Small Tract Rd; dm/cabins $20/68;) A rare Southeastern Alaska hostel of sorts, this place is a 20-minute walk outside town – follow Mud Bay Rd and when it veers right, continue straight onto Small Tract Rd for 1.5 miles. The complex consists of eights cabins (most sleep four) clustered around a grassy common area.

A restroom/shower building also has laundry facilities, and there is a common, fully equipped kitchen reminiscent of a mess hall.

It's ideal for backpackers on a budget.

Chilkat State Park Campground CAMPGROUND $
(Mud Bay Rd; tent & RV sites $15) Seven miles southeast of Haines toward the end of Chilkat Peninsula, this campground has good views of Davidson and Rainbow Glaciers spilling out of the mountains into the Lynn Canal. There are 35 tree-enveloped drive-in campsites and, a bit lower, four walk-ins on the beach.

Enter the campground by turning right off Mud Bay Rd and driving for a couple of miles along a dirt access road.

Salmon Run Campground & Cabins CABIN $
(907-766-3240; Mile 6.5, Lutak Rd; tent & RV sites $17-35, cabins $65-85;) About a mile past the ferry terminal is this private campground on a hillside above Lynn Canal. There are

A VALLEY FULL OF EAGLES

The **Alaska Chilkat Bald Eagle Preserve** was created in 1982 when the state reserved 48,000 acres along the Chilkat, Klehini and Tsirku Rivers to protect the largest-known gathering of bald eagles in the world. Each year from October to February, more than 4000 eagles congregate here to feed on spawning salmon. They come because an upwelling of warm water prevents the river from freezing, thus encouraging the late salmon run. It's a remarkable sight – hundreds of birds sitting in the bare trees lining the river, often six or more birds to a branch.

The best time to see this wildlife phenomenon is during the Alaska Bald Eagle Festival (p136). If the rain, snow and sleet of November is not on your Alaskan agenda, then you can still see eagles during the summer from the Haines Hwy, where there are turnouts for motorists to park and look for birds. The best view is between Mile 18 and Mile 22, where you'll find spotting scopes, interpretive displays and viewing platforms along the river. The numbers are not as mind-boggling as in early winter but 400 eagles live here year-round and more than 80 nests line the rivers.

There are several operators who tour the area by boat and land, including Alaska Nature Tours and Chilkat River Adventures.

1. Ice pools on Mendenhall Glacier (p110) 2. Remote cabin in the Alaskan wilderness 3. St Michael's Cathedral (p100), Sitka

Juneau & Southeast Alaska Highlights

You can't drive to Juneau, or to most of Southeast Alaska, and that seems only proper. This watery, mountainous region, filled with fjords, thousands of islands, impressive glaciers and small but interesting ports, is best explored at the casual pace of a cruise ship or – for independent travelers – a state ferry.

Icing on the Lake

It's big, it's blue and it's still active, tossing icebergs into Mendenhall Lake. No wonder Mendenhall Glacier (p110) is Juneau's most popular attraction. Paddle up to it, helicopter over it, hike toward it, or strap on crampons and walk on top of it.

Russian Culture

Nowhere is Alaska's Russian heritage so well preserved as in Sitka, the state's finest (and oldest) colonial relic, replete with 19th-century emplacements, an old Bishop's House (p99) and the onion dome of the emblematic St Michael's Cathedral (p100), Alaska's finest Russian Orthodox church.

Rustic Cabins

The floatplane lands on an isolated lake and you step out to a small A-frame cabin. It's one of the nearly 150 US Forest Service cabins scattered across Southeast Alaska, your personal slice of wilderness for the next three days.

Emerald Maze

Alaska's gold rushes weren't just about gold: they were as much about struggle, adventure and life-changing experiences. Today, you can relive the drama in the museums and saloons of Juneau and Skagway or empathize far more physically by hiking the 33-mile Chilkoot Trail (p70).

17 tent sites and 18 RV sites with central restroom/showers, plus two small cabins that come with heating and bunks but no indoor plumbing or kitchen facilities.

Aspen Suites Hotel HOTEL **$$**
(907-766-2211; www.aspenhotelsak.com/haines; 409 Main St; r $179; P ❄ @ ☎) One of six Aspen hotels in Alaska, this slick building offers rooms more akin to studio apartments, all equipped with kitchenettes and comfortable sofas. There's coffee on tap at reception, a small fitness room and a clean, polished sheen to the whole operation.

Alaska Guardhouse Lodging B&B **$$**
(907-766-2566; www.alaskaguardhouse.com; 15 Seward Dr; r $145-170; P) What used to jail insubordinate soldiers is now housing less troublesome visitors in typical small-town Alaska comfort. Four large bedrooms, a pleasant living room and an enclosed sun porch with rocking chairs all give way to views of mountains and water. Fort Seward's old fire hall is next door; you'll recognize it by the giant tower.

Beach Roadhouse B&B **$$**
(907-766-3060; www.beachroadhouse.com; 717 Beach Rd; r/cabins $115/145; P) This B&B is what Alaska is all about. The large cedar home is perched above Lynn Canal and surrounded by impressive pines for a tranquil, woodsy setting. Two rooms are large and include kitchenettes. The three cabins are even larger with full kitchens and lofts that sleep three to four persons.

Perhaps the best amenity of this roadhouse is just a few yards away: the start of the charming Battery Point Trail (p132).

Lynn View Lodge LODGE **$$**
(907-766-3713; www.lynnviewlodge.com; 1299 Lutak Rd; r $105-145, cabins $109; P) Three miles north of town and 1 mile south of the ferry terminal, this basic lodge has a great view of Lynn Canal and a long, covered porch to relax on and soak up the scenery. Accommodations range from one room with shared bath, to two suites with private bath, to three small cabins. Car rental is available for $79 a day.

Hotel Halsingland HOTEL **$$**
(907-766-2000; www.hotelhalsingland.com; 13 Fort Seward Dr; r $119; @) The grand dame of Haines hotels is the former bachelor officers' quarters and overlooks Fort Seward's parade ground. A National Historic Landmark, the hotel has 35 rooms which are comfortably modern, but, at the same time, agreeably old school. Many still have their original fireplaces and classic claw-foot bathtubs.

The wood-paneled communal areas emanate a pleasant air of refinement, emulated in the verging-on-posh restaurant (p138) and sedate bar.

House No 1 B&B B&B **$$**
(907-766-2856; www.housenumberone.com; Fort Seward; r $130-160) Built in 1904, this grand and roomy place was once the chief surgeon's house and the walls are adorned with historic photos. The five rooms have private baths, chunky radiators, bright vistas and beautiful period fireplaces. Rooms come with a large American breakfast and use of the kitchen.

There's a fine wooden porch out front overlooking the water.

Captain's Choice Motel MOTEL **$$**
(907-766-3111; www.capchoice.com; 108 2nd Ave N; s/d $144/155) Haines' default motel has the best view of the Chilkat Mountains and Lynn Canal and a huge sundeck to enjoy it on. The wood-paneled rooms are simple but spacious enough to include a microwave, small refrigerator, coffeemaker and TV. A light breakfast is offered in the morning, and courtesy transportation to the ferries and airport is available.

Eating

Rusty Compass Coffeehouse CAFE **$**
(116 Main St; panini $10-13; 6:30am-4pm Mon-Sat, 9am-2pm Sun) Hands-on, megafriendly coffee and sandwich bar that could hold its own in Seattle, let alone Haines. It backs up its expertly made coffee with fresh baked goods made on-site and substantial panini and soups. The small interior is a mix of buzzing conversation and flickering laptops.

Sarah J's CAFE **$**
(132 2nd Ave; breakfast $6-9, sandwiches $9-10; 6:30am-5pm Mon-Fri, 7am-3pm Sat & Sun) Sarah's relocated from Fort Seward to the town center, but it maintains its ephemeral roots in a food truck with a little awning tacked on the side. As with all Alaskan food trucks, the food is formidable, with great breakfast burritos, homemade granola, organic smoothies, baked goods, perky coffee and more.

Mountain Market & Cafe DELI $
(3rd Ave, at Haines Hwy; sandwiches $7-9; 7am-7pm Mon-Sat, 8am-6pm Sun;) The center of Haines' unlikely hip and healthy eating scene, Mountain Market stocks health foods, while its deli is loaded with vegetarian options, baked goods, great homemade soup, espresso drinks and indoor seating.

Bonus: the cafe roasts its own coffee, which you can buy in bags.

★ Fireweed Restaurant BISTRO $$
(37 Blacksmith St; salads $10-19, pizzas $14-30; 4:30-9pm Tue-Sat;) This clean, bright and laid-back bistro is in an old Fort Seward building and its copious salads are an ideal antidote to the Southeast's penchant for grease. A quick scroll down the menu will reveal words like 'organic,' 'veggie' and 'grilled' as opposed to 'deep fried' and 'captain's special.'

Vegetarians and carnivores alike can indulge in sandwiches, burgers and the town's best pizza, all washed down with beer served in icy mugs. The locals love it.

Chilkat Bakery & Restaurant THAI, AMERICAN $$
(907-766-3653; cnr 5th Ave & Dalton St; mains $12-20; 7am-3pm & 5-8pm Thu-Tue, 7am-3pm Wed) Baked goods, Thai food, Mexican *comida* and American chow; the Chilkat is a peddler of numerous genres and the masters of at least two of them – the Thai food and the cakes and pastries are pretty good.

It occupies a white clapboard house with a long front porch decorated with flower baskets, just off the main drag. Decor is megacasual.

Bamboo Room CAFE $$
(907-766-2800; 11 2nd Ave; mains $15-25; 7am-10pm) A typical Alaskan restaurant of well-worn booths and Formica tables, the Bamboo likes to claim it has the best fish and chips in the world. No chance of that, but the blueberry pancakes with whipped cream aren't bad and it's hard to pass up a plate of steamed Dungeness crabs served whole.

Commander's Room MODERN AMERICAN $$$
(907-766-2000; 13 Fort Seward Dr; mains $27-32; 5:30-9pm Wed-Mon) Located in Hotel Halsingland (p136) is Haines' most upscale restaurant. Begin the evening with a drink (and maybe some duck confit) in its cozy Officer's Club Lounge and then venture into the Commander's Room, where you'll find white tablecloths, a fine wine list and a chef who has a herb garden out back.

In July and August the salmon and halibut are flown in daily, or try the stout-braised lamb shank served with a lemon-mint gremolata.

Drinking & Nightlife

Possibly the best drinking scene for a town of its size in the whole of North America. Tiny Haines (population 1700-ish) has its own microbrewery and its own microdistillery, and they're both excellent.

★ Port Chilkoot Distillery DISTILLERY
(907-766-3434; www.portchilkootdistillery.com; 34 Blacksmith St; 2-8pm Mon-Sat) A fantastic resource in such a tiny town, this microdistillery is not just a token gesture; it's inventive enough to compete with anything in the lower 48.

Housed in Fort Seward's former bakery with a small on-site shop and tasting room, it serves a wide array of spirits, from recently matured bourbon to absinthe, gin and vodka.

A full menu of cocktails is available for those who like their poison mixed with fruitier flavors. Try a Bee's Knees made with lemon, honey and the homemade 50 fathoms gin.

Fogcutter Bar BAR
(Main St; 10am-midnight) Haines is a hard-drinking town, and this is where a lot of locals belly up to the bar and spout off.

Shopping

Despite a lack of cruise-ship traffic, or maybe because of it, Haines supports an impressive number of local artists and has enough galleries to fill an afternoon.

Extreme Dreams Fine Arts ARTS & CRAFTS
(www.extremedreams.com; Mile 6.5, Mud Bay Rd; 10am-5pm) At the Chilkat State Park entrance is this wonderful gallery packed with the work of 20 local artists, from watercolors and weavings to handblown glass, cast silver and beautiful beads.

The gallery also has a climbing wall because it's the studio of artist John Svenson, a renowned mountain climber who has scaled the highest peak on almost every continent.

DON'T MISS

HAINES BREWING COMPANY

Surely one of the finest small breweries in the US, the **Haines Brewing Company** (☎907-766-3823; www.hainesbrewing.com; Main St, cnr 4th Ave; ⏲noon-7pm Mon-Sat), founded in 1999, runs a lovely tasting room in what passes for downtown Haines. The beautiful wood and glass structure serves all of the locally brewed favorites, including Spruce Tip Ale, Elder Rock Red and the potent Black Fang stout (8.2% alcohol content).

It's no small wonder that Haines hosts the Great Alaskan Craftbeer & Home Brew Festival (p133).

Wild Iris ARTS & CRAFTS

(22 Tower Rd) This art gallery is the most impressive of a growing number on the edge of Fort Seward. Outside the home is a beautiful Alaskan garden; inside, a fine selection of original jewelry, silk-screened prints, cards, pastels and other local art. Entry is on Portage St.

Dejon Delights FOOD

(☎907-766-2505; 37 Portage St; ⏲10am-6pm Thu-Tue, 8am-7pm Wed) This shop in Fort Seward turns out some of the best smoked fish in the Southeast, such as salmon that is first marinated in stout beer.

Sea Wolf Art Studio ARTS & CRAFTS

(www.tresham.com; Fort Seward; ⏲hours vary, May-Sep) Housed in a log cabin in the middle of Fort Seward's old parade ground is Tresham Gregg's gallery. Gregg is one of Haines' best-known Alaska Native artists, and he combines the imagery of the spiritism, animism and shamanism of Northwest Coast Indians to create wood carvings, totems, masks, bronze sculpture and talismanic silver jewelry.

Babbling Book BOOKS

(☎907-766-3356; 223 Main St; ⏲11am-5pm Mon-Sat, noon-5pm Sun) Small bookstore stuffed full with plenty of Alaska-themed books, cards and calendars, while its walls serve as the noticeboard for Haines' cultural scene.

Information

MEDICAL SERVICES

Haines Health Center (☎907-766-6300; 131 1st Ave S)

MONEY

First National Bank Alaska (123 Main St; ⏲10am-5pm Mon-Fri) For all your presidential-portrait needs.

TOURIST INFORMATION

Alaska Division of Parks (☎907-766-2292; 219 Main St, Suite 25; ⏲8am-5pm Mon-Fri) For information on state parks and hiking; above Howser's IGA (there's no sign).

Haines Convention & Visitors Bureau (☎907-766-2234; www.haines.ak.us; 122 2nd Ave; ⏲8am-5pm Mon-Fri, 9am-4pm Sat & Sun) Has restrooms, free coffee and racks of free information for tourists. There is also a lot of information on Canada's Yukon for those heading up the Alcan.

Getting There & Away

AIR

There is no jet service to Haines, but **Alaska Seaplanes** (☎907-766-3800, 907-789-3331; www.flyalaskaseaplanes.com) will take you to Juneau seven times a day ($125). The airport is 3 miles northwest of town just off the Haines Hwy.

BUS

Amazingly no buses serve Haines. You'll need to either thumb it north or take the ferry to Skagway and get a bus north from there.

CRUISE SHIP

Cruise ships tie up at the **Port Chilkoot Dock**, adjacent to Fort Seward and a quarter-mile from Main St. A free shuttle loops around the town when ships are in.

FERRY

State ferries depart daily from the inconveniently located **Alaska Marine Highway Ferry Terminal** (☎907-766-2111; 2012 Lutak Rd) 4 miles north of town for Skagway ($32, one hour) and Juneau ($47, 5½ hours).

Haines-Skagway Fast Ferry (☎907-766-2100; www.hainesskagwayfastferry.com; round-trip adult/child $73/36.50; ⏲May-Sep) uses a speedy catamaran to cruise down Taiya Inlet to Skagway in 45 minutes. The 80ft cat departs Haines from the Port Chilkoot Dock , close to the town center, five to six times a day in peak season.

Getting Around

BUS

Haines Shuttle (☎907-766-3768; www.hainesshuttle.com) meets every ferry at the terminal and will run you into town for $10. It also provides service to the airport and various local trailheads.

CAR

To visit Alaska Chilkat Bald Eagle Preserve (p133) on your own, you can rent a car at **Captain's Choice Motel** (p137), which has compacts for around $79 a day (plus tax) with unlimited mileage.

Skagway

907 / POP 890

At first sight, Skagway appears to be solely an amusement park for cruise-ship day-trippers, a million of whom disgorge onto its sunny boardwalks every summer. But, haunted by Klondike ghosts and beautified by a tight grid of handsome false-fronted buildings, this is no northern Vegas. Skagway's history is very real.

During the 1898 gold rush, 40,000 stampeders passed through the nascent settlement; they were a sometimes-unsavory cast of characters who lived against a backdrop of brothels, gunfights and debauched entertainment wilder than the Wild West. Today, the main actors are seasonal workers, waitstaff posing in period costume and storytelling national-park rangers. Indeed, most of the town's important buildings are managed by the National Park Service (NPS) and this, along with Skagway's location on the cusp of a burly wilderness with trails (including the legendary Chilkoot) leading off in all directions, has saved it from overt Disneyfication. Dive in and join the show.

Sights

Skagway's best sights are managed by the National Park Service and are a stimulating diversion from the town's copious popcorn makers and jewelry stores.

★Klondike Gold Rush National Historical Park Museum & Visitor Center — MUSEUM

(907-983-9200; www.nps.gov/klgo; Broadway St, at 2nd Ave; 8:30am-5:30pm May-Sep) FREE The NPS center is in the original 1898 White Pass & Yukon Route depot. The center is spread over two interconnecting buildings. One contains a small museum explaining some of the Klondike background with an emphasis on the two routes out of Skagway: Chilkoot Pass and White Pass. The other space is a visitor center staffed by park rangers.

At the visitor center you can sign up for free walking tours (displayed on a blackboard) and view a fabulous 25-minute film, *Gold Fever: Race to the Klondike*. There are usually about four tours on any given day.

Skagway Museum — MUSEUM

(907-983-2420; cnr 7th Ave & Spring St; adult/child $2/1; 9am-5pm Mon-Sat, 1-4pm Sun) Skagway Museum is not only one of the finest in a town filled with museums, but it's one of the finest in the Southeast. It occupies the entire 1st floor of the venerable century-old McCabe Building, a former college, and is devoted to various aspects of local history, including Alaska Native baskets, beadwork and carvings, and, of course, the Klondike gold rush.

The display that draws the most looks is the small pistol Soapy Smith (Skagway's most notorious gold-rush-era gangster) kept up his sleeve.

Jeff Smith's Parlor — MUSEUM

(2nd Ave & Broadway St; tours $5) Soapy Smith's old den of iniquity has been renovated by the National Park Service to keep the rose-tinted legend of the erstwhile conman alive. Entry is by tour only (except on weekends when it's open house 9am to 5pm), with overviews of the small interior decorated in period style given by NPS rangers.

Mascot Saloon Museum — MUSEUM

(Broadway St, at 3rd Ave; 8:30am-5:30pm May-Sep) FREE The only saloon in Alaska that doesn't serve booze – but it did during the gold rush, and plenty of it. Built in 1898 the Mascot was one of Skagway's 80 to 100 saloons during its heyday as 'the roughest place in the world.' The NPS has turned it into a small museum, with a mock-up of the bar as it used to be complete with life-sized mannequins.

Gold Rush Cemetery & Reid Falls — CEMETERY

Visitors who become infatuated with 'Soapy' Smith and Frank Reid can walk out to this wooded cemetery, a 1.5-mile stroll northeast on State St, where Smith, Reid and many others are buried. Follow State until it curves into 23rd Ave and take the track on the right just before crossing the bridge over the Skagway River. Soapy's modest grave is close to the entrance. Reid's more extravagant stone monument is nearby.

From Reid's gravestone, it's a short hike uphill to lovely **Reid Falls**, which cascades 300ft down the mountainside.

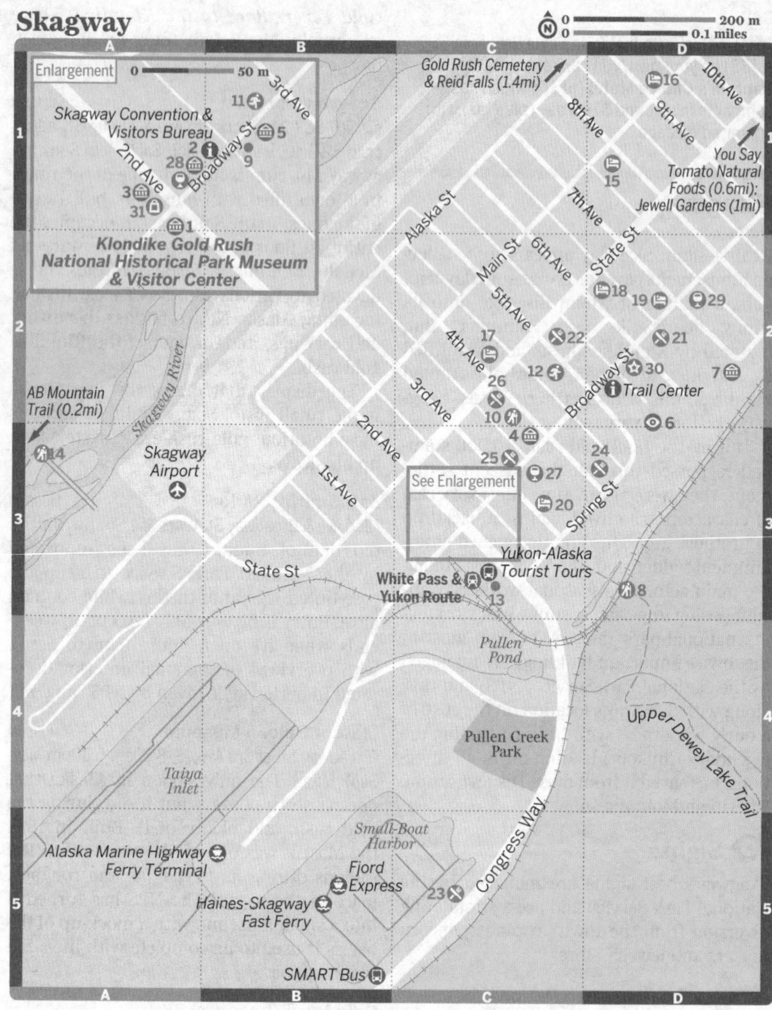

Dyea HISTORIC SITE

In 1898 Skagway's rival city, Dyea (die-*ee*) was the trailhead for Chilkoot Trail (p145), the shortest route to Lake Bennett, where stampeders began their float to Dawson City. After the White Pass & Yukon Route railroad (p144) was completed in 1900, Dyea quickly died. Today it's a few old crumbling cabins, the pilings of Dyea Wharf, and Slide Cemetery, where 47 men and women were buried after perishing in an avalanche on the Chilkoot Trail in April 1898.

To explore the ghost town, pick up the Dyea Townsite *Self-Guided Walking Tour* brochure from the NPS center. The guide will lead you along a mile loop from the town-site parking area past what few ruins remain. Or join a ranger-led walk, which meets at the parking area at 3pm Monday to Thursday.

Dyea is a 9-mile drive along winding Dyea Rd, whose numerous hairpin turns are not for timid RVers. But it's a very attractive drive, especially at Skagway Overlook, a turnoff with a viewing platform 2.5 miles from Skagway. The overlook offers an excellent view of Skagway, its waterfront and the peaks above the town. Just before crossing

Skagway

Top Sights
1 Klondike Gold Rush National Historical Park Museum & Visitor Center ... A1

Sights
2 Arctic Brotherhood Hall ... A1
3 Jeff Smith's Parlor ... A1
4 Junior Ranger Activity Center ... C3
5 Mascot Saloon Museum ... B1
6 Moore Homestead Museum ... D2
7 Skagway Museum ... D2

Activities, Courses & Tours
8 Dewey Lakes Trail System ... D3
9 Klondike Tours ... B1
10 Packer Expeditions ... C2
Red Onion Saloon Tours ... (see 28)
11 Skagway Float Tours ... B1
12 Sockeye Cycle ... C2
13 White Pass & Yukon Route Railroad ... C3
14 Yakutania Point & Smuggler's Cove ... A3

Sleeping
15 At the White House ... D1
16 Mile Zero B&B ... D1
17 Morning Wood Hotel ... C2
18 Sgt Preston's Lodge ... D2
19 Skagway Inn ... D2
20 Westmark Hotel ... C3

Eating
21 Bites on Broadway ... D2
22 Lemon Rose Bakery ... C2
Olivia's Bistro ... (see 19)
23 Skagway Fish Company ... C5
24 Starfire ... D3
25 Sweet Tooth Cafe ... C3
26 Woadie's South East Seafood ... C2

Drinking & Nightlife
27 Bonanza Bar & Grill ... C3
28 Red Onion Saloon ... A1
29 Skagway Brewing Company ... D2

Entertainment
30 Days of '98 Show ... D2

Shopping
31 Alaska Geographic Museum Store ... A1
Mountain Shop ... (see 10)

the bridge over the Taiya River, you pass the Dyea Campground.

Jewell Gardens GARDENS
(907-983-2111; www.jewellgardens.com; Klondike Hwy; adult/child $12.50/6; 9am-5pm May-Sep) If the crowds are overwhelming you, cross the Skagway River to Jewell Gardens. Located where Henry Clark started the first commercial vegetable farm in Alaska, the garden is a quiet spot of flower beds, ponds, giant vegetables and a miniature train. There is also a pair of glassblowing studios where artists give fascinating demonstrations while making beautiful glassware. Call for glassblowing times and then hop on a Smart bus that will drop you off at the entrance.

Arctic Brotherhood Hall HISTORIC BUILDING
(Broadway St, at 2nd Ave) The most outlandish building of the seven-block historical corridor along Broadway St, and possibly the most photographed building in Alaska, is this defunct fraternal hall that was a club for prospectors, now home of the Skagway Convention & Visitors Bureau. Nearly 9000 pieces of highly decorative driftwood cover the facade; they were attached in 1899 and extensively renovated, piece by piece, in 2005.

Junior Ranger Activity Center MUSEUM
(Broadway St, at 4th Ave; 10am-3pm Mon-Fri;) FREE At the Pantheon Saloon, built in 1903, kids are the customers. The historic bar is now home to the Klondike Gold Rush National Historical Park's Junior Ranger Program, where children and their parents can touch and examine artifacts, dress up as stampeders and shoulder a miner's pack on their way to earning a Junior Ranger badge.

Moore Homestead Museum NOTABLE BUILDING
(5th Ave & Spring St; 10am-5pm) FREE The founder of Skagway was not a gold-hungry Klondike stampeder but the savvy Captain William Moore, who arrived in the area on a hunch in 1887 and built himself a small cabin in the then uninhabited woods. The log cabin (the oldest structure in town) still stands alongside Moore's newer homestead built on the eve of the gold rush in 1897. The NPS has turned them into small museums.

Moore's land was effectively over-run in 1897 when thousands of Klondike-bound gold-seekers stampeded in and set about building their own city. They even had the audacity to change place's name from 'Mooresville' to 'Skaguay'. Moore wasn't happy, but he had the last laugh staying in town and ultimately setting up a profitable sawmill when everyone else hedged their bets with Klondike.

Activities

Cycling

Sockeye Cycle MOUNTAIN BIKING

(907-983-2851; www.cyclealaska.com; 381 5th Ave; bikes per 2/8hr $20/45) This affiliate of Haines' leading bike shop rents hybrids and mountain bikes and offers several bike tours from Skagway. Its three-hour Rainforest Tour ($89) begins with transportation to Dyea, followed by a guided tour of the area.

The Klondike Tour takes you up to Klondike Pass (elevation 3295ft) on the Klondike Hwy so you can freewheel 15 miles back to town, stopping to view waterfalls. The same trip is also offered with a ride up on the White Pass & Yukon Route ($209).

Hiking

The 33-mile Chilkoot Trail (p70) is Southeast Alaska's most popular hike. Less daunting are a couple of trail systems that originate downtown and two more that you can reach by train. There is no USFS office in Skagway, but the NPS Visitor Center (p139) has a free brochure entitled *Skagway Trail Map*. You can also get backcountry information and any outdoor gear you need (including rentals) at the excellent Mountain Shop (p147).

Packer Expeditions HIKING

(www.packerexpeditions.com; 355 4th Ave) If bear paranoia, fear of heights or plain old loneliness have dissuaded you from undertaking the Chilkoot Trail (p70) on your own, fear not: this outfit can offer all levels of support, from camping-equipment rental to full-on guides who'll carry your gear.

AB Mountain Trail HIKING

The AB Mountain Trail ascends 5.5 miles to the 5100ft summit of AB Mountain. Also known as the Skyline Trail, its official name comes from the 'AB' pattern that appears on its south side when the snow melts every spring. The first 30 minutes is along a well-defined trail through a hemlock forest to a view of Skagway.

After that the trail is considerably more challenging, especially above the tree line, requiring a full day to reach the summit. Watch the weather and consider something lower if the summit is obscured.

Arctic Brotherhood Hall (p141)

Dewey Lakes Trail System HIKING

This series of trails leads east of Skagway to a handful of alpine and subalpine lakes, waterfalls and historic sites. From Broadway, follow 3rd Ave southeast to the railroad tracks. On the east side of the tracks are the trailheads to Lower Dewey Lake (0.7 miles), Icy Lake (2.5 miles), Upper Reid Falls (3.5 miles) and Sturgill's Landing (4.5 miles).

Plan on taking an hour round-trip for the hike to Lower Dewey Lake, where there are picnic tables, camping spots and a trail circling the lake. At the lake's north end is an alpine trail that ascends steeply to Upper Dewey Lake, 3.5 miles from town, and Devil's Punchbowl, another 1.25 miles south of the upper lake. For those who want to stay the night, Skagway Recreation Center has a **cabin** (907-983-2679; www.skagwayrecreation.org; cabins $35) at Upper Dewey Lake, and there is also a run-down free-use shelter that does not require reservations.

The hike to Devil's Punchbowl is an all-day trip or an ideal overnight excursion; stay at the Dewey Lake cabins. There are also campsites at Sturgill's Landing overlooking Taiya Inlet.

Laughton Glacier Trail HIKING

At Mile 14 of the White Pass & Yukon Route (p144) is a 1.5-mile hike to the USFS **Laughton Glacier Cabin** (877-444-6777; www.recreation.gov; cabins $45). The cabin overlooks the river from Warm Pass but is only a mile from Laughton Glacier, an impressive hanging glacier between the 3000ft walls of the Sawtooth Range. The alpine scenery and ridge walks in this area are well worth the train ticket.

There are two excursion trains from Skagway, so this could be a possible day hike, but it's far better to carry a tent and spend a night in the area.

Denver Glacier Trail HIKING

This trail begins at Mile 6 of the White Pass & Yukon Route, where the USFS has renovated a WPYR caboose into the Denver Caboose, a rental cabin of sorts. The trail heads up the east fork of Skagway River for 2 miles, then swings south and continues another 1.5 miles up the glacial outwash to Denver Glacier.

Most of the trail is overgrown with brush, and the second half is particularly tough hiking. White Pass & Yukon Route will drop hikers off at the caboose.

Yakutania Point & Smuggler's Cove HIKING

The Skagway River footbridge, at the foot of the airport runway on 1st Ave, leads to a couple of easy strolls. To reach Yakutania Point, turn left at the far side of the bridge and follow the mile-long trail to picnic areas with lovely views. Sheltered Smuggler's Cove with its fire pit lies a quarter-mile further on.

You can make a loop by hiking up a dirt road behind the cove and descending through the woods to a pet cemetery before heading back to the bridge.

Rafting

Skagway Float Tours RAFTING

(907-983-3688; www.skagwayfloat.com; 209 Broadway St; 9am-6:30pm Mon-Sat, to 4pm Sun) Fancy some bliss on the river? Try the three-hour tour of Dyea that includes a 45-minute float down the placid Taiya River (adult/child $75/55); there are two per day at 9am and 1:30pm. The Hike & Float Tour ($95/75) is a four-hour outing that includes hiking 2 miles of the Chilkoot Trail then some floating back; there are several per day.

Tours

★ White Pass & Yukon Route Railroad RAIL

(800-343-7373; www.wpyr.com; 231 2nd Ave; May-Sep) This epic gold-rush-era railroad has departures from Skagway, AK; Fraser, British Columbia; and Carcross and Whitehorse, Yukon. The line was built across White Pass between 1898 and 1900 just in time to catch the coattails of the gold rush. In WWII it was used to transport troops to Whitehorse in Canada.

It closed in 1982 (after a highway was built), but reopened in 1986 as a tourist train. The journey in old-fashioned carriages is absolutely magnificent.

The trip is available from Monday to Saturday (May to September), leaving Skagway at 12.10pm and arriving in Fraser at 2:15pm. A bus leaves Fraser at 3pm and arrives in Whitehorse at 5:30pm. Total cost is $129.

The railroad also operates a hiker's shuttle bringing those who have completed the Chilkoot Trail back to Skagway from Lake Bennett. It operates Tuesday, Wednesday, Thursday and Saturday ($95). Check website for times.

Klondike Tours TOURS
(☎907-983-2075; www.klondiketours.com; cnr Broadway St & 3nd Ave) Offers all number of reasonably priced tours, from gold-panning to ziplining.

Red Onion Saloon Tours HISTORY
(☎907-983-2222; www.redonion1898.com; cnr Broadway St & 2nd Ave) Given time even brothels become vaguely respectable. This beloved saloon (p147), once a house of sin, is living proof. Tours of the upstairs bedrooms are strangely popular. 'The Quickie' is $10 for 20 minutes and offered throughout the day, while the 'Ghosts and Goodtime Girls Walking Tour' ($39.95) is a two-hour stroll around the town's infamous haunts culminating in the brothel museum, where you'll raise a champagne toast.

Expect to be joined by large number of cruise-ship tourists along with a humorous and witty guide.

Aiaska 360 TOURS
(☎907-983-3175; www.alaska3sixty.com; Mile 1.7, Klondike Hwy; 2hr tours $50) The renamed Klondike Gold Fields offers tours of a former working gold dredge, which was in Dawson before being moved to Skagway, where it has hit the mother lode. There is also a gold-panning show with a crack at finding dust yourself, a brewpub, and the inevitable snack shacks and gift shops on-site.

Gold Rush Trail Camp HISTORY
(☎907-983-3333; Mile 3, Klondike Hwy; adult/child $59/44) Reaffirming Skagway's obsession with humorous historical reenactments, this mock-up camp offers a miners' show, a turn at gold-panning and a salmon bake. It's clearly aimed at the cruise-ship market.

Bookable through most of Skagway's travel agencies.

Sleeping

The bulk of Skagway's visitors arrive and leave on cruise ships, meaning the town isn't particularly well set up for overnight accommodations. There are several B&Bs, a couple of mediocre hotels and three so-so campgrounds, but, alas, no longer a hostel.

Skagway levies an 8% sales and bed tax on all lodging.

Morning Wood Hotel HOTEL $
(☎907-983-3200; 444 4th Ave; r with shared/private bath $90/150; 📶) A buoyant hotel with a handsome, if typical, false-fronted wooden exterior. Inside, the rooms (located at the rear) aren't fancy, but at least they're spanking new and come with deluxe bathroom accessories and sharp color accents. There's an affiliated restaurant and bar.

Cheaper economy rooms have shared bathrooms.

Denver Caboose CABIN $
(☎877-444-6777; www.recreation.gov; cabins $45) This wonderfully unique accommodation comprises an old caboose donated by the White Pass & Yukon Railway to the USFS to use as a cabin sleeping up to six people. It sits at Mile 6 of the railway at the trailhead to the Denver Glacier. The train will stop here on request.

Dyea Campground CAMPGROUND $
(☎907-983-2921; tent & RV sites $10) Located a half-mile from the Chilkoot trailhead in Dyea, about 9 miles north of Skagway, this 21-site campground is operated by the NPS on a first-come, first-served basis. There are vault toilets and tables but no drinking water.

Skagway Inn INN $$
(☎907-983-2289; www.skagwayinn.com; Broadway St, at 7th Ave; r $149-249; @📶) In a restored 1897 Victorian building that was originally one of the town's brothels (what building still standing in Skagway wasn't?) this beautiful downtown inn features 10 rooms, four with shared baths. All are small but filled with antique dressers, iron beds and chests, and named after the 'ladies' who worked here. Breakfast is included, as are ferry/airport/train transfers.

Chilkoot Trail Outpost B&B $$
(☎907-983-3799; www.chilkoottrailoutpost.com; Mile 8.5, Dyea Rd; cabins $165-195; 📶) Hitting the 'Koot? Start with a good night's sleep at this excellent if unconventional B&B located a half-mile from the trailhead. The cabins are comfortable and equipped with microwaves, refrigerators and coffeemakers. In the morning you can fuel up on a buffet breakfast at the main lodge (included).

There are bicycles available, and the screened-in gazebo is strategically located at a waterfall.

Westmark Hotel HOTEL $$
(☎907-983-6100; www.westmarkhotels.com; 3rd Ave & Spring St; r from $149; 📶) The town's largest hotel has a cozy reception area and

CHILKOOT PASS V WHITE PASS: EVERY STAMPEDER'S DILEMMA

Two rugged mountain barriers faced stampeders on their way to the Klondike gold fields in 1897–98: White Pass, between Skagway and Lake Bennett, and Chilkoot Pass, between Dyea and Lake Bennett. For many hopefuls, the decision about which one to cross came down to a coin toss. Neither route was easy. A feverish prospector who had tried both described one as 'hell' and the other as 'damnation'. Another proclaimed: 'Whichever way you go, you will wish you'd gone the other'.

White Pass, at 2864ft, is the lower of the two mountain crossings, though the 1897 route was significantly longer in mileage (44 miles). Furthermore, with a more gradual gradient than Chilkoot, it was accessible by horse. However, the pass was invariably muddy, narrow and treacherous. Indeed, so many packhorses died on the trail during the frigid winter of 1897–98, worked to death by their cruel, inexperienced owners, that it became known as Dead Horse Pass. Jack London, who summited White Pass on his way to Dawson in 1897, described the tragic scenes which saw more than 3000 horse carcasses left abandoned in the snow.

The 33-mile **Chilkoot Trail** (☎907-983-9234; www.nps.gov; Broadway St, Skagway) between Dyea and Lake Bennett is higher and steeper than White Pass, and merciless winds often greeted prospectors at the 3525ft summit. Since horses couldn't ascend, stampeders had to lug all their own gear up the steepest section, the so-called golden stairs, climbing in single file up narrow steps carved into the ice. However, thanks to a long history of native use, the Chilkoot was, at least, an established trail and, as a result, was far more popular. It is estimated that around 30,000 people crossed Chilkoot Pass during the gold rush (all carrying a mandatory one tonne of supplies) compared to around 5000 who tackled White Pass. Nevertheless, the Chilkoot quickly fell out of favor in April 1898 after an avalanche killed over 60 people.

Today, the Chilkoot remains an established trail protected as part of the Klondike Gold Rush National Historical Park (p139). Up to 3000 people hike it in any given season.

A railway line was built through White Pass in 1900, causing the trail to be quickly abandoned. Nevertheless, you can still pick out parts of the erstwhile path – narrow and overgrown – from the train line close to the US–Canada border crossing. See p70 for more on hiking the Chilkoot Trail.

a quite refined (for Skagway) restaurant and cafe. Downsides: the rooms in sprawling wooden blocks are small and motel-like, you can only get wi-fi in the lobby, and checkout is an ungenerous 10am.

It's run by Holland America cruise lines.

Sgt Preston's Lodge MOTEL **$$**
(☎907-983-2521; www.sgtprestonslodge.com; 370 6th Ave; s $90-115, d $100-151; @) This motel in an old army barracks is one of Skagway's better bargains and the 38 rooms are nicer than outside appearances indicate. It's just far enough from Broadway St to escape most of the cruise-ship crush. Courtesy transportation and complimentary coffee provided.

At the White House INN **$$**
(☎907-983-9000; www.atthewhitehouse.com; cnr 8th Ave & Main St; r incl breakfast $149-169; 📶) A large, historic nine-room inn filled with antiques, remembrances of the Klondike and colorful comforters on every bed. Rooms are spacious and bright, even on a rainy day, and have cable TV and phone. In the morning you wake up to a breakfast of fresh-baked goods and fruit served in a sun-drenched dining room.

Mile Zero B&B B&B **$$**
(☎907-983-3045; www.mile-zero.com; 901 Main St; r $135-145; @📶) A purpose-built B&B that's more like a motel with the comforts of home. Six large rooms have their own private entrance on a wraparound porch. If you hook the fish of your dreams, there's a BBQ area where you can grill it for dinner.

Eating

Bites on Broadway CAFE **$**
(☎907-983-2166; 648 Broadway St; sandwiches $11; ⏲6am-6pm Mon-Fri, to 4pm Sat, to 2pm Sun) Skagway's best bona fide coffee shop shares space with a gift store and sells some energy-elongating sweet snacks to

complement its cups of joe, apple crumb cake and rhubarb coffee cake among them.

You can also build your own sandwich for around $11.

You Say Tomato Natural Foods HEALTH FOOD $

(2075 State St; pastries $3; ⏲10:30-7:30pm Mon-Fri, noon-6:30 Sat & Sun; ✎) Located in a replica of the Whitehorse Railroad Depot is this natural-foods store with (expensive) organic produce. There's also a bakery on-site. It's a mile from the town center.

Sweet Tooth Cafe CAFE $$

(315 Broadway St; breakfast $10-17; ⏲6:30am-2:30pm) Skagway's quick-turnover, always-busy diner plays heavy on the gold-rush theme. Expect to get your coffee refill poured by a lady dressed like Katherine Ross in *Butch Cassidy and the Sundance Kid*. Beyond the theatrics, the food is reliable diner fare. Breakfasts are best (porridge, eggs, pancakes etc), but also make note of the cinnamon buns and eclairs.

Woadie's South East Seafood SEAFOOD $$

(☎907-983-3133; State St & 4th Ave; mains $14-19; ⏲11:30am-7pm Mon-Thu, noon-6pm Fri & Sat) A food cart with its own deck and awning, equipped with picnic tables, delivers the town's best fish at a lightning pace. Report to the window and place your order for fresh oysters, crab or halibut. It allows BYO booze.

Starfire THAI $$

(☎907-983-3663; 4th Ave, at Spring St; lunch $12-15, dinner $14-19; ⏲11am-10pm; ✎) Skagway's token Thai restaurant is authentic and good, with a small lunch menu and a large, varied dinner menu. Order spicy drunken noodles or curry dishes in five colors (purple is Fire with Flavor!) and enjoy it with a beer on the outdoor patio, so pleasant and secluded you would never know Skagway's largest hotel is across the street. Good for vegetarians.

Poppies AMERICAN $$

(Klondike Hwy; mains $8-16; ⏲11am-3pm; ✎) Located inside a greenhouse at Jewell Gardens (p142), this restaurant has the best salads in town because the greens are grown just outside and probably picked that afternoon. Most of the other dishes also begin with organic ingredients and, best of all, are served with a view of the gardens in full bloom and AB Mountain looming overhead.

Olivia's Bistro SEAFOOD $$

(Broadway St, at 7th Ave; mains $14-27; ⏲10am-9pm; ✎) A charming bistro in the Skagway Inn (p145). The menu features wild game and seafood and whatever is growing in the lovely garden outside. How can you top that? With a serving of homegrown rhubarb crisp for dessert. Portions aren't huge, but they're creatively cooked, and besides, you need room for dessert.

Skagway Fish Company SEAFOOD $$$

(☎907-983-3474; Congress Way; mains $18-52; ⏲11am-9pm) Overlooking the harbor, with crab traps on the ceiling, this is a culinary homage to fish. You can feast heartily on halibut stuffed with king crab, shrimp and veggies, or king-crab bisque, but surprisingly, what many locals rave about are its baby back ribs. Its bar has the best view in town.

Drinking & Nightlife

In 1898 Skagway had 80 saloons. These days there are significantly less, although you *will* find a microbrewery and the still-rowdy Red Onion Saloon.

★Skagway Brewing Company MICROBREWERY

(www.skagwaybrewing.com; cnr 7th Ave & Broadway St; burgers $15; ⏲10am-10pm Mon-Fri, 11am-10pm Sat & Sun) Skagway's sole microbrewery offers stampeders such choices as Prospector Pale Ale, Boomtown Brown and Chilkoot Trail IPA. There's a full menu with nightly dinner specials, and a quiet outdoor deck in the back to escape the rowdiness at the front. It lures tired hikers like Klondike miners into a bordello.

Red Onion Saloon BAR

(www.redonion1898.com; Broadway St, at 2nd Ave; ⏲4-10pm Mon-Fri, noon-10pm Sat & Sun Apr-Oct) Skagway's most beloved brothel at the turn of the century is now its most famous saloon.

The 'RO' is done up as a gold-rush saloon, complete with mannequins leering down at you from the 2nd story to depict pioneer-era working girls.

When bands are playing here, it'll be packed, noisy and rowdy – but always fun. It also has the best pizza in town.

Facetious tours (p144) of the upstairs brothel rooms run daily throughout the summer.

Bonanza Bar & Grill BAR

(☎907-983-6214; 320 Broadway St; ⏲10am-2am) Bonanza has a go at being a local 'dive', but, since the lion's share of the clientele who sit sinking beer and fish and chips at the bar have just stepped off a cruise ship, it's not exactly a throwback to the days of 'Soapy' Smith.

Still, if you just want cold suds, slim prices, and burgers delivered to your canteen booth without the gangsterism of yore, go and join the melee.

☆ Entertainment

Days of '98 Show THEATER

(☎907-983-2545; www.thedaysof98show.com; 598 Broadway St, cnr 6th Ave; adult/child $25/12.50) This melodramatic show, held in the old Eagle's fraternity hall, is almost as long-standing as the events it portrays (it's been running since 1923). The evening show begins with 'mock gambling,' then moves on to a show focusing on Soapy and his gang.

Up to four shows are offered daily, but call ahead as the schedule is heavily dependent on the cruise ships.

Shopping

Skagway is chock-a-block with stores aimed at milking the cruise-ship crowds. Few of them are locally owned, and most of them ply tacky souvenirs like Alaska mugs that are actually made in China. The town seems to have a curious jewelry-store fetish, too.

★Alaska Geographic Museum Store BOOKS

(Broadway St & 2nd Ave; ⏲8:30am-5:30pm May-Sep) NPS bookstore selling classic Klondike tomes and essential Chilkoot Trail maps ($8.50).

Mountain Shop SPORTS & OUTDOORS

(☎907-983-2544; 355 4th Ave; ⏲9am-7pm) Very handy outdoor outfitters where you can stock up on all your backcountry needs, eg bear spray, water-purification tablets.

Information

MONEY

Wells Fargo (Broadway St, at 6th Ave; ⏲9:30am-5pm Mon-Fri) Occupies the original office of National Bank of Alaska.

TOURIST INFORMATION

Klondike Gold Rush National Historical Park Museum & Visitor Center (p139) For general info on Skagway's historical sites, museums and free walking tours. Run by the National Park Service.

Skagway Convention & Visitors Bureau (☎907-983-2854; www.skagway.com; cnr Broadway St & 2nd Ave; ⏲8am-6pm Mon-Fri, to 5pm Sat & Sun) For information on lodging, tours, restaurant menus and what's new, visit this bureau housed in the can't-miss **Arctic Brotherhood Hall** (p142) – think driftwood.

Trail Center (☎907-983-9234; www.nps.gov/klgo; Broadway St, btwn 5th & 6th Aves; ⏲8am-5pm Jun-Sep) If you're stampeding to the Chilkoot Trail (p70), you'll need to stop off here the day before to pick up trail passes, get the latest trail and weather conditions, and watch a mandatory bear-awareness video. Expert rangers from both the US NPS and Parks Canada are there to answer any questions.

Getting There & Away

AIR

Skagway's tiny **airport** (Terminal Way) receives no jet flights. Currently the only operator is **Alaska Seaplanes** (☎907-983-2479, 907-789-3331; www.flyalaskaseaplanes.com; Terminal Way) with seven daily flights to Juneau ($135, 45 minutes).

BUS

Yukon-Alaska Tourist Tours (☎866-626-7383, Whitehorse 867-668-5944; www.yukonalaskatouristtours.com) offers a bus service to Whitehorse (one way $70), departing the train depot in Skagway at 2pm daily.

CRUISE SHIP

Cruise ships (and there are a lot of them in summer) dock five minutes' walk from the town center, either next to the small-boat harbor or in Taiya Inlet at the far end of Terminal Way.

FERRY

There is a daily state ferry from Skagway to Haines ($32, one hour), Juneau ($59, 6½ hours) and back again. In Skagway, the ferry departs from the **Alaska Marine Highway Ferry Terminal** (☎907-983-2229; www.ferryalaska.com) at the southwest end of Broadway St.

Haines-Skagway Fast Ferry (☎888-766-2103; www.hainesskagwayfastferry.com; one way adult/child $36/18) provides speedy transportation on a catamaran to Haines only. The boat departs from the Skagway small-boat harbor between one and seven times per day.

Alaska Fjordlines runs the **Fjord Express** (☎800-320-0146; www.alaskafjordlines.com), which departs Skagway at 8am and arrives in

Juneau at 11am, and includes snacks, a wildlife tour and a bus to downtown Juneau or the airport. A one-way ticket costs $169. Departure is from the small-boat harbor.

Getting Around

BUS

The city operates the **Smart bus** (907-983-2743; single rides/day passes $2/5; 7am-9pm May-Oct), which moves people (primarily cruise-ship passengers) from the docks up Broadway St and to Jewell Gardens and the Alaska 360 gold dredge on the edge of town. Call ahead for an airport or ferry pickup.

TAXI

Chilkoot Trail Dyea Transport (907-617-7551; trumooreservices@outlook.com) Very reliable taxi service to the Chilkoot trailhead (including early starts). Owner Ann Moore can also help out with other Skagway transport conundrums.

Yakutat

907 / POP 700

Isolated on the strand that connects the Southeast to the rest of Alaska, Yakutat is becoming something of a tourist destination; although, admittedly, still a minor one. The main reason is improved transportation. You still can't drive to the most northern Southeast town, but there is now a twice-monthly Alaska Marine Highway ferry and – since 2015 – a couple of small cruise ships stopping by. Yakutat also claims to be the smallest town in the world with a regular jet-plane service, courtesy of Alaska Airlines.

So what does tiny Yakutat have to offer curious tourists? Big waves, the world's largest tidal glacier and world-class fishing. The waves rolling in from the Gulf of Alaska have made Yakutat the unlikely (and frigid) surf capital of the Far North. The little-visited Hubbard Glacier creaks and crashes 30 miles to the north, and the sea- and river-fishing are phenomenal even by Alaskan standards.

Sights

★ **Hubbard Glacier** GLACIER

Just 30 miles north of Yakutat is Hubbard Glacier, the longest tidewater glacier in the world. The 8-mile-wide glacier is easily Alaska's most active. The riptides and currents that flow between Gilbert Point and the face of the glacier, a mere 1000ft away, are so strong that they cause Hubbard to calve al-

Hubbard Glacier

most continuously at peak tides. The entire area, part of the 545-sq-mile Russell Fjord Wilderness, is one of the most interesting places in Alaska and usually visited through flightseeing or boat tours.

The 76-mile-long glacier captured national attention by galloping across Russell Fiord in the mid-1980s, turning the long inlet into a lake. Eventually Hubbard receded, reopening the fjord, but in 2002 it again surged across Russell Fjord, and it came close to doing it a third time in 2011.

Tours

Yakutat Charter Boat Co TOUR
(907-784-3433; www.alaska-charter.com) Runs a four-hour tour of the area for $180 per person including a visit to the Hubbard Glacier. It can also organize one-day ocean-fishing charters from $300 per person.

Sleeping

Glacier Bear Lodge LODGE $$
(907-784-3202; www.glacierbearlodge.com; 812 Glacier Bear Ave; s/d $145/205;) Has 31 comfortable rooms, and a good restaurant and lounge. It also provides a shuttle to and from the airport. Heavily oriented toward fishing.

Eating

You best bet for a good meal is the dining room at the Glacier Bear Lodge, open daily for breakfast, lunch and dinner, including local fish and steak. There's a local grocery store that sells coffee and doughnuts.

Shopping

Situk River Fly Shop SPORTS & OUTDOORS
(www.situk.com; 101 The Hanger; 10am-7pm) Thrumming with the fishing energy and general pulse of Yakutat is Situk River Fly Shop, where you'll find tackle and other gear, as well as area information. The website and blog are excellent sources of news and happenings.

Icy Waves Surf Shop SPORTS & OUTDOORS
(907-784-3226; www.icywaves.com; 635 Haida St; hours vary) Yakutat has its own surf shop. All aspiring wave-riders should pitch in here first.

Information

USFS Yakutat Ranger Station (907-784-3359; 712 Ocean Cape Rd) For info on cabins in the area.

Getting There & Away

AIR

Alaska Airlines has one daily flight south to Seattle via Juneau and one heading north to Anchorage via Cordova.

Yakutat Airport (997 Airport Rd) is 3.5 miles southeast of what passes for the town center.

FERRY

The **Alaska Marine Highway Ferry Terminal** (www.dot.state.ak.us/amhs; Max Italio Dr) is right in town. The twice-monthly MV *Kennicott* ferry travels south to Juneau ($110, 16 hours) and north to Whittier ($165, 22 hours). Book ahead.

Anchorage & Around

Includes ➡

Best Places to Eat

- ➡ Snow City Café (p169)
- ➡ Jack Sprat (p183)
- ➡ Bear Tooth Grill (p171)
- ➡ Turkey Red (p190)

Best Places to Stay

- ➡ Copper Whale Inn (p165)
- ➡ Hatcher Pass Lodge (p189)
- ➡ Wildflower Inn (p165)
- ➡ Eklutna Lake State Recreation Area (p186)
- ➡ Hotel Alyeska (p182)

Why Go?

Once you realize that Anchorage isn't simply a big city on the edge of the wilderness but rather a big city in the wilderness, it starts to make sense. The town manages to mingle hiking trails and traffic jams, small art galleries and Big Oil like no other city. Among big chain stores and mini-malls, there are more than 100 miles of city trails meandering in hidden greenbelts and a creek downtown where anglers line up to catch trophy salmon.

Towering behind the municipality is the nation's third-largest state park, the half-million-acre Chugach. The wilderness is never far away, which is why Anchorage's young population (the median age is 33) is an active one. Stay for a few days, explore the cycling trails, patronize the art galleries and dine in Alaska's best restaurants, and you'll understand why half the state's population chooses to live in and around this city.

When to Go

Anchorage

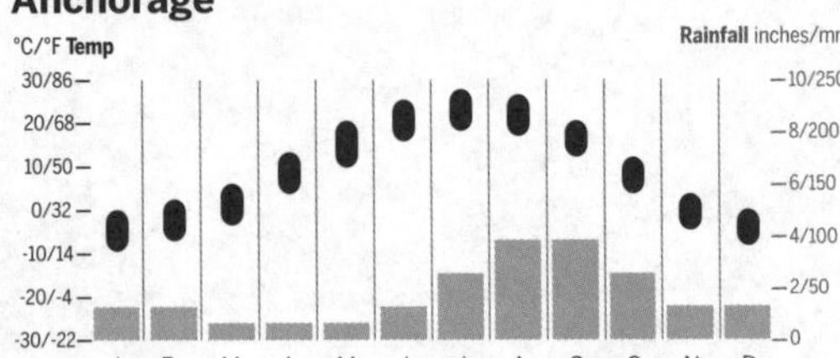

Mar Anchorage comes alive for the Iditarod Sled Dog Race and Fur Rendezvous festival.

May The weather is nice, and the crowds and high prices are yet to arrive.

Jul The best month to see or catch a king salmon in Anchorage's Ship Creek.

Anchorage & Around Highlights

1. **Anchorage Museum** (p156) Enjoying Alaskan art and culture at this world-class facility.
2. **Tony Knowles Coastal Trail** (p160) Pedaling along Anchorage's shoreline with the Alaska Range in the distance.
3. **Girdwood** (p179) Taking the tram, going on a stroll and savoring a gourmet meal in this little ski town.
4. **Eklutna Lake** (p153) Biking and kayaking the glacier blue, mountain-ringed lake just outside Anchorage.
5. **Palmer** (p187) Gazing at 100lb produce in this colonial farming town surrounded by peaks.
6. **Flattop Mountain Trail** (p153) Bagging your first Alaskan peak on this short but steep trail.
7. **Ship Creek Viewing Platform** (p160) Watching anglers reel in king salmon just blocks from city office buildings.

HIKING & PADDLING IN & AROUND ANCHORAGE

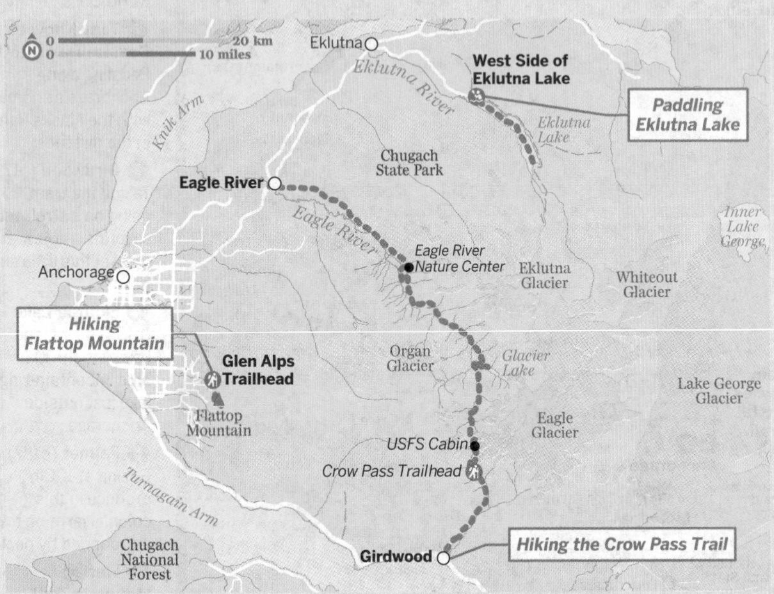

HIKING THE CROW PASS TRAIL

START GIRDWOOD
END EAGLE RIVER
DURATION/DISTANCE TWO DAYS/ 24 MILES
DIFFICULTY MEDIUM

One of the best backpacking adventures near Anchorage is the 24-mile Crow Pass Trail. Part of the Iditarod National Historic Trail (p185), it was once used by gold miners and mushers. This classic alpine crossing begins at Crow Pass trailhead in Girdwood, climbs Crow Pass and wanders past Raven Glacier. You then enter Chugach State Park and descend Eagle River Valley, ending north of Anchorage at the Eagle River Nature Center (p186). The trail is well maintained but requires fording Eagle River, which is tricky when the water is high. Bring trekking poles and a partner.

Armed with a decent light backpack and blessed with some reasonably good weather, you could potentially cover this trail in one long, challenging, adventurous Alaskan summer day. Heck, they stage a mountain race here every summer with the winner usually smashing it out in less than 3½ hours. But why rush? The alpine scenery is remarkable, the mining ruins along the trail are interesting, and the hike is reasonably demanding. Plan on taking two days, or even three, because this is why you come to Alaska – to wander in the mountains.

You must have a stove; campfires are not allowed in the state park. Near Mile 3 of the trail is a USFS cabin (p182) in a beautiful alpine setting. At the other end of the trail are yurts and a cabin ($65) rented out by the Eagle River Nature Center.

The Crow Pass trailhead is reached 7 miles up Crow Creek Rd in Girdwood. To return to Anchorage, you can catch bus 102 of the People Mover (p179) from the Eagle River Transit Center near the Glenn Hwy.

Take advantage of Anchorage's proximity to stunning wilderness. Backed by Chugach State Park, the city's easy access to the lake- and mountain-filled backcountry is unparalleled.

HIKING FLATTOP MOUNTAIN

START GLEN ALPS TRAILHEAD
END GLEN ALPS TRAILHEAD
DURATION/DISTANCE 2½ HOURS/1.7 MILES
DIFFICULTY MEDIUM TO HARD

One of the most popular trails in Anchorage's seductive front range is Flattop Mountain, a somewhat squat and easily identifiable peak. Its namesake summit is big as a football field, with views of Anchorage, Cook Inlet, and on a clear day, Denali.

What this hike lacks in length it makes up for in its pure quad-killing ascent; you'll gain 1350ft in 1.7 miles. Sure, this is the first peak every Anchorage kid summits, but these are *Alaskan* kids we're talking about. Bring sturdy shoes, plenty of water and a hat and jacket; there's very little protection along the trail and it can get windy.

The hike begins at Glen Alps Trailhead and begins to climb almost as soon as you leave the parking lot. The first section is through a wind-twisted grove of hemlock, but you soon emerge to talus slopes. There's a brief respite at a saddle before your final push to the summit. You'll need to scramble the last few hundred feet; the trail here is marked by spray-painted rocks.

The summit, while obvious, is marked with a flag and plenty of photo-snapping hikers. You can continue along the ridgeline or even down the back side where the trail connects with Upper Dearmon Rd. Regardless of which way you head down, it's steep.

The Flattop Mountain Shuttle (p179) travels to and from Glen Alps daily.

PADDLING EKLUTNA LAKE

START WEST SIDE OF EKLUTNA LAKE
END WEST SIDE OF EKLUTNA LAKE
DURATION/DISTANCE HALF-DAY/UP TO 14 MILES ROUND-TRIP
DIFFICULTY EASY TO MEDIUM

This 7-mile-long lake is the largest in Chugach State Park and is excellent grounds – er, waters – for exploring. It's close enough to Anchorage for a day trip, where you can truly feel like you're escaping civilization for an afternoon. There's a great biking/hiking path along the north side of the lake, but with so few opportunities to kayak near Anchorage it'd be a shame to pass up the opportunity.

Rent kayaks from a shack near shore on the lake's west side. From here, you can launch into the water and begin your exploration east. The lake is ringed by deciduous forest, with glacial streams pouring in from the peaks above. Look for wildlife.

The paddle to the end of the lake and back can be ambitious, especially if there's wind; you can also buy a pedal/paddle package and have mountain bikes waiting for you at the end of the lake to ride back. Otherwise, the shoreline is a pleasant place to explore on its own; Eklutna glacier has retreated, but you can still catch glimpses on a short hike from the shore.

The lake is 10 miles from the Glenn Hwy on Eklutna Lake Rd.

Eklutna Lake (p186)

DAY TRIPS FROM ANCHORAGE

GIRDWOOD

Plenty of fun awaits you in the glacier-embraced Girdwood valley (p179). Alaska's biggest ski resort offers year-round activities, including hiking, mountain biking, tram rides and berry picking, and even Anchorage-ites drive down here just to dine in one of several excellent restaurants. It's about 37 miles south of Anchorage.

☆ Best Things to See/Do/Eat

Alyeska Resort Tram Take the tram up the slopes to explore alpine territory and take in sweeping views of Turnagain Arm. You can have lunch at the cafe in the Upper Tram Terminal – if you can take your eyes off the scenery.

Winner Creek Trail This mellow 5.5-mile (round-trip) walk makes for an excellent little day hike, taking you to a hand-tram over a rushing glacial stream. It's a mostly flat walk in a pleasant, mossy forest.

Jack Sprat Don't miss dinner at this popular-with-locals restaurant serving organic dishes in a sunroom and on a sun-drenched deck. There's an extensive wine list, and dessert is always worth it.

☆ How to Get There

Bus Seward Bus Lines can drop you off on the way to Seward from Anchorage.

Car A road trip down Turnagain Arm is worth it just for the drive itself; you can hire a car in Anchorage.

Train Alaska Railroad provides the most relaxing way to reach Girdwood, aboard the Coastal Classic.

HATCHER PASS

An incongruous blend of mine tailings and alpine meadows that make you want to frolic, Hatcher Pass (p189) is a worthy day trip from Anchorage. The spiky geography of the Talkeetna Mountains makes for excellent scenery and exploring.

☆ Best Things to See/Do/Eat

Independence Mine State Historical Park The main attraction here is this abandoned gold mine from the 1930s, which sprawls across 272 acres. Surrounded by gorgeous mountains, the mine is a great place to photograph.

Reed Lakes Trail Take a full day to hike this trail, one of the region's best. In a glowing green alpine valley, the Lower and Upper Lakes glitter like clear sapphire jewels, and the sound of waterfalls adds even more magic to the surrounds.

Hatcher Pass Lodge Stop here for a hot meal; you'll have excellent views of the valley below in cozy surrounds. If you have the time, consider staying the night in one of the adorable cabins, and warm up in the sauna.

☆ How to Get There

Car The only way to reach Hatcher Pass is your own vehicle, which you can rent in Anchorage.

Bus Valley Transit can get you as far as Palmer, but you'll still need a car for the remaining 20 or so miles.

EAGLE RIVER

A bedroom community north of Anchorage, Eagle River (p184) is a suburb saved by sprawl thanks to those steep mountains enclosing it. Look past the big-box stores to the mountains beyond; they hold a lot of promise.

☆ Best Things to See/Do/Eat

Eagle River Nature Center Be sure to drive out Eagle River Rd to this excellent spot. A family friendly center, it has guided hikes along the excellent surrounding trails and viewing copes to spot Dall sheep.

Eagle & Symphony Lakes A great day hike along a fairly mellow path that follows the South Fork of Eagle River through a valley filled with wildflowers. The lakes are a great destination for a day hike, but even weekend alpinists can use the lakes as a base for exploring the mountains and valleys beyond.

Pizza Man Stop in for a hot slice – or maybe a whole pie. A favorite with locals, this busy place is the best in town for replenishing all those calories you burned while hiking. Plenty of beers on tap will help you exaggerate your wildlife-encounter tales, on the off chance you didn't run into bear that day.

☆ How to Get There

Car It's an easy drive up the Glenn Hwy from Anchorage.

Bus Public transportation, including Anchorage's People Mover, stops here.

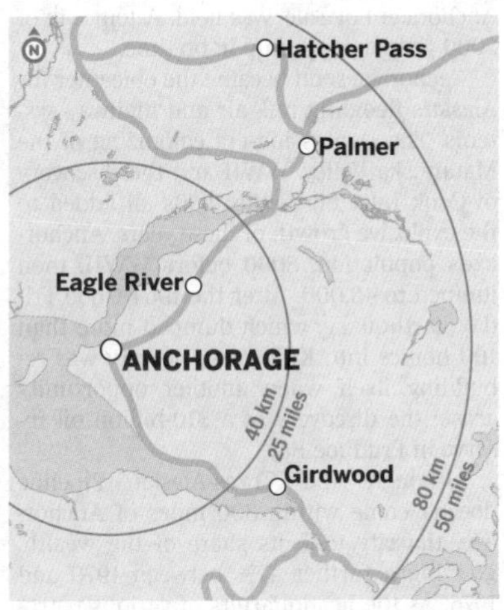

Anchorage is an urban center surrounded by nearly limitless opportunities to explore. When you've had your fill of city life, use Anchorage as a base to discover nearby communities and adventures.

History

Though British explorer Captain James Cook sailed past the site in 1779 in search of the elusive Northwest Passage, and hopeful gold prospectors had been visiting Ship Creek since the 1880s, Anchorage wasn't founded until 1915. That was the year the Alaska Railroad called the area home and the 'Great Anchorage Lot Sale' was held. A tent city of 2000 people popped up in no time.

Anchorage soon became the epicenter for Alaska's fledgling rail, air and highway systems. The Depression-era colonizing of the Matanuska Valley, WWII and the discovery of Cook Inlet oil in the 1950s all added to the explosive growth of these years. Anchorage's population, 8000 before WWII, then jumped to 43,000. After the 1964 Good Friday Earthquake, which dumped more than 100 homes into Knik Arm, the city was rebuilding itself when another opportunity arose: the discovery of a $10-billion oil reserve in Prudhoe Bay.

Although the Trans-Alaska Pipeline doesn't come within 300 miles of Anchorage, the city took its share of the wealth, growing a further 47% between 1970 and 1976. As the headquarters of various petroleum and service companies, Anchorage still manages to gush with oil money.

This city of stage plays and snowy peaks also has serious pork-barrel power. During the late 1970s, when a barrel of crude oil jumped more than $20 and Alaska couldn't spend its tax revenue fast enough, Anchorage received the lion's share. It used its political muscle to revitalize downtown Anchorage with the Sullivan Arena, Egan Civic Center and stunning Alaska Center for the Performing Arts. While downtown saw a recent boom, with the Dena'ina Center and a museum expansion, dwindling oil revenue has residents and business on edge with threats of a major recession.

ANCHORAGE

☎907 / POP 299,037

Locals like to say that Anchorage is only 30 minutes from Alaska: wedged between 5000ft peaks and an inlet filled with salmon and whales, the Big Apple of the north is unlike any other city.

At first glance the traffic, strip malls and suburban sprawl can feel off-putting. But inside those strip malls are top-notch restaurants serving fresh seafood and locally grown produce, and the two roads that lead in and out of town spool right into some of the most majestic wilderness in the world. This is a city where bears are seen wandering bike paths, moose munch on neighborhood gardens, and locals pull salmon from a creek within blocks of hotels and office buildings.

Dive into this city of parks, museums and restaurants and you'll see why almost half the state's population calls it home.

Sights

Downtown Anchorage

★**Anchorage Museum** MUSEUM
(Map p166; www.anchoragemuseum.org; 625 C St; adult/child $15/7; 9am-6pm summer;) This world-class facility is Anchorage's cultural jewel. The West Wing, a four-story, shimmering, mirrored facade, adds 80,000 sq ft to what was already the largest museum in the state. The museum's flagship exhibit is the Smithsonian Arctic Studies Center (with more than 600 Alaska Native objects, such as art, tools, masks and household implements), which was previously housed in Washington, DC.

It's the largest Alaska Native collection in the state and it's surrounded by large video screens showing contemporary Alaska Native life. Nearby is the Listening Space, where you can listen to storytellers and natural sounds from arctic Alaska.

The museum also contains the **Imaginarium Discovery Center** (Map p166; ☎907-929-9200; 625 C St; adult/child $15/7; 9am-6pm Mon-Sat), a hands-on science center for children that was previously housed in a separate downtown location. On the 1st floor of the original East Wing you will still find the Art of the North Gallery, with entire rooms of Alaskan masters Eustace Ziegler and Sydney Laurence. On the 2nd floor, the Alaska History Gallery is filled with life-size dioramas that trace 10,000 years of human settlement, from early subsistence villages to modern oil dependency.

There are also galleries devoted to traveling art exhibits, a planetarium and the Kid-Space Gallery, which is designed for young children (and their parents) to explore the worlds of art, history and science through hands-on play. Clearly, this is a place where you can spend an entire afternoon.

Oscar Anderson House HISTORIC BUILDING

(Map p166; www.aahp-online.net; 420 M St; adult/child $10/5; ⌚noon-4pm Tue-Sun Jun-Aug) Housed in the city's oldest wooden-framed home, this little museum overlooks the delightful Elderberry Park. Anderson was the 18th American settler to set foot in Anchorage, and he built his house in 1915. Today it's the only home museum in Anchorage, and despite past budget problems, it's open as a reminder that until fairly recently there wasn't a single building in this city that was a century old.

Delaney Park PARK

(Map p166) Known locally as the Delaney Park Strip, this narrow slice of well-tended grass stretches from A to P Sts between W 9th and W 10th Aves; there's an impressive playground near the corner of E St. The park was the site of the 50-ton bonfire celebrating statehood in 1959 and Pope John Paul II's 1981 outdoor Mass. Today it hosts festivals like Summer Solstice and Pridefest, not to mention Frisbee games any time the weather is nice.

4th Avenue Market Place/Village of Ship Creek Center MARKET

(Map p166; 333 W 4th Ave; ⌚8am-6pm Mon-Fri, from 9am Sat & Sun) FREE This shopping mall contains an array of native and crafty gift shops – in a few, you can watch artists at work. Outside, walls are painted with a historic timeline of Anchorage, while inside are displays devoted to the 1964 Good Friday Earthquake. The Alaska Experience Theatre (p176) shows films about the 49th state throughout the day. On the bottom floor, an indoor market (10am to 6pm Friday to Saturday) feels like an extension of the weekend market across the street, with homemade crafts and food.

Fraternal Order of Alaska State Troopers Law Enforcement Museum MUSEUM

(Map p166; www.alaskatroopermuseum.com; 245 W 5th Ave; ⌚10am-4pm Mon-Fri, from noon Sat) FREE Most of us would rather avoid the police. But who can resist a museum devoted solely to the state's troopers? Displays are dedicated to law enforcement, starting from when Alaska was a territory. The storefront museum has exhibits that range from a beautifully restored 1952 Hudson Hornet cop car to state-issued sealskin cop boots.

Stop by its gift shop for a T-shirt that proclaims 'Alaska: 367 Troopers, 570,000 square miles' to impress the next cop who pulls you over at home.

> **CULTURE PASS TICKET**
>
> Anchorage's top two attractions, the Alaska Native Heritage Center (p158) and the Anchorage Museum, can both be enjoyed at a discount with a special joint-admission ticket. The Culture Pass Joint Ticket is $29.95 per person and includes admission to both museums as well as shuttle transportation between them. You can purchase the joint pass from the ticket offices at either location.

Rooftop PARK

(Rooftop Park; Map p166; 245 W 5th Ave; 👪) Anchorage's newest park sits on top of a parking garage downtown, but don't let its urban setting dissuade you from visiting. There's a synthetic ice rink, basketball court and plenty of sunshine.

Resolution Park PARK

(Map p166) At the west end of 3rd Ave, this small park is home to the Captain Cook Monument, built to mark the 200th anniversary of the English captain's 'discovery' of Cook Inlet. If not overrun by tour-bus passengers, this observation deck has an excellent view of the surrounding mountains.

Midtown Anchorage & Spenard

Alaska Heritage Museum MUSEUM

(Map p162; ☎907-265-2834; www.wellsfargohistory.com/museums/anchorage; 301 W Northern Lights Blvd; ⌚noon-4pm Mon-Fri) FREE Inside the midtown Wells Fargo bank, this museum is home to the largest private collection of Alaska Native artifacts in the state and includes costumes, baskets and hunting weapons. There are also original paintings covering the walls, including several by Sydney Laurence, and lots of scrimshaw. The museum's collection is so large that there are displays in the elevator lobbies throughout the bank. You can call to book a guided tour.

Alaska Aviation Heritage Museum MUSEUM

(Map p158; www.alaskaairmuseum.org; 4721 Aircraft Dr; adult/child $15/8; ⌚9am-5pm) On the south shore of Lake Hood (the world's

Greater Anchorage

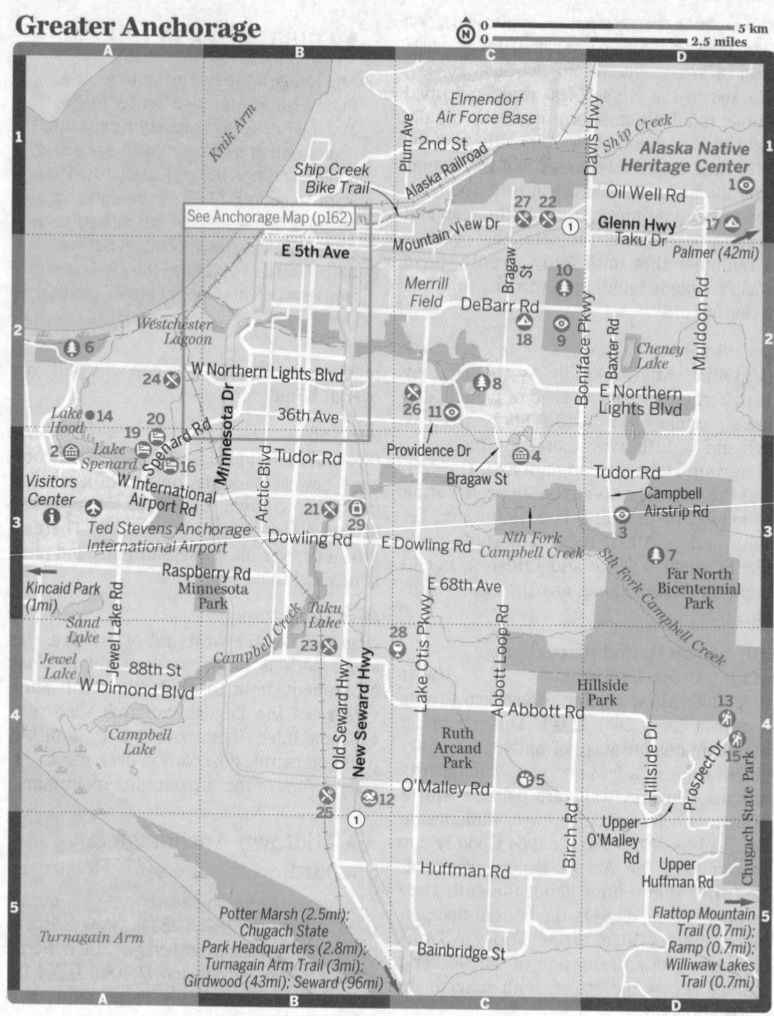

busiest floatplane lake), this museum is a tribute to Alaska's colorful Bush pilots and their faithful planes. Housed within are 25 planes along with historic photos and displays of pilots' achievements, from the first flight to Fairbanks (1913) to the early history of Alaska Airlines.

You can view early footage of Bush planes in the museum's theater or step outside to its large observation deck and watch today's pilots begin their own quest for adventure with a roar on Lake Hood.

Greater Anchorage

★ Alaska Native Heritage Center CULTURAL CENTER

(Map p158; ☎907-330-8000; www.alaskanative.net; 8800 Heritage Center Dr; adult/child $25/17; ⏲9am-5pm) If you can't travel to the Bush region to experience Native Alaska culture firsthand, visit this 26-acre center and see how humans survived – and thrived – before central heating. This is much more than just a museum: it represents a knowledge bank of language, art and culture that will survive no matter how many sitcoms are crackling

Greater Anchorage

Top Sights
1 Alaska Native Heritage Center............... D1

Sights
2 Alaska Aviation Heritage Museum....... A3
3 Alaska Botanical Garden D3
4 Alaska Native Medical Center............... C3
5 Alaska Zoo C4
6 Earthquake Park A2
7 Far North Bicentennial Park................. D3
8 Goose Lake C2
9 Mann Leiser Memorial Greenhouses C2
10 Russian Jack Springs Park.................... C2
11 University of Alaska Anchorage........... C2

Activities, Courses & Tours
12 H2Oasis.. B4
13 Prospect Heights Trailhead.................. D4
14 Regal Air A2
Rust's Flying Service ....(see 2)
15 Wolverine Peak Trail............................. D4

Sleeping
16 Alex Hotel & Suites A3
17 Centennial Park Campground............... D1
18 Golden Nugget RV Park.........................C2
Lake Hood Inn ....(see 19)
19 Lakefront Anchorage Hotel....................A3
20 Lakeshore Inn & Suites..........................A3
Long House Alaskan Hotel............(see 19)
Puffin Inn ....(see 19)
Spenard Hostel...............................(see 19)

Eating
21 Arctic Roadrunner..................................B3
22 Hula Hands C1
23 PHOnatik B4
24 Rustic Goat..A2
25 South Restaurant & Coffee House........B4
26 Turkish Delight..C2
27 West Berlin C1

Drinking & Nightlife
28 Midnight Sun Brewing Company C4

Shopping
Alaska Native Heritage Center.......(see 1)
29 Alaska Wild Berry Park B3
ANC Auxiliary Craft Shop............... (see 4)

through the Alaskan stratosphere. It's a labor of love, and of incalculable value.

The main building houses meandering exhibits on traditional arts and sciences – including kayaks and rain gear that rival the best offerings of outdoors department store REI. It also features various performances, among them the staccato Alaghanak song, lost for 50 years: the center collected bits and pieces of the traditional song from different tribal elders and reconstructed it. Outside, examples of typical structures from the Aleut, Yupik, Tlingit and other tribes are arranged around a picturesque lake. Docents explain the ancient architects' cunning technology: check out wooden panels that shrink in the dry summers (allowing light and air inside) but expand to seal out the cold during the wet winter. Dog-cart rides and private and audio tours are all available for an extra charge.

Alaska Zoo ZOO

(Map p158; www.alaskazoo.org; 4731 O'Malley Rd; adult/child $15/7; 9am-9pm;) The unique wildlife of the Arctic is on display at this zoo, the only one in North America that specializes in northern animals, including snow leopards, Amur tigers and Tibetan yaks. Alaskan native species, from wolverines and moose to caribou and Dall sheep, are abundant. What kids will love watching, however, are the bears. The zoo has all Alaskan species, but the polar bears are clearly the star attraction. Note that hours vary outside June, July and August.

Far North Bicentennial Park PARK

(Map p158) Comprising 4000 acres of forest and muskeg in east central Anchorage, this park features 20 miles of trails. In the center of the park is the Bureau of Land Management's (BLM's) Campbell Tract, a 700-acre wildlife preserve where it's possible to see moose and bears in the spring and brilliant fall colors in mid-September. There is an active grizzly population, and it's wise to steer clear of salmon streams during the twilight hours.

There are several entrances to the park. Take O'Malley Rd east to Hillside Dr and follow the signs, or take Campbell Airstrip Rd off of Tudor Rd. You can also enter off of Elmore Rd.

Kincaid Park PARK

At the western 'nose' of the peninsula and southern terminus of the Tony Knowles Coastal Trail (p160) is this beloved 1400-acre park populated by mountain bikers in the summer and Nordic skiers in the winter. Trails wind through a rolling terrain of forested hills where there are views of Mt Susitna and Denali on a clear day and fiery sunsets in the evening. From certain spots on the coastal trail you can stand directly under incoming jets.

Follow Raspberry Rd west to the parking lot and trailheads.

Ship Creek Viewing Platform VIEWPOINT
(Map p162) FREE From mid- to late summer, king, coho and pink salmon spawn up Ship Creek, the historical site of Tanaina Indian fish camps. At the overlook you can cheer on those love-starved fish humping their way toward destiny, and during high tide see the banks lined with anglers trying to hook them in what has to be one of the greatest urban fisheries anywhere in the USA. Take C St north, cross Ship Creek Bridge and turn right on Whitney Rd.

Nearby is the **Bait Shack** (Map p162; ☎907-522-3474; www.thebaitshackak.com; 212 W Whitney Rd; ⏰10am-8pm), which will rent you the rod, reel, waders and tackle needed to catch a trophy king.

Alaska Native Medical Center GALLERY
(Map p158; www.anmc.org; 4315 Diplomacy Dr; ⏰24hr) FREE This hospital has a fantastic collection of Alaska Native art and artifacts: take the elevator to the top floor and wind down the staircase past dolls, basketry and tools from all over Alaska. It's an informal presentation but a worthy visit.

University of Alaska Anchorage UNIVERSITY
(Map p158; www.uaa.alaska.edu; Providence Dr; 🚌1, 3, 13, 36, 45, 102) UA-Anchorage is the largest college campus in Alaska. The Campus Center is home to a small art gallery and the bookstore, which has a good selection of Alaskana, clothing that says 'Alaska' on it and used microbiology texts. A planetarium shows films on space ($10 if bought at www.UAAtix.com), and an arena is home to sports, live music and a burger joint with a deck that faces the mountains.

There are trails from the campus that connect to Goose Lake and Chester Creek Greenbelt.

Russian Jack Springs Park PARK
(Map p158; 🚌8, 45, 15) Named after the original homesteader of the site, this 300-acre park is south of Glenn Hwy on Boniface Pkwy. The park has tennis courts, hiking and cycling trails, and a picnic area. Near the DeBarr Rd entrance, you'll find the **Mann Leiser Memorial Greenhouses** (Map p158; ☎907-343-4717; ⏰8am-3pm) FREE, a toasty oasis of tropical plants, exotic birds and fish.

Earthquake Park PARK
(Map p158) For decades after the 1964 earthquake, this park remained a barren moonscape revealing the tectonic power that destroyed nearby Turnagain Heights. Today Earthquake Park, at the west end of Northern Lights Blvd on the Knik Arm, is being reclaimed by nature; you'll have to poke around the bushes to see evidence of tectonic upheaval. A nice stop if you're biking the Coastal Trail.

Alaska Botanical Garden GARDENS
(Map p158; ☎907-770-3692; www.alaskabg.org; 4601 Campbell Airstrip Rd; adult/child $12/8; ⏰daylight) The garden is a colorful showcase for native species, where gentle paths lead you through groomed herb, rock and perennial gardens in a wooded setting. The mile-long Lowenfels-Hoersting Family Nature Trail – built for tanks during WWII – is a great place to learn your basic Alaskan botany or just to stroll and watch the bald eagles pluck salmon from Campbell Creek. Guided tours are offered by appointment.

Goose Lake PARK
(Map p158; UAA Dr; 🚌3, 45) You'll stop complaining about global warming once you experience an 85°F (29°C) Anchorage afternoon at Goose Lake. Just off Northern Lights Blvd, this is the city's most developed lake for swimming, with lifeguards.

Activities

Cycling

Anchorage has 122 miles of paved paths that parallel major roads or wind through the greenbelts, making a bicycle the easiest and cheapest way to explore the city. If you run out of gas before the end of the ride, all People Mover buses are equipped with bike racks.

Anchorage is also a haven for mountain biking, with the most popular areas being Kincaid Park (p159), Far North Bicentennial Park (p159) and Powerline Pass Trail in Chugach State Park.

★ **Tony Knowles Coastal Trail** CYCLING
(Map p166) Anchorage's favorite trail is the scenic 11-mile Tony Knowles Coastal Trail. It begins at the west end of 2nd Ave downtown and passes Elderberry Park before winding through Earthquake Park, around Point Woronzof and finally to Point Campbell in Kincaid Park (p159). There are good views of Knik Arm and the Alaska Range, and the Anchorage Lightspeed Planet Walk (p163).

Downtown Bicycle Rental CYCLING
(Map p166; ☎907-279-5293; www.alaska-bike-rentals.com; 333 W 4th Ave; 3/24hr rental $16/32; ⊙8am-10pm) Has road, hybrid and mountain bikes as well as tandems, trailers and even clip-in pedals and shoes. Locks, helmets and bike maps are free, and the staff are a wealth of information on where to ride.

Ship Creek Bike Trail CYCLING
(Map p162) This ribbon of asphalt runs 2.6 miles from the Alaska Railroad depot along the namesake creek and into the Mountain View neighborhood. Here you can watch aggressive anglers fish for salmon as you wind through woods and industry.

Campbell Creek Trail CYCLING
Campbell Creek Trail features some of the newest paved path in Anchorage, stretching 7 miles from Far North Bicentennial Park, under the Seward Hwy, to Dimond Blvd, with most of the ride in the Campbell Creek Greenbelt. Look for salmon swimming up the creek and joyful boaters rafting down.

Chester Creek Bike Trail CYCLING
This scenic 4-mile path through the Chester Creek Greenbelt connects with the coastal trail at Westchester Lagoon and follows a mountain-fed stream to Goose Lake.

Pablo's Bicycle Rental CYCLING
(Map p166; ☎907-277-2453; www.pablobicyclerentals.com; 415 L St; per 3/24hr $20/54; ⊙8am-8pm) Bicycles, including tandems, kids' trailers and hybrids.

Hiking

Though there are dozens of trails in town, outdoors enthusiasts head to 773-sq-mile Chugach State Park for the mother lode. You can access an array of trails from the Glen Alps and Prospect Heights entrances; parking at each is $5.

McHugh Lake Trail HIKING
This 13-mile trail originates at McHugh Creek Picnic Area, 15 miles south of Anchorage at Mile 111.8 of the Seward Hwy. The route follows the McHugh Creek valley and in 7 miles reaches Rabbit and McHugh Lakes, two beautiful alpine pools reflecting the 5000ft Suicide Peaks.

A forest fire in 2016 burned much of the forest along this trail, but you can see signs of regrowth, including carpets of wildflowers beneath the blackened trees. The first 3 miles feature some good climbs, and the round-trip trek makes for a long day. It's better to haul in a tent and spend the afternoon exploring the open tundra country and nearby ridges.

Williwaw Lakes Trail HIKING
This relatively flat 13-mile hike begins at Glen Alps and leads to a handful of alpine lakes at the base of stunning Mt Williwaw. The trail makes a pleasant overnight hike and many consider it the most scenic outing in the Hillside area of Chugach State Park.

Walk half a mile to the Powerline Pass Trail and turn right, continuing 300yd to the Middle Fork Loop Trail. Follow it across the south fork of Campbell Creek, then north for 1.5 miles to the middle fork of the creek. At the junction, make a right on Williwaw Lakes Trail.

Rendezvous Peak Route HIKING
A 4-mile trek to the top of this 4050ft peak from Alpenglow Ski Area at Arctic Valley. From the parking lot, a short trail leads along the right-hand side of the stream up the valley to the northwest. It ends at a pass where a short ascent to Rendezvous Peak is easily seen and climbed.

This climb rewards hikers with incredible views of Denali, Cook Inlet and the city far

THE MOST DIVERSE NEIGHBORHOOD IN THE US

New York, San Francisco...Anchorage? With its lack of a port, relatively short history and somewhat inconvenient location, Anchorage does not at first glance appear to be the type of place that caters to a diverse population. But over 90 languages are spoken in the city's schools and, in 2010, Anchorage's Mountain View neighborhood was found to be the most diverse census tract in the US. After Native Alaskans, Asians/Pacific Islanders make up the bulk of the neighborhood's diversity.

The northeast Mountain View neighborhood is not necessarily set up for tourists, but it's worth a visit to sample one of the many restaurants that reflect its diversity. Cycle the Ship Creek Bike Trail to its end in Mountain View, and wander along Mountain View Dr and its ethnic grocery stores and small restaurants until you find a place that sounds appetizing.

Anchorage

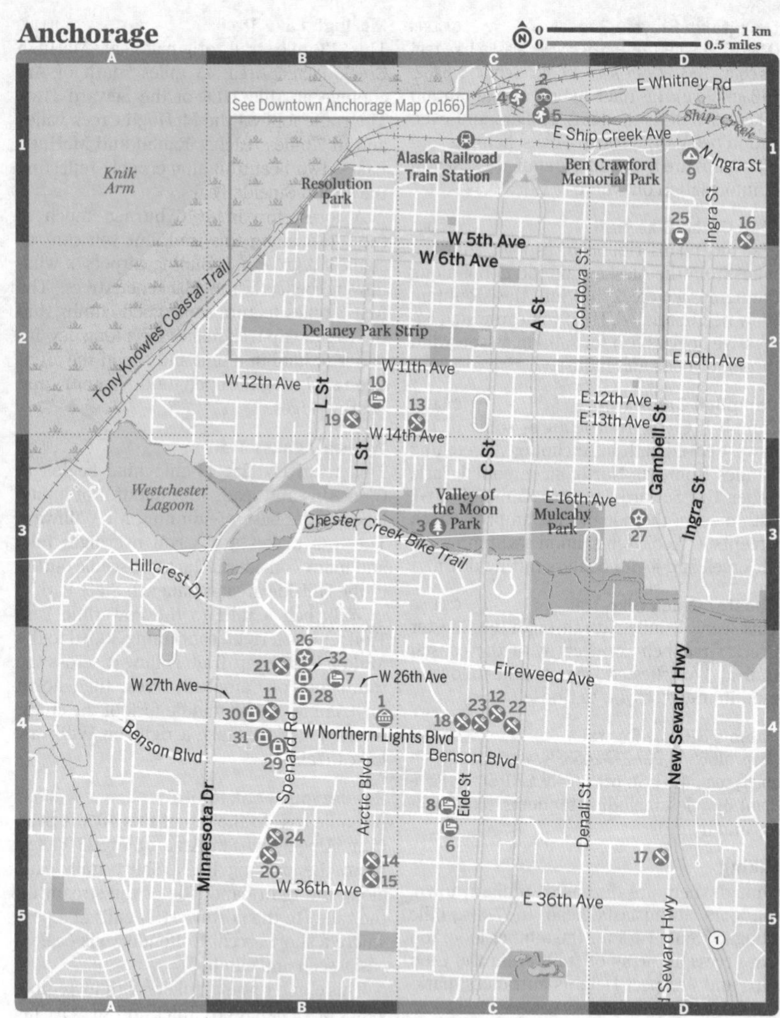

below. From Glenn Hwy, exit onto Arctic Valley Rd (Fort Richardson) and follow signs to Arctic Valley; a 7-mile gravel road leads to the Alpenglow Ski Area parking lot. Parking costs $5.

Ramp HIKING

The 14-mile round-trip hike starts at Glen Alps and takes you past alpine summits and through tranquil tundra. Hike half a mile to the Powerline Pass Trail. Turn right and follow the power line 2 miles, turn left and head downhill across the south fork of Campbell Creek.

Continue to a valley on the other side. Hike up the alpine valley to Ship Lake Pass, which lies between the 5240ft Ramp and the 4660ft Wedge. You can also take a mountain bike along the Powerline Pass Trail until it intersects with Campbell Creek.

Wolverine Peak Trail HIKING

(Map p158) This strenuous but rewarding 9.5-mile round-trip ascends the 4455ft triangular peak, visible from Anchorage. The trail begins at **Prospect Heights Trailhead** (Map p158), on an old homesteader road that crosses the south fork of Campbell Creek.

Anchorage

Head east; the road becomes a footpath that ascends above the treeline and eventually fades out. From there, it's 3 miles to Wolverine Peak.

From Seward Hwy, go 4 miles east on O'Malley Rd, turn left on Hillside Dr and follow signs to Prospect Heights.

Anchorage Lightspeed Planet Walk WALKING

(Map p166) **FREE** A massive sun sits at the corner of 5th Ave and G St, marking the start of this built-to-scale model of the solar system that stretches along the Coastal Trail. There are colorful interpretive displays for each planet; the first four planets can be reached within a few blocks of the sun but Pluto is out in Kincaid Park (p159).

The scale is set so that walking pace mimics the speed of light, but it'll take you all day to reach marble-sized Pluto at that pace. Travel faster than the speed of light by renting a mountain bike.

Tours

Bicycle Tours

Alaska Trail Guides CYCLING

(907-317-5707; www.alaskatrailguides.com; half-day $80-125, full day $180-200) Alaska's singletrack and winter trails can be intimidating for an outsider; enter Alaska Trail Guides. This operator will set you up with all the gear you need (think hand warmers and headlamps to go along with your fat bike in winter). More leisurely paved-trail tours are also on offer, including a Bike & Brew ride ending at a brewery.

Custom tours and tours to Girdwood (transport included) are also available.

Arctic Bicycle Club BICYCLE

(907-566-0177; www.arcticbike.org) Alaska's largest bicycle club. It sponsors a wide variety of road- and mountain-bike tours during the summer. Its website includes a list of Alaska cycle shops.

City Tours

Anchorage City Trolley Tours BUS

(Map p166; 907-775-5603; www.alaskatrolley.com; 546 W 4th Ave; adult/child $20/10; tours 9am-8:15pm) One-hour rides in a bright-red trolley past Lake Hood, Earthquake Park and Cook Inlet, among other sights. Tours depart on the hour (adult/child $20/10).

Gray Line BUS

(Map p166; 888-425-1737; www.graylineofalaska.com; Hilton Anchorage, 500 W 3rd Ave) Offers a handful of excursions to Anchorage surrounds by bus, rail and plane. The two-hour

DON'T MISS

GHOSTLY TOURS

In Anchorage you can sign up for a city tour, a tour on a trolley or a walking tour with a guide dressed (somewhat) like Captain Cook. Or you can be really brave and join a **ghost tour** (Map p166; ☎907-274-4678; www.ghosttoursofanchorage.com; per person $15; ⏰7:30pm Tue-Sun). Oooooh! Now that's scary.

These tours are a hit with out-of-towners, who can't seem to get enough grizzly Alaskan tales of murder and mayhem.

Anchorage Flightseeing Safari ($116) whisks you high above the city on a floatplane from Lake Hood to Turnagain Arm and the Chugach Mountains.

Flightseeing Tours

They're costly and never as long as you wish, but flightseeing tours are a stunning way to spend an hour or two. If you've got the cash, these tours provide an eagle's eye view of the wilderness and mountains, imparting a sense of scale that's difficult to appreciate from the ground. Regal Air and Rust's Flying Service are two long-standing companies with good tours on offer.

Rust's Flying Service SCENIC FLIGHTS
(Map p158; ☎907-243-1595; www.flyrusts.com; 4525 Enstrom Circle) Offers a three-hour Denali flight that includes flying the length of the magnificent Ruth Glacier ($425), a Denali glacier landing ($495) and a three-hour Prince William Sound tour ($365 to $395). Also offers bear-watching and fly-in fishing. All flights have a 3% transportation fee.

Regal Air SCENIC FLIGHTS
(Map p158; ☎907-243-8535; www.regal-air.com; 4506 Lakeshore Dr) Flying out of Lake Hood, Regal Air's three-hour Denali tour is $425, while a 1½-hour tour of Knik Glacier is $265. There are several more stunning tours on offer.

Day Tours

Have a leftover day? Go on an adventure. There are few places in Alaska that somebody in Anchorage isn't willing to whisk you off to in a day.

★Alaska Railroad RAIL
(Map p166; ☎907-265-2494; www.akrr.com; 411 W 1st Ave) Has many one-day tours from Anchorage that begin with a train ride. Its nine-hour Spencer Glacier Float Tour (per person $242) trundles to Spencer Lake and includes a gentle raft trip among icebergs. The Glacier Quest Cruise ($223) rumbles to Whittier and includes a four-hour boat cruise in Prince William Sound; watch glaciers calve while feasting on king crab cakes.

Alaska Photo Trek PHOTOGRAPHY
(Map p166; ☎907-350-0251; www.alaskaphototreks.com; 531 W 4th Ave) Unleash your wildlife paparazzo with year-round tours that cater specifically to shutter snappers. Led by professional photographers, tours range from the 2½-hour Anchorage PhotoWalk ($50) to a one-day brown bear flightseeing tour ($1504), to a glacier helicopter tour ($1990). Optimum light and wildlife-sighting probability are taken into account. The twilight photo tour is especially nice in Alaska's long evenings.

Big Swig Tours FOOD & DRINK
(☎907-268-0872; www.bigswigtours.com) Anchorage has nearly a dozen breweries, and this is one way to see several of them. There are three tours on offer: Anchorage Brews ($99), Anchorage Bike and Brew ($199) and Hops on the Rails ($299). The former two take you around the city for tastings and local insight while the latter sends you on an excursion with the railroad.

Phillips Cruises & Tours BOATING
(Map p166; ☎907-276-8023; www.phillipscruises.com; 519 W 4th Ave) Takes you by bus to Whittier and then on a boat past 26 glaciers in Prince William Sound. The five-hour cruise (adult/child $179/119) is offered daily and includes a hot lunch. Bus service from Anchorage tacks on a couple of hours on either side and costs an extra $60/30, but it's worth it if you don't have your own transport.

Also offers an excellent rail-and-cruise combo that combines a trip along Turnagain Arm on the Alaska Railroad with a glacier cruise.

Alaska's Finest Tours & Cruises BUS
(☎907-764-2067; www.akfinest.com) Offers a six-hour tour of Turnagain Arm that includes a boat cruise to the face of Portage Glacier and the Alaska Wildlife Conservation Center ($199). Don't bother with the Best of Anchorage tour, which takes you to some of the kitschiest sites in the city.

Festivals & Events

Anchorage Fur Rendezvous CULTURAL
(www.furrondy.net; late Feb & early Mar) FREE The place to get fresh-trapped furs is still the 'Rondy,' but most folks prefer to sculpt ice, ride the Ferris wheel in freezing temperatures, or watch the 'Running of the Reindeer.' When Rondy ends, the famed 1049-mile Iditarod Trail sled-dog race (p187) to Nome begins. Better stay another week.

Spenard Jazz Fest MUSIC
(www.spenardjazzfest.org; early Jun) For three days cool, trendy and local jazz musicians stage concerts and workshops throughout Anchorage. One event includes a hike up to the top of Flattop (p153), where a live band plays on the summit.

Sleeping

Several hostels in town help bring the cost of sleeping down, but Anchorage is expensive. Note that most of the hostels rent to long-term tenants in the off-season and aren't always available for travelers.

Chugach State Park has several public campgrounds, but none are close to town.

Tack on the city's 12% sales-and-bed tax to the prices given here.

Downtown Anchorage

Bent Prop Inn HOSTEL $
(Map p166; 907-276-3635; www.bentpropinn.com; 700 H St; dm/r $35/89; @) This excellent downtown hostel is friendly and relaxed, with eight private rooms that share bathrooms, and 14 dorm rooms with either four or eight bunks as well as lockers. Key-card access, a large kitchen and eating area, laundry, city-center location and super-friendly management make this hostel one of the best budget sleeps in Anchorage.

Ship Creek RV Park CAMPGROUND $
(Map p162; 907-277-0877; www.bestofalaskatravel.com; 150 N Ingra St; tent sites $19-29, RV sites $39-49) It's a bit of an odd location right next to the train tracks, but there's wi-fi throughout the campground and the price is right for a downtown spot.

★ **Copper Whale Inn** INN $$
(Map p166; 907-258-7999; www.copperwhale.com; cnr W 5th Ave & L St; r $199-240, ste $279; @) An ideal downtown location and a bright and elegant interior make this inn one of the best midrange places in Anchorage. The suite has a full kitchen. Two relaxing waterfall courtyards make it easy to consume that novel, while many rooms and the breakfast lounge give way to views of Cook Inlet. Are those beluga whales out there?

Wildflower Inn B&B $$
(Map p162; 907-274-1239; www.alaska-wildflower-inn.com; 1239 I St; r $159-169;) Housed in a historic home, a duplex built in 1945 for Federal Aviation Administration (FAA) families, this B&B offers three large rooms, pleasant sitting areas and a full breakfast in the morning featuring treats such as caramelized French toast. For anybody who packed their walking shoes, the location is ideal, just three blocks south of Delaney Park.

Arctic Fox B&B $$
(Map p166; 907-274-1239; www.arcticfoxinn.com; 327 E 2nd Ct; r $125-169, ste $169-299) Built as a seven-unit apartment complex, this downtown B&B now has six rooms and five apartment-style suites, one with two bedrooms. All have been remodeled into sleek, modern digs. There are several decks with views of the port. It's one of Anchorage's best midrange deals.

Oscar Gill House B&B $$
(Map p166; 907-279-1344; www.oscargill.com; 1344 W 10th Ave; r $120-150; ; 7A) This historic clapboard home was built in 1913 in Knik by former Anchorage Mayor Oscar Gill and later moved to its midtown location. The quaint and friendly B&B offers three guest rooms (two that share a bathroom) and a fantastic breakfast that ranges from sourdough French toast to smoked-salmon quiche. There's parking.

City Garden B&B B&B $$
(Map p166; 907-276-8686; www.citygarden.biz; 1352 W 10th Ave; r $125-175; ; 7A) One of several B&Bs located on a two-block stretch of 10th Ave, this is an open, sunny, gay- and lesbian-friendly place with more cutting-edge art than antiques. The nicest of the three rooms has a private bathroom.

Anchorage Downtown Hotel BOUTIQUE HOTEL $$
(Map p166; 907-258-7669; www.theanchoragedowntownhotel.com; 826 K St; r $120-168;) With fun murals on the walls, this edge-of-downtown hotel is a pleasant place to stay. The 16 colorful and comfortable rooms feature private baths, coffeemakers and small refrigerators. The free parking is convenient.

Downtown Anchorage

Downtown Anchorage

Top Sights

1 Anchorage Museum E3

Sights

2 4th Avenue Market Place/Village of Ship Creek Center E2
3 Bear & Raven Adventure Theater D2
Captain Cook Monument .... (see 9)
4 Delaney Park C4
5 Fraternal Order of Alaska State Troopers Law Enforcement Museum E2
6 Frontierland Park D4
7 Imaginarium Discovery Center E3
8 Oscar Anderson House B2
9 Resolution Park B2
10 Rooftop E2

Activities, Courses & Tours

11 Alaska Photo Trek D2
12 Alaska Railroad D1
13 Anchorage City Trolley Tours D2
14 Anchorage Lightspeed Planet Walk D3
Downtown Bicycle Rental .... (see 2)
15 Ghost Tours of Anchorage B2
Gray Line .... (see 25)
16 Pablo's Bicycle Rental B2
17 Phillips Cruises & Tours D2
18 Tony Knowles Coastal Trail C1

Sleeping

19 Anchorage Downtown Hotel B4
20 Anchorage Grand Hotel D1
21 Arctic Fox F2
22 Bent Prop Inn C3
23 City Garden B&B A4
24 Copper Whale Inn B2
25 Hilton Anchorage D2
26 Historic Anchorage Hotel D2
27 Hotel Captain Cook C2
28 Oscar Gill House A4
29 Susitna Place A3
30 Voyager Inn C2

Eating

31 10th & M Seafoods B4
32 Brown Bag Sandwich Co D2
33 Club Paris D2
34 Ginger D2
35 Humpy's Great Alaskan Alehouse D3
36 Marx Bros Café D2
37 Orso C2
Snow City Café .... (see 15)

Drinking & Nightlife

38 49th State Brewing C2
39 Bernie's Bungalow Lounge D3
40 Bubbly Mermaid E2
Crow's Nest .... (see 27)
41 Crush C2
42 Glacier BrewHouse C2
43 Side Street Espresso C2
44 Williwaw D3

Entertainment

45 Alaska Center for the Performing Arts D3
Alaska Experience Theatre .... (see 2)
46 Cyrano's Theatre Company E2
47 Egan Civic Center D2
48 Mad Myrna's G3

Shopping

49 Anchorage Market & Festival E2
50 Oomingmak Musk Ox Producers Co-op C3
51 Ulu Factory E1

Hilton Anchorage HOTEL **$$**
(Map p166; ☎907-272-7411; www.hiltonanchorage.com; 500 W 3rd Ave; r $199; @☎≋) The Hilton has the best location of any of the luxury hotels, right in the heart of the downtown scene. Two restaurants, a fitness center with a pool, two 1000lb bears in the lobby, 606 rooms and lots of elegance. If you're going to pay this much, ask for a room with a view of Cook Inlet.

Anchorage Grand Hotel LUXURY HOTEL **$$**
(Map p166; ☎907-929-8888; www.anchoragegrand.com; 505 W 2nd Ave; r $199; @☎) This converted apartment building rests on a quiet street with 31 spacious suites that include full kitchens and separate living and bedroom areas. Many overlook Ship Creek and Cook Inlet, and its downtown location is convenient to everything.

Voyager Inn HOTEL **$$**
(Map p166; ☎907-277-9501; 501 K St; r $245; @☎) A 40-room hotel with a great location downtown. Each room comes with a kitchenette, and some have peek-a-boo inlet views. There's a junior suite ($255). Guests also have access to the fitness center at the Hotel Captain Cook across the street. There's an evening reception with complimentary drinks.

Susitna Place B&B **$$**
(Map p166; ☎907-274-3344; www.susitnaplace.com; 727 N St; r $115-145, ste $175-200; ☎) On the edge of downtown, this 4000-sq-ft home sits on a bluff overlooking Cook Inlet and Mt Susitna in the distance. Four rooms have

shared bathrooms while the Susitna suite comes with fireplace, whirlpool bath and private deck.

Historic Anchorage Hotel BOUTIQUE HOTEL $$$
(Map p166; 907-272-4533; www.anchoragehistorichotel.com; 330 E St; r/ste from $220/280;) This boutique hotel was established in 1916, only a year after the city was founded, though the current building is from 1936. It's luxurious, loaded with amenities ranging from an excellent continental breakfast (served in an atmospheric old saloon) to free newspapers, and has an ideal downtown location.

Hotel Captain Cook HOTEL $$$
(Map p166; 907-276-6000; www.captaincook.com; 939 W 5th Ave; s/d $295/315; @) The grand dame of Anchorage accommodations still has an air of an Alaskan aristocrat, right down to the finely dressed door staff. There are plenty of plush services and upscale shops: hot tubs, a fitness club, beauty salon, jewelry store and four restaurants, including the famed Crow's Nest bar on the top floor.

Midtown Anchorage & Spenard

Spenard Hostel HOSTEL $
(Map p158; 907-248-5036; www.alaskahostel.org; 2845 W 42nd Ave; tent sites/dm $22/33; @; 7, 36) Two blocks from Spenard Rd, this friendly and laid-back hostel has been an Anchorage mainstay for nearly 25 years. It has a laundry, no lockout and three kitchens. Campsites are in the yard and a little cramped. Also for rent: mountain bikes ($5 per hour) and store bags ($2/5 per day/week). Consider booking ahead in July and August.

Bent Prop Inn Midtown HOSTEL $
(Map p162; 907-222-5220; www.bentpropinn.com; 3104 Eide St; dm $30-35;) The micro-dorms here are the best deal in town: in converted one-bedroom apartments, these come with four beds, a private kitchen and a living room – it's like dorms meet the suite life. Regular dorms are co-ed and have six beds. There are two kitchens, coin-operated laundry and big-screen TV. The one private apartment goes for $149.

Base Camp Anchorage Hostel HOSTEL $
(Map p162; 907-274-1252; www.basecampanchorage.com; 1037 W 26th Ave; dm/r $32/82; @; 3, 7) Conveniently located in the thick of midtown action, this great little hostel has a coin-operated laundry, a kitchen, lockers, luggage storage and bicycle rental ($15 per day). The large dorm rooms (including female-only) have two bunk beds, so you're never crowded. Outside you'll find a tipi, garden, sauna and, often, live music. Buses stop on Spenard Rd, a block away.

Arctic Adventure Hostel HOSTEL $
(Map p162; 907-562-5700; www.arcticadventurehostel.com; 337 W 33rd Pl; dm/r $33/58;) The welcome isn't always the warmest, but in a city with so few budget options Arctic Adventure Hostel is a decent standby. The private rooms (with shared bathroom) are a screamin' deal for two people, and the kitchen is huge – a great place to cook a big spread.

Lakeshore Inn & Suites MOTEL $$
(Map p158; 907-248-3485; www.lakeshoremotorinn.com; 3009 Lakeshore Dr; s/d/ste $159/169/220;) This tidy motel's rooms are more spacious than the exterior would have you believe, with high ceilings and large windows. It offers a free courtesy shuttle to and from the airport as well as a pleasant breakfast area.

Lake Hood Inn B&B $$
(Map p158; 907-258-9321; www.lakehoodinn.com; 4702 Lake Spenard Dr; r $169-189;) This spotless upscale home, with four guest rooms, is adorned with airplane artifacts, from a Piper propeller that doubles as a ceiling fan to a row of seats from a Russian airline. Outside are decks where you can watch a parade of floatplanes lift off the lake. Headsets on the lakeside deck even let you listen to radio control.

Alex Hotel & Suites HOTEL $$
(Map p158; 907-243-3131; www.alexhotelalaska.com; 4615 Spenard Rd; r $249-265;) A bit of a quirky place close to the airport. Prices are based on vacancy and the rooms are a bit shabby, but there's an international clientele and a 24-hour airport shuttle. A gym was being constructed when we visited, so you can pump iron on your holiday. The staff is welcoming.

Long House Alaskan Hotel HOTEL $$
(Map p158; 907-243-2133; www.longhousehotel.com; 4335 Wisconsin St; s/d $139/155;) Near Spenard Rd, this log hotel has large, if simple, rooms that are well priced. It of-

fers guest laundry facilities, tile floors in the bathrooms, in-room fridges, microwaves, TV, coffee service and 24-hour shuttle to the airport. And to top it off, the staff are really friendly.

Puffin Inn MOTEL **$$**
(Map p158; 907-243-4044; www.puffininn.net; 4400 Spenard Rd; r $212-252;) Anchorage's best late-night-airport-arrival motel. It has four tiers of fine rooms, from 26 sardine-can economy rooms ($160) to full suites with hot tubs and hideaway kitchens, all accessible via free 24-hour airport shuttle.

Lakefront Anchorage Hotel HOTEL **$$$**
(Map p158; 907-243-2300; www.millennium hotels.com/usa/destinations/anchorage; 4800 Spenard Rd; r $239-340;) A large, 250-room resort with a woodsy lodge feel overlooking Lake Spenard. PETA members take note: there are stuffed animals, trophy mounts and large fish everywhere. All rooms are large with king or full beds. There's a decent pub with a great deck for imbibing on sunny evenings. Free shuttle to airport and downtown Anchorage.

Greater Anchorage

Golden Nugget RV Park CAMPGROUND **$**
(Map p158; 907-333-2012; www.goldennugget camperpark.com; 4100 DeBarr Rd; RV sites $43-50; ; 15) If you're pulling a trailer or driving an RV, this is Anchorage's largest commercial campground, with 215 sites in all. Everything you could possibly need is here: showers, laundry, souvenir shop, bus stop.

Centennial Park Campground CAMPGROUND **$**
(Map p158; 907-343-6986; 8300 Glenn Hwy; tent & RV sites $25; ; 3, 75) It's 5 miles from downtown but is pleasant, with 88 sites, wi-fi, good rates and 'the hottest showers in town.'

Eating

The Anchorage dining scene ranges from fast food and espresso stands to farm fresh and superhip. Even the fanciest restaurants are generally low-key, so you can enjoy your salmon in your sandals.

The bustling city also boasts a variety of international cuisines, from Polynesian to Mexican to Vietnamese. Best of all, Anchorage restaurants and bars are smoke-free.

Downtown Anchorage

★ **Snow City Café** CAFE **$**
(Map p166; 907-272-2489; www.snowcity cafe.com; 1034 W 4th Ave; breakfast $8-15, lunch $10-15; 6:30am-3pm Mon-Fri, to 4pm Sat & Sun;) Consistently voted best breakfast by *Anchorage Press* readers, this busy cafe serves healthy grub to a clientele that ranges from the tattooed to the up-and-coming. For breakfast, skip the usual eggs and toast and try a 'crabby' omelet or a sockeye smoked-salmon Benedict.

Fire Island Rustic Bakeshop BAKERY **$**
(Map p162; www.fireislandbread.com; 1343 G St; 7am-6pm Wed-Sun) Stop in at Anchorage's most beloved bakery for a sandwich or choose a loaf of artisan bread for a picnic. Just don't forget dessert, which ranges from warm-out-of-the-oven cookies to fruit tarts. There's a small neighborhood location at 2530 E 16th Ave.

Brown Bag Sandwich Co SANDWICHES **$**
(Map p166; www.akbrownbag.com; 535 W 3rd Ave; sandwiches $10; 10am-2:30am Mon-Thu, to 3am Fri, 11am-3am Sat) Delicious, funky and popular, Brown Bag has a diverse selection of creative and loaded sandwiches. Go hungry, leave full. At night the low-ceilinged 'bassment' becomes a casual cocktail bar, often with a DJ spinning.

New Sagaya City Market MARKET **$**
(Map p162; www.newsagaya.com; 900 W 13th Ave; 6am-9pm Mon-Sat, 8am-9pm Sun) Eclectic and upscale, this is a grocery store with lots of organic goodies, a great deli specializing in Asian fare, and seating indoors and outdoors. There's also a larger midtown branch at 3700 Old Seward Hwy.

10th & M Seafoods MARKET **$**
(Map p166; www.10thandmseafoods.com; 1020 M St; 8am-6pm Mon-Fri, from 9am Sat) This market sells the freshest seafood in a city that loves its seafood fresh. Staff will also butcher and ship your king salmon or 200lb halibut.

Lucky Wishbone AMERICAN **$**
(Map p162; 1033 E 5th Ave; burgers $6-15; 10am-10pm Mon-Thu, to 11pm Fri & Sat) Down-home, pan-fried chicken is the main draw at this busy diner. No frills, just deep-fried goodness, cheap and delicious burgers and massive milkshakes.

ANCHORAGE FOR CHILDREN

Anchorage is exceptionally kid-friendly – more than 40 city parks boast playscapes.

Frontierland Park (Map p166; 10th Ave & E St) Close to downtown, this park is a local favorite.

Valley of the Moon Park (Map p162; Arctic Blvd & W 17th St) Makes a delightful picnic spot next to Chester Creek.

Goose Lake (p160) A great place to swim on a hot summer day (yes, Alaska has those).

Rooftop (p157) An urban rooftop park with a synthetic skate rink, table tennis and basketball court.

Imaginarium Discovery Center (p156) Inside the Anchorage Museum, this award-winning center features creative, hands-on, Alaska-themed exhibits that include live marine animals in a touch tank, a simulated earthquake and a planetarium. Included with museum entrance fee.

Bear & Raven Adventure Theater (Map p166; www.bearsquare.net; 315 E St; per group $10; ⊙noon-10pm) This mini-amusement park is a cheesy but easy downtown break from shopping. It offers two 'special effects' movies (think snow falling from the ceiling), one about the Iditarod sled-dog race and one about bears (adult/child $15/13 for both). Virtual 'rides' (reeling in a salmon, for example) ought to satisfy the little ones.

H2Oasis (Map p158; www.h2oasiswaterpark.com; 1520 O'Malley Rd; adult/child $25/20; ⊙10am-8pm) Qualifying as surreal, Anchorage's original water park is a $7-million, three-level amusement zone with palm trees, water slides, a wave pool and the 505ft Master Blaster, one very wet roller coaster. Feel free to just watch from the grown-ups-only hot tubs.

Ginger FUSION $$

(Map p166; ☎907-929-3680; www.gingeralaska.com; 425 W 5th Ave; lunch $11-18, dinner $19-32; ⊙11:30am-2pm Mon-Fri, & 11am-2:30pm Sat & Sun, 5-10pm daily) Sleek and trendy, Ginger's menu is a fusion of Pacific Rim cuisine and classic Asian dishes. The end result is an artistic endeavor like banana and lemongrass soup or spicy tuna tower, served in surroundings that are elegant but still Alaska casual. The bar stocks fine wines and locally brewed beer, as well as a wide selection of sake.

Humpy's Great Alaskan Alehouse PUB FOOD $$

(Map p166; www.humpys.com; 610 W 6th Ave; mains $14-30; ⊙11am-2am Mon-Thu, to 2:30am Fri, 10am-2:30am Sat, to 2am Sun; 📶) A beloved Anchorage beer place, with almost 60 beers on tap. It also has ale-battered halibut, gourmet pizzas, outdoor tables and live music most nights. The kitchen usually closes at midnight on weeknights and 1am on Friday and Saturday.

Orso MEDITERRANEAN $$

(Map p166; ☎907-222-3232; www.orsoalaska.com; 737 W 5th Ave; dinner $16-30; ⊙5-10pm, bar to 11pm) The walls are a smoked-salmon color and the wooden floors are covered with Asian rugs, there's modern art all around and soft jazz floating into both dining levels and the bar. Mains are Mediterranean grill with an Alaskan twist, and the lamb shank served with creamy polenta has stayed on the menu from the day Orso opened.

Marx Bros Café MODERN AMERICAN $$$

(Map p166; ☎907-278-2133; www.marxcafe.com; 627 W 3rd Ave; dinner $38-46; ⊙5:30-10pm Tue-Sat) Old-school Anchorage fine dining with innovative cooking and a 500-bottle wine list are the reasons this 14-table restaurant (located in a historic home built in 1916) is so popular. The menu changes nightly, but the beloved halibut macadamia always stays put. In summer book your table a week in advance.

Club Paris STEAK $$$

(Map p166; ☎907-277-6332; www.clubparisrestaurant.com; 417 W 5th Ave; lunch $12-21, dinner $30-43; ⊙11am-midnight Mon-Sat, from 4pm Sun) This longtime restaurant – it survived the 1964 earthquake – is old-school fine dining and serves some of the best steaks in Anchorage. If there's room on your credit card –

and in your stomach – try the 4in-thick filet mignon.

Midtown Anchorage & Spenard

Middle Way Cafe CAFE $
(Map p162; www.middlewaycafe.com; 1200 W Northern Lights Blvd, Suite G; lunch & brunch $8-15; 7am-6pm Mon-Fri, from 8am Sat & Sun;) This veggie-friendly cafe serves healthy breakfasts and organic salads, soups and sandwiches in a cozy, artsy atmosphere. Many vegan and gluten-free options, as well as espresso and smoothies.

Yak & Yeti TIBETAN $
(Map p162; www.yakandyetialaska.com; 3301 Spenard Rd; mains $9-13; 11am-2:30pm Mon-Fri, 5-9pm Wed-Sat) Billing itself as 'Himalayan' cuisine, Yak & Yeti serves delicious Indian, Nepalese and Tibetan dishes, including *momos* (Tibetan dumplings), curries and spiced meats. No alcohol is served, but you can bring your own. The homemade chai is perfect on a rainy day. The owners also run a **cafe** (Map p162; 1360 W Northern Lights Blvd; mains $8-13; 10am-8pm Mon-Thu, to 9pm Fri & Sat, 11am-7pm Sun;) in the Northern Lights mall.

Fromagio's Artisan Cheese SANDWICHES $
(Map p162; www.fromagioscheese.com; 3555 Arctic Blvd; sandwiches $11; 11am-6pm Tue-Sat, noon-5pm Sun) A cheesemonger that serves gourmet sandwiches. Stop in for lunch, sample some exotic cheeses and then grab some for a picnic while on your hike.

Pho Lena ASIAN $
(Map p162; www.pholena.com; 3311 Spenard Rd; mains $9-16; 11am-10pm Mon-Fri, from noon Sat, from 3pm Sun) An Anchorage favorite, Pho Lena serves up more than the namesake soup: Thai, Lao and other Vietnamese specialties are all available in the tiny Spenard restaurant. There are a few other branches around the city.

Charlie's Bakery CHINESE $
(Map p162; 2729 C St; mains $10-15; 11am-8:30pm Mon-Sat) The most authentic Chinese food you'll find in Anchorage, sold next to French baguettes and wedding cakes. The dim sum is particularly loved, and there are extra specials on Saturdays.

Ray's Place VIETNAMESE $
(Map p162; www.raysplaceak.com; 32412 Spenard Rd; mains $8-15; 10am-3pm & 5-9pm Mon-Fri;) This Vietnamese restaurant does great cold noodle salads, stir-fries and huge bowls of pho, and stocks Vietnamese beer.

Taco King MEXICAN $
(Map p162; www.tacokingak.com; 113 W Northern Lights Blvd; dinner $7-11; 10am-11pm Mon-Sat, to 10pm Sun) Anchorage's beloved taco shop is so good and so affordable it now has six more locations, including one on Spenard near the airport. The original is still the busiest.

Spenard Food Truck Festival FAST FOOD $
(Map p162; cnr W 26th Ave & Spenard Rd; 11am-2pm Thu) If you're in town on Thursday, check out the Food Truck Festival in Spenard, in Chilkoot Charlie's (p173) parking lot. It's an eclectic mix of Asian cuisine, sandwiches, ice cream and Alaskan seafood as well as live music.

New Central Market MARKET $
(Map p162; www.newcentralmarket.com; 555 W Northern Lights Blvd; 9am-8pm) A touch of Asia in the heart of Anchorage.

★ **Bear Tooth Grill** TEX-MEX $$
(Map p162; www.beartoothgrill.net; 1230 W 27th St; burgers $13-17, mains $11-22; 11am-11:30pm Mon-Fri, 9:30am-11:30pm Sat & Sun) A popular hangout with an adjacent theater. It serves excellent burgers and Alaska seafood as well as Mexican and Asian fusion dishes. The microbrews are fresh and the cocktails are the best in town – if you're up for a splurge, lash out on *el Cielo* (the sky) margarita. Has an excellent Mexican-leaning brunch menu (with matching cocktails).

Rustic Goat BISTRO $$
(Map p158; 907-334-8100; www.rusticgoatak.com; 2800 Turnagain St; pizzas $14-16, mains $18-32; 6am-10pm Mon-Thu, to 11pm Fri, 7am-11pm Sat, to 10pm Sun) This sweet little bistro is in the suburban Turnagain neighborhood, but it feels like a city loft. Old-growth timbers support two stories of windows that look out to the Chugach Mountains. The assorted menu includes wood-fired pizzas, steaks and salads. In the morning it's a casual coffee shop.

Moose's Tooth Brewpub PIZZA $$
(Map p162; www.moosestooth.net; 3300 Old Seward Hwy; large pizzas $16-25; 10:30am-midnight Mon-Fri, from 11am Sat & Sun;) An Anchorage institution serving two-dozen custom-brewed beers, including monthly specials. This is *the* place to refuel after climbing

Flattop, with nearly 40 gourmet pizzas on the menu, including plenty of veggie pies.

VIP Restaurant KOREAN $$
(Map p162; 555 W Northern Lights Blvd; barbecue $17-22; ⏲11am-9:30pm Mon-Sat) Of the many Korean restaurants in Anchorage, VIP is the most popular. Try the barbecue, which comes with your choice of sizzling tender meat and about 20 side dishes, and then follow all that spice with an imported beer.

Turkish Delight TURKISH $$
(Map p158; ☎907-258-3434; 2210 E Northern Lights Blvd; mains $15-28; ⏲11am-9pm Tue-Sat) Dark and atmospheric, this strip-mall surprise serves up Mediterranean favorites such as delicious baba gahnoush, kebabs and fresh, warm pita bread. Be sure to save room for baklava and Turkish coffee.

Jen's Restaurant EUROPEAN $$$
(Map p162; ☎907-561-5367; www.jensrestaurant.com; 701 W 36th Ave; lunch $13-26, dinner $22-45; ⏲11:30am-2pm Mon-Fri, 6-10pm Tue-Sat) This fine restaurant in midtown has dazzled the critics with innovative, Scandinavian-accented cuisine emphasizing fresh ingredients and elaborate presentation. The dining room features a constantly changing exhibition of Alaskan artists while the wine bar stays open to 11pm with music.

Greater Anchorage

PHOnatik VIETNAMESE $
(Map p158; 901 E Dimond Blvd; mains $8-12; ⏲11am-11pm Mon-Sat, noon-8pm Sun) This busy southside joint serves up Alaska-size bowls of excellent pho, great for warming up after a chilly Hillside hike. Options range from vegetarian to oxtail pho, spring rolls and banh mi.

West Berlin GERMAN $
(Map p158; 4133 Mountain View Dr; mains $10-14; ⏲11am-3pm & 5-9pm Mon-Sat, noon-8pm Sun) Fresh-baked pretzel buns, homemade schnitzel and a long list of imported German beers make this Mountain View spot a worthy visit.

Hula Hands HAWAIIAN $
(Map p158; 4630 Mountain View Dr; mains $10-16; ⏲11am-9pm Mon-Fri, from noon Sat, noon-8pm Sun) Represents Anchorage's large Polynesian population with *poke* (cubed raw fish mixed with shoyu, sesame oil salt, chili pepper), taro-leaf wraps and pulled pork. The shaved ice is a citywide favorite.

Arctic Roadrunner BURGERS $
(Map p158; 5300 Old Seward Hwy; burgers $5-8; ⏲10:30am-9pm Mon-Sat) Since 1964 this place has been turning out beefy burgers and great onion pieces and rings. If your timing is right, you can eat outdoors while watching salmon spawn up Campbell Creek.

South Restaurant & Coffee House BISTRO $$
(Map p158; ☎907-770-9200; www.southak.com; 11124 Old Seward Hwy; breakfast & lunch $8-13, dinner $18-39; ⏲7am-10pm Mon-Thu, to 11pm Fri & Sat, 8am-10pm Sun; 📶) South Restaurant has a drinks menu emphasizing creative gin cocktails. Food options run from small plates and salads to butter burgers and Bristol Bay salmon. The attached coffee shop has great baked goods and is a sunny spot to sip a cuppa. Hours vary between the two establishments.

Drinking & Nightlife

With its young and lively population, Anchorage has a lot to do after the midnight sun finally sets. The city has nearly a dozen breweries, a distillery and a micro-cidery – more than enough for everyone. The free *Anchorage Press* has events listings.

Bubbly Mermaid WINE BAR
(Map p166; 417 D St; ⏲11am-late Mon-Fri, from 10am Sat & Sun) Perch like a mermaid (or merman) at the prow of the boat that the Bubbly Mermaid uses for a bar as you pour champagne and local oysters down your throat. It's small, intimate and unique. Bubbly is $8 to $12; oysters $3 a pop.

Midnight Sun Brewing Company BREWERY
(Map p158; www.midnightsunbrewing.com; 8111 Dimond Hook Dr; ⏲11am-8pm) One of a growing handful of brewpubs in Anchorage, Midnight Sun sits in a loft in an industrial/suburban neighborhood on the south side of the city. Besides its excellent brews, it has a tasty menu that includes creative bruschetta and Taco Tuesdays. Refuel on the sunny little deck after a hike or mountain-bike ride in the Chugach.

Crush WINE BAR
(Map p166; ☎907-865-9198; www.crushak.com; 328 G St; ⏲11am-10pm Mon-Thu, to 11pm Fri & Sat) This swanky wine bar serves 'bistro bites,' a menu of appetizers, salads and small plates, as well as more than 40 wines by the glass. Nibble, swirl and sip.

Bernie's Bungalow Lounge LOUNGE
(Map p166; www.bernieslounge.com; 626 D St; ⏲11am-1am Mon-Fri, 2pm-2:30am Sat & Sun) Pretty people, pretty drinks: this is the place to see and be seen. Its outdoor patio, complete with a water-spewing serpent, is the best in Anchorage, and on summer weekends it rocks late into the night with DJs up in the VIP room.

Crow's Nest LOUNGE
(Map p166; 939 W 5th Ave; ⏲5pm-midnight Mon-Sat) There's upscale dining at the Crow's Nest, at the top of the Hotel Captain Cook, but most come for a drink made by the award-winning bartenders and the million-dollar view of Cook Inlet.

Williwaw BAR
(Map p166; www.williwawsocial.com; 609 F St; ⏲11am-late) It almost feels like you're in the big city when you spend a sunny evening at the rooftop bar surrounded by Anchorage's downtown buildings. A hidden speakeasy mixes upscale drinks (entry requires a password – note the payphone in the lobby), and there are live musical acts every weekend on the 1st floor. By day, a coffee shop serves up espressos.

Glacier BrewHouse BREWERY
(Map p166; ☎907-274 2739; http://glacierbrewhouse.com; 737 W 5th Ave; lunch $13-19, dinner $18-32; ⏲11am-10pm Mon-Fri, to 11pm Sat & Sun) Grab a table overlooking the three giant stainless-steel brewing tanks and enjoy wood-fired pizzas and rotisserie-grilled ribs and chops with a pint of oatmeal stout. But be prepared to wait for that table, as this place is popular.

Raven GAY & LESBIAN
(Map p162; 708 E 4th Ave; ⏲1:30pm-2am) One of a couple of gay and lesbian bars in Anchorage.

Side Street Espresso COFFEE
(Map p166; 412 G St; light fare $4-7; ⏲7am-3pm Mon-Sat; 📶) A long-standing shop that serves espresso, bagels and muffins between its art-covered walls.

49th State Brewing BREWERY
(Map p166; www.49statebrewing.com; 717 W 3rd Ave; lunch $15-19, dinner $13-30; ⏲11am-1am) The two-level rooftop deck overlooks Cook Inlet, Sleeping Lady, and Denali in the distance, and it's the place to throw back a cold one on a sunny evening. Inside has a sports-bar feel, but the menu is a bit more creative with specialties such as a yak quesadilla and crab-stuffed jalapeños. There's often live music in the adjacent theater.

LGBTIQ+ ANCHORAGE

The weeklong Pridefest (mid-June) is a gay-pride celebration that includes a Queer Film Festival, Drag Queen Bingo, a parade through downtown and a party at Delaney Park.

It's not West Hollywood, but Anchorage does have a handful of gay- and lesbian-friendly bars and lodgings, and several straight bars are regarded as gay- and lesbian-friendly: try Mad Myrna's (p176), Raven, Bernie's Bungalow Lounge and the Moose's Tooth Brewpub.

☆ Entertainment

Live Music

Chilkoot Charlie's LIVE MUSIC
(Map p162; www.koots.com; 2435 Spenard Rd; ⏲11:45am-2:30am Mon-Thu, 10:30am-3am Fri & Sat, to 2:30am Sun) More than just Anchorage's favorite meat market, 'Koots,' as the locals call it, is a landmark. The sprawling, wooden edifice has 10 bars, four dance floors and a sawdust-strewn floor. Many live acts perform here and there's at least one fun thing happening every night of the week.

Cinemas

Bear Tooth Theatrepub CINEMA
(Map p162; ☎907-276-4200; www.beartooththeatre.net; 1230 W 27th Ave) Cruise into this very cool venue (check out the mural on the lobby ceiling) where you can enjoy great microbrews, wine and dinner while watching first-run movies as well as foreign and independent films ($4). It often hosts live music and other special events.

Theater & Performing Arts

★Cyrano's Theatre Company THEATER
(Map p166; ☎907-274-2599; www.cyranos.org; 413 D St) This small off-center playhouse is the best live theater in town, staging everything from *Hamlet* to *Archy and Mehitabel* (comic cockroach and a cat characters), Mel Brooks' jazz musical based on the poetry of Don Marquis and

1

4

JOHN T. ROBERTS/SHUTTERSTOCK ©

3

JON MANJEOT/SHUTTERSTOCK ©

EQROY/SHUTTERSTOCK ©

AKPHOTOC/SHUTTERSTOCK ©

1. Anchorage Museum (p156)
This world-class museum, with sculptures by Rachelle Dowdy outside, houses the largest Alaska Native collection in the state.

2. Anchorage (p156)
The Big Apple of the north is unlike any other city – a city where bears wander footpaths, moose munch on gardens and locals pull salmon from streams near office buildings.

3. Eklutna Lake (p153)
The gorgeous 7-mile long Eklutna Lake offers lots of recreational opportunities, including kayaking, biking and hiking.

4. Flattop Mountain Trail (p153)
One of the most popular trails near Anchorage, particularly with families, the Flattop Mountain trail leads to a summit with views of Anchorage and, on a clear day, Denali.

an ever-changing lineup of original shows. Shows typically run Thursday to Sunday.

Mad Myrna's DANCE

(Map p166; 907-276-9762; 530 E 5th Ave; 4pm-2:30am) A fun, cruisy bar with two dances floors, Drag Diva shows, a cabaret, and dance music most nights after 9pm.

Alaska Center for the Performing Arts PERFORMING ARTS

(Map p166; tickets 907-263-2787; www.myalaskacenter.com; 621 W 6th Ave) This center impresses tourists with the 40-minute film *Aurora: Alaska's Great Northern Lights* (adult/child $13/7), screened on the hour from 9am to 9pm during summer in its Sydney Laurence Theatre.

It's also home to the **Anchorage Opera** (907-279-2557; www.anchorageopera.org), **Anchorage Symphony Orchestra** (907-274-8668; www.anchoragesymphony.org), **Anchorage Concert Association** (907-272-1471; www.anchorageconcerts.org) and **Alaska Dance Theatre** (907-277-9591; www.alaskadancetheatre.org).

Egan Civic Center CONCERT VENUE

(Map p166; 907-263-2800; www.anchorageconventioncenters.com; 555 W 5th Ave) Try this place for top-drawer musical groups, trade shows and other big events.

Alaska Experience Theatre CINEMA

(Map p166; 907-272-9076; www.alaskaexperiencetheatre.com; 333 W 4th Ave; movies $8-10; 9am-4pm) More a tourist trap than a movie house, with IMAX-style nature films and a 15-minute theatrical simulation of the 1964 Good Friday Earthquake.

Sullivan Arena CONCERT VENUE

(Map p162; 907-279-0618; www.sullivanarena.com; 1600 Gambell St) The 'Sully' hosts large musical acts and sporting events.

Sports

Anchorage Bucs BASEBALL

(907-561-2827; www.anchoragebucs.com; general admission $5) This semipro team of the Alaska Baseball League plays at Mulcahy Ball Park, where living legend Mark McGuire once slammed a few homers.

Also taking the same field is arch-rival **Anchorage Glacier Pilots** (907-274-3627; www.glacierpilots.com; general admission $5).

Shopping

★ **Dos Manos** ARTS & CRAFTS

(Map p162; 1317 W Northern Lights Blvd; 11am-6pm Mon-Sat, to 5pm Sun) Billing itself as a 'funktional' art gallery, Dos Manos sells locally crafted art and jewelry, and very cool Alaska-themed T-shirts. A recent expansion allows room for large works of fine art. A great place to get a locally made souvenir.

Spenard Farmers Market MARKET

(Map p162; www.spenardfarmersmarket.org; cnr W 26th Ave & Spenard Rd; 9am-2pm Sat) One of a handful of farmers markets around town, this one features handmade arts and crafts, plus locally grown produce and Alaska seafood. A festive vibe with live music on Saturday mornings in Chilkoot Charlie's parking lot.

REI SPORTS & OUTDOORS

(Map p162; 1200 W Northern Lights Blvd; 10am-9pm Mon-Fri, 9am-7pm Sat, 10am-7pm Sun) Anchorage's largest outdoor store has everything you might ever need, from wool socks to backpacks to kayaks to camp chairs. Besides being able to repair your camp stove or bicycle tire, it will also rent canoes, bear containers, tents and bicycles.

Oomingmak Musk Ox Producers Co-op CLOTHING

(Map p166; www.qiviut.com; 604 H St; 8am-8pm Mon-Fri, 10am-6pm Sat & Sun) Handles a variety of very soft, very warm and very expensive garments made of arctic musk-ox wool, hand-knitted in Inupiaq villages.

Anchorage Market & Festival ARTS & CRAFTS

(Map p166; www.anchoragemarkets.com; cnr W 3rd Ave & E St; 10am-6pm Sat, to 5pm Sun;) This was called the 'Saturday Market' until it became so popular it opened on Sundays. It's an open market with live music and more than 300 booths stocked with hot food, Mat-Su Valley veggies, and souvenirs ranging from birch steins to birch syrup and T-shirts that proclaim your love of Alaska.

ANC Auxiliary Craft Shop ARTS & CRAFTS

(Map p158; 4315 Diplomacy Dr; 10am-2pm Mon-Fri, from 11am 1st & 3rd Sat of month) Located on the 1st floor of the Alaska Native Medical Center, it has some of the finest Alaska Native arts and crafts available to the public. But it has limited hours and does not accept credit cards.

Title Wave Books BOOKS
(Map p162; www.wavebooks.com; 1360 W Northern Lights Blvd; 10am-8pm Mon-Sat, 11am-7pm Sun;) A fabulous bookstore, with 25,000 sq ft of used books, including many on Alaska.

Alaska Mountaineering & Hiking SPORTS & OUTDOORS
(AMH; Map p162; www.alaskamountaineering.com; 2633 Spenard Rd; 9am-7pm Mon-Fri, to 6pm Sat, noon-5pm Sun) Staffed by experts and stocked with high-end gear, AMH is the place for serious adventurers.

Dankorage POT SHOP
(Map p162; 907-279-3265; www.dankorage.com; 2812 Spenard Rd; 10am-10pm Mon-Sat, noon-6pm Sun) Weed shops have sprouted across Anchorage since the state legalized recreational marijuana in 2014. One of more than half-a-dozen weed shops in Anchorage, Dankorage bills itself as 'pretty dope'. You can buy joints, edibles and a selection of strains, and all the things you need to smoke out of. You'll need ID to enter.

Alaska Native Heritage Center ARTS & CRAFTS
(Map p158; www.alaskanative.net; 8800 Heritage Center Dr; 9am-5pm) A gift shop stocking jewelry, carvings and other 'artifacts'. There are booths where craftspeople make fresh knickknacks while you watch.

Alaska Wild Berry Park GIFTS & SOUVENIRS
(Map p158; www.alaskawildberryproducts.com; 5525 Juneau St; 10am-9pm) FREE If the Flattop Mountain hike is overly ambitious for your kids, head to this giant jam and gift shop. It's definitely a tourist trap, but who can resist a 20ft chocolate waterfall? You can sample and purchase jams, jellies and chocolates made in Alaska.

Ulu Factory ARTS & CRAFTS
(Map p166; www.theulufactory.com; 211 W Ship Creek Ave; 9am-6pm Mon-Fri, from 10am Sat & Sun) The *ulu* (oo-loo) is to Alaska what the rubber alligator is to Florida: everybody sells them. Still, it's a tool many Alaskans actually use, and this shop is interesting. Demonstrations teach you how to use the cutting tool.

Information

INTERNET ACCESS

Internet access and wi-fi are widely available all over Anchorage at hotels, restaurants, bars and even gift shops.

ZJ Loussac Public Library (907-343-2975; 3600 Denali St; 10am-9pm Mon-Thu, to 6pm Fri & Sat, 1-5pm Sun; 2, 36, 60) This large library has free internet terminals (one hour per day) as well as wi-fi.

MEDIA

Tourist freebies are available everywhere: the *Official Anchorage Visitors Guide* and *Anchorage Daily News' Alaska Visitor's Guide* are all packed with useful information.

In 2014 the independent, online-only news site Alaska Dispatch bought the long-running, award-winning *Anchorage Daily News* and named the combined outlet Alaska Dispatch News (www.alaskadispatch.com).

MEDICAL SERVICES

Alaska Regional Hospital (907-276-1131; www.alaskaregional.com; 2801 DeBarr Rd; 24hr; 13, 15) Near Merrill Field.

Anchorage Planned Parenthood Clinic (800-769-0045; 4001 Lake Otis Pkwy) Offers contraceptives, medical advice and services.

First Care Medical Center (907-248-1122; 3710 Woodland Dr, Suite 1100; 7am-11pm; 7) Walk-in clinic just off Spenard Rd in midtown.

Providence Alaska Medical Center (907-562-2211; http://alaska.providence.org/; 3200 Providence Dr; 24hr; 1, 3, 13, 36, 45, 102) The largest medical center in the state.

MONEY

Key Bank (907-257-5502; 601 W 5th Ave; 9am-5pm Mon-Fri) Downtown.

Wells Fargo (907-265-2805; 301 W Northern Lights Blvd; 10am-6pm Mon-Sat) The main bank is in midtown.

POST

Post office (Map p166; 320 W 5th Ave; 10am-2pm & 3-6pm Mon-Fri) This one's downtown in the 5th Avenue Mall, but there are nearly a dozen more in town.

TOURIST INFORMATION

Alaska Public Lands Information Center (Map p166; 907-644-3661; www.alaskacenters.gov; 605 W 4th Ave, Suite 105; 9am-5pm) In the Federal Building (you'll need photo ID). The center has handouts for hikers, mountain bikers, kayakers, fossil hunters and just about everyone else, on almost every wilderness area in the state. There are also excellent wildlife displays, free movies, fun dioramas, and ranger-led walks (11am and 3:15pm).

Anchorage Convention & Visitors Bureau (907-276-4118; www.anchorage.net) Has a useful website. Ring before your trip and ask to be posted a guide.

DON'T MISS

RIDING THE ALASKA RAILROAD

In a remote corner of the Alaskan wilderness, you stand alongside a railroad track when suddenly a small train appears. You wave a white flag in the air – actually yesterday's dirty T-shirt – and the engineer acknowledges you with a sound of the whistle and then stops. You hop on board to join others fresh from the Bush: fly-fishers, backpackers, a hunter with a dead moose, locals whose homestead cabin can be reached only after a ride on the *Hurricane Turn*, one of America's last flag-stop trains.

This unusual service between Talkeetna and Hurricane along the Susitna River is only one aspect that makes the Alaska Railroad so unique. At the other end of the rainbow of luxury is the railroad's GoldStar Service, two lavishly appointed cars that in 2005 joined the *Denali Star* and *Coastal Classic* trains as part of the Anchorage–Fairbanks and Anchorage–Seward runs. The 89ft double-decked dome cars include a glass observation area on the 2nd level with 360-degree views and a bartender in the back serving your favorite libations. Sit back, sip a chardonnay and soak in the grandeur of Denali.

Take your pick, rustic or relaxing, but don't pass up the Alaska Railroad. There's not another trip like it.

The railroad was born on March 12, 1914, when the US Congress passed the Alaska Railroad Act, authorizing the US president to construct and operate the line. With the exception of the train used at the Panama Canal, the US government had never before owned and operated a railroad.

It took eight years and 4500 men to build a 470-mile railroad from the ice-free port of Seward to the boomtown of Fairbanks, a wilderness line that was cut over what were thought to be impenetrable mountains and across raging rivers. On a warm Sunday afternoon in 1923, President Warren Harding – the first US president to visit Alaska – tapped in the golden spike at Nenana.

The Alaska Railroad has been running ever since. The classic trip is to ride the railroad from Anchorage to Fairbanks, with a stop at Denali National Park. Many believe the most scenic portion, however, is the 114-mile run from Anchorage to Seward, which begins by skirting the 60-mile-long Turnagain Arm, climbs an alpine pass and then comes within a half-mile of three glaciers.

There are far cheaper ways to reach Seward, Fairbanks or points in between. But in the spirit of adventure, which is why many come to Alaska, a van or bus pales in comparison to riding the Alaska Railroad.

Log Cabin & Downtown Information Center (Map p166; ☎907-257-2363; www.anchorage.net; 524 W 4th Ave; ⌚8am-7pm) Has pamphlets, maps, bus schedules, city guides in several languages and a lawn growing on its roof.

Visitors Center (Map p158; ☎907-266-2437; Anchorage International Airport; ⌚9am-4pm) Two visitor-center kiosks are located in the baggage-claim areas of both airport terminals.

ℹ Getting There & Away

AIR

The vast majority of visitors to Alaska, and almost all international flights, fly into **Ted Stevens Anchorage International Airport** (ANC; Map p158; www.dot.state.ak.us/anc; 📶; 🚌7).

Alaska Airlines (☎800-252-7522; www.alaskaair.com) provides the most intrastate routes to travelers, generally through its contract carrier, Ravn Air, which operates services to Valdez, Homer, Cordova, Kenai and Kodiak.

BUS

Anchorage is a hub for various small passenger and freight lines that make daily runs between specific cities. Always call first; Alaska's volatile bus industry is as unstable as an Alaska Peninsula volcano.

Alaska Park Connection (☎800-266-8625; www.alaskacoach.com) Offers daily service from Anchorage north to Talkeetna ($65, 2½ hours) and Denali National Park ($90, six hours), and south to Seward ($65, three hours).

Alaska/Yukon Trails (☎907-479-2277, 907-888-5659; www.alaskashuttle.com) Runs a bus up the George Parks Hwy to Denali ($75, six hours) and Fairbanks ($99, nine hours).

Homer Stage Lines (☎907-868-3914; http://stagelineinhomer.com) Will take you to Homer ($90, 4½ hours) and points in between.

Interior Alaska Bus Line (☎800-770-6652; www.interioralaskabusline.com) Has regular services between Anchorage and Glennallen ($70, three hours), Tok ($115, eight hours) and Fairbanks ($160, 17 hours), and points in between.

Seward Bus Line (☎907-563-0800; www.sewardbuslines.net) Runs between Anchorage and Seward ($40, three hours) twice daily in summer. For an extra $5, you can arrange an airport pickup/drop-off.

TRAIN

Alaska Railroad (☎800-544-0552; www.akrr.com) From its downtown depot, the Alaska Railroad sends its *Denali Star* north daily to Talkeetna (adult/child $101/51), Denali National Park ($167/84) and Fairbanks ($239/120). The *Coastal Classic* stops in Girdwood ($80/40) and Seward ($89/45), while the *Glacial Discovery* connects to Whittier ($105/53). You can save 20% to 30% traveling in May and September.

Getting Around

TO/FROM THE AIRPORT

People Mover bus 7 offers hourly service between downtown and the airport (adult/child $2/1; 6:15am to 10:40pm Monday to Friday, 8:35am to 8:10pm Saturday, 10:35am to 6:05pm Sunday). Pickup is at the south (domestic) terminal. You can call **Eagle River Shuttle** (☎907-694-8888, 907-338-8888; www.alaskashuttle.net) for door-to-door service around Anchorage ($40 to $45) or Eagle River ($60). Plenty of hotels and B&Bs also provide a courtesy-van service. Finally, an endless line of taxis will be eager to take your bags and your money. Plan on a $25 fare to the downtown area.

BUS

Flattop Mountain Shuttle (Map p166; ☎907-279-3334; www.hike-anchorage-alaska.com; 333 W 4th Ave; round-trip $23) Takes you to the trailhead for Anchorage's most climbed peak: Flattop. It departs Downtown Bicycle Rental at 12:30pm daily, returning at 4:30pm.

Valley Mover (☎907-892-8800; www.valley-mover.org; 1-way/day pass $7/10) Offers about a dozen round-trips a day between Eagle River, the Mat-Su Valley and Anchorage.

People Mover (☎907-343-6543; www.peoplemover.org; 1-way adult/child $2/1; ⏲6am-midnight Mon-Fri, 8am-8pm Sat, to 7pm Sun) Anchorage's excellent bus system. Pick up a schedule at the **Downtown Transit Center** (Map p166; www.muni.org; cnr W 6th Ave & G St) or call for specific route information. An unlimited day pass ($5) is available at the transit center.

CAR & MOTORCYCLE

All the national concerns (Avis, Budget, Hertz, Payless, National etc) have counters in the airport's south terminal.

Midnight Sun Car & Van Rental (☎907-243-8806; www.ineedacarrental.com; 4211 Spenard Rd; ⏲6am-1am) The best of the Spenard cheapies, with compacts for $70 per day, $425 per week.

MotoQuest (☎907-272-2777; www.motoquest.com; 4346 Spenard Rd; ⏲9am-5pm) Rents out Harley-Davidsons and BMW bikes (per day $170 to $250). Sure, it's pricey, but still much better value than traditional psychotherapy.

TAXI

Alaska Yellow Dispatch (☎907-222-2222)

SOUTH OF ANCHORAGE

Girdwood

☎907 / POP 1842

Some 37 miles south of Anchorage, Alyeska Hwy splits off at Mile 90 Seward Hwy and heads 3 miles east to Girdwood, a small hamlet with a city-like list of things to do and see. Encircled by mighty peaks brimming with glaciers, Girdwood is a laid-back antidote to the bustle of Anchorage. Home to the luxurious Alyeska Ski Resort and the fabled Girdwood Forest Fair (p182), Girdwood is a dog-and-kid kind of town, with excellent hiking, fine restaurants and a feel-good vibe that will have you staying longer than anticipated.

Sights

Alyeska Resort Tram CABLE CAR

(☎907-754-2275; www.alyeskaresort.com; adult/child $29/15; ⏲9am-9pm; 👪) The Alyeska Ski Resort Tram offers the easiest route to the alpine area during the summer. The resort offers a Dine & Ride combo (adult/child $39/25) that lets you wander the alpine terrain and then grab a bite at the Bore Tide Deli located in the Upper Tram Terminal.

Girdwood Center for Visual Arts GALLERY

(www.gcvaonline.org; 194 Olympic Mountain Loop; ⏲10am-6pm) FREE In town this center serves as an artisan cooperative during the summer and is filled with the work of those locals who get inspired by the majestic scenery that surrounds them.

Crow Creek Mine MINE

(www.crowcreekmine.com; Mile 3.5 Crow Creek Rd; adult/child $10/5; ⏲9am-6pm; 👪) Girdwood was named for James Girdwood, who staked the first claim on Crow Creek in

1896. Two years later the Crow Creek Mine was built, and today you can still see some original buildings and sluices at this working mine. You can even learn how to pan for gold and then give it a try yourself (adult/child $20/10), or pitch the tent and spend the night ($10). It's a peaceful little place and worth a visit just to walk around.

Activities

Hiking

Ringed by mountains and served by a year-round tram up into them, Girdwood is a great place for a hike. Several trails are perfect for kids, but there's no shortage of steep, quad-busting climbs either.

Winner Creek Trail HIKING

(👪) This is an easy, pleasant hike that winds 5.5 miles (round-trip) through lush forest, ending in a dramatic gorge. The first half of the trail is a boardwalk superhighway and at the end you'll cross the gorge on an ultrafun hand-tram. The most popular trailhead is behind the Alyeska Prince Hotel, toward the bottom of the tram.

From the gorge you can connect to the Iditarod National Historic Trail for a 7.7-mile loop.

Alyeska Glacier View Trail HIKING

Take the Alyeska Resort Tram to the easy, 1-mile Alyeska Glacier View Trail, in an alpine area with views of the tiny Alyeska Glacier. You can continue up the ridge to climb the so-called summit of Mt Alyeska, a high point of 3939ft. The true summit lies further to the south, but is not a climb for casual hikers.

Cycling

The Indian–Girdwood Trail – a paved path that leads out of the valley and along the Seward Hwy above Turnagain Arm, dubbed Bird-to-Gird – is the most scenic ride here.

If you like a rush, check out the Alyeska Resort Single Track Trails, for downhill mountain-bike fun.

Alyeska Resort Single Track Trails MOUNTAIN BIKING

Mountain bikers will love these elevated tread singletracks, suitable for beginners as well as adrenaline addicts. The tram and chairs 3, 4 and 6 will carry cyclists and their wheels all the way up to Glacier Bowl if they choose and then a variety of intermediate and advanced trails lead them downhill. A day pass for the lifts is $30.

You can purchase a day pass or rent downhill bikes with pads and helmet at Alyeska Daylodge Rental Shop.

Indian–Girdwood Trail CYCLING

Running 13.3 miles one way from Indian to Girdwood, this paved cycling path parallels the highway and train tracks as it winds along Turnagain Arm. Look for the bore tide, beluga whales and Dall sheep.

Alyeska Daylodge Rental Shop CYCLING

(☎907-754-2111; 104 Alberg Ave; bikes per day $100) Rents full-suspension downhill setups. Opens late June through September.

Tours

Spencer Whistle Stop Train GLACIER

(☎907-265-2494; www.akrr.com; Brundle Rd) Ride the Alaska Railroad to Spencer Glacier, where you can hike a 3.4-mile trail to the face of the glacier or join a guided walk with a United States Forestry Service Ranger. Whistle Stop hikers have from 1:25pm to 4:40pm to complete the hike and meet the train for the return. Or you can camp overnight at a group campsite. The round-trip fares from Girdwood and Anchorage include transport (adult/child $123/62); save money by catching the train directly at Portage station (adult/child $80/40).

Girdwood's tiny rail depot is off the Seward Hwy; turn off at Toadstool Dr just north of the main Girdwood turnoff. Make a right on Brundle Rd; you can't miss it.

Ascending Path HIKING

(☎907-783-0505; www.ascendingpath.com; 1000 Arlberg Ave) This climbing-guide service has a three-hour glacier hike on Alyeska Glacier ($139), and tours that combine guided hikes with an Alaska Railroad trip to Spencer Glacier ($379). The company also offers a three-hour rock-climbing outing designed for beginners (adult/child $129/89), or summer ice climbing ($403). The Ascending Path yurt is behind Hotel Alyeska, near the base of the tram.

Alpine Air SCENIC FLIGHTS

(☎907-783-2360; www.alpineairalaska.com; Girdwood airport) Has a 30-minute glacier tour ($270) and an hour-long tour in which the helicopter lands on the ice ($385).

★Hotel Alyeska TOURS

(☎907-754-2111; www.alyeskaresort.com; 1000 Arlberg Ave) Whether you want to golf, paraglide, downhill mountain bike or do a yoga

WORTH A TRIP

TURNAGAIN ARM

The drive out of Anchorage along Turnagain Arm is well worth the price of a train ticket or rental car. Sure, it might be quicker (and probably cheaper) to fly, but staying on the ground will make you appreciate just how close to the wilderness Anchorage really is.

The 127 miles of the Seward Hwy is all Scenic Byway, and there are plenty of turnoffs for gawking and snapping photos. The mileposts along the highway show distances from Seward (Mile 0) to Anchorage (Mile 127). The Turnagain Arm section of this road is from Anchorage to just past the Portage Glacier turnoff (Mile 79).

Expect lots of traffic, a frightening percentage of which involves folks who have (1) never seen a Dall sheep before, and (2) never driven an RV before; it's a frustrating and sometimes-deadly combination.

If you're lucky (or a planner), you'll catch the bore tide (p182), which rushes along Turnagain Arm in varying sizes daily.

Potter Marsh (Mile 117) was created in 1916, when railroad construction dammed several streams. You can stretch your legs along the 1500ft boardwalk while spying on ducks, songbirds, grebes and gulls.

Chugach State Park Headquarters (907-345-5014; Mile 115, Seward Hwy; 10am-4pm Mon-Fri) is housed in the Potter Section House, a historic railroad workers' dorm with a snowplow train outside.

Turnagain Arm Trail, an easy 11-mile hike, begins at Potter Trailhead (Mile 115). Originally used by Alaska Natives, the convenient route has since been used by Russian trappers, gold miners and happy hikers. The trail, with a mountain goat's view of Turnagain Arm, alpine meadows and beluga whales, can also be accessed at the McHugh Creek (Mile 112), Rainbow (Mile 108) and Windy (Mile 107).

Indian Valley Mine (www.indianvalleymine.com; Mile 104, Seward Hwy; $1; 9am-6pm), a lode mine originally blasted out in 1901, still produces gold. You can buy bags of ore ($10, $50 or $100) and see for yourself. The wonderful proprietors are extremely knowledgeable on the history and science of Alaskan gold mining; ask about the potato retort.

The **Brown Bear Motel** (907-653-7000; www.brownbearalaska.com; Mile 103, Seward Hwy; r $67;) has six clean rooms and plenty of cheap beer in the adjoining Brown Bear Saloon, which can get hopping at night. There are also two cabins out back ($100 and $120) with kitchens.

Bird Ridge Trail starts with a wheelchair-accessible loop at Mile 102, then continues with a steep, popular and well-marked path that reaches a 3500ft overlook at Mile 2; this is a traditional turnaround point for folks in a hurry. Or you can continue another 4 miles to higher peaks and even better views from sunny Bird Ridge, a top spot for rock climbing.

Bird Creek State Campground (907-269-8700; www.dnr.alaska.gov; Mile 101, Seward Hwy; campsites $20) is popular for fishing, hiking and, best of all, the sound of the bore tide rushing by your tent. Remind children and the forgetful to stay off the deadly mudflats, which act as quicksand and are subject to extremely strong tides. Two rustic cabins are also available; reserve in advance.

Seward Hwy continues southeast past Girdwood (p179) and a few nifty tourist attractions to what's left of Portage, which was destroyed by the 1964 Good Friday Earthquake and is basically a few structures sinking into the nearby mudflats.

The **Wetland Observation Platform** (Mile 81) features interpretive plaques on the ducks, arctic terns, bald eagles and other wildlife inhabiting the area.

Alaska Wildlife Conservation Center (907-783-2025; www.alaskawildlife.org; Mile 79, Seward Hwy; adult/child $15/10; 8am-7pm) is a nonprofit wildlife center where injured and rescued animals are on display. Particularly of interest are the wood bison, the only herd in the US, which are part of a program to reintroduce the extinct-in-Alaska breed. It's also a good spot to see a bear or moose if you haven't yet.

CATCHING THE BORE TIDE

One attraction along the Turnagain Arm stretch of the Seward Hwy is unique among sights already original: the bore tide. The bore tide is a neat trick of geography that requires a combination of narrow, shallow waters and rapidly rising tides. Swooping as a wave sometimes 6ft in height (and satisfyingly loud), the tide fills the arm in one go. It travels at speeds of up to 15mph, and every now and then you'll catch a brave surfer or kayaker riding it into the arm.

So, how to catch this dramatic rush? First, consult a tide table, or grab a schedule, available at any Anchorage visitor center. The most extreme bore tides occur during days with minus tides between -2ft and -5.5ft, but if your timing doesn't hit a huge minus, aim for a new or full-moon period. Once you've determined your day, pick your spot. The most popular is Beluga Point (Mile 110), and a wise choice. If you miss the tide, you can always drive further up the arm and catch it at Bird Point (Mile 96).

session on the alpine slopes, this resort has the (expensive) tour for you.

Festivals & Events

Girdwood Forest Fair FAIR
Girdwood's Forest Fair combines local art and live music in a gorgeous wooded setting. The beer garden backs onto a glacial stream, and there's a fun hippie vibe. It's held the first weekend of July each year.

Sleeping

B&Bs make up the bulk of Girdwood's lodging and are the only midrange option. The Alyeska/Girdwood Accommodations Association can find last-minute rooms. Girdwood has a 12% bed tax.

Alyeska/Girdwood Accommodations Association ACCOMMODATION SERVICES
(907-222-4845; www.alyeskagirdwoodaccommodations.net) A large collection of B&Bs. The only midrange option in Girdwood.

Alyeska Accommodations ACCOMMODATION SERVICES
(907-783-2000; www.alyeskaaccommodations.com; 140 Olympic Mountain Loop; r $120-450) Sublets massive, privately owned (and decorated) condos, many with full kitchens, hot tubs and saunas. If you need something smaller, it also rents out rooms and cabins.

Alyeska Hostel HOSTEL $
(907-783-2222; www.alyeskahostel.com; 227 Alta Dr; dm/s/d $25/60/80;) A cozy, no-shoes guesthouse with a private cabin ($100), private studio, six bunks and killer mountain views. The one dorm room sleeps six; make sure you book ahead. It has a shared kitchen and a friendly atmosphere.

Girdwood Campground CAMPGROUND $
(907-343-8373; tent sites $10) Eighteen walk-in sites in the woods with an excellent, in-town location. It has a cooking pavilion, outhouses and a bear-proof locker. From the Alyeska Hwy, turn right on Egloff Dr and follow the road past the ball field.

USFS Cabin CABIN $
(907-783-3242; www.recreation.gov; cabins $65) Three miles up the Crow Pass trail, on a beautiful alpine lake. Book well in advance.

★ **Ski Inn** INN $$
(907-783-0002; www.akskiinn.com; 189 Hightower Rd; dm/d/apt $39/175/280;) A comfortable place offering a range of accommodation from a four-bed dorm to a two-bedroom apartment and everything in between. It's clean, affordable and one of the few places where pets are welcome. All stays include breakfast. Some rooms have shared bathrooms.

Bud & Carol's B&B B&B $$
(907-783-3182; www.budandcarolsbandb.com; 211 Brighton Rd; r $140;) Located at the base of the ski hill, this B&B offers two very clean rooms with private bathroom and a fully equipped kitchen stocked with all you need for a hearty continental breakfast.

Hotel Alyeska RESORT $$$
(907-754-2111; www.alyeskaresort.com; 1000 Arlberg Ave; d $279-299, ste $349;) This place earned four stars from AAA because it deserved them – from bathrobes and slippers in every room to the whirlpool with a view, this place is swanky. For something less swanky, you can park your RV in the day lodge for $10 a night.

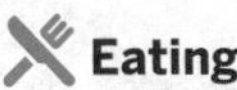

Eating

For such a tiny place, Girdwood has an amazing selection of restaurants, which often pull their patrons in from Anchorage. Since it's part of the municipality of Anchorage, all restaurants and bars are refreshingly smoke-free.

Bake Shop BAKERY $
(www.thebakeshop.com; Olympic Mountain Loop; breakfast $6-10, lunch $7-11; ⏲7am-7pm) Always busy, this bright and art-filled place serves wholesome omelets with fresh-baked breads and sourdough pancakes, all of which you can enjoy at one of the large wooden tables. One of the giant cinnamon rolls is big enough to share with a friend – or not.

Girdwood Picnic Club BREAKFAST $
(194 Hightower Rd; breakfast $9-12, lunch $11-13; ⏲7am-4pm) A family-friendly joint that feels a little like your grandma's living room, if her living room was at a ski resort. Breakfasts are ample and a great way to fuel up before a day of adventure.

Crow Creek Mercantile MARKET $
(150 Hightower Rd; ⏲7am-midnight) Girdwood's tiny grocery store also has some ready-to-eat items.

Chair 5 Restaurant PIZZA $$
(www.chairfive.com; 5 Lindblad Ave; medium pizzas $16-20, dinner $17-30; ⏲11am-1am) The kind of bar and restaurant skiers love after a long day on the slopes. It features more than 60 beers, including a dozen on tap, 16 types of gourmet pizza, big burgers and a lot of blackened halibut. The bar closes late.

★ **Jack Sprat** MODERN AMERICAN $$$
(☎907-783-5225; www.jacksprat.net; 165 Olympic Mountain Loop; brunch $9-17, dinner $20-35; ⏲5-10pm Mon-Fri, 10am-10pm Sat & Sun; ☑) Creative fresh cuisine at the base of the ski hill. Many dishes are vegetarian friendly and made from organically grown ingredients. Homemade almond-milk lattes and the constant favorite *bibimbap* (a Korean-influenced bowl with kimchi, rice, pork and eggs) are only two of the many reasons to eat here. It has a wine list and outdoor seating. Reservations recommended.

Seven Glaciers Restaurant SEAFOOD $$$
(☎907-754-2237; dinner $39-59; ⏲5-9pm) Sitting 2300ft above sea level is the best of Alyeska Resort's six restaurants and bars. The hotel tram will take you to an evening of gourmet dining and absolutely stunning views that include Turnagain Arm and, yes, seven glaciers. The menu is a meat-lover's paradise, with duck, local pork and plenty of Alaska seafood. Tram tickets are included with dinner reservation.

Double Musky Inn CAJUN $$$
(☎907-282-7833; www.doublemuskyinn.com; Crow Creek Rd; dinner $22-45; ⏲5-10pm Tue-Thu, from 4:30pm Fri-Sun) Folks drive down from Anchorage for the French pepper steak – New York strip encrusted in cracked pepper and covered with a spicy burgundy sauce – which is why you might have to wait (reservations are not accepted) two hours on weekends. The cuisine is Cajun accented, hence the masks and Mardi Gras beads hanging from the ceiling. The desserts are divine.

Drinking & Nightlife

Girdwood Brewing Company BREWERY
(www.girdwoodbrewing.com; 2700 Alyeska Hwy; ⏲noon-8pm) This place serves fresh-brewed beer with stunning mountain views. It's cozy and companionable – a perfect spot for your après-ski socializing. If you're hungry, check ahead to see if there's a food truck (schedule is online).

Information

INTERNET ACCESS

Girdwood Laundromall (158 Holmgren Pl; ⏲8am-9:30pm; 📶) Voted the number-one laundromat in the US by American Coin-Op Magazine, this place also has themed coin-op showers ($7) complete with nature sounds, plus free wi-fi and an ATM.

Scott & Wesley Gerrish Library (250 Egloff Dr; ⏲10am-6pm Tue & Thu-Sat, 1-8pm Wed; 📶) Girdwood's library has 10 terminals for free internet access, as well as wi-fi.

MEDICAL SERVICES

Girdwood Clinic (☎907-783-1355; 131 Lindblad Ave; ⏲10am-6pm Tue-Sat) Offers basic medical care. Call for urgent care on Sunday.

MONEY

There are ATMs at the Tesoro Station, Laundromall, Alyeska Resort and Crow Creek Mercantile.

TOURIST INFORMATION

Girdwood Chamber of Commerce (www.girdwoodchamber.com) A great website for pretrip planning.

USFS Glacier Ranger Station (☎907-783-3242; Ranger Station Rd; ⏲8am-5pm Mon-Fri) Has topo maps; a viewing scope; and information on area hikes, campgrounds and public-use cabins.

WORTH A TRIP

PORTAGE VALLEY

As you drive down the Seward Hwy past Girdwood and along the tip of Turnagain Arm, a couple of valleys sing a dazzling siren song with wide silty rivers, hanging glaciers packed tight into towering peaks, and fields of wildflowers. One of these, Portage Valley, is set for exploring, and you can take a very short side trip (though it's worth a full day).

Portage Glacier Access Rd leaves Seward Hwy at Mile 79, continuing 5.4 miles to the **Begich-Boggs Visitors Center** (907-783-2326; adult/child $5/free; 9am-6pm;) en route to Whittier (on the other side of the Anton Memorial Tunnel).

The building, with its observation decks and telescopes, was designed to provide great views of Portage Glacier. But ironically (and to the dismay of thousands of tourists) the glacier has retreated so fast you can no longer see it from the center. Still, inside are neat high-tech wildlife displays and the excellent movie *Voices from the Ice*.

Most people view the glacier through **Gray Line** (888-425-1737; www.graylinealaska.com; adult/child $39/19) cruise boat *MV Ptarmigan* which departs from a dock near the Begich-Boggs Center five times daily during summer. The one-hour (adult/child $39/19) tour cruises up to Portage Glacier's face. If you have a pair of hiking boots, Portage Pass Trail (p212), a mile-long trek to the pass, will provide a good view of Portage Glacier. The trail begins near the tunnel on the Whittier side, so it's a $12-per-car fare to drive through and then return.

The multiuse Trail of Blue Ice parallels Portage Glacier Access Rd and meanders through forest on a wide gravel (and occasionally boardwalk) trail, connecting Portage Lake to the Seward Hwy. Another interesting hike is **Byron Glacier View Trail** (), a single, flat mile to an unusually ice-worm-infested snowfield and grand glacier views.

There are two USFS campgrounds: **Black Bear Campground** (Mile 3.7 Portage Glacier Access Rd; tent & RV sites $14) is beautiful and woodsy – and caters more to tent campers – while **Williwaw Campground** (www.recreation.gov; Mile 4.3 Portage Glacier Access Rd; tent & RV sites $18-28) is stunningly located beneath Explorer Glacier and receives more of an RV crowd. Both campgrounds are extremely popular, although sites at Williwaw can be reserved in advance through National Recreation Reservation Service (www.recreation.gov).

Getting There & Away

BUS

Glacier Valley Transit (907-382-9909; www.glaciervalleytransit.com) Known simply as 'The Shuttle,' Girdwood's bus service operates from Alyeska Resort to the Seward Hwy by donation ($1 recommended). In summer there's another shuttle that travels to Crow Creek Mine a half-dozen times at midday.

Magic Bus (907-230-6773; www.themagicbus.com) An accommodating charter-bus service that leaves Anchorage at 9:30am and departs from Girdwood for the return trip at 6:30pm (one way/round-trip $30/50).

Seward Bus Lines (907-563-0800; www.sewardbuslines.net) Can arrange transport to Seward and Anchorage from Girdwood ($35 to $45).

TRAIN

Alaska Railroad (907-265-2494; www.akrr.com) is pricey, but you can hop on the Alaska Railroad in Anchorage for a day trip to Girdwood. On its way to Seward, the *Coastal Classic* (one way adult/child $80/40) arrives at Girdwood at 8am daily in summer and at 9pm on its return to Anchorage. The *Glacier Discovery* (one way adult/child $66/33) arrives in Girdwood at 10:55am and 7:40pm.

NORTH OF ANCHORAGE

Eagle River

907 / POP 25,995

As you drive out of Anchorage, you'll soon parallel Knik Arm, while the Chugach Mountains stay to your right. Small communities dot either side of the road, but Eagle River and Eklutna offer the best access to the mountains.

Both communities are worthy of a day trip from Anchorage (p156), but to escape the hustle of the city, you can use these small towns as a base for exploring both Anchorage and the wilds around it.

Eagle River has something of a city center; the Eagle River Town Square is off Business Blvd, and has just about every business you'll need. The **Bear Paw Festival** (www.bearpawfestival.com; 11800 Business Blvd; mid-Jul;) is worth the trip just for the 'Slippery Salmon Olympics,' which involves racing with a Hula Hoop, serving tray and, of course, a large dead fish.

Most people, however, come here for the drive down Eagle River Rd or to take a hike.

Activities

Iditarod National Historic Trail HIKING
(32750 Eagle River Rd) The National Historic Iditarod Trail is a 24-mile trek used by gold miners and sled-dog teams until 1918, when the Alaska Railroad was finished. It's a two- to three-day hike through superb mountain scenery to Girdwood (where it's known as the Crow Pass Trail), and is the region's best backpack adventure.

Pitch a tent at Rapids Camp or Echo Bend (Mile 3), or rent one of two yurts ($65 per night) close by. For a shorter outing you can turn around at the Perch, a very large rock in the middle of wonderland, then backtrack to the Dew Mound Trail at Echo Bend and loop back to the Nature Center, making this a scenic 8-mile trip.

Eagle River Road SCENIC DRIVE
This stunning side trip into the heart of the Chugach Mountains follows the Eagle River for 13 miles. The road is paved and winding, and at Mile 7.4 there is a put-in for rafts to float the Class I and II section of the river. The road ends at the Eagle River Nature Center (p186).

South Fork Valley Trail HIKING
Meandering through an alpine valley alongside a rushing stream, this mellow trail takes you back to two lakes. At 4.8 miles from the trailhead is Eagle Lake, a silty glacier blue. Just above it is Symphony Lake, which is smaller and clear. The surrounding valleys make great bases for exploration, and it's worth it to spend a night out here.

To reach the trailhead, take the Eagle River Loop/Hiland Dr exit off the Glenn Hwy. Follow Hiland Dr 7.5 miles, take a left onto South Creek Rd and then a right onto W River Dr. You'll see the trailhead.

Rodak Nature Trail HIKING
(32750 Eagle River Rd) Several trails depart from the Eagle River Nature Center, with Rodak Nature Trail being the easiest. Children will love the mile-long interpretive path, as it swings by an impressive overlook straddling a salmon stream and a huge beaver dam. Albert Loop Trail is a slightly more challenging 3-mile hike through boreal forest and along Eagle River.

Thunderbird Falls HIKING
() Thunderbird Falls, near Eklutna, is a rewarding 2-mile round-trip walk with a gorgeous little waterfall for the grand finale. Anchorage's People Mover bus 102 stops at the trailhead, off the Thunderbird Falls exit of Glenn Hwy.

Sleeping

Eagle River doesn't have a lot to choose from, but there are a few B&Bs, an excellent campground and some chain-style motels. There's a 12% bed tax.

Lifetime Adventures ACCOMMODATION SERVICES
(907-764-4644; www.lifetimeadventures.net) Manages four campgrounds, including the Eagle River Campground.

Eagle River Campground CAMPGROUND $
(907-746-4644; www.lifetimeadventure.net; Hiland Rd exit; tent sites $20) At Mile 11.5 of Glenn Hwy, with beautiful walk-in sites. The river runs closest to the shady sites in the 'Rapids' section.

This is one of the most popular campgrounds in the state; around half the sites can be reserved up to a year in advance.

Alaska Chalet B&B B&B $$
(907-694-1528; www.alaskachaletbb.com; 11031 Gulkana Circle; ste $95-135;) This excellent value, European-style B&B is within walking distance of downtown Eagle River.

The clean guest quarters are separate from the main house and include kitchenettes, and the host speaks German.

Eating

Pizza Man PIZZA $$
(16410 Brooks Loop; medium pizzas $18-23; 11am-midnight Mon-Sat, from noon Sun) An Eagle River establishment, Pizza Man is the place to go to replace those carbs you burned off on the nearby trails.

There are more than two-dozen beers on tap to wash the pizza down.

Drinking & Nightlife

Jitters COFFEE
(www.jitterseagleriver.com; 11401 Old Glenn Hwy; snacks $5-10; ⏲5:30am-9pm Mon-Fri, 6am-7pm Sat, 7am-7pm Sun;) The best place to stop after a rainy hike. It serves soup, sandwiches and pastries in a warm environment.

Information

MEDICAL SERVICES

Acute Family Medicine Clinic (☎907-622-4325; 11470 Business Blvd; ⏲8am-5pm Mon-Fri, 9am-4pm Sat) Offers walk-in service.

TOURIST INFORMATION

Chugiak-Eagle River Chamber of Commerce (www.cer.org) Has a semi-useful website.

Eagle River Nature Center (☎907-694-2108; www.ernc.org; 32750 Eagle River Rd; vehicles $5; ⏲10am-5pm;) At the end of Eagle River Road, this log-cabin center offers wildlife displays, telescopes for finding Dall sheep, guided hikes on most Saturdays and Sundays, and heaps of programs for kids.

Getting There & Away

Eagle River is right off the Glenn Highway, about a 20-minute drive from downtown Anchorage. Having your own wheels is the easiest way to get there, as public transport in town is nil.

Eklutna

☎907 / POP 54

In one direction, just west of the Eklutna Lake Rd exit at Mile 26.5 of the Glenn Hwy, you have the 350-year-old Alaska Native village of Eklutna, home to Eklutna Village Historical Park. In the other direction is the gorgeous 7-mile-long Eklutna Lake, which offers lots of recreation opportunities, including kayaking, biking and hiking. It's worth every minute once the sky suddenly opens, unveiling a stunning valley with a glacier-and-peak-ringed lake, the largest body of water in Chugach State Park, at its center. Eklutna Lake is 10 miles east of the highway on Eklutna Lake Rd.

Sights

Eklutna Village Historical Park HISTORIC SITE
(☎907-688-6026; www.eklutnahistoricalpark.org; tour adult/child $5/2.50; ⏲10am-5pm Mon-Sat) One of the most interesting anthropological sites in the region, where the uneasy marriage of the Athabascan and Russian Orthodox cultures is enshrined. The interior of St Nicholas Church is modeled after Noah's ark while outdoor altars abound, including a heartfelt lean-to for St Herman, patron saint of Alaska. The most revealing structures, however, are the 80 brightly colored spirit boxes in the nearby Denáina Athabascan cemetery. Invest your time in one of the half-hour tours.

Activities

This slice of Chugach State Park is a recreational paradise, with more than 27 miles of hiking and mountain-biking trails.

Lakeside Trail MOUNTAIN BIKING, HIKING
() This trail is a flat 13 miles to the end of the lake, passing two excellent free backcountry camping areas: Eklutna Alex Campground (Mile 9) and Kanchee Campground (Mile 11). East Fork Trail diverts from the main trail at Mile 10.5 and runs another 5.5 miles to a great view of Mt Bashful, the tallest mountain (8005ft) in the park.

Keep going past the Lakeside Trail terminus to view Eklutna Glacier. All-terrain vehicles can use the trails Sunday through Wednesday, hikers and cyclists anytime. The glacier has receded in recent years; keep looking.

Bold Ridge Trail HIKING
To reach the alpine treeline, hike this steep 3.5-mile trail that begins 5 miles along the Lakeshore Trail and continues to a saddle below Bold Peak (7522ft), where there are views of the valley, Eklutna Glacier and even Knik Arm. People with the energy can scramble up nearby ridges. To actually climb Bold Peak requires serious equipment.

Twin Peaks Trail HIKING
This route to the mountains is 2.6 miles from the parking lot, but steep. It takes you 1800ft up through lush forest into alpine meadows presided over by the imposing eponymous peaks. Berries, wildlife and great lake views make scrambling toward the top downright enjoyable.

Sleeping

★ **Eklutna Lake State Recreation Area** CAMPGROUND $
(www.dnr.alaska.gov; tent sites $15) Has a popular campground at the west end of the lake and is a beautiful place to spend a night. But even with 60 sites it's often filled. There's also a rustic cabin ($60).

WORTH A TRIP

IDITAROD TRAIL HEADQUARTERS

Near Wasilla, the town of Knik boasts a rich sled-dog history, since it's the home of many Alaskan mushers (and checkpoint 4 on the Iditarod race route). For more information about this uniquely Alaskan race, stop in at **Iditarod Trail Headquarters** (☎907-376-5155; www.iditarod.com; 2100 Knik-Goosebay Rd; ⊙8am-7pm). The log-cabin museum's most unusual exhibit is Togo, the famous sled dog that led his team across trackless Norton Sound to deliver serum to diphtheria-threatened Nome in 1925 – a journey that gave rise to today's Iditarod.

He's been stuffed and is now on display. Outside, you can get a short sled-dog ride (around US$10, from 9am to 5pm) on a wheeled dogsled. The Iditarod, a famous 1100-mile dogsled race to Nome, begins in Anchorage – but only for the sake of appearances. At the end of a short run in Anchorage, the teams wave goodbye to the cameras, pack up their dogs and sleds, and drive to snowier country up north for the 'restart.' Wasilla serves as the second official starting point for the race, though the lack of snow often pushes the restart north to Willow or even further north.

Alaska Wilderness Cabins CABIN **$**
(☎907-688-6201; www.goalaskan.com; Eklutna Lake Rd; cabins/r $50/75) Offers accommodations ranging from its cozy Eklutna room with a view of the lake to three cabins without electricity or running water.

Getting There & Away

Eklutna village is just west of the Eklutna Lake Rd extension at Mile 26.5 of the Glenn Hwy. The lake is 10 miles in the other direction. No public transport runs here; to reach the village or the lake you'll need your own wheels.

Palmer

☎907 / POP 5937

Filled with old farming-related buildings, Palmer at times feels more like the Midwest than Alaska, except that it's ringed by dramatic mountains. Many downtown venues exude 1930s ambience, with antique furniture and wood floors. Sure, Palmer is subjected to the same suburban sprawl as anywhere else, but its charm lies in its unique history and living agricultural community. For those who want to skip the city hassles and high prices of Anchorage, Palmer is an excellent option with just enough choices in lodging, restaurants and sights to keep you satisfied for a day or two.

History

Born during President Roosevelt's New Deal, Palmer was one of the great social experiments in an era when human nature was believed infinitely flexible. The mission was to transplant 200 farming families, who were refugees from the Depression-era Dust Bowl (the worst agricultural disaster in US history), to Alaska, where they would cultivate a new agricultural economy.

Trainloads of Midwesterners and their Sears & Roebuck furniture were deposited in the Matanuska and Susitna Valleys, both deemed suitable by the government for such endeavors. Nearly everything was imported, from building materials (and plans) to teachers. Soil, rich by Alaskan standards, enjoyed a growing season just long enough for cool-weather grains and certain vegetables. There was little margin for error, however, and any unexpected frost could destroy an entire year of seed and sweat.

Original buildings stand throughout Palmer, many of which have been refurbished and maintain their hearty wooden farm feel. Descendants of the original colonists, who refer to themselves as Colony children or grandchildren, still inhabit Palmer and have wonderful stories to tell.

Sights

Knik Glacier GLACIER
Trekkies take note: Knik Glacier is best known as the setting where a portion of *Star Trek VI* was filmed. You can get a partial view of the ice floe at Mile 7 of Knik River Rd off Old Glenn Hwy, but the best way to experience it is on either an air- or jet-boat ride up the Knik River. Knik Glacier Tours has three-hour tours departing twice a day

that include an overland safari before the boat ride.

Colony House Museum MUSEUM

(907-745-1935; www.palmerhistoricalsociety.org; 316 E Elmwood Ave; adult/child $2/1; 10am-4pm Tue-Sat) This friendly museum is run by enthusiastic Colony descendants. Take the time for a guided tour, and you'll leave with an appreciation of the enormity of the colonizing project. The museum itself was a 'Colony Farm House' built during the original settlement of Palmer, and its eight rooms are still furnished with artifacts and stories from that era.

To bring their living-room piano to Alaska, members of one pioneer family left behind their luggage and stuffed their clothes in it, the only way to make their weight allotment. Rumor has it a sock or two is still stuffed inside.

Matanuska Valley Agricultural Showcase GARDENS

(723 S Valley Way; 8am-7pm Jun-Aug) FREE A garden next to the visitor center that features flowers and the area's famous oversized vegetables. But you have to be passing through in August if you want to see a cabbage bigger than a basketball. Every Friday during summer is Friday Fling.

Friday Fling MARKET

(www.fridayfling.org; 723 S Valley Way; 10am-5pm Jun-Aug) An open-air market with local produce, art, crafts, food and live music. Held every Friday in summer.

Musk Ox Farm FARM

(907-745-4151; www.muskoxfarm.org; 12850 E Archie Rd; adult/child $11/5; 10am-6pm) The Musk Ox Farm is home to a domesticated herd of these big, shaggy beasts. These ice-age critters are intelligent enough to have evolved a complex social structure that allows survival under incredibly harsh conditions. Qiviut (kiv-ee-oot), the incredibly warm, soft and pricey material ($55 for 2oz of raw qiviut or $95 for an ounce of yarn) made from the musk ox's undercoat, is harvested here. Tours are given every 30 minutes.

Fine sweaters and hats are for sale in the gift shop. And yes, you'll probably get to pet the musk ox too.

Pyrah's Pioneer Peak Farm FARM

(907-745-4511; www.pppfarm.net; Mile 2.8 Bodenberg Loop Rd; by appointment Mon-Sat) South of Palmer, Pyrah's Pioneer Peak Farm is the largest pick-your-own-vegetables place in the Mat-Su Valley, with would-be farmers in the fields from July to early October picking everything from peas and potatoes to carrots and cabbages.

Reindeer Farm FARM

(www.reindeerfarm.com; 5561 S Bodenburg Loop Rd; adult/child $9/7; 10am-6pm) The Reindeer Farm is one of the original Colony farms and a great place to bring the kids. Here they will be able to pet and feed the reindeer, and are encouraged to think the reindeer are connected to Santa. There are also elk, moose and bison to take photos of, and horseback-riding tours. Rubber boots are provided. There's a small snack shack for munchies on the picnic tables.

Palmer Museum of History & Art MUSEUM

(723 S Valley Way; 9am-6pm) FREE The log cabin that used to be just a visitor center is now more museum than brochures, with local art and interesting displays on Palmer's agricultural past. Some of the valley's famous produce grows outside at the Matanuska Valley Agricultural Showcase.

Activities

There is some great hiking in the Mat-Su area and a more complete list of hikes is available from the Mat-Su Trails & Parks Foundation (www.matsutrails.org).

Knik Glacier Tours ADVENTURE

(907-745-1577; www.knikglacier.com; adult/child $125/65) Has three-hour tours departing twice per day. Take a 4-mile overland safari and then finish with either a jet- or air-boat ride up the Knik River.

Government Peak Recreation Area HIKING

(10690 N Mountain Trails Dr) A chalet and parking area offer easy access to a collection of mountain-bike trails and a steep hike to the top of Government Peak in the Talkeetna Mountains. It's a steep 3.5-mile climb to the top, where you are rewarded with sweeping views that include Knik Glacier in the distance. A more gentle hike is the 1.5-mile Blueberry Knoll.

From Palmer-Fishook Rd, take a left onto Egderton Parks Rd just before you climb into Hatcher Pass. Take your first right onto Mountain Trails Dr.

WORTH A TRIP

HATCHER PASS

A side trip from Palmer (or even a base) is the photogenic Hatcher Pass. This alpine passage cuts through the Talkeetna Mountains and leads to meadows, ridges and glaciers. Gold was the first treasure people found here; today it's footpaths, ski trails, abandoned mines and popular climbs that outshine the precious metal.

The main attraction of Hatcher Pass is **Independence Mine State Historical Park** (Mile 18 Hatcher Pass Rd; per person $3), which holds a huge 272-acre abandoned gold mine sprawled out in a gorgeous alpine valley. The 1930s facility, built by the Alaska-Pacific Mining Company (APC), was for 10 years the second-most-productive hard-rock gold mine in Alaska. At its peak, in 1941, APC employed 204 workers here, blasted almost 12 miles of tunnels and recovered 34,416oz of gold, today worth almost $18 million. The mine was finally abandoned in 1955.

Today you can explore the structures, hike several trails and take in the stunning views at Hatcher Pass. It's $5 to park and another $3 per person to enter.

In the park **Visitors Center** (9am-5pm) you'll find a map of the park, a simulated mining tunnel, displays on the ways to mine gold (panning, placer mining and hard rock) and guided tours at 1pm and 3pm (included with park entry fee). From the center, follow Hardrock Trail past the dilapidated buildings, which include bunkhouses and a mill complex that is built into the side of the mountain and looks like an avalanche of falling timber. Make an effort to climb up the trail to the water-tunnel portal, where there is a great view of the entire complex and a blast of cold air pouring out of the mountain.

Hatcher Pass also offers some of the best alpine hiking in the Matanuska-Susitna areas. The easy, beautiful **Gold Mint Trail** begins at Mile 14 of Fishhook–Willow Rd, where you'll find a small campground (tent sites $15). The trail follows the Little Susitna River into a gently sloping mountain valley, and within 3 miles you spot the ruins of Lonesome Mine. Keep hiking and you'll eventually reach Mint Glacier.

With two alpine lakes, lots of waterfalls, glaciers and towering walls of granite, the 7-mile **Reed Lakes Trail** – 9 miles to the upper lake – is worth the climb, which includes some serious scrambling. Once you reach upper Reed Lake, continue for a mile to Bomber Glacier, where the ruin of a B-29 bomber lies in memorial to six men who perished there in a 1957 crash. Around mile 14 of Hatcher Pass Rd, a road to Archangel Valley splits off from Fishhook–Willow Rd and leads to the Reed Lakes trailhead, a wide road. If you've got a 4WD, you can (theoretically) drive the first 3 miles of the **Craigie Creek Trail**, posted along the Fishhook–Willow Rd just west of Hatcher Pass. It's better, however, to walk the gently climbing old road up a valley and past several abandoned mining operations to the head of the creek. It then becomes a very steep trail for 3 miles to Dogsled Pass, where you can access several wilderness trails into the Talkeetna Mountains.

If the weather is nice and you have the funds, it's hard to pass up spending the night at the pass at **Hatcher Pass Lodge** (907-745-5897; www.hatcherpasslodge.com; Mile 17.5 Hatcher Pass Rd; cabins $150;). The lodge is inside the state park, and is a highly recommended splurge. Aside from spectacular views at 3000ft, the lodge has 11 cabins, a (pricey) restaurant and bar, and a sauna built over a rushing mountain stream.

Lazy Mountain Trail HIKING

A great hike near Palmer is the climb to the top of 3720ft Lazy Mountain. The 2.5-mile trail is very steep at times, but makes for a pleasant trek that ends in an alpine setting with good views of Matanuska Valley farms. Take Old Glenn Hwy across the Matanuska River, turn left onto Clark-Wolverine Rd and then right onto Huntley Rd; follow it to the Equestrian Center parking lot and the trailhead, marked 'Foot Trail.' Plan on three to five hours for the round-trip.

Matanuska Peak Trail HIKING

The 8-mile Matanuska Peak (also called Byers Peak) Trail is steep, traversing the south slope of Lazy Mountain. As you ascend Matanuska Peak, you'll climb 5670ft in 4 miles – be prepared for a long day. You'll be richly rewarded for your hard work, however, by the views of the Knik and Matanuska Rivers, and Cook Inlet.

Take Old Glenn Hwy from Palmer toward Butte and turn left onto Smith Rd at Mile 15.5. Drive 1.4 miles until it ends at the parking lot.

Pioneer Ridge Trail HIKING

Pioneer Ridge Trail is a 5.7-mile route that climbs the main ridge extending southeast from Pioneer Peaks (6400ft). You'll climb through forest until you reach alpine tundra at 3200ft. From the ridge, South Pioneer Peak is a mile to the northwest, and North Pioneer Peak is 2 miles. Don't scale any peaks without rock-climbing experience and equipment.

The trailhead is on the right at mile 3.8 of Knik River Rd.

Festivals & Events

Alaska State Fair CULTURAL

(www.alaskastatefair.org; per day adult/child $13/9) A rollicking 12-day event that ends on Labor Day, the first Monday in September. There's live music and prized livestock from the surrounding area, as well as horse shows, a rodeo, a carnival and the giant cabbage weigh-off to see who grew the biggest one in the valley (in 2012 a world record was set: 138lb!). If greased pigs and Spam-sponsored recipe contests aren't enough to get you here, try this: berry-pie cook-offs.

Colony Days FAIR

(www.palmerchamber.org) Every June, Palmer's Chamber of Commerce hosts a celebration of the town's origins as a farming colony. The down-home festival features a parade, market, sidewalk art and tractor pull.

Sleeping

If you arrive late, the Palmer Visitor Center has a courtesy phone outside with direct lines connected to area accommodations. There is also the Mat-Su B&B Association (www.alaskabnbhosts.com), which lists almost 30 B&Bs in the area, including nine in Palmer. Add 5% tax to the prices here.

Hatcher Pass B&B B&B $$

(907-745-6788; www.hatcherpassbb.com; Mile 6.6 Palmer-Fishhook Rd; cabin s/d $139/189;) This B&B, 8 miles from Palmer, offers five button-cute log cabins – two large and a few tiny – with kitchenettes and fridges stocked with everything you need for a CYOB (cook your own breakfast). The prices go down the longer you stay.

Colony Inn HISTORIC HOTEL $$

(907-745-3330; 325 E Elmwood Ave; r $100;) What was constructed in 1935 as the Matanuska Colony Teacher's Dorm is now a quaint inn. The 12 rooms are spacious (especially the corner rooms), well kept and equipped with TVs, pedestal sinks and whirlpool tubs. There's an inviting parlor for reading, furnished with antiques. Check in at the **Valley Hotel** (907-745-3330; 606 S Alaska St; r $102;).

Knik River Lodge LODGE $$

(877-745-4575; www.knikriverlodge.com; 29979 E Knik River Rd; cabins $259;) Almost two-dozen clean and cozy one-room cabins line up in tidy rows facing the Knik River (steep discounts for shoulder season). An excellent restaurant is on site, and the lodge also operates a tour company that features helicopter tours of Knik Glacier.

Alaska's Harvest B&B B&B $$

(907-745-4263; www.alaskasharvest.com; 2252 Love Dr; r $119-169;) Seven bathrooms for seven bedrooms. This grand home sits on a 15-acre sheep farm and has uninterrupted views of Pioneer Peak over the trees, many from private balconies. Trails wind through the woods. The rooms range from the Fox Hole (a cozy closet-turned-bunk-bed) to the Pioneer Suite (sleeps nine). Each has a kitchenette and comes with continental breakfast.

Eating

Hearty cuisine, often utilizing locally grown produce, makes Palmer's expanding restaurant scene unique in Alaska.

★ **Turkey Red** FUSION $$

(907-756-5544; www.turkeyredak.com; 550 S Alaska St; lunch $8-13, dinner $15-33; 7am-9pm Mon-Sat;) A bright and colorful cafe serving fresh dishes made from scratch including wonderful fresh-baked breads and desserts. Vegetarians won't go hungry here, and much of the produce is organic and locally grown. Lunch is good, but the menu really shines at dinner.

Inn Café & Steakhouse CAFE $$

(☎907-746-6118; 325 E Elmwood Ave; lunch $12-16, dinner $20-30; ⏲11am-7pm Mon-Wed, to 9pm Thu-Sat) This former teachers' dorm houses a pleasant restaurant with the kind of creaky wood-floored ambience expected in Palmer.

Lunch includes a wide selection of sandwiches and burgers, and dinner features lots of steak and seafood.

Colony Kitchen BREAKFAST $$

(1890 Glenn Hwy; breakfast $9-14, dinner $12-23; ⏲6am-9pm) If you like your breakfast big, you'll be stoked: not only is your most important meal huge, but it's served all day.

You'll eat beneath stuffed birds suspended from the ceiling (hence its other name, the Noisy Goose Café).

Palmer City Alehouse AMERICAN $$

(www.alaskaalehouse.com; 320 E Dahlia St; mains $13-19; ⏲11am-10pm) Housed in the renovated Palmer Trading Post, this is basically a sports bar in a cool building.

If you're not into the game, head for the delightful outdoor area, where every seat has a view of the mountains and there's live music many nights in summer.

The menu includes beer, pizza and meals for hearty appetites.

Drinking & Nightlife

Bleeding Heart Brewery BREWERY

(16013 Outer Springer Loop Rd; ⏲4-8pm Thu & Fri, from noon Sat, 2-6pm Sun) One of two breweries in Palmer, Bleeding Heart takes advantage of its neighboring farms to create brews like the namesake Bleeding Heart IPA, which incorporates Alaska-grown beets to give it that sexy red color.

Vagabond Blues COFFEE

(www.vagblues.com; 642 S Alaska St; light meals $6-11; ⏲6am-8pm Mon-Sat, 7am-7pm Sun; 📶) 🌿 The cultural heartbeat of Palmer is this cozy coffee shop, with local art on the walls and often live music at night.

It has healthy sandwiches, soups and salads.

ℹ Information

INTERNET ACCESS

Palmer Library (655 S Valley Way; ⏲10am-8pm Mon & Wed, to 6pm Tue & Thu, to 2pm Fri & Sat) An excellent library with free internet access.

MEDICAL SERVICES

Mat-Su Regional Hospital (☎861-6000; 2500 S Woodworth Loop) Gleaming on a hill near the intersection of the Parks and Glenn Hwys.

MONEY

Wells Fargo (705 S Bailey St; ⏲10am-6pm Mon-Fri, to 5pm Sat)

TOURIST INFORMATION

Gateway Visitors Center (☎907-746-5000; www.alaskavisit.com) Once there's funding, a two-story center will be located at Mile 36 of the Glenn Hwy, just before Palmer if you're coming from Anchorage. In the meantime, the website is an excellent planning tool. You'll find info on Palmer and Wasilla and all the adventure between there and Denali.

Palmer Visitor Center (☎907-745-2880; www.palmerchamber.org; 723 S Valley Way; ⏲9am-6pm) Within the Palmer Museum of History & Art; has pamphlets, books, maps, helpful staff and free coffee inside.

ℹ Getting There & Around

From Eklutna Lake Rd, Glenn Hwy continues north, crossing Knik and Matanuska Rivers at the northern end of Knik Arm, and at Mile 35.3 reaching a major junction with the George Parks Hwy. At this point, Glenn Hwy curves sharply to the east and heads into Palmer, 7 miles away. If you're driving, a much more scenic way to reach Palmer is to leave Glenn Hwy just before it crosses Knik River and follow Old Glenn Hwy into town.

Valley Transit (☎907-864-5000; www.valleytransitak.com; single-zone ride $3; ⏲8am-6pm Mon-Fri) serves nine 'zones,' or communities, in the area, including Palmer and Wasilla. A bus ride is $3 per zone; it'll therefore cost you $6 to get to Wasilla. This is an on-demand service, so you must call ahead; it's based on availability. It also runs a fixed commuter service to/from Anchorage ($7 one-way).

Alaska Cab (☎907-746-2727) and **R & B Taxi** (☎907-775-7475) provide service around town, as well as to Wasilla ($30) and Anchorage ($80).

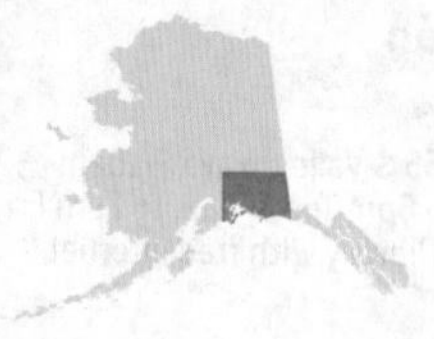

Prince William Sound

Includes ➡

Best Places to Eat

➡ Roadside Potatohead (p201)

➡ Baja Taco (p207)

➡ Harborside Pizza (p207)

Best Places to Stay

➡ Orca Adventure Lodge (p206)

➡ Best Western Valdez Harbor Inn (p200)

➡ Reluctant Fisherman Inn (p207)

➡ Inn at Whittier (p214)

Why Go?

This island-speckled sound named for an 18th-century British prince is home to precipitous fjords, sheer-sided coastal mountains, numerous boom-crashing tidal glaciers, remarkable bird and animal life, and three very unique 'villages' that guard the gates to endless adventure possibilities. Local cruise-ship traffic is light, lending the region a genuine remoteness.

The best base for travelers is Valdez, a tough town hemmed in by dramatic mountains that's hailed for its helicopter-skiing and blue-water paddling. Connected to the road network via the Richardson Hwy, Valdez has survived two 20th-century disasters – an oil spill and an earthquake. More isolated Cordova is a fishing community with a quaint downtown, excellent bird-watching and access to great day hikes in the Chugach Mountains. On the western edge of the Sound, Whittier, a bizarre city born out of wartime necessity, is hideous, gorgeous, evocative and eerie. It's easily reached by car from Anchorage.

When to Go

Valdez

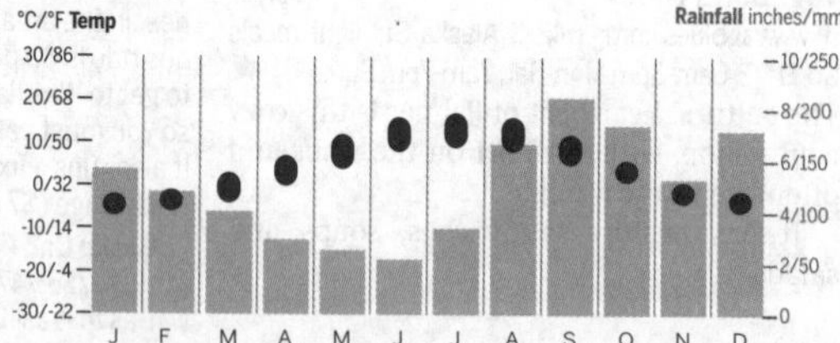

Apr & May Tail end of the heli-skiing season, massive bird migrations and pre-season discounts.

Jun Things dry out (kind of), hotels open and the wildlife kicks into overdrive.

Jul Whale-watching picks up, the salmon are running and the sun shines bright.

History

Prince William Sound was long a crossroads of Alaska Native cultures; the region has been inhabited at various times by coastal Chugach Inuit people, Athabascans originally from the Interior, and Tlingits who traveled up from Alaska's panhandle. The first European to arrive was Vitus Bering, a Danish navigator sailing for the tsar of Russia, who

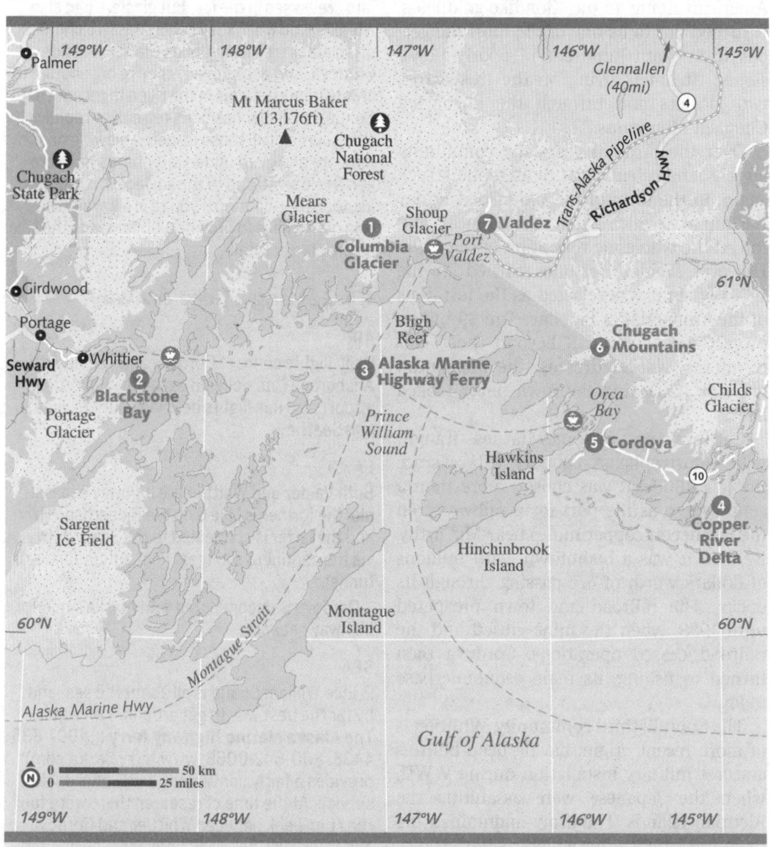

Prince William Sound Highlights

❶ **Columbia Glacier** (p195) Listening to the snap-crackle-and-pop of icebergs as you blue-water paddle around one of Alaska's largest tidal glaciers.

❷ **Blackstone Bay** (p212) Heading out from Whittier to kayak or sightsee amid wildlife, waterfalls, icebergs and the fantastical forces of nature.

❸ **Alaska Marine Highway Ferry** (p360) Taking a cheap 'cruise' on a state ferry in an area where few cruise ships venture.

❹ **Copper River Delta** (p205) Exploring the birds and bears of this huge continuous wetland by boat, raft, car or bike.

❺ **Cordova** (p202) Chilling in a bar, bakery or snack-shack listening to fishers lamenting about the one that got away.

❻ **Heli-skiing** (p198) Experiencing the ultimate in white-knuckle Alaskan adventure with a winter heli-skiing trip in the Chugach Mountains.

❼ **Valdez Earthquake History** (p195) Visiting the museums and old town site in Valdez and learning about the catastrophic power of the 1964 earthquake.

anchored his ship near Kayak Island, east of Copper River, in 1741.

The Sound's three major towns have rather divergent modern histories. Valdez was settled in 1897, when 4000 gold prospectors took what had been billed as the 'All-American Route' to the Klondike goldfields. It turned out to be one of the most dangerous trails, with hundreds of poorly provisioned dreamers dying on the trek across two glaciers and through the uncharted Chugach Mountains.

Over the next 60 years the community largely languished until catastrophe struck again, in the form of the 1964 Good Friday Earthquake, which killed over 30 locals and forced the wholesale relocation of the town. However, Valdez' fortunes turned in the 1970s when it was selected as the terminus of the Trans-Alaska Pipeline. The $9-billion project was a windfall beyond those early miners' wildest dreams; the population grew by 320% and the town never looked back.

Cordova's past is somewhat less fraught with catastrophe. A cannery village since the late 1800s, it was chosen more than a century ago as the port for a railway from the Kennecott copper mines near McCarthy. By 1916 it was a boomtown, with millions of dollars worth of ore passing through its docks. The railroad and town prospered until 1938, when the mine closed and the railroad ceased operations. Cordova then turned to fishing, its main economic base today.

The Sound's third community, Whittier, is of more recent origin, having been built as a secret military installation during WWII, when the Japanese were assaulting the Aleutian Islands. The army maintained the town until 1968, after which, as in Cordova, fishing became the main industry. Tourism now puts food on many residents' plates. Whittier is the Sound's only regular cruise-ship stop.

In recent decades the most monumental event in the Sound has been the *Exxon Valdez* oil spill, which dumped at least 11 million gallons of petroleum into the sea, killing countless birds and marine mammals, and devastating the fishing industry for several years. Though fishing – and the environment – has largely rebounded, oil is still easy to find beneath the surface of beaches, and certain species are not expected to recover.

ℹ Safe Travel

By definition, glaciers move at a glacial pace, so you'd think they'd be harmless. In glacier-strewn Prince William Sound, however, they can be a real hazard. Not only have trekkers and mountaineers been killed when they've plunged into crevasses in the ice, but glaciers can also wreak havoc when they calve. Massive chunks often crack free from Childs Glacier, outside Cordova, and occasionally they're big enough to create mini tsunamis in the river. In recent years Columbia Glacier has been retreating rapidly (the source of all those icebergs glowing on the horizon) and giant underwater bergs have broken free only to pop to the surface in a random location. Use caution if you're in a kayak. The rule of thumb is to provide a buffer twice the size as the glacier is tall.

ℹ Getting There & Away

AIR

Daily flights connect Cordova and Valdez with Anchorage (but not with each other). Cordova airport also has flights heading south to Juneau and Seattle.

LAND

Both Valdez and Whittier are highway accessible; the former is Mile 0 on the Richardson Hwy and the latter is connected to the Seward Hwy via the continent's longest joint automobile-rail tunnel.

Cordova is unconnected with Alaska's main highway network.

SEA

Prince William Sound is all about the sea, and by far the best way to get around is on water. The **Alaska Marine Highway ferry** (☎907-835-4436, 800-642-0066; www.ferryalaska.com) provides a fairly convenient, fairly affordable service. At the time of research there were four runs per week between Whittier and Cordova and three runs per week between Whittier and Valdez, and Valdez and Cordova. The Valdez–Cordova run (which goes via Whittier) takes all day.

Remember, the ferry is more than just transport: it's an experience. There's something transcendent about bundling up on deck and watching the mountain-riddled, fjord-riven watery world unfold.

Valdez

☎907 / POP 4022

There are two Valdezs. The cool contemporary town – an irresistible lure for adventure sportspeople redolent of Boulder, Colorado or Bend, Oregon – and the town that existed pre-1964, before the second-strongest earthquake in recorded history sent its docks sliding into the sea.

Valdez was quickly rebuilt on more stable ground 5 miles to the west before it was hit again, this time by a human-made disaster, the catastrophic *Exxon Valdez* oil spill of 1989 that killed marine life, disrupted ecosystems and ruined livelihoods.

It is a testament to Valdez' feisty Alaskan spirit that it has managed not only to survive, but bounce back, despite its isolation from the lucrative cruise-ship economy. Founded by gold-rush-era prospectors in 1897, the town has tough antecedents and it still draws in the brawny and brave, who love to fish in its iceberg-punctuated seas and heli-ski in the precipitous mountains that surround it.

Sights

★Columbia Glacier GLACIER

The big daddy of Prince William Sound's glaciers is also one of the world's fastest moving, though, like many ice floes in Alaska, it is rapidly retreating – peeling back an estimated 19 miles since 1980. Spilling forth from the Chugach Mountains, it ends with a face as high as a football field. The voyage to see the Columbia is a popular day trip out of Valdez, either in a boat or on a kayaking excursion.

★Valdez Museum MUSEUM

(907-835-2764; www.valdezmuseum.org; 217 Egan Dr; adult/child $8/free; 9am-5pm) This lovingly curated museum includes an ornate, steam-powered antique fire engine, a 19th-century saloon bar and the ceremonial first barrel of oil to flow from the Trans-Alaska Pipeline.

There are disturbing photos taken during the six minutes when Valdez was shaken to pieces by the 1964 Good Friday Earthquake, and an exhibit featuring correspondence from stampeders attempting the grueling All-American Route from Valdez to the inland goldfields. Equally thought-provoking is an exhibit about work behind the scenes

THE EXXON VALDEZ

The *Exxon Valdez* crashed into Bligh Reef in 1989, spilling some 11 million gallons of oil into the delicate ecosystem of Prince William Sound. But to this day, the communities, industries and environment in the area have yet to fully recover from one of modern history's worst human-made environmental disasters.

It is getting better, but most experts say the ecosystem has suffered permanent damage. On the 25th anniversary of the spill in 2014, it was estimated that up to 21,000 gallons of oil were still present in the Sound. The disaster financially crippled the commercial fisheries and tourism industries in places like Valdez and Cordova. And while commercial salmon and halibut fishing have returned to the region, the herring population has never fully recovered.

There is some positive news. Many studies show rebounds in animal populations decimated by the spill, which stretched over 1000 miles and killed anywhere from 100,000 to 250,000 seabirds, 2800 sea otters, and obliterated huge populations of salmon and herring. Sea-otter populations are at pre-spill levels, but a pod of orcas remains at risk of extinction.

Exxon claims to have spent some $4.3 billion in cleanup costs and legal settlements. In 2008 the US Supreme Court took a knife to the original jury award of $5 billion, cutting it to just $507 million plus $470 million in interest due.

And whatever happened to the captain, Joseph Hazelwood? He was acquitted from the drunken-boating charges and slapped with 1000 hours of community service and a $50,000 fine. Most onlookers argue, however, that it was really Exxon's lack of security protocols and onboard-collision avoidance radar that led to the disaster.

Other legacies of the disaster are more inspiring. Long-recommended security measures have finally been enacted at oil-processing facilities across the nation. All tankers built post-1990 have, by law, had to be double-hulled. Manufacturers were given 25 years to make the changeover and, in 2015, double hulls became mandatory in the US. Similarly, tugs must always escort tankers passing through Prince William Sound. And the *Exxon Valdez* itself, which was initially repaired and renamed *Exxon Mediterranean* after the oil spill, was finally sold for scrap in 2012.

Valdez

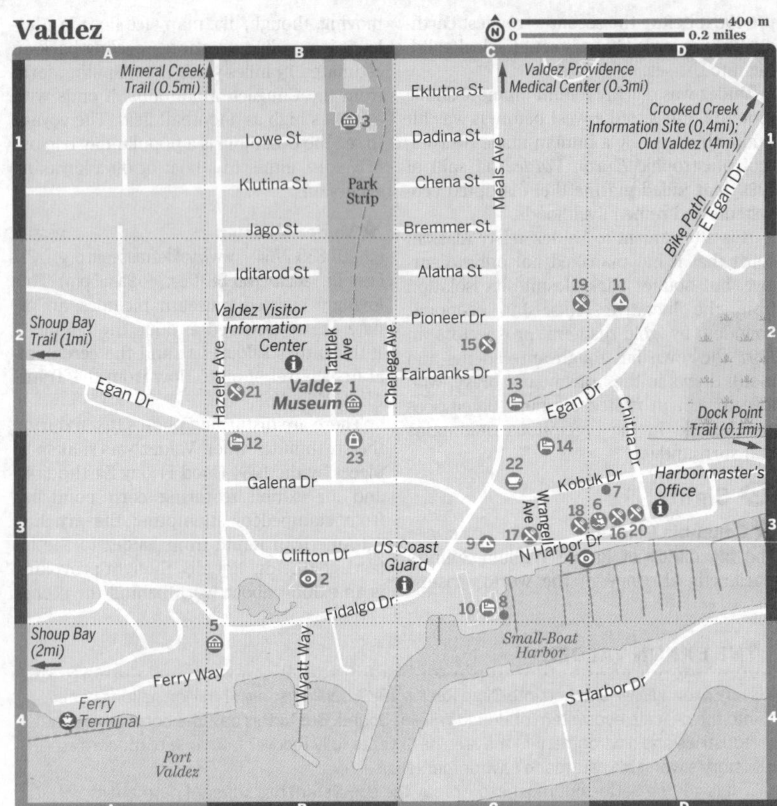

at the museum that seeks to show how historical material is preserved and archived.

Maxine & Jesse Whitney Museum MUSEUM
(907-834-1690; www.mjwhitneymuseum.org; 303 Lowe St; 9am-7pm;) FREE For a small town Valdez has several wonderful museums, including this one, the private collection of an American couple who settled in Alaska in 1947 and became enthusiastic horders of Alaska Native art, artifacts and taxidermy. It's all incredibly well put together with written commentaries that debate and question rather than preach. Enjoy the ivory and baleen artwork, moose-antler furniture, natural-history displays and very creative stuffed animals.

Small-boat Harbor HARBOR
Valdez' harbor is a classic: raucous with gulls and eagles, reeking of fish guts, sea salt and creosote, and home to all manner of vessels. The benches and long boardwalk are ideal for watching lucky anglers weighing in 100lb or 200lb halibut, and for taking in the fairy-tale mountainscape in the background.

Nearby is the **Civic Center** (Fidalgo Dr), which has more picnic tables, a small lake and the short Overlook Trail.

Old Valdez HISTORIC SITE
Old Valdez is like a wilder, starker, less trammeled version of Italy's Pompeii. This is where the town stood before the devastating 1964 earthquake pretty much wiped it out. Today there isn't much left of the original town, bar some street signs, a few overgrown foundations and a smattering of interpretive boards.

The Earthquake Memorial, listing the names of the dead, is reached by turning off the highway onto the unsigned gravel road just south of Mark's Repair. On the day of the quake, Valdez' post office was here; in

Valdez

mere moments the ground sank so far that nowadays high tides reach the spot.

Markers show where many of the buildings used to stand, although the lots themselves have largely been returned to nature. One-hour guided walking tours of Old Valdez are organized by the Valdez Museum (p195) on selective days throughout the summer. Check the museum website for dates.

Valdez Museum Annex MUSEUM
(☎907-835-5407; 436 Hazelet Ave; $8, free with Valdez Museum ticket; ⏲9am-5pm) This annex of the Valdez Museum (p195) is dominated by a scale model of the Old Valdez township. Each home destroyed in the Good Friday Earthquake has been restored in miniature, with the family's name in front. In the theater, stick around to check out the film *Between the Glacier and the Sea,* including a collection of first-hand accounts of the 1964 earthquake.

The exhibits on the earthquake and subsequent tsunamis and fires are moving, and there is a decent collection of pioneer-era artifacts.

Activities

Hiking

One good day hike and another potential two-day excursion start from Valdez town. There are several other excellent trails in Keystone Canyon (p198), starting roughly 12 miles from Valdez on the Richardson Hwy.

Mineral Creek Trail HIKING
A great walk away from town is the trek to the old Smith Stamping Mill. Built by WL Smith in 1913, the mill required only two men to operate it and used mercury to remove the gold from the ore. To reach the trailhead, turn onto Mineral Creek Rd from Hanagita St.

The marginal road bumps for 5.5 miles along a velvety green valley adorned with dozens of precipitous waterfalls. The last mile is on a narrower trail often rendered a scramble by landslides. Bears and mountain goats are commonly visible on this hike.

Shoup Bay Trail HIKING
This verdant stunner has views of Port Valdez, Shoup Glacier and the impressive Gold Creek Delta. Turn around when you reach Gold Creek Bridge at Mile 3.5 to make this a somewhat-challenging day, or go another seven steep, difficult and not always perfectly maintained miles along the water (and sometimes through it), bearing right to follow Shoup Bay to its tidewater glacier.

A free campsite and two reservable public-use cabins, Kittiwake (p200) and Moraine, are at the end of the trail, near a noisy kittiwake rookery. **McAllister Creek Cabin** (☎907-269-8400; www.dnr.alaska.gov; cabin $70) is accessible by boat only. The trailhead is at a parking lot at the western terminus of Egan Dr. Bring mosquito repellent and prepare to get wet feet.

Keystone Canyon Pack Trail HIKING

One of three interconnecting trails in Keystone Canyon that were once part of the abortive All-American Route to the Klondike goldfields, the 'pack trail' was later part of a wagon trail that followed a telegraph line from Valdez to Eagle in the Interior. This part of the trail was abandoned in the 1910s, but renovated and cleared 90 years later.

The trail starts 12 miles from Valdez on the Old Richardson Hwy Loop and ascends through spruce and hemlock forest via a series of switchbacks. There are views of Keystone Canyon before the trail descends to Horsetail Falls and the intersection with the **Goat Trail**. Parts of the route have guide-ropes to assist hikers through steep sections.

Dock Point Trail HIKING

Not so much a hike as an enjoyable stroll through Dock Point Park with the Duck Flats on one side and Port Valdez on the other. The 1-mile loop offers views of the peaks and the water, proximity to eagle nests, as well as salmonberry and blueberry picking.

John Hunter Memorial Trail HIKING

A mile past the Solomon Gulch Fish Hatchery on Dayville Rd, this 1.7-mile trail (one way) is a steep uphill hike on an unremarkable gravel road (underneath lies the Alaska Pipeline).

At a fork at the top, a left turn leads to an overlook with views of Port Valdez, while a right turn meanders up to Solomon Lake, whose dam is the source of 80% of Valdez' power.

Paddling

The waters around Valdez are a kayaker's paradise. People sticking to the bay will be rewarded with views of seagulls fighting over cannery offal for the first hour or so and it's worthwhile heading out with a guided outfit or water taxi. Independent kayakers should

HELI-SKIING

Valdez is legend. It has some of the steepest, deepest, gnarliest and burliest snow-riding terrain anywhere in the world.

At inland ski resorts in, say, Colorado, dry powder barely clings to 50-degree inclines; here in the coastal Chugach Mountains, the sopping-wet flakes glue to angles of 60-plus-degrees, creating ski slopes where elsewhere there'd be cliffs. Factor in 1000in of snow per winter and mountains that descend 7000ft from peak to sea, and you've got a ski bum's version of Eden.

The season lasts only from February to the end of April. And because helicopters often get grounded due to poor weather (or you need to find safe terrain because of avalanche danger), it's recommended that you schedule at least five days for a trip, expecting that you'll get three or four days of great turns.

The operations will provide you with a knowledgeable guide, along with avalanche equipment including a beacon, shovel, probe and air-bag pack. Expect an average of six runs a day. That's more than enough to leave your quads pulverized.

Heli-skiing is for advanced and expert skiers only. And while your guides know this terrain well, avalanches do happen (though the heavy maritime snow generally creates consistent, stable snow pack). It still pays to know how to use your beacon and have some understanding of safe backcountry travel – your guides will give you tutorials when you get there. Get up-to-date avalanche information at www.avalanche.org.

Points North Heli Adventures (☎907-424-7991; www.alaskaheliski.com; Orca Adventure Lodge; 7-day all-inclusive $5975) Based in Cordova where it organizes all-inclusive ski-lodging packages out of the Orca Adventure Lodge (p207).

H2O Heli-Guides (☎907-835-8418; www.alaskahelicopterskiing.com; 300 Airport Rd) Has seven-day helicopter-skiing packages with or without lodging from $5729 in the Chugach Mountains from late February to late April.

Valdez Heli-Ski Guides (☎907-835-4528; www.valdezheliskiguides.com; Mile 35, Richardson Hwy) If extreme skiing down 6200ft runs tickles your fancy, check out these guys, who offer a day of heli-skiing (usually six runs) for $1350, plus lodge-ski packages for three to seven days for $4744 to $11,076. For advanced skiers only. Accommodation is in the lovely Tsaina Lodge (p200).

be aware of no-go zones around the pipeline terminal and moving tankers; contact the **US Coast Guard** (☎907-831-0546; 235 Fidalgo Dr) for current regulations.

Only experienced paddlers should attempt to paddle the open water from Valdez Arm to the Columbia Glacier, a multiday trip. Anadyr Adventures can arrange for a drop-off and pickup near the glacier, or a full-on guided trip.

★Anadyr Adventures KAYAKING
(☎907-835-2814; www.anadyradventures.com; 225 N Harbor Dr) Anadyr Adventures is what Alaska is all about – rugged but accessible trips into the wilderness with fun, experienced guides who are mad about the great outdoors. There's a choice of sea or lake kayaking, some involving a transfer. The rub? With the ever-changing glaciers, you never quite know what you're going to get.

Trips range from a day at Columbia Glacier ($299) to several days on the water aboard a 'mothership' (two days $1550). For those with less time, try the half-day trip to the nearby Valdez Glacier ($140), which involves kayaking on an iceberg-filled lake and climbing into blue ice caves during a walk on the glacier.

Shoup Bay KAYAKING
Protected as a state marine park, this bay off Valdez Arm makes for a great kayaking trip from Valdez, with overnighting at McAllister Creek Cabin (p197). The bay is home to a retreating glacier.

It's 10 miles to the bay and another 4 miles up to the glacier. You must enter the bay two hours before the incoming tide to avoid swift tidal currents.

Rafting

The glacial Lowe River, 12 miles from Valdez, cuts through impressive Keystone Canyon. A popular trip is to raft the relatively easy class III rapids through sheer canyon walls and cascading waterfalls. The highlight is a stop to look at Bridal Veil Falls, which drops 900ft from the canyon walls. **Pangaea Adventures** (☎907-835-8442; www.alaskasummer.com; 107 N Harbor Dr) offers a three-hour raft down the river for $89.

Tours

VS Helicoptors SCENIC FLIGHTS
(☎907-831-0643; www.vshelicopters.com; 300 Airport Rd) A fantastic way to see the glaciers and peaks around Valdez is by helicopter. Tours are $250 to $595 for up to 2½ hours for three people or less, and well worth every cent: you'll be up close to wildlife (including bears and goats), calving glaciers and historic mines. The quirkiest tour? Fly-out yoga in the wilderness!

Stan Stephens Glacier & Wildlife Cruises BOATING
(☎907-835-4731,866-867-1297; www.stanstephenscruises.com; 112 N Harbor Dr; ⏲May-Sep) The biggest tour operator in town runs large vessels on six-hour journeys to Columbia Glacier (adult/child $132/66) and 8½-hour trips (adult/child $165/82) to Mears Glacier (which you can generally get closer to).

Lunch and lots of tummy-warming tea are included.

Lu-Lu Belle Glacier Wildlife Cruises BOATING
(☎800-411-0090; www.lulubelletours.com; Kobuk Dr; adult/child $130/75; ⏲tours depart 1pm daily) The dainty and ornately appointed MV *Lu-Lu Belle* is all polished wood, leather and Asian rugs. The daily cruise into Columbia Bay passes Glacier Island for puffin-watching and can get within a half-mile of the glacier, conditions permitting. Cruises last approximately seven hours, but the captain is flexible. If whales are spotted, he'll hang around. There's a small cafe on board.

Festivals & Events

Gold Rush Days CULTURAL
(www.valdezgoldrushdays.org; ⏲Jul/Aug) A five-day festival in late July or early August, this hometown rocker includes a parade, bed races, dances, a free fish feed and a portable jailhouse that's pulled through town by locals, who arrest people without beards and other innocent bystanders.

Sleeping

The town has a good selection of accommodations, including a couple of business-like hotels, some more-spartan motels and copious popular RV parks and campgrounds. Curiously, there's no hostel.

Valdez' 6% bed tax is not included in quoted rates.

Bear Paw RV Campground CAMPGROUND $
(☎907-835-2530; www.bearpawrvpark.com; 101 N Harbor Dr; tent sites $20-25, RV sites $40-45; P 📶) This mega-popular park has two sites. The main one (where you check-in) is right downtown in a big barren parking

lot behind the small-boat harbor (on Wyatt Way). The more wooded Bear Paw II welcomes recreational vehicles (RVs) and tents, is right on the water and is for adults only. People rave about the spotlessly clean shower and bathroom blocks, strong wi-fi and friendly management.

Eagle's Rest RV Park CAMPGROUND $
(907-800-553-7275; www.eaglesrestrv.com; 139 E Pioneer Dr; tent sites $27, RV sites $38-50, cabins $135-155;) On the edge of town, this RV park has nice views, plus showers and laundry. The small wooden cabins have cable TV and coffee machines.

Kittiwake Cabin CABIN $
(907-269-8400; www.alaskastateparks.org; cabins $70) This reservable public-use cabin is located at the end of the rough 11-mile Shoup Bay Trail (p197), near a noisy kittiwake rookery. There's another similar cabin (Moraine) nearby. Both cabins sleep eight.

Valdez Glacier Campground CAMPGROUND $
(907-835-2282; Airport Rd; tent sites $15-20, RV sites $20-40) Located 6 miles out of town toward the Valdez Glacier, this spot has 101 pleasant wooded sites and a foaming waterfall. It's part-owned by the military and there's a firing range next door (read: occasional noise). Hot showers (free for campers) are a huge bonus.

Robe Lake Lodge LODGE $$
(907-831-2339; www.robelakelodge.com; Mile 6, Richardson Hwy; d/q/whole lodge $189/209/1099; P) This large traditional house 6 miles outside Valdez has six small rooms (all with shared bath). The place is built out of full scribe logs with massive beams crossing the vaulted ceilings. The hot tub has a view of the absurdly pretty Robe Lake – as does the wraparound balcony – but you can also warm up in the sauna.

Continental breakfast is served in the great room, and if you rent the whole place out (a popular option with families and hunting groups) you have access to the full kitchen. There are also trails to the lake, and a canoe for paddling around.

Best Western Valdez Harbor Inn HOTEL $$
(907-835-3434; www.valdezharborinn.com; 100 N Harbor Dr; r $169-179, ste $194-209; P) This is a strong pick if you are looking for comfort on the waterfront. The independently run hotel has the standard business-savvy rooms you'd expect from the Best Western chain, with a few pictures of jumping orcas to remind you you're in Alaska. There's also a fitness room, free airport shuttle and a pretty substantial breakfast included.

Mountain Sky Hotel BUSINESS HOTEL $$
(907-835-4445; www.mountainskyhotel.com; 100 Meals Ave; d/ste $189/209; P) This business hotel is set in an inordinately large parking lot, but has OK rooms (despite the old-school TVs) and good views (if you can see past the parking lot). For comfort, it's not the top midrange choice, but the staff are friendly, it's uncluttered and clean, and the spa suites have romantic tubs. It also has the Valdez Bistro.

Keystone Hotel HOTEL $$
(907-835-3851, 888-835-0665; www.keystonehotel.com; 401 W Egan Dr; s/d $125/132; P) The Keystone looks like one of those utilitarian container hotels aimed at oil workers in the Arctic. Not surprisingly it was conceived during the pipeline boom years. However, give this industrial prefab structure a chance. The small rooms are clean and the staff are friendly. Small continental breakfast included.

Totem Inn HOTEL $$
(907-835-4443, 888-808-4431; www.toteminn.com; 144 E Egan Dr; cabin/ste $204/249; P) Since a fire took out its restaurant and main lodge, the Totem has been reduced to offering upscale suites and a row of lesser-endowed tin-box cabins (popular with fishers). The one-bedroom suites have full kitchens; some have sofa-beds. The cabins are staler and overpriced.

Tsaina Lodge BOUTIQUE HOTEL $$$
(907-835-3535; www.tsainalodge.com; Mile 35, Richardson Hwy; d $279-299; P) Something of an apparition 35 miles east of Valdez on the Richardson Hwy is this gorgeous boutique hotel that is taken over by the heli-skiing set in the winter, but open to all-comers in the summer. The design is modern and minimalist throughout, with outstanding deluxe beds and linens. There's also a lounge (with fireplace), fine-dining restaurant and bar on-site.

Take note TV addicts – there aren't any.

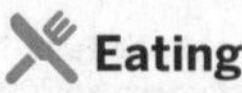

Eating

Valdez has Prince William Sound's best stash of restaurants, with a couple of inventive newer places awakening the food scene

THE DAY THE EARTH MOVED

On March 27, 1964, Valdez was hit by the second-strongest earthquake in human history. The quake, which registered a magnitude of 9.2 on the Richter scale, prompted a huge underwater landslide that caused Valdez' entire city dock to break off and collapse into the sea. A tsunami and fire destroyed much of what survived the initial 4½-minute-long tremor. All 32 people on the dock that day were killed. However, the SS *Chena*, a ship that was unloading its cargo at the time, miraculously survived despite being thrown 30ft into the air by the waves.

Following the quake it was revealed that the city of Valdez, founded in the late 1890s by gold prospectors, had been sited on unstable ground. It was thus decided to move the town en masse to safer terrain several miles to the west. The move, which involved drawing up a brand-new townsite on a square flat grid, took three years to plan and execute. Over 30 surviving houses from what was left of the semi-ruined town were ultimately towed over to the new site at the mouth of Mineral Creek. The old townsite was quickly abandoned and, over time, it has returned largely to nature. Today, the only evidence of its once-bustling streets is a poignant memorial and a series of small markers denoting where important buildings once stood.

from its former drowsiness. The local specialty is – guess what? – fish.

★ Roadside Potatohead AMERICAN **$**
(907-835-3058; www.theroadsidepotatohead.com; 255 N Harbor Dr; burritos $10-11; 7am-8pm May-Sep) An offshoot of a legendary wilderness food cart in McCarthy, this Valdez incarnation sits on foundations rather than wheels in a fine harborside location. It knocks out the kind of carb-heavy menu often necessary in these rugged parts; its specialty is fries (including the signature rosemary and garlic fries) and all their associated accompaniments, such as the ever-popular pulled pork po'boy.

Old Town Burgers BURGERS **$**
(E Pioneer Dr; burgers $8-15; 5am-10pm) A super-popular burger and breakfast joint with indoor picnic tables, lightning-fast service, free coffee and – often – a line out the door. It does all the diner favorites as well as fish tacos, and halibut and chips, but the real stars are the burgers and curly fries. No booze.

Rogue's Garden MARKET **$**
(354 Fairbanks Dr; sandwiches $8-10; 7:30am-6pm Mon-Fri, 9am-5pm Sun;) A health-food market – in small-town Alaska? Enjoy it while you're here, especially the tip-top deli, where you can customize your sandwich or smoothie. There's a small seating area if it's cold outside.

Valdez Bistro SOUTHERN US, KOREAN **$$**
(907-835-4445; 100 Meals Ave; mains $9-21; 6am-10pm) Southern American and Korean cuisine engage in an unlikely dance at this casual open-all-hours restaurant in the Mountain Sky Hotel. Though not endowed with typical bistro airs, it is the only Valdez restaurant with an executive chef and certainly the only one that puts *bulgogi* (Korean barbecued beef) on the same menu as gumbo and shrimp 'n' grits.

Auntie Yum Yum's Real Thai Food THAI **$$**
(N Harbor Dr; mains $12-18; 11am-7pm) Of Valdez' smattering of summer food carts this is the best. After digging into its lashings of pad Thai noodles (with pork or shrimp), any hike will seem easy. It usually sets up opposite the harbor with some picnic tables outside.

Mike's Palace ITALIAN **$$**
(201 N Harbor Dr; mains $14-34; 11am-10pm Sun-Thu, 11am-11pm Fri & Sat;) Palace? Mike's is more like a *ristorante* in the rough, but in a totally good way. The theme is American-Italian with a few attempts at Mexican (which are probably best left alone) and some better stabs at seafood.

First order a super-cold draft beer in a chilled glass, then peruse the extensive menu, which contains a whole page of creative (and huge) pasta dishes as well as pizzas and veal parmigiana. For hungry hikers who manage to polish off all this, an ambrosial tiramisu awaits.

Fat Mermaid PIZZA **$$**
(907-835-2788; 143 N Harbor Dr; sandwiches $12-13, pizzas $14-24; 6:30am-1am) First things first: the Fat Mermaid has got

Valdez' best selection of beers, with drafts from three different Alaskan breweries. Second, the food's quite adventurous too, with an eclectic menu featuring funked-out sandwiches like a taste-bud-popping wasabi chicken, inventive pizzas and a standard assortment of seafood. Then there's the outdoor deck – perfect on a long summer's evening for gazing wistfully at the mountains.

Drinking & Nightlife

There's a dearth of bars in Valdez. Even the standard Alaskan dives are missing. Most of the restaurants serve good cold beer. Keep your ear to the ground for word of summer house parties.

Latte Dah Espresso COFFEE
(130 Meals Ave; ⏲6am-4pm Mon-Sat, to 2pm Sun) Don't bother with any fact-gathering opinion polls. This is the best coffee in town – Kaladi Brothers, no less (Alaska's finest) perfectly pulled into your 8oz or 12oz cup in a dinky little cafe with a warm, friendly vibe a block back from the harbor.

Shopping

Prospector SPORTS & OUTDOORS
(☎907-835-3538; www.prospectoroutfitters.com; 200 Egan Dr; ⏲9am-8pm Mon-Sat, noon-6pm Sun) Just the kind of outfitters' shop you want and need somewhere like Valdez. It sells all the outdoor essentials, including that fleece you'd forgotten and that camping food you were craving.

Information

MEDICAL SERVICES

Valdez Medical Clinic (☎907-835-4811; 912 Meals Ave) Provides walk-in care.

Valdez Providence Medical Center (☎907-835-2249; 911 Meals Ave) Has an emergency room.

MONEY

Wells Fargo (☎907-835-4381; 337 Egan Dr; ⏲10am-5pm) Bank and ATM.

TOURIST INFORMATION

Valdez Visitor Information Center (☎907-835-2984; www.valdezalaska.org; 309 Fairbanks Dr; ⏲9am-6pm Mon-Fri, 10am-7pm Sat & Sun) Has a few interesting historical photos and plenty of free maps and brochures. There's also an unstaffed information booth at the airport.

Crooked Creek Information Site (☎907-835-4680; Mile 0.9, Richardson Hwy; ⏲8am-5pm May-Sep) Staffed by US Forest Service (USFS) naturalists, this place half a mile outside town on the Richardson Hwy offers great advice about outdoor activities.

Harbormaster's Office (☎907-835-4981; 300 N Harbor Dr; ⏲8am-10pm Jun-Aug, 8:30am-5pm Sep-May) Has showers ($4).

Getting There & Away

AIR

The small **Valdez Airport** (Airport Rd) is four miles northeast of town. There are two or three daily flights to Anchorage ($185, 45 minutes) with **Ravn Alaska** (☎907-835-2636; www.flyravn.com).

BOAT

Alaska Marine Highway ferries (p194) sail regularly to Whittier ($78) and Cordova ($58). They run every two to three days in the summer. The Cordova run takes all day. The Ferry Terminal is in the town center.

BUS

Soaring Eagle Transit (☎907-822-4545; www.gulkanacouncil.org) runs a summer shuttle between Valdez and Anchorage ($130, 6¼ hours) via Glennallen ($65, 2¼ hours) on Tuesday, Thursday and Saturday. There's no office in Valdez. Book in advance.

Cordova

☎907 / POP 2200

Cordova is about as real as Alaska gets. Detached from the state's primary road network and rarely visited by cruise ships, this small mainland fishing community feels more like an island floating in a brawny wilderness, with the impenetrable Chuguch Mountains on one side and the bird-rich Copper River Delta on the other.

Roll in on an airplane or a ferry, and you'll find yourself disgorged into an eccentric little fishing village where everyone knows everyone else, patrons prop up grimy bars in yellow oilskins, and no one gives a hoot about image or pretense.

Outside its gritty harbor, Cordova has a network of clearly marked trails beloved by locals, one of the US's dinkiest ski areas, incredible bird-watching potential and a festival dedicated to ice worms.

Within an hour of docking and landing, you'll quickly ascertain that this town has yet to sell its soul to tourism. All the more reason to visit today.

Sights

Cordova Museum MUSEUM
(907-424-6665; 601 1st St; $1 donation; 10am-5pm Tue-Sat) Cordova's Museum is located in the impressive Cordova Center (p210). It features local artwork and a colorful overview of the city's history. There's a plush gift store next door.

Small-boat Harbor HARBOR
In Cordova, the standard greeting among locals is 'Been fishing?' Unsurprisingly, the harbor is the community's heart, humming throughout the season as fishers frantically try to meet their quota before the runs are closed.

Watching over the hubbub is the **Cordova Fisherman's Memorial**, a quiet place dominated by artist Joan Bugbee Jackson's sculpture *The Southeasterly* (1985), and spotted with flower bouquets.

The fishing fleet is composed primarily of seiners and gillnetters, with the method used by the fishers determining the species of salmon they pursue.

The former primarily target pink salmon, while the latter, generally one-person operations, go for kings and reds early in the season and silvers later on.

Ilanka Cultural Center CULTURAL CENTER
(907-424-7903; 110 Nicholoff Way; 10am-5pm Mon-Fri) FREE This compact museum operated by local Alaska Natives has a small but high-quality collection of Alaska Native art from all over the state. Don't miss the intact killer-whale skeleton – one of only five in the world – with flippers that could give you quite a slap.

Also on display is artist Mike Webber's Shame Pole, a totem pole that tells the grim tale of the oil spill, spitting back the famous words of Exxon's then top official Don Cornett: 'We will make you whole again.' This place also has a wonderful gift shop and offers classes on such crafty subjects as scrimshaw and spruce-root weaving. Call for a schedule.

Salmon Canneries FACTORY
Every summer Cordova's population swells with young idealists, opportunists and stragglers hoping to make a mint by canning salmon on 16-hour shifts.

Whether you're curious about the effects of sleep deprivation on adventurous teenagers or just want to see how some of the finest salmon in the world is processed, ask at the Chamber of Commerce (p211) about canneries offering tours.

You can watch your own catch get processed at **Northern Fish Alaska** (northernfishalaska.com), a smaller-scale operation that packs salmon and ships it to your home.

Prince William Sound Science Center MUSEUM
(907-424-5800; www.pwssc.org; 300 Breakwater Ave; 8:30am-5:30pm Mon-Fri;) FREE This dockside research facility offers themed 'Discovery Packs' for kids, which include information on the birds, flora and geology of Cordova.

Inside the building there's not much for visitors to see save a few interesting brochures, but the researchers are happy to answer questions about local ecology.

Activities

Devoid of cruise ships, Cordova doesn't have much in the way of organized activities. DIYers, however, will have a field day. Borrow a bike, grab some binoculars and/or join a community hike.

Hiking

Cordovans cherish their trail network. More than 35 miles of trails are accessible from the small road network surrounding the town. Several of these paths lead to USFS cabins.

As in much of the Southeast, the hiking is excellent, combining lush forest with alpine terrain, an expansive river delta rich in birdlife and tons of glaciers.

★Heney Ridge Trail HIKING
Cordova's most popular trail – as it incorporates multiple ecosystems and is only 5 miles from town – is this fairly easy 3.7-mile (one-way) route beginning by a bridge near the end of the Whitshed Rd.

The first stretch winds around reedy Hartney Bay, followed by a mellow 2-mile climb to the tree line through forests and wildflowers (and, in rainy weather, lots of mud – rubber boots are recommended).

It's another steep mile up to the ridge, where you'll enjoy a gorgeous view.

Cordova

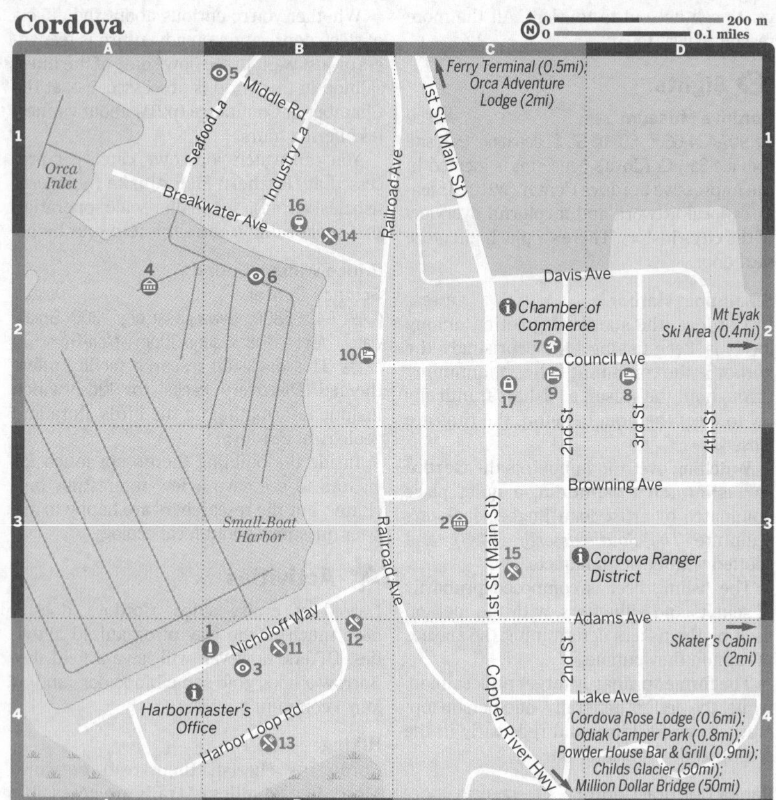

Sheridan Mountain Trail HIKING

This trail starts near the picnic tables at the end of Sheridan Glacier Rd, which runs 4.3 miles from the turnoff at Mile 13 of Copper River Hwy. Most of the 2.9-mile route is a moderate climb, which passes through mature forests before breaking out into an alpine basin.

From there, the view of mountains and the Sheridan and Sherman Glaciers is stunning, and it only gets better when you start climbing the surrounding rim. This trail isn't the best maintained of routes, putting it into the 'difficult' category.

Crater Lake & Power Creek Trails HIKING

For remarkable views of the pancake-flat Copper River Delta glimmering behind Cordova's guardian mountains, climb the 2.4-mile Crater Lake Trail, which begins on Eyak Lake across from Skater's Cabin. The trail ascends steeply through mossy forest to a lookout at the 1-mile mark, beyond which the path flattens out. As it's on a south-facing slope, the path is often snow-free by late May.

Once at the lake (frozen until early summer) you can continue on the 4½-mile ridge route (the Alice Smith Intertie), which descends to the Power Creek Trail. The entire 12-mile loop makes for an ideal overnight backpacking trip. Halfway along the ridge is a free-use shelter, while at Mile 4.2 of the Power Creek Trail is the USFS Power Creek Cabin. Arrange to be dropped off at the Power Creek trailhead and hike all the way back into town via the Mt Eyak Trail.

McKinley Lake & Pipeline Lakes Trails HIKING

The 2.5-mile McKinley Lake Trail begins at Mile 21.6 of the Copper River Hwy and leads to the head of the lake and the remains of

Cordova

the Lucky Strike gold mine. There are two USFS cabins: McKinley Lake Cabin, just past the trailhead, and McKinley Trail Cabin, at Mile 2.4.

The abandoned Lucky Strike mine is accessible via an unmaintained trail behind McKinley Trail Cabin. Departing from the midway point of the McKinley Lake Trail is the Pipeline Lakes Trail, which loops back to the Copper River Hwy at Mile 21.4.

Almost all of this marshy 2-mile trail has been boardwalked to provide easier access to several small lakes packed with grayling and cutthroat trout, but if it's rainy consider bringing rubber boots.

Saddlebag Glacier Trail HIKING

You reach this trail via a firewood-cutting road at Mile 25 of Copper River Hwy. It's an easy 3-mile walk through cottonwoods and spruce, emerging at Saddlebag Lake. Outstanding views of surrounding peaks and cliffs (and maybe mountain goats) are made even more fabulous by the namesake glacier, which litters the lake with icebergs.

Cycling

Most of Cordova's trails are too muddy and steep to ride; an exception is the Saddlebag Glacier Trail.

However, if you have a few days, the Copper River Hwy itself is a straight, though sometimes windy, mountain-biking route. The road is flat and paved up to Mile 12. There were no official bike rentals in Cordova at the time of research; ask around at your hotel or B&B.

Bird-Watching

The **Copper River Delta** and the rich waters of Prince William Sound attract an astonishing number and variety of birds. Spring migration is the busiest, and that is when the town hosts the Copper River Delta Shorebird Festival (p210). Stop at the **Cordova Ranger District** (USFS Office; 877-444-6777; 612 2nd St; 8am-5pm Mon-Fri) for a birding checklist and advice about where to break out the binoculars.

A favorite birding area is Hartney Bay, 6 miles southwest of Cordova along Whitshed Rd, where as many as 70,000 shorebirds congregate during spring migration. Bring rubber boots and plan to be there two hours before or after high tide for the best fall and spring viewing conditions. Sawmill Bay, at Mile 3 of Whitshed Rd, is also a prime bird-watching spot.

Another good place for bird- and wildlife-watching is Alaganik Slough. Turn south on Alaganik Slough Rd at Mile 17 of Copper River Hwy and travel 3 miles to the end, where a picnic area and boardwalk offer great views of dusky Canada geese, bald eagles and other feathered friends.

Paddling

The Copper River flows for 287 miles, beginning at Copper Glacier near Slana in the Interior and ending in the Gulf of Alaska, east of Cordova. Most of the river is for experienced rafters, as rapids, glaciers and narrow canyons give it a white-water rating of Class II to III much of the way. The 20-mile stretch between Million Dollar Bridge and Flag Point, at Mile 27 of the

Copper River Hwy, is considerably wider and slower. Below Flag Point, the river becomes heavily braided, which inevitably means dragging your boat through shallow channels.

For skiff rentals to remote lodges check at the small-boat harbor.

For blue-water paddlers, Orca Adventure Lodge is the only kayak operation working in town. Rent kayaks ($65 per day) here for a fun day trip up the coast to Nelson Bay.

Skiing

Mt Eyak Ski Area SKIING
(☎907-424-7766; www.mteyak.org; 6th St; lift ticket $30; ⌚mid-Nov–mid-May) Hardly anyone comes to Cordova specifically to ski, which means the small but much-cherished Mt Eyak ski area, just a quick walk from town, is utilized primarily by locals. It features an 800ft drop, an average 118in of natural snow annually, and runs that accommodate everyone from novice snowboarders to world-class skiers.

The most famous attraction is the vintage single-seater ski lift salvaged from Sun Valley, Idaho, the oldest working chairlift in North America.

During the summer (when the chairlift doesn't operate), the ski run doubles up as a mountain trail, which connects with the Crater Lake Trail (via a short intertie) and the summit of Mt Eyak.

Festivals & Events

Iceworm Festival CULTURAL
(www.cordovachamber.com; ⌚Feb) Cordova's famous homegrown, tongue-in-cheek event is held on the second weekend of February. It includes the crowning of a Miss Iceworm, the Survival Suit Race, in which participants don survival suits and plunge into the harbor, and a parade that culminates with a giant ice-worm float.

Ice worms spend their entire lives on ice, and if they warm up too much they disintegrate (read: melt). These little critters feed on snow algae, and thread through tiny cracks in the ice.

Their coloring tends to mimic glacial ice: white or blue. They're just mysterious enough that not only did they became the topic of a Robert Service poem, 'Ballad of the Ice-worm Cocktail,' but they've also captured the attention of NASA, which has been studying what makes the worms such excellent survivors.

Sleeping

There aren't a lot of tourists in Cordova and thus accommodation is thin on the ground, with one good B&B, a motel and a reasonable hotel in the town itself, plus a few other options – including campgrounds – scattered around. The town tacks an additional 12% in bed and sales tax onto rates.

Skater's Cabin CABIN $
(☎907-424-7282; Eyak Lake; cabin 1st/2nd/3rd night $25/60/110) In a beautiful Eyak Lake setting, 2 miles east of town on Lake Ave, with a scoop of gravel beach and a woodstove, this one-room cabin can be booked through the **Bidarki Recreation Center** (☎907-424-7282; cnr 2nd St & Council Ave; $10; ⌚8am-1pm & 4-8pm Mon-Fri, noon-8pm Sat). There are no bunks, but a few tables and chairs, so bring your sleeping pad, food and water. There's an outhouse on-site and a fire pit with grill on the beach.

You'll have to scavenge your own wood. The escalating prices for further nights are to deter multiday use so more people can enjoy it.

Shelter Cove Campground CAMPGROUND $
(☎907-424-7282; Orca Rd; tent & RV sites $20) Several raised tent platforms and a dozen RV sites set back from the road, a half-mile north of the ferry terminal, are a good option for those leaving on an early-morning ferry. There are no showers or sinks, just an outhouse.

Odiak Camper Park CAMPGROUND $
(☎907-424-7282; Whitshed Rd; tent/RV sites $5/25) A half-mile from town, this is basically a gravel parking lot with a restroom and a view. It's popular with seasonal fishers. Make reservations at the Bidarki Recreation Center.

Orca Adventure Lodge LODGE $$
(☎866-424-6722, 907-424-7249; www.orcaadventurelodge.com; Orca Rd; d/ste $165/220; P ☎) Artfully encased in the erstwhile Orca Cannery two miles north of downtown where the road ends, this self-contained waterfront lodge caters to wilderness lovers with daily adventure-tour packages. Most rooms have ocean views plus there's a ravishing on-site restaurant (guests only), games area and plenty of local info.

It's particularly popular with fishers, but it also organizes kayaking and wildlife photography excursions along with trips by boat to see the Childs Glacier. It's a professional but very friendly operation.

Northern Nights Inn APARTMENT **$$**
(907-424-5356; www.northernnightsinn.com; cnr 3rd St & Council Ave; r from $110; P) Run out of a 1910 heritage home, the NN offers four old-school rooms in the house itself along with accommodations in a self-contained apartment down on the harborside. Both options are economical and full of homespun Cordova charm. The apartment comes complete with kitchen, two bedrooms and a large open-plan lounge with views over the clustered fishing fleet in the harbor.

Reluctant Fisherman Inn HOTEL **$$**
(800-770-3272, 907-424-3272; www.reluctantfisherman.com; cnr Railroad & Council Aves; r $135-185; P) As close to luxurious as Cordova gets, this fishy place overhangs Orca Inlet and is affiliated with the eponymous restaurant and bar. Some of the tidy rooms complete with parquet floors and fish-prints have been remodeled; all are shipshape. Pay a little extra for a harbor view.

Cordova Rose Lodge INN **$$**
(907-424-7673; www.cordovarose.com; 1315 Whitshed Rd; r $155; P) This spot has a higgledy-piggledy assortment of structures, including a lighthouse and rooms in a large barge, docked – sort of – on Odiak Slough. Rooms are small and quaint and adorned with seafaring themes. All come with breakfast and have use of a communal living room, kitchen and sauna.

Prince William Motel MOTEL **$$**
(907-424-3201; www.princewilliammotel.com; 501 2nd St; r/ste $140/160; P) There are eight rooms with kitchenettes and eight more with full kitchens at this utilitarian but perfectly comfortable motel. Regular remodeling has kept the place up-to-date and the service is amicable.

Eating

★Baja Taco MEXICAN **$**
(907-424-5599; Harbor Loop Rd; tacos $4.50, mains $12-18; 7am-9pm) Alaska has a remarkably healthy quota of scruffy-in-a-good-way food trucks, some of which have sprung more permanent foundations. A case in point is Baja Taco, an antediluvian school bus grafted onto the side of a bedraggled wooden cabin that sports an all-over-the-map menu of juicy treats from dawn till dusk.

Of the many highlights are the breakfast muffins, the rich yogurt and granola, and – best of all – the Mexican-style *migas* (eggs and fried tortilla strips).

Little Cordova Bakery CAFE, BAKERY **$**
(907-424-5623; 210 Breakwater Ave; snacks $2-5; 5:30am-2:30pm Thu-Sat, to 4:30pm Sun & Wed) Up with the larks to provide sweetness and caffeine for early-morning fishing trawlers, this tiny bakery (no seating) offers a gorgeous mélange of almond pastries, cinnamon buns, fresh bread and jolting cups of joe.

Harborside Pizza PIZZA **$**
(907-424-3730; 131 Harbor Loop Rd; pizza & pasta $6-17, per slice $3.50-7; 11am-9pm) Expanded to include a slick sit-down eating space, this emporium of fine pizza is still insanely popular, meaning it can be hard to get a seat on a busy night when half of Cordova piles in. Phone ahead, or arrive early.

AC Value Center SUPERMARKET **$**
(106 Nicholoff Way; 7:30am-10pm Mon-Sat, 8am-9pm Sun) A supermarket with a deli, drip-coffee flasks, ATM and Western Union. It also sells camping and fishing gear.

WILDERNESS CABINS

There are 15 United State Forest Service (USFS) cabins located in the Cordova area, and they're much easier to reserve than those in other Southcentral Alaskan parts. Three are best accessible by boat or plane: Tideman Slough bunks six in the wilderness of the Copper River flats; Softuk Bar sleeps six on a remote beach 40 miles southeast of Cordova; and popular Martin Lake, 30 minutes east of town by floatplane, has a rowboat and sleeps six people. Two others are along the McKinley Lake Trail and a third is on the Power Creek Trail. Hinchinbrook Island, 20 minutes from Cordova by plane and, at most, two hours by boat, has three more cabins: Shelter Bay, Double Bay and Hook Point. The other cabins are further afield. Check with the Cordova Ranger District (p205) for more details.

CHRISTOPHER BOSWELL/SHUTTERSTOCK ©

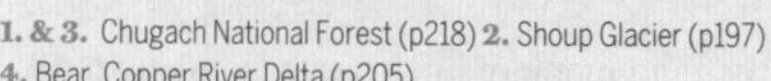

1. & 3. Chugach National Forest (p218) **2.** Shoup Glacier (p197) **4.** Bear, Copper River Delta (p205)

KEVIN SMITH / DESIGN PICS/GETTY IMAGES ©

Prince William Sound Wild Explorer

Prince William Sound is massive. It's wild. It's everything Alaska was meant to be. Beyond the villages of Cordova, Valdez and Whittier, out-of-this-world terrestrial and maritime adventures await. Grab your backpack, put on your rain jacket and hold on tight for some of the best hiking and paddling around.

Shoup Bay (p199)

Once used as a rough route to the Klondike goldfields, the Valdez Glacier still throws up the rusty remains of equipment abandoned by prospectors past. Paddle silently past icebergs on its glacial lake before landing for a walk on the moraine-covered ice itself, where you can peer into glassy crevasses and examine chilly blue ice caves.

Chugach National Forest (p218)

Basically all the mountains, islands, fjords and glaciers of Prince William Sound fall within the boundaries of this 10,780-sq-mile forest, the second largest in the US, after Tongass National Forest in Southeast Alaska. Trek, paddle or – even better – heli-ski to corners seldom visited.

Copper River Delta (p205)

Just outside Cordova, the mountains step back and make room for the sky. Here you'll find the 700,000-acre Copper River Delta, a wildlife-rich wilderness with amazing opportunities for birding, fishing, hiking and rafting. Along the 60-mile Copper River Hwy, you can trek up the Sheridan Mountain Trail, Saddlebag Glacier Trail and more.

Harriman Fjord

Hire a guide in Whittier (p211) to take you on a paddle through a sea of ice on Blackstone Bay, where seven glaciers dump icebergs and jettison chilly waterfalls into Prince William Sound. Arrive in a water taxi, or kayak direct from Whittier and make it a multiday trip with some camping thrown in. Plan to get wet.

DON'T MISS

SHOREBIRD FESTIVAL

On the first weekend of May, the Copper River Delta Shorebird Festival (www.copperriverdeltashorebirdfestival.com) celebrates the largest avian migration in the USA, as some five million shorebirds throng the delta – the biggest continuous wetland on the Pacific coast – en route to their Arctic breeding grounds.

The festival draws birders from the world over, and features presentations and workshops by international experts plus field trips to the prime viewing areas. Non-birders, don't scoff: this event fills every hotel room in town.

Powder House Bar & Grill AMERICAN **$$**
(907-424-3529; Mile 2, Copper River Hwy; mains $8-20; 11am-8pm Sun-Thu, to 9pm Fri & Sat) Overlooking Eyak Lake on the site of the original Copper River & Northwestern Railroad powder house, this is a fun place with live music, excellent beer, soup and sandwiches for lunch, and quality steak and – the highlight – seafood dinners, especially razor clams. Due to its out-of-town location it's 95% local and has that lived-in aroma of old carpets and cooking oil.

There are tranquilizing lake views from the deck.

Reluctant Fisherman Restaurant SEAFOOD **$$**
(907-424-3272, 800-770-3272; www.reluctantfisherman.com; cnr Railroad & Council Aves; meals $19-32; 7am-10pm) The only Cordova restaurant worth putting a clean shirt on for, the RF sits next to its affiliated hotel (p207) and enjoys excellent harbor views and a decent bar scene. The seat-yourself dining space is best for its fresh seafood dishes, some of which have subtle Asian influences.

OK Restaurant ASIAN, AMERICAN **$$**
(616 1st St; lunch $13-15, dinner $15-23; noon-10pm) The OK restaurant is just...OK, if you have a hankering for Chinese...or Japanese...or Korean...or American. The catch-all menu even includes Mongolian beef, and you can wash it all down with pie à la mode.

Drinking & Nightlife

Cordova's bars are primarily trawled by fishing-boat workers fresh off the trawlers.

Reluctant Fisherman Bar BAR
(cnr Railroad & Council Aves; noon-10pm) One of Cordova's less dive-y bars, the best thing about this establishment, besides a healthy selection of microbrews on tap, is its harbor-view deck. It's part of the eponymous hotel and restaurant.

Anchor Bar BAR
(Breakwater Ave; noon-2am) Across from the small-boat harbor, this is your basic Alaskan watering hole that's open 'as long as there are fish.' Also serves basic food.

Entertainment

Cordova Center ARTS CENTER
(907-424-6665; 601 1st St) What a cultural resource! The handsome Cordova Center would make a town 10 times the size proud. Aside from a museum and library, the facility shelters a 206-seat theater that attracts traveling acting groups and film festivals, and has sent Cordova's cultural life onto a different plane.

Shopping

Fill up your backpack with a couple of unique souvenirs from Cordova, such as a locally made fleece jacket with Tlingit or Haida trim.

Copper River Fleece CLOTHING
(800-882-1707; www.copperriverfleece.com; 504 1st St; 10am-6pm Mon-Sat) You'll see plenty of people around town sporting the high-quality, unique fleece jackets, vests and hats here. Colorful trim is the company's signature, and most of the sewing is done upstairs above the shop.

Information

MEDICAL SERVICES

Cordova Community Medical Center (907-424-8000; 602 Chase Rd) Provides emergency services.

MONEY

Wells Fargo (907-424-3258; 515 1st St; 10am-5pm Mon-Fri) Has a 24-hour ATM.

TOURIST INFORMATION

Chamber of Commerce (907-424-7260; www.cordovachamber.com; 404 1st St; 10am-4pm Mon-Fri) If you find it open, you can get visitor info here, or just call and leave a message – the friendly folks will call you back.

Harbormaster's Office (☎907-424-6400; Nicholoff Way; ⏲8am-5pm) Has $5 showers and a small book swap.

ℹ Getting There & Away

AIR

There are two daily flights to Anchorage with either **Alaska Airlines** (p429) or **Ravn Alaska** (p430) and one daily flight to Yakutat, which subsequently carries on to Juneau and Seattle **Merle K Smith Airport** (Copper River Hwy) is 12km east of Cordova. Most accommodations offer a free shuttle service; phone ahead to check.

BOAT

The **Alaska Marine Highway** (☎907-424-7333, 800-642-0066; www.ferryalaska.com) has ferries to Whittier ($81, 6½ hours) every other day in spring and summer. The ferry to Valdez ($58, 14 hours) goes via Whittier and takes all day.

ℹ Getting Around

Compact Cordova can be easily explored on foot, but the problem for travelers exploring the outlying Copper River area is finding transportation. Then again, this is small-town Alaska. With a bit of initiative, you might be able to borrow a bike, share a lift or join in a community hike. Ask around.

Hitchhiking along the Copper River Hwy is possible. The road is well-trafficked up until the airport at Mile 12. Note that the Copper River Hwy to Childs Glacier and the Million Dollar Bridge is closed at the Mile 36 Bridge.

Whittier

☎907 / POP 200

Whittier is both beautiful and ugly, a wonderfully weird Cold War anachronism set on the edge of some sublime coastal wilderness where rugged fjords dispatch tumbling glaciers into Prince William Sound. Even by Alaskan standards, this is a bizarre outpost. The 'town' is dominated by two Cold War military installations: the hopelessly ruined Buckner building and the equally incongruous Begich Towers, a 14-story skyscraper that houses most of Whittier's population.

Founded in 1941 as a deep-water military base, Whittier was heavily fortified in the early years of the Cold War, before the military pulled out in the 1960s. In danger of becoming a ghost town, the settlement somehow survived and is now a popular cruise-ship port and day-trip destination from Anchorage (a shared road-rail tunnel links it to the Seward Hwy). Serious outdoor enthusiasts revere it for its kayaking, fishing and glacier-viewing – inclement weather and ugly architecture be damned!

👁 Sights

Prince William Sound Museum MUSEUM
(100 Whittier St; $5; ⏲10am-8pm) Whittier's history goes back to – well – 1941, so you might be surprised to hear that it has a museum. Bivouacked next to a grocery store beneath the Anchor Inn, it does a good, if modest, job of chronicling 75 years of Whittier's pioneer settlement, WWII military activity and subsequent Cold War building 'spree.'

After a few opening salvos, the story (told mainly with photos and extended captions) strays away from Whittier to cover the War in the Pacific – more specifically the American-Japanese battles in the Aleutian Islands during WWII.

Begich Towers LANDMARK
(100 Kenai St) Part of Whittier's bizarreness stems from the fact that most of its inhabitants live in the same building, the 14-story Begich Towers. The Begich started life as the Hodge building in 1956 when it was constructed to house newly arrived military personnel living temporarily in a trailer park.

Abandoned by the military in 1960, it was subsequently purchased by the City of Whittier in 1972 and has since housed up to 150 people, along with a grocery store, post office and community center. An underground tunnel links it to the local elementary school.

You can wander into the main lobby where there's a photo display tracking Whittier's history.

Buckner Building RUINS
(Blackstone Rd) You can't miss this ugly Cold War creation that melds into the surrounding landscape like a moose on a catwalk. Hailing from an architectural school best described as 'brutalist,' the ginormous Buckner was constructed in 1953 to act as a kind of mini-city for Whittier's military personnel – a function that it fulfilled for less than a decade. When the military pulled out of Whittier in 1960 the building was abandoned.

It has since fallen into disrepair, a victim of vandalism, asbestos and a lack of sufficient funds to do it up. Today it remains in limbo, too expensive to renovate but apparently too 'historic' to pull down.

Activities

Hiking

Portage Pass Trail HIKING

Whittier's sole USFS-maintained trail is a superb afternoon hike, providing good views of Portage Glacier (where Alaska Natives once portaged goods between Turnagain Arm and Prince William Sound), Passage Canal and the surrounding mountains and glaciers. Clearly marked in its early stages, the trail proceeds along an old roadbed and is easily reachable on foot from town.

To reach the trailhead, head west out of town toward the road/rail tunnel on a paved path that parallels the main road. Just before the tunnel a road branches left over the railroad tracks and dead-ends at a small parking area. From the marked trailhead, a good path climbs steadily along the flank of a mountain for around a mile, finishing at a promontory (elevation 750ft) that offers views of Portage Glacier and Passage Canal to the east. The trail then descends for a half-mile to Divide Lake and Portage Pass. At this point the trail ends, and a route through alder trees continues to descend to a beach on Portage Lake. It's a 2-mile hike one way from the trailhead to the lake, and it's well worth bashing some brush at the end. There are great views from the shores of Portage Lake and plenty of places to set up camp on the alluvial flats.

Horsetail Falls Trail HIKING

One in a trio of lovely trails accessible from town, the Horsetail Falls Trail starts at the end of the Reservoir Rd behind the Buckner Building and winds up the mountainside on a series of boardwalks through a mixture of forest and muskeg to a wooden platform high above Whittier. It's just over a mile in length, and delivers a priceless view.

The Horsetail Falls are only visible in the distance.

Shotgun Cove Trail HIKING

The Shotgun is more of a dirt road than a trail in its initial stages tracking along a delightful stretch of coast with waterfalls, a kittiwake colony and the Billings Glacier visible on the opposite side of Passage Inlet.

From the northeast corner of the Buckner Building, follow Salmon Run Rd for half a mile to the Lu Young Park Picnic Area, where king and silver salmon run during June and late August. Beyond here an undulating dirt road continues along the coast. It's 1½ miles to Second Salmon Run where a trail alongside the creek leads up to a waterfall. The dirt road ends just past the creek, whereupon the rough-and-ready **Emerald Cove Trail** continues for several more miles, partly on boardwalks through a mixture of forest and muskeg. About a mile in, a side trail leads down to a beach.

Paddling

★Blackstone Bay KAYAKING

One of the kayaking highlights of Alaska, Blackstone Bay is named, somewhat ominously, for a visiting 19th-century miner who froze to death in a snowstorm. There are seven glaciers in the bay, two of which touch the salt water, including the giant Blackstone. Other glaciers jettison foaming cascades of fresh water into the bay's icy depths.

Wildlife is a common sight as you negotiate the moving sea of ice and there are beaches for camping on the north and south shores.

Boat and kayaking trips to the bay are two-a-dime in Whittier. Experienced kayakers sometimes paddle here all the way from Whittier, but it's easier to arrange a water-taxi drop-off.

Sound Paddler KAYAKING

(Prince William Sound Kayak Center; ☎907-472-2452; www.pwskayakcenter.com; 101 Billings St; ⏲7am-8pm) This well-run operation has been outfitting kayakers since 1981. Perry and Lois Solmonson rent kayaks including outer rain gear (single/double/triple $70/120/150, discounted for multiple days) and run guided tours. The day-long excursions to Blackstone Bay ($625 for two people; hefty discount if you can rustle up six people) are top flight.

They also have escorts for multiday trips. These aren't guided tours: while escorts will suggest camping spots and routes, you're in charge of your own trip, including food and gear. It's a neat option for independent-minded folks who don't have the experience to feel comfortable spending a week on the water solo.

Alaska Sea Kayakers KAYAKING

(☎877-472-2534, 907-472-2534; www.alaskaseakayakers.com; The Triangle; ⏲7am-7pm) Rents out kayaks (single/double $65/80 per day), and arranges water taxis and multiday tours to places like Harriman Fjord, Nellie Juan Glacier and Whale Bay. It has booking offices at the harbor and the Triangle. Guided sea-kayaking trips include three-hour tours to the kittiwake colony across the passage ($89), half-day trips ($145 to $235) and a Blackstone Bay full-day trip ($345).

Lazy Otter Charters KAYAKING
(☎907-694-6887, 800-587-6887; www.lazyotter.com; Harbor View Rd; ⏰6:30am-7pm) Lazy Otter operates out of a very pleasant cafe on the harbor and offers all the adventurous water activities you could hope for, including a guided kayaking trip (with water-taxi transfer) to Blackstone Bay ($325 per person). It also runs a water taxi for experienced indie kayakers and rents out fiberglass kayaks (singles/doubles $55/95 per day).

Tours

Historical Walking Tour HISTORY
Pick up a map at the Anchor Inn (p214) or the Inn at Whittier (p214) and follow the self-guided seven-stop tour through the Whittier Army Port Historical District. You'll find information signs on the walls of each building, including the Buckner Building and Begich Towers (p211). The walk will deposit you at the Prince William Sound Museum (p211), which rounds off the story nicely.

Phillips Cruises & Tours BOATING
(☎907-276-8023, 800-544-0529; www.26glaciers.com; Harbor View Rd) Packs in 26 glaciers on a speedy five-hour boat ride for $159/99 per adult/child. There's a slightly less harried 3¾-hour Blackstone Bay cruise for $109/69 per adult/child, or the ironically named Sunset cruise for $99/69 per adult/child (the sun barely sets in the summer). A hot meal is included with all trips.

The Philips office is right on the cruise dock. Many of its clientele are cruisers.

Major Marine Tours BOATING
(☎800-764-7300, 907-274-7300; www.majormarine.com; Harbor Loop Rd) One of two competing boat-tour operators in Whittier with offices on the cruise dock, Major employs a USFS ranger on every cruise. It does a five-hour tour of glacier-riddled Blackstone Bay for $119/59.50 per adult/child. A slightly longer tour visits Surprise Glacier and cruises through the Esther Passage for $149/74.50 per adult/child.

Sleeping

Since most people visit Whittier on cruise ships or on day trips from Anchorage, there isn't much demand for overnight accommodations. The only real hotels are the posh Inn at Whittier and the not-so-posh

BORN IN WORLD WAR II

Understanding how Whittier was born is key to unraveling the complexities of this odd non sequitur.

Shortly after the Japanese attack on the Aleutian Islands during WWII, the US began looking for a spot to build a secret military installation. The proposed base needed to be not only an ice-free port, but also as inaccessible as possible, lost in visibility-reducing cloud cover and surrounded by impassable mountains. They found it all right here.

And so, in this place that would be considered uninhabitable by almost any standard, surrounded by 3500ft peaks and hung with sloppy gray clouds most of the year, Whittier was built. A supply tunnel was blasted out of solid granite, one of Alaska's true engineering marvels, and more than 1000 people were housed in a single tower, the Buckner Building. It wasn't picturesque, but it was efficient.

The army maintained Whittier until 1968, leaving behind not only the Buckner Building, now abandoned, but also the 14-story Begich Towers.

A labyrinth of underground tunnels connects the apartment complex with schools and businesses, which certainly cuts down on snow-shoveling time. The structure has also given rise to a unique society, where 150-odd people, though virtually isolated from the outside world, live only a few feet from one another – high-rise living in the middle of the wilderness. It's a must-see attraction for cultural anthropologists.

For years Whittier was accessible only by train or boat, despite being only 11 miles from the most traveled highway in Alaska. But in 2000, the Anton Anderson Memorial Tunnel was overhauled for auto traffic and, since then, one of the most abnormal places imaginable has been easily accessible – though normalization seems yet to happen.

Anchor Inn. For something a bit different, you can rent rooms in one of two apartments in the skyline-hogging Begich Towers. The town campground is little more than an afterthought. There's a 5% room tax.

June's Whittier Condo Suites CONDO **$$**
(☎888-472-6001, 907-841-5102; www.juneswhittier condosuites.com; 100 Kenai St, Suite 1506; condos $165-265;) This option offers an insight into the local lifestyle, putting you up in comfortable, homey suites on the 14th and 15th floors of Begich Towers (p211). There are 10 suites in all, including the rather grandly named 'Presidential Suite.' With full kitchens and living rooms, they are more suited to longer stays.

Anchor Inn MOTEL **$$**
(☎907-472-2354; www.anchorinnwhittier.com; 100 Whittier St; s/d $120/140;) This multipurpose venue has cinder-block walls and overlooks the railway tracks, with snow-capped mountains in the background. In many ways, it's quintessential Whittier: industrial, austere and anachronistic. Notwithstanding, the rooms are clean and spacious with fridges, but no microwaves or coffee machines. To make up for it, there's an attached restaurant, bar, laundry and grocery store. Added bonus – the town museum is downstairs.

Inn at Whittier HOTEL **$$$**
(☎907-472-3200; www.innatwhittier.com; Harbor Loop Rd; r $169-299; P) This Cape Cod–stylized inn at the secluded end of the harbor is the best in town pretty much by default. The rooms are rather plain, but the views more than compensate – make sure you spend the $20 extra for a water view. Families can rent a two-story town-house suite or cozy junior suites with fireplaces and peaked ceilings.

Attached is a high-end restaurant and Whittier's best stab at a swank bar.

WILDERNESS CABINS

There are five USFS cabins accessible by boat from Whittier. Pigot Bay and Paulson Bay are the closest, with excellent salmon fishing and good views; Harrison Lagoon has the best access for the mobility-impaired, plus some great tide pools; Shrode Lake comes with a boat; and Coghill Lake is a scenic spot with good fishing and berry picking. For bookings visit www.recreation.gov.

Eating

Vardy's Ice Cream & Pizza Parlor ICE CREAM, PIZZA **$**
(The Triangle; ice cream $3-6; 11am-9pm) Under the same ownership as Swiftwater Seafood Cafe, this place is sheltered two doors away in a white clapboard bungalow and serves a casual assortment of ice cream, pizzas and various sweet treats. It's a welcome addition to this tiny community.

Swiftwater Seafood Cafe SEAFOOD **$$**
(www.swiftwaterseafoodcafe.com; The Triangle; mains $10-18; 11:30am-9pm Sun-Thu, to 10pm Fri & Sat) This tiny hole in the wall has a walk-up counter where you order your food and pay before eating. Halibut and chips and red seafood chowder are the signature dishes, but there's also crab cakes, fried zucchini, burgers and calamari, and bread pudding for dessert. Service is exceedingly friendly.

Peruse the photos of famous Alaskan shipwrecks as you wait or head to the outside patio to watch weighty clouds amass over the harbor.

Wild Catch Cafe SEAFOOD **$$**
(☎907-472-2252; 12 Harbor Loop Rd; burgers $14-16; 6am-7pm) The 'wild catch' at this place appears primarily in its salmon burgers, and halibut and chips. The menu is inscribed on a big blackboard and there are two eating options – take-out from a cafe window, or sit down indoors. It also does Whittier's best breakfast, stuffed into a burrito and washed down with Alaska-roasted Kaladi Brothers coffee.

Ask about the boxed lunches – great for fishing trips.

Inn at Whittier Restaurant SEAFOOD **$$$**
(☎907-472-3200; Harbor Loop Rd; breakfast & lunch $9-20, dinner $23-36; 7am-9pm) A hotel dining room with glorious views of the Sound (cloudy or not) that cooks up steaks, seafood and a spicy cajun shrimp Alfredo that's out of this world. Have a martini at the posh lounge attached to the restaurant.

Shopping

Log Cabin Gifts ARTS & CRAFTS
(☎907-472-2501; The Triangle; 11am-6pm) Looking like a museum to Alaskan eccentricities, this genuine log cabin is adorned with reindeer antlers and Alaska Native art. The knickknacks, including lots of

high-quality leatherwork, are handmade by owner Brenda Tolman.

Information

MONEY

Anchor Inn (907-472-2354; www.anchorinnwhittier.com; 100 Whittier St; 9am-10pm;) Has an ATM.

TOURIST INFORMATION

Pay for boat launches and overnight parking at the **Harbormaster's Office** (Harbor View Rd; 7am-7pm). It also has pay phones and showers ($4).

There's no official tourist office, but there are bundles of leaflets at the Anchor Inn (along with a coin-op laundry and showers). Begich Towers (p211) contains the police and fire stations, medical clinic and a church.

Getting There & Away

The only way into Whittier by land is via the Anton Anderson Memorial Tunnel, which is shared between cars and trains.

BOAT

Alaska Marine Highway (800-642-0066; www.ferryalaska.com; The Triangle) runs regular ferries across Prince William Sound. Departure times and schedules vary, but in the height of the summer, there are sailings several times a week to Valdez ($78, six hours) and Cordova ($81, 6½ hours). The ferry terminal is beside the Triangle. Both trips are super-scenic – think Dall's porpoises, Steller sea lions and a kittiwake rookery. Twice a month a ferry departs from Whittier, crosses the Gulf of Alaska and docks in Juneau ($252, 39 hours).

BUS

Bus transport to Whittier is limited and normally only operates around the once- or twice-weekly cruise ships.

Park Connection (800-266-8625; www.alaskacoach.com) has plush coaches that whisk people between Anchorage and Whittier when there's a ship in dock (usually Saturdays). One-way tickets for the two-hour journey cost $65; book online.

CAR

Whittier Access Rd, also known as Portage Glacier Access Rd, leaves the Seward Hwy at Mile 79, continuing to Whittier through the claustrophobic Anton Anderson Memorial Tunnel, which at 2.7 miles long is the longest 'railroad-highway' tunnel in North America. Negotiating the damp one-lane shaft as you skid across the train tracks is almost worth the steep price of admission (per car/RV $13/22), which is charged only if you're entering Whittier; if you bring your car into town on the Alaska Marine Highway ferry you can exit through the tunnel for free. Eastbound and westbound traffic alternate every 30 minutes, with interruptions for the Alaska Railroad. Bring a magazine.

Whittier has car rentals with **Avis** (907-440-2847; www.avis.com; Lot 8, Small-boat Harbor; 8am-8pm).

TRAIN

The **Alaska Railroad** (907-265-2494, 800-544-0552; www.akrr.com) *Glacier Discovery* train runs daily to and from Anchorage (2½ hours, $83) from late May to mid-September from Whittier's train station, little more than a platform and an awning next to the cruise dock.

Kenai Peninsula

Includes ➡

Best Places to Eat

- La Baleine (p253)
- The Cookery (p234)
- Saltry (p254)
- Flats Bistro (p246)

Best Places to Stay

- Exit Glacier Campground (p238)
- Alaska Paddle Inn (p234)
- Across the Bay Tent & Breakfast (p260)
- Tutka Bay Wilderness Lodge (p253)

Why Go?

The Kenai Peninsula offers some of the most accessible wilderness adventures in Alaska. There are multiday hikes through the snow-capped Kenai Mountains and mind-blowing paddles through glaciated fjords. You'll camp on never-seen-before lost coves in remote corners of Kenai Fjords National Park (p236) and Kachemak Bay State Park (p262), and battle some of the biggest fish around. And in every forgotten corner you'll be close to the natural world, the mountains, the lakes, the rivers and the people that make Alaska wild.

Approximately the size of Belgium, the peninsula is a top pick for first-time Alaska explorers. The eastern peninsula is dominated by large ice fields, the jutting Kenai Mountains and the icy waters of Resurrection Bay. To the west it flattens out, with rolling hills, large lakes and a long coastline. There are several worthwhile towns, such as Seward, Hope and Homer that provide interesting cultural attractions and rip-roaring nightlife.

When to Go

Hope

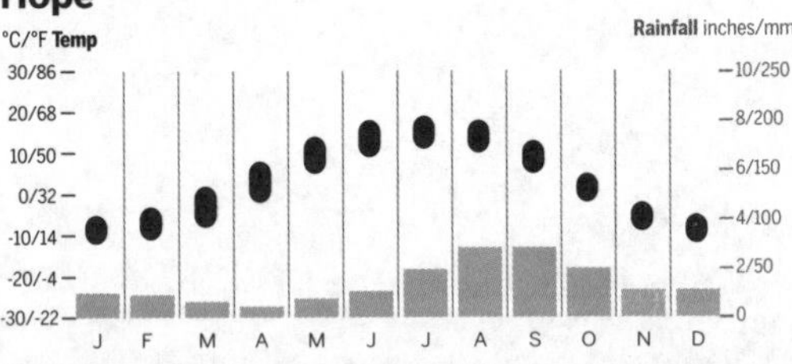

May Beat the crowds for the best deals and excursions into the desolate wilderness.

Jul Hook a salmon as it jumps upstream at the height of the summer season.

Sep The cruise crowds thin, and it's time for berry picking.

History

For millennia, Dena'ina people made the Kenai Peninsula their home, as did Alutiiqs in the south and Chugaches in the east. They largely subsisted as many modern residents do – by pulling fish from the area's bountiful waterways. In 1741 Vitus Bering, a Dane sailing for the Russians, was the first European to lay eyes on the peninsula; in 1778 British explorer Captain James Cook sailed up the inlet that would bear his name, landing north of the present-day city of Kenai and claiming the

Continued on p224

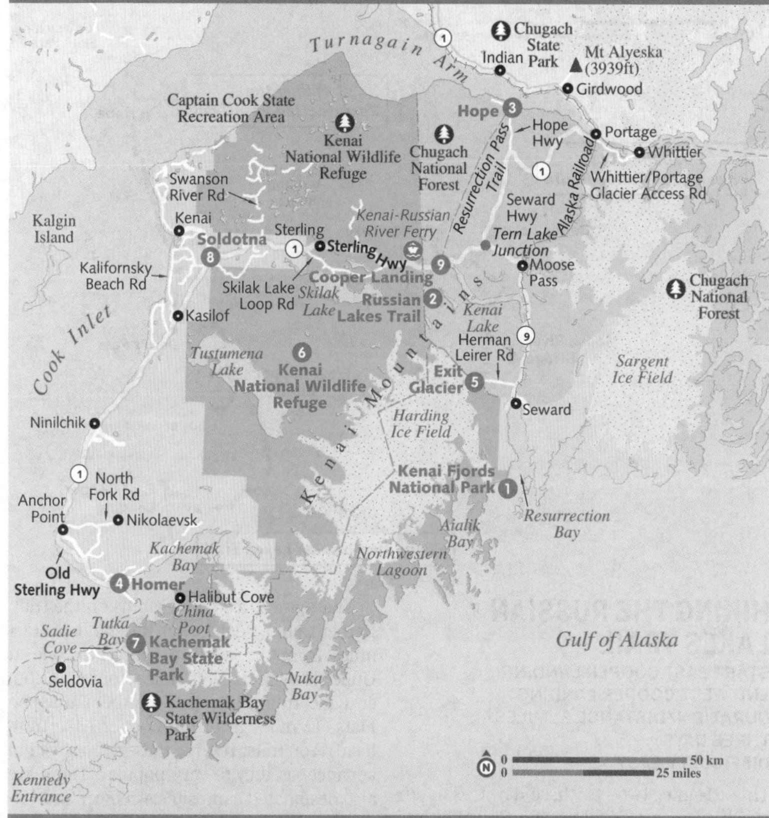

Kenai Peninsula Highlights

1. **Kenai Fjords National Park** (p236) Watching whales breach from your perch in a kayak.

2. **Russian Lakes Trail** (p239) Hiking from cabin to cabin among magnificent mountains.

3. **Hope** (p224) Rafting whitewater by day and then boogieing to bluegrass by night.

4. **Homer** (p247) Feasting on art, culture and home brews in this peace-loving town.

5. **Exit Glacier** (p237) Driving right up to the toe of a glacier.

6. **Kenai National Wildlife Refuge** (p240) Canoeing from lake to lake on the lookout for moose and caribou.

7. **Kachemak Bay State Park** (p263) Taking in the quiet coves and excellent hiking across the bay from Homer.

8. **Soldotna** (p242) Reeling in your first (or third) king salmon.

9. **Cooper Landing** (p239) Choosing between fishing, hiking or rafting in this little mountain town.

HIKING & PADDLING IN THE KENAI PENINSULA

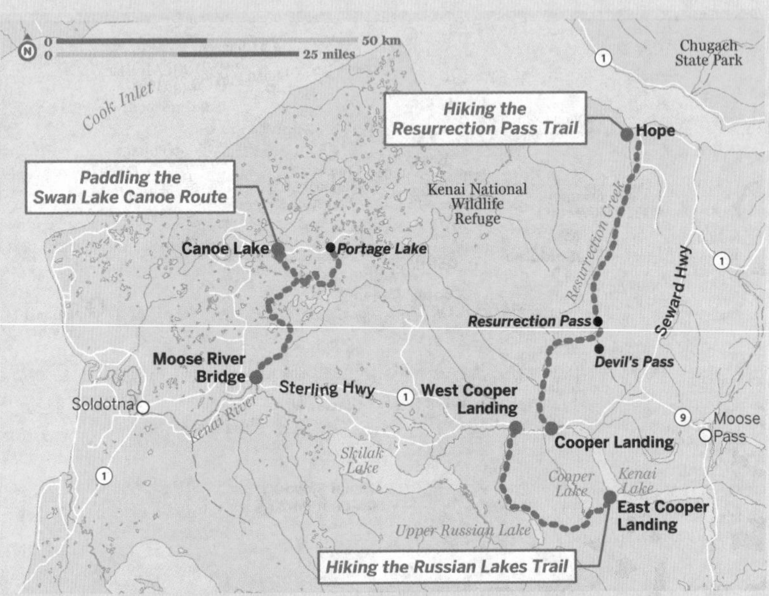

HIKING THE RUSSIAN LAKES TRAIL

START EAST COOPER LANDING
END WEST COOPER LANDING
DURATION/DISTANCE 21 MILES/ THREE DAYS
DIFFICULTY EASY

This 21-mile, two- to three-day trek is an excellent way to explore the Chugach National Forest on the Kenai Peninsula without overextending yourself. The popular and relatively flat trail is kid-friendly, and the 3.4 miles between the western trailhead and Barber Cabin are wheelchair accessible.

The trail is well maintained and well-marked, and most of the hike is a pleasant forest walk broken up by patches of wildflowers, ripe berries, lakes and streams. You can easily connect the trail with the Resurrection Pass Trail to the north and the Resurrection River Trail (p237) to the south.

There are three USFS cabins on the trail: Barber Cabin, near Lower Russian Lake (3.4 miles from the western trailhead); one at Upper Russian Lake (9 miles from the Cooper Lake trailhead); and another at Aspen Flats (12 miles from the Cooper Lake trailhead). You must reserve these cabins well in advance, as they're very popular. There are also designated campsites at Lower and Upper Russian Lakes.

Highlights of the hike include getting an eyeful of the supremely impressive glaciated mountains that stab the sky across from Upper Russian Lake, the possibility of experiencing a firsthand encounter with moose or bears – or both – and the chance to catch your own fish-shaped dinner. The trek offers excellent angling opportunities for fishing folk who are willing to carry in a rod and reel. Dolly Varden, rainbow trout and salmon are found in the upper portions of the Russian River; rainbow trout in Lower Russian Lake, Aspen Flats and Upper Russian Lake; and Dolly Varden in Cooper Lake near

The Kenai Peninsula is a recreational playground, with all types of wilderness adventure on offer. Well-maintained trails, excellent public-use cabins and even two canoe routes offer nearly limitless exploration opportunities.

the Cooper Lake trailhead. Check ahead for restrictions.

This is serious bear country, so you should take precautions while hiking, setting up camp, and cooking and storing food to prevent any unfortunate encounters. Bear spray is prudent, and so is making a whole lot of noise. The best bear sighting is from afar.

You can start the hike from either end, though it is easiest to begin this trek from the Cooper Lake trailhead, the higher end of the trail. To get there, turn off at Mile 47.8, Sterling Hwy onto Snug Harbor Rd; the road leads south 12 miles to Cooper Lake and ends at a marked parking lot and the trailhead.

The western trailhead is on a side road marked 'Russian River USFS Campground' at Mile 52.7, Sterling Hwy. From there it's just under a mile's hike to the parking lot at the end of the campground road – the beginning of the trail. There is a small fee if you leave a car here. If you're planning to camp at Russian River the night before starting the hike, keep in mind that the campground is extremely popular during the salmon season in June and July. This portion of the trail is generally full of anglers during fishing season.

HIKING RESURRECTION PASS TRAIL

START HOPE
END COOPER LANDING
DURATION/DISTANCE 38.5 MILES/ FOUR DAYS
DIFFICULTY MODERATE

Located in the Chugach National Forest, the 38.5-mile Resurrection Pass Trail (www.dnr.alaska.gov/parks/aktrails) was carved by prospectors in the late 1800s and today is the most popular hiking and cross-country biking route on the Kenai Peninsula. The Resurrection Pass Trail's mild climb from 500ft to only 2600ft has made it an increasingly popular trail for mountain bikers, who can ride the entire route in one day. For those on foot, the trip can be done in three days by a strong hiker, but most people prefer to do it in four to five days to make the most of the immense beauty of the region.

The trail is also the first leg of a trek across the Kenai Peninsula. By linking Resurrection Pass, Russian Lakes and Resurrection River Trails in Chugach National Forest, you can hike 71 miles from Hope to Seward and cross only one road. It's a rare feat but, if you have the time and endurance, a worthy one.

You can start from either end, but the climb is more friendly if you start in Hope. From here, the trail climbs gently through birch forest and along Resurrection Creek before reaching a wide alpine valley. Look for beaver dams (and beavers); be sure to filter your water since wildlife use this corridor.

At mile 17 the trail forks at Devil's Pass, and you can exit on the Devil's Creek Trail. It makes a nice option for a shorter trip (27 miles from the Hope trailhead). The Devil's Pass trailhead is at mile 39 of the Seward Hwy.

The trail continues on to Juneau Lake, where you'll see an occasional floatplane land. The final few miles into Cooper Landing are set off by thundering Juneau Falls and then a series of switchbacks down to the Sterling Hwy, which you can hear before you see.

There are eight USFS cabins along the route, but you must reserve them well in advance. Most hikers take a tent and stay in designated backcountry campsites at Mile 4, Wolf Creek (Mile 5.3), Caribou Creek (Mile 7), Mile 9.6, Mile 12.6 and East Creek (Mile 14.6). Most sites have bear-resistant food lockers, but pack a camp stove as fallen wood is scarce during summer.

The northern trailhead is 20 miles from the Seward Hwy and 4 miles south of Hope on Resurrection Creek Rd. Hope, a historic mining community founded in 1896 by gold seekers, is a charming, out-of-the-way place to visit, but be warned: Hope Hwy is not an easy road for hitchhiking (if you choose to travel in this potentially risky way).

From Hope Hwy, go south at the Resurrection Pass trail signs onto Resurrection Creek Rd, passing the fork to Palmer Creek Rd. The southern trailhead is on the Sterling Hwy, near Cooper Landing.

PADDLING THE SWAN LAKE CANOE ROUTE

START CANOE LAKE
END MOOSE RIVER BRIDGE
DURATION/DISTANCE 3 DAYS/60 MILES
DIFFICULTY EASY; CLASS I WATER

In the northern lowlands of the Kenai National Wildlife Refuge, there is a chain of rivers, lakes, streams and portages that make up the Swan Lake canoe route. The trip is perfect for novice canoeists, as rough water is rarely a problem and portages do not exceed half a mile. Fishing for rainbow trout is good in many lakes, and wildlife is plentiful; a paddle on this route could result in sightings of moose, bears, beavers and a variety of waterfowl. This land also belongs in large part to the mosquito, so bring plenty of bug dope and a mosquito net at a minimum.

This easy and popular route connects 30 lakes with forks in the Moose River for 60 miles of paddling and portaging. The

WILDNERDPIX/SHUTTERSTOCK ©

Canoeing, Swanson River

JOSEPH SOHM/SHUTTERSTOCK ©

Seward Highway (p224), Kenai Peninsula

entire route would take only a week but a common three-day trip is to begin at the west entrance on Swan Lake Rd and end at Moose River Bridge on Sterling Hwy. The topography is relatively flat, which makes portages fairly easy but views a little unexciting.

You have a few options for this journey. Your first put in is at Canoe Lake and you'll then meander south through Contact, Martin, Spruce and Otter Lakes. At Otter, you can fork southwest or southeast; this itinerary takes the latter route to Rock and then Loon Lake (though another route to the Moose River Bridge is a fork at Spruce Lake). From there you'll travel north to Swan Lake where you can end your journey, or carry on north through several more lakes to the east entrance.

Bring a map and have your route planned out beforehand, as the many options can feel confusing and lakes can look the same. Portages are marked by signs; once you train your eyes to find them they'll become obvious.

To reach the Swan Lake canoe route, travel to Mile 84, Sterling Hwy, east of Soldotna, and turn north on Robinson Lake Rd, just west of the Moose River Bridge. Robinson Lake Rd turns into Swanson River Rd, which leads to Swan Lake Rd, 17 miles north of the Sterling Hwy. East on Swan Lake Rd are two entrances for the canoe route. The west entrance for the Swan Lake route is at Canoe Lake, and the east entrance is another 6 miles beyond, at Portage Lake.

Throughout the summer months, Alaska Canoe & Campground (p243) rents canoes and runs a shuttle service for people paddling the Swan Lake canoe route. Alaska Canoe's campground (tent sites/cabins $20/175) is near the takeout along Sterling Hwy, and it makes a nice place to stay overnight if you find yourself arriving late on the last day.

DAY TRIPS FROM SEWARD

KENAI FJORDS NATIONAL PARK

Calving tidewater glaciers, mountains crashing straight into the sea, an abundance of marine wildlife, a massive ice field and a drive-up glacier: the Kenai Fjords National Park (p236) is a recreational wonderland, with sites that are both relatively easy to access and among Alaska's best. Hiking, kayaking, whale-watching or just gazing at the scenery are some of the most popular activities.

☆ Best Things to See/Do

Exit Glacier This small glacier is one of two dozen spilling from the Harding Ice Field. A road leads to its toe, so it's easy to reach by car or shuttle.

Aialik Bay A snug bay packed with several tidewater glaciers, Aialik is popular with kayakers.

Kayaking Some of the park's most stunning sights are in the fjords, where tidewater glaciers deposit house-sized icebergs and harbor seals haul out on them.

Harding Ice Field If your quads are up to the challenge, hike to this remnant of the Pleistocene Ice Age, where the views of the surrounding valleys and fjords are unlike anything you'll see elsewhere.

☆ How to Get There

Boat Water-taxis, tours of the fjords, or kayaks are all great ways to explore the park.

Bus Exit Glacier Shuttle runs an hourly bus to and from Exit Glacier.

Car Exit Glacier is a gorgeous 9-mile drive from Seward with plenty of photo ops.

MOOSE PASS

The tiny little town of Moose Pass (p231) is easy to miss, as it's just a quick blur along the Seward Hwy. But there are a few great hikes in the area and it's worth a day trip from Seward. One good campground also makes a pleasant overnight if you want to escape Seward's summer crowds.

☆ Best Things to See/Do

Primrose Trail The northern trailhead for reaching the stunning Lost Lake, the Primrose Trail winds through mossy forest and past a huge waterfall before climbing above the treeline to fresh-aired alpine meadows. The lake is a worthy destination for a long day hike or a peaceful overnight.

Ptarmigan Creek Trail This mellow trail leads to a blue alpine lake framed by imposing peaks. It's a rewarding hike that is manageable for kids, and extends 4 miles along the lakeshore.

Crescent Lake Cabin A public cabin maintained by the Forest Service, this little abode is surrounded by towering peaks. A night spent reading by the shore of the mountain lake will restore your soul.

☆ How to Get There

Bus Buses en route to Seward will drop you off in Moose Pass.

Car Your own wheels are the best way to access Moose Pass's many trailheads.

COOPER LANDING

The brilliant turquoise waters of Kenai River slice through verdant peaks in Cooper Landing (p239), creating a fishing and adventure wonderland. Come here to pull vibrant salmon from the rivers, raft the rapids or explore the numerous trails.

☆ Best Things to See/Do

Fishing When the salmon are running, this place is a magnet. Anglers stand elbow-to-elbow to reel in some of the world's best fish in an incongruous mountain scene called 'combat fishing.' Don't be afraid to join in.

Hiking Miles of excellent trails lead to mountain lakes, public-use cabins, waterfalls and alpine scenery. Some of the best trails on the peninsula originate here, and they are well worth an afternoon, if not a few days, of your time.

Rafting The Kenai River's mellow rapids and gorgeous scenery make for a pleasant float. There are plenty of operators in Cooper Landing happy to guide you down the river. You'll never hit anything more than a Class III rapid.

☆ How to Get There

Bus Buses traveling between Anchorage, Homer and Soldotna call at Cooper Landing.

Car Although small, Cooper Landing is a major summer destination, and your own wheels are the best way to get from town to river to campground.

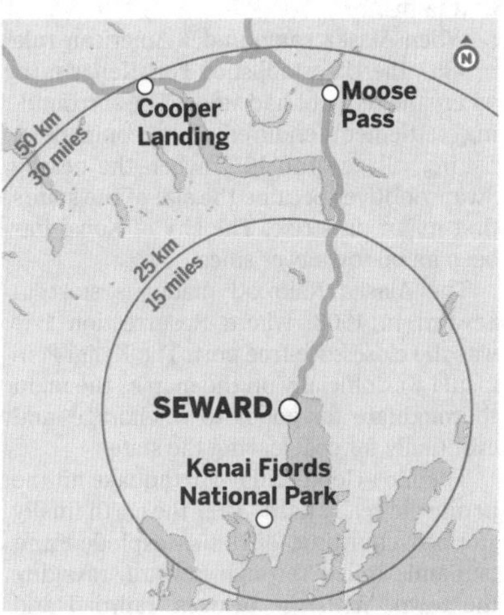

At Mile 0 of the Seward Hwy, and the gateway to Kenai Fjords National Park, Seward is an excellent base for exploring the many hiking trails, small towns, glaciers, peaks and other adventures in the region. Explore with lunch, rain gear and a curious eye, and you'll be rewarded with magnificent sights and activities.

Continued from p217
area for England. Despite that, the first white settlement on the peninsula was Russian – St Nicholas Redoubt, founded at the mouth of the Kenai River as a fur trading post in 1791. Russian Orthodox missionaries arrived soon thereafter and many of the local Alaska Natives were converted to that faith.

When Alaska came under American rule in 1867, the US established Fort Kenay near where the redoubt had stood. The surrounding settlement endured as a commercial fishing village until 1957, when the nearby Swanson River became the site of the state's first major oil strike. The city of Kenai has been an oil town ever since.

The Alaska Railroad made its start in Seward in 1903, where Resurrection Bay was the closest ice-free port. The Kenai Peninsula was officially on the map as the main thoroughfare for goods to Anchorage, and eventually for coal leaving the state.

The 1964 Good Friday Earthquake hit the peninsula really hard. After the earth finally stopped churning, oil tanks exploded and tsunamis rolled through Seward, ravaging the town. With the bridges, railroad and boat harbor gone, Seward was suddenly cut off from the rest of the state. Homer suffered badly, too: the quake dropped the Spit by 6ft and leveled most of the buildings. It took six years and almost $7 million to rebuild.

Since then tourism has boomed on the Kenai Peninsula, turning the region into Alaska's premier playground for visitors and locals, and a key engine of the region's economy.

SEWARD HIGHWAY

Hope

907 / POP 189

Hope has beautiful views of Turnagain Arm, a quaint and historic downtown, wonderful gold-rush-era relics, and incredible camping and hiking opportunities.

Life here moves a little slower. It's close enough to Anchorage to attract a weekend city crowd, but tucked away enough to stay tiny and quiet. It's authentic, pioneering, friendly and esoteric. Most tourist services close October to May.

Sights

Hope-Sunrise Mining Museum MUSEUM
(907-782-3740; Old Hope Rd; by donation; noon-4pm) FREE This small grouping of log cabins preserves relics from early miners and homesteaders with a great deal of respect. Creaky buildings give a feel for life at the turn of the 20th century; a quick guided tour by one of the town's children is worth the tip for history buffs and anyone with a little extra time. A new Quonset hut shows 10-minute films about the history of the area.

Activities

Gold-Panning

There are about 125 mining claims throughout the Chugach National Forest. Some of the more serious prospectors actually make money, but most are happy to take home a bottle with a few flakes of gold in it.

The Hope area provides numerous opportunities for the amateur panner, including a 20-acre claim that the US Forest Service (USFS) has set aside near the Resurrection Pass trailhead for recreational mining.

Hiking

The northern trailhead of the legendary 39-mile Resurrection Pass Trail (p219) is near the end of Resurrection Creek Rd.

Just before Porcupine Campground, two fine trails lead to scenic points overlooking Turnagain Arm.

Hope Point HIKING
This is a steep trail, following an alpine ridge 5 miles for incredible views of Turnagain Arm. Begin at an unmarked trail along the right-hand side of the small Porcupine Creek. Except for an early-summer snowfield, you'll find no water after Porcupine Creek.

Gull Rock Trail HIKING
A flat 5-mile (one-way), four- to six-hour walk to Gull Rock, a rocky point 140ft above the Turnagain shoreline. The trail follows an old wagon road built at the turn of the 19th century, and along the way you can explore the remains of a cabin and a sawmill.

Note that the trailhead has moved from Porcupine Campground to just before it.

Rafting

Sixmile Creek is serious white water, with thrilling – and dangerous – rapids through

Hope

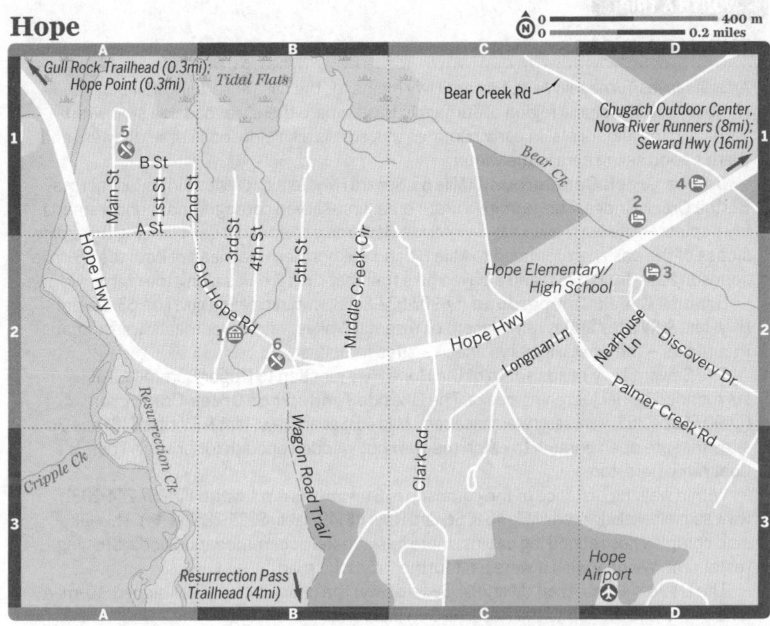

deep gorges that survivors describe as 'the best roller coaster in Alaska.' The first two canyons are rated Class IV; the third canyon is a big, bad Class V. It's a four- to five-hour round-trip. Dress warmly and bring extra clothes.

Nova River Runners RAFTING
(☎907-746-5753; www.novalaska.com; Hope & Seward Hwys) It does twice-daily trips down Sixmile, costing $105 for the Class III–IV canyons, and $155 if you continue for the Class V.

Chugach Outdoor Center RAFTING
(☎907-277-7238; www.chugachoutdoorcenter.com; Mile 7.5, Hope Hwy) Offers guided rafting trips down Sixmile twice daily during summer. The two-canyon run is $109 per person; to defy death on all three canyons it's $165 per person. It offers a float on Turnagain Pass for $85.

Sleeping

Near the end of Resurrection Creek Rd, just before and just after the Resurrection Pass trailhead, are many underdeveloped camping spots beneath a verdant canopy. The town charges a 3% lodging tax.

Hope

Sights
1 Hope-Sunrise Mining Museum B2

Sleeping
2 Bowman's Bear Creek Lodge D1
3 Discovery Cabins D2
4 Hope's Hideaway D1

Eating
Bowman's Bear Creek Lodge ...... (see 2)
5 Seaview Cafe A1
6 Tito's Discovery Cafe B2
Turnagain Kayak and Coffeehouse .... (see 4)

Coeur d'Alene Campground CAMPGROUND $
(Mile 6.4, Palmer Rd; tent sites free) FREE A gorgeous informal campground at the end of a narrow, winding back road set high in an alpine valley. The sites are for tents only, and RVs shouldn't try to drive up the road.

Porcupine Campground CAMPGROUND $
(☎907-224-3374; www.reserveamerica.com; Mile 17.8, Hope Hwy; tent & RV sites $18) This highly recommended waterfront campground is set in a shimmering birch forest near the trailheads for Hope Point and Gull Rock. A few of the sites (notably 4, 6, 8 and 10) have

WORTH A TRIP

TURNAGAIN PASS

After it leaves Turnagain Arm, Seward Hwy heads for the hills. Near Mile 68 it begins climbing into the alpine region of Turnagain Pass, where there's a roadside stop with garbage cans and toilets. In early summer, this area is a kaleidoscope of wildflowers and there's good skiing here in the winter.

Bertha Creek Campground (Mile 65, Seward Hwy; tent & RV sites $14) is just across Bertha Creek Bridge. This primitive first-come, first-served campground is understandably popular – site No 6 even has a waterfall view. You can spend a day climbing the alpine slopes of the pass here, or head to Mile 64 and the northern trailhead of both the 23-mile Johnson Pass Trail (p231) and a paved bike trail that runs 8 miles along the highway.

Granite Creek Campground (☎907-522-8368; www.recreation.gov; Mile 63, Seward Hwy; tent & RV sites $14) is reminiscent of Yosemite Valley: wildflower meadows, dramatic mountains – the works. Reserve ahead – sites fill up fast.

The Seward Hwy heads south of the Hope Hwy junction to Upper Summit Lake, surrounded by neck-craning peaks. The lakeside **Tenderfoot Creek Campground** (☎907-522-8368; www.reserveamerica.com; Mile 46, Seward Hwy; tent & RV sites $18) has 35 sites that are open enough to catch the view but wooded enough for privacy. There's a boat ramp here, too.

Within walking distance of the campsite is **Summit Lake Lodge** (☎907-244-2031; www.summitlakelodge.com; Mile 45.8, Seward Hwy; r $149, cabin $235-285; ⊜📶). This lakeside complex has refined log cabins, more basic motel accommodation and a bustling restaurant. We only wish it were a bit further from the road.

The **Devil's Pass Trail** (Mile 39.4, Seward Hwy) is a difficulty, very well signed, 10-mile hike over a 2400ft gap to the Resurrection Pass Trail.

At Tern Lake Junction (p238) – also known as 'The Y' – is the turnoff for the Sterling Hwy, which runs another 143 miles to Homer.

transcendent waterfront views and private trails down the bluff to the beach. It books up quickly.

Discovery Cabins CABIN $
(☎907-782-3730; www.advenalaska.com/cabins.htm; Discovery Dr; r $95) Set above gurgling Bear Creek, this cozy collection of spruce cabins brings you closer to the zen-entranced forest surrounding Hope. There's a hot tub on-site. You have to share bathrooms, but with little porches looking onto the creek, it doesn't matter.

Hope's Hideaway CABIN $$
(☎907-782-3111; www.hopeshideaway.com; 19796 Hope Hwy; cabins $120-175) Two clean and cozy cottages make for a relaxing and warm stay. The kitchens are fully stocked, and each cabin is basically a small home. The proprietors are friendly and run group kayaking tours; ask if they have space for individual travelers.

Bowman's Bear Creek Lodge CABIN $$
(☎907-782-3141; www.bowmansbearcreeklodge.com; Mile 15.9, Hope Hwy; cabins incl dinner $250; ⊜📶) This place has seven hand-hewn log cabins (all but one with shared bathroom) surrounding a beautiful pond and burbling creek. You'll love the cozy fires and sauna. Room rates include a five-course meal at the excellent restaurant.

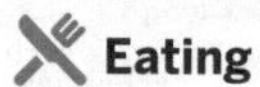

Eating

Turnagain Kayak and Coffeehouse BREAKFAST $
(☎907-764-1910; 19796 Hope Hwy; breakfast $9-11; ⏲7:30am-3:30pm) Breakfast sandwiches, smoothies and hot coffee; this little coffee shop is a great place to warm up on a rainy day. It also books kayak tours; independent travelers can see if there's a spot on a group tour.

Seaview Cafe SEAFOOD $$
(www.seaviewcafealaska.com; B St; mains $10-20; ⏲4-9pm Sun & Wed, to 11pm Thu-Sat) Serves up good beer, chowder and burgers. It attracts some of Alaska's best acts for weekend jams (Thursday, Friday and Saturday nights). Also rents RV/tent sites $10/25 with views of the Arm and noise from the bar.

Bowman's Bear Creek Lodge AMERICAN $$$
(☎907-782-3141; Mile 15.9, Hope Hwy; dinner $50; ⏲from 7pm) This creekside lodge features a fabulous Alaska-casual-cuisine prix-fixe

menu with homemade desserts, seafood specials and a friendly, intimate dining room. One seating per night at 7pm; reservations are required before 3pm.

Information

INTERNET ACCESS

Hope Sunrise Library (907-782-3121; Old Hope Rd; by donation; vary;) This library is in a one-room 1938 schoolhouse complete with cozy wood stove. Don't miss its gift shop next door, which sells locally made crafts to help support this grassroots facility. It also offers internet access. It's open when the neon sign says 'open'.

TOURIST INFORMATION

Hope Chamber of Commerce (www.hopealaska.info) A good website for pre-planning.

Getting There & Away

Hope remains idyllic in part because of its isolation. Though the **Seward Bus Line** (907-224-3608; www.sewardbuslines.net) and **Homer Stage Line** (907-868-3914; www.stagelineinhomer.com) will drop you off (and pick you up) at the junction of the Hope and Seward Hwys, the only way to get to the town proper is by driving, hitching, pedaling or plodding.

Seward

907 / POP 2787

Perched on the edge of Resurrection Bay, Seward offers out-of-this-world views of water, sky, mountain and forest, and is easily accessed by road, boat and rail. Because of its size (and its history as a railroad port), there is plenty of nightlife and lots of good restaurants in the picturesque old-time downtown area.

Just a jump from town, you have access to Kenai Fjords National Park, superb sea kayaking, birding and whale-watching, and hikes that can take you to the top of the Harding Ice Field or across the whole Kenai Peninsula.

The body of the city is divided into two centers: the newer, touristy harbor and the historic downtown. Lowell Point stretches to the south of town, and other amenities can be found just north along the Seward Hwy.

History

Seward got its start in 1903, when settlers arrived and plotted construction of a northbound rail line. Once the Alaska Railroad was completed two decades later, this ice-free port would become the most important shipping terminal on the Kenai Peninsula. The city also served as the start of the 1200-mile Iditarod National Historic Trail to Nome, along a major dogsled thoroughfare via the Interior and the Bush. In WWII the town got another boost when the US Army built Fort McGilvray at Caines Head, just south of town.

Sights

★Alaska Sealife Center AQUARIUM

(Map p228; 800-224-2525; www.alaskasealife.org; 301 Railway Ave; adult/child $25/13; 9am-9pm Mon-Thu, 8am-9pm Fri-Sun;) A fitting legacy of the *Exxon Valdez* oil-spill settlement, this $56-million marine research center is more than just one of Alaska's finest attractions. As the only cold-water marine-science facility in the Western Hemisphere, it serves as a research and educational center and provides rehabilitation for injured marine animals. Plan to spend the better part of a great afternoon here.

Kids will love the tidepool touch tank, where they can hold sea anemones and starfish, as well as the ship's helm and the massive two-story tanks where you can see seals, birds and more both above and below the water. An outdoor observation platform offers a fabulous view of the mountains ringing Resurrection Bay where you can watch salmon thrash their way up a fish ladder.

It's worth including an Encounter tour (per person $75): you'll get face to face with the creatures you normally only see behind the glass with deeper dives into the lives of octopus, puffins or marine mammals.

Small-Boat Harbor HARBOR

(Map p228) The small-boat harbor at the northern end of 4th Ave hums during the summer with fishing boats, charter vessels, cruise ships and a number of sailboats. At its heart is the **Harbormaster's Office** (Map p228; 907-224-3138; 4th Ave; 8am-5pm). Look for the huge anchors outside. Radiating outward from the docks are seasonal restaurants, espresso bars and tourist services.

Seward Community Library & Museum MUSEUM

(Map p228; www.cityofseward.us; 239 6th Ave; museum adult/child $4/free; 10am-5pm Tue-Sat, 1-5pm Sun) This eclectic museum has an excellent Iditarod exhibit, a rare 49-star US flag, and relics of Seward's Russian era,

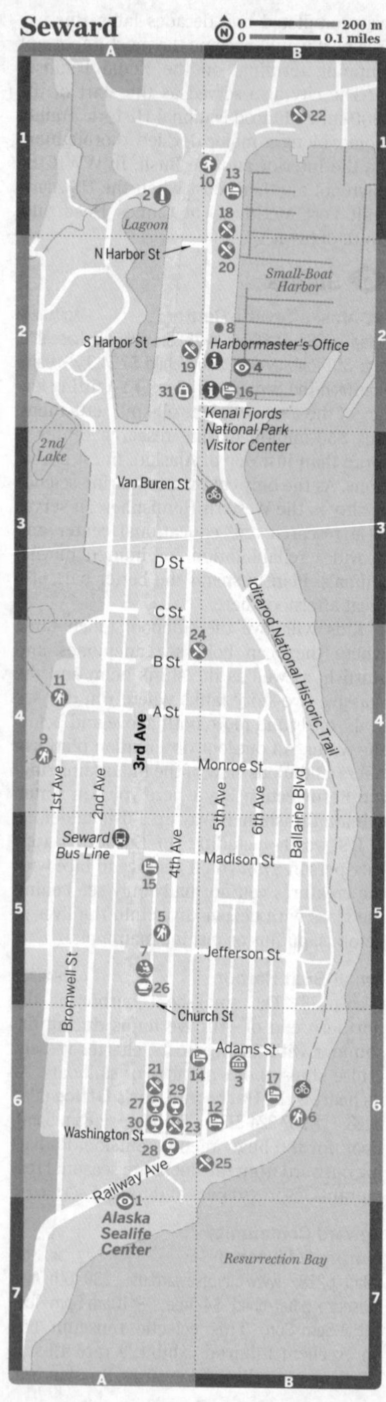

Seward

Top Sights

1 Alaska Sealife Center A7

Sights

2 Benny Benson Memorial A1
3 Seward Community Library & Museum B6
4 Small-Boat Harbor B2

Activities, Courses & Tours

5 Exit Glacier Guides A5
6 Iditarod National Historic Trail B6
7 Kayak Adventures Worldwide A5
8 Kenai Fjords Tours B2
Major Marine Tours ....(see 8)
9 Mt Marathon Trail A4
10 Seward Bike Shop B1
Sunny Cove Kayaking ....(see 8)
11 Two Lakes Trail A4

Sleeping

12 Best Western Edgewater Hotel B6
13 Harbor 360 Hotel B1
14 Hotel Seward B6
15 Moby Dick Hostel A5
16 Safari Lodge B2
17 Seward Front Row B&B B6

Eating

18 Chinooks B1
19 Lighthouse Cafe and Bakery A2
20 Ray's Waterfront B2
21 Sea Bean Cafe A6
22 Smoke Shack B1
23 The Cookery A6
24 Woody's Thai Kitchen A4
25 Zudy's Cafe B6

Drinking & Nightlife

26 Resurrect Art Coffee House Gallery A5
27 Seward Alehouse A6
28 Seward Brewing Company A6
29 Thorn's Showcase Lounge A6
30 Yukon Bar A6

Shopping

31 Fish House A2

the 1964 Good Friday Earthquake and the 1989 oil spill. There are also lots of amusing antiques, including an ancient electric hair-curling machine, plus movies and a children's section.

The staff are enthusiastic and knowledgeable, and worth engaging. The library is a good place to relax on a rainy day (and entrance is free).

Benny Benson Memorial MONUMENT
(Map p228) This humble monument at the corner of the Seward Hwy and Dairy Hill Lane honors Seward's favorite son, Benny Benson. In 1926 the orphaned 13-year-old Alaska Native boy submitted his design for the Alaska state flag, arguably the loveliest in the Union.

His stellar design (you can see one of his first at the library) includes the North Star, symbolizing the northernmost state, the Great Bear constellation for strength, and a blue background representing the sky and the forget-me-not, Alaska's state flower.

Activities

Dog Sledding

Seward Helicopter Tours DOG SLEDDING
(☎907-362-4354; www.sewardhelicopters.com; per person $519) Transports you by helicopter to an alpine glacier, where you'll be met by lots of dogs and a genuine snow-sledding adventure, even in July.

Hiking

★ **Lost Lake Trail** HIKING
(Map p232) This challenging 7-mile trail to an alpine lake is one of the most scenic hikes the Kenai Peninsula has to offer in midsummer. The trailhead is in Lost Lake subdivision, at Mile 5.3 of the Seward Hwy.

Clemens Memorial Cabin (p233) is 4.5 miles up the trail (book way ahead). It has amazing views of Resurrection Bay and is also a good winter destination. The final 2 miles are above the treeline, making the shores of Lost Lake a wondrous place to pitch a tent.

If you'd rather not return the same way, continue around the east side of Lost Lake to the Primrose Trail, an 8-mile alpine trek ending at Primrose Landing Campground at Mile 17.2 of the Seward Hwy. Plan on seven to 10 hours for the round-trip to Lost Lake, and bring a camp stove, as wood is hard to come by.

Caines Head State Recreation Area HIKING
(Lowell Point; Map p232) This 6000-acre preserve, 5.5 miles south of Seward on Resurrection Bay, contains WWII military facilities (bring a flashlight for exploring), a 650ft headland, trails to Tonsina Beach (2.3 miles), North Beach (5 miles) and Fort Gilvany (7.8 miles) and two public-use cabins. There's a $5 day-use fee for the recreation area, paid at the trailhead.

Time your trips with low tide.

Mt Marathon Trail HIKING
(Map p228; www.mmr.seward.com) This steep, punishing trail is the scene of a grueling race every 4th of July. Don't take the Racer's Trail, at the west end of Jefferson St, without someone who's been up before. Instead, take the so-called Jeep Trail at the end of Monroe St, where you'll still have access to the peak and a heavenly bowl behind the mountain.

According to local legend, grocer Gus Borgan wagered $100 in 1909 that no one could run Mt Marathon in an hour, and the race was on. Winner James Walters clocked in at 62 minutes, losing the bet but becoming a legend. The 3.1-mile suffer-fest quickly became a celebrated Fourth of July event and today is Alaska's most famous footrace. It pits runners from all over the world against the 3022ft-high peak. Be careful: the runner's trail is painful – think Stairmaster with a view – and every summer several tourists who didn't know what they were in for are rescued.

Iditarod National Historic Trail HIKING
(Map p228) This legendary trail to Nome begins at the foot of Ballaine Blvd. Here, a memorial marks Mile 0 and a paved bike path heads 2 miles north along the beach. A more interesting segment of the trail for hikers, however, can be reached by heading east 2 miles on Nash Rd, which intersects the Seward Hwy at Mile 3.2.

From here you can follow the Iditarod National Historic Trail through woods and thick brush for a 4-mile hike to Bear Lake. Nearby is the unmarked trailhead for the **Mt Alice Trail**, a fairly difficult and highly recommended 2.5-mile climb to the alpine summit. Bald eagles, blueberries and stunning views can be had elsewhere, but it's the solitude – this trail is relatively unused – and afternoon light that make Mt Alice great. Back at Bear Lake, you can either backtrack to town or forge on another 11 miles to rejoin the Seward Hwy.

Two Lakes Trail HIKING
(Map p228; cnr 1st Ave & A St) This easy 1-mile loop circumnavigates pleasant Two Lakes Park, through woods and picnic grounds, across a creek and around the two promised lakes at the base of Mt Marathon. Unsatisfied hikers can access the Jeep Trail nearby, which climbs Mt Marathon, for a much more intense climb.

Glacier Trekking

★Exit Glacier Guides HIKING

(Map p228; ☎907-224-5569; www.exitglacier guides.com; 405 4th Ave; ⊙8am-5:30pm) Exit Glacier Guides gives you the chance to tread upon Seward's backyard glacier. Its six-hour ice-hiking trip costs $130 per person, gears you up with crampons and ropes, ascends partway up the Harding Ice Field Trail and then heads out onto the glacier for crevasse exploration and interpretive glaciology.

It also offers helicopter tours, hiking tours and a historic downtown tour as well as overnight journeys.

Mountain Biking

Popular with hikers, the Lost Lake Trail (p229) is single-track riding that is sometimes steep and technical but highly rewarding nonetheless. Local cyclists say the Iditarod National Historic Trail and the Resurrection River Trail are also good rides.

Seward Bike Shop CYCLING

(Map p228; 411 Port Ave; cruisers full/half-day $28/18, mountain bikes full/half-day $38/25; ⊙10am-6pm) Rents out bikes and has the latest details on local biking trails.

Paddling

You can paddle right out from Seward's shores in Resurrection Bay, though it's better, if more expensive, to go to Kenai Fjords National Park (p236). Resurrection Bay lacks tidewater glaciers and ample wildlife but can still make for a stunning day on the water. **Sunny Cove Sea Kayaking** (Map p228; ☎907-224-4426; www.sunnycove.com; small-boat harbor) offers a big Kenai Fjord day trip for $425, trips to Fox Island with a paddle and salmon bake ($209), and a hike and paddle combo for $119 to $139. **Kayak Adventures Worldwide** (Map p228; ☎907-224-3960; www.kayakak.com; 328 3rd Ave) runs half-day kayak adventures for $75 or longer trips to Aialik Bay for $399 to $505. **Miller's Landing** (Map p232; ☎907-331-3113; www.millerslandingak.com; cnr Lowell Rd & Beach Dr; ⊙5:30am-11pm) rents kayaks.

Ziplining

Stoney Creek Canopy Adventures ZIP LINE

(Map p232; ☎907-224-3662; www.stoneycreekca.com; 13037 Knotwood St; adult/child $149/119) Accessed from Mile 6.5 of the Seward Hwy, this three-hour canopy zip line takes you whizzing past giant Sitka spruce and mirror ponds. There are eight zip runs in all, plus three suspension bridges and two rappels.

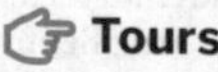

Tours

Painted Whale CULTURAL

(☎907-521-0311; www.sewardmurals.com; per adult/child $18/free) Seward is the mural capital of Alaska, and the Painted Whale offers tours from one of the artists herself. Follow artist Justine for a 1½-hour walking tour of Seward's main murals. Tours are offered Tuesday to Saturday, but times weren't set at the time of research. Call ahead.

Adventure 60 North KAYAKING

(Map p232; ☎907-224-2600; www.adventure60.com; 31872 Herman Leirer Rd) This is a reputable kayaking and adventure outfitter, with guided kayak tours of Resurrection Bay (half/full day $68/130), stand-up paddleboard tours as well as guided hikes.

Major Marine Tours BOATING

(Map p228; ☎907-274-7300; www.majormarine.com; small-boat harbor, Seward; ⊙7am-9pm) Major Marine Tours includes a national-park ranger on every boat. It has a half-day Resurrection Bay tour (per adult/child $79/39.50), a full-day Northwestern Fjords (per person $224), and an assortment of semicustomized trips for birders, whale-watchers and more. With most tours, you can add a prime rib and salmon buffet feast for $19.

Kenai Fjords Tours BOATING

(Map p228; ☎888-749-1016; www.kenaifjords.com; small-boat harbor) This long-running operation offers a wide variety of options, including a six-hour national-park tour (per adult/child $159/80). Instead of having a naturalist on board, the captain rocks the mic. A few options offer a lunchtime salmon bake on Fox Island.

Prices range from $79 to $198 for four- to nine-hour tours. Children are half price. Smaller vessels are available for more intimate tours, often adapted to the interests of the group.

⁂ Festivals & Events

Mt Marathon Race CULTURAL

(http://mmr.seward.com; ⊙Jul) This Fourth of July race attracts runners who like to test themselves by running up a near vertical peak, and fans who like to drink beer and yell. It's one of the oldest trail races in the US, and well worth watching.

WORTH A TRIP

MOOSE PASS

Moose Pass is serious about a few things: the scenery, the hiking trails and obeying the speed limit. This drive-through town is easy to miss but is worth a stop for a day of hiking.

Traveling south on the Seward Hwy after Tern Lake Junction, you'll pass a number of worthwhile hikes, roadside inns and viewpoints.

Set on nine gorgeous acres, the **Inn at Tern Lake** (907-288-3667; www.innatternlake.com; Mile 36, Seward Hwy; r $175-200;) has four guest rooms and a patio with lovely lake views. The rooms are folksy and warm, and there's a separate living area for guests. It has a golf practice hole (on the airstrip) and a tennis court, and stand-up paddleboards are available.

Four miles south of the junction is the trailhead for the **Carter Lake Trail** (Mile 33, Seward Hwy), a steep 1.9-mile 4WD track providing quick access to subalpine terrain and Carter Lake, where you can continue another mile to some excellent campsites and Crescent Lake. Sturdy hikers can press on another 4 miles to **Crescent Lake Cabin** (907-288-3178; www.recreation.gov; cabin $65). If you're not driving, Seward-bound buses can drop you here. You'll also find the southern trailhead for the **Johnson Pass Trail** (Mile 33, Seward Hwy), a 23-mile trail that heads north to Turnagain Pass, and can be done as a single-day bike or a two-day backpack.

At Mile 29.4 the village of Moose Pass relaxes along the banks of Upper Trail Lake. Founded during the Hope-Sunrise gold rush of the late 19th century, Moose Pass (named by a mail carrier who couldn't get past one of the critters) came into its own when the original Iditarod National Historic Trail was cut around the lake in 1910–11. Today the small town is known for its lively **Summer Solstice Festival** (www.moosepasssportsmensclub.com/events.html; Jun).

Just south of Moose Pass are a few sleeping options close enough to Seward to use as a base, but far enough out to escape the crowds.

Renfro's Lakeside Retreat (907-288-5059; www.renfroslakesideretreat.com; 27177 Seward Hwy; RV sites $25-40, cabins $140-200;) has mediocre RV sites but fabulous lakeside cabins with fire pits and lofts with views. Nearby, the USFS-run Trail River Campground (p233) has 91 lovely sites among tall spruce trees along Kenai Lake and Lower Trail River.

After departing Moose Pass, the highway winds through national forest. At Mile 23, the **Ptarmigan Creek Trail** (Mile 23, Seward Hwy) leads 3.5 miles from the campground to Ptarmigan Lake. Here you'll find turquoise, trout-filled waters that reflect the mountains. A 4-mile trail continues around the north side of the lake, which is brushy in places and wet in others; plan on five hours for the round-trip. The **Ptarmigan Creek Campground** (907-522-8368; www.reserveamerica.com; Mile 23, Seward Hwy; tent sites $14) has 16 sites that were once shady but now resemble a clear-cut in places due to the spruce beetle.

The **Victor Creek Trail** (Mile 19.7, Seward Hwy) on the east side of the highway is a fairly steep path that ascends 3 miles to good views of the surrounding mountains.

If everywhere else is full, head to **Primrose Landing Campground** (907-743-9500; Mile 17.2, Seward Hwy; tent sites $14), which is a quiet and wooded spot with a rushing creek and wonderful views of Kenai Lake. It's also where the **Primrose Trail** (Primrose Rd) begins. This trail leads south to Lost Lake, and traverses to Mile 5 of the Seward Hwy. About 2 miles up the path is an unmarked side trail to the right, which leads to a magnificent waterfall – the source of that roaring you can hear as you hike.

The **Grayling Lake Trail** (Mile 13.2, Seward Hwy;), accessed from a parking lot at Mile 13.2, leads walkers for two pleasant miles to Grayling Lake, a beautiful spot with views of Snow River and excellent grayling fishing. Side trails connect Grayling Lake with Meridian and Leech Lakes. This is an excellent hiking trail for the kids.

Seward Music & Arts Festival MUSIC
(www.sewardfestival.com; 913 Port Ave; Sep;) Held the last weekend in September in the railroad/cruise-ship depot, this summer's-end celebration brings together an eclectic mix of local artists and musicians, and is particularly kid-friendly, with circus training and mural-painting.

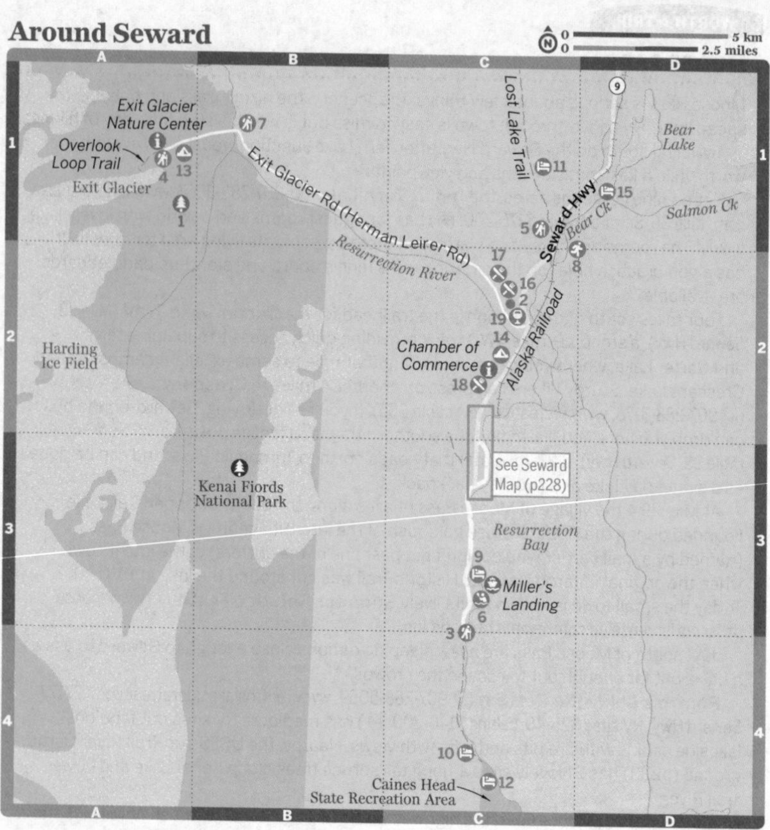

Around Seward

Sights
1 Kenai Fjords National Park....................A1

Activities, Courses & Tours
2 Adventure 60 North..............................C2
3 Caines Head State Recreation Area.....C4
4 Harding Ice Field Trail..........................A1
5 Lost Lake Trail.......................................C1
Miller's Landing.............................(see 6)
6 Miller's Landing......................................C3
7 Resurrection River Trail........................B1
8 Stoney Creek Canopy Adventures.......C2

Sleeping
9 Alaska Paddle Inn..................................C3
10 Callisto Canyon Cabin..........................C4
11 Clemens Memorial Cabin......................C1
12 Derby Cove Cabin..................................C4
13 Exit Glacier Campground......................A1
14 Forest Acres Campground....................C2
Miller's Landing.................................(see 6)
15 Stoney Creek Inn...................................D1

Eating
16 Exit Glacier Salmon Bake.....................C2
17 Resurrection Roadhouse......................C2
18 Safeway..C2

Drinking & Nightlife
19 Pit Bar..C2

Silver Salmon Derby CULTURAL
(www.seward.com; daily/full event $10/50; ⊙mid-Aug) This event draws big crowds, all vying for prizes in excess of $150,000. Don't be caught with a huge salmon and no derby ticket!

Sleeping

Above and beyond the listed rates you have to add 11% in Seward sales and bed taxes (outside city limits the tax is 3%). Kenai Fjords National Park maintains a free, drive-up campground near Exit Glacier. There are lots of informal campsites along Herman Leirer/Exit Glacier Rd.

Among Seward's midrange places, dozens are B&Bs and vacation rentals; you can book through Alaska's Point of View, even at the last minute.

Alaska's Point of View ACCOMMODATION SERVICES
(907-224-2424; www.alaskaspointofview.com) You can call to book B&Bs, cabins, apartments and more, even at the last minute.

Resurrection River Cabin CABIN
(877-444-6777, 518-885-3639; www.recreation.gov; free) FREE This public-use cabin is 6.5 miles from the southern trailhead of the Resurrection River Trail. It's first-come, first-serve.

Clemens Memorial Cabin CABIN $
(Map p232; 907-224-3374; www.recreation.gov; cabins $65) Located 4.5 miles up the Lost Lake Trail, this renovated public-use cabin sleeps eight and is located at the treeline, providing spectacular views of Resurrection Bay. It's always booked, so reserve at least six months ahead.

Moby Dick Hostel HOSTEL $
(Map p228; 907-224-7072; www.mobydickhostel.com; 430 3rd Ave; dm $25, r $70-90;) Right in the middle of the town, this rambling hostel has a great big kitchen table for sharing tales, brightly painted walls and four dorm rooms sleeping up to six, with decent bunks and enough room to move about. It will help book tours. The private rooms are a decent buy for couples.

Callisto Canyon Cabin CABIN $
(Map p232; www.alaskastateparks.org; cabins $70) A public-use cabin located just off the tidal trail, a half-mile before you reach Derby Cove in Caines Head State Recreation Area. It can be reached on foot or by kayak.

Miller's Landing CAMPGROUND $
(Map p232; 866-541-5739; www.millerslandingak.com; cnr Lowell Rd & Beach Dr; tent/RV sites $27/37, cabins $50-150) This touristplex offers everything from campsites to kayak rentals to fishing charters. The waterfront location is hard to beat, though it's a good mile-long slog south of downtown.

Trail River Campground CAMPGROUND $
(www.recreation.gov; Mile 24, Seward Hwy; tent & RV sites $18) Run by the USFS, this spot has nearly 100 lovely sites among tall spruce trees along Kenai Lake and Lower Trail River. Both RVs and tents are welcome, though there's no electricity or hookups for RVs.

Derby Cove Cabin CABIN $
(Map p232; www.alaskastateparks.org; cabins $70) This is just off the tidal trail between Tonsina Point and North Beach in Caines Head State Recreation Area, 4 miles from the Lowell Point trailhead. This public-use cabin can be accessed on foot at low tide, or by kayak any time.

Kayaker's Cove HOSTEL $
(907-224-2662; www.kayakerscove.com; dm/cabins $20/60;) Located 12 miles southeast of Seward near Fox Island in a lush little cove, this place is accessible by kayak or water-taxi only. There's a shared kitchen, and you'll need to bring your own food. You can kayak for $25 per day. Book online and bring firewood.

Forest Acres Campground CAMPGROUND $
(Map p232; 907-224-4055; cnr Hemlock St & Seward Hwy; tent/RV sites $10/20) Located 2 miles north of town just off the Seward Hwy on Hemlock St. It has quiet sites shaded by towering spruce.

Stoney Creek Inn B&B $$
(Map p232; 907-224-3940; www.stoneycreekinn.net; Stoney Creek Ave; d $159-174;) This secluded place has five rooms sharing a common area, and comes with a fantastic sauna and hot tub next to a deliciously icy-cold salmon stream. The barbecue area is a great place to grill up your catch.

Seward Front Row B&B B&B $$
(Map p228; 907-224-3080; swannest@seward.net; 227 Ballaine Blvd; r $169-$259;) This waterfront B&B has fabulous two-story views of Resurrection Bay from the large living room. There are two well-done rooms (neither with ocean views). Next door is a six-person vacation rental perfect for families. Book six months ahead.

Hotel Seward HISTORIC HOTEL $$
(Map p228; 907-224-8001; www.hotelsewardalaska.com; 221 5th Ave; standard r with/without bath $200/170, deluxe $250-300;) This historic hotel is very Alaskan, with major

taxidermy in the lobby and a variety of rooms that range from stinky to a splurge. The historic wing has low-slung ceilings, smallish rooms and will give you the sense of living in a fisherperson's flophouse. The deluxe rooms in the new wing have expansive views, and some even come with fireplaces.

★ Alaska Paddle Inn B&B $$$

(Map p232; ☎907-362-2628; www.alaskapaddleinn.com; 13745 Beach Dr; r from $199;) Two custom-built rooms and two gorgeous houses overlook a private beach and Resurrection Bay on Lowell Point. Arched ceilings, walk-in tiled showers and gas fireplaces make this place one of the coziest and classiest places in Seward. The Main House ($280 per night) is cozy, while Spruce House ($295 to $395) is larger and better for groups.

Orca Island Cabins YURT $$$

(☎907-362-9014; www.orcaislandcabins.com; yurt per person $325) In Humpy Cove, 9 miles southeast of Seward, this privately owned place has a gathering of seven yurts with private bathrooms and kitchens. All have propane-powered ranges, water-heaters and solar power. These are a great choice for those who want to rough it without roughing it *too* much. The price includes water-taxi, stand-up paddleboard and kayak rentals.

Harbor 360 Hotel HOTEL $$$

(Map p228; ☎888-514-8687; www.harbor360hotel.com; small-boat harbor; r $289-329;) Half the rooms face the water in this harbor-front hotel, and a few have balconies. Rooms are clean and comfortable, and it has a pool and a hot tub. It feels a little corporate, but is still warm and inviting.

Safari Lodge LODGE $$$

(Map p228; ☎907-224-5232; www.saltwatersafari.com; 120 4th Ave; d $199-289;) Facing the small-boat harbor, these cozy and modern rooms are some of the best waterfront spots in town. All rooms have bay views, cushy beds, large bathrooms and tasteful Alaskan appointments, including the occasional deer head. Each room has its own patio.

Best Western Edgewater Hotel HOTEL $$$

(Map p228; ☎907-224-2700; www.bestwestern.com; 202 5th Ave; d $269-349;) Some of the most comfortable rooms in town are found in this chain hotel that faces the bay. There's a slightly odd configuration for the bathrooms (with the sink in the room), but the bay views are spectacular. The handsome wood furniture and jumping orca photos provide a fleeting glimpse of Alaska.

Eating

Zudy's Cafe CAFE $

(Map p228; ☎907-224-4710; 501 Railway Ave; breakfast $5-8, lunch $10-17; 8am-7pm) Breakfast, lunch, espresso and wine, all housed in a historic building with incredible views of Resurrection Bay. The signature baked good is the 'duffin,' a doughnut muffin. Trust us, it works.

Lighthouse Cafe and Bakery BAKERY $

(Map p228; ☎907-224-6091; 1210 4th Ave; breakfast & lunch $3-8, dinner $5-12; 6am-2pm Mon-Thu, 5am-2pm & 5-8pm Fri-Sun) This busy joint has plenty of warm, fresh-baked goods to start your day. On weekends there's an Indian buffet dinner for $15.

Sea Bean Cafe CAFE $

(Map p228; www.seabeancafe.com; 225 4th Ave; light meals $7-12; 7am-9pm;) Serves hot paninis, wraps, Belgian waffles, ice-cream, smoothies and espressos.

Smoke Shack BARBECUE $

(Map p228; ☎907-224-4987; 411 Port Ave; breakfast $9-16 lunch $11-16; 8am-3pm) Housed in a cozy rail car, this joint has a decent breakfast and pulled pork for lunch. All pork and chicken is smoked in-house.

Safeway SUPERMARKET $

(Map p232; Mile 1.5, Seward Hwy; 5am-midnight) Has sushi, espressos, a sandwich bar and all the groceries you need.

★ The Cookery BISTRO $$

(Map p228; ☎907-422-7459; www.cookeryseward.com; 209 5th Ave; mains $16-25; 5-10pm Tue-Sun) Seward's best restaurant serves excellent land-based cuisine, but local seafood is where it really shines. Start off with local oysters and bubbly, and then delight in whatever fresh seafood is on the menu.

Chinooks SEAFOOD $$

(Map p228; ☎907-224-2207; 1404 4th Ave; mains $14-35; 11:30am-10pm) Seward's best waterfront eatery, this airy, steel-walled spot features a good selection of creative plates featuring local seafood such as smoked scallop, mac 'n' cheese and puttanesca. The cocktails (and mocktails) are delicious and creative.

Exit Glacier Salmon Bake SEAFOOD $$
(Map p232; Herman Leirer Rd; mains $13-28; 5-10pm) Its motto – 'cheap beer and lousy food' – is wrong on the second count. Locals like the salmon sandwich, which you can adorn with pickles from a barrel. It's a quarter mile from the Seward Hwy turnoff.

Woody's Thai Kitchen THAI $$
(Map p228; 907-422-0338; 800 4th Ave; mains $13-15; noon-9pm Tue-Sun) Locally loved, this little Thai bistro is a welcome break from the bucket o' halibut. And while the ambience is a little spartan, you'll love the excellent Thai dishes, with perfectly cooked fresh veggies and generous portions.

Resurrection Roadhouse PIZZA $$
(Map p232; www.sewardwindsong.com; Herman Leirer Rd; breakfast & lunch $9-14, dinner $18-46; 6am-10pm) This local favorite is home to pizza, burgers and sweet-potato fries that are well worth traveling for, plus the best deck in town on sunny evenings. It also has a vast range of on-tap brews. It's about 1 mile west of the Seward Hwy on Exit Glacier/Herman Leirer Rd. The bar is open until midnight.

Ray's Waterfront SEAFOOD $$$
(Map p228; 907-224-5606; www.rayswaterfrontak.com; small-boat harbor; lunch $16-25, dinner $17-45; 11am-10pm) Ray's has amazing views, popular seafood dishes and attentive service in a fine-dining atmosphere that retains its Alaskan vibe. The bar is a friendly place to rehydrate.

Drinking & Nightlife

Seward has no shortage of welcoming watering holes, most featuring a mix of young and old, locals and tourists. Almost all the bars are downtown.

★Resurrect Art Coffee House Gallery CAFE
(Map p228; 320 3rd Ave; 7am-7pm;) Located in an old high-ceilinged church, this place serves espressos and snacks next to a massive soapstone wood stove. It also carries a great collection of local art and often hosts live music and performances. The best place to read the paper and check out the view is from the airy choir loft.

> **DON'T MISS**
>
> **MURALS**
>
> Seward is the undeniable mural capital of Alaska. There are more than two dozen public paintings in town – mostly on buildings in the downtown area. Enjoy historic treatments of Exit Glacier (it really was that big), tributes to the Mt Marathon Race and more politically charged pieces. See www.sewardmuralsociety.com for details or sign up for an excellent 1½-hour tour with the Painted Whale (p230).

Stop by here for First Friday art walks – local art shows held on the first Friday of each month at galleries around town.

Seward Brewing Company BREWERY
(Map p228; 907-422-0337; www.sewardbrewery.com; 139 4th Ave; 11:30am-10pm) You'll find homecrafted brew at this expansive restaurant and taphouse. The food ($12 to $21) is just as good as the beer; it's a departure from standard pub grub and includes Alaskan faves such as salmon poke, halibut curry and fried rockfish.

Thorn's Showcase Lounge LOUNGE
(Map p228; 208 4th Ave; 10am-midnight Mon-Thu, to 1am Sat & Sun) This curio-bedecked plush leather lounge serves the strongest drinks in town – try its white Russians – and is said to have the best halibut around (mains $14 to $18). The Jim Beam collection is valued at thousands of dollars; can you spot the pipeline bottle?

Seward Alehouse BAR
(Map p228; 215 4th Ave; noon-2am) This fun pub has a good selection of beers on tap and a dance-party-starting jukebox.

Yukon Bar BAR
(Map p228; 907-224-3063; 201 4th Ave; noon-2am) There are hundreds of dollars pinned to this bar's ceiling and almost nightly live music in the summer. It's festive.

Pit Bar BAR
(Map p232; Mile 3.5, Seward Hwy; to 5am) Just past Exit Glacier Rd, this is where the crowd heads when the bars close in town.

Shopping

Fish House SPORTS & OUTDOORS
(True Value; Map p228; 1303 4th Ave; 6am-9pm) This hardware store sells fishing licenses,

quality camping gear and has the town's best collection of rubber boots.

Information

MEDICAL SERVICES

Providence Seward Medical Center (907-224-5205; 417 1st Ave) At the west end of Jefferson St.

MONEY

First National Bank of Anchorage (907-224-4200; 303 4th Ave; 10am-5pm Mon-Thu, 9am-6pm Fri) One of two banks in town. There are ATMs in Safeway and the Yukon Bar.

TOURIST INFORMATION

Chamber of Commerce (Map p232; 907-224-8051; www.seward.com; 2001 Seward Hwy/3rd Ave; 9am-6pm Mon-Fri, to 5pm Sat, 10am-4pm Sun) At the entrance to town, this helpful place provides everything from trail maps to local menus, plus lots of good advice.

Harbormaster's Office (p227) Has showers for $2 (available 24 hours). Boat launches start at $10.

Kenai Fjords National Park Visitor Center (p239) In Seward's small-boat harbor; has information on hiking and camping, and issues free backcountry permits.

USFS Ranger Station (907-224-3374; 29847 Seward Hwy; 8am-4:30pm Mon-Fri) Has maps and information about Seward's outstanding selection of trails, cabins and campgrounds.

Getting There & Away

BUS

Homer Stage Line (907-868-3914; www.stagelineinhomer.com) Runs Monday, Wednesday and Friday from Seward (9am) to Homer ($100), with stops in Soldotna ($65) and Cooper Landing ($65).

Park Connection (800-266-8625; www.alaskacoach.com) Has a daily service from Seward to Denali Park (one-way $155) via Anchorage (one-way $65).

Seward Bus Line (Map p228; 907-224-3608; www.sewardbuslines.net; 539 3rd Ave) Departs at 9:30am and 2pm daily en route to Anchorage ($40). It also offers service at 9:30am to Whittier ($60, minimum two passengers).

Seward Shuttle (http://www.cityofseward.us) When cruise ships are in town, the free shuttle runs between the ferry terminal and downtown every 30 minutes.

TRAIN

Alaska Railroad (907-265-2494; www.akrr.com; 408 Port Ave; one-way/round-trip $105/168) Offers a daily run to Anchorage from May to September. It's more than just public transportation: it's one of the most famous rides in Alaska, complete with glaciers, steep gorges and rugged mountain scenery.

Kenai Fjords National Park

Kenai Fjords National Park (Map p232; 907-224-2125; www.nps.gov/kefj) was created in 1980 to protect 587,000 acres of Alaska's most awesome, impenetrable wilderness. Crowning the park is the massive Harding Ice Field; from it, countless tidewater glaciers pour down, carving the coast into dizzying fjords.

With such a landscape – and an abundance of marine wildlife – the park is a major tourist attraction. Unfortunately, it's also an expensive one. That is why road-accessible Exit Glacier is its highlight attraction. Hardier souls can ascend to the Harding Ice Field from the same trailhead, but only experienced mountaineers equipped with skis, ice axes and crampons can investigate the 900 sq miles of ice.

The majority of visitors either take a quick trip to Exit Glacier's face or splurge on a tour-boat cruise along the coast. For those who want to spend more time in the park, the coastal fjords are a blue-water kayaker's dream. The park is free.

Activities

Hiking

Harding Ice Field Trail HIKING

(Map p232) This strenuous and yet extremely popular 4-mile trail (six- to eight-hour round-trip) follows Exit Glacier up to Harding Ice Field. The 700-sq-mile expanse remained undiscovered until the early 1900s, when a map-surveying team discovered that eight coastal glaciers flowed from the exact same system.

Today you can rediscover it via a steep, roughly cut and sometimes slippery ascent to 3500ft. Beware of bears; they're common here. Only experienced glacier-travelers should head onto the ice-field proper.

The trek is well worth it for those with the stamina, as it provides spectacular views of not only the ice field but Exit Glacier and the valley below. The upper section of the route is snow-covered for much of the year; bring a jacket and watch for ice-bridges above creeks. Camping up here is a great idea, but

WORTH A TRIP

EXIT GLACIER

The marquee attraction of Kenai Fjords National Park is Exit Glacier, named by explorers crossing the Harding Ice Field who found the glacier a suitable way to 'exit' the ice and mountains.

From the Exit Glacier Nature Center (p239), the **Outwash Plain Trail** is an easy three-quarter-mile walk to the glacier's alluvial plain – a flat expanse of pulverized silt and gravel, cut through by braids of gray meltwater. The **Edge of the Glacier Trail** leaves the first loop and climbs steeply to an overlook at the side of the glacier before returning. Both trails make for a short hike that will take one or two hours; you can return along the half-mile nature trail through cottonwood forest, alder thickets and old glacial moraines before emerging at the ranger station. Note how the land becomes more vegetated the further you get from the ice, the result of having had more time to recover from its glacial scouring. Signs indicate how far the glacier extended.

If you have the time and legs for it, the hike up to the Harding Ice Field is well worth it; where else can you see a large remnant of the Pleistocene Ice Age?

the free, tiny public-use cabin at the top is for emergencies only.

Resurrection River Trail HIKING

(Map p232) This 16-mile trail accesses a 72-mile trail system connecting Seward and Hope. The continuous trail is broken only by the Sterling Hwy and provides a wonderful wilderness adventure through streams, rivers, lakes, wooded lowlands and alpine areas.

It's difficult and expensive to maintain, so expect to encounter natural hassles such as downed trees, boggy patches and washed-out sections. Resurrection River Cabin (p233) is 7 miles from the trailhead, and cannot be reserved.

The southern trailhead is at Mile 8 of Exit Glacier Rd. The northern trailhead joins the Russian Lakes Trail 5 miles from Cooper Lake or 16 miles from the Russian River Campground off the Sterling Hwy. The hike from the Seward Hwy to the Sterling Hwy is a 40-mile trip, including Exit Glacier.

Paddling

Blue-water paddles out of Resurrection Bay along the coastline of the park are for experienced kayakers only; others should invest in a drop-off service. You'll be rewarded, however, with wildlife encounters and close-up views of the glaciers from a unique perspective.

With several glaciers to visit, **Aialik Bay** is a popular arm for kayakers. Many people hire water-taxis to drop them near Aialik Glacier, then take three or four days to paddle south past Pedersen Glacier and into Holgate Arm, where they're picked up. The high point of the trip is Holgate Glacier, an active tidewater glacier that's the main feature of all the boat tours.

Northwestern Lagoon is more expensive to reach but much more isolated, with not nearly as many tour boats. The wildlife is excellent, especially the seabirds and sea otters, and more than a half-dozen glaciers can be seen. Plan on three to four days if you're being dropped inside the lagoon.

Most companies can arrange drop-off and pick-up; it's about $300 for the round-trip to Aialik Bay; prices decrease or increase depending on distance.

Miller's Landing KAYAKING

(Map p232; ☎907-331-3113; www.millerslandingak.com; Lowell Point; ⏰5:30am-11pm) Rents out kayaks (single/double $45/55) and equipment, and also provides a water-taxi service as far as Aialik Bay ($315 per person, four-person minimum).

Kayak Adventures Worldwide KAYAKING

(☎907-224-3960; www.kayakak.com) A highly respected, eco-oriented operation that guides educational half- and full-day trips out of Seward. Trips to Aialik Bay start at $399 and include a water-taxi and a guided paddle to Aialik Glacier.

Sunny Cove Sea Kayaking KAYAKING

(☎907-224-4426; www.sunnycove.com) It doesn't rent out kayaks, but does arrange a multitude of different trips, including a popular $425 Kenai Fjords day trip.

WORTH A TRIP

TERN LAKE JUNCTION TO COOPER LANDING

From **Tern Lake Junction** (Mile 37, Seward Hwy) it's only 58 miles to Soldotna, not much more than an hour's drive. Yet this stretch contains so many hiking, camping and canoeing opportunities that it would take you a month to enjoy them all. Surrounded by the Chugach National Forest and Kenai National Wildlife Refuge, the Sterling Hwy and its side roads pass a dozen trails, 20 campgrounds and an almost endless number of lakes, rivers and streams.

Mileposts along the highway show distances from Seward, with Tern Lake Junction at Mile 37 the starting point of the Sterling Hwy.

During July and August, be prepared to stop at a handful of campgrounds before finding an available site.

At the roadside **Sunrise Inn & Cafe** (907-595-1222; www.alaskasunriseinn.com; Mile 45, Sterling Hwy; r $129-179; 7am-10pm;) there are 10 cozy rooms facing the parking lot. The bar and restaurant – with its gorgeous patio – are worth a stop.

Around the corner on Quartz Creek Rd, **Alaska Horsemen Trail Adventures** (907-595-1806; www.alaskahorsemen.com; Mile 45, Sterling Hwy; cabin $125-175; 8am-7pm) gives you the full cowpoke treatment, with big stetsons and trail coats for guests, a mess hall, basic spruce cabins and horseback rides along Quartz and Crescent Creeks (per half-/full day $129/229). Pricier guided overnight trips include rafting (called the 'Saddle Paddle') and/or flightseeing or custom fishing trips.

Just past Sunrise Inn, **Quartz Creek Campground** (www.recreation.gov; Mile 0.3, Quartz Creek Rd; tent & RV sites $18) on the shores of Kenai Lake is crazily popular with RVs and anglers during salmon runs. The campground is so developed that the sites are paved.

The **Crescent Creek Trail** (Mile 3.3, Quartz Creek Rd), about half a mile beyond the **Crescent Creek Campground** (www.recreation.gov; Mile 3, Quartz Creek Rd; tent sites $14), which is itself 3 miles up Quartz Creek Rd from Alaska Horsemen, leads 6.2 miles to the outlet of Crescent Lake and the USFS's **Crescent Saddle Cabin** (907-288-3178; www.recreation.gov; cabins $60). It's an easy walk or bike ride and has spectacular autumn colors in September. Anglers can fish for Arctic grayling in the lake during the summer. The Carter Lake Trail (p231) connects the east end of the lake to the Seward Hwy, with a rough path along the south side of the lake between the two trails.

Tours

The easiest and most popular way to view the park's dramatic fjords, glaciers and abundant wildlife is from a cruise ship. Several companies offer the same basic tours: wildlife cruises (three to five hours) take in Resurrection Bay without really entering the park. Don't bother taking the short cruise, unless you are really trying to avoid seasickness. Much better tours (eight to 10 hours) explore Holgate Arm or Northwestern Lagoon.

Scenic Mountain Air SCENIC FLIGHTS
(907-362-6205; www.sewardair.com) For flightseeing trips, contact Scenic Mountain Air at Seward airport for flights over the fjords. Prices start at $129 per person for a 30-minute flight over Bear Glacier, and go up to $389 for a 1½-hr flight that takes you to Northwestern Glacier.

Sleeping

★ **Exit Glacier Campground** CAMPGROUND
(Map p232; Exit Glacier Rd; tent sites free) The only formal campground in the park. It has great walk-in sites for tents only and a bear-proof food-storage area. Other campsites are dotted along Exit Glacier Rd – look for small turnoffs in the alders.

Public-Use Cabins CABIN $
(www.recreation.gov; cabins $75) There are two cabins along the fjords, as well as countless other informal campsites that line the kayak-accessible beaches of Aialik Bay and Northwestern Lagoon.

Aialik Cabin is on a beach that's perfect for hiking, beachcombing and whale-watching, while Holgate Arm Cabin has a spectacular view of Holgate Glacier. You'll want to reserve these well in advance.

Kenai Fjords Glacier Lodge CABIN $$$
(☎800-334-8730; www.kenaifjordsglacierlodge.com; cabins per person from $850) On gorgeous Pedersen Lagoon, this lodge has 16 rustic-chic cabins (with private bathrooms and electricity) connected by a network of boardwalks. The all-inclusive price is a better deal for longer stays and includes transportation from Seward, gourmet meals, glacier cruises and guided kayaking.

Information

Exit Glacier Nature Center (Map p232; 9am-8pm) At the Exit Glacier trailhead; has interpretive displays, sells postcards and field guides, and is the starting point for ranger-guided hikes.

Kenai Fjords National Park Visitor Center (Map p228; ☎907-224-3175; 1212 4th Ave, Seward; 9am-7pm) Located in Seward's small-boat harbor; has info on hikes and paddles in the park.

Getting There & Away

To reach the coastal fjords, you'll need to take a tour or catch a water-taxi with **Miller's Landing** (Map p232; ☎907-331-3113; www.millerslandingak.com; Lowell Point). It's a couple of miles outside south of town, so you can walk or take a taxi. Getting to Exit Glacier is a bit easier. If you don't have a car, the **Exit Glacier Shuttle** (☎907-224-5569; www.exitglaciershuttle.com; round trip $15; 9:30am-5pm Mon-Thu, from 8:30am Fri-Sun) runs hourly shuttle to the glacier between 9:30am and 4:30pm. The van scoops passengers up in downtown Seward and at the small-boat harbor. **Glacier Taxi** (☎907-224-5678; www.glaciertaxicab.com) charges $60 (round trip) from Seward whether it's one passenger or a full car.

STERLING HIGHWAY

At Tern Lake Junction, the paved Sterling Hwy turns off from the Seward Hwy, heading westward through the forests and mountains of the Kenai National Wildlife Refuge (p242) to Soldotna and then bending south along Cook Inlet toward Homer.

Cooper Landing

☎907 / POP 293

After skirting the north end of Kenai Lake, you enter scenic Cooper Landing (Mile 48.4). This picturesque outpost – named for Joseph Cooper, a miner who worked the area in the 1880s – is best known for its rich and brutal combat salmon fishing along the Russian and Kenai Rivers. While rustic log-cabin lodges featuring giant fish freezers are still the lifeblood of this town, the trails, rafting and kayaking opportunities attract a very different sort of tourist.

Sights

K'Beq Interpretive Site ARCHAEOLOGICAL SITE
(☎907-395-7290; www.kenaitze.org; Mile 52.6, Sterling Hwy; 10am-4pm Thu-Sun) FREE This riverfront site, run by the local Kenaitzie tribe, is a refreshing reminder of what this area was like before the flood of sport fishers. A quarter-mile boardwalk winds past an ancient house pit and other archaeological relics, while interpretive panels address berry picking, steam-bath building and more traditional methods of catching fish on the Kenai. Several guided tours depart throughout the day, and of course there's a gift shop.

Activities

Fishing

Most of the fishing on the Upper Kenai is for rainbow trout, Dolly Varden, and silver and sockeye salmon. Expect to pay at least $150 for a half-day on the water and more than $200 for a full day.

Hiking

Cooper Landing is the starting point for two of the Kenai Peninsula's loveliest multiday trails: the 39-mile Resurrection Pass Trail (p219) to Hope; and the 21-mile **Russian Lakes Trail** (Mile 52.6, Sterling Hwy;), a favorite for fishers and families. This is serious bear country. It is recommended that you bring good bear protection and make a lot of noise while hiking in the area.

Tours

Kenai Kayak Company KAYAKING
(☎907-521-0244; www.kenaikayakco.com) Offers two-hour guided tours on Kenai Lake in double kayaks (per person $75).

Alaska Rivers Company RAFTING
(☎888-595-1226; www.alaskariverscompany.com; Mile 50, Sterling Hwy; 7:30am-10:30pm) Runs guided raft trips down the Kenai River (per half-/full day $56/155). These are mostly float trips, but the longer paddle bumps over some Class III rapids. It also offers stand-up paddleboard tours on Kenai Lake; a two-hour beginner tour is $65 per person and regular tours per half-/full day are $125/225.

Alaska River Adventures RAFTING
(☎907-595-2000; www.alaskariveradventures.com; Mile 48, Sterling Hwy; ⏲7am-7pm) Runs scenic three-hour floats on the Kenai (per person $59). Extend the trip with an intro to gold prospecting for $289 per person. It also offers guided hiking, fishing and flightseeing packages.

Sleeping

Russian River Campground CAMPGROUND $
(www.recreation.gov; Mile 52.6, Sterling Hwy; s/d tent & RV sites $18/28) Located where the Russian and Kenai Rivers merge, this place is beautiful and incredibly popular when red salmon are spawning; you'll want to reserve one of the 80 sites. It costs $12 just to park here, and there's a three-day limit for stays.

Cooper Creek Campground CAMPGROUND $
(☎907-522-8368; www.reserveamerica.com; Mile 50.7, Sterling Hwy; tent & RV sites $18-28) This campground, nestled in a cottonwood and spruce grove, has 28 sites on both sides of the highway, including some right on the Kenai River. Good luck hooking one of those.

Hutch B&B B&B $$
(☎907-595-1270; www.arctic.net/~hutch; Mile 48.5, Sterling Hwy; r $105-129, cabins $225;) In a three-story, balcony-ringed lodge, the big, simple, clean rooms are the best deal in town, and its small mess hall the cutest. Nightly campfires and common sitting areas add a social angle.

Drifters Lodge CABIN $$$
(☎907-595-5555; www.drifterslodge.com; Mile 48.3, Sterling Hwy; cabins $325-375, r $200-250;) Six tidy and fresh cabins come with memory-foam mattresses, river views and kitchenettes, while five smaller rooms share bathrooms and leafy views. A brook babbles next to the sauna, and there's a nightly campfire. Drifters also takes folks out on the river – a float costs $50 to $75 and fishing trips are $200 to $300. It focuses on all-inclusive trips.

Eating

Cooper Landing Grocery MARKET $
(Mile 48.2, Sterling Hwy; ⏲10am-8pm) Snacks, sweatshirts and s'mores supplies.

Gwin's Lodge AMERICAN $$
(☎907-595-1266; www.gwinslodge.com; Mile 52, Sterling Hwy; mains $10-30; ⏲11am-9pm) Established way back in 1952 (that's ancient for Alaska), this chunky-log roadhouse serves up generous portions with the friendliest waiters in Cooper Landing. It has upped the local scene with live music on weekends, which attracts summer employees and tourists alike. It can make you a box lunch to take on the river ($13).

Information

Chamber of Commerce (☎907-595-8888; www.cooperlandingchamber.com; Mile 48.7 Sterling Hwy; ⏲11am-5pm) You'll find a few brochures here, but the website is actually more informative.

Getting There & Away

If you're without wheels, your best option for reaching Cooper Landing is **Homer Stage Line** (☎907-868-3914; www.stagelineinhomer.com), which runs daily buses through here from both Anchorage and Homer. From either end, it's $65 per person one-way and stops at **Wildman's** (☎907-595-1456; www.wildmans.org; Mile 47.5, Sterling Hwy; ⏲6am-11pm).

Kenai National Wildlife Refuge

Once west of the Resurrection Pass southern trailhead, you enter the Kenai National Wildlife Refuge, managed by the US Fish & Wildlife Service. Originally called the Kenai National Moose Range, 1.73 million acres was set aside by President Roosevelt in 1941, and the 1980 Alaska Lands Act increased that acreage to the almost 2 million acres that it now encompasses. It supports impressive populations of Dall sheep, moose, caribou and bear, and has attracted hunters from around the world since the early 1900s.

Highlights of the area include camping along Skilak Lake or canoeing through the Kenai National Wildlife Canoe Trail System. A massive forest fire burned more than 300 sq miles in the refuge in 2014, including much of the northern shore of Tustumena Lake, but signs of life are showing.

Activities

Russian River Ferry BOATING
(Mile 55, Sterling Hwy; per adult/child $11/5.50) This ferry, west of the confluence of the Kenai and Russian Rivers, transports tens of thousands of anglers across the water every summer to some of the finest fishing anywhere. The separate parking fee is $12.

COMBAT FISHING

In a place that's mostly natural and wild, there are few sights more unnatural than what happens each summer wherever Alaska's best salmon rivers meet a busy road. When the fish are running, the banks become a human frenzy – a ceaseless string of men, women and children hip-to-hip, hundreds of fishing rods whipping to and fro, the air filled with curses and cries of joy. This is combat fishing.

As with any form of combat, there are subtle rules that guide the chaos. Among them: don't wade out in front of other anglers, or snap up their spot on the bank if they briefly step away. (On the other hand, don't let the glares of the earlier arrivals dissuade you from taking your proper place in the fray.) Try to give your neighbor space – and whatever you do, don't foul your line with theirs. Most importantly, if you get a bite, shout, 'Fish on!' so others can reel in their lines and give you room to wrestle your catch. In combat fishing, you don't 'play' a fish; you land it fast, so others can rejoin the fight.

Hiking

As the highway heads southwest toward Soldotna, the mountains will fade back. You can still hit up a few good hiking trails before that happens, though.

Skyline Trail HIKING

(Mile 61, Sterling Hwy) This route ascends above the treeline for 1 mile, which is a decent turnaround point. After that it follows a ridge on an unmarked and unmaintained route for 6.5 miles before connecting with the Fuller Lakes Trail. Those who want to hike both trails should plan to stay overnight at Upper Fuller Lake, where there are several good campsites.

Fuller Lakes Trail HIKING

(Mile 57, Sterling Hwy) This 3-mile hike leads to Fuller Lake just above the treeline. The well-marked trail begins with a rapid ascent to Lower Fuller Lake, where you cross a stream and continue over a low pass to Upper Fuller Lake.

At the lake, the trail follows the east shore and then branches; the fork to the left leads up a ridge and becomes a route to the Skyline Trail.

Skilak Lake Road

Skilak Lake Rd, a scenic 19-mile loop off the Sterling Hwy, is a bit too rough for low-clearance vehicles outside summer. It provides access to an assortment of popular recreational opportunities.

Seven Lakes Trail HIKING

(Engineer Lake, Mile 9.5, Skilak Lake Rd) A 4.4-mile hike to the Sterling Hwy from Engineer Lake. The trail is easy walking over level terrain and passes Hidden and Hikers Lakes before ending at Kelly Lake Campground (p242). The trail was shortened when Skilak Lake Rd cut off access to the three northern lakes, so you only pass four.

Kenai River Trail HIKING

(Mile 0.6, Skilak Lake Rd) A half mile down this trail are wonderful views of the Kenai River Canyon. There are really two trailheads; the main 'upper' trail starts at mile 0.6 of Skilak Lake Rd, and the other at mile 2.3.

Skilak Lookout Trail HIKING

(Mile 5.5, Skilak Lake Rd) Ascends 2 miles to a knob (elevation 1400ft) that has a panoramic view of the mountains and lakes. Plan on four to five hours for the round-trip.

Sleeping

There are five well-marked campgrounds along Skilak Lake Rd, and many more spread throughout the refuge. Some, such as Hidden Lake and Upper Skilak, cost $10 to $14 while others are free. The campgrounds are well marked, running from east to west:

CAMPGROUND	SITES	LOCATION
Hidden Lake	44	Mile 3.6
Upper Skilak Lake	25	Mile 8.4
Lower Ohmer Lake	3	Mile 8.6
Engineer Lake	4	Mile 9.7
Lower Skilak Lake	14	Mile 14

If you choose to stay on the Sterling Hwy past the Skilak Lake Rd junction, a side road at Mile 69 leads south to the **Peterson Lake Campground** (Mile 69, Sterling Hwy; tent sites free) FREE and **Kelly Lake Campground** (Mile 69, Sterling Hwy; tent sites free) FREE, near one end of the Seven Lakes Trail. **Watson Lake Campground** (Mile 71.3 Sterling Hwy; tent sites free) FREE has three sites. Four miles down the highway is the west junction with Skilak Lake Rd.

At Mile 81, the Sterling Hwy divides into a four-lane road, and you soon arrive in the small town of **Sterling** (pop 5600), where the Moose River empties into the Kenai.

Izaak Walton Recreation Site (www.dnr.alaska.gov; Mile 82, Sterling Hwy; tent & RV sites $15), at the confluence of the Kenai and Moose Rivers, is popular among anglers during the salmon runs and with paddlers ending their Swan Lake route canoe trip at the Moose River Bridge.

Swanson River Road, at Mile 85 of the Sterling Hwy, heads north for 18 miles, with Swan Lake Rd heading east for 12 miles at the end of Swanson River Rd. The roads offer access to the Swanson River and Swan Lake canoe routes, and three campgrounds: **Dolly Varden Lake Campground** (Mile 14, Swanson River Rd; tent sites free) FREE, **Rainbow Lake Campground** (Mile 16, Swanson River Rd; tent sites free) FREE and **Swanson River Campground** (www.alaska.org/detail/swanson-river-campground; tent sites free) FREE at the very end of the road. Even without a canoe, you'll enjoy exploring the trails that connect prized fishing holes.

Across the Sterling Hwy from Swanson River Rd is the entrance to Scout Lake Rd, where you'll find the **Morgans Landing State Recreation Area** (www.dnr.alaska.gov/parks/aspunits/kenai/morgldcamp.htm; Lou Morgan Rd; tent & RV sites $15). This is a particularly scenic area on the bluffs overlooking the Kenai River, a 3.5-mile drive from the Sterling Hwy.

There are 16 **public use cabins** (877-444-6777; www.recreation.gov; cabin $35-45) in the refuge. Get more information at the Refuge Headquarters.

Information

Kenai National Wildlife Refuge Headquarters & Visitor Center (907-262-7021; https://kenai.fws.gov; 1 Ski Hill Rd; 9am-5pm) In Soldotna, this is the Refuge Headquarters.

Getting There & Away

Entrance to the refuge is easy by car, though you'll need your own. You can rent a car in Anchorage (p179) or Soldotna.

Soldotna

907 / POP 4617

The Kenai River runs right through town, making this one of the peninsula's premier fishing outposts. That said, with its strip malls and fast-food chains, Soldotna is ugly as ugly gets, and its flat nearby topography offers very little for hikers, bikers or adventurers.

Most years, you'll be competing with hundreds of anglers for prime shoreline. But the opportunity to hook some of the biggest salmon in the state makes it worthwhile – note that past king salmon closures have serious anglers looking elsewhere, so check in advance to make sure numbers are high enough.

Situated where the Sterling Hwy crosses the Kenai River, Soldotna sprawls in every direction, including practically to the city of Kenai, some 12 miles northwest along the Kenai Spur Hwy. The intersection of the Spur Hwy and the Sterling Hwy is referred to as the 'Y.'

Sights

Kenai National Wildlife Refuge Headquarters & Visitor Center PARK

(907-262-7021; https://kenai.fws.gov; 1 Ski Hill Rd, Soldotna; 9am-5pm) Opposite Kalifornsky Beach Rd near the Kenai River is the junction with Funny River Rd. Follow signs to Ski Hill Rd, following it for a mile to reach this excellent, kid-friendly information center that has an exhibit hall, bookstore and 2.2 miles of trails that wrap around the nearby lake.

There are displays on the life cycles of salmon, daily wildlife films and naturalist-led outdoor programs.

Soldotna Homestead Museum MUSEUM

(907-262-3832; 461 Centennial Park Rd; by donation; 10am-4pm Tue-Sat, from noon Sun) FREE This museum includes a wonderful collection of homesteaders' cabins spread through six wooded acres in Centennial Park. Ask for a free guided tour to discover the stories of early homesteaders who were awarded plots here after WWII.

It also has a one-room schoolhouse, a torture-chamber collection of early dental tools, an excellent natural-history display with archaeological finds, and a replica of the $7.2-million check the US paid Russia for Alaska.

DON'T MISS

EXPLORING THE REFUGE CANOE TRAIL SYSTEM

One of only two wilderness canoe systems established in the US (the other is the Boundary Waters, Minnesota), the **Kenai National Wildlife Refuge Canoe Trail System** (www.fws.gov) offers yet another unique experience for the Alaskan visitor. Divided into two areas, the Swan Lake and the Swanson River routes, the system connects 120 miles of lakes and water trails in an undulating landscape. Expect as much portaging as paddling.

Swan Lake is the more popular area, covering 60 miles and 30 lakes, and connecting to the Moose River. The Swanson River route requires longer portages and isn't as well marked as Swan Lake, but you'll be rewarded for effort with solitude and excellent trout fishing. This route covers 80 miles, 40 lakes and 46 miles of the Swanson River.

Several outfitters can rent you canoes and paddles: try **Alaska Canoe & Campground** (☎907-262-2331; www.alaskacanoetrips.com; 35292 Sterling Hwy, Sterling; canoe per 12/24hr $45/55, kayak $35/45), which also rents out rafts and kayaks.

Activities

From mid-May through September, runs of red, silver and king salmon make the lower Kenai River among the hottest sport-fishing spots in Alaska. King salmon levels on the Kenai River have been lower than normal since 2009, and the Alaska Department of Fish & Game (p425) heavily restricted king salmon fishing on the river in 2013 and 2014. Check ahead for openings, bank closures and the latest news.

If you're green to the scene but want to wet a line, first drop by the visitors center (p244) where staff members will assist you in determining where to fish and what to fish for. They can also hook you up with a guide, who'll charge you up to $300 a day but will vastly improve your chances of catching dinner – and of not violating the river's multilayered regulations.

Rather go it alone? From the shore, you've still got a shot at catching reds (from mid-July to early August) and silvers (late July through August). Try casting from the 'fishwalk' below the visitors center or from city campgrounds. If you don't have your own rod, you can pick up inexpensive gear from **Trustworthy Hardware** (☎907-262-4655; 44370 Sterling Hwy; ⊙8am-7pm Mon-Fri, 9am-6pm Sat, 10am-6pm Sun).

Sleeping

Spending the night in Soldotna is a catch-22: outside fishing season there's no reason to stay here; in season, there's nowhere to stay – just about every campsite and room is taken. What's left will cost you dearly. Make reservations. The chamber of commerce can locate last-minute rooms. The Kenai Peninsula B&B Association (www.kenaipeninsulabba.com) has listings for the entire peninsula.

Swiftwater Park Campground CAMPGROUND $
(☎907-262-5299; www.ci.soldotna.ak.us; 675 Swiftwater Park Rd; tent & RV sites $21) Run by the city, this campground doesn't have a boardwalk but is still a good place for pulling in prized salmon. If you just want to fish, it's $8 to park for the day.

Centennial Park Campground CAMPGROUND $
(☎907-262-5299; www.ci.soldotna.ak.us; cnr Sterling Hwy & Kalifornsky Beach Rd; tent & RV sites $21) Maintained by the city, this 176-site campground has boardwalked fishing access to the Kenai River. The day-use fee is $8.

Kenai River Lodge HOTEL $$
(☎907-262-4292; www.kenairiverlodge.com; 393 Riverside Dr; r $199-220; 🅟📶) All rooms face the river, and there's a private fishing hole right outside – though the road noise can be a bit much. All rooms come with coffee, microwave and fridge, and there's an excellent bar on site.

Diamond M Ranch RESORT $$
(☎866-283-9424; www.diamondmranch.com; Mile 16.5, Kalifornsky Beach Rd; tent sites $38-65, RV sites $53-95, r $52-186, cabins $132-219; 🅟📶) Nearly 20 years ago, this was just the Martin family farm – but with anglers constantly asking to camp in their field, the Martins converted it to a tourist megaplex, complete with kids' programs, walking tours, movie nights and horse rides. An extensive

campground, cabins and full B&B share the 80-acre farm. Look for caribou on the Kenai River Flats.

Soldotna B&B Lodge B&B $$$
(877-262-4779; www.alaskafishinglodges.us; 399 Lovers Lane; r $157-267;) This is the town's top luxury spot, drawing blue-chip anglers and honeymooners. It has plush rooms, custom adventure and fishing packages, and some rooms without bathrooms. It offers breakfast in a riverfront sunroom and a private fishing hole for reds.

Eating & Drinking

Odie's Deli DELI $
(44315 Sterling Hwy; breakfast & lunch $9-15; 8am-8pm Mon-Fri, 9am-4pm Sat) A surprisingly hip little deli serving breakfast until 10:30am. You can build your own sandwiches on homemade bread.

Moose is Loose CAFE $
(44278 Sterling Hwy; snacks $2-7; 6:30am-4:30pm Tue-Sat) This Moose comes with coffee and goodies galore, including a huge array of fresh doughnuts.

St Elias Brewing Company PIZZA $
(www.steliasbrewingco.com; 434 Sharkathmi Ave; dinner $8-14; 11am-10pm Sun-Thu, to 11pm Fri & Sat) Stone-fired pizzas and sandwiches served in an echoing brewery with a big patio. Delicious. Beer-lovers should order the sampler. Expect the service to be mediocre.

Mykel's SEAFOOD $$
(907-262-4305; www.mykels.com; 35041 Kenai Spur Hwy; mains $14-37; 11am-11pm) This is Soldotna's fanciest place, with high-backed leather booths and dishes such as chargrilled salmon with mushroom risotto.

The Bridge BAR
(907-260-2000; 393 Riverside Dr; noon-midnight Sun-Thu, to 1am Fri & Sat) This excellent and welcoming bar looks over the Kenai River from the second story of the Kenai River Lodge. Enjoy a drink on the deck and watch anglers pull in salmon below you.

Kenai River Brewing Co BREWERY
(www.kenairiverbrewing.com; 308 Homestead Lane; noon-8pm) Enjoy handcrafted ales in a large, airy building.

Information

MEDICAL SERVICES

Central Peninsula Hospital (907-714-4404; 250 Hospital Pl) Just west of the Kenai Spur Hwy.

MONEY

Wells Fargo (44552 Sterling Hwy; 10am-6pm Mon-Fri, to 5pm Sat) Has cash.

TOURIST INFORMATION

Soldotna Chamber of Commerce & Visitors Center (907-262-9814; www.visitsoldotna.com; 44790 Sterling Hwy; 9am-7pm;) Has internet plus up-to-date fishing reports and a nice boardwalk along the river

Getting There & Away

Homer Stage Line (907-868-3914; www.stagelineinhomer.com) buses pass through daily en route to Anchorage and Homer. It stops at the Soldotna Chamber of Commerce & Visitors Center.

City of Kenai

907 / POP 7745

At first blush, Kenai is a sorry sight. It's not convenient or especially picturesque, existing primarily as a support community for the drilling operations at Cook Inlet.

It's long been a rare bird: a major Alaskan town with minimal tourism. Lately, though, this faded boomtown has taken some hesitant steps toward wooing visitors with the excellent salmon fishing at the mouth of the Kenai River.

The first Russian Orthodox Church on mainland Alaska today presides over a replica of the 1867 fort, which hasn't fully realized its potential as adorable tourist magnet. And then there's the view: Mt Redoubt (the volcano that erupted steam and ash in December 1989) to the southwest, Mt Iliamna at the head of the Aleutian Range and the Alaska Range to the northwest. Nice.

North of town, around Mile 19 of the Kenai Spur Hwy, is Alaska's largest concentration of oil infrastructure outside Prudhoe Bay.

Sights

Kenai Beach BEACH
Down below the bluffs is an oddity in Alaska: a sweeping, sandy beach, ideal for picnicking, Frisbee-chucking and other waterfront

fun. There are stellar views of the volcanoes across the inlet, and from July 10 to 31 you can watch hundreds of frantic fishers dip-net for sockeye salmon at the mouth of the Kenai River.

Sadly, unless you've lived in Alaska for the past year, you can't participate.

Kenai Visitors & Cultural Center CULTURAL CENTER
(907-283-1991; www.visitkenai.com; 11471 Kenai Spur Hwy; 9am-6pm Mon-Fri, 10am-5pm Sat, from noon Sun) FREE This excellent visitors center is among Kenai's main attractions. The museum features historical exhibits on the city's Russian heritage, offshore drilling and a room full of stuffed wildlife staring down from the rafters. It also has quality Alaska Native art from around the state. Free movies about the city's strange history are screened.

Captain Cook State Recreation Area PARK
By following the Kenai Spur Hwy north for 36 miles, you'll first pass the trailer parks and chemical plants of the North Kenai industrial district before reaching this uncrowded state recreation area that encompasses 4000 acres of forests, lakes, rivers and beaches along Cook Inlet.

The area offers swimming, camping and the beauty of the inlet in a setting that is unaffected by the stampede for salmon to the south.

The Kenai Spur Hwy ends in the park after first passing Stormy Lake, where you'll find a bathhouse and a swimming area along the water's edge. Discovery Campground has 53 sites on the bluff overlooking Cook Inlet, where some of the world's greatest tides ebb and flow. The fishing in Swanson River is great, and this is a fine place to end the Swan Lake canoe route.

Activities

Kenai River Estuary BIRDWATCHING
(Boat Launch Rd) This beautiful estuary with its own viewing platform is an excellent spot for bird-watching. Get here by heading 1 mile south of town along the bike path on Bridge Access Rd, then turning west onto Boat Launch Rd.

Sleeping

Finding last-minute rooms during summer's salmon runs can be more challenging than hauling in a 70-pounder, but for help log onto the website of Kenai Peninsula B&B Association (www.kenaipeninsulabba.com). If you're on a tight budget, head north along the Kenai Spur Hwy, where several motels cater to oil workers and offer lower rates. Kenai adds 10% in bed-and-sales tax.

Discovery Campground CAMPGROUND $
(907-522-8368; www.dnr.alaska.gov; tent & RV sites $15) Has 53 campsites near the beach in Captain Cook State Recreation Area.

Uptown Motel MOTEL $$
(907-283-3660; www.uptownmotel.com; 47 Spur View Dr; r $149-199;) The rooms here are clean and the very cool lobby is full of antiques, including an old barber's chair and cash register.

OLD TOWN KENAI

'Old Town' is an odd amalgam of historic structures and low-rent apartments, all stupendously situated high above the mouth of the Kenai River. You can pick up a free Walking Tour pamphlet at the visitors center.

Near Cook Inlet, the US military established Fort Kenay in 1867 and stationed more than 100 personnel here. What stands today is a replica constructed as part of the Alaska Centennial in 1967. It's not open to the public.

Across Mission Ave from the fort is the ornate Russian Orthodox Church, a white-clapboard structure topped with baby-blue onion domes. Built in 1895, it's the oldest Orthodox church on mainland Alaska. It was renovated in 2009. Staff at the visitors center can call to check the hours for you. West of the church overlooking the water is St Nicholas Chapel, built in 1906 on the burial site of Father Igumen Nicolai, Kenai's first resident priest.

Head southeast on Mission Ave, and you'll be traveling along the Bluff, a good vantage point to view the mouth of the Kenai River or the mountainous terrain on the west side of Cook Inlet. Look for belugas in the late spring and early summer.

Eating

Veronica's Cafe CAFE $

(604 Petersen Way; sandwiches $13; ⏲11am-3:30pm Mon-Thu, to 8pm Fri & Sat) In an Old Town log building dating from 1918, Veronica's serves espressos and healthy sandwiches and hosts open mics, folk jams and live bands. There's a warm wooden sun porch filled with flowers – the best place in town to relax with a sandwich.

Charlotte's Restaurant CAFE $

(115 Willow St; sandwiches $12-14; ⏲7am-3pm Mon-Fri, from 8am Sat) Grab sandwiches or just some fresh-baked goodies for your beach picnic.

★ **Flats Bistro** BISTRO $$

(☎907-335-1010; www.theflatsbistro.com; 39847 Kalifornsky Beach Rd; lunch $14-22, dinner $18-38; ⏲11:30am-10pm) Enjoy grand views of the Kenai River Flats as you sup on fresh Alaska seafood, house-made pasta or local greens. The dining is both comfortable and elegant, and it's Kenai's best place to dine.

Louie's Restaurant STEAK $$

(☎907-283-3660; 47 Spur View Dr; breakfast & lunch $12-15, dinner $19-29; ⏲5am-10pm) Under stuffed moose and elk heads in the Uptown Motel, Louie's serves the best surf-and-turf in the city.

Information

INTERNET ACCESS

Kenai Community Library (☎907-283-4378; 163 Main St Loop; ⏲9am-7pm Mon-Thu, to 6pm Fri, to 5pm Sun; 📶) Has free internet access; bring an ID.

MONEY

Alaska USA Bank (230 Bidarka St; ⏲10am-6pm Mon-Sat) Has a 24-hour ATM.

Getting There & Away

Kenai has the main airport on the peninsula and is served by **Ravn Alaska** (☎907-266-8394, 800-866-8394; www.flyravn.com), which offers multiple daily flights between Anchorage and Kenai. The round-trip fare is about $300 with ongoing service to other rural destinations.

Getting Around

For taxis, **Alaska Cabs** (☎907-283-6000) serves Kenai and Soldotna.

Ninilchik

☎907 / POP 867

This appealing little village is well worth spending a night at. The community is among the oldest on the Kenai Peninsula, having been settled in the 1820s by employees of the Russian-American Company. Many stayed even after imperial Russia sold Alaska to the US, and their descendants form the heart of the present community.

Sights

Old Russian Church CHURCH

Reached via a posted footpath behind the Village Cache Gift Shop, or from the highway on Orthodox Ave, the historic bluff-top structure was built in 1901. It sports five golden onion domes, and commands an unbelievable view of Cook Inlet and the volcanoes on the other side. Adjoining it is a prim Russian Orthodox cemetery of white-picket cribs.

Old Ninilchik Village HISTORIC SITE

The site of the original community, this is a postcard scene of faded log cabins in tall grass and beached fishing boats against the spectacular backdrop of Mt Redoubt.

Festivals & Events

Kenai Peninsula State Fair CULTURAL

(www.kenaipeninsulafair.com) The main event in Ninilchik is the Kenai Peninsula State Fair, the 'biggest little fair in Alaska,' which takes place annually in mid-August. Has live bands, food stalls and more.

Sleeping & Eating

Ninilchik View State Campground CAMPGROUND $

(www.dnr.alaska.gov/parks/aspunits/kenai/ninilvwcamp.htm; Mile 135.5, Sterling Hwy; tent & RV sites $15) By far the best of Ninilchik's public campgrounds, it's set atop a wooded bluff with a view of the old village and Cook Inlet. A stairway leads down to the beach.

Ninilchik River Campground CAMPGROUND $

(www.dnr.alaska.gov/parks/aspunits/kenai/ninilrvcamp.htm; Mile 134.9, Sterling Hwy; tent & RV sites $15) This campground has great river access and some pleasant trails.

Rosco's Pizza PIZZA $$

(15915 Sterling Hwy; pizza $12-25; ⏲11am-9pm) Hand-tossed dough made from scratch makes this a perfect place to fill up after a day of clam slamming.

Information

Ninilchik General Store (907-567-3378; Mile 135.7, Sterling Hwy; 7am-10pm Mon-Sat, to 8pm Sun) Has an ATM, lots of fishing and camping gear, and you will find a few tourist-oriented brochures posted out the front of the store.

Getting There & Away

Ninilchik is right along the Sterling Hwy, so buses traveling to or from Homer should drop you off there. It's more difficult to arrange a pickup, so it's best if you have your own wheels.

Homer

907 / POP 5631

As the Sterling Hwy descends into Homer, a panorama of mountains sweeps across the horizon. The Homer Spit juts into a glittering Kachemak Bay, and just when you think the view might unwind forever, it ends with dramatic Grewingk Glacier.

Hearing travelers' tales, you half expect to find lotus-eaters and mermaids lounging about. At first, though, Homer's appeal isn't evident. It sprawls and is choked with tourists, it lacks legendary hikes and it has a windswept waterfront that makes kayaking a slog. And then there's the Homer Spit – a tourist trap you may love to hate.

Stick around, however, and Homer will make you a believer. For one thing, there's that panorama, and the promise that it holds. And the vibe: the town is a magnet for radicals, artists and folks disillusioned with mainstream society, who've formed a critical mass here, dreaming up a sort of utopian vision for their city, and striving – with grins on their faces – to enact it.

Sights

★Alaska Islands & Ocean Visitor Center MUSEUM

(Map p248; 907-235-6961; www.islandsandocean.org; 95 Sterling Hwy; 9am-5pm) FREE More a research facility and museum than a visitor center, this impressive place has numerous cool interactive exhibits. The best is a room that's a replica seabird colony, complete with cacophonous bird calls and surround-view flocking.

There's also a decent film about ship-based marine research, a hands-on discovery lab, a pole that shows Homer's tides in real time, and a slate of daily educational programs and guided walks (they even have loaner binoculars for free).

★Pratt Museum MUSEUM

(Map p248; 907-235-8635; www.prattmuseum.org; 3779 Bartlett St; adult/child $10/5; 10am-6pm) There's lots of local art and Alaska Native artifacts, but a more impressive feature is the interactive displays on the area's wildlife, designed to mesmerize both kids and ex-kids. More sobering is the Storm Warning Theater, with harrowing tales about fishing on Kachemak Bay, where making a living can end your life.

More light-hearted and whimsical, and perhaps the coolest aspect of the museum, is the Forest Ecology Trail, where artists can contribute to the 'Facing the Elements' exhibit. Paths wind through the trees, and you'll stumble upon small exhibits, be they mirrors, rocks or pottery. A must-do. Take a walk around the grounds, where art installations glitter in the forest.

The Pratt also offers 1½-hour **harbor tours** (Map p250; Homer Spit Rd; per person $10) throughout summer at 3pm Monday and Thursday, leaving from the Salty Dawg Saloon (p255).

Fireweed Gallery GALLERY

(Map p248; 907-235-3411; www.fireweedgallery.com; 475 E Pioneer Ave; 10am-6pm Mon-Sat, to 4:30pm Sun) This gallery can get good local wares, and has more than just art to hang on your walls: sculptures, carvings, baskets and more are all on offer.

Bunnell Street Gallery GALLERY

(Map p248; 907-235-2662; www.bunnellstreetgallery.org; 106 W Bunnell Ave; 11am-6pm Mon-Sat, noon-4pm Sun) The town's best gallery, with monthly shows of fine art. You can also buy stunning jewelry and pottery.

Carl E Wynn Nature Center NATURE RESERVE

(Map p250; 907-235-5266; www.akcoastalstudies.org; Skyline Dr; adult/child $8/5; 10am-6pm) Situated on the bluffs above Homer, this moose-ridden 140-acre reserve is highly recommended for families and anyone interested in the area's ethnobotany – though the price tag is a little steep.

Homer

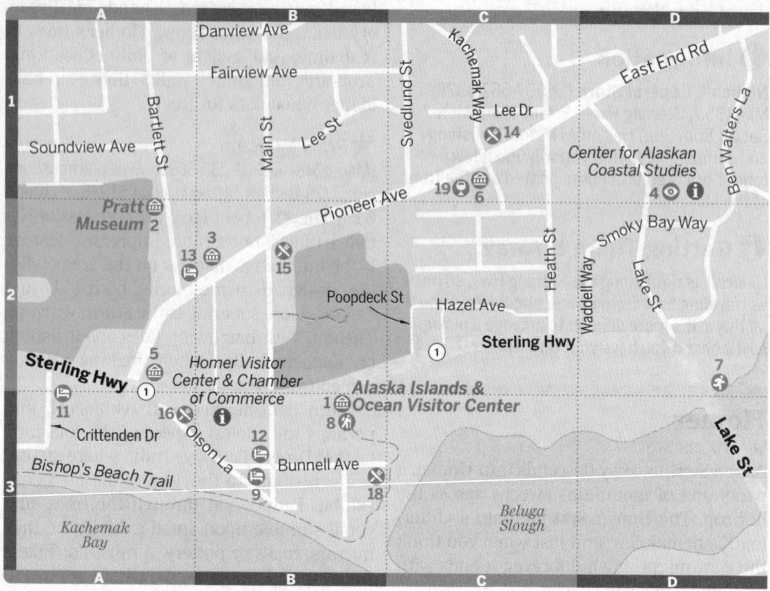

With a few short interpretive nature trails, one of them boardwalked and wheelchair accessible, this is a grand place to learn which plants can be used to heal a cut, condition your hair or munch for lunch. Naturalist-led hikes leave at 10am and 2pm daily in summer. It also has a slate of lectures and other programs; call the center for a schedule.

Homer Spit AREA

(Map p250) Generally known as 'the Spit,' this long needle of land – a 4.5-mile sandbar stretching into Kachemak Bay – is viewed by some folks as the most fun place in Alaska. Others wish another earthquake would come along and sink the thing. Regardless, the Spit throbs all summer with tourists.

They mass here in unimaginable density, gobbling fish and chips, purchasing alpaca sweaters, arranging bear-watching trips, watching theatrical performances and – oh yeah – going fishing in search of 300lb halibut. The hub of all this activity is the small-boat harbor, one of the best facilities in Southcentral Alaska and home to more than 700 boats. Close by is the **Seafarer's Memorial** (Map p250), which, amid all the Spit's hubbub, is a solemn monument to residents lost at sea.

Beachcombing, bonfiring, bald-eagle watching (they seem as common here as pigeons in New York City) and observing recently docked fishers angling for cute tourists at the Salty Dawg Saloon are all favorite activities. You can also go clamming at Mud Bay, on the east side of the Spit. Blue mussels, an excellent shellfish overlooked by many people, are the most abundant.

If you'd rather catch your dinner than buy it, try your luck at the **Fishing Hole**, just before the Pier One Theater. The small lagoon is the site of a 'terminal fishery,' in which salmon are planted by the state and return three or four years later to a place where they can't spawn. Sportsman's Supply & Rental (p256), close by, rents out rods ($10 to $20) as well as rakes and shovels (each $5) for clamming.

Art Shop Gallery GALLERY

(Map p248; www.artshopgallery.com; 202 W Pioneer Ave; ⏲10am-6pm Mon-Sat, noon-4pm Sun) Alaska art, on every wall. You'll find plenty of watercolors and other mediums here.

Ptarmigan Arts GALLERY

(Map p248; ☎907-235-5345; www.ptarmiganarts.com; 471 E Pioneer Ave; ⏲10am-6pm) Local cooperative gallery with stained class, wood carvings and pottery.

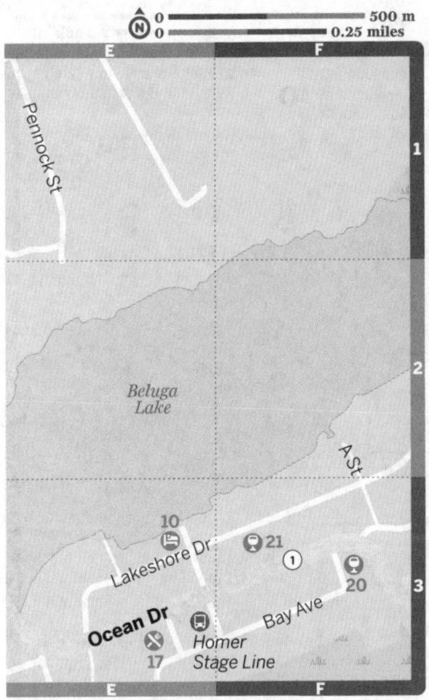

Homer

Top Sights
1 Alaska Islands & Ocean Visitor Center ... B3
2 Pratt Museum ... A2

Sights
3 Art Shop Gallery ... B2
Bunnell Street Gallery ... (see 12)
4 Center for Alaskan Coastal Studies ... D1
Fireweed Gallery ... (see 6)
5 Homer Council of the Arts ... A2
6 Ptarmigan Arts ... C1

Activities, Courses & Tours
7 Alaska Ultimate Safaris ... D2
8 Bishop's Beach Trail ... B3
Emerald Air Service ... (see 10)

Sleeping
9 Driftwood Inn ... B3
10 Homer Floatplane Lodge ... E3
11 Ocean Shores Motel ... A3
12 Old Town B&B ... B3
13 Pioneer Inn ... A2

Eating
14 Cosmic Kitchen ... C1
15 Duncan Diner ... B2
16 Fat Olives ... A3
17 Homer Farmers Market ... E3
18 Two Sisters Bakery ... B3

Drinking & Nightlife
19 Alibi ... C1
20 Grace Ridge Brewing Company ... F3
21 Homer Brewing Company ... F3

Center for Alaskan Coastal Studies CULTURAL CENTER
(Map p248; 907-235-6667; www.akcoastalstudies.org; 708 Smokey Bay Way; 9am-5pm Mon-Fri) FREE This nonprofit organization devoted to promoting appreciation of Kachemak Bay's ecosystem, runs the Carl E Wynn Nature Center and the Peterson Bay Field Station ($140 day tour), both of which offer guided hikes and educational programs throughout the summer.

It also operates the **Yurt on the Spit** (Map p250; Homer Spit Rd; per person $7; noon-5pm), right behind Mako's Water-Taxi, which does a daily 'Creatures of the Dock' tour at 1pm and 4pm ($5).

Activities

Cycling

Though Homer lacks formal mountain-biking trails, the dirt roads in the hills above town lend themselves to some great rides, especially along Diamond Ridge Rd and Skyline Dr. For an easy tour, head out E End Rd, which extends 20 miles east to the head of Kachemak Bay. There's also good biking to be had in Seldovia, an easy day or overnight trip from Homer by water-taxi.

Fishing

There are more than two dozen charter captains working out of the Spit, and they charge anywhere from $225 to $350 for a full-day halibut and salmon trip – half-day trips run around $160 and your fishing license is usually extra.

A good option to go with is Rainbow Tours (p256). The biggest distinction between the charter operations is vessel size: bigger boats bounce around less when the waves kick, meaning greater comfort and less mal de mer.

Around Homer

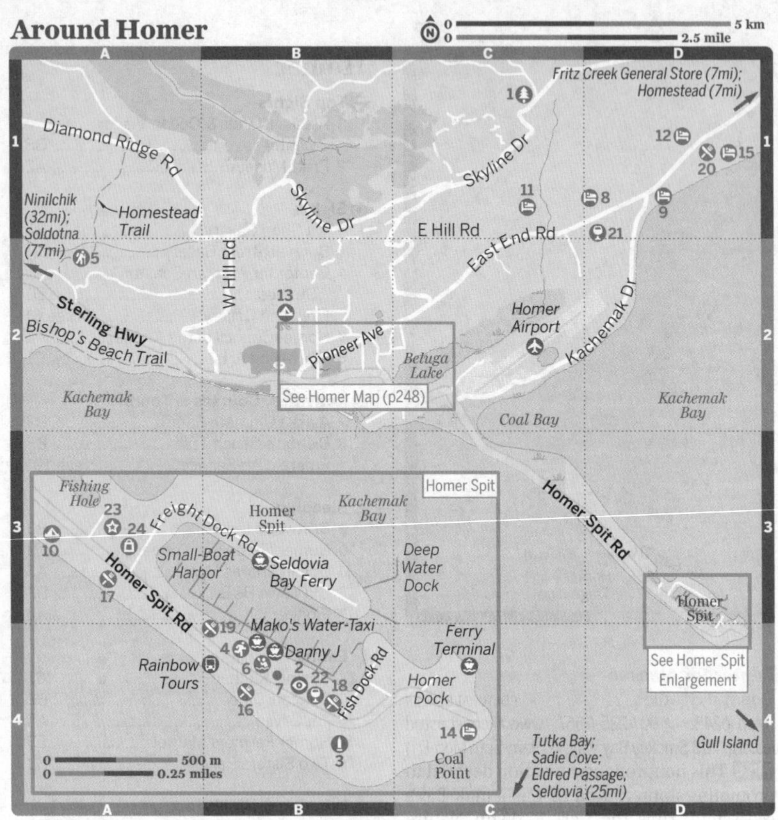

Around Homer

Sights
1 ACarl E Wynn Nature Center C1
2 Homer Spit B4
3 Seafarer's Memorial B4

Activities, Courses & Tours
4 Bald Mountain Air B4
5 Homestead Trail A2
Pratt Museum Harbor Tours .... (see 22)
6 True North Kayak Adventures B4
7 Yurt on the Spit B4

Sleeping
8 Bear Creek Lodging D1
9 Glacier View Cabins D1
10 Homer Spit Public Camping A3
11 Homer Stay & Play C1
12 Juneberry Lodge D1
13 Karen Hornaday Memorial Campground B2
14 Land's End Resort C4
15 Seaside Farm D1

Eating
16 Finn's Pizza B4
17 Homer Spit Oyster Bar A3
18 La Baleine B4
19 Little Mermaid B4
20 Wasabi's D1

Drinking & Nightlife
Bear Creek Winery .... (see 8)
21 Down East Saloon D1
22 Salty Dawg Saloon B4

Entertainment
23 Pier One Theatre A3

Shopping
24 Sportsman's Supply & Rental A3

Hiking

For all its natural beauty, Homer has few good public trails (though hiking across Kachemak Bay is awesome). For a map of short hiking routes around town, pick up the *Walking Guide to the Homer Area* at the visitor center.

Homestead Trail HIKING

(Map p250) This 6.7-mile trek from Rogers Loop Rd (accessed 1 mile north of town on the Sterling Hwy) is probably the best in town, taking you via boardwalk and singletrack to large meadows with panoramic views of Kachemak Bay, and Mt Iliamna and Mt Redoubt on the other side of Cook Inlet.

They maintain cross-country trails here in winter.

Bishop's Beach Trail HIKING

(Map p248) This hike is a leisurely waterfront trek from Homer. The views of Kachemak Bay and the Kenai Mountains are superb, while the marine life that scurries along the sand at low tide is fascinating. It's great for beachcombing.

Start right behind the Islands & Ocean Visitor Center down the road from Two Sisters Bakery.

Diamond Creek Trail HIKING

This trailhead is opposite Diamond Ridge Rd, 5 miles north along the Sterling Hwy. The trail begins by descending along Diamond Creek, then hits the beach. Check a tide book, and leave before low tide and return before high tide. High tides will cover most of the sand and force you to scramble onto the base of the nearby cliffs.

You can walk the 7 miles into town and eventually meet up with Bishop's Beach Trail.

Paddling

Though, theoretically, you could spend a wavy day paddling in the vicinity of the Spit, you'll find infinitely better scenery, more varied wildlife and far more sheltered waters across the bay in the Kachemak Bay State Park (p262). Due to fast currents and massive waves, attempting the wide-open crossing is a poor idea; you're better off taking your kayak across on a water-taxi or renting one from the various companies that maintain fleets of kayaks on the far side, such as True North Kayak Adventures.

True North Kayak Adventures KAYAKING

(Map p250; ☎907-235-0708; www.truenorthkayak.com) Based on Yukon Island and with an office on Homer Spit, it runs half-day paddles amid the otters, with eagles overhead, for $115 (water-taxi included). Once you've spent all that time crossing the bay, however, it makes more sense to spring for the full-day paddle ($160), or at least the three-quarter-day ($140).

There are also several multiday options that cross Eldred Passage into Tutka Bay or Sadie Cove. For experienced kayakers, it rents rigid single/double kayaks for $40/60 per day. And jumping on trend, stand-up paddleboard adventures are also on offer in a stunning glacier lake ($225).

Bear Viewing

Due largely to the density of tourists visiting Homer, the town has become a major departure point for bear-watching trips to the famed bruin haven of Katmai National Park, located on the Alaska Peninsula 100-plus miles southwest by floatplane. Due to the distances involved, these trips cost a pretty penny: expect to pay at least $500 for a day trip. However, that may be a small price to pay for the iconic Alaskan photo: a slavering brown bear, perched atop a waterfall, snapping its fangs on an airborne salmon.

Alaska Ultimate Safaris SCENIC FLIGHTS

(Map p248; ☎888-696-2327; www.alaskaultimatesafaris.com; Beluga Lake; flights from $375) Locals Kirsten and Eric whisk you away in a helicopter for either a 'Fire' or 'Ice' tour that sweeps across volcanoes (per person $670) or glaciers (per person $375). They also specialize in bear viewing in Katmai and Lake Clark, as well as remote hiking.

Bald Mountain Air BEAR VIEWING

(Map p250; ☎907-235-7969; www.baldmountainair.com; Homer Spit Rd; per person $675-695) Runs floatplane trips to the park headquarters at Brooks Camp in Katmai National Park, where countless bears converge to snag salmon ascending Brooks River – and where countless tourists converge to watch them. Also flies 'where no-one else goes' in June and August to spot bears when they aren't at Brooks Camp.

Emerald Air Service BEAR VIEWING

(Map p248; ☎907-235-4160; www.emeraldairservice.com; 2144 Lakeshore Dr; per person $745) Run by respected naturalists this floatplane operator offers a wilderness-oriented experience, bypassing Brooks Camp and seeking out bears along isolated Katmai beaches and salmon streams. Expect about 4 miles of walking.

Festivals & Events

Kachemak Bay Shorebird Festival CULTURAL
(www.kachemakshorebird.org) Brings hundreds of birders and 100,000 shorebirds to Mud Bay in early May, making it the largest bird-migration site along the Alaskan road system. The tidal flats of Homer become the staging area for thousands of birds, including one-third of the world's surfbirds.

Kachemak Bay Wooden Boat Festival CULTURAL
(www.kbwbs.org) Held in September, this boaters' fest celebrates the craft, design and history of wooden boatbuilding, and is rounded out by tall tales of drama on the high seas.

Sleeping

There are B&Bs galore. Homer adds a 7.5% sales tax to lodging.

Seaside Farm HOSTEL $
(Map p250; ☎907-235-7850; www.seasidealaska.com; E End Rd; sites/dm/r/cabins $15/35/65/95) Located 5 miles from the city center, this is more like Burning Man than a regulation youth hostel. Run by Mossy Kilcher, pop star Jewel Kilcher's aunt, Seaside Farm has a meadow campground with views of Grewingk Glacier, somewhat dingy dorms and basic cabins.

The outdoor cooking pavilion is patrolled by roosters, and impromptu jam sessions often spark up around the campfire.

Karen Hornaday Memorial Campground CAMPGROUND $
(Map p250; 360 Fairview Ave; tent/RV sites $13/20) Below the bluffs just north of downtown, this is the best family camping option in Homer. It has private, wooded sites with impressive views of the Bay and baseball field.

Homer Spit Public Camping CAMPGROUND $
(Map p250; Homer Spit Rd; tent/RV sites $13/20) On the west beach of Homer Spit a catch-as-catch-can tent city springs up every night of the summer. It's a beautiful spot, though often windy (make sure you add weight to your tent if you leave). It can get crowded and sometimes rowdy. The self-registration stand is right across the road from Sportsman's Supply (p256).

Homer Stay & Play B&B $$
(Map p250; ☎907-399-1475; www.homerstayandplay.com; Paradise Pl; r $115-165; 📶) The best part about staying here isn't the panoramic views of Kachemak Bay or the fresh baked breakfasts: it's the owners' enthusiasm for all things Homer. Stay here and be treated to a good dose of local flavor; as much as possible, from the soap to the salad, comes from the area.

Juneberry Lodge B&B $$
(Map p250; ☎907-235-4779; www.juneberrylodge.com; 40963 China Poot St; r $130-165; 📶) This large log-and-stone home has four rooms, including one with adorable sleeping cubbies tucked into the eaves, perfect for families. The house belonged to a gold-miner's daughter, and her original sourdough start for breakfast is from 1897.

Land's End Resort HOTEL $$
(Map p250; ☎800-478-0400; www.lands-end-resort.com; r $189-289 lodges $399-600; 🚭📶🏊) This multiplex is as close as you can get to the mountains across Kachemak Bay. At the end of the spit, it offers tidy little economy rooms and three-story 'lodges' (read: condos), and more in-between. If you're going to splurge for this place, make sure you splurge for a view. It also has a sauna, a hot tub and an endless pool.

Old Town B&B B&B $$
(Map p248; ☎907-235-7558; www.oldtownbedandbreakfast.com; 106 W Bunnell Ave; d $90-130; 🚭📶) Built in 1937, this historic B&B has just three rooms. The Mabel Suite has ocean views and a private bathroom. All come with hardwood floors, great paintings and a fresh feel that makes this a top pick in downtown.

Otter Cove Resort CABIN $$
(☎800-426-6212; www.ottercoveresort.com; cabins $125) Located on Eldred Passage, Otter Cove Resort has affordable camping-style cabins (with electricity) near the Sadie Knob Trail. It rents out kayaks ($70 to $85) and guides paddling trips of one or more days. Round-trip transportation is $70 to $85. There's a cook shack on site, and no restaurant, so bring your own food.

Glacier View Cabins CABIN $$
(Map p250; ☎907-299-1519; www.glacierviewcabins.com; 59565 E End Rd; cabins $140-175;

) These log cabins sit in a sort of suburban utopia: a wide expanse of lawn has views of Kachemak Bay over neighborhood rooftops. While they feel a bit modular, the spruce cabins have nice kitchens, and there are grills on every porch and plenty of fire pits.

Homer Floatplane Lodge LODGE $$
(Map p248; 907-235-4160; www.floatplanelodge.com; 2144 Lakeshore Dr; r $125-200;) Aviation buffs will love the waterfront rooms at this cozy grouping of log cabins right on Beluga Lake. Spruce walls, ample porches and kitchenettes make this a great spot for families.

Pioneer Inn MOTEL $$
(Map p248; 907-235-5670; www.pioneerinnhomerak.com; 244 W Pioneer Ave; r $139-159;) Super-friendly, this central motel is tidy and warm. A few rooms have larger kitchenettes and living rooms – and you can get at least partial ocean views from much of the motel.

Driftwood Inn INN $$
(Map p248; 907-235-8019; www.thedriftwoodinn.com; 135 W Bunnell Ave; RV sites $49-57, r $99-265, cottage $300;) Everything is on offer here: cheery European-style rooms with or without bathrooms, snug, cedar-finished 'ships' quarters,' two sprawling vacation houses with remarkable waterfront views, and a great patio area. It's an excellent deal for the price, and larger groups can have an entire cottage (complete with kitchen and living area) all to themselves.

Ocean Shores Motel MOTEL $$
(Map p248; 800-770-7775; www.oceanshoresalaska.com; 3500 Crittenden Dr; d $159-219;) This motel-style lodge has spacious rooms – many with flat-screens and modern bed treatments, and several with kitchenettes. The decks and awesome views make this a strong contender in the midrange motel category. Those down by the ocean cost the most; the cheaper ones are up on the hill. The motel has opened a bar/restaurant, The Kannery Grill.

Bear Creek Lodging B&B $$
(Map p250; 907-235-8484; www.bearcreekwinery.com; Bear Creek Dr; ste $200-275;) On a hillside at the Bear Creek Winery, this place has two suites (each with a kitchenette), a hot tub overlooking the fruit vineyard and koi pond, and a complimentary bottle of vino beside each bed. No kids allowed.

★ **Tutka Bay Wilderness Lodge** LODGE $$$
(907-274-2710; www.withinthewild.com; r per person for 2 nights $3800) Tutka Bay Wilderness Lodge is an all-inclusive resort with chalets, cottages and rooms surrounding the lodge house, where guests enjoy meals with a sweeping view of the inlet and Jakolof Mountain. The accommodations are very comfortable, the food is excellent and the amenities include a sauna, deepwater dock, boathouse and hiking trails.

Activities range from sea kayaking to a renowned maritime cuisine cooking school. There's a two-night minimum and the cost includes water taxi, massages and the choice between a deep sea-fishing charter or bear viewing.

Sadie Cove Wilderness Lodge LODGE $$$
(907-235-2350; www.sadiecove.com; r per person $550) Located just to the north of Tutka Bay in Sadie Cove. This wilderness lodge offers cabins, sauna, icy-cold plunge pool for use after or during your sauna, and Alaskan seafood dinners, but it's not quite as elegant – or pricey – as some other options in the area.

Eating

★ **La Baleine** SEAFOOD $
(Map p250; 907-299-6672; www.labaleinecafe.com; 4460 Homer Spit Rd; breakfast $8-15 lunch

HOMER ART GALLERIES

The cold, dark season of unemployment has inspired a saying in these parts: 'If you're starving, you might as well be an artist.' Just browsing these great galleries is a treat, and on the first Friday of the month, many break out the wine and cheese, and stay open late for a series of openings all over town. This is just the tip of the iceberg – grab a free *Downtown Homer Art Galleries* flyer at the visitor center, which has many more gallery listings, or stop by the **Homer Council of the Arts** (Map p248; 907-235-4288; www.homerart.org; 355 W Pioneer Ave; 1-5pm Mon-Fri), with its own awesome gallery and information on various tours, artist-in-residence programs and guerrilla installations throughout town.

$13-15; ⌚5am-4pm Tue-Sun) Hands down some of the best food in Homer, if not the entire Kenai Peninsula. As much of it as possible is organic or made in-house, the seafood is freshly caught and the greens and mushrooms locally foraged. Come here for breakfast (we like the homemade corned-beef hash) and then come back for lunch. Coffee is free with breakfast, and boxed meals are also available.

It was just opening a few nights per week for dinner when we visited; call ahead if you fancy a later meal.

Homer Farmers Market MARKET **$**
(Map p248; www.homerfarmersmarket.org; Ocean Dr; snacks $2-10; ⌚2-5pm Wed, 10am-3pm Sat) Pick up fresh produce, peruse homemade crafts kiosks or just chow down on kettle corn.

Cosmic Kitchen MEXICAN **$**
(Map p248; 510 E Pioneer Ave; burritos & sandwiches $6-11; ⌚9am-6pm Mon-Fri, to 3pm Sat; 📶) With excellent burritos, burgers and a salsa bar, this joint is the place to go for a filling meal on the cheap; it's probably the best bargain in town. It also serves breakfast until 3pm and has a deck for sunny evenings.

Finn's Pizza PIZZA **$**
(Map p250; Homer Spit Rd; slice $6, pizza $20-28; ⌚noon-9pm) Finn's wood-fired pizzas are best enjoyed with a pint of ale in the sunny upstairs solarium. Is there anything better than an excellent pizza and unobstructed views of the bay? We don't think so. You can also get soup, salad and polenta.

Two Sisters Bakery BAKERY **$**
(Map p248; ☎907-235-2280; www.twosistersbakery.net; 233 E Bunnell Ave; light meals $4-7, dinner mains $17-25; ⌚7am-6pm Mon-Tue, to 9pm Wed-Sat) This quintessential Homer institution has great fresh-baked bread and light snacks. There is a lilting air to the open-kitchen that seems pulled straight from Johnny Depp's classic *Chocolat*.

Homer Spit Oyster Bar SEAFOOD **$**
(Map p250; 3851 Homer Spit Rd; oysters $3; ⌚11am-10pm) The oysters are fresh as can be; unfortunately the service is also pretty fresh and more than a little salty. Still, the deck is lovely on a sunny afternoon, and the sake goes down smoothly. It also serves soup, grilled cheese and salad.

Fritz Creek General Store DELI **$**
(Mile 8.2, E End Rd; sandwiches $8-12; ⌚7am-9pm Mon-Sat, 10am-8pm Sun) What is an excellent deli doing all the way out on East End Rd? Serving some of the best beef brisket sandwiches in Homer.

Duncan Diner CAFE **$**
(Map p248; 125 E Pioneer Ave; breakfast & lunch $6-11; ⌚7am-2pm) This busy downtown place fries up home-style breakfast among home-style decor.

Saltry SEAFOOD **$$**
(☎906-226-2424; www.thesaltry.com; lunch $17-20, dinner $23-28; ⌚lunch 1:30pm & 3pm; dinner 6pm & 7:30pm; 🖉) In the village of Halibut Cove on Ismailof Island, Saltry makes for the ultimate date, with an outdoor deck over the aquamarine inlet and excellent seafood and vegetarian cuisine. After eating, check out the galleries in Halibut Cove.

Catch the **Danny J** (Map p250; ☎907-226-2424; www.thesaltry.com; Homer Spit; per person noon/evening tour $63/38) boat service to Halibut Cove.

Little Mermaid BISTRO **$$**
(Map p250; ☎907-399-9900; www.littlemermaidhomer.com; 4246 Homer Spit Rd; lunch $10-20, dinner $16-38; ⌚11am-9pm Thu-Tue) Local ingredients, fresh seafood and a simple but creative menu make this little joint a locals' favorite. If it's carbs you're after, its hand-tossed pizzas are the best. Don't skip dessert.

Fat Olives ITALIAN **$$**
(Map p248; ☎907-235-8488; www.fatoliveshomer.com; 276 Ohlson Lane; dinner $17-25; ⌚11am-10pm) Housed in the old 'bus barn,' this chic and hyperpopular pizza joint and wine bar serves affordable appetizers such as prosciutto-wrapped Alaskan scallops and delicious mains such as wood-oven-roasted rack of lamb. Almost everything is fresh and homemade.

Wasabi's JAPANESE **$$$**
(Map p250; ☎907-226-3663; www.wasabisrestaurant.com; 57217 E End Rd; mains $8-32; ⌚5-10pm) With some of the best views in town, this playful and modern sushi house offers innovative cocktails, finely constructed rolls and some of the freshest fish you could imagine.

WORTH A TRIP

NIKOLAEVSK & NORMAN LOWELL STUDIO

Tucked inconspicuously down a winding road from Anchor Point sits one of several Russian Old Believer Villages on the Kenai Peninsula. The Old Believers are members of a sect that split from mainstream Russian Orthodoxy in the 1650s, defending their 'old beliefs' in the face of what they considered heretical reforms. Long considered outcasts in Russia, they fled communism in 1917, ending up in Brazil, then Oregon, and then – in 1968 – Alaska, where they finally felt they could enjoy religious freedom while avoiding the corruptive influences of modernity.

Alaska's Old Believers are hardcore traditionalists, speaking mainly Russian, marrying in their teens, raising substantial broods of children, and living simply. The men – usually farmers or fishers – are forbidden from trimming their beards; the women typically cover their hair and are garbed in long dresses. The Old Believers tend to keep to themselves, inhabiting a handful of isolated villages on the Kenai Peninsula, of which Nikolaevsk is the most prominent.

To get there, head 10 miles east on North Fork Rd, which departs from the Sterling Hwy in the heart of Anchor Point and winds through hillbilly homesteads and open, rolling forest. Right before the pavement ends, hang a left at Nikolaevsk Rd. Two miles later, you'll enter the village.

On your way back, stop at the **Norman Lowell Studio** (www.normanlowellgallery.net; Normal Lowell Rd, Anchor Point; 9am-5pm Mon-Sat) in Anchor Point. This spacious gallery features the work of the self-taught homesteading painter. While it can get a little cheesy, many of the Alaskan wildland paintings are quite powerful – and certainly masterfully crafted.

Drinking & Nightlife

Salty Dawg Saloon BAR
(Map p250; Homer Spit Rd; ⌚10am-5am) Maybe the most storied bar on the Kenai Peninsula, the Salty Dawg isn't just a tourist trap. Locals love the cavernous lighthouse tavern, back patio and pool table. Come evening, the sea shanties start in earnest.

Homer Brewing Company BREWERY
(Map p248; www.homerbrew.com; 1411 Lakeshore Dr; ⌚noon-7pm Mon-Sat, to 6pm Sun) This tasting room has picnic tables and fresh Jakalof Bay oysters Friday and Saturday. Try the Broken-Birch Bitter ale and then grab a growler to go.

Grace Ridge Brewing Company BREWERY
(Map p248; 3388 B St; ⌚noon-8pm) A brewery in Homer with a modern little taproom and local art on the walls. A rotating special is the Lemon Tart Ale – don't knock it till you've tried it.

Down East Saloon BAR
(Map p250; 3125 E End Rd; ⌚10am-2am) This spacious bar is where locals head to listen to live music. The view is killer, but you'll likely be paying more attention to whichever Homer talent is on stage.

Alibi BAR
(Map p248; www.alibi-homer.com; 453 E Pioneer Ave; ⌚4pm-late) Catering to a younger crowd, the Alibi has DJs, karaoke and occasional dance parties. The large picture windows reveal the bay, and locals say the food isn't bad; it's one of the few places in town where you can find late-night grub.

Bear Creek Winery WINE BAR
(Map p250; www.bearcreekwinery.com; Bear Creek Dr; ⌚10am-6pm) Wineries are scarcer than vineyards in Alaska, but this impressive family-run operation bottles some fine berry-based wines. Tastings are $5 (credited to your purchase), and it offers tours at 11am Monday, Wednesday, Friday and Saturday. If you want to make some cash, Bear Creek will buy your berries.

Entertainment

Pier One Theatre THEATER
(Map p250; ☎907-226-2287; www.pieronetheatre.org; Homer Spit Rd) Live drama and comedy are performed in a 'come-as-you-are' warehouse next to the Fishing Hole on the spit. Shows start at 7:30pm.

Shopping

Sportsman's Supply & Rental SPORTS & OUTDOORS
(Map p250; ☎907-235-2617; 1114 Freight Dock Rd; ⏲6am-midnight) Rents out fishing rods ($10 to $20) and sells other camping and fishing gear. You can also shower ($7) here and do laundry.

Information

INTERNET ACCESS

Homer Public Library (500 Hazel Ave; ⏲10am-6pm Mon, Wed, Fri & Sat, to 8pm Tue & Thu;) Homer's excellent library is arty and airy, with a decidedly Homer-esque selection of magazines. Internet access is free, and it has a great kids' section for rainy days.

MEDICAL SERVICES

Homer Medical Clinic (☎907-235-8586; 4136 Bartlett St; ⏲8:30am-5pm Mon-Fri, from 10am Sat) Next door to South Peninsula Hospital; for walk-in service.

South Peninsula Hospital (☎907-235-8101; 4300 Bartlett St; ⏲24h) North of the Pratt Museum.

MONEY

Wells Fargo (88 Sterling Hwy; ⏲10am-6pm Mon-Fri, to 5pm Sat) Has an ATM.

TOURIST INFORMATION

Homer Visitor Center & Chamber of Commerce (Map p248; ☎907-235-7740; www.homeralaska.org; 201 Sterling Hwy; ⏲9am-6pm Mon-Fri, 10am-4pm Sat & Sun) Has countless brochures and a funky mosaic on the floor. It's operated by the chamber of commerce, however, and only provides info on members. Also has courtesy phones to book rooms or tours.

Getting There & Away

AIR

Ravn Alaska (p246) provides daily flights between Homer and Anchorage from Homer's airport, 1.7 miles east of town on Kachemak Dr. The advance-purchase fare runs at about $125 one-way, or $205 for the round-trip. **Smokey Bay Air** (☎907-235-1511; www.smokeybayair.com; 2100 Kachemak Dr) offers flights to Seldovia for $62 each way.

Homer Airport (Map p250; 3720 Faa Rd) Commercial flights operate here.

BUS

Homer Stage Line (Map p248; ☎907-868-3914; www.stagelineinhomer.com; 1242 Ocean Dr) Runs from Homer to Anchorage, and between Homer and Seward.

Homer Trolley (☎907-299-6210; www.homertrolley.com; $15 day pass; ⏲11am-6pm) Hop-on-hop-off bus trolley between downtown and the spit.

FERRY

The Alaska Marine Highway provides a thrice-weekly service from Homer to Seldovia (each way $34, 1½ hours) and Kodiak ($85, 9½ hours), with a connecting service to the Aleutians.

The **ferry terminal** (Map p250; ☎907-235-8449; www.ferryalaska.com) is found at the end of Homer Spit.

Rainbow Tours (Map p250; ☎907-235-7272; Homer Spit Rd; 1-way/round-trip $49/69) offers the inexpensive Rainbow Connection shuttle from Homer to Seldovia. It departs at 9am, gets to Seldovia an hour later and then returns to take you back to Homer at 5pm. It'll transport your bike for $5 and your kayak for $10.

The **Seldovia Bay Ferry** (Map p250; ☎907-435-3299; www.seldoviabayferry.com; Lot 21, Freight Dock Rd; 1-way $40) takes passengers to Seldovia twice a day, with departures from Homer at 9am and 11am.

Many water-taxi operations shuttle campers and kayakers between Homer and points across Kachemak Bay. Though the companies are good and work closely together, the most respected is **Mako's Water-Taxi** (Map p250; ☎907-235-9055; www.makoswatertaxi.com; Homer Spit Rd). It usually charges $80 to $90 per person round-trip with a two-person minimum.

Getting Around

BICYCLE

Cycle Logical (☎907-226-2925; www.cyclelogicalhomer.com; 3585 E End Rd; ⏲10am-6pm Tue-Sat, by appointment Mon) Rents mountain, fat and city bikes for $35 to $69 per day.

Homer Saw & Cycle (☎907-235-8406; 1532 Ocean Dr; ⏲9am-5:30pm Mon-Fri, 11am-5pm Sat) Rents out mountain bikes and hybrids ($25 per 24 hours).

CAR & MOTORCYCLE

Polar Car Rental (☎907-235-5998; 1563 Homer Spit Rd) To obtain an affordable rental car, this small dealer has cars of all sizes at $65 a day.

TAXI

Kostas Taxi (☎907-399-8008) can get you anywhere around town for a reasonable fare.

Seldovia

☎907 / POP 276

Normally visited as a quick overnight from Homer, this waterfront village is just 15 miles from Homer by boat. While touring the boardwalk and compact center will take a few hours, the nearby adventures in Kachemak Bay could easily extend your trip.

The town is sleepy and secluded, esoteric and at times frustrating – plan for an extra day to get in or out. A new generation of end-of-the-worlders are moving in, and although Seldovia relies in part on fishing, it's making its best stab at becoming a tourist destination. It's a process that's happening in fits and starts: the hiking, skiing, paddling and biking possibilities here are excellent. And while the accommodations are plush, the culinary offerings are limited and the galleries feel a bit desperate.

All in all, you'll find a village with quaintness to spare, but little tourist infrastructure, which may be the best thing about the place.

History

One of the oldest settlements on Cook Inlet, Russians founded the town in the late 18th century and named it after their word *seldevoy,* meaning 'herring bay.' By the 1890s Seldovia had become an important shipping and supply center for the region, and the town boomed right into the 1920s with salmon canning, fur farming, a theater and, of course, a (short-lived) herring industry.

But then the highway came, stretching as far as the tip of the Homer Spit. After it was completed in the 1950s, Seldovia's importance as a supply center began to dwindle.

Sights

Historic Boardwalk WATERFRONT

(Main St) Two hundred feet south of the boat harbor is Seldovia's historic boardwalk. Overlooking the slough, this atmospheric collection of shops, inns and flowers is worth a quick stroll.

Seldovia Village Tribe Visitor Center MUSEUM

(☎907-234-7898; www.svt.org; cnr Airport Ave & Main St; ⊙noon-5pm) This visitors center and museum showcases Seldovia's Alaska Native heritage – a unique blend of Alutiiq (Eskimo) and Tanaina (Indian) cultures. The small, tidy museum covers the history of Alaska Natives in the area, and its subsistence display is informative and interesting. This is also the place to buy souvenirs.

Outside Beach BEACH

(Jakolof Bay Rd) This beach is an excellent place for wildlife sightings and a little beachcombing. To reach it, follow Anderson Way out of town for a mile, then head left at the first fork to reach the picnic area at Outside Beach Park.

You stand a good chance of spotting eagles, seabirds and possibly even otters here. At low tide, you can explore the sea life among the rocks, and on a clear day the views of Mt Redoubt and Mt Iliamna are stunning.

St Nicholas Orthodox Church CHURCH

(tinetteh@ptialaska.net; Church St) Seldovia's most popular attraction is this onion-domed church, which overlooks the town from a hill just off Main St. Built in 1891 and restored in the 1970s, the church is open only during services and by appointment. Though there is no resident clergyman, occasionally a visiting priest conducts services.

Activities

Berry Picking

Seldovia is known best for its blueberries, which grow so thick just outside town that from late August to mid-September you often can rake your fingers through the bushes and fill a two-quart bucket in minutes. You'll also come across plenty of low-bush cranberries and salmonberries, a species not found around Homer. Be aware, however, that many of the best berry areas are on tribal land; before setting out, stop at the **Seldovia Native Association** (☎907-234-7625; https://.snai.org; Main St; day-use/camping permits $5/10; ⊙9am-5pm Mon-Fri), which will sell you a day-use permit for $5.

Hiking

The **Otterbahn Trail** was famously created by local high-school students, who dubbed it the 'we-worked-hard-so-you-better-like-it trail.' The trailhead lies behind Susan B English School, off Winifred Ave. Lined with salmonberries and affording great views of Graduation Peak, it skirts the coastline most of the way and reaches Outside Beach in 1.5

4

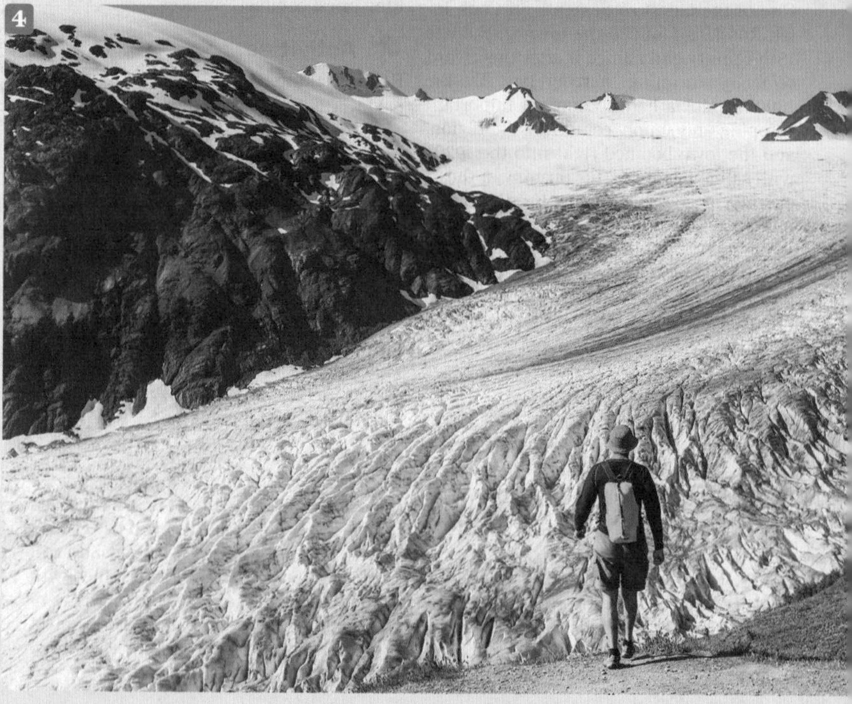

JAY YUAN/SHUTTERSTOCK ©

GALYNA ANDRUSHKO/SHUTTERSTOCK ©

3

JAY YUAN/SHUTTERSTOCK ©

1. Resurrection Bay
Orca whales are frequently spotted at the mouth of Resurrection Bay near Seward (p227).

2. Cooper Landing (p239)
An area best known for salmon fishing along the Russian and Kenai rivers.

3. Homer (p247)
Homer Spit (p249) juts out into Kachemak Bay.

4. Kenai Fjords National Park (p236)
A hiker at the edge of Exit Glacier, part of the massive Harding Ice Field in Kenai Fjords National Park.

miles. Make sure you hike it at tides below 17ft, as the last stretch runs across a slough that is only legally passable when the water is out (property above 17ft is private).

Two trails start from Jakolof Bay Rd. You can either hike down the beach toward the head of Seldovia Bay at low tide, or you can follow a 4.5-mile logging road to reach several secluded coves. There is also the **Tutka/Jakolof Trail**, a 2.5-mile trail to a campsite on the Tutka Lagoon, the site of a state salmon-rearing facility. The posted trail departs from Jakolof Bay Rd about 10.5 miles east of town.

The town's steepest hike is the rigorous **Rocky Ridge Trail**, where 800ft of climbing will be rewarded with remarkable views of the bay, the town and Mt Iliamna. The trail starts (or ends) on Rocky St and loops back to the road to the airport, covering about 3 miles.

Cycling

Seldovia's nearly carless streets and outlying gravel roads make for ideal biking; mountain bikes can be brought over from Homer. Those looking for a fairly leisurely ride can pedal the 10-mile Jakolof Bay Rd, which winds along the coast nearly to the head of Jakolof Bay. For a more rigorous experience, continue on another 6 miles beyond the end of the maintained road, climbing 1200ft into the alpine country at the base of Red Mountain.

In the past, fit cyclists could also depart from Jakolof Bay Rd for an epic 30-mile round-trip ride along the rough Rocky River Rd, which cuts across the tip of the Kenai Peninsula to Windy Bay. In recent years washouts have made the road largely impassable; inquire about current conditions.

Paddling

There are some excellent kayaking opportunities in the Seldovia area. Just north, Eldred Passage and the three islands (Cohen, Yukon and Hesketh) that mark its entrance are prime spots for viewing otters, sea lions and seals, while the northern shore of Yukon Island features caves and tunnels that can be explored at high tide. Even closer are Sadie Cove, and Tutka and Jakolof Bays, where you can paddle in protected water amid interesting geological features, row up to oyster farmers to buy straight from the source, and camp in secluded coves.

Kayak'Atak KAYAKING
(☎907-234-7425; www.alaska.net/~kayaks; single/double kayaks 1st day $35/50, subsequent days $15/35) Rents out kayaks and can help arrange transportation throughout the bay. It also offers various guided tours starting from $80, some including a 'gourmet lunch.' Make reservations in advance.

Thyme on the Boardwalk OUTDOORS
(☎907-440-2213; www.thymeontheboardwalk.com; Main St) This flower shop on the old Boardwalk rents stand-up paddleboards and kayaks (each $30 per hour). It has a nice vacation rental upstairs.

Tours

Mako's Water-Taxi BOAT, AIR
(☎907-235-9055; www.makoswatertaxi.com; drop-off at Homer Spit Rd, Homer; round-trip $150) Has an excellent tour that takes you by boat, car and plane. Mako's drops you at Jakolof Bay, from where you'll be driven to Seldovia. You return to Homer via a short flightseeing trip. It's a good deal.

Central Charters BOATING
(☎907-235-7847; www.centralcharter.com; drop-off at Homer Spit Rd, Homer; one-way/round-trip $39/69) Does a daily seven-hour tour from Homer, leaving at 10:30am, circling Gull Island, and dropping you in Seldovia to enjoy the village for a few hours.

Sleeping

For free camping, head to Sandy Beach accessed north of town on the Otterbahn Trail. Be sure to camp in the grass above the high-tide line.

★ **Across the Bay Tent & Breakfast** CABIN $
(☎summer 907-350-4636, winter 907-345-2571; www.tentandbreakfastalaska.com; tent/cabin per person $80/85;) Located 8 miles from town on Jakolof Bay, this is something a little different. Its cabin-like tents include a full breakfast, and for $120 per day you can get a package that includes all your meals – dinner could consist of fresh oysters, beach-grilled salmon or halibut stew with a side of garden-grown greens. Bring your sleeping bag.

The offbeat resort also organizes guided kayak trips ($95 to $115).

Seldovia Wilderness RV Park CAMPGROUND $
(☎907-234-7643; tent/RV sites $10/15) About a mile out of town, this is a city-maintained

Seldovia

campground on spectacular Outside Beach. You can pay for your site at the ferry terminal or harbormaster's office.

Seldovia Harbor Inn GUESTHOUSE **$$**
(☎907-202-3095; www.seldoviaharborinn.com; 273 Main St; ste $155-165; wifi) Two updated suites overlook either the harbor or the mountains. They are basically furnished apartments, with full kitchens, private bedrooms and great decks. There's a warm coffee shop downstairs.

Seldovia Boardwalk Hotel HOTEL **$$**
(☎907-234-7816; www.seldoviaboardwalkhotel.com; 234 Main St; r $149-159; nonsmoking, wifi) These are the best hotel digs in town. The 12 bright and cheery rooms have brand new everything, expansive windows and flat-screen TVs. A lot of care has been taken in the decor, and it shows.

Seldovia Rowing Club B&B B&B **$$**
(☎907-234-7614; www.seldoviarowingclubinn.wordpress.com; Boardwalk; r $135) Located on the Historic Boardwalk, this place (the first B&B in Southcentral Alaska) has homey suites decorated with quilts, antiques and owner Susan Mumma's outstanding watercolors. She serves big breakfasts and often hosts in-house concerts.

Even if you aren't staying here, stop by in the afternoon to see the artist at work or inquire about drawing classes.

Dancing Eagles CABIN **$$**
(☎907-360-6363; www.dancingeagles.com; Main St; cabin $195; wifi) Large windows look onto the harbor from this weather-beaten waterfront cabin just south of the harbor. It sleeps up to six in its cramped loft and private bedroom. There's a full kitchen, great decks and a wood-burning stove.

Sea Parrot Inn INN **$$**
(☎844-377-7829; www.seaparrotinn.com; 226 Main St; r $99-125; nonsmoking, wifi, pets) They aren't the best rooms in town, but they are affordable, and you get fine harbor views, a nice deck, wood floors and a social atmosphere (thanks to a shared common area). Laundry (wash and dry $10.50) and showers (10 minutes $8.50, with soap and towel) are also available for campers. There's a cafe downstairs.

Bridgekeeper's Inn B&B B&B **$$**
(☎907-234-7535; www.thebridgekeepersinn.com; 223 Kachemak Dr; r $140-150; nonsmoking) A cozy place with private bathrooms and full breakfasts;

one room has a balcony overlooking the salmon-filled slough.

Eating

Restaurants are packed when the ferry gets in. Time your visit well.

Linwood Bar & Grill PUB FOOD $$
(253 Main St; mains $10-17; grill noon-10pm) The only real bar in town has an awesome deck overlooking the harbor. The food is simple and well prepared, though a bit overpriced. The bar stays open well after the kitchen closes.

Information

MEDICAL SERVICES

Seldovia Village Tribe Health & Wellness (907-435-3262; 206 Main St; 8:45am-5pm Mon, Wed & Thu)

MONEY

Linwood Bar & Grill has an ATM, but there are no banks in town.

TOURIST INFORMATION

Harbormaster's Office (907-234-7886; Harbor; 8am-9pm) Has toilets and pamphlets.

Seldovia Chamber of Commerce (www.seldoviachamber.org) Great website for pre-trip planning.

Seldovia Village Tribe Visitor Center (p260) Sells day-use permits and has information about the surrounding Native lands.

Getting There & Away

AIR

Smokey Bay Air (888-482-1511; www.smokeybayair.com; 2100 Kachemak Dr; 1-way $62) Has a 12-minute scenic flight from Homer.

FERRY

Alaska Marine Highway ferries provide service two to three times per week between Homer and Seldovia ($34, 1½ hours) with connecting service throughout the peninsula and the Aleutians. The **Seldovia ferry terminal** (www.ferryalaska.com; $34) is at the north end of Main St.

Seldovia Bay Ferry (907-435-3299; www.seldoviabayferry.com; $40) has two departures per day to Homer from Seldovia, at 9am and 4:30pm.

Getting Around

The main area of town is easily walked. You can also rent a bike in Homer and bring it on the ferry.

UWE BERGWITZ/SHUTTERSTOCK ©

Grewingk Glacier

For rides out to Jakolof Bay Rd or to the airport, try **Halo Cab** (☎907-399-4229).

Kachemak Bay State Park

Across from Homer Spit, an alluring wonderland sprawls south: a luxuriantly green coastline, sliced by fjords and topped by sparkling glaciers and rugged peaks. This is Kachemak Bay State Park, which, along with Kachemak Bay State Wilderness Park to the south, includes 350,000 acres of idyllic wilderness accessible only by bush plane or boat. It was Alaska's first state park, and according to locals, it remains the best.

The most popular attraction is **Grewingk Glacier**, which can be seen from Homer. Viewing the glacier at closer range means a boat trip to the park and a very popular one-way hike of 3.5 miles. Outside the glacier, you can easily escape into the wilds by hiking or kayaking. More than 40 miles of trails, plenty of sheltered waterways, numerous campsites, good backcountry skiing, and a few enclosed accommodation options make this a highly recommended outing for a day or three.

Sights

Peterson Bay Field Station NATURE RESERVE

(☎907-235-6667; www.akcoastalstudies.org)
Though technically it's outside the park, this field station operated by the Center for Alaskan Coastal Studies (p265) provides an excellent introduction to the ecology and natural history of the area.

In summer, staff members lead day-long educational tours of the coastal forest and waterfront tidepools; the best intertidal beasties are seen during extremely low, or 'minus,' tides. Inside the station, too, you can get up close and personal with a touch tank full of squishy sea creatures. It costs $155/90 per adult/child, which includes the boat ride over from Homer Spit. If you want to overnight here, the station has bunks and yurts.

Activities

Hiking

The park has some of the region's best hikes, especially around Grewingk Glacier. Plan to spend a full day, if not a few days, exploring the lakes, streams and peaks.

Glacier Lake Trail HIKING

The most popular hike in Kachemak Bay State Park is this 3.5-mile, one-way trail that begins at the Glacier Spit trailhead, near Rusty Lagoon Campground. The level, easy-to-follow trek crosses the glacial outwash and ends at a lake with superb views of Grewingk Glacier. Camping on the lake is spectacular, and often the shoreline is littered with icebergs (and day-trippers).

At Mile 1.4 you can connect to the 6.4-mile Emerald Lake Trail, with a hand-tram and access to the face of the glacier. If you don't have time for the entire hike, there are excellent views less than a mile from the tram.

Lagoon Trail HIKING

Departing from the Saddle Trail is this 5.5-mile route that leads to the ranger station at the head of Halibut Cove Lagoon. Along the way it passes the Goat Rope Spur Trail, a steep 1-mile climb to the alpine tundra. You also pass the posted junction of Halibut Creek Trail.

The Lagoon Trail is considered a difficult hike and involves fording Halibut Creek, which should be done at low tide. At the ranger station, more trails extend south to several lakes, as well as Poot Peak and the Wosnesenski River.

Emerald Lake Trail HIKING

This steep, difficult 6.4-mile trail begins at Grewingk Lake Trail and leads to Portlock Plateau. You'll witness firsthand the reclamation of the wasted forest (due to spruce bark beetle damage) by brushy alder and birch, considered delicacies by local wildlife. You also get to use a hand tram to cross Grewingk Creek.

At Mile 2.1 a spur trail reaches the scenic Emerald Lake, and there are great views of the bay from the plateau. In spring, stream crossings can be challenging.

Poot Peak HIKING

Poot Peak is a difficult, slick, rocky ascent of 2600ft. The trailhead begins at the Halibut Cove Lagoon, where a moderate 2.6-mile climb along the China Poot Lake Trail takes you to a campsite on the lake.

From there, the trail to the peak diverges after the Wosnesenski River Trail junction. For a little over a mile you'll clamber upward through thinning forest until you reach the Summit Spur, where the route climbs even more precipitously to the mountain's lower summit, 2100ft in elevation. From here, reaching the very top involves scaling a shifting wall of scree, a feat that should be attempted only by those who have some rock-climbing experience. In wet weather, it should be avoided altogether. Getting from the lake to the summit and back will take the better part of a day.

Grace Ridge Trail HIKING

This is a 7-mile trail that stretches from a campsite at Kayak Beach trailhead to deep inside Tutka Bay in the state park. Much of the hike runs above the treeline along the crest of Grace Ridge, where, needless to say, the views are stunning. It starts on an old road in thick alder.

There's also access from the Sea Star Cove public-use cabin. You could hike the trail in a day, but it makes a great two-day trek with an overnight camp.

Alpine Ridge Trail HIKING

At the high point of the Saddle Trail you will reach the posted junction for this 2-mile 'stairway to heaven' to an alpine ridge above the glacier. The climb can be steep at times but is manageable for most hikers with day packs. On a nice day, the views of the ice and Kachemak Bay are stunning.

Saddle Trail HIKING

This mile-long trail starts in Halibut Cove; it connects to the Glacier Lake Trail for a nice loop.

Paddling

You can spend three or four days paddling the many fjords of the park, departing from Homer and making overnight stops at Glacier Spit or Halibut Cove. Think twice before crossing Kachemak Bay from Homer Spit, however; the currents and tides are powerful and can cause serious problems for inexperienced paddlers.

St Augustine Charters KAYAKING

(☎907-299-1894; www.homerkayaking.com; half-/full-day incl water-taxi $110/150) Offers many guided tours from its Peterson Bay office, including multiday paddling and trekking trips through state parks, camping at seaside sites. 'Paddle Hike Dine' ($215) is a popular day of kayaking and hiking, ending with dinner at Saltry (p254) in Halibut Cove.

LOUISE HEUSINKVELD/GETTY IMAGES ©

Eagles in China Poot Bay, Kachemak Bay State Park

Seaside Adventures KAYAKING
(907-235-6672; www.seasideadventure.com; per person $150) A tiny family-run outfit, Seaside Adventures will show you the bay in a kayak complete with running commentary about local flora and fauna. It also has two adorable little cabins for rent (from $150).

Sleeping

Camping is permitted throughout Kachemak Bay State Park. Moreover, numerous free, primitive camping areas have been developed, usually at waterfront trailheads or along trails. Consult **Alaska State Parks** (907-269-8400; www.dnr.alaska.gov/parks) for the locations and facilities.

Alaskan Yurt Rentals YURT $
(907-299-6879; www.alaskanyurtrentals.com; yurts $75) There are eight yurts for rent in the park, maintained by a private operator. All are near the ocean and equipped with bunks and wood stoves and are an excellent way to cozy up for a night or two.

Center for Alaskan Coastal Studies YURT $
(Peterson Bay Field Station; 907-235-6667; www.akcoastalstudies.org; 9am-5pm Mon-Fri) This organization reserves bunks in yurts (per person $35 or $120 for an entire yurt) close to its Peterson Bay Field Station, just outside the park. Lodgers can use the kitchen at the field station.

Public-Use Cabins CABIN $
(907-262-5581; www.alaskastateparks.org; cabins $45-70) There are six cabins that can be reserved in the park (five in Halibut Cove and one in Tutka Bay).

Three are in Halibut Cove: Lagoon Overlook, with a pair of bunk-beds; Lagoon East Cabin, which has disabled access; and Lagoon West Cabin, a half-mile west of the public dock. China Poot Lake Cabin is a 2.4-mile hike from Halibut Cove on the shore of what's also called Leisure Lake. Moose Valley Cabin is about 2.5 miles from the Halibut Cove Lagoon Ranger Station and only sleeps two ($35). Sea Star Cove Cabin, on the south shore of Tutka Bay, is convenient to the Tutka Lake Trail. China Poot Cabin is accessible by kayak or water-taxi. Make reservations for any of them months in advance.

Information

Center for Alaskan Coastal Studies (Map p248; 907-235-6667; www.akcoastalstudies.org; 708 Smokey Way; 9am-5pm Mon-Fri) Has maps and information about the park, both at its downtown Homer headquarters off Lake St and at its yurt on Homer Spit behind Mako's Water-Taxi. National Geographic's *Trails Illustrated* map of the park is an excellent resource, depicting hiking routes, public-use cabins, docks and campsites, and it's available at both.

Getting There & Away

A number of water-taxis offer drop-off and pick-up service (round-trip $60 to $80). Because boat access to some of the trailheads is tidally dependent, you'll need to work with them to establish a precise rendezvous time and location – and then be sure to stick to it.

Getting Around

Ashore Water Taxi (907-235-2341; www.homerwatertaxi.com) Charges $75 per person with a two-person minimum to any place in the park.

Mako's Water-Taxi (907-235-9055; www.makoswatertaxi.com) For most cross-bay destinations from Homer Spit, it charges $75 with a two-person minimum. To Seldovia, the boat costs $250 one-way, so grab all your friends and fill 'er up. It can also give you the lowdown on possible hikes and paddles in the park – and about the logistics of getting over and back.

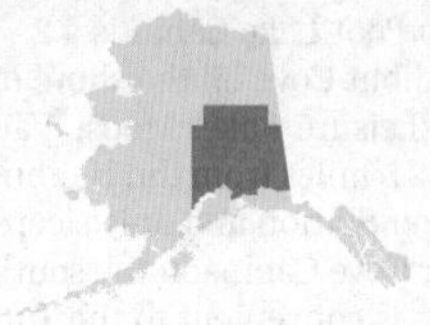

Denali & the Interior

Includes ➡

Best Places to Eat

- ➡ Sheep Mountain Lodge (p322)
- ➡ LuLu's Bread and Bagels (p306)
- ➡ Prospectors Pizzeria & Ale House (p286)
- ➡ 229 Parks (p287)

Best Places to Stay

- ➡ Wonder Lake Campground (p282)
- ➡ Ultima Thule (p328)
- ➡ Ma Johnson's Hotel (p329)
- ➡ EarthSong Lodge (p285)

Why Go?

Alaska literally translates as 'mainland,' but a more poetic etymology would be 'The Land.' And with that in mind, the great Alaskan Interior is, truly, The Land: a vast expanse of boreal forest, alpine tundra and jagged mountains cut by braided rivers and slithering tongues of frost-white glaciers.

Interspersed throughout this region, which is larger than many US states (and small countries), are tiny villages, thriving towns and lonely roadhouses, where a population of trappers, hunters, guides, rangers, teachers, truckers and plain old folk live amid one of the world's great wilderness playgrounds.

The big name in this region is Denali National Park, blessed with the continent's mightiest mountain, abundant megafauna and easy access. But there's so much more: routes that are destinations in and of themselves, clapboard settlements and a myriad of parks that will redefine your very notion of natural beauty.

When to Go

Fairbanks

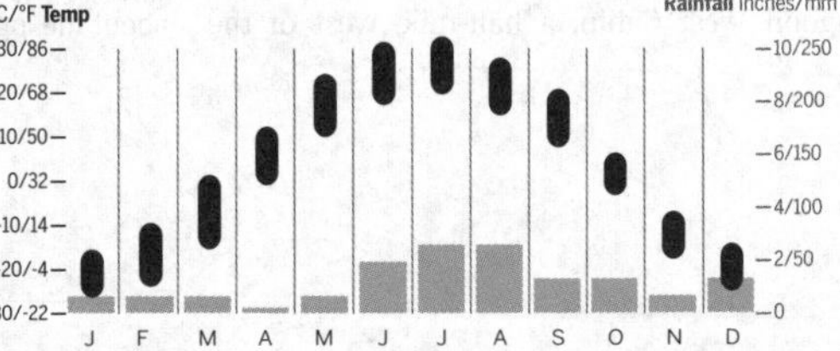

May The best month to visit Denali National Park for clear views of Denali.

Jun The tundra comes alive with millions of migratory birds.

Sep High probability of seeing the northern lights in Fairbanks.

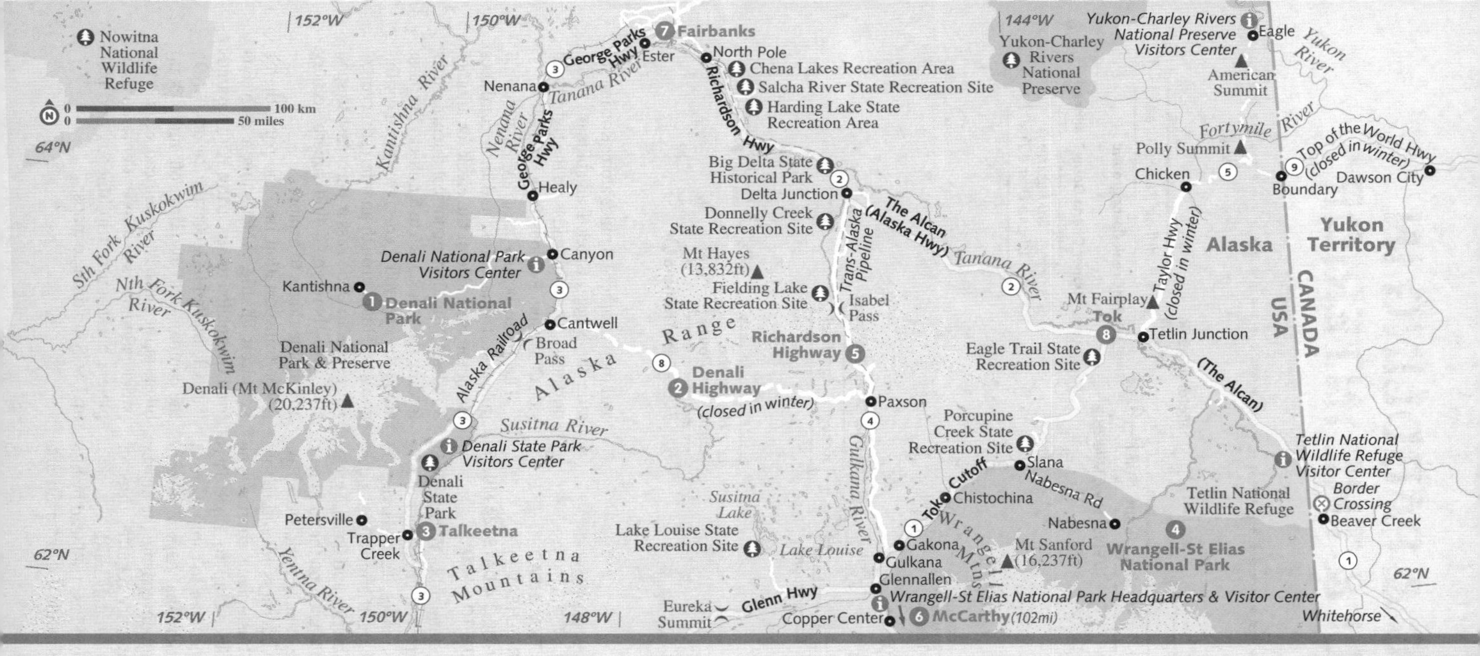

Denali & the Interior Highlights

1 **Denali National Park** (p272) Spotting caribou near the country's largest mountain.

2 **Denali Highway** (p296) Hiking or bird-watching on this lonely, scenic wonder.

3 **Talkeetna** (p289) Enjoying a beer and a perfect summer day in this artsy town.

4 **Wrangell-St Elias National Park** (p327) Stepping into the great expanse of the nation's largest national park.

5 **Richardson Highway** (p324) Driving this awe-inspiring track over mountain passes and river valleys.

6 **McCarthy** (p328) Exploring glaciers and copper mines around this quirky 'burg.

7 **Fairbanks** (p298) Beholding the northern lights from the Interior's largest town.

8 **Tok** (p314) Discovering the strange theme park/junkyard that is Mukluk Land.

HIKING & PADDLING IN DENALI & THE INTERIOR

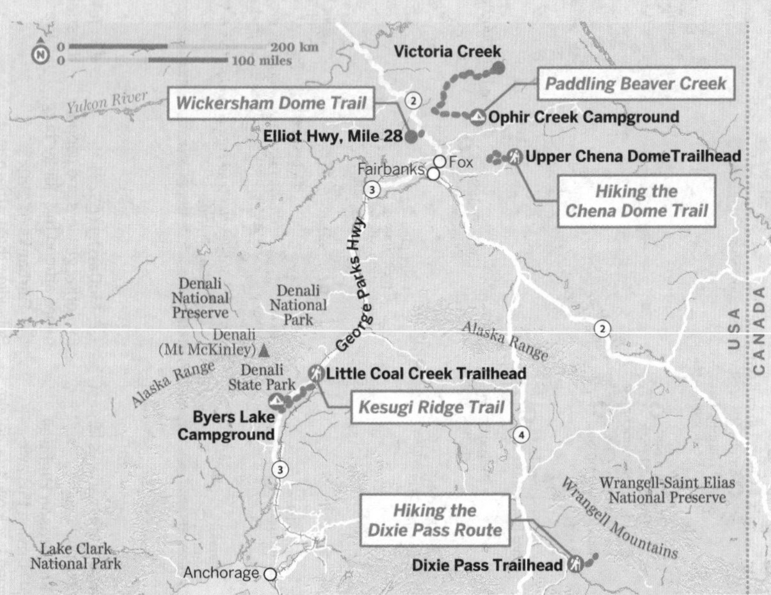

HIKING THE DIXIE PASS ROUTE

START DIXIE PASS TRAILHEAD
END DIXIE PASS TRAILHEAD
DURATION/DISTANCE 3-4 DAYS/24 MILES
DIFFICULTY MEDIUM TO HARD

Even by Alaskan standards, **Wrangell-St Elias National Park** is a large tract of wilderness. At 20,625 sq miles, it's the largest US national park, contains the most peaks over 14,500ft in North America and has the greatest concentration of glaciers on the continent.

Within this huge, remote park, Dixie Pass provides the best wilderness adventure that doesn't require a bush-plane charter. The trek from the trailhead up to Dixie Pass and back is 24 miles. Plan to camp there at least one or two additional days to take in the alpine beauty and investigate the nearby ridges. Such an itinerary requires three or four days and is moderately hard.

You reach the Dixie Pass trailhead by hiking 2.5 miles up Kotsina Rd from Strelna and then another 1.3 miles along Kotsina Rd after the Nugget Creek Trail splits off to the northeast. The trailhead is on the right-hand side of Kotsina Rd; look for a marker.

The route begins as a level path for 3 miles to Strelna Creek, and then continues along the west side of the creek for another 3 miles to the first major confluence. After fording the creek, it's 5 to 6 miles to the pass; along the way you'll cross two more confluences and hike through an interesting gorge. The ascent to Dixie Pass is fairly easy to spot, and once there you'll find superb scenery and alpine ridges to explore.

For transportation into the park, there's Kennicott Shuttle, which runs a daily bus from Glennallen to McCarthy. With a round-trip Glennallen-to-McCarthy ticket ($149), the company will also drop off and pick up hikers at the Dixie Pass trailhead. Stop at the park headquarters in Copper Center to complete a backcountry trip itinerary and pick up USGS quadrangle maps.

If you're into grand, sweeping landscapes, vast tracts of boreal forest, and fields of alpine tundra, welcome to paradise. All of these hikes are for experienced trekkers only.

HIKING THE CHENA DOME TRAIL

START UPPER CHENA DOME TRAILHEAD
END UPPER CHENA DOME TRAILHEAD
DURATION/DISTANCE 3-4 DAYS/ 29.5 MILES
DIFFICULTY HARD

Fifty miles east of Fairbanks in the Chena River State Recreation Area, the 29.5-mile **Chena Dome** loop trail makes an ideal three- or four-day alpine romp. The trail circles the Angel Creek drainage area, with the vast majority of it along tundra ridgetops above the treeline. That includes climbing Chena Dome, a flat-topped peak near Mile 10, which, at 4421ft, is the highest point of the trail. The scramble to the top is a steep affair, so get ready for a serious huff.

An intriguing aspect of the trek is the remains of a military plane that crashed into the ridge in the 1950s. The trail winds past the site near Mile 8.5. Other highlights are views from Chena Dome and picking blueberries in August. In clear, calm weather you can even see Denali from spots along the trail.

From either end of the trail, you'll have to ascend for about 3 miles through pine forests before emerging past the treeline into open swathes of alpine tundra. From there, the trail follows the ridgelines – keep an eye out for cairns that mark the way.

Pack a stove (open fires aren't permitted), and carry at least 3 quarts (3L) of water per person (refill bottles from small pools in the tundra). There's a free-use shelter at Mile 17, while a 1.5-mile and 1900ft descent from the main trail will bring you to Upper Angel Creek Cabin, which can be used as a place to stay on the third night; reserve online with Alaska Division of Parks (http://dnr.alaska.gov/parks).

It's easier to hike the loop by beginning at the northern trailhead at Mile 50.5, Chena Hot Springs Rd. The trailhead is 0.7 miles past Angel Creek Bridge. The southern trailhead is at Mile 49.

KESUGI RIDGE TRAIL

START LITTLE COAL CREEK TRAILHEAD
END BYERS LAKE CAMPGROUND
DURATION/DISTANCE 3-4 DAYS/27 MILES
DIFFICULTY MEDIUM TO HARD

With Denali National Park offering no marked long-distance trails, aspiring hikers in search of a three- or four-day backcountry adventure head south to smaller **Denali State Park** and the Kesugi Ridge/ Troublesome Creek trail.

Established in 1970, 325,240-acre Denali State Park is more heavily forested than the national park and harbors Alaska's largest concentration of black bears. Essentially a wilderness, the park is bisected north–south by the George Parks Hwy, making access to its various trailheads easy. The Kesugi Ridge trail forms the backbone of the park and is part of the Talkeetna Mountain Range. Averaging 3000ft to 4000ft above sea level, the ridge is situated above the treeline amid tundra landscapes speckled with small lakes; it offers what many claim to be the best views of Denali in the state.

Most hikers start at Little Coal Creek trailhead on the George Parks Hwy and proceed north to south. The initial 2.5-mile climb to the ridge on the Little Coal Creek trail is steep, but views of Denali will inspire you to dig deep. Once up on the ridge beware of sudden changes in weather. Most of the path is marked by intermittent cairns. After passing Eight-Mile Divide and Stonehenge Hill, you'll encounter the intersection with the Ermine Hill trail, a handy escape hatch if you're tired or weather-beaten.

Soon after this the path descends briefly below the treeline before ascending again to open tundra. Many hikers come off the ridge at the Cascade trail intersection, descending 3.4 miles through forest to the Byers Lake campground on the George Parks Hwy (27.4 miles total hike). If you wish to continue, descend on the Troublesome Creek trail, aptly named due to its regular wash-outs and large bear population. The final 6 miles are in forest. Check ahead for current trail status, and bring bear spray and mosquito repellent.

The four trailheads that give access to the Kesugi Ridge trail are all conveniently located on the arterial George Parks Hwy that runs between Anchorage and Fairbanks. They are Little Coal Creek (Mile 163.9), Ermine Hill (Mile 156.5), Byers Lake (Mile 147) and Upper Troublesome Creek (Mile 137.6). All have parking facilities. Alaska/Yukon Trails (p315) runs a regular shuttle bus along the George Parks Hwy and may be able to help out with transport if you can coordinate times beforehand.

PADDLING BEAVER CREEK

START OPHIR CREEK CAMPGROUND
END VICTORIA CREEK
DURATION/DISTANCE 6-9DAYS/111 MILES
DIFFICULTY MEDIUM, CLASS I WATER

Beaver Creek is the adventure for budget travelers with time and a yearning to paddle through a roadless wilderness. The moderately swift stream, with long clear pools and frequent rapids, is rated Class I and can be handled by canoeists with expedition experience. The creek flows past hills forested with white spruce and paper birch below the jagged peaks of the White Mountains.

The scenery is spectacular, the chances of seeing another party remote and you'll catch so much grayling you'll never want to eat another one. You can also spend a night in the Borealis-Le Fevre Cabin, a BLM cabin on the banks of Beaver Creek, but on many a night, you'll be utterly surrounded by pure wilderness.

To get there, at Mile 57 of Steese Hwy go north on US Creek Rd for 6 miles, then northwest on Nome Creek Rd to the Ophir Creek Campground. You can put in at Nome Creek and paddle to its confluence with Beaver Creek. Most paddlers plan on six to nine days to reach Victoria Creek, a 111-mile trip, where gravel bars are used by bush planes to land and pick up paddlers.

Those who continue their expedition, however, will stay on Beaver Creek as it spills into Yukon Flats National Wildlife Refuge and meanders through a marshy area. There are portions of river width here that are so large, paddlers may not see their opposite shores (the land you do spot may well be literal islands in the stream). Eventually the water flows north into the Yukon River, where, after two or three days, you'll pass under the Yukon River Bridge on the Dalton Hwy and can be picked up there. This is a 399-mile paddle and a three-week expedition – the stuff great Alaskan adventures are made of.

WICKERSHAM DOME TRAIL

START ELLIOT HWY, MILE 28
END ELLIOT HWY, MILE 28
DURATION/DISTANCE 1 DAY/7 MILES
DIFFICULTY MEDIUM

Hiking in Alaska's interior generally demands time and can be immensely challenging to novices, but the Wickersham Dome Trail is an excellent intermediate-difficulty track that you can tackle as an easy day trip from Fairbanks. On good days, this 7-mile out-and-back cops you great views of the region once you reach the eponymous dome. On any day, you'll get a good taste of the boreal hinterland of interior Alaska.

The hike is located within the White Mountains, north of Fairbanks. Drive out to Mile 28 on the Elliot Hwy, where it splits from the Steese Hwy outside Fox, and look for the **trailhead** (Mile 28, Elliott Highway), which is marked by a signed parking area. The trail is pretty straightforward, and is part of the larger Summit Trail; going to Wickersham Dome makes for a solid day-trip option.

Relative to other hikes in the Interior, this trek is rewarding for the more casual hiker, but it still helps to be in decent shape before heading out. Wickersham Dome has an elevation of 1007ft (306m), and to get there, you'll first have to undergo gradual but steady elevation gain. Along the way you'll be surrounded by alpine vegetation, including gorgeous wildflowers and berry bushes. On that note, berry pickers often come here during the summer.

Eventually the trail coils around the crest of Wickersham Dome. This is the steepest huff, but once you make the top, you'll have an uninterrupted view of the Interior rolling all the way to the Brooks Range (assuming it's a clear day). Kick back, relax and remember the walk back to the parking area is downhill. Or continue along the Summit Trail, which crests similar ridges and has its own slate of sweet views.

Wickersham Dome Trail

History

If archaeologists are correct, Interior Alaska was the corridor through which the rest of the continent was peopled, as waves of hunter-gatherers migrated across the Bering land bridge to points south. Ancestors of the region's present Alaska Native group, the Athabascans, are thought to have been here at least 6000 years.

It wasn't until the 1800s that the first white people began to trickle in. The newcomers were mainly traders: Russians, who established posts along the lower Yukon and Kuskokwim Rivers; and Britons, who began trading at Fort Yukon, on the upper Yukon River, in the 1840s. Later came prospectors, whose discoveries transformed this region, beginning with the first major gold rush in the Fortymile district in the 1880s. Similar rushes, for gold and also copper, subsequently gave rise to many Interior communities.

Transportation projects brought the next wave of growth. In 1914 Congress agreed to fund the building of the USA's northernmost railroad, from Seward to Fairbanks. At the peak of construction, 4500 workers labored along the route, and their base camps became boom towns.

Three decades later, during WWII, the building of the Alcan had the same effect on the eastern Interior. Tok and Delta Junction got their starts as highway construction camps, while Fairbanks saw a second boom in its economy and population. Another three decades after that came the biggest undertaking the Interior has ever seen: the laying of the $8 billion Trans-Alaska Pipeline, which transects Alaska, running from Valdez to the Arctic Ocean at Prudhoe Bay.

Safe Travel

Getting lost in the backcountry is a real possibility, as national and state parks, national forest and Bureau of Land Management (BLM) areas have few marked trails. Come prepared with a compass, topographic map, GPS (optional), enough food and water to get you by for a few extra days and, most importantly, the skills to use your equipment properly. Long sleeves and light pants will help fend off mosquitoes, while our bear tips should prevent any unpleasant encounters with these creatures. Glacier travel and mountaineering are dangerous endeavors. If you don't know how to self-arrest and perform a crevasse rescue (or don't know what these things are), you should go with a qualified guide.

DENALI NATIONAL PARK & PRESERVE

In our collective consciousness, Alaska represents the concept of the raw wilderness. But that untamed perception can be as much a deterrent as a draw. For many travelers, in-depth exploration of this American frontier is a daunting task.

Enter **Denali National Park & Preserve** (907-683-9532; www.nps.gov/dena; George Parks Hwy; $10;) : a parcel of land both primeval and easily accessible. Here, you can peer at a grizzly bear, moose, caribou, or even wolves, all from the comfort of a bus.

On the other hand, if independent exploration is your thing, you can trek into 6 million acres of tundra, boreal forest and ice-capped mountains – a space larger than Massachusetts.

This all lies in the shadow of Denali, once known as Mt McKinley and to native Athabascans as the Great One. Denali is North America's highest peak, rightly celebrated as an icon of all that is awesome and wild in a state where those adjectives are ubiquitous.

History

The Athabascan people used what is now Denali National Park & Preserve as hunting grounds, but it wasn't until gold was found near Kantishna in 1905 that the area really began to see development. With the gold stampede came the big-game hunters, and things weren't looking very good for this amazing stretch of wilderness until a noted hunter and naturalist, Charles Sheldon, came to town.

Sheldon, stunned by the destruction, mounted a campaign to protect the region. From this, Mt McKinley National Park was born. Later, as a result of the 1980 Alaska National Interest Lands Conservation Act, the park was enlarged by 4 million acres, and renamed Denali National Park & Preserve.

In 1923, when the railroad arrived, 36 visitors enjoyed the splendor of the new park. Nowadays some 400,000 visitors are received annually. A number of unique visitor-management strategies has been created to deal with the masses, and generally they've been successful. The park today is still the great wilderness it was decades ago.

Sights

Park Road

Park Road begins at George Parks Hwy and winds 92 miles through the heart of the park, ending at Kantishna, an old mining settlement and the site of several wilderness lodges. Early on, park officials envisaged the onset of bumper-to-bumper traffic along this road and wisely closed almost all of it to private vehicles. During the summer, motorists can only drive to a parking area along the Savage River at Mile 15, one mile beyond the Savage River Campground (p283). To venture further along the road you must walk, cycle, be part of a tour or, most popularly, take a park shuttle or tour bus.

It's worth noting that you can *still* have an awesome Denali experience just by driving to the checkpoint that marks the end of car traffic. While wildlife isn't as prevalent in this outer membrane of the park road, it's not entirely absent either. The end of the line for car traffic is itself a suitably jaw-dropping river valley, so it's not like you can't find some great trekking areas in Denali's drivable park area.

Still, the majority of visitors opt to enter the park via a shuttle or tour bus, and with good reason: as lovely as the park's car zone is, the landscape beyond is simply one of the great wilderness spaces of North America. If you're planning on spending the day riding the buses (it's an eight-hour round-trip to the Eielson Visitor Center (p274), the most popular day trip in the park), pack plenty of food and drink. It can be a long, dusty ride, and in the park there are only limited services at the Toklat River Contact Station (p274) and Eielson Visitor Center. Carry a park map so you know where you are and can scope out ridges or riverbeds that appeal for hiking.

Denali MOUNTAIN

What makes 20,310ft Denali (formerly Mt McKinley) one of the world's great scenic mountains is the sheer independent rise of its bulk. Denali begins at a base of just 2000ft, which means that on a clear day you will be transfixed by over 18,000 feet of ascending rock, ice and snow. By contrast, Mt Everest, no slouch itself when it comes to memorable vistas, only rises 12,000 feet from its base on the Tibetan Plateau.

Despite its lofty heights, the mountain is not visible from the park entrance or the nearby campgrounds and hotel. Your first glimpse of it comes between Mile 9 and Mile 11 on Park Rd – *if* you're blessed with a clear day. The rule of thumb stressed by the National Park Service (NPS) rangers is that Denali is hidden two out of every three days, but that's a random example – it could be clear for a week and then hidden for the next month. While the 'Great One' might not be visible for most of the first 15 miles of Park Rd, this is the best stretch to spot moose because of the proliferation of spruce and especially willow, the animal's favorite food. The open flats before Savage River are good for spotting caribou and sometimes brown bears.

DENALI PLANNING GUIDE

Consider making reservations at least six months in advance for a park campsite during the height of summer, and at least three months ahead for accommodations outside the park. The park entrance fee is $10 per person, good for seven days.

There's only one road through the park: the 92-mile unpaved Park Rd, which is closed to private vehicles after Mile 15 in summer. Shuttle buses run from the middle of May until September past Mile 15. Sometimes, if the snow melts early in April, visitors will be allowed to proceed as far as Mile 30 until the shuttle buses begin operation. The park entrance area, where most visitors congregate, extends a scant 4 miles up Park Rd. It's here you'll find the park headquarters, visitor center and main campground, as well as the Wilderness Access Center (p288), where you pay your park entrance fee and arrange campsites and shuttle-bus bookings to take you further into the park. Across the lot from the WAC sits the Backcountry Information Center (p279), where backpackers get backcountry permits and bear-proof food containers.

There are few places to stay within the park, excluding campgrounds, and only one restaurant. The majority of visitors base themselves in the nearby communities of Canyon, McKinley Village, Carlo Creek and Healy.

Denali National Park – Park Road

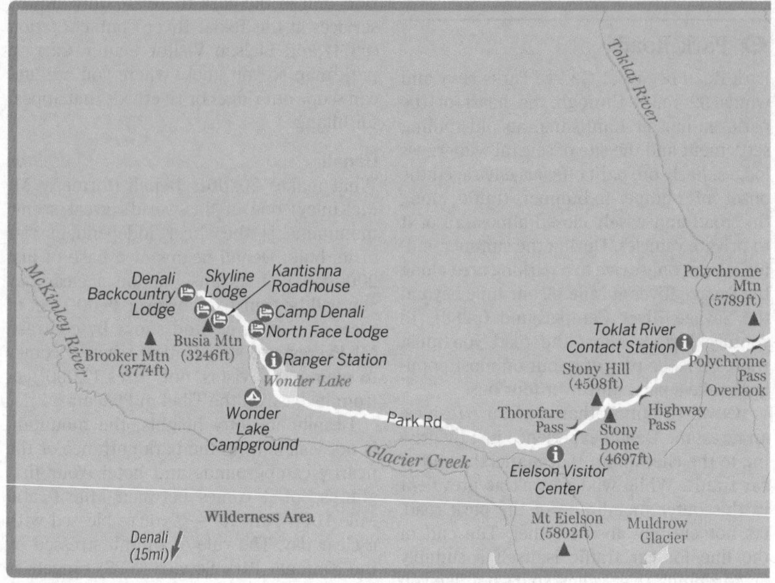

Savage River to Eielson Visitor Center

From Savage River, the road dips into the Sanctuary and Teklanika Valleys, and Denali disappears behind the foothills. Igloo Creek Campground (p283) is the unofficial beginning of 'bear country'.

After passing through the canyon formed by the Igloo and Cathedral Mountains, the road ascends to 3880ft **Sable Pass** (Mile 39.05). The canyon and surrounding mountains are excellent places to view Dall sheep, while the pass is known as a prime habitat for Toklat brown bears.

Given the prevalence of big brown bears and other wildlife, the area around Sable Pass is permanently closed to hikers and backpackers. From here, the road drops to the bridge over the **East Fork Toklat River** (Mile 44). Hikers can trek from the bridge along the riverbanks both north and south.

Polychrome Pass Overlook (Mile 46, Park Rd) is a rest stop for the shuttle buses, and is named for its exposed bands of multihued rock strata. This scenic area, at 3500ft, has the sort of dramatic views of the Toklat River that will inevitably win over all of your social media followers, plus trails and social paths that lead to the ridgelines. If you're nervous about making a steep ascent to high altitude, this is a good jump-off point, as the pass is pretty elevated.

In contrast, the next major stop for shuttle buses, the **Toklat River Contact Station** (Mile 53, Park Rd; 9am-7pm late May–mid-Sep) FREE, is a deep valley depression. Here you'll find toilets and a large tented store selling books and souvenirs (ready to hike into the park? Don't forget a plush grizzly bear puppet!), as well as scopes to check out Dall sheep on the neighboring hills. Again, this is a good jumping-off point for hikers – while you're not on top of the ridges, you'll still have incredible views of them from the Toklat riverbed, which also attracts local wildlife.

Eielson Visitor Center (907-683-9532; www.nps.gov/dena/planyourvisit/the-eielson-visitor-center.htm; Mile 66, Park Rd; 9am-7pm Jun–mid-Sep) FREE, on the far side of Thorofare Pass (3900ft), is the most common turning-around point for day-trippers taking the shuttle or tour buses into the park. While it's undoubtedly a remote spot – and a dramatic one, wedged into the side of the mountain like a north-country Frank Lloyd Wright installation – it's also a well-appointed visitor facility, with helpful rangers onsite and plenty of interpretive displays (and toilets:

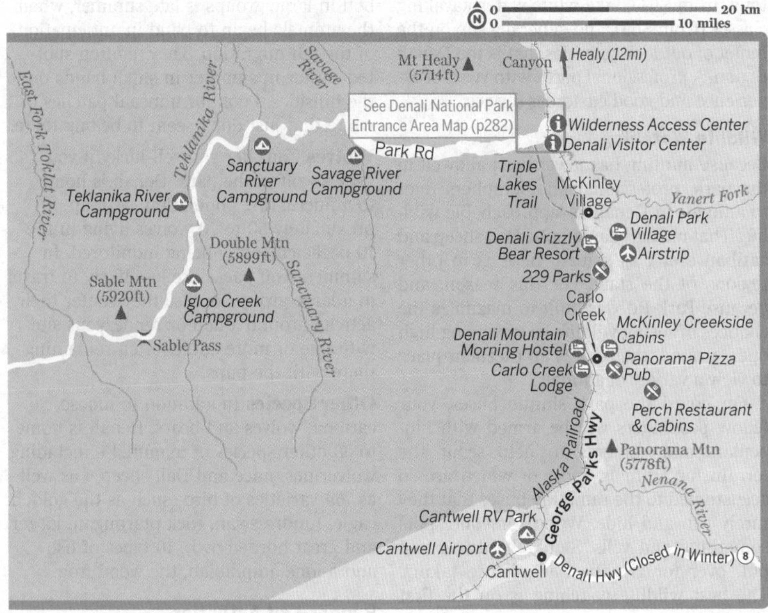

sweet, sweet, toilets). A walkway extends around the center, affording mind-boggling views of the Toklat River, nearby mountains and, if the weather gods are smiling upon you, Denali itself. There's also a mountain viewing area within the visitor center with a helpful diagram of the ranges.

From Eielson, you'll find trails leading down to the bed of the river and up to the ridgelines that buttress the mountains. There's also a very easy loop trail (around half a mile, with nary an elevation gain) that leads out to a tongue of land, once again offering the sort of views you've only seen on the covers of paperback fantasy novels.

Eielson to Kantishna

Past Eielson, Park Rd drops to the valley, passing a sign for **Muldrow Glacier** (Mile 74.4). At this point, the glacier lies about a mile to the south, and the terminus of the 32-mile floe of ice is clearly visible, though you might not recognize it because the ice is covered with a mat of plant life. If the weather is cloudy and the mountain and the surrounding peaks are hidden, the final 20 miles of the bus trip are still an enjoyable ride through rolling tundra, passing small glacier-made lakes known as kettle ponds. Study the pools of water carefully to spot beavers or waterfowl.

Wonder Lake Campground (p282), only 26 miles from Denali, sees the beauty of the mountain doubled on a clear day as the peak reflects in the lake's surface. Sadly, the heavy demand for the 28 campsites and the numerous overcast days caused by Denali itself prevent the majority of visitors from ever seeing this remarkable panorama. If you do experience the reddish sunset on the summit reflecting in the lake's still waters, cherish the moment.

The campground is on a low rise above the lake's southern end. The famous McKinley-reflected-in-the-lake photos are taken along the northeast shore, 2 miles beyond the campground.

Kantishna (Mile 90) is mainly a destination for people staying in the area's private lodges. The buses turn around here after a 40-minute rest, and begin the long trip back to the Wilderness Access Centre.

Activities

Denali Outdoor Center OUTDOORS
(Map p282; ☎888-303-1925; www.denalioutdoorcenter.com; Mile 238.9, George Parks Hwy) You can rent bicycles (half/full day $25/40) at this Canyon fixture, go on a kayak or raft

tour (from $94), take white-water kayaking classes (from $65), and generally sup on the buffet of outdoor activities that is the Denali region. A professional outfit with years of experience and good customer service.

Wildlife Watching

Because hunting has never been allowed in the park, professional photographers refer to animals in Denali as 'approachable wildlife.' That means bear, moose, Dall sheep and caribou aren't as skittish here as in other regions of the state. For this reason, and because Park Rd was built to maximize the chances of seeing wildlife by traversing high open ground, the park is an excellent place to view a variety of animals.

On board the park shuttle buses, your fellow passengers will be armed with binoculars and cameras to help scour the terrain for animals, most of which are so accustomed to the rambling buses that they rarely run and hide. When someone spots something and yells 'Stop!', the driver will pull over for viewing and picture taking. The best wildlife watching is on the first morning bus.

Bears In the area of the park that most people visit (north of the Alaska Range), there are an estimated 300 to 350 grizzly bears and around 200 black bears. Grizzlies tend to inhabit tundra areas, while black bears stick to the forests. With most of Denali's streams fed by glaciers, the fishing is poor and bears must rely on vegetation for 85% of their diet. As a result, most male grizzlies here range from only 300lb to 600lb, while their cousins on the salmon-rich coasts can easily top 1000lb. There's no guarantee of seeing a grizzly, but most park bus drivers say they spot around five to eight per day along the road.

Moose Around 1800 moose roam the park, and they are almost always found in stands of spruce and willow shrubs (their favorite food). Backpackers should be wary when plowing blindly through areas of thick ground cover, especially in early September, when the bulls clash over breeding rights to the cows. Make no mistake: a moose can be just as dangerous as a bear.

Caribou All the park's caribou belong to the Denali herd – one of 32 herds in Alaska – which presently numbers around 1760 animals. The best time to spot caribou in large groups is late summer, when the animals begin to band in anticipation of the fall migration. They're often spotted earlier in summer in small bands on the hillsides. Look for unusual patches of white that just don't seem to belong there.

Wolves Consider yourself lucky if you spot a wolf in the park. Denali is home to a fluctuating population, with approximately 50 to 70 wolves living in the 10 packs currently being monitored. In summer, wolf packs are less likely to travel in a large group because they center their activity around a den or rendezvous site, with one or more adults often remaining there with the pups.

Other Species In addition to moose, caribou, wolves and bears, Denali is home to 33 other species of mammal – including wolverines, mice and Dall sheep – as well as 159 varieties of bird (such as the golden eagle, tundra swan, rock ptarmigan, jaeger and great horned owl), 10 types of fish and a lone amphibian, the wood frog.

Ranger-Led Activities

If you're hesitant about venturing into the wilds on your own, or merely looking to kill some time until your desired backcountry unit opens, Denali offers a daily slate of worthwhile free ranger-led hikes and presentations. See www.nps.gov/dena/planyourvisit/ranger-programs.htm for more information.

Discovery Hikes HIKING

(☎907-683-9532; www.nps.gov/dena/planyourvisit/discovery-hikes.htm; ⏲Jun 8-Sep) National Park Service (NPS) rangers lead moderate to strenuous three- to five-hour hikes deep into the heart of the park on a daily basis during summer. The location varies from day to day; you can find the schedule at the Denali Visitor Center (p288) or online. Sign up at the center one or two days in advance and then reserve a shuttle ticket at the WAC (p288).

Shuttles leave at 8am. Note that hiking is off trail, so be sure to have sturdy footwear and to pack rain gear, food and water. Rangers will turn away unprepared hikers. This is an all-day affair; the bus ride to the hiking departure point can take up to four hours, to hike for three to five hours, and then a similar-length bus ride back to the park entrance.

SCALING THE MOUNTAIN

So, has gazing at lordly Denali from the seat of an aircraft infected you with summit fever? If so, you're suffering from a century-old sickness.

James Wickersham, the US district judge in Alaska, made the first documented attempt to scale Denali, reaching the 7500ft mark of the 20,310ft peak in 1903. His effort inspired a rash of ensuing bids, including Dr Frederick Cook's 1906 effort (which he falsely claimed was a success) and the 1910 Sourdough Expedition, where four Fairbanks miners, carrying only hot chocolate, doughnuts and a 14ft spruce pole, topped out on the North Peak only to realize it was 850ft lower than the true, more southerly summit.

Success finally came in 1913 when Hudson Stuck, Henry Karstens, Robert Tatum and Walter Harper reached the top on June 7. From there they saw the spruce pole on the North Peak to verify the claims of the Sourdough Expedition.

The most important date for many climbers, however, is 1951. That year, Bradford Washburn arrived and pioneered the West Buttress route, by far the preferred avenue to the top. Not long after, Talkeetna's two most famous characters – Ray 'the Pirate' Genet and Don Sheldon – began to have an impact on the climbing world. Genet was an Alaskan mountaineer who made a record 25 climbs up Denali, while Sheldon was a legendary glacier pilot. The two worked closely in guiding climbers to the top and, more importantly, rescuing those who failed. Sadly, the town lost both in quick succession, with Sheldon dying of cancer in 1975 and Genet freezing to death on Mt Everest four years later.

Nowadays, Denali's storied mountaineering history adds considerably to the mythic business of scaling the peak. Between 1200 and 1300 climbers attempt it each year, spending an average of three weeks on the slopes. About 80% use the West Buttress route, which involves flying in a ski plane from Talkeetna to the 7200ft Kahiltna Glacier and from there climbing for the South Peak, passing a medical/rescue camp maintained by mountaineering clubs and the National Park Service (NPS) at 14,220ft.

In a good season (April through July), when storms are not constantly sweeping across the range, more than 50% of expeditions will be successful. In a bad year, that rate falls below 40%, and several climbers may die. Particularly grim was the annus horribilis of 1991, when 11 lives were lost.

The most solemn way to appreciate the effect of the mountain is to visit the cemetery (p290) in Talkeetna, a restful spot set among tall trees on 2nd St, just off Talkeetna Spur Rd near the airport. Don Sheldon's grave is the most prominent, with the epitaph 'He wagered with the wind and won.' The Mt McKinley Climber's Memorial includes a stone for Ray Genet, despite the fact that his body was never removed from the slopes of Mt Everest. The most touching sight, however, is a memorial with the names and ages of all the climbers who've died on Denali and neighboring peaks.

If you're a seasoned alpinist you can mount an expedition yourself, or be among the 25% of Denali climbers who are part of guided ascents. If you're looking for a local guiding company, try Alaska Mountaineering School (p291), which charges $8300 to lead you up the mountain. Another acclaimed company with a high success rate is Seattle-based **Alpine Ascents** (☎206-378-1927; www.alpineascents.com). Its trips start at $8400 excluding meals, lodging and flights to Alaska. Book at least a year in advance.

Sled-Dog Demonstrations DOG SLEDDING
(Map p282; www.nps.gov/dena/planyourvisit/sled-dog-demonstrations.htm; Park Headquarters; ⏲10am, 2pm & 4pm May–mid-Sep) FREE Denali is the only US national park where rangers conduct winter patrols with dog teams. In summer the huskies serve a different purpose: amusing and educating the legions of tourists who sign up for the park's free daily tours of the sled-dog kennels, and dog demonstrations. During warm months, the dogs briefly pull rangers in an ATV for the crowds.

Day-Hiking

Even for those who have neither the desire nor the equipment for an overnight trek, hiking is the best way to enjoy the park and to see the land and its wildlife. You can hike virtually anywhere that hasn't been closed to prevent an impact on wildlife.

For a day-hike (which doesn't require a permit), ride the shuttle bus and get off at any valley, riverbed or ridge that grabs your fancy. Check in at the Backcountry Information Center or Wilderness Access Center (p288) for suggestions.

Here's an important reminder for shuttle bus riders: while you can hop on any shuttle bus heading back to the park gates, those buses are often packed. It's generally easier to get yourself on a bus if you try to board at a recognized bus stop (Toklat River p274, Polychrome Pass p274, the Eielson Visitor Center p274, etc), where your name will be placed on a list and park staff will do what they can to get you on board. While many people flag a bus down from the road on a daily basis, you may well find yourself waiting for hours in cold rain for a bus with an empty seat. Obviously, the larger your group, the greater the risk of finding a bus with no room.

Park Entrance Area HIKING

(www.nps.gov/dena/planyourvisit/dayhiking.htm) A few short, well-maintained trails web the park entrance area.

The **Horseshoe Lake Trail**, accessed by the railroad crossing at Mile 1.2 of Park Rd, is a leisurely 1.5-mile walk through the woods to the lake overlook, followed by a steep trail to the water's edge and beaver dam at the end. The **Taiga Loop Trail**, also commencing from the railroad tracks, turns west from the Horseshoe Lake Trail and leads to both the Mt Healy Overlook Trail (p279) and the Rock Creek Trail.

The moderate, 2.3-mile **Rock Creek Trail** leads west to the Park Headquarters and dog kennels (p277). You can hike this trail downhill from the headquarters end, where the trail begins just before Park Rd. From here it crosses Rock Creek but doesn't stay with the stream. Instead, it climbs a gentle slope of mixed aspen and spruce forest, breaks out along a ridge with scenic views of Mt Healy and George Parks Hwy and then begins a

A MOUNTAIN BY ANY OTHER NAME

The Athabascans called it Denali or the 'Great One'. Their brethren to the south in the Susitna Valley called it Doleika, the 'Big Mountain'. The Aleuts meanwhile referred to it as Traleika. The first European to spot the peak, George Vancouver, didn't bother to call it anything, while Ferdinand von Wrangell, a prominent Russian administrator in the 19th century, wrote 'Tenada' on his maps. So why was North America's highest peak called McKinley for over a century?

During the gold-rush days, the mountain was known locally as Densmore's Mountain, in honor of a local prospector. But soon afterwards, it was dubbed Mt McKinley for William McKinley, an Ohioan who was running for – and later became – president of the United States. This was no high-minded attempt to commemorate McKinley's political legacy; the man who came up with the name, William Dickey, was a gold miner who wanted to flip the bird at rival silver miners. McKinley ran for office against William Jennings Bryan, a politician who wanted to use silver instead of gold as the backing standard for American currency. McKinley was a strong defender of the gold standard – as was, unsurprisingly, Dickey the gold prospector, who was known for getting into arguments with silver miners. Rarely has such a grand natural feature been named with such petty motivation.

In 1975, the state of Alaska, via its Board of Geographic Names, changed the name of the mountain to Denali, and sent an official request to Washington DC asking for the nation to do the same. That authority is vested in the United States Board on Geographic Names, but the agency had its hands tied by Ohio congress members and senators (remember, William McKinley was from Ohio), who apparently thought the federal government was slacking when it came to insulting Native Americans.

This impasse continued until 2015, when then president Barack Obama ordered his Secretary of the Interior, Sally Jewell, to rename the mountain 'Denali'. The Secretary of the Interior has the power to name geographic features if the Board of Geographic Names is dragging its heels, and apparently 40 years qualifies. Some Ohio Republicans opposed the rename, while Alaskans (and most of the rest of the universe) felt like the mountain finally had a name worthy of its grandeur.

rapid descent to its end at the Taiga Loop Trail.

The **Roadside Trail** parallels Park Rd and takes you 1.5 miles from the Denali Visitor Center (p288) to the dog kennels next to the park headquarters. The 1.6-mile **McKinley Station Trail** takes you from the visitor center to the Wilderness Access Centre (p288) and also connects with the **Jonesville Trail** to Canyon.

Mt Healy Overlook Trail HIKING

(Map p282; www.nps.gov/dena/planyourvisit/overlook.htm) This is the longest maintained trail in the park's entrance area, and is proof that even at the entrance, there's some great wilderness hiking to be found. One of the steepest official hikes in the park, it yields some fantastic views from the top of Mt Healy. Plan on the route taking three to five hours.

The trail veers off the Taiga Loop Trail and makes a steep climb up Mt Healy, ascending 1700ft in 2.5 miles.

Although you begin in a forest of spruce, alder and aspen, higher up you enter alpine tundra – a world of moss, lichen, wildflowers and incredible views. Keep an eye out for the large hoary marmots (a northern cousin of the groundhog) and pikas (a small relative of the rabbit).

From the overlook (3425ft), hardy hikers can climb another mile to the high point of Healy Ridge (4217ft), or another 2 miles to the summit of Mt Healy (5714ft).

Triple Lakes Trail HIKING

(www.nps.gov/dena/planyourvisit/triple.htm) When it opened in 2011, this 9.5-mile trail (four to five hours one- way) quickly gained a reputation as the entrance area's best day hike, as well as the longest official trail in the park. The terrain and vegetation are more varied than on other trails, and there's a palpable feeling that you've truly entered the wilds.

From the McKinley Station Trail (p278) the path begins after a bridge crossing of Hines Creek. The trail is flat at first and the forest cover unusually lush. In about a mile you begin to climb switchbacks, eventually reaching a ridgetop affording yodel-inspiring views of the Alaska Range and the valleys formed by Hines Creek and the Nenana River.

After a long run along the ridgeline, the path begins to descend, first to the Triple Lakes and then to George Parks Hwy. After crossing the highway bridge, it's a short walk to McKinley Village Lodge, where you can catch a shuttle ($5) back to the Denali Visitor Center (p288).

Savage Alpine Trail HIKING

(907-683-9532; www.nps.gov/dena/planyourvisit/dayhiking.htm) This 4-mile trail begins at Savage River (Mile 15), ascends 1200ft to a windy alpine ridge with fabulous views and descends to the Mountain Vista day-use area (Mile 13), where you can catch a park shuttle.

Savage River Loop Trail HIKING

(www.nps.gov/dena/planyourvisit/savagecanyon.htm) You can get to this trailhead by car (Mile 14), but you're better off taking the free Savage River Shuttle Bus as the small parking lot often fills up. The 2-mile loop is wheelchair accessible for the first half mile and runs north from Park Rd on either side of the river.

Backpacking

The park is divided into 87 backcountry units, and for 41 of these only a regulated number of backpackers (usually four to six) are allowed in at a time. You may spend a maximum of seven nights in any one unit, and a maximum of 30 consecutive nights in the backcountry. For more information download *A Denali Backpacking Guide* from the national park's website (www.nps.gov/dena).

Permits are needed if you want to camp overnight and you can obtain these at the **Backcountry Information Center** (BIC; Map p282; 907-683-9532/90; Mile 0.5, Park Rd; 9am-6pm late May–mid-Sep), where you'll also find wall maps with the unit outlines and a quota board indicating the number of vacancies in each. Permits are issued only a day in advance, and the most popular units fill up fast. It pays to be flexible: decide which areas you're aiming for, and be prepared to take any zone that's open. If you're picky, you might have to wait several days.

After you've decided where to go, the next step is to watch the required backcountry orientation video, followed by a brief safety talk that covers, among other things, proper use of the bear-resistant food containers (BRFCs) you'll receive free of charge with your permit. The containers are bulky, but they work – they've reduced bear encounters dramatically since 1986. It's also worth noting that you're required to carry out dirty toilet paper (you bury your waste), so be sure to take at least a dozen ziplock bags. Finally, after receiving your permit, buy the topographic maps ($8) for your unit and head over to the WAC (p288) to purchase a ticket for a camper bus ($34) to get you out to the starting point of your hike.

For an overview of the different units in the park, check out the park's website for the brilliant Backcountry Camping and Hiking Guide. Its unit-by-unit descriptions include access points, possible hiking corridors, dangers and, maybe best of all, pictures from the area.

Cycling

No special permit is needed to cycle on Park Rd, but cycling off-road is prohibited. Camper buses and some shuttle buses will carry bicycles, but only two at a time and only if you have a reservation. Many cyclists ride the bus in and cycle back out, carrying their gear and staying at campsites they've reserved along the way. It's also possible to take an early morning bus in, ride for several hours and catch a bus back the same day. The highest point on the road is Highway Pass (3980ft). The entrance area is at 1585ft. Note that the park road is narrow, but buses are used to cyclists, and drivers generally do a grand job of giving riders a decent berth.

Ziplining

Denali Park Zipline OUTDOORS
(Map p282; 907-683-2947; www.denalizipline.com; 238 George Parks Hwy; adult/child $139/99) This well-regarded course will take you across six sky bridges and seven zip lines that whoosh over the boreal forest and swathes of tundra. The entire adventure takes around three hours.

Courses

Murie Science & Learning Center OUTDOORS
(Map p282; www.nps.gov/rlc/murie; Mile 1.5, Park Rd; 9am-4:30pm May–mid-Sep;) Representing eight of Alaska's arctic and subarctic parks, this center is *the* place to come for information on research taking place within the park and around the state. During the summer there are presentations and half-day 'Denali-ology' courses, as well as multi-day field seminars (coordinated with Alaska Geographic), teacher training and youth camps.

THE STAMPEDE TRAIL AND THE MAGIC BUS

The Stampede Trail was an overgrown, semi-abandoned mining road in April 1992 when an idealistic 24-year-old wanderer called Chris McCandless made camp in an abandoned bus west of Healy, equipped with little more than a rifle, 10lb of rice and a copy of Louis L'Amour's *Education of a Wandering Man* in his bag. His quest: to attempt to survive on his own in the unforgiving Alaskan wilderness.

McCandless' death a few months later, in August 1992, was famously chronicled in the book *Into the Wild* by Jon Krakauer in 1996. But it was Sean Penn's cinematic rendering of the book in 2007 that brought the story to international attention and turned the Stampede Trail and the so-called 'Magic Bus' into a pilgrimage site for a stream of romantic young backpackers.

The deluge of hikers has led to problems. Thanks to two dangerous river crossings along the Stampede Trail's muddy if relatively flat route, some of the amateur hikers have found they've bitten off more than they can chew. As a result, search-and-rescue teams are called out five or six times a year to aid stranded or disorientated travelers and, in 2010, a Swiss woman tragically drowned while trying to cross the Teklanika River.

Today the Magic Bus – a 1946 International Harvester (number 142) abandoned by road builders in 1961 – continues to sit incongruously amid the taiga-tundra in an increasingly deteriorating state. A plaque in memory of McCandless adorns the faded interior, which is filled with graffiti scribbled by travelers from around the world inspired by his story. Many of them stay the night inside.

If you're hiking to the bus, it's approximately 28 miles from the start of the Stampede Trail, which begins 2 miles north of Healy (the first 8 miles are accessible in a vehicle). Go prepared, preferably in a group, and take extreme precautions when crossing the Savage and Teklanika Rivers (and if they're flowing high, don't cross them at all). Bears are common in the area and the mosquitoes are savage. Alternatively, you can take an ATV tour along the trail in summer, or head out in winter on a dogsledding trip from EarthSong Lodge (p285).

A replica of bus 142 sits outside the 49th State Brewing Company (p287) in Healy.

Denali Education Center ADVENTURE SPORTS
(☎907-683-2597; www.denali.org; Mile 231, George Parks Hwy; 🚻) 🌿 This enthusiastic nonprofit outfit offers day and extended educational backpacking programs, including a number specifically designed for seniors and youths.

Tours

Some travelers confuse Denali's shuttle buses and tour buses. The former are purely for getting around the park. The latter ply the same routes, but with drivers who give narrated tours. If you're lucky and get a congenial driver on a park shuttle, you can get the lowdown on what's what without paying the extra cost of a tour.

Narrated tours include a packed lunch. See www.nps.gov/dena for more information and www.reservedenali.com for reservations.

Aramark NATURAL HISTORY, WILDLIFE
(☎800-622-7275; www.reservedenali.com) Offers a variety of natural-history and wildlife tours throughout the park.

Tundra Wilderness Tour WILDLIFE
(☎800-622-7275; www.reservedenali.com; adult/child $112.75/51.50) 🌿 This narrated bus tour is a seven- to eight-hour trip that heads to the Toklat River (at Mile 53) and focuses on wildlife viewing. That endeavor is aided by the presence of dropdown video screens on the bus – your driver will take footage of the local wildlife and project said content onto the screens.

Natural History Tour ECOTOUR
(☎800-622-7275; www.reservedenali.com; adult/child $80.75/35.50) This four- to five-hour trip rolls out to the Teklanika River (Mile 30) and includes multiple stops focusing on the park's history and ecosystems. At Primrose Ridge, you'll get to see an Alaskan Native presentation on indigenous land stewardship.

ATVs

Denali ATV Adventures ADVENTURE
(Map p282; ☎907-683-4288; www.denaliatv.com; Mile 238.6, George Parks Hwy; 2hr one-/two-person ATV tours from $115/175) This friendly outfit offers four different butt-busting rides on all-terrain vehicles in the surrounding wilderness (two tours are offered year-round, and two are seasonal). Note that you're not allowed to make this kind of cacophony in the national park. Instead, the trips skirt the park's fringes.

There's a ton of add-on cross-experience tours available; you can combine an ATV trip with a zipline experience, a visit to a husky kennel, etc. Visit the website for more details.

Flightseeing

Most flightseeing tours around Denali leave from Talkeetna, but some companies also operate out of the park area.

Kantishna Air Taxi SCENIC FLIGHTS
(☎907-644-8222; www.katair.com) Based at Skyline Lodge (p283), this operation flies out of Kantishna, the park entrance and Anchorage. Hour-long flightseeing excursions around Denali are $270 per person from Kantishna.

River Rafting

Thanks to Denali tourists, the Nenana River is the most popular white-water-rafting area in Alaska. The river's main white-water stretch begins near the park entrance and ends 10 miles north, near Healy. It's rated class III and IV, and involves standing waves, rapids and holes with names such as 'Coffee Grinder' in sheer-sided canyons. South of the park entrance, the river is much milder, but to many it's just as interesting as it veers away from both the highway and the railroad, increasing your chances of sighting wildlife.

Rafting companies offer similar guided trips on both stretches, in which either the guide does all the work or you help paddle. Advance reservations (no deposit) are accepted, and all trips include dry suits and shuttle pick-ups. The canyon and the easier 'wilderness' paddles go for about $95, and last around three hours.

Denali Raft Adventures RAFTING
(Map p282; ☎907-683-2234; www.denaliraft.com; Mile 238.6 George Parks Hwy; trips from $94) Saunter down the Nenana River between Canyon and Healy on class II to IV rapids with this well-regarded, experienced outfitter. It offers five trips aimed at all levels of experience.

Sleeping

You should definitely reserve something in midsummer – even if it's just a campsite – before showing up. Note the Denali Borough charges a 7% accommodations tax on top of listed prices (except for campsites). High-end accommodation in and around the park generally feels overpriced, as you're often at the mercy of select concessionaires.

Denali National Park Entrance Area

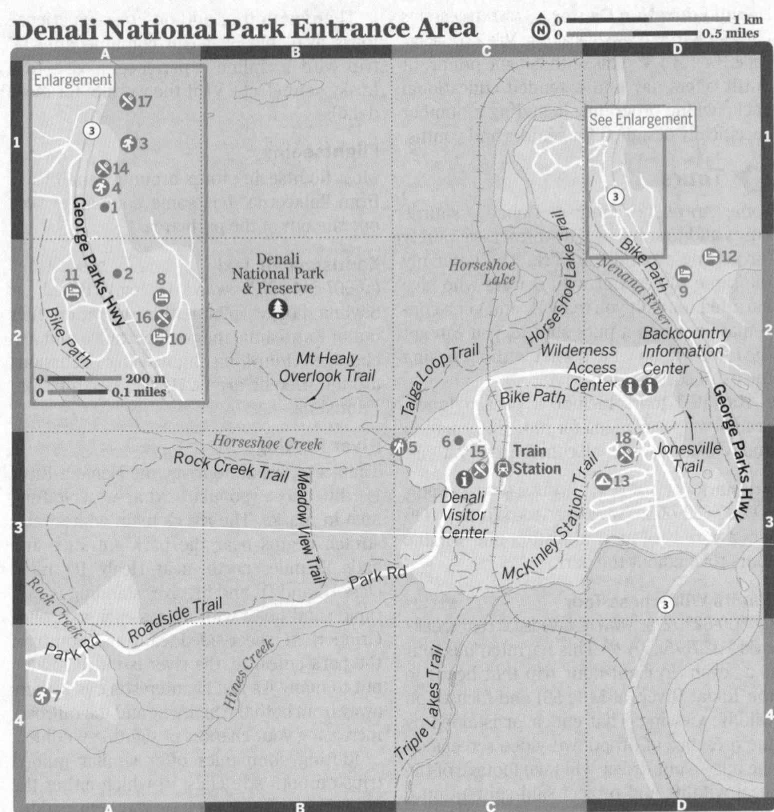

Within the Park

Kantishna excepted, lodgings are not available inside park boundaries, so if you want overnight shelter within the park you'll need a tent or RV (recreational vehicle).

★Wonder Lake Campground CAMPGROUND $

(www.nps.gov/dena; Mile 85, Park Rd; tent sites $16) This is the jewel of Denali campgrounds, thanks to its eye-popping views of the mountain. The facility has 28 sites for tents only, but does offer flush toilets and piped-in water. If you're lucky enough to reserve a site, book it for three nights and then pray that Denali appears during one of the days you're there.

Teklanika River Campground CAMPGROUND $

(www.nps.gov/dena; Mile 29, Park Rd; campsites $25; P) There are 53 sites, flush toilets, piped-in water and evening programs at this campground, popular with tenters, RVers and the occasional wolf or two.

You can drive to the campground, which is located past Mile 15, but you must stay a minimum of three days if you do, and you can't use your vehicle until you're ready to return to the park entrance. For $35, you can buy a Tek Pass that allows you to access the park bus system.

Sanctuary River Campground CAMPGROUND $

(www.nps.gov/dena; Mile 22, Park Rd; tent sites $15) This official park campground is nicely set on the banks of a large glacial river in an area that is great for day-hiking. The seven sites can only be reserved in person at the WAC (p288) two days in advance, and there's no piped-in water.

Riley Creek Campground CAMPGROUND $

(Map p282; www.nps.gov/dena; Mile 0.25, Park Rd; tent sites $24, RV sites $24-30) At the

Denali National Park Entrance Area

park's main entrance, and within earshot of George Parks Hwy, this is Denali's largest and most developed campground. It's open year-round and has 147 sites for tents and RVs, piped-in water, flush toilets and evening interpretive programs. Walk-ins have their own section in C lot.

The location is convenient for access to Riley Creek Mercantile (p286), the WAC (p288), visitor center (p288) and many hikes.

Savage River Campground CAMPGROUND $
(www.nps.gov/dena; Mile 14, Park Rd; campsites $24-30) Despite its name, this park campground is a mile short of the eponymous river and close to the Mountain Vista rest area. It's one of only two campgrounds with a view of the mountain. The 32 sites can accommodate both RVs and tents, with such amenities as flush toilets, piped-in water and evening presentations.

Igloo Creek Campground CAMPGROUND $
(www.nps.gov/dena; Mile 34, Park Rd; tent sites $15) This small, waterless, seven-site camping area marks the beginning of true bear country. The day-hiking around here is excellent, especially the numerous ridges around Igloo and Cathedral Mountains that provide routes into alpine areas.

Sites can only be reserved in person at the WAC (p288) two days in advance.

Kantishna

Park Rd ends at this privately owned island of land, an old gold-mining enclave that was outside the park's original boundary but was enveloped by additions in 1980. Kantishna provides the ultimate lodging location. Many options include meals and round-trip transportation from the park entrance.

Skyline Lodge LODGE $$$
(907-644-8222; www.katair.com/skyline-lodge; s/d $364.25/434.25) This five-room, solar-powered lodge serves as Kantishna Air Taxi's (p281) base of operations. Guests have use of a common area, dining room, bath and shower block, and decks overlooking the Kantishna Valley. Add $70 per person for three meals a day.

Camp Denali LODGE $$$
(907-683-2290; www.campdenali.com; cabins per person without bath per minimum 3-night stay $1800) Verging on legendary, Camp Denali has been the gold standard among Kantishna lodges for the last half century. Widely spread across a ridgeline, the camp's simple, comfortable cabins elegantly complement the backcountry experience while minimizing impact on the natural world.

Think of it as luxury camping, with gourmet meals, guided hikes, free bicycle and canoe rentals, killer views of the mountain, and staff so devoted to Denali that you'll come away feeling like the beneficiary of a precious gift. If you can't handle the outhouses or the seven-minute walk to the bathroom, book the nearby, affiliated **North Face Lodge** (s/d $725/1250) with en-suite rooms for the same price.

Kantishna Roadhouse LODGE $$$
(907-374-3041; www.kantishnaroadhouse.com; d incl meals per person $427) Owned by park concessionaire Doyon, Kantishna

Roadhouse has clean modern cabins, a beautiful dining room, bar and guided activities. Room rates include round-trip transport from the park entrance and various guided activities. Note there is a two-day minimum stay and draconian cancellation policies.

Denali Backcountry Lodge LODGE **$$$**
(☎888-602-3323; www.alaskacollection.com/lodging/denali-backcountry-lodge; cabins incl meals per person from $545) The last lodge on Park Rd, this is a great-looking place on the banks of Moose Creek with comfortable modern cabins and common areas. Transport, meals and guided activities are included. The setting is as beautiful as the cabins are pricey.

Canyon

Canyon is as close as the Denali area comes to a 'village'. In essence, it's a convenient service center consisting of a thin strip of wooden shops, accommodations, gas stations and stores clustered either side of the George Parks Hwy, roughly a mile north of the park entrance area (a walking path links the two). The western side of the road is dominated by two cruise-line-owned hotels, including the Denali Princess Wilderness Lodge. The eastern side harbors a skinny line of shops, restaurants and outdoor-adventure specialists.

Denali Park Salmon Bake Restaurant & Cabins CABIN **$$**
(Map p282; ☎907-683-2733; www.denalinationalparklodging.net; Mile 238.5, George Parks Hwy; cabins without/with bath from $74/149; P 📶) These standard cabins come with TV, heater and bath, and are on the dingy side of clean. The economy rooms have shared bathroom and a shingle exterior with a white tarpaulin roof cover, giving the place a bit of a work-camp atmosphere. Notwithstanding, Salmon Bake is a big player in Canyon, running a popular bar, restaurant (p286) and shuttle bus.

For a step up in quality (and price), these folks also operate the Crow's Nest cabins.

Denali Princess Wilderness Lodge HOTEL **$$$**
(Map p282; ☎800-426-0500; www.princesslodges.com; Mile 238.5 George Parks Hwy; r from $249; P 📶) The high-roofed, perennially busy reception hall at this giant 'lodge' carries the slightly antiseptic essence of a cruise ship, which is fitting as 80% of its guests are cruisers bussed up from the coast. The splayed grounds constitute a medium-sized resort overlooking the choppy Nenana River and exhibit multiple restaurants, shops, hot tubs and accommodations blocks.

It's all very comprehensive, but oddly lacking in soul. Then again, there are places around the park that charge around this much for four walls and a pit toilet, so if comfort's your thing, go for it.

Crow's Nest CABIN **$$$**
(Map p282; ☎907-683-2723; www.denalicrowsnestcabins.com; Mile 238.5, George Parks Hwy; cabins $249-299; 📶) Rustic but proud might describe the feel of the Nest's rooms, arranged in terraced rows that afford better and better views the higher you go. Beds are fluffy and comfortable and cabins have pleasant terraces and en-suite bathrooms. The lodge runs a free shuttle bus into the park (5am to 10pm).

Grande Denali Lodge HOTEL **$$$**
(Map p282; ☎855-683-8600; www.denalialaska.com; r $399-479; P 📶) The pro here is the location, perched like an eagle's nest over the George Parks Hwy and high above the cacophony of Canyon. The con is the price, which doesn't really match the plain, unimaginative rooms. Solution: linger in the lodge's comfy communal areas and admire the stupendous view.

The affiliated **Denali Bluffs Hotel** (Map p282; www.denalialaska.com/denali-bluffs-hotel; Mile 238, George Parks Hwy; r $300-380; 📶) is further down the hillside.

McKinley Village

Six miles south of the park entrance, McKinley Village (Mile 229–231, George Parks Hwy) sits at a cozy bend of the Nenana River. Though small, the area is far less commercialized than Canyon and is served by a courtesy bus ($5, 6am to 10pm) running between the Denali Park Village lodge (in McKinley Village), Canyon and the park's visitor center and WAC. If you need to withdraw money, Denali Park Village has an ATM in the lobby.

Denali Grizzly Bear Resort CABIN **$$**
(☎866-583-2696; www.denaligrizzlybear.com; Mile 231.1, George Parks Hwy; campsites $27, tent cabins $38-44, dry cabins $78-105, cabins $122-329, hotel r $249; 📶) The 'Grizzly' spans pretty much every price range and configuration, including wooded campsites by the Nenana River, platform tent-cabins, and

well-spaced cabins in various styles. Some cabins are modern and come with private bath, river views and kitchen, while others have tons of Alaskan character (including one log cabin that was dismantled and brought in from Fairbanks).

There's also the on-site Cedar Hotel, with river-facing rooms and cabin-like interiors. Note that dry cabins do not have running water or toilets. Communal amenities include hot showers and laundry facilities.

Denali Park Village LODGE **$$$**
(☎800-276-7234; www.denaliparkvillage.com; Mile 231, George Parks Hwy; r from $379; P) This log-cabin-style complex is still a fine place to enjoy a deckside drink overlooking the Nenana River. Rooms sport a liberal use of wood, but overall it's a generic-looking place with online deals making it much more attractive at times.

The lodge runs a courtesy shuttle to the Denali Visitor Center, WAC and Canyon. It's free for guests and $5 for everyone else.

Carlo Creek

Located 12 miles south of the park entrance (Mile 224, George Parks Hwy), this is one of the best places to stay near Denali, especially for independent travelers looking for a chilled-out experience that includes a gorgeous mountain backdrop. Most of the businesses here are family run, with some now seeing the second or third generation taking over.

There's good hiking nearby – stop in at the Denali Mountain Morning Hostel to get the lowdown on area tramps. The hostel, Perch Restaurant & Cabins and Panorama Pizza Pub all offer shuttle services to the park. It's definitely nice to have wheels, though, if you decide to stay here.

Denali Mountain Morning Hostel HOSTEL **$**
(☎907-683-7503; www.hostelalaska.com; Mile 224.1, George Parks Hwy; dm & tents $34, cabins $85-170; P) Perched beside the gurgling Carlo Creek, this is the area's only true hostel. That's cool – it makes up in quality for a lack of hostel quantity. The setting is a dream – mountains to one side, a stream running through it all. The hostel features a hotchpotch of tent-cabins, log cabins and platform tents. Only open during summer.

There's a fire pit, and visitors can cook meals and swap tales in the 'octagon' – the hostel's common area. Laundry facilities are available and the hostel offers free shuttle services to/from the park's Wilderness Access Center throughout the day.

Carlo Creek Lodge CABIN **$$**
(☎907-683-2576; www.denaliparklodging.com; cabins without bath $84-90, with bath $120-149; P @) The 32-acre grounds here, nestled amidst the mountains, are nothing short of spectacular, and the hand-hewn log cabins are filled with genuine old-Alaskan charm. Maintained by the descendants of the original homesteaders who settled this scenic little plot by the creek, the lodge has a fresh feel but still a healthy respect for tradition.

Communal amenities include a laundry room, spiffy shower block, barbecue and cooking areas.

McKinley Creekside Cabins CABIN **$$**
(☎907-683-2277; www.mckinleycabins.com; cabins $169-229; P) This is a friendly, well-run place with the most modern cabins in Carlo Creek. Given that the grounds aren't well treed, it's best to get a creek-side cabin so you can enjoy the warble of the water and the wide-open views from your porch. The popular cafe at the front of the premises serves some tasty home-cooked fare, including breakfasts. Larger cabins are available for $369.

Healy

Healy (Mile 249.5, George Parks Hwy), a pleasant decentralized community about 12 miles north of the park entrance, has a range of lodging options, but you'll need your own vehicle if you plan to stay here.

★**EarthSong Lodge** CABIN **$$**
(☎907-683-2863; www.earthsonglodge.com; Mile 4, Stampede Rd; cabins $175-255; P) North of Healy, off Mile 251 on the George Parks Hwy, this spotlessly clean lodge is pretty much on its own in green fields above the treeline. The private-bath cabins have an appealing at-home styling, with decorative touches such as sprays of wildflowers and hand-carved ornaments.

Breakfast and dinner are available in the adjacent Henry's Coffeehouse and there are sleddog demos, a nightly slide show and dogsled and cross-country-skiing tours in winter. The lodge is just a short climb away from stunning views of the mountain, and just in case you wanted to know more about that peak, proprietor Jon Nierenberg, a former

Denali ranger, quite literally wrote the book on hiking in the park's backcountry.

Denali Dome Home B&B B&B **$$**
(907-683-1239; www.denalidomehome.com; 137 Healy Rd; r $245;) This is not a yurt but a huge, intriguing geodesic house on a 5-acre lot, offering a fantastic B&B experience. There are seven modern rooms (with partial antique furnishings), an open common area with fireplace, and a small business area. Also: it's a dome home! How cool is that?

The owners are absolute oracles of wisdom when it comes to Denali, and do a bang-up job with breakfast. They also offer car rental.

Denali Park Hotel MOTEL **$$**
(866-683-1800; www.denaliparkhotel.com; Mile 247, George Parks Hwy; r $149-154;) 'Moose in the grounds!' is a regular cry at this hotel, which is actually more like a motel in terms of facilities and appearance. The communal areas are a different matter, encased inside a couple of old Alaska Railroad carriages and impossible to miss from the main road.

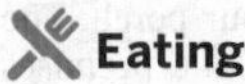

Eating

Groceries are limited and expensive in the Denali area, so stock up before you arrive. Inside the park itself there are no restaurants, except Morino Grill. Luckily, the neighboring towns are not far apart, so there's a good variety of eating and drinking options to choose from. You can easily stuff yourself wandering around the Canyon area.

Note that many restaurants either close or have considerably reduced hours in winter.

Within the Park

Morino Grill BURGERS **$**
(Map p282; Mile 1.5, Park Rd; mains $8-13; 11am-6pm;) This cafeteria-style establishment is the only eatery within the park. It has burgers, paninis and veggie chili, as well as seafood chowder and reindeer stew. There's a cafe and to-go section at the front, but the sandwiches are pricier than at the Mercantile.

Riley Creek Mercantile DELI **$**
(Map p282; Mile 0.2, Park Rd; sandwiches $5-8; 7am-11pm;) The Mercantile has a decent selection of groceries, as well as fresh coffee, deli sandwiches and wraps. There's also a small selection of camping supplies, such as gas, head nets and trail mix.

Canyon

★**Black Bear Coffee House** CAFE **$**
(Map p282; 907-683-1656; www.blackbeardenali.com; Mile 238.5, George Parks Hwy; mains $6-13; 6am-8pm;) Serving coffee worthy of a hip Seattle-based barista, along with jolly decent coconut cake and strong wi-fi, this place is a knee-weakening apparition to people who've been living off camping food for the last few weeks.

★**Prospectors Pizzeria & Ale House** PIZZA **$$**
(Map p282; 907-683-7437; http://prospectorspizza.com; Mile 238.9, George Parks Hwy; pizza $20-31, mains $15-19; 11am-11pm, bar to 1am;) Perennially busy and with good reason! Set in the Old Northern Lights Theater building, this cavernous alehouse-cum-pizza-parlor has quickly become one of the most popular eating establishments in the park area. In addition to a menu with two-dozen oven-baked pizza choices, there are some 50 beers available on tap from almost all of Alaska's small breweries.

★**Moose-AKa's** EASTERN EUROPEAN **$$**
(Map p282; 907-750-4961, 907-687-0003; www.facebook.com/Mooseakas; Mile 238.9, George Parks Hwy; mains $9-24; 10am-10pm Tue-Sun, from 5pm Mon;) There are lots of young Eastern Europeans working the tourism season in Alaska, and this restaurant is testimony to the fact. Started by a Serbian former season worker turned American, Moose-AKa's serves fried crepes, schnitzel, Russian salad, stuffed peppers and of course, moussaka. It's vegan- and vegetarian-friendly, and a great departure from the usual burgers and pizza.

Denali Park Salmon Bake AMERICAN **$$**
(Map p282; 907-683-2733; www.thebakerocks.com; Mile 238.5, George Parks Hwy; mains $16-30; 11am-3am) The better-on-the-inside 'Bake' offers some quirky starters, such as Yak-a-dilla (locally raised yak quesadilla), and a well-regarded halibut and chips. The bar is open 24/7 and there's a free 24-hour shuttle. Popular and *very* casual.

Overlook Bar & Grill AMERICAN **$$$**
(Map p282; 907-683-2723; www.denalicrowsnestcabins.com; Mile 238.5, George Parks Hwy; breakfast $15-18, dinner mains $19-64; 6-10:30am & 5pm-midnight;) This restaurant serves locally sourced breakfasts and dinners – think blueberry sourdough pancakes

in the morning, and prosciutto-wrapped halibut in the evening. It's good, but hey, anything tastes nice when matched with those valley views.

McKinley Village

★229 Parks AMERICAN $$$
(☎907-683-2567; www.229parks.com; Mile 229, George Parks Hwy; dinner mains $23-42; ⏱8-11am & 5-10pm Tue-Sun;) South of McKinley Village, this stylish timber-frame hideaway is quintessentially modern Alaskan: locally owned, organic and fervently committed to both the community and environment.

Everything is made on-site, including the bread and butter, and the menu changes daily, though it usually features local game dishes and a veritable cornucopia of vegetarian options.

And don't worry if you can't finish every mouthful: scraps go to feed local sled dogs. Reservations definitely recommended.

Carlo Creek

Perch Restaurant & Cabins AMERICAN $$
(☎907-683-2523; www.denaliperchresort.com; Mile 224, Parks Hwy; breakfast $8-13, dinner mains $14-28; ⏱6-11am & 5-11pm) It's called the Perch for a reason, as the restaurant sits high on a moraine above Carlo Creek, with an almost-eye-level view of the surrounding peaks.

It's just a quick jaunt from the highway, however, and on a sunny day a meal or drink on the deck should be mandatory. Try the steak, the salmon, or the enormous cinnamon rolls.

There's a free shuttle to and from the park. Perch also offers **cabins** (cabins incl breakfast buffet $89-180; P).

Panorama Pizza Pub PIZZA $$
(☎907-683-2623; Mile 224, George Parks Hwy; 12in pizzas $16-23; ⏱5-10pm, bar to 2am;) This eatery was once the family's gift shop but now offers good beer, burgers and pizza pies, with midsummer salads coming from a Healy-based organic grower.

Later at night the place becomes more pub than pizzeria, with locals, travelers and seasonal workers congregating for live music, open mics and pub quizzes.

Panorama shares a free shuttle with Perch Restaurant & Cabins so you can get here even if you aren't staying in Carlo Creek.

Healy

Miner's Market & Deli DELI $
(Mile 248, George Parks Hwy; ⏱6am-9pm) A surprisingly good selection of groceries (including fresh produce) can be purchased at this market attached to a gas station. The deli even sells breakfast, sandwiches and Prospectors Pizzeria slices.

Rose's Café DINER $$
(☎907-683-7673; Mile 249.5, George Parks Hwy; mains $7-20; ⏱7am-9pm;) This classic breakfast, burger and pie joint is a good option if you're in Healy. The covered outdoor seating area out the back and authentic diner-style counter seating add to its *Nighthawks*-meets-*Easy Rider* appeal.

Drinking & Nightlife

★49th State Brewing Company BREWERY
(www.49statebrewing.com; Mile 248.4, George Parks Hwy; ⏱11pm-1:30am) You can have the *best* evening out in Denali at this multifarious place which is 1) a brewpub brewing its own fine ales; 2) a wonderful flame-grilled restaurant; 3) a live-music venue; and 4) a dedicated purveyor of dozens of whiskeys. A celebratory atmosphere is generated at the communal tables both inside and out, where fun games shorten the wait for your food.

Also out front is the famous Magic Bus from the Sean Penn film *Into the Wild*. The actual bus used by Chris McCandless is 28 miles along the nearby Stampede Trail. Brewery tours with free tastings take place on Fridays at 4pm.

Entertainment

Charles Sheldon Center ARTS CENTER
(☎907-683-2597; www.denali.org/campus; Mile 231, George Parks Hwy) At the back of the Denali Park Village in McKinley Village, this community center holds local talks and speeches, art shows and theatrical and musical performances, all designed to 'inspire personal connections to Denali.'

Shopping

Cannabis Cache MARIJUANA
(Map p282; ☎907-683-2633; www.denaliscache.com; Mile 238.9, George Parks Hwy; ⏱10am-9pm Mon-Sat & from noon Sun May-Sep) This popular pot shop sells a wide range of edibles and smokeables.

Denali Mountain Works SPORTS & OUTDOORS
(Map p282; ☎907-683-1542; www.denalimountainworks.com; Mile 239, George Parks Hwy; ⊙9am-9pm) This jam-packed Canyon store sells camping gear, clothing and pretty much anything you'd need for a few days in the backcountry. It also rents out tents, stoves and other outdoor gear, and has dehydrated meals.

Alaska Geographic Bookstore BOOKS
(Map p282; ☎907-274-8440; Mile 1.5, Park Rd; ⊙8am-6pm) This inviting bookstore has field guides, topographic maps, coffee-table books and Alaskan literature.

Information

MEDICAL SERVICES

Canyon Clinic (☎907-683-4433, 907-455-6875; Mile 238.6, George Parks Hwy; ⊙9am-6pm) Only open during summer months but on call 24 hours.

Interior Community Health Center (☎907-683-2211; Mile 0.5, Healy Spur Rd) In the Tri-Valley Community Center in Healy.

MONEY

There are ATMs in most of Canyon's big hotels. The closest full-service bank is in Healy.

TOURIST INFORMATION

Denali Visitor Center (Map p282; ☎907-683-9532; www.nps.gov/dena; Mile 1.5, Park Rd; ⊙8am-6pm late May–mid-Sep) The place to come for an executive summary of Denali National Park & Preserve, with quality displays on the area's natural and human history.

Wilderness Access Center (WAC; Map p282; ☎907-683-9532; Mile 0.5, Park Rd; ⊙5am-7pm late May–mid-Sep) There's a general-purpose info desk, cafe, snack and gear shop, but the WAC's main function is as the park's transport hub and campground-reservation center.

Getting There & Away

Located on George Parks Hwy, about 240 miles north of Anchorage and 120 miles south of Fairbanks, Denali is easy to access without your own vehicle.

BUS

Alaska/Yukon Trails (☎907-479-2277, 907-888-5659; www.alaskashuttle.com) heads north from Anchorage ($65), departing between 7am and 7:30am depending on where you board the bus, and arriving at Denali around 1pm. From Fairbanks ($55), it leaves southbound around 8:45am, hitting the park around noon. Check its website or call ahead for pick-up points.

Park Connection (☎800-266-8625; www.alaskacoach.com) runs two buses a day from major Canyon hotels to Anchorage ($90, departing 7am and arriving 1:30pm, and departing 1:45pm and arriving 9pm) and one a day to Seward ($155, departing 7am and arriving 5:45pm; buses leave Seward at 10:30am and arrive at the park at 8:30pm). From Anchorage, the buses leave at 6:30am (arriving 12:30pm) and 3pm (arriving 8:30pm) for Denali ($90).

Anchorage-bound Park Connection buses will also stop in Talkeetna ($65; about 2½ hours from the park). If you're arriving on a cruise line in Whittier, you can hop on a Park Connection bus at 9:45am that will have you in Anchorage for the 3pm bus to Denali, which arrives at 8:30pm; total fare from Whittier is $155.

TRAIN

The most enjoyable way to arrive or depart from the park is aboard the **Alaska Railroad** (☎800-544-0552; www.alaskarailroad.com), with its viewing-dome cars that provide sweeping views of Denali and the Susitna and Nenana Valleys along the way. All trains arrive at the depot beside the visitor center (p288), only staying long enough for passengers to board. The northbound *Denali Star* departs from Denali at 4pm and reaches Fairbanks at 8pm; the reverse leaves Fairbanks at 8:15am and arrives at Denali at 12:10pm. The southbound *Denali Star* departs Denali at 12:30pm and gets into Anchorage at 8pm; the reverse departs Anchorage at 8:15am and arrives at Denali at 3:40pm. The one-way fare to/from Anchorage starts at $167; to/from Fairbanks starts at $73.

Getting Around

The area between Canyon and McKinley Village is well served by public transport. North or south, you may need your own car, though Denali Mountain Morning Hostel (p285) in Carlo Creek provides limited transport to the Wilderness Area Center, as does Panorama Pizza Pub (p287).

From Canyon, it's a not-unpleasant 2-mile walk to the park entrance area.

Within the park itself is a good system of free and paid shuttle buses.

WITHIN THE PARK

Shuttle buses are big, clunky, school-bus-style affairs aimed at wildlife watchers and day-hikers, with the occasional bus also carrying bicycles. The drivers are concessionaire employees, not NPS naturalists, but most provide unofficial natural-history information en route. Day-hikers don't need a backcountry permit and can get off anywhere (and multiple times) along Park Rd. After hiking, flag down the next bus that comes along and produce your bus-ticket stub.

Due to space considerations, you might have to wait a bus or two during peak season. The bus to Wonder Lake heads into the park as early as 5:45am, but the usual ones to Toklat or Eielson start running around 7am. The last returning bus (from Eielson) leaves around 6:30pm; check carefully when the last bus from your destination returns. Also note the exact schedule changes every year. It's wise to reserve a seat as far in advance as possible. The cost varies, and there are three-for-two passes, allowing three days of travel for the price of two. Sample return fares include Savage River (Mile 14, free), Toklat River (Mile 53, $26.50), Eielson Visitor Center (Mile 66, $34), Wonder Lake (Mile 85, $46.75) and Kantishna (Mile 92, $51).

Camper buses ferry overnight campers, backpackers and cyclists, offering ample space to stow gear. To take these buses you must have a campsite or backcountry unit reserved along Park Rd, or be toting a bicycle. If you don't have a campground booking, you can't ride *in* on the camper bus, but you can probably hitch a ride *back* on one. The buses cost $34 to anywhere along the road. As with shuttle buses, it's good to reserve as far ahead as possible.

The free Riley Creek Loop Bus makes a circuit through the park entrance area, picking up at the visitor center every half hour and stopping at the Murie Science & Learning Center, Horseshoe Lake trailhead, WAC, park headquarters and Riley Creek Campground. The park also has a free Dog Sled Demo Bus, which departs the visitor center for the park headquarters 40 minutes before each sled-dog demonstration.

OUTSIDE THE PARK

The useful Salmon Bake Shuttle runs from the park's WAC (p288) and visitor center to Healy via Canyon's hotels. It's particularly handy for those wishing to enjoy an evening microbrew at 49th State Brewing Company (p287). Tickets are $5 for a day pass. Buses run 4:30am to 3:30am.

Many other restaurants and lodges run their own shuttle buses, which means you can get about reasonably well without your own vehicle. Some charge $5 while others are free if you're staying or eating (or if the driver can't be bothered charging you). Some have regular pick-ups, while others will come for any potential customer at any time. For more information, inquire at the WAC.

GEORGE PARKS HIGHWAY

This ribbon of highway, drizzled ever so lovingly over vast stretches of wilderness, offers one of Alaska's top road journeys. From a beginning at the junction with Glenn Hwy (35 miles north of Anchorage), the Parks Hwy runs 327 miles to Fairbanks, Alaska's third-largest city. Along the way it's a veritable Denali Alley, with a state park, national park and highway named after the Great One. And while there's no doubt about everyone's final destination, the rest is no mere sideshow. There are views that won't be outdone later, a half-dozen local-favorite hikes and paddles, and one spunky former boomtown that's now most everyone's idea of a good time.

Mileposts along the highway indicate distances from Anchorage.

Talkeetna

907 / POP 876

It takes a few things to climb Denali, and among them are extensive logistical infrastructure and being a special kind of crazy. When those two elements collide, you get a town like Talkeetna: a hub for climbers, tourists, and idiosyncratic Alaskans with a slightly crunchier take on the state's 'Do what you will' libertarian mindset. Fact: in 1997, the town elected a cat named Stubbs as its mayor.

The name Talkeetna comes from the Athabascan language, and means 'Place of Many Gift Stores.' Kidding! It actually means 'Riverside food cache,' but we think our jokey take works, as 'downtown' Talkeetna is a strip of gift shops, guide services, restaurants and old-school saloons. And it's awesome: artsy, playful, infused with community spirit, but also self-aware enough to market itself to the thousands who come here seeking a view of Denali and a dip in the funky energy that permeates the mountain's main climbing base.

Sights

Fairview Inn HISTORIC BUILDING

(101 Main St; 11am-2:30am) Though not an official museum, the Fairview Inn might as well be. Founded in 1923 to serve as the overnight stop between Seward and Fairbanks on the newly constructed Alaska Railroad, the inn is listed on the National Register of Historic Places. As it is officially a bar, you need to be 21 or over to get in.

Its old plank-floored saloon is classic Alaska: its walls are covered with racks of antlers, various furry critters and lots of local memorabilia. One corner holds Talkeetna's only slot machine; another is devoted to President Warren G Harding. When the railroad was finished in 1923, Harding arrived in Alaska and rode the rails to the Nenana River, where he hammered in the golden spike. Talkeetna locals swear (with grins on their faces) that he stopped at the Fairview Inn on the way home, was poisoned and wound up dying in San Francisco less than a week later. Ever since, the Fairview has remained a fine place to be poisoned.

Talkeetna Riverfront Park PARK

FREE Three rivers – the Talkeetna, Susitna and Chulitna – come together here like an aquatic Voltron to form the Big Susitna River (which is technically the Susitna River), which eventually empties into Cook Inlet. This is a good spot to view Denali, assuming conditions are clear. There are public restrooms on-site.

Talkeetna Cemetery CEMETERY

(E 2nd St; 24hr) FREE This beautiful cemetery is rife with wildflowers, so much so that it feels more like a secret garden than a space for the dead. Among the interred bodies are bush pilots and memorial stones to mountain climbers who perished trying to climb Denali.

Talkeetna Historical Society Museum MUSEUM

(907-733-2487; www.talkeetnahistoricalsociety.org; off D St; $5; 10am-6pm May-Sep, 11am-4pm Sat & Sun Oct-Apr) A block south of Main St, look for this small complex of restored buildings that includes the town's 1936 schoolhouse, a fully furnished trapper's cabin and a train depot. There are exhibits devoted to bush pilots, trapping and mining artifacts, but the real highlights are the talks about Denali given by park rangers using fantastic scale models of the mountain.

Pick up the museum's *Historic Walking Tour* brochure if you want to head out and explore more old buildings around town.

Activities

Hurricane Turn Train RAIL

(800-544-0552; www.alaskarailroad.com; round-trip from Talkeetna adult/child $104/52; Thu-Mon mid-May–mid-Sep) Sometimes called the 'Local' or the 'Bud Car,' this flagstop train (one of the last still running in America) provides a local rural service from Thursday through Sunday (and some major holidays) in summer.

Departure from Talkeetna is at 1pm for the trip north to Hurricane Gulch, where the train turns around and heads back the same day.

The train takes you within view of Denali and into some remote areas, and because it goes slower and is less noisy than the *Denali Star*, your chances of spotting wildlife are greater.

You also have a better opportunity to mingle with local residents, many of whom use this line to access hunting locations, or simply enjoy it as a nostalgic journey from another era.

During the winter, the train operates once a week (on Thursdays) and travels between Anchorage and Hurricane Gulch, north of Talkeetna.

Sun Dog Kennel DOG SLEDDING

(907-733-3355; www.sundogkennel.com; $75) Ever wondered how sled dogs are trained and raised? Take a tour of the kennels owned by pro-mushers (dogsled keepers) Holden and Gerald Sousa, play with the puppies and, if you want, take a sled-dog ride over local trails. Call or book online to make reservations.

Hiking & Cycling

One of the easiest but most scenic walks in the area begins at the end of Main St, on the sandy banks of the Talkeetna River. There are pinch-yourself views of Denali across the waterway on a clear day.

Just south of town, a cycling/walking route parallels Talkeetna Spur Rd almost 14 miles back to Glenn Parks Hwy. At Mile 12 (2 miles south of town), the road begins to climb and, behind you, Denali suddenly fills half the sky.

Just a little further is the turn for Comsat Rd, which quickly leads to the Talkeetna Lakes Park Day-Use Area, offering short hikes around X and Y Lakes.

From the lakes you can either retrace your route back to town or continue up Comsat Rd and take the first left at Christiansen Lake Rd.

In a short while, you'll pass Christiansen Lake (where you can swim) and then reach a dead-end at a lookout with views over the river flats and, if you're lucky, to Denali in the distance.

The trail past the stop sign leads to Beaver Rd, which eventually runs into F St. You can follow this road back to Talkeetna Spur Rd just south of town. Pick up a copy of *Talkeetna Town & Trail Map* for a rough map of this and other routes.

Belle's Interpretive Trail WALKING

FREE All around town, you'll see interpretive signs marking the route of this trail, which winds past some of Talkeetna's more important historical sites. It's a flat, easily walkable route; ask at the Talkeetna Historical Society for a map.

Tours

Climbing

Alaska Mountaineering School CLIMBING

(907-733-1016; www.climbalaska.org; 13765 3rd St) This local guiding company leads several expeditions up Denali; the cheapest trip (up the West Buttress) costs $8300. It also offers mountaineering courses (from $2600), backpacking trips ($675) and helicopter hikes ($1375), among other trips.

Flightseeing

Many flightseeing tours to Denali depart from Talkeetna, both because it's an intrinsically exhilarating experience and because flights are actually cheaper from here than from within Denali National Park. Plan on spending anywhere between $220 and $460 per person for a flight; with a larger group, you may be able to wrangle a discount.

Sheldon Air Service FLIGHTSEEING

(907-733-2321; www.sheldonairservice.com; 22703 S Terminal Ave; tours $210-365) Sheldon offers a slate of three air tours, with glacier landings costing $90 extra. It also offers charter flights that follow Iditarod race mushers from the sky (p396; $550).

Talkeetna Air Taxi SCENIC FLIGHTS

(907-733-2218; www.talkeetnaair.com; 14212 E 2nd St; tours $210-325; 9am-5pm) Offers four different trips year-round to see Denali from every conceivable angle, starting with the one-hour South Face tour. You can land on a glacier for around $95 more, depending on the tour.

K2 Aviation SCENIC FLIGHTS

(907-733-2291; www.flyk2.com; 14052 E 2nd St; flightseeing tours $220-460; 7:30am-9pm) Aside from standard flightseeing tours, this company teams up with a Denali National Park concessionaire to offer fly-in day-hiking trips ($495).

Fishing

Fishing around Talkeetna is amazing, with runs of every species of Pacific salmon plus grayling, rainbow trout and Dolly Varden.

Phantom Salmon Charters FISHING

(907-733-2400; www.phantomsalmoncharters.com; 22228 Talkeetna Spur Rd; 9am-6pm Mon-Fri, 7am-7pm Sat & Sun) Arranges custom fishing charters in covered, heated boats along the region's three rivers. Pop into the office for details, or call or email to ask about rates.

Nature & River Tours

Talkeetna River Guides RAFTING

(907-733-2677; www.talkeetnariverguides.com; 13521 N Main St) To get out onto Talkeetna's many nearby waterways, Talkeetna River Guides will put you in a raft for a placid two-hour float on the Talkeetna River ($79) or a four-hour float on the Chulitna River through Denali State Park ($129). The guides are a fun-loving, youthful bunch, but fair warning: they do all the paddling – this isn't an active rafting trip.

Want to pop into the office? Look for the big yurt on Talkeetna's main street.

Alaska Nature Guides WALKING

(907-733-1237; www.alaskanatureguides.com; nature walks/hikes/rafting trips from $59/99/239) Offers various nature adventure tours around Talkeetna and Denali State Park; options include helicopter-assisted hikes ($443), hiking and rafting trips, and simple nature walks around the region's forests and lakes.

Mahay's Jet Boat Adventures BOATING

(907-733-2223; www.mahaysjetboat.com; adult/child from $75/57) This company offers three jetboat tours along local rivers; the longest (adult/child $175/132) ventures into the white water in Devil's Canyon via Denali State Park. It's a tourist trap, but it's a fun one. If you want a more active adventure, look elsewhere.

Ziplining

Denali Zipline Tours ZIP LINE

(855-733-3988, 907-733-3988; www.denaliziplinetours.com; 13572 Main St; adult/child $149/119) This zipline strung up in Talkeetna's forest canopy has nine lines and three high-flying suspension bridges, meaning you can stay up in the trees for three hours. It's the most northerly zipline in North America.

Sleeping

Talkeetna Roadhouse HISTORIC HOTEL $

(907-733-1351; www.talkeetnaroadhouse.com; 13550 E Main St; dm $23, d $60-90, tr $77-102, 2-person cabins $112-160;) The real Alaskan deal, this roadhouse dates from 1917 and maintains five small private rooms, a bunkroom, a couple of rustic cabins out back, and walls covered with Alaskan history dating back to frontier days. In keeping with the old-time setting, it's shared bath all the way. Cabin rates rise or fall based on the number of guests.

River Park Campground CAMPGROUND $
(off Main St; tent sites $10) This informal place (with self check-in) at the end of Main St is a popular camping spot for seasonal workers and backpackers living on the extreme cheap. No RVs and no hookups, but there is a public toilet onsite.

Talkeetna Hostel International HOSTEL $
(907-733-4678; www.talkeetnahostel.com; 22159 S I St; camping/dm/r $15/25/65;) This friendly, basic hostel has two small dorms and a private room. It's a popular base for Denali trekkers and the usual backpacking community, all of whom give it solid reviews. You can also camp on the hostel grounds and chill out in the main common area, which is full of tourist info.

★Denali Fireside Cabins & Suites CABIN $$
(907-733-2600; www.denalifireside.com; 22647 Talkeetna Spur Rd; ste $189, cabin $209-229;) Upscale, centrally located (for town) and embellished with only-in-Alaska decor, this place is a jolly good deal for the price, and far more intimate than the large lodges beloved by cruise passengers. The separate cabins look sparkling new and are equipped with fireplaces, decks and kitchenettes.

Meandering Moose Lodge LODGE $$
(907-733-1000; www.meandering-moose-lodging.com; 14677 E Cabin Spike Ave; cabins with breakfast $90-175, B&B r $90-150;) Sitting 2 miles northeast of the town center, this collection of cabins – all with amusing moose-themed titles – balances rustic charm and creature comforts. Private log cabins hold plenty of extra space in funky hideaway lofts, and feature full kitchens and bathrooms (except the lowest-priced ones, which share).

The B&B cabin features modern rooms, a shared living space and kitchen, and an interior design that wouldn't be out of place in a high-end suburb.

There's a shuttle service from Talkeetna and its train station.

Talkeetna Eastside Cabins CABIN $$
(907-903-6202; www.talkeetnaeastsidecabins.com; 22102 S H St; yurt/cabin/home $130/170/200, r $130-155;) You're spoiled for accommodation choice here. Options include a rustic-chic cabin, tastefully appointed rooms in a main house, a comfy entire-home rental, and our favorite option – a pretty yurt that perfectly fits the quirky Talkeetna outdoors vibe.

Talkeetna Alaskan Lodge RESORT $$$
(907-733-9500, 888-602-3323; www.alaskacollection.com; 23601 Talkeetna Spur Rd; r $200-265, ste from $300;) This high-end Alaska Native Corporation–owned lodge has a hillside setting with excellent views of the Alaska Range. Rooms are spacious and quietly stylish, and cruise-ship guests (a big chunk of the clientele) and noncruise-ship guests are housed in different buildings. Check the massive stuffed bear in the lobby.

Eating

You won't go hungry for food or choice in Talkeetna, and just to make it easy, almost everything is crowded onto a few blocks of Main St.

★Flying Squirrel Bakery Café AMERICAN $
(907-733-6887; www.flyingsquirrelcafe.com; Mile 11, Talkeetna Spur Rd; mains $7-13, pizza $13-22; 8am-9pm Thu-Sat, 9am-5pm Sun, 8am-5pm Mon & Wed;) Located a little ways outside of town, this Flying Squirrel soars above the competition (see what we did there?). There's no official menu, just a rotating list of seasonal pizzas, breads, sandwiches and baked goods that are expertly crafted and delicious to boot; there are plenty of vegan options. Often hosts art events and the occasional acoustic music performance.

★Talkeetna Roadhouse BREAKFAST $
(907-733-1351; www.talkeetnaroadhouse.com; 13550 E Main St; breakfast $9-14, dishes $5-7; 7am-4pm;) The oldest of old-school Talkeetna establishments, the Roadhouse is decked out in frontier-era kitsch and dishes out the best breakfast in town. The restaurant also doubles as a bakery, cooking up giant cinnamon rolls in the morning, and lasagna, pasties and salads during the day. The long table seating is great for meeting other travelers.

★Mountain High Pizza Pie PIZZA $$
(☎907-733-1234; www.pizzapietalkeetna.com; Main St; pizzas $12-25; ⏱11am-10pm; 🍴) Cold beers, outdoor patio, excellent pizzas and live music all come together in a pretty purple building that houses one of Talkeetna's better chill-out spots. There are plenty of toppings, from reindeer sausage to garlic oil to fresh basil. Did we mention the beer and live music?

Twister Creek Restaurant GASTROPUB $$
(☎907-733-2537; www.denalibrewingcompany.com; 13605 E Main St; mains $13-32; ⏱11am-10pm May-Sep, noon-9pm Sun-Thu, to 10pm Fri & Sat Oct-Apr) At the showcase restaurant for the Denali Brewing Company, you can pair your microbrews with cod sandwiches, burgers, Thai curry and reindeer meatloaf. There are better dining options in town, but this is a brewpub that hosts live music, so it's pretty popular.

★Wildflower Café SANDWICHES $$$
(☎907-733-2694; www.talkeetnasuites.com; 13578 E Main St; sandwiches $16, mains $29-38; ⏱11am-9pm Sun-Thu, to 10pm Fri & Sat; 🍷) This is one of the better dining options located on the Talkeetna main drag. Indulge with delicious burgers, fantastic fish and chips, daily specials that utilize Alaskan ingredients, and a deck facing Main St. There's also a good salad-menu selection if you need to fill up on greens.

Foraker Restaurant AMERICAN $$$
(☎907-733-9500; 23601 Talkeetna Spur Rd; mains $20-39; ⏱6:30-11am & 5-9pm; P🍷) Located within the Talkeetna Alaskan Lodge, the Foraker boasts jaw-dropping views of the Alaska Range from its elevated deck. Otherwise, the fine dining here is good, and puts an emphasis on fresh fish and seasonal Alaskan ingredients.

Drinking & Nightlife

Pretty much every joint in town will serve you a beer, and most of them have fine outdoor perches for people-watching.

★Fairview Inn BAR
(101 Main St; ⏱11am-2:30am) One of Talkeetna's most impressive historic buildings (p289) also happens to be its best bar. There's tons of old Alaskan history hanging from the walls, creaking floorboards, whiffs of sawdust, frequent live music, and a clientele of tourists and locals who will wear flannel and wolf T-shirts until the sun goes supernova. God bless this place.

Denali Brewing Company BREWERY
(☎907-733-2537; www.denalibrewingcompany.com; 13605 E Main St; ⏱11am-10pm) Beer from this popular local microbrewery has already found its way right across the state, but there's something about sipping from the source, and that's right here in Talkeetna. There's an outdoor garden facing Main St, where you can relax and enjoy whatever tipple you choose – it even carries local mead (honey wine).

Denali Brewing Company also has a **tap room** (☎907-733-2536; 37083 Talkeetna Spur Rd; ⏱11am-8pm) located off Talkeetna Spur Rd.

Entertainment

Denali Arts Council PERFORMING ARTS
(☎907-733-7929; www.denaliartscouncil.org; cnr D & E 1st Sts, Sheldon Community Arts Hangar) Based in the Sheldon Community Arts Hangar across from the museum, this outfit runs theatrical performances and an arts program throughout the summer. It also sponsors a family-friendly live outdoor music show in the Village Park (corner of Main St and Talkeetna Spur Rd) on Friday evenings.

Shopping

Kahiltna Gold Birch Syrup FOOD & DRINKS
(☎907-373-1309; www.alaskabirchsyrup.com; 38139 S Talkeetna Spur; ⏱10am-6pm May-Sep) Birch syrup is *kind* of like maple syrup – viscous, light amber to deep brown, sweet – but it's more difficult to make, and it's only available in select spots, like this little shop located near the beginning of the Talkeetna Spur Rd. Come here for tons of birch and syrupy goodies, Alaska souvenirs and a small tour of the facilities.

Information

MONEY

There are ATMs in **Nagley's** (☎907-733-3663; www.nagleysstore.com; 13650 E Main St; ⏱7:30am-9pm) and Twister Creek Restaurant (p293).

TOURIST INFORMATION

Walter Harper Talkeetna Ranger Station (☎907-733-2231; cnr 1st & B Sts; ⏱8am-5:30pm daily mid-April–mid-Sep, 8am-4:30pm Mon-Fri other months) Whether you're intrigued or boggled by high-altitude alpinism, this ranger station provides an excellent window into that rarefied world. In addition to coordinating the numerous Denali expeditions during spring and summer, the station functions as a visitor center, with maps, books, photos and video presentations about the Alaska Range. Hosts frequent ranger-led activities.

Getting There & Away

Talkeetna is an easy day trip from Anchorage. It can be reached by turning at Mile 98.7 on George Parks Hwy onto Talkeetna Spur Rd. This 14-mile paved road ends at the junction with Main St. Check the noticeboard outside the post office (behind Sheldon Community Arts Hangar) for information on shared rides.

Arriving by train is a good option. It's a gentle half-mile stroll from the station to Talkeetna's main drag.

BUS

Alaska Bus Guy (☎907-720-6541; www.alaskabusguy.com) Runs vans to Anchorage ($89; two hours), leaving at 3:30pm; the bus leaves Anchorage for Talkeetna at 6am.

Alaska/Yukon Trails (☎907-479-2277; www.alaskashuttle.com) Has buses departing from Talkeetna Roadhouse daily at 10:15am heading for Denali Park ($65, 2½ hours) and continuing on to Fairbanks ($92, 6½ hours). They also leave at 4:15pm for Anchorage ($62, 2½ hours).

TRAIN

From mid-May to mid-September, the **Alaska Railroad** (☎800-544-0552; www.alaskarailroad.com) train *Denali Star* leaves Anchorage at 8:15am and stops at Talkeetna (three hours; adult/child $101/51) and Fairbanks (Talkeetna to Fairbanks 6½ hours; adult/child $141/71). Talkeetna to Denali takes four hours and costs adult/child $95/48

Getting Around

Sunshine Transit (☎907-354-3885; fare $3) This community shuttle runs from town out to the George Parks Hwy, making stops anywhere passengers request. Buses run about every 20 to 30 minutes from 7:30am to 7pm Monday to Friday and 10am to 6pm Saturday.

Denali State Park

At 325,240 acres, Denali State Park is the fourth-largest state park in Alaska and is roughly half the size of Rhode Island. The park covers the transition zone between the coastal region and the spine of the Alaska Range, and among the dense forests you can look forward to distant views of towering peaks, including Denali and the glaciers on its southern slopes.

The park, which is run through by the George Parks Hwy, is largely undeveloped, but does offer a handful of turnouts, trails, rental cabins and campgrounds that can be reached from the main road. That said, you need to be better prepared for any hiking and backpacking adventures than at the same-named national park to the north. At the height of summer, experienced backpackers may want to consider this park as a hassle-free and cheaper alternative to its NPS-managed sibling

Activities

The excellent hiking trails and alpine routes crossing the park are popular with locals. Keep in mind that in the backcountry open fires are allowed only on the gravel bars of major rivers. Pack a stove if you plan to camp overnight.

The Chulitna River runs through the park. Floats can be arranged in Talkeetna.

Byers Lake Loop Trail HIKING
(Mile 147, George Parks Hwy) If you only have a few hours, but really want to get away from it all, head out on this easy 4.8-mile hike around the lake. The path begins at Byers Lake Campground, passes six hike-in campsites on the other side and then returns to the original campground after a bridge crossing.

If you want to go for a paddle across the lake, you can rent canoes or kayaks at the Byers Lake Campground through **Southside River Guides** (☎907-733-7238; www.denaliriverguides.com; Mile 147, George Parks Hwy; per hr/day $15/45).

Sleeping

Byers Lake Campground CAMPGROUND $
(Mile 147, George Parks Hwy; tent sites/cabins $20/70; P) In addition to its 70 sites, this campground offers walk-in sites along the loop trail around the lake, and the state park's Byers Lake cabins 1, 2 and 3. You can drive to cabin 1, cabin 2 is a half-mile hike from there, while cabin 3 is a further 70yd beyond that. Cabins can be reserved in advance online at the Division of Parks and Outdoor Recreation.

Denali Viewpoint North Campground CAMPGROUND $
(Mile 162.7, George Parks Hwy; tent sites $15) This handy outpost in the north of the park

(closer to the national park) has 20 sites around a parking lot and a few walk-in sites in a level glade up a slope.

Mt McKinley Princess Wilderness Lodge HOTEL $$
(907-733-2900; www.princesslodges.com; Mile 133, George Parks Hwy; r from $129;) More isolated, spread out and economical than other Princess lodges, the McKinley retains a laid-back rustic atmosphere that's not a million miles from a national park lodge. The view of the iconic mountain (should it reveal itself) from the main building's deck is probably worth the room rate alone.

Throw in hot tubs, a small cardio room and wooded grounds with four short trails and you'll quickly forget how crowded this lodge can get.

McKinley View Lodge HOTEL $$
(907-733-1555; www.mckinleyviewlodge.com; Mile 134.5, George Parks Hwy; r $100-120; cafe 8am-8pm) Charming is the word at this highway stop older than the highway itself. The place was first homesteaded in 1962 and is now run by Jean Carey Richardson, a children's author and daughter of the original owner. Come here for quaint economical rooms, decent cafe grub (mains $10 to $17) and a fork-dropping Denali (McKinley) view.

Information

Denali State Park Visitors Center (http://dnr.alaska.gov/parks/units/denali1.htm; Mile 147, George Parks Hwy; 8am-5pm Thu-Sun) At the Alaska Veterans' Memorial, just north of Byers Lake Campground. Volunteer staff are well informed about the area, and maps and brochures are available for sale.

Division of Parks and Outdoor Recreation (907-745-3975; http://dnr.alaska.gov/parks) Manages the state-parks system. The number given is for the Denali State Park ranger station.

Getting There & Away

The entrance to the park is at Mile 132.2 of the George Parks Hwy. The park is about 30 miles north of the turnoff for Talkeetna.

Cantwell & Broad Pass

The northern boundary of Denali State Park is at Mile 168.5, George Parks Hwy. Situated at Mile 203.6, Broad Pass (2300ft) is a dividing line: rivers to the south drain into Cook Inlet, while waters to the north flow to the Yukon River. The area is at the treeline and worth a stop for some hiking. The mountain valley, surrounded by tall white peaks, is unquestionably one of the most beautiful spots along George Parks Hwy or the Alaska Railroad – both use the low gap to cross the Alaska Range.

North from the pass, George Parks Hwy descends 6 miles to Cantwell (population 211), at the Denali Hwy junction. The 'town' is 2 miles west of the George Parks Hwy and Denali Hwy junction, on the extension of the Denali Hwy.

Sleeping

Cantwell RV Park CAMPGROUND $
(907-888-6850; www.cantwellrvpark.wordpress.com; off Denali Hwy; tent sites/RV/cabin $18/28.50/65;) This friendly, well-run RV park has on-site showers, tent sites and laundry facilities. The owners are happy to watch your pets as well (for an additional fee, of course).

Getting There & Away

Cantwell is located about 25 miles south of the main entrance to Denali National Park. There is no public transportation here.

Nenana

907 / POP 376

The only significant town encountered between Denali National Park and Fairbanks is Nenana (nee-*na*-nuh, like 'banana'), which lies at the confluence of the Nenana and Tanana (*tan*-uh-naw, not like 'banana') Rivers. Though the big industry is barging freight downstream, for visitors and northerners the community is most famous for the Nenana Ice Classic, an eminently Alaskan game of chance in which prognosticators guess when the ice will break up on the Nenana River.

Historically, this was little more than a roadhouse until it was chosen as the base for building the northern portion of the Alaska Railroad in 1916. On July 15, 1923, President Warren G Harding arrived to hammer in a golden spike on the northern side of the Tanana. The sickly Harding missed the spike the first two times, or so the story goes, but finally drove it in to complete the railroad.

Sights

Alaska Railroad Museum MUSEUM
(907-787-9784; 900 A St; 9:30am-6pm; P) FREE This little museum was a railroad depot back in the day, and displays railroad memorabilia and local artifacts ranging from ice tongs to animal traps. You can rent a room here, too (why not?), for $99 to $129; the rooms are cozy, and hey, how many times do you get to sleep above a history museum?

Alfred Starr Nenana Cultural Center CULTURAL CENTER
(415 River Front St; 10am-6pm; P) FREE This riverfront center informs visitors about local culture and history, and includes exhibits on the old riverboat trade and frontier days, plus a small but excellent collection of Athabascan artifacts and costumes.

Sleeping & Eating

Denali View Lodge LODGE $$
(907-832-5238; www.denaliviewlodge.com; 817 A St; r $115-199;) Modern rooms have that whole 'new student housing' vibe, but they're clean, and the more expensive ones are decked out in local art. The knowledgeable owners love Nenana and are happy to help you explore the region.

Monderosa Bar & Grill AMERICAN $$
(907-832-5243; Mile 309, George Parks Hwy; mains $10-24; 10am-10pm Mon-Fri, from noon Sat & Sun) Best burger in Alaska? That's the Monderosa's claim to fame, and while we haven't eaten *every* burger in the state, this one is a contender. Other winners off the menu include a chicken sandwich with melted pepperjack and jalapeños and a fine burrito. The bar has pool tables, cold beer and locals partaking of all of the above. Cash only.

Information

Nenana Valley Visitor Center (907-832-5435; www.nenana.org; 487 A St; 8am-6pm) A small visitor center located in a cabin with a sod roof.

Getting There & Away

Nenana is about 57 miles southwest of Fairbanks and 68 miles north of Denali. Most shops and businesses can be found off A St, which runs four blocks from the helpful Nenana Visitor Center, at the entrance to town, to the train station beside the river.

DENALI HIGHWAY

Still appearing ominously as a dotted line on maps, this 135-mile road was opened in 1957 as the only route to the national park. Now a secondary route, during the summer the road sees a steady flow of hikers, hunters, mountain bikers, anglers, bird-watchers, and adventurers. A highway in only the titular sense, Denali is basically a gravel road from Cantwell on George Parks Hwy to Paxson on Richardson Hwy.

As scenery and wildlife goes, this drive is absolutely stunning – you'll pass vast blankets of tundra and may spot grazing herds of caribou. Enjoy the views, because the road itself, though passable in a standard car, is slow going. Expect to average 30mph, taking six hours from end to end. Watch out for potholes and stretches of 'washboard' road if it's been raining.

Sights

Tangle Lakes Archaeological District ARCHAEOLOGICAL SITE
(http://dnr.alaska.gov/mlw/tlad) An enormous swath of land totaling some 226,660 acres, this district sandwiches the Denali Hwy between Mile 15 and Mile 32. Within the protected grounds are over 900 archaeological sites, many of which are thousands of years old. Three excellent hiking trails can be found within the district (a fourth was closed at the time of research).

Activities

Crazy Dog Kennels DOG SLEDDING
(www.dogsleddenali.com; Mile 42; kennel tours/dogsled rides per person $35/55) On the MacLaren River's far side is the summer operation of two-time Yukon Quest champ John Schandelmeier and his wife, Zoya DeNure, an Iditarod finisher. Passionate about their pups, they run the only dog yard in Alaska that rescues unwanted sled dogs and turns them into racers.

They have comfortable cabins on-site that run $90 to $100. Email to contact John and Zoya and arrange bookings.

Hiking

Several potential hiking trails – none signposted – branch off the highway in the dozen-or-so miles after Gracious House Lodge, a roadhouse at Mile 82. Use topographical maps and ask at lodges for clear directions and the latest on conditions.

MacLaren Summit Trail HIKING

(Mile 37) Starting across the road from the Osar Lake Trail, this 3-mile, mostly dry route runs north across the tundra to MacLaren Summit. This trail crosses federally protected land, so you can't bushwhack off the route.

Landmark Gap Trail HIKING

(Mile 24.6) This 3-mile trail leads north to Landmark Gap Lake, at an elevation of 3217ft. You can't see the lake from the highway, but you can spot the noticeable gap between the Amphitheater Mountains.

Swede Lake Trail HIKING

(Mile 16.2) From a trailhead on the southern side of the highway, this path (mostly used by motorized vehicles and mountain bikers) runs south about 10 miles to the Middle Fork of the Gulkana River. From here there's access to the Alphabet Hills and Dickey Lake.

Osar Lake Trail HIKING

(Mile 37) On the southern side of the highway, this easy 8-mile trail leads to Osar Lake and wide views of the MacLaren River valley. In August and September you'll be sharing the path with hunters.

Paddling

At Mile 118, pull in to begin a float down the silt-choked **Nenana River** if you have your own kayak or raft. The river can be paddled in class I to II conditions from here to George Parks Hwy, 18 river miles distant. Novices should pull out at that point, as after the highway it gets way hairier.

Delta River Canoe Route CANOEING

This 35-mile paddle starts at Tangle Lakes Campground and ends a few hundred yards from Mile 212.5 of the Richardson Hwy. After crossing Round Tangle Lake, the route continues to Lower Tangle Lake, where you must make a portage around a waterfall.

Below the falls is a set of class III rapids that you must either line for 2 miles or paddle if you're an experienced hand. Be warned, though, that every year canoeists damage their boats beyond repair on these rapids and have to hike 15 miles back to the Denali Hwy. After the rapids, the remainder of the route is a much milder trip, though there are still class II sections.

For a more thorough overview and map, download the *Delta National Wild and Scenic River* brochure from the BLM website (www.blm.gov).

Upper Tangle Lakes Canoe Route CANOEING

Though an easier and shorter paddle than the Delta River Canoe Route, this one does require four portages (unmarked but easy to work out in the low-bush tundra). The route starts at the Delta Wayside at Mile 21.7 of the Denali Hwy, and then passes through Upper Tangle Lake before ending at Dickey Lake, 9 miles to the south. There is a 1.2-mile portage into Dickey Lake.

From here, experienced paddlers can continue by following Dickey Lake's outlet to the southeast into the Middle Fork of the Gulkana River. For the first 3 miles the river is shallow and mild, but then it plunges into a steep canyon where canoeists have to contend with class III and IV rapids. Most canoeists choose to line their boats, though some make a portage. Allow seven days for the 76-mile trip from Tangle Lakes to Sourdough Creek Campground on the Gulkana River off the Richardson Hwy.

All paddlers trying this route must have topo maps. The useful BLM brochure *Gulkana National Wild River Floater's Guide* can be downloaded from the BLM website (www.blm.gov).

Tours

Denali Jeep Excursion DRIVING

(Map p282; ☎907-683-5337; www.denalijeep.com; Mile 238.6, George Parks Hwy; adult/child $169/99; ⏲tours depart 7:30am & 6:30pm summer) These jeep tours offer the opportunity to experience the highway for those without their own car. The five-hour trips go roughly halfway along the entire route from Cantwell. Jeeps travel in convoy with a guide and are equipped with CBs to aid communication. You can either handle the driving yourself, or travel as a passenger.

Sleeping

Clearwater Mountain Lodge B&B $

(☎907-203-1057; www.clearwatermountainlodge.com; Mile 82; r without/with breakfast $86/100, cabin $147; P) Accommodation skews toward the expensive when you get this deep into the bush, but the Clearwater is both reasonably priced and nicely appointed, with cozy rooms decorated with quilty Alaskan art and furs. You can also tent camp on the ground ($10). Breakfasts are delicious, and we want to come back for more of them.

Brushkana Creek Campground CAMPGROUND $

(907-822-3217; Mile 104.3, Denali Hwy; tent sites $12; P) If you can't find your own little hideaway tent spot off the highway, this campground offers 22 not-very-private sites, a picnic shelter, drinking water and a meat rack for the hunters who invade the area in late summer and fall.

★**Denali Highway Cabins** CABIN $$

(907-987-0977; www.denalihwy.com; Denali Hwy; tent cabin $195, cabins with breakfast $250-295;) A couple of hundred feet from the junction with Richardson Hwy, this place is pure Alaskan gold. It's got pedigree (it's the oldest running lodge on the highway), authority (it's run by naturalist Dr Audubon Bakewell, co-author of the *Birding in Alaska* guide) and fine accommodation.

The modern log cabins, each with a private balcony, sit along the Gulkana River, and feature real flush toilets, among other civilized comforts. There are also surprisingly cozy prefab tents and a communal 'great room' with books, grand piano and painting easel. The owners welcome guests on their highly regarded birding and river tours.

Tangle River Inn LODGE $$

(907-822-3970; www.tangleriverinn.com; Mile 20, Denali Hwy; r without/with bath $95/125, cabins $170, dm $48; P) Though at first it may appear to be a truck stop, this is in fact a well-run lodge with a good range of sleeping options. There are private cabins, family rooms and a bunkhouse (groups only) spread across the gravel hilltop. The restaurant serves tasty home-style meals with tranquil views of Sugarloaf Mountain and the Tangle Lakes thrown in for free.

The lodge is popular with anglers but come June, bird-watchers flock from all corners of the world to set their binoculars on Arctic warblers, wheateaters and golden plovers, among many other winged worthies.

MacLaren River Lodge LODGE $$

(907-331-3518; www.maclarenlodge.com; Mile 42, Denali Hwy; r with shared bath/cabins/r $$60/100/150;) The lodge sits on the edge of the MacLaren River and features a bar and restaurant open for breakfast, lunch and dinner. Some of the lodging is set inside Whitney's Cabin, the oldest cabin on the Denali Hwy, while the rooms are remodeled Atco units.

FAIRBANKS REGION

Fairbanks sits at the crossroads of a number of the region's major highways, and as such, there are several day trips and longer adventures to be had in the outlying areas. Along the Steese and Elliot Hwys you'll find plenty of good hiking and paddling. This being Interior Alaska, the minute you leave the suburbs, you are enfolded by the wilderness.

Fairbanks

907 / POP 32,751

Fairbanks is the only 'city' in the interior, and the largest settlement for hundreds of miles, but it has many characteristics of a small town. Everyone seems to know everyone, and 'everyone' includes some truly fascinating characters – sled-dog breeders, crusading environmentalists, college students, gun nuts, military personnel, outdoor enthusiasts, bush pilots, and the rest of the usual Alaska cast of oddities.

Because the city sits at the nexus of some truly epic routes – north to the Arctic, east to Canada and south to Denali – you'll almost inevitably end up spending time here, and that time is rarely boring.

This is a spread-out burg that's admittedly heavy on ugly strip malls, but the residential streets of compact downtown are pretty as a picture, and during winter, this is ground zero for viewing the aurora borealis.

History

The city was founded in 1901, as a result of a journey ET Barnette undertook up the Tanana River on the SS *Lavelle Young*. Barnette was hauling supplies to the Tanacross goldfields, but a detour up the shallow Chena River stranded him at what is now the corner of 1st Ave and Cushman St. Barnette could have been just another failed trading-post merchant in the Great White North, but local miners convinced him to set up shop. The following year the Italian prospector Felix Pedro (who had incidentally been one of Barnette's first customers) struck gold 12 miles north.

A large boomtown sprang to life amid the hordes of miners stampeding into the area, and by 1908 more than 18,000 people resided in the Fairbanks Mining District. In the ensuing decade, other gold rushes largely drained the population, but ironically the city's gold-mining industry was to outlast any other in the state.

While WWII and the construction of the Alcan and military bases produced the next boom in the city's economy, nothing affected Fairbanks quite like the Trans-Alaska Pipeline. From 1973 to 1977, when construction of the pipeline was at its height, the town was bursting at its seams as the principal gateway to the North Slope.

The aftermath of the pipeline construction was just as extreme. The city's population shrank and unemployment crept towards 25%.

By the late 1990s, however, the city was on the rebound – thanks to tourism and, once again, gold. Just north of town is the Fort Knox Gold Mine – Alaska's largest. In 2010 Fort Knox produced 349,729oz of gold and employed more than 400 workers.

Sights

★University of Alaska Museum of the North — MUSEUM

(Map p300; ☎907-474-7505; www.uaf.edu/museum; 907 Yukon Dr; adult/child $12/7; ⊙9am-7pm) In an architecturally abstract, igloo- and aurora-inspired edifice sits one of Alaska's finest museums, with artifact-rich exhibits on the geology, history, culture and trivia of each region of the state. You are greeted by an 8ft 9in, 1250lb stuffed bear and signposted around very well laid-out exhibits, which examine the state's regions as geographic *and* cultural units.

Upstairs, the Rose Berry Alaska Art Gallery covers 2000 years of northern works, including ancient ivory carvings, wood masks and contemporary photographs.

Morris Thompson Cultural & Visitors Center — CULTURAL CENTER

(Map p304; ☎907-459-3700; www.morristhompsoncenter.org; 101 Dunkel St; ⊙8am-9pm late May-early Sep, to 5pm mid-Sep–mid-May; P) There are a few contenders for 'best visitor center in Alaska' but this one, an ingenious mix of museum, info point and cultural center, has to be in the running. Inside are exhibits on Alaskan history and Alaska Native culture, as well as daily movies and cultural performances. Outside, on the grounds, don't miss the historic cabin and moose-antler arch.

The on-site Tanana Chiefs Conference Cultural Programs are designed to share Native culture with the wider world, and also ensure it survives to the next generation.

There are one-hour cultural performances (1pm, 3pm and 5pm), live craft-making demonstrations (schedule varies; call ahead) and the opportunity to make your own crafts under the guidance of Native artists.

Creamer's Field Migratory Waterfowl Refuge — NATURE RESERVE

(Map p300; ☎907-452-5162; www.creamersfield.org; 1300 College Rd; suggested donation $5; ⊙visitor center 9:30am-5pm Jun-Aug, trails 24hrs year-round; P 🚻) Birds have been migrating through this idyllic little stretch of farmland for millennia, and when the local dairy finally shut its doors, the community rallied to preserve the land. More than 100 species can now be seen in summer, including thousands of sandhill cranes during August.

The Farmhouse Visitor Center has a handbook to help you get the most out of the short trails through the nearby boreal forest and wetlands (bring bug spray). Volunteers also lead one-hour nature walks at 10am Monday through Saturday, and at 7pm on Wednesday, from June through August.

Large Animal Research Station — WILDLIFE RESERVE

(☎907-474-5724; www.uaf.edu/lars; 2220 Yankovich Rd; guided walk $10; ⊙guided walks 10am, noon & 2pm) If you can't make a trip to the Arctic for a little wildlife observation, consider visiting this research station that tends herds of musk ox, reindeer and caribou. The station studies the animals' unique adaptations to the sub-Arctic climate, and viewing areas outside the fenced pastures allow a free look at the herds any time.

To see the facility itself, you must partake in a 45-minute guided walk. When you're done, check out the on-site shop that sells qiviut hats and scarves. Qiviut is musk-ox wool spun very fine, an incredibly warm, soft and – fair warning – expensive natural fiber.

Fountainhead Antique Auto Museum — MUSEUM

(Map p300; ☎907-450-2100; www.fountainheadmuseum.com; 212 Wedgewood Dr; adult/child

Fairbanks

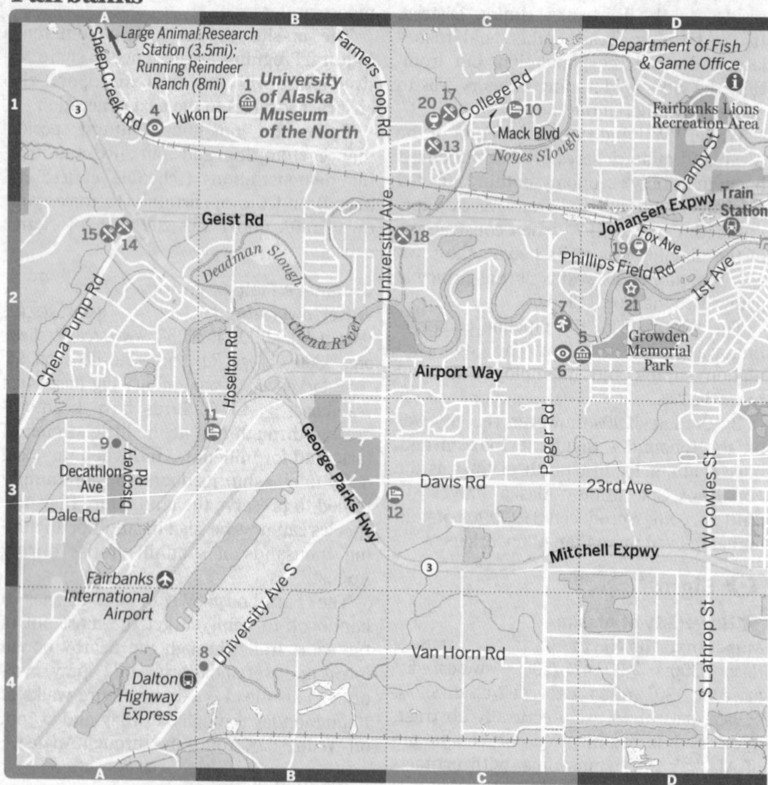

$10/5; ⏲10am-8pm Sun-Thu, 11am-6pm Fri & Sat; P) For a state with so few highways, this is a surprisingly comprehensive collection of 70 working antique vehicles, highlighting the evolution of the automobile from the late 19th century, as well as motor-vehicle history in Alaska.

Gearheads will love this place.

Georgeson Botanical Garden GARDENS
(Map p300; ☎907-474-1944; www.georgesonbotanicalgarden.org; 117 W Tanana Dr; suggested donation $5; ⏲8am-8pm; P) The severe Arctic and wild interior of Alaska are blessed with rainbows of wildflowers, which are all on display here.

The Georgeson Botanical Garden is a perfect picnic spot, as well as a 5-acre kaleidoscope of flowers, herbs, fruits and gigantic vegetables.

Golden Heart Plaza SQUARE
(Map p304; Between 1st Ave & Lacey St) FREE This square is meant to serve as a natural nexus point for downtown activity in Fairbanks. Within the riverside square, you'll see a clock tower, winter wildflowers, historical plaques, paved pedestrian paths that lead to the river, and an 18ft statue of an Alaskan family – Malcolm Alexander's *Unknown First Family.*

Fairbanks Community & Dog Mushing Museum MUSEUM
(Map p304; ☎907-457-3669; https://fairbankscommunitymuseum.wordpress.com; 535 2nd Ave; ⏲10am-7pm Mon-Fri, 11am-3pm Sun) FREE A small but packed museum that traces the city's history through old photos, newspaper clippings and historical artifacts from daily life.

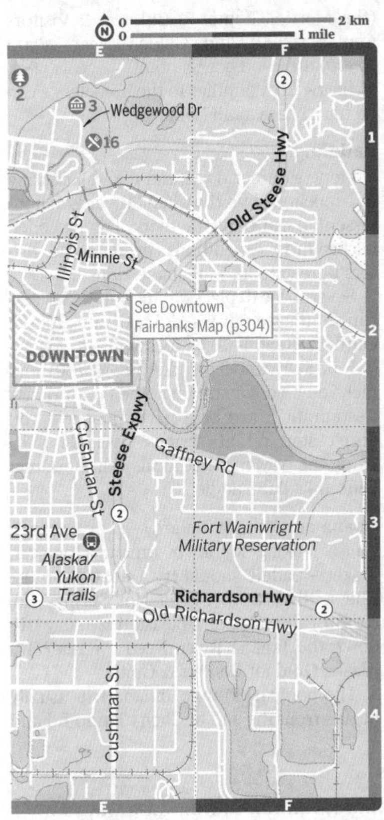

Fairbanks

One room focuses exclusively on sled-dog history and culture. The museum is located on the second floor of the Co-op Plaza Building.

Pioneer Park HISTORIC SITE
(Map p300; ☎907-459-1087; Airport Way; stores & museums noon-8pm late May-early Sep, park 5am-midnight; P) Like many cities with little surviving history, Fairbanks attempts to recreate the 'old' days in a historical theme park. Suffice to say, it doesn't always work. The most prominent sight in the rather dowdy 44-acre Pioneer Park is the *SS Nenana*, a hulking stern-wheeler that once plied the Yukon River. Many of the old homes and stores are relocated historic buildings.

You'll find dusty exhibitions on the olden days scattered here and there. Most interesting is the **Pioneer Air Transportation Museum** (Map p300; ☎907-451-0037; www.pioneerairmuseum.org; 2300 Airport Way; admission $4; noon-8pm May-Sep; P), which boasts some vintage planes. A miniature train, the **Crooked Creek & Whiskey Island Railroad**, gives rides (adult/child $2/1) around the park for an overview from noon to 7:45pm.

To get to Pioneer Park, take the Metropolitan Area Commuter Service Blue or Red Line bus.

Activities

Fairbanks has plenty to keep outdoor enthusiasts enthusiastic. Much of the best trekking and paddling, however, is well out of town. In winter the rivers freeze up, making ideal ski-touring trails.

Cycling

Fairbanks has a decent network of cycle routes in and around the city, and cycling is a feasible way to get around if you don't have a car. One of the more popular and scenic rides (about 17 miles long) is to head north on Illinois St from downtown, and then loop around on College Rd and Farmers Loop Rd/University Ave. You can pick up a free *Bikeways* map at the Morris Thompson Cultural & Visitors Center (p299), and should consider downloading the **Fairbikes** (☎907-687-6884; www.fairbikes.com) app and participating in the city's bike-share program.

Alaska Outdoor Rentals & Guides CYCLING
(Map p300; ☎907-457-2453; www.canoealaska.com; 1101 Pegger Rd; kayak per 8hrs/day $55/85, bike 4/24hrs from $20/35; ⊙11am-7pm) Located on the river behind Pioneer Park (p301), this small hut rents out mountain bikes, canoes, kayaks, SUP boards and other gear.

Hiking

Chena Riverwalk WALKING
FREE To soak up Fairbanks, talk a stroll along this series of paved pedestrian paths, which hugs the Chena for about 3.5 miles between Pioneer Park and Airport Way (the Morris Thompson Cultural & Visitors Center (p299) and Golden Heart Plaza (p300) are good access points). Locals of all stripes – from families to the homeless – can be found here at all hours.

Paddling

On long summer days (and nights), floating or canoeing down the Chena River is a quintessential Fairbanks activity. For extended backcountry expeditions, head to the visitors bureau (p309) for suggestions.

Several local places rent out boats and run shuttles to put-ins and take-outs: Alaska Outdoor Rentals & Guides will set you up (kayak/SUP/canoe per day $55/55/80) and pick you up downstream at the Pump House Restaurant. You'd be a party pooper if you didn't stop off at various riverside pubs along the way, in what locals call the 'Great Fairbanks Pub Paddle'.

Chena and Tanana Rivers CANOEING
Those looking for an overnight – or even longer – paddle should try a float down the Chena River from Chena Hot Springs Rd, east of Fairbanks, or a pleasant two-day trip down the Tanana River. Need a rental? Try Alaska Outdoor Rentals & Guides.

The popular 60-mile Tanana trip usually begins from the end of Chena Pump Rd and

THE NORTHERN LIGHTS

Fairbanks' best attraction is also its furthest flung: the aurora borealis, better known as the northern lights, which take place 50 to 200 miles above Earth. As solar winds flow across the upper atmosphere, they hit gas molecules, which light up much like the high-vacuum electrical discharge of a neon sign. The result is a solar-powered light show of ghostly, undulating colors streaming across the sky. In the dead of winter, the aurora can be visible for hours. Other evenings 'the event,' as many call it, lasts less than 10 minutes, with the aurora often spinning into a giant green ball and then fading. Milky green and white are the most common colors of the lights; red is rare. In 1958 the sky was so 'bloody' with brilliant red auroras that fire trucks rushed to the hills surrounding Fairbanks, expecting to find massive forest fires.

This polar phenomenon has been seen as far south as Mexico, but Fairbanks is the undisputed aurora capital. Somebody in northern Minnesota might witness fewer than 20 'events' a year, and in Anchorage around 150, but in Fairbanks you can see the lights an average of 240 nights a year. North of Fairbanks, the number begins to decrease, and at the North Pole the lights are visible for fewer than 100 nights a year.

Regrettably, from May to mid-August there's too much daylight in Alaska to see an 'event'. In late summer, the aurora generally begins to appear in the Interior, and can be enjoyed if you're willing to be awake at 2am. By mid-September the lights are dazzling and people are already asking, 'Did you see the lights last night?' As any Alaskan will tell you, the main benefit to an outhouse is the view you get of the aurora when nature calls at three in the morning.

The best viewing is in Fairbanks' outlying hills, away from city lights, or at the University of Alaska Fairbanks.

finishes in the town of Nenana, from where you can return with your canoe to Fairbanks on the Alaska Railroad.

Gold-Panning

If you've been bitten by the gold bug, Fairbanks is an ideal area to try your hand at panning. Get handouts and up-to-date information at the Alaska Public Lands Information Center in the visitors bureau (p309).

Popular places include the **Discovery Claim** on Pedro Creek off the Steese Hwy (across from the Felix Pedro Monument), and several other locations further up the highway.

Recreational gold-panning can be done as part of the Gold Dredge No 8 tour.

Wildlife Watching

Running Reindeer Ranch WILDLIFE WATCHING
(☎907-455-4998; www.runningreindeer.com; Ivans Alley; adult/child $55/35) Reindeer, if you didn't know, are domesticated caribou. Now that you've got the bar trivia handy, come to this ranch, where you can take a one-hour nature walk into the boreal forest with the resident family's own reindeer herd, watching the beasts snuff the ground, munch lichen, and generally be cute. Reservations required – they don't want drop-ins.

Tours

Alaskan Tails of the Trail DOG SLEDDING
(☎907-455-6469; www.maryshields.com; 2699 Waldheim Dr; adult/child $50/30) Well-known musher and writer Mary Shields (the first woman to complete the Iditarod sleddog race) offers an intimate two-hour glimpse into the life of a dog team and the Alaskans who raise and love them. You're asked to call first to confirm space and then make an online reservation.

The kennels are just north of the Large Animal Research Station (p299) on the UAF campus. Transportation is available to the kennels from downtown for $20, round-trip.

Northern Alaska Tour Company TOURS
(Map p300; ☎907-474-8600; www.northernalaska.com; 3820 University Ave S) Offers all sorts of packages, including a three-day tour ($1339 per person, based on double occupancy) that involves a drive up or down the Dalton Hwy (with a flight going the other way).

Northern Alaska Tour Co SCENIC FLIGHTS
(☎907-474-8600; www.northernalaska.com) The Arctic Circle may be an imaginary line, but it's become one of Fairbanks' biggest draws, with small air-charter companies doing booming business flying travelers on sightseeing excursions across it. This company offers flights to the Dalton Hwy (starting from around $480), day flights to Barrow ($900) and van tours across the Arctic Circle ($220), among many other options.

Riverboat Discovery BOATING
(Map p300; ☎907-479-6673; www.riverboatdiscovery.com; 1975 Discovery Dr, Mile 4.5, Airport Way; adult/child $64.95/39.95; ⊙tours 9am & 2pm) This 3½-hour tour navigates the Chena River on a historic stern-wheeler, stopping at a replica Athabascan village as well as the riverfront home and kennels of the late Susan Butcher, four-time winner of the Iditarod sleddog race. The boat leaves from **Steamboat Landing**, a replica of a historic trading post (if trading posts were massive tourist gift shops).

There's a '40 below' room on the boat, where you can experience the intense cold of an Alaskan interior winter day; the chamber is cooled to, you guessed it, 40 below zero.

Gold Dredge No 8 CULTURAL
(☎907-479-6673; http://golddredge8.com; 1803 Old Steese Hwy N; adult/child $40/25; ⊙tours 10:30am & 1:45pm) The arrival of the Alaska Railroad in 1923 prompted major mining companies to bring their money and their three-story-high mechanized dredges to the region. The behemoths worked nonstop, making mincemeat of the terrain. The most famous of these, Gold Dredge No 8, a five-deck, 250ft dredge, ran from 1928 to 1959 and uncovered 7.5 million ounces of gold.

Now listed as a national historic site, this is probably the most viewed dredge in the state. Despite the official address, it's off the Old Steese Hwy at Mile 10, Goldstream Rd.

Note that individual travelers must join a scheduled tour to enter, which includes an opportunity to do some recreational gold-panning.

Festivals & Events

World Eskimo-Indian Olympics CULTURAL
(www.weio.org; ⊙2nd-last weekend Jul) Taking place at the **Carlson Center** (Map p300;

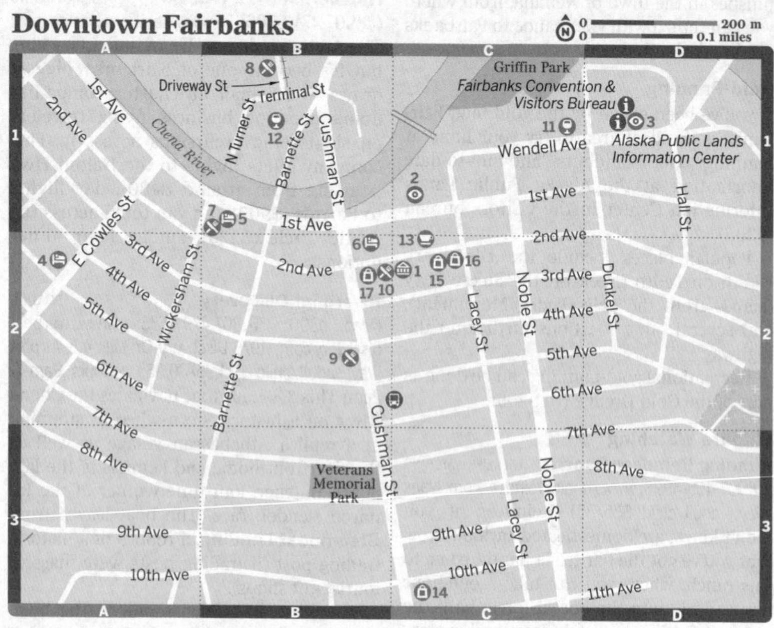

Downtown Fairbanks

Sights

1 Fairbanks Community & Dog Mushing Museum C2
2 Golden Heart Plaza C1
3 Morris Thompson Cultural & Visitors Center D1

Sleeping

4 Alaska Heritage House B&B A2
5 Bridgewater Hotel B1
6 Springhill Suites B2

Eating

7 Big Daddy's BBQ & Banquet Hall B1
8 LUNCH Cafe & Eatery B1
9 McCafferty's Coffee House B2
10 Soapy Smith's Pioneer Restaurant B2

Drinking & Nightlife

11 Midnite Mine C1
12 The Big I B1
13 Venue C2

Shopping

14 Alaska House Art Gallery C3
15 Bad Mother Vintage C2
16 Big Ray's C2
17 Lost & Found B2
Two Street Gallery .... (see 1)

Box Office 907-451-7800; http://carlson-center.com; 2010 2nd Ave), this four-day event attracts indigenous people from across the Far North, who display their athletic prowess in contests such as the Alaska High Kick and test their pain thresholds in games such as the Knuckle Hop. There's also dancing, cultural performances and plenty of traditional regalia.

Summer Solstice Celebrations CULTURAL

(www.downtownfairbanks.com; Jun) Festivities take place on or around June 21, when the sun shines for almost 23 hours, and include foot races, arts-and-crafts booths and the Midnight Sun Festival and Midnight Sun Baseball Game.

Sleeping

Fairbanks has more than 100 B&Bs, many in the downtown area; drop by the visitors bureau (p309) for brochures. There is an 8% bed tax. You'll also find some cheap motels downtown, which mostly seem to emit a sleazy vibe. Chain hotels can be found both downtown and in the strip-mall suburbs; they're comfortable and overpriced.

Sven's Basecamp Hostel HOSTEL, CAMPGROUND **$**

(Map p300; 907-456-7836; www.svenshostel.com; 3505 Davis Rd; tent sites $9, tipis/tents/cabins/treehouses $30/35/75/100;) Sven, from Switzerland, welcomes all kinds of travelers and vagabonds to this fine, multifarious hostel. This is where you'll meet some of Alaska's most intrepid, sweatiest explorers and hear plenty of travel tales. Accommodations are in cabins, shared tents, a plush treehouse or your own tent. Showers are coin-operated and there's table football, books, a movie room and kitchen.

Billie's Backpackers Hostel HOSTEL **$**

(Map p300; 907-479-2034; www.alaskahostel.com; 2895 Mack Blvd; tent site/dm $25/35;) An easy-breezy international scene makes this place regularly full in summer. Billie's has typical hostel amenities such as showers, laundry and kitchen, but it also offers nice touches such as a mosquito-netted communal tent for campers and free use of bicycles.

The hostel is off the MACS Red Line and not far from the university. The owners are incredibly nice and very flexible with check-in times, leaving luggage and so on.

Alaska Heritage House B&B B&B **$$**

(Map p304; 907-456-4100; www.alaskaheritagehouse.com; 410 Cowles St; r $130-220;) Probably the fanciest B&B in town, Heritage House was built in 1916 by Arthur Williams as a way to lure his future wife up to the Great White North to marry him. The home is on the national historic register, and each room has its own flair.

Bridgewater Hotel HOTEL **$$**

(Map p304; 907-456-3642; www.fountainheadhotels.com; 723 1st Ave; r $145; mid May-mid Sep;) Your best affordable option in what passes for downtown in Fairbanks, the Bridgewater is on the Chena River and abuts a pretty riverside walking path. Rooms, while unlikely to blow your mind, will keep you comfortable and there's a decent buffet breakfast and a handy free 'around town' shuttle.

It's part of a small family-run chain of four local hotels.

Springhill Suites HOTEL **$$$**

(Map p304; 907-451-6552; www.marriott.com; 575 1st Ave; r from $254;) A northerly branch of the Marriott empire, Springhill Suites is renovated and boasts clean, bland rooms spiced up with local artwork. You can't beat the location on the Chena River smack downtown for convenience. Amenities include an indoor pool and fitness center.

Pike's Waterfront Lodge LODGE **$$$**

(Map p300; 877-774-2400; www.pikeslodge.com; 1850 Hoselton Rd; r from $259, cabins $289;) This upscale lodge has an enviable position on the green banks of the Chena River. Room decor tilts toward the matronly, but there's also a row of spiffy log cabins with their own lawn.

Service is quick and friendly, local artwork adorns the public spaces, and amenities include a steam room, sauna, exercise facilities and the popular Pike's Landing (p306), with its Alaskan-sized deck facing the river.

In 2003, the Iditarod dogsled race finished here due to lack of snow further south. The event is memorialized in a pleasant iris garden.

Eating

Downtown

LUNCH Cafe & Eatery CAFE **$**

(Map p304; 907-455-8624; http://lunchcafeandeatery.com; 206 Driveway St, Suite A; mains $6-14; 8am-4pm;) Great coffee and an eclectic menu, featuring everything from Korean *bibimbap* (rice bowls) and falafel croquettes to pita sandwiches and organic salads, are the name of the game at LUNCH. The friendly spot is a magnet for young Fairbanks families and professionals.

Spice It Up INDIAN **$**

(907-388-7777; www.facebook.com/spiceitupfairbanks; mains $8-14) Track this excellent food truck down and don't let them leave until you've tried their curries or tandoori platters, served with heaped plates of yellow rice. The friendly owner takes a ton of pride in his food, and caters to an obsessively loyal fan base. They are very good at posting their schedule on Facebook.

McCafferty's Coffee House CAFE $
(Map p304; ☎907-456-6853; 408 Cushman St; baked goods $3-7; ⏰7am-6pm Mon-Thu, to 11pm Fri, 9am-11pm Sat, 9am-4pm Sun; 📶) Espresso emporium with good daily soups and baked goods. Striking up a conversation with the person at the next table is almost obligatory. Live music adds atmosphere on Friday and Saturday nights.

Big Daddy's BBQ & Banquet Hall BARBECUE $$
(Map p304; ☎907-452-2501; www.bigdaddysbarb-q.com; 107 Wickersham St; mains $9-19; ⏰11am-10pm Mon-Sat, noon-9pm Sun) This must be, as the owners claim, the northernmost Southern barbecue in the USA, and if you like slow-smoked ribs, juicy brisket, bowls of baked beans and creamy mac 'n' cheese, it does not disappoint. Wash it all down with one of the cold beers on tap, and roll yourself out the door when you finish.

Soapy Smith's Pioneer Restaurant AMERICAN $$
(Map p304; ☎907-451-8380; 543 2nd Ave; mains $10-24) It would be easy to dismiss Soapy Smith's as a gold rush-dusted twist on the themed family restaurant. But while there's tons of Alaska kitsch on the walls, there's something that feels sincere about this restaurant's execution – it's as close as Fairbanks gets to a gold-miners' mess hall. Cuisine is burger-style grub, along with some Alaskan reindeer sausage and halibut.

University Area

★LuLu's Bread and Bagels BAKERY $
(Map p300; ☎907-374-3804; www.lulusbagels.com; 364 Old Chena Pump Rd, Chena Pump Plaza; baked goods $2-5; ⏰6am-6pm Tue-Fri, 7am-5pm Sat & Sun) The coffee is carefully brewed and delicious; the baked goods, from rosemary bread to quiche, are gorgeous; and the bagels just get the day started *right*. All baked goods and breads are created on-site – no plastic-wrapped supermarket bagels sneak onto this menu.

Hot Licks ICE CREAM $
(Map p300; ☎907-479-7813; www.hotlicks.net; 3453 College Rd; cones from $3.50; ⏰noon-10pm Sun-Thu, to 11pm Fri & Sat Jun-Aug) There's no more quintessential Fairbanks summer solstice moment than buying a double scoop of this homemade ice-cream – which includes Alaskan-themed flavors such as wild berry and Silver Gulch stout – and watching the sun never set. For perhaps obvious reasons, Hot Licks is only open from spring until the end of August.

Pita Place MIDDLE EASTERN $
(Map p300; ☎907-687-2456; www.pitasite.com; 3300 College Rd; mains $5-9.25; ⏰11am-7pm Tue-Sat; 🌱) A humble food stand with a couple of pews indoors, picnic tables outside and delicious (and unexpected) Middle Eastern cuisine. The pitas are filled with falafel and made entirely from scratch, or you can grab hummus, tahini and other dips.

Lemongrass THAI $$
(Map p300; ☎907-456-2200; 388 Old Chena Pump Rd, Chena Pump Plaza; mains $14-38; ⏰11am-4pm & 5-10pm) Ignore the out-of-the-way, strip-mall setting – Lemongrass not only serves good Thai food, but good *Northern* Thai food. If that doesn't mean anything to you, there's still plenty of pad thai and green curry on the menu, but you can also find simmering bowls of *khao soi* (a type of noodle soup).

Wolf Run Restaurant AMERICAN, FUSION $$$
(Map p300; ☎907-458-0636; 3360 Wolf Run; mains $24-38; ⏰11am-10pm Tue-Thu & Sun, to 11pm Fri & Sat, 5-10pm Mon) Set in an old timber house that has been spruced up for guests, Wolf Run has long been known for its generous, super-sweet dessert plates, but also excels at gourmet food with a strong Middle Eastern influence. Of note are the meze plates, including a fine hummus dish, plus treats such as salmon on a cedar plank.

There's an outside patio, should the weather cooperate.

Airport Way & Around

Pho House AK VIETNAMESE $
(Map p300; ☎907-456-1086; 400 College Rd; mains $6-14; ⏰11am-8:30pm Tue-Sun, noon-7:30pm Mon; 🌱👶) If it's a cold night in Fairbanks, or you're hungover – actually, if you're just hungry – head to this family-friendly spot, which represents the flavors of Vietnam with *banh mi* sandwiches, steaming bowls of *pho* and other Vietnamese staples.

Pike's Landing AMERICAN $$$
(Map p300; ☎907-479-6500; 4438 Airport Way; mains $18-36; ⏰11am-11pm) For fine dining riverfront style, head to this restaurant, which has a cozy-cabin main dining room, a huge deck that looks out over the water and solid American-Alaskan mains: prime-

rib sandwiches, roasted salmon, coconut shrimp and the like. Reservations for dinner are a good idea.

Around Fairbanks

Turtle Club RIBS $$

(907-457-3883; Mile 10, Old Steese Hwy; mains $23-37; 5pm-2am) Drive about 10 miles out of town to the Turtle Club, which does not serve turtle and is not a club, but does boast a packed parking lot. Folks roll up for the prime rib, a local specialty – big, thick, juicy protein that gets you through an Alaskan winter night. Gloriously old school.

Silver Gulch Brewery BURGERS $$

(907-452-2739; www.silvergulch.com; Mile 11, Old Steese Hwy; mains $15-36; 4-10pm Mon-Fri, 11am-11pm Sat, 11am-10pm Sun) This cavernous, slightly overdone brewpub – the northernmost microbrewery in the US – makes jolly good beer, and plenty of people come just for the pub grub. Said food is fine; it doesn't match the beer for quality, but down a few and you won't care.

Drinking & Nightlife

The Big I BAR

(Map p304; 907-456-6437; 122 Turner St; 10am-2am Sun-Thu, to 3:30am Fri, 9am-2am Sat;) This excellent dive has a large outdoor drinking area, sassy bartenders, grizzled locals and lots of bush kitsch lining the walls, which look like they haven't been scrubbed since the time of the Bering land bridge. Live music acts liven up the scene on some nights.

Marlin BAR

(Map p300; 907-479-4646; 3412 College Rd; 4pm-2am Mon-Thu, to 3:30am Fri & Sat) Step into this dark cavern of a dive bar and discover a magic land of beards, flannel, punk stickers, more beards, tattoos, Fairbanks' edgiest musical acts, fantastic piercings, a sweet outdoor deck, and beards. One of our favorite spots for a live show in the area.

Midnite Mine BAR

(Map p304; 907-456-5348; 308 Wendell Ave; 10am-2am Sun-Thu, to 3am Fri & Sat) One of the best bonuses of this basement-level dive, with its dusty floors, beardy clientele, strong drinks and sports on the TV, is its downtown location. Had a few overly hopped Northwest IPAs? Walk your butt home from the Mine. Or stay for another – it's always a scene inside.

Venue CAFE

(Map p304; 907-374-3044; https://fairbanksalaska.com/venue; 514 2nd Ave; 8am-5pm;) Need a cool spot to sit down, drink coffee, check email and check out local art, crafts and music? Venue's got your back. The cafe area sits across from a gallery of local artistic goodness, and the wi-fi is strong. Huzzah. It also hosts music and performance events, natch.

Hoodoo Brewing Co BREWERY

(Map p300; 907-459-2337; www.hoodoobrew.com; 1951 Fox Ave; 3-8pm Tue-Fri, from 11am Sat) This Pacific Northwest-style brewery has an on-site tasting room that's kitted out in modern, minimalist decor. Get the sampler, which includes a stout, IPA and some pale blondes with interesting Germanic flavors (pale blonde *beers*. C'mon). There's a refined, non-pub-like atmosphere inside, especially on Saturday afternoon when they run free brewery tours (4pm).

Entertainment

Palace Theatre & Saloon THEATER

(Map p300; 907-452-7274; www.akvisit.com/the-palace-theatre; 2300 Airport Way, Pioneer Park; adult/child $22/11; show 8:15pm) Pioneer Park comes alive at night in this historical theater with honky-tonk piano, cancan dancers and other acts in the Golden Heart Revue, which recreates frontier-era Alaska for audiences.

Shopping

Lost & Found MUSIC

(Map p304; 551 2nd Ave; 11am-7pm Mon-Fri, to 8pm Sat) This little shop looks like an Alaskan closet that suddenly exploded into the world's coolest record collection, a nexus of vinyl that would make Nick Hornby characters nod in silent respect. The whole vibe of the place is enhanced by weird little odds, ends and doodads peppered throughout the store.

Alaska House Art Gallery ARTS & CRAFTS

(Map p304; 907-456-6449; www.thealaskahouse.com; 1003 Cushman St; 11am-6pm Tue-Sat) In a log building at the southern end of downtown, this gallery specializes in indigenous and Native-themed creations. Artists can often be found on the premises, demonstrating their talents or telling

WORTH A TRIP

ELLIOT HIGHWAY

From the crossroad with the Steese Hwy at Fox, just north of Fairbanks, the Elliot Hwy extends 154 miles north and then west to Manley Hot Springs (p311), a small settlement near the Tanana River. Along the way are a number of free campgrounds as well as public-use cabins (per cabin $25) that need to be reserved through the **BLM** (BLM; 907-474-2200; www.blm.gov) in Fairbanks.

The first half of the highway is paved, the rest is gravel, and there's no gas and few services until you reach the end. Diversions along the way are comparatively few, but the leisurely, scenic drive, coupled with the disarming charms of Manley Hot Springs, makes it a worthwhile one- or two-day road trip.

At Mile 11 is the **Lower Chatanika River State Recreation Area**, a 400-acre unmaintained park offering fishing, boating and informal camping opportunities along the Chatanika River.

At Mile 28, look for the Wickersham Dome trailhead parking lot and an information box. From here, trails lead to two public-use cabins. **Lee's Cabin** is a 7-mile hike in and overlooks the White Mountains. **Borealis-Le Fevre Cabin** is a 20-mile hike over the White Mountains Summit Trail.

At Mile 49.5, you'll enter (probably without realizing it) the 'settlement' of Joy (population 30), named for Joy Griffin, an original homesteader. Stop at the tumbledown wooden shop-cum-cafe known variously as **Wildwood General Store** or Arctic Circle Trading Post, which sells Arctic-themed souvenirs, coffee and rather nice muffins. Stock up as there aren't many more places like this further north.

Ten miles before the junction with the Dalton Hwy, at Mile 62, a 500yd spur road on the right leads to the public-use **Fred Blixt Cabin**.

Livengood (*lye*-ven-good), 2 miles east of the highway at Mile 71, has no services and is little more than a maintenance station with a scattering of log shanties. Here, the Elliot Hwy swings west and, 2 miles later, at the junction of the Dalton Hwy, the pavement ends and the road becomes a rutted, rocky lane. Traffic evaporates and until Manley Hot Springs you may not see another vehicle.

The rustic, privately managed **Tolovana Hot Springs** (907-455-6706; www.tolovanahotsprings.com; GPS: N 65°16.111', W 148°51.285'; 2-/4-/6-person cabins $65/125/160) can be accessed on a taxing 11-mile overland hike south from Mile 93. Facilities consist of outdoor wood tubs bubbling with 125°F (51°C) to 145°F (62°C) water, outhouses, a drinking-water barrel and three cabins that must be reserved in advance. The trailhead isn't signposted, so contact the managers for directions.

At Mile 110, a paved side road runs 11 miles to the small Athabascan village of **Minto** (population 180), which isn't known for welcoming strangers.

Beyond Minto, the Elliot Hwy briefly becomes winding and hilly, and then suddenly, at Mile 120, there's chip sealing for the next 17 miles. Hutlinana Creek is reached at Mile 129, and a quarter-mile east of the bridge (on the right) is the start of an 8-mile creekside trail to **Hutlinana Warm Springs**, an undeveloped thermal area with a rock-wall pool. The springs are visited mainly in winter; in summer, the buggy bushwhack seems uninviting.

From the bridge it's another 23 miles southwest to Manley Hot Springs.

stories. If you want an original piece of local art, this is a great spot to start your search.

Bad Mother Vintage VINTAGE
(Map p304; 907-456-1719; 511 2nd Ave; 11am-6pm) What's cool about this vintage shop is how Alaskan it is. Sure, there are outfits and clothes that edge into hipster territory, but most of them are functional too – the sort of cute but conventional clothes you could wear on a hike and then to a bar. It also sells accessories and local art and crafts.

Two Street Gallery ART
(Map p304; 907-455-4070; www.2streetgallery.com; 535 2nd Ave; 11am-6pm Mon-Fri, to 5pm Sat, to 4pm Sun) This excellent gallery showcases a well-laid-out collection of work by local artists. Both the prints and original artwork on display are often quite reasonably priced, which is a nice bonus. A great

spot for a unique souvenir, located in the downtown Co-op Plaza Building.

Information

MEDICAL SERVICES

Fairbanks Memorial Hospital (907-452-8181; www.foundationhealth.org; 1650 W Cowles St) Emergency care; south of Airport Way.

MONEY

Most strip-mall areas have a bank and ATM, and more bank branches and ATMs are popping up downtown.

Key Bank of Alaska (100 Cushman St) Has an ATM.

TOURIST INFORMATION

Alaska Public Lands Information Center (Map p304; 907-456-0527; www.alaskacenters.gov; 101 Dunkel St, Fairbanks; 8am-6pm) Located in the Morris Thompson Cultural & Visitors Center, this is the place to head if you're planning on visiting any state or national parks and reserves in the region. Pick up one of its detailed free brochures on the Steese, Elliot, Taylor and Denali Hwys.

Department of Fish & Game Office (Map p300; 907-459-7206; 1300 College Rd)

Fairbanks Convention & Visitors Bureau (Map p304; 907-456-5774; www.explorefairbanks.com; 101 Dunkel St; 8am-9pm late May-early Sep, to 5pm late Sep–mid-May)

Getting There & Away

AIR

Alaska Airlines (p429) flies direct to Anchorage, where there are connections to the rest of Alaska, the lower 48 and overseas, on a daily basis. There are also handy direct flights to Seattle with Delta and Alaska. For travel into the Bush, try **Ravn Alaska** (www.flyravn.com), **Warbelow's Air Ventures** (907-474-0518; www.warbelows.com; 3758 University Ave S) or **Wright Air Service** (907-474-0502; www.wrightairservice.com; 3842 University Ave).

BUS

Interior Alaska Bus Line (p321) leaves at 9:30am from the downtown **Transit Park** (Map p304; cnr Cushman St & 5th Ave) on Sunday, Wednesday and Friday for Delta Junction ($60, two hours) and Tok ($95, 5½ hours), where you can transfer to a bus for Glennallen and Anchorage. At Whitehorse you can catch the company's bus to Skagway. **Alaska/Yukon Trails** (Map p300; 907-479-2277; www.alaskashuttle.com) leaves daily around 8:45am from various points in Fairbanks (including the hostels) and travels down the George Parks Hwy to Denali ($55, three hours), Talkeetna ($92, seven hours) and Anchorage ($99, 10 hours). The company also has a 7am service to Whitehorse ($385, nine hours) via the Taylor Hwy.

Want to see the Arctic? The Dalton Highway Express (p372) runs all the way up to Deadhorse.

CAR & MOTORCYCLE

If you're driving to Fairbanks from Canada, you'll likely be coming up the Alcan Hwy. It's a good 590 miles (950 km) from Whitehorse (Canada) to Fairbanks, with little en route, save for Tok and a few other highway service communities. From Anchorage, it's 360 miles to Fairbanks up George Parks Hwy.

TRAIN

Alaska Railroad (907-458-6025; www.alaskarailroad.com) leaves Fairbanks daily at 8:15am from mid-May to mid-September. The train gets to Denali National Park & Preserve (adult/child $73/37) at noon, Talkeetna (adult/child $141/71) at 4:40pm, Wasila (adult/child $239/120) at 6:15pm and Anchorage (adult/child $239/120) at 8pm. The **station** (907-458-6025; www.alaskarailroad.com; 1031 Alaska Railroad Depot Road; 6:30am-3pm) is at the southern end of Danby St. **MACS** Red Line buses run to and from the station.

Getting Around

TO/FROM THE AIRPORT

Small, modern and well laid out, **Fairbanks International Airport** (Map p300; 907- 474-2500; www.dot.state.ak.us/faiiap) is at the west end of Airport Way, 4 miles from town. MACS Yellow Line buses swing by seven times a day Monday to Friday (three times on Saturday) between 7:30am and 7:15pm, charging $1.50 and taking you past some Airport Way motels en route to the Transit Park. The 15-minute taxi ride to the city is $18. Most of the main hotels along Airport Way and in downtown have airport shuttles. Free phones are available in the baggage claim.

CAR

All the national rental agencies (Avis, National, Budget, Payless, Hertz) have counters at the airport. However, to drive on the unpaved roads around Fairbanks, including the Dalton Hwy, you'll need to contact **Arctic Outfitters** (907-474-3530; www.arctic-outfitters.com; 3820 University Ave, Fairbanks International Airport east ramp). Expect to pay $200 a day, and note that rental taxes are very high (18%) and so are gas prices.

PUBLIC TRANSPORTATION

MACS (Metropolitan Area Commuter Service; ☎907-459-1010; http://fnsb.us/transport ation/Pages/MACS.aspx) is the fixed-route bus system for the Fairbanks region. There are nine lines, which run from roughly 6:30am to 9:30pm Monday to Friday, with limited service on Saturdays and no service on Sundays. The **Transit Park** is the system's central hub. Blue and Red Line buses run in loops linking the university district and downtown. The Green Line route heads to North Pole, and the Yellow Line to the airport. The fare on all routes is $1.50, or you can purchase an unlimited day pass for $3. Schedules are posted on bus stops and online.

TAXI

Uber is popular in Fairbanks. Otherwise, try **Yellow Cab** (☎907-455-5555).

Chena Hot Springs Road

This fireweed-lined, forest-flanked corridor parallels the languid Chena River 56 miles to the Chena Hot Springs Resort, the closest (and most developed) hot springs to Fairbanks. The road out here is paved and in good condition, so you've got a chance to penetrate some backcountry without wrecking your rental car.

From Mile 26 to Mile 51 the road passes through **Chena River State Recreation Area**, a 397-sq-mile preserve encompassing the valley and nearby alpine areas. Some of the Fairbanks area's best hiking, canoeing and fishing can be found here, usually just steps from the road.

Sights

Aurora Ice Museum MUSEUM
(☎907-451-8104; https://chenahotsprings.com/icemuseum; Mile 56.5, Chena Hot Springs Rd, Chena Hot Springs Resort; adult/youth $15/10; ⊙tours 11am, 1pm, 3pm, 5pm & 7pm) The interior of this building is kept to a frosty 25°F (-3.8°C) throughout the year. Visitors can marvel at a slate of ice sculptures while on a tour, or order a $15 appletini from the requisite on-site ice bar. Just remember the ice loo is only for show.

Activities

Dogsledding

Just Short of Magic DOG SLEDDING
(☎907-750-0208; http://justshortofmagic.com; 5157 Chena Hot Springs Rd; half/full hour mushing $65/95) The enthusiastic proprietors of this recommended spot love their dogs, and lead a variety of tours, including a two-hour intro-to-mushing school ($200).

They've also got a yurt on-site that functions as a B&B ($100).

Hiking

Angel Rocks Trail HIKING
A moderate two- to three-hour, 3.5-mile loop trail that leads to Angel Rocks, large granite outcroppings near the north boundary of Chena River State Recreation Area. The elevation gain is a modest 900ft.

The trail is also the first leg of the **Angel Rocks–Chena Hot Springs Traverse**, a more difficult, 8.3-mile trek that ends at the Chena Hot Springs Resort. Roughly halfway along the traverse is a free-use shelter.

The posted trailhead for Angel Rocks is just south of a rest area at Mile 49. The lower trailhead for the Chena Dome Trail (p269) is practically across the road.

Granite Tors Trail Loop HIKING
The 15-mile Granite Tors Trail Loop – accessed from the Tors Trail State Campground, at Mile 39.5 – ascends into an alpine area with unusual tors (isolated pinnacles of granite rising out of the tundra). The first set is 6 miles from the trailhead, but the best group lies 2 miles further along the trail.

This eight- to 10-hour trek gains 2700ft in elevation. There's a free-use shelter midway.

Paddling

Chena River CANOEING
With no white water and comparatively few other hazards, the peaceful Chena River offers a variety of day and multiday canoeing possibilities, with access points all along Chena Hot Springs Rd.

Thermal Baths

Chena Hot Springs THERMAL BATHS
(☎907-451-8104; www.chenahotsprings.com; Mile 56.5 Chena Hot Springs Rd; pass adult/child $15/12; ⊙7am-midnight) The burbling Chena Hot Springs were discovered by gold miners in 1905 and quickly became the area's premier soaking spot. At the heart of a 40-sq-mile geothermal area, the springs produce a steady stream of water that, at 156°F (69°C), must be cooled before you can even think about bathing in it.

Access to the hot springs is via Chena Hot Springs Resort (p312), which has aging indoor and outdoor facilities. The pure hot-spring water is for adults only; kids are allowed in an outdoor hot tub.

Chena Hot Springs Road

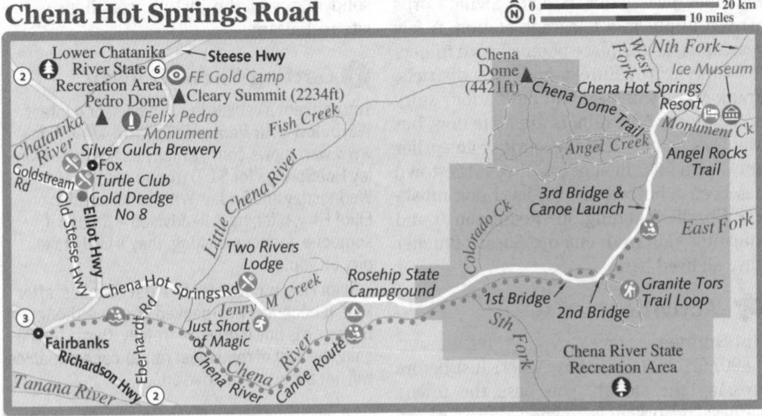

Tours

Geothermal Renewable Energy Tours ECOTOUR
(907-451-8104; www.chenahotsprings.com/renewables; Mile 56.5, Chena Hot Springs Rd; 2pm & 4pm) FREE The US's biggest oil state hides a potentially rich source of geothermal energy, as these tours at Chena Hot Springs Resort will demonstrate. The Chena plant was inaugurated in 2006 and these tours will enlighten you to the ins and outs of the valuable renewable resource. Tours are free, but you have to be a guest at the resort.

Sleeping

Rosehip State Campground CAMPGROUND $
(907-269-8400; www.reserveamerica.com; Mile 27, Chena Hot Springs Rd; campsites $15, cabins $35-60; P) The largest of the area's three campgrounds, Rosehip has a nature trail, nine public-use cabins, and well-spaced campsites, some located right on the riverbank.

Chena Hot Springs Resort RESORT $$$
(907-451-8104; www.chenahotsprings.com; Mile 56.5, Chena Hot Springs Rd; campsites $20, yurts with outhouse $65, r $209-309 restaurant mains $20-35; P) This come-as-you-are complex is a good example of what happens when a so-so property monopolizes the accommodation options in a given area and overprices their mediocre rooms. On the plus side, they're super into renewable energy thanks to the geothermal power of the springs.

The resort manages a lot of local tourism infrastructure, including access to the hot springs and the ice museum.

Eating

Two Rivers Lodge PUB FOOD $$$
(907-488-6815; http://tworiverslodge.com; 4968 Chena Hot Springs Rd; mains $24-37; 5-10pm Tue-Sun) Steak, seafood and poultry are the focus at this rustic lodge, which is fully kitted out Interior Alaska style, complete with hunting trophies, a lounge that's good for drinks, and a deck for those long Alaskan summer days.

Information

Alaska Division of Parks & Outdoor Recreation (907-269-8400; http://dnr.alaska.gov/parks) Contact to arrange camping permits at state parks.

Getting There & Away

Chena Hot Springs Resort runs a shuttle service from Fairbanks ($195 round-trip, two-person minimum), but you'd be better off renting a car. Hitchhiking is not too grand of an effort, thanks to heavy summer usage of the Chena River State Recreation Area.

Manley Hot Springs

907 / POP 89

At the end of a long, lonely road, the well-kept town of Manley Hot Springs is full of friendly people, tidy log homes and luxuriant gardens. Located between Hot Springs Slough and the Tanana River, the community was first homesteaded in 1902 by JF

Karshner, just as the US Army Signal Corps arrived to put in a telegraph station. A few years later, as the place boomed with miners from the nearby Eureka and Tofty districts, Frank Manley arrived and built a four-story hotel. Most of the miners are gone now, but Manley's name – and the spirit of an earlier era – remains. In modern times, the town has been a hotbed of high-level dog mushing: Charlie Boulding, Joe Redington Jr and four-time Iditarod champ Susan Butcher have all lived here.

Activities

Hot Springs THERMAL BATHS
(907-672-3213; per hr $5; 24hr) Just before crossing the slough, you pass the town's namesake, privately owned hot springs. Bathing takes place inside a huge, thermally heated greenhouse, which brings to mind a veritable Babylonian garden of grapes, Asian pears and hibiscus flowers.

Deep in this jungle are three spring-fed concrete tubs, each burbling at different temperatures. Pay your entrance fee (which gives you sole access to the springs for an hour), hose yourself down and soak away in this deliriously un-Alaskan setting. Heed the signs to not pick the fruit, but do call ahead to reserve a time slot.

Manley Boat Charters BOATING
(907-672-3271; boat rental per hr $75) Across the slough and 3 miles beyond the village is the broad Tanana River, just upstream from its confluence with the Yukon. Frank Gurtler can take you fishing or just show you the sights along the waterway.

Sleeping & Eating

Manley Lodge HISTORIC HOTEL **$$**
(Manley Roadhouse; 907-672-3161; www.manleylodge.com; 100 Front St; r without/with bath from $110/140, cabin $130; P) Facing the slough, this antique-strewn, century-old establishment has clean, uncomplicated rooms and is the social center of town. There's a bit of a frontier vibe to the spot, and, while it's certainly expensive for what you get, the friendly, take-no-guff-but-give-none-either attitude is appreciated.

Manley Lodge AMERICAN **$$**
(907-672-3161; www.manleylodge.com; 100 Front St; mains $17-26; 8am-8pm) Steak, ribs, salmon and pizza, plus big omelets and pancake platters in the morning, make up the solid mains at the historic roadhouse's on-site restaurant.

Getting There & Away

You can rent a vehicle in Fairbanks, or contact **Warbelow's Air Ventures** (907-474-0518; www.warbelows.com), which has flights to Manley Hot Springs for $170 (round-trip) on Monday, Wednesday and Friday. With so little traffic on Elliot Hwy, hitching is ill-advised – though if someone *does* come along, they'll likely take pity on you.

Elliot Hwy is paved for the first 73 miles; after that, it becomes well-packed gravel. Although the route is fine if driven carefully, this is technically the sort of road most rental-car companies will not allow you to drive on.

THE ALCAN-ALASKA HIGHWAY

One of the most impressive engineering feats of the 20th century, the Alcan stretches 1390 miles from Dawson Creek in British Columbia to Delta Junction in Alaska. A drive up (or down) the Alaska Hwy is one of those once-in-a-lifetime road trips that many folks dream of.

The highway was famously punched through the wilderness in a mere eight months in 1942, as part of a WWII effort to protect Alaska from expansionist Japan. Commonly known as the Alcan, short for 'Alaska–Canada Military Hwy,' it remains the only year-round overland route that links the 49th state to the Lower 48.

Approximately 300 of its miles, paved and well maintained, are within Alaska, between Fairbanks and the Yukon Territory border. The 98-mile stretch from Delta Junction to Fairbanks is 'technically' the Richardson Hwy, but most figure this to be the final leg of the Alcan and we, too, treat it as such.

Delta Junction

907 / POP 934

For most visitors, Delta Junction is notable for a technicality: it proclaims itself the end of the Alcan, as the famous highway joins Richardson Hwy here to complete the route to Fairbanks. The town began as a construction camp and picked up its name as it lies at the junction of the two highways. Most travelers use the town as a fuel and grocery stop, with a quick visit to the historic Sullivan Roadhouse, and Rika's Roadhouse and Landing. The big Deltana Fair takes place on the last weekend of July.

Sights

Big Delta State Historical Park PARK
(907-451-2695; http://dnr.alaska.gov/parks/units/deltajct/bigdelta.htm; Mile 274.5, Richardson Hwy; 8am-8pm; P) FREE This 10-acre historical park on the Tanana River preserves **Rika's Roadhouse and Landing**, an important crossroads for travelers, miners and soldiers on the Fairbanks–Valdez Trail from 1909 to 1947. You can easily spend a couple of hours wandering the pretty grounds and exploring buildings stocked with displays of turn-of-the-century farming and roadhouse life.

Sullivan Roadhouse HISTORIC BUILDING
(907-895-5068; junction Alaska & Richardson Hwys; 9am-6pm; P) FREE This classic log structure (on the National Register of Historic Places) was built in 1906 to serve travelers along the Fairbanks–Valdez Trail. In 1997 the cabin was moved, log by log, from Fort Greely to its present location and now serves as a museum with a collection of exhibits dedicated to travel in Alaska in the early 1900s – the roadhouse era.

Sleeping

Delta Junction is blessed with scads of nearby campgrounds and no bed tax.

Clearwater State Recreation Site CAMPGROUND $
(907-895-4599; 1415 Clearwater Rd; tent sites $15; P) With 17 wooded and well-spaced sites, most overlooking the peaceful Clearwater Creek, this is a lovely little spot to spend a night. The site is 13 miles northeast of Delta Junction. Clearwater Creek has good grayling fishing and some paddling options.

Quartz Lake State Recreation Area CAMPGROUND $
(907-451-2695; http://dnr.alaska.gov/parks/aspunits/northern/qtzlkcamp.htm; Mile 277.8, Richardson Hwy; tent sites/cabins $15/45; P) Covering 600 acres north of town (3 miles from the Richardson Hwy), this area has two camping areas and 103 tent sites. Both are accessible by road, and there is additional primitive camping at Bluff Point, accessible by a 3-mile trail starting near the lake. There are a few public-use cabins onsite as well.

★ **Garden B&B** B&B $$
(907-895-4633; www.alaskagardenbandb.com; 3103 Tanana Loop Extension; r without/with bath $89/109, cabin $129-149; P Wi-Fi) Located on what is possibly the neatest-looking farm you'll ever see, the Garden B&B grows its own vegetables (many of which find their way onto your breakfast plate) and tends a flower garden that looks as lush as a jungle. The rooms are instantly inviting – the cabins have kitchenettes – and the hosts are lovely.

Kelly's Alaska Country Inn MOTEL $$
(907-895-4667; www.kellysalaskacountryinn.com; 1616 Richardson Hwy; s/d $129/139; P Wi-Fi) Two blocks north of the visitor center, Kelly's has spacious, clean rooms, some with kitchenettes. It's old school, and either dated or charming depending on your tolerance for roadside Americana.

Eating

★ **Buffalo Center Drive-In** BURGERS $$
(907-895-4055; Mile 265.5, Richardson Hwy; mains $9-16; 11am-10pm Mon-Sat, from noon Sun Jun-Aug; P) At this novel Alaskan drive-in they bring heaped burger baskets out to your car, or you can enjoy them on an adjacent patio. The patties and relishes are excellent – the setting may be casual, but these are gourmet-level burgers. It also serves excellent fish and chips and ice-cream. Cash only.

Cave AMERICAN $$
(907-895-1074; 1596 Richardson Hwy; mains $10-27; 4-10pm Wed-Mon; P) Located in a strip mall, the Cave has a nice outdoor deck and a decent menu of chicken wings, prime rib steaks, salmon and pasta. It advertises itself as a wine bar, and there is indeed a decent selection of vino (and beer), so drink up, thirsty travelers.

Information

Delta Junction Visitor Center (907-895-5063; www.deltachamber.org; Mile 1422, Alaska Hwy; 8am-8pm) More a gift shop than a visitor center, this place at the junction of the Richardson and Alaska Hwys is usually jammed with RVers clamoring to purchase 'End-of-the-Alaska-Highway' certificates ($1). Take a glance at the giant, 'life-sized' mosquito statues.

Getting There & Away

Alaska/Yukon Trails (Map p300; ☎907-479-2277; www.alaskashuttle.com) Passes through on its way to/from Fairbanks and Dawson City (Sunday, Tuesday and Friday), or Whitehorse (Monday, Wednesday and Saturday).

Interior Alaska Bus Line (☎800-770-6652; www.interioralaskabusline.com) Stops in Delta Junction at 10:30am and 3:30pm on Monday, Wednesday and Friday on its run between Fairbanks ($40) and Tok; the bus picks up from the **IGA** (☎907-895-4653; www.igafoodcache.com; Mile 266, Richardson Hwy; ⏲6:30am-9pm Mon-Sat, 8am-8pm Sun). From Tok you can continue to Glennallen and Anchorage.

Tok

☎907 / POP 1258

If you've just stumbled carsick out of your bruised Buick after several hundred miles on the Alcan, Glenn or Taylor Hwys, Tok (pronounced *Toke*) might – briefly – seem like heaven on Earth. But after you've spent a night at one of its cheap motels, exhausted its oversized visitor center and given a cursory glance to the crapshoot of kitschy gift shops and eating joints, there's little reason to linger.

The town was born in 1942 as a construction camp for the highway, and was called Tokyo Camp until anti-Japanese sentiment caused locals to shorten it to Tok. From here, the rest of the state beckons: the Alcan heads 206 miles northwest to Fairbanks; the Tok Cutoff and Glenn Hwy reaches 328 miles southwest to Anchorage; and the Taylor Hwy curls back 161 miles to Eagle.

Sights

★Mukluk Land AMUSEMENT PARK

(www.muklukland.net; Mile 1317, Alaska Hwy; adult/child $5/2; ⏲2-8pm; P) It's hard to miss Mukluk Land. The entrance, after all, is marked by a giant red boot. But more importantly: you *shouldn't* miss Mukluk Land. Is it a theme park? Sure – this is Disney World... if Disney World were made by Alaska backwoods folks working with whatever they had at their fingertips. There may be no better manmade roadside attraction in the state.

At first glance, this looks like a junkyard. But within said junkyard is an odd tour of Tok and the Interior, with 'exhibits' ranging from an outhouse museum to World War II military vehicles, to pump-house generators, to a Santa Claus rocket ship (trust us), to several abandoned houses filled with a creepy doll collection that must surely be a portal to Hell. Funhouse games – Skee-ball, electronic darts, minigolf, and the like – abound, and of course, there's a bounce house in the middle of everything. Run by a retired schoolteacher and his wife, Mukluk Land even publishes its own newspaper, and hosts curious tourists and kids from Tok on a daily basis.

Sleeping & Eating

There is no bed tax in Tok. Hurray! You'll find a few campgrounds and roadside motels in the area.

Main Street Motel MOTEL $

(☎907-883-6246; www.mainstreetmotelalaska.com; Mile 1312.7, Alcan Hwy; r from $85; P 📶) Ask Alcan truckers to name the best accommodation in Tok and they'll probably surprise you with this boring-looking motel box that seems like a four-out-of-10 from the outside, but scores 10 out of 10 on most internal barometers, including friendliness, cleanliness and – important if you're on the Alcan – its welcoming 24-hour reception.

Moon Lake State Recreation Site CAMPGROUND $

(☎907-883-3686; http://dnr.alaska.gov/parks/aspunits/northern/moonlksrs.htm; Mile 1332, Alaska Hwy; tent sites $20; P) Fifteen campsites sit next to placid Moon Lake, 17 miles west of Tok. The lake has the closest thing to a sandy beach for miles around, so if it's deep summer (or another time of year and you're insane), you can bring some swim clothes and take a dip.

Caribou Cabins CABIN $$

(☎907-883-8080; www.cariboucabins.info; Borealis Ave; cabins from $159; P) Fancy a little woodsy privacy? Head to these cabins, which have a quilted, cozy kind of comfort. All cabins have front porches and TVs and microwaves, and some come with a hot tub and private bath.

Mooseberry Inn B&B $$

(☎907-388-5525; 3 Mae's Way; r from $135; P 📶) Just 2.5 miles west of Tok, this B&B has rustic yet surprisingly sharp and modern rooms, private balconies and big breakfasts served in a homey family atmosphere, making it one of the best options outside town. The friendly owner speaks German.

Fast Eddy's DINER $$
(907-883-4411; www.fasteddysrestaurant.com; Mile 1313.3, Alaska Hwy; burgers $8-12, pizzas $14-22; 6am-11pm;) One of the most famous eateries on the Alcan, Eddy's delivers decent diner food with a smile; we're a sucker for the pizzas. Portions will keep you or a small country fed.

Information

Tok Mainstreet Visitors Center (907-883-5775; Mile 1314, Alaska Hwy; 10am-7pm) Tok's main 'sight' is its visitor center, but it's a good one with ultra-friendly staff and info on pretty much everywhere and everything within a 500-mile radius.

Getting There & Away

Tok is about 110 miles southeast of Delta Junction and 85 miles northwest of the Canadian border.

Alaska/Yukon Trails (907-479-2277; www.alaskashuttle.com) Runs a charter service from Fairbanks to Dawson City, but needs at least two passengers to depart. The fare from Tok is $125.

Interior Alaska Bus Line (p321) Passes through Tok on Monday, Wednesday and Friday, stopping at the Three Bears Outpost at Mile 1313. From there, buses leave at 1:45pm, heading northwest to Fairbanks ($80, four hours) and southwest to Anchorage ($115, seven hours).

TAYLOR HIGHWAY

The twisty, turny, bush-as-all-get-out Taylor Hwy is the only road leading to what we like to think of as the 'bird towns': the gold-mining tourist trap of Chicken, and the sleepy, historic village of Eagle, perched on the banks of the Yukon River.

This is a road that traces and embraces a series of mountain ridges and ranges. Wildfires in 2004 and 2005 scarred many sections of the scenic drive, but the large swaths of burnt spruce create a 'Seussical' landscape, scenic in its own way.

The route was once infamously rough, but these days the only white-knuckle stretch is the last 65 miles from Jack Wade Junction to Eagle.

The highway closes in winter (generally from October to May), when you can still get to Eagle by plane, snow machine or dogsled.

Chicken

907 / POP 17

A place to buy gas, a gift shop, a few businesses selling coffee and beer – dusty Chicken was once a thriving mining center, but these days it's a bit of an overrated tourist attraction. The town's name allegedly originated at a meeting of resident miners in the late 1800s. As the story goes, the men voted to dub their new tent-city 'Ptarmigan,' since that chicken-like bird (now the Alaskan state bird) was rampant in the area. Trouble is, no-one could spell it.

In retrospect, the naming was a savvy move. Nowadays, folks flock here for 'I got laid in Chicken' caps and similar tat. There's an isolated, end-of-the-world feeling to Chicken that attracts a certain kind of self-imposed exile; we've found said exiles can either be friendly or distinctly chilly when dealing with outsiders.

Activities

The nearby Fortymile River is a popular recreational kayak route. Chicken Gold Camp rents out kayaks for $40 per half-day. Shuttle services are also available. The bridge over South Fork (Mile 75.3) marks the most popular access point for the Fortymile River.

Dominating the town's skyline is the **Pedro Gold Dredge**, which worked creeks in the area from 1959 to 1967.

Chicken Gold Camp offers gold-panning (four hours $10) near the dredge, and more advanced recreational mining down the road at a working claim where you can sluice your way to riches (per day $25 to $60). It's not unheard of for visitors to come away with an ounce of gold after a day's work.

Festivals & Events

Chickenstock Music Festival MUSIC
(www.chickenstockmusicfest.com; Jun;) This excellent, family-friendly quirk of a music festival attracts thousands of visitors – seriously – to tiny Chicken. Bluegrass and Americana music reigns supreme.

Sleeping & Eating

Chicken Gold Camp CABIN, CAMPGROUND $
(907-782-4427; www.chickengold.com; tent sites $16, RV sites $30-36, cabin $90-135, apt $150; cafe 7:30am-7:30pm;) On a spur road to the right as you enter Chicken, this camp offers workaday cabins and a gravel camping area. It's a friendly, family-run place, and the

DENALI & THE INTERIOR CHICKEN

cafe and saloon in the Chicken Creek Outpost are good hangouts.

Goldpanner CABIN, CAMPGROUND **$**

(907-505-0231; www.townofchicken.com; Mile 66.8, Taylor Hwy; tent sites $20, RV sites $32-40, 2-/4-person cabins $129/149, r $169; gift shop & restaurant 8am-10pm;) Just before Chicken Creek is another gravel lot featuring cabins, rooms, a gas station, a gift shop, and the only flush toilets in Chicken. There's a small restaurant on-site (the Chicken Burger Barn), open for breakfast, lunch and dinner, serving (imagine that) burger and fish fare.

Chicken Creek Cafe, Saloon & Mercantile Emporium DINER **$$**

(www.chickenalaska.com; breakfast & dinner $12-18; cafe 7am-8pm; P) This row of clapboard buildings across from Chicken Gold Camp makes the most of the chicken kitsch. The gift shop is extensive, the saloon has hats from every corner of the world, and the cafe, unsurprisingly, features lots of chicken on the menu (try the pot pie!), plus that wilderness staple – cinnamon buns.

Hours are pretty fungible. The saloon stays open depending on how busy it is – although don't expect it to rock out too late.

Getting There & Away

The Alaska/Yukon Trails (p310) bus stops at the Chicken Creek Cafe on its way between Fairbanks and Dawson City on Sunday, Tuesday and Friday. Otherwise, it's a good 90 minutes (80 miles) from here to Tok.

Fortymile River

Historic Fortymile River, designated as Fortymile National Wild River, offers an excellent escape into scenic wilderness for paddlers experienced in lining their canoes around rapids. It's also a step back into Alaska's gold-rush era; the river passes abandoned communities, including Franklin, Steele Creek and Fortymile, as well as some present-day mining operations.

Activities

All mile markers listed here apply to the Taylor Hwy.

Many paddlers put in at the West Fork Bridge (Mile 49) or South Fork Bridge (Mile 75) and push to the O'Brien Creek Bridge (Mile 112). If you're coming from the South Fork, expect the trip to take three days; along the way you'll cross Class III rapids. Starting at the West Fork the trip takes four to five days; again, rapids are in the Class II to III range.

For a greater adventure, continue paddling the Fortymile into the Yukon River; from here, head north to Eagle at the end of the Taylor Hwy. From O'Brien Creek Bridge, the trip is 90 miles, and you may cross Class IV water.

See the 'Fortymile Wild and Scenic River' pages on the **BLM** (BLM; 907-474-2200; www.blm.gov/ak; 8:30am-5pm) website for route planning, maps and more; you can also check out www.alaska.org/detail/fortymile-river for more information.

Eagle Canoe Rentals, in Eagle, is the closest place to get an expedition-worthy canoe or raft.

Getting There & Away

You'll need your own car to reach the bridge waysides that serve as put-in points for accessing the river. Chicken is located around Mile 65 on the Taylor Hwy. There are put-in points at Mile 49 and 75.

Eagle

907 / POP 85

This quaint hamlet of log cabins and clapboard houses arrayed against the backdrop of the Yukon River is one of the better-preserved boomtowns of the Alaskan mining era.

The original settlement, today called Eagle Village, was established by the Athabascans long before Francois Mercier arrived in the early 1880s and built a trading post in the area. A permanent community of miners took up residence in 1898, and in 1900 President Theodore Roosevelt issued a charter that made Eagle the first incorporated city of the Interior.

The gold strikes of the early 1900s, most notably at Fairbanks, began drawing residents away from Eagle. At one point, it's said, the population of Eagle dipped to nine residents, seven of whom served on the city council. When the Taylor Hwy was completed in the 1950s, the town's population increased to its present level.

Sights

Residents say Eagle has the state's largest 'museum system,' boasting five restored turn-of-the-20th-century buildings. If you're spending a day here, the best way to see the buildings and learn the town's history is to take the two-hour **Eagle Historical Society** (907-547-2325; cnr 3rd & Chamberlain; tour $7; 9am) walking tour.

Fort Egbert HISTORIC SITE

(24hr; P) FREE Back in 1899, this fort was established as a means of providing some federal law enforcement in the lawless heart of gold-rush territory. The base didn't last long; Egbert was closed and abandoned in 1911. Some historical buildings remain standing; ask at the Yukon-Charley Rivers National Preserve Visitor Center or Eagle Historical Society if you want to peek inside them.

Activities

During its heyday, Eagle was an important riverboat landing for traffic moving up and down the Yukon. Today it's a departure point for the many paddlers who float along the river through the Yukon-Charley Rivers National Preserve. The 165-mile trip extends from Eagle to Circle, at the end of the Steese Hwy northeast of Fairbanks. Most paddlers take six to 10 days, though some require as few as three.

It's not a difficult paddle, but it must be planned carefully. Kayakers and canoeists should come prepared for insects, but can usually camp either in public-use cabins or on open beaches and river bars, where winds keep the bugs at bay. They also need to be prepared for extremes in weather; freezing nights can be followed by daytime temperatures of 90°F (32°C).

Eagle Canoe Rentals (907-547-2203; www.eaglecanoerentals.com; A St; by appointment) rents canoes and can also arrange transportation. The **Yukon-Charley Rivers National Preserve Visitor Center** (www.nps.gov/yuch; 8am-5pm) in Eagle is also worth contacting.

Sleeping

Eagle Campground CAMPGROUND $

(907-883-5121; tent sites $10; P) This basic campground consists of rustic sites arranged around a forest north of Fort Egbert. We're not sure why – well, maybe because it was a totally isolated patch of ominous pine trees – but this spot sort of gave us the willies come evening.

Riverside Hotel HOTEL $$

(907-547-7000; www.riversidehoteleaglealaska.com; Front St; s/d $120/135; P) The writings on the tin at this big hotel: it's on the river, and it has everything from a decent restaurant (open 7am to 6pm; mains $12 to $18) to an on-site grocery store. Rooms are surprisingly modern and quite nice, and a decent rate given how overpriced things can be in remote Alaska.

Falcon Inn B&B B&B $$

(907-547-2254; www.falconinnlodgelogcabins.com; 220 Front St; s/d from $140/165;) While this place may be a B&B in name (and you do get breakfast), it also rents entire, nicely appointed log cabins. Try to score a seat on a deck overlooking the Yukon River.

Getting There & Away

From Jack Wade Junction, the Taylor Hwy continues north 90 miles on a highway that's unpaved, dusty, full of lurching turns, potholes, stretches of washboard and lovely views. If you're leaving from Chicken, the drive takes about three hours. There are no buses. Check at the Tok Mainstreet Visitors Center (p315) for the latest road conditions.

TOK CUTOFF & GLENN HIGHWAY

The quickest path from the Alcan to Anchorage, the paved Tok Cutoff and Glenn Hwy offers some of the best hiking, boating and gawk-worthy scenery in the state. The rugged 328-mile route is graced by both the Wrangell and Chugach Mountains. Glennallen and Palmer are significant-sized communities along the way.

Tok Cutoff

Narrow, forest flanked and almost surreally isolated (in a region where surreal isolation isn't that uncommon), the Tok Cutoff runs 125 miles from Tok to Gakona Junction. There it meets the Richardson Hwy, which heads 14 miles south to Glennallen, the eastern terminus of the Glenn Hwy. There are glorious views of towering Mt Sanford and the Wrangell Mountains on a clear day. The Cutoff is a lonely road; services and gas stations are pretty spaced out. Plan accordingly.

GALYNA ANDRUSHKO/SHUTTERSTOCK ©

1. Kennicott Glacier (p330) 2. Moose, Denali National Park & Preserve (p272) 3. Denali Highway (p296)

Denali & the Interior Highlights

Visitors often come to the Interior for Denali National Park, but they stay for the rest. There are few places in Alaska where wildlife is so commonly spotted, where pure wilderness is so easily accessed, or where so many legendary highways criss-cross, offering unique adventure after adventure to the willing.

Wilderness Park

There's more untracked wilderness and wildlife at Wrangell-St Elias National Park (p327) than at Denali National Park, and only a fraction of the visitors. A junction of several mountain ranges, the park is an adventure playground with world-class glacier trekking, backcountry hiking and paddling.

Legendary Wildlife

Having a close encounter with Alaska's wildlife (p413) is on the bucket list of every visitor. Whether it's a grizzly bear or a moose, a Dall sheep or one of hundreds of bird species you're wanting to see, this region won't disappoint.

Rough Riding

It's a bouncy ride along the dirt of the 135-mile Denali Hwy (p296) – a marvelous landscape of glaciers, braided river valleys, chain lakes and panoramas of the Alaska Range – but that just means you'll be sharing the road with fewer vehicles.

The Great One

The tallest mountain in North America, Denali (p273) sets the stage for one of the world's toughest climbs and most stunning alpine landscapes. Take in views of the mountain from stops along the Park Rd or splash out on a bush-plane flight around the summit.

Sleeping

Porcupine Creek State Recreation Site CAMPGROUND $
(907-822-3973; Mile 64.2, Tok Cutoff; tent sites $20; P) Just north of the Nabesna Rd junction is the 240-acre Porcupine Creek State Recreation Site, offering 12 wooded sites in a scenic spot along the creek. A mile north along the highway you'll find a historical marker and the first views of Mt Sanford (16,237ft), a dormant volcano.

Eagle Trail State Recreation Site CAMPGROUND $
(907-883-3686; Mile 109.5, Tok Cutoff; tent sites $15; P) The first public campground on Tok Cutoff, Eagle Trail State Recreation Site, near Clearwater Creek, has 35 sites, drinking water and toilets. The historic Old Slana Cutoff Hwy, which at one time extended from Tok to Valdez, now provides a leisurely 20-minute nature walk in the vicinity of the campground. Look for the posted trailhead near the covered picnic shelters.

Gakona Lodge LODGE $$
(907-822-3482; www.gakonalodge.com; Mile 2, Tok Cutoff; r $89-119, cabins with bath $129-169; P) In a state full of cool roadhouses, the Gakona is an exemplar of the genre. This lovely log roadhouse dates from 1905 and is listed on the National Register of Historic Places. Even if you aren't staying the night, the friendly owners will let you snoop around. There are 10 small rooms, three big cabins and lots of good-natured service.

In addition to accommodation, the roadhouse has a dining room, a bar and, according to some, a resident ghost. Fishing tours are offered on the Klutina and Gulkana Rivers, which offer some of Alaska's best salmon fishing.

Getting There & Away

Depending on where you're coming from, the Tok Cutoff either begins or ends at Gakona Junction, where it merges with the Richardson Hwy. From Gakona Junction, you can follow the Richardson Hwy 14 miles south to the Glenn Hwy junction. Otherwise, it's about 125 miles to Tok, where you can then hop on the Alcan-Alaska Hwy.

Glenn Highway

In a state with no shortage of amazing road trips, the Glenn is one of Alaska's most jaw-dropping drives, running through mountain valleys that look as if they were freshly carved by a higher power. Appropriately, most of this corridor has been declared a National Scenic Byway. Along the route, outdoor opportunities abound: great alpine hiking around Eureka Summit, easy access to the humbling Matanuska Glacier, and some of the state's best white water in the nearby Matanuska River. Note there is a 5% bed tax in this area.

Glennallen

907 / POP 483

Glennallen (the name is a combo of two early explorers: Edwin Glenn and Henry Allen) is a small, strung-out community that sits at the confluence of two of Alaska's most important highways: the Glenn and the Richardson. Turnoffs for the Denali and Edgerton Hwys are also close by. Unfortunately this geographic importance has done little to enliven Glennallen's appeal, which is limited to a gas station, a visitor center and a smattering of so-so eating and sleeping providers. If you overnight here, admire the views of the icy Wrangell Mountains, top up your gas tank and use the ATM, before heading off somewhere more interesting.

Sleeping & Eating

Northern Nights Campground CAMPGROUND $
(907-822-3199; www.northernnightscampground.com; Mile 188.7, Glenn Hwy; tent/RV sites $25/40; 8am-8pm; P) Sites don't have much privacy, but this is a clean, well-run, centrally located campground. There are also showers, laundry, strong free wi-fi and complimentary coffee in the morning.

Antler's Rest B&B B&B $$
(907-259-4107; www.antlersrest.com; 3rd St; r summer/winter $135/95; P @) A lovely, pristine and very private B&B tucked away behind Glennallen's busy crossroads. Expect large rooms, a relaxing lounge and formidable breakfasts. It's about a mile north of Omni Park Place.

Caribou Hotel MOTEL $$
(907-822-3302; www.caribouhotel.com; Mile 187, Glenn Hwy; r from $150; P) In a town with little competition, or panache, the Caribou often gets a bad rap. But if you think of it as a staging post rather than a romantic getaway, the dated rooms and utilitarian

motel decor will be a little easier to swallow. Granted, it's a tad overpriced. There's an average restaurant on-site.

Tok Thai THAI **$$**
(cnr Glenn & Richardson Hwys; mains $12-15; ⌚6am-6pm; P) Bangkok-style street food is the last thing you expect to see at a dusty road junction in freezing cold or (depending on the season) sweltering hot, mosquito-ridden Alaska. Thus, all hail Tok Thai's well-worn purple food truck. Judging by its pad thai noodles – a good barometer for any Thai restaurant – the food's quite good, and cheap.

Information

Copper River Valley Visitor Center (907-822-5555; junction Glenn & Richardson Hwys; ⌚9am-7pm) This center is useful if you need a stack of brochures.

Getting There & Away

For hitchhikers, Glennallen is notorious as a place for getting stuck when trying to thumb a ride north to the Alcan. Luckily, buses are available.

Interior Alaska Bus Line (800-770-6652; www.interioralaskabusline.com) Passes through town at 9:45am and 5pm every Monday, Wednesday and Friday en route between Anchorage ($70, four hours) and Tok ($65, three hours), where you can connect to Fairbanks. Book ahead.

Kennicott Shuttle (907-822-5292; www.kennicottshuttle.com) Vans run to and from McCarthy in Wrangell-St Elias National Park daily in summer (round-trip same day/different day $109/149, four hours, 7am). You'll need to make a reservation.

Soaring Eagle Transit (907-822-4545; www.soaringeagletransit.com) Connects to Anchorage ($65) and Valdez ($65) on Tuesday, Thursday and Saturday. It also has a local shuttle linking Glennallen with Copper Center and Gulkana ($5).

Tolsona Creek to Matanuska Glacier

West of Glennallen, the Glenn Hwy slowly ascends through woodland into wide-open high country, affording ridiculously gorgeous views of the Chugach and Talkeetna Mountains, and limitless hiking opportunities. If you're driving, anticipate plenty of stops to get out and coo over the scenery.

From Eureka Summit (Mile 129.3), the highway's highest point (3222ft), you can see both Gunsight Mountain and the Chugach Mountains to the south. The Nelchina Glacier spills down in the middle here and the Talkeetna Mountains strut to the northwest.

From here the Glenn Hwy begins to descend, and the surrounding scenery fires the imagination as the Talkeetna Mountains loom in the distance and you pass the sphinx-like rock formation known as the Lion's Head (Mile 114). A half-mile further, the highway reaches the first viewpoint of Matanuska Glacier. To the north is Sheep Mountain, aptly named as you can often spot Dall sheep on its slopes.

Activities

Sheep Mountain Lodge Trails HIKING
The lodge (Mile 113.5) maintains a network of easy-to-follow trails in the overlooking hills. The paths are open to all, not just guests, and outstanding views of the Chugach Mountains and the chance to see Dall sheep are among the highlights. Nonguests can park in the lodge's gravel lot or at the nearby airstrip.

Chickaloon-Knik Nelchina Trail System HIKING
Once a gold-miner's route used before the Glenn Hwy was built, today this network of dirt roads and rough trails extends to Palmer and beyond, and is popular with backpackers and off-road vehicles alike. The system is not maintained regularly and hikers attempting any part of it should have extensive outdoor experience and the appropriate topographic maps.

There are five to six main hikes, ranging from two to three hours (8.5 miles) for the trail to **Knob Lake**, to three to four days (32 miles) for the **Belanger Pass & Syncline Mountain Trail**. The latter can also be mountain biked in one long day.

The trailhead rest area is also a popular vantage point for bird-watchers. With a bit of patience you might be able to get the fixed spotting scopes to reveal a variety of raptors resting in the trees in the wide valley below. In particular, be on the lookout for the hawk owl, which is visible during the day.

Tours

Majestic Heli-Ski SKIING
(800-559-8691; www.majesticheliski.com; 16162 W Glenn Hwy) As winter adventures go, it's

tough to beat a heli-ski adventure in the Chugach Mountains. Of course, you pay for the privilege: a one-day package costs $1250, while a one-week ski expeditions starts at $9450 – but all dining is covered, and you're housed in a lovely lodge with mountain views. The operator is based at Mile 114.9.

Blue Ice Aviation SCENIC FLIGHTS
(www.blueiceaviation.com; 16288 Glenn Hwy) The good-natured folks who run this operation, at Mile 115, can take you on flightseeing tours ($270 per hour), customized fly-in backpacking tours ($470 to $570) and fly-in skiing adventures ($550 to $650 round-trip). We like these guys for their name alone (blue ice is a feature on glaciers, but it's also pilotspeak for leaked sewage from a commercial airliner).

The owners prefer bookings through the website.

Sleeping & Eating

Lake Louise State Recreation Area CAMPGROUND $
(907-441-7575; Lake Louise Rd; tent sites $20) At Mile 160, a 19-mile spur road runs north to this scenic recreation site popular among Alaskans keen on swimming, boating and angling for grayling and trout. There are 52 campsites in two campgrounds, and a few lodges and numerous private cabins around the lake as well.

★**Sheep Mountain Lodge** LODGE $$
(907-745-5121; www.sheepmountain.com; 17701 W Glenn Hwy; r with shared bath $99, cabins $169-199; P) Among the finest and most scenically situated lodges along the highway (Mile 113.5), Sheep Mountain features a cafe, a bar, a sauna (free for cabin guests), comfortable log cabins and a bunkhouse dorm with free showers. The lodge also maintains a lovely network of easy trails in the surrounding hills.

However, the real seeling point of Sheep Mountain Lodge is the **restaurant** (mains $14-22; 8am-8:30pm;). It is, to be succinct, fantastic. Creamy chowders, perfectly grilled burgers, creative salads and gorgeous fish and chips are all delicious, but save room for the desserts, which will knock you out to gastro-stuffed sleepyland.

Eureka Lodge DINER $$
(907-822-3808; www.eurekalodge.com; Mile 128, Glenn Hwy; mains $10-18; 7am-8pm Wed-Mon) A typical roadside Alaska diner where taxidermic animals stand guard over truck drivers tucking into home cooking. The lodge is at a high point on the Glenn Hwy, meaning the weather can go through four different seasons by the time you finish your cheeseburger. Grab a massive muffin and the cheapest coffee in Alaska (25¢!) for the road.

It also rents basic rooms ($115 to $125) if you're too knackered to press on to Glennallen.

Getting There & Away

This segment of the Glenn Hwy is located about 70 miles west of Glennallen. To really explore, you need your own vehicle. Interior Alaska Bus Lines runs from Anchorage to Tok (departs 5:55am Monday, Wednesday and Friday) and can drop you off at Eureka Lodge at 8:30am ($45). Buses from Tok leave at 1:45pm on the same days and arrive at Eureka Lodge at 6:15pm.

Matanuska Glacier to Palmer

One of Alaska's most accessible ice tongues, Matanuska Glacier really does look as if it's about to lick the Glenn Hwy as it stretches from its source in the Chugach Mountains. Well, to be clear, the glacier *did* look like it was about to lick the highway, but climate change seems to be shrinking this outcrop of ice faster than it can replenish itself. Sigh.

Beyond the glacier, almost 12 miles past Sutton, is the junction with the Fishhook-Willow Rd, which provides access to Independence Mine State Historical Park in Wasilla. The highway then descends into the agricultural center of Palmer.

From Palmer, the Glenn Hwy merges with the George Parks Hwy and continues south to Anchorage, 43 miles away.

Sights

★**Matanuska Glacier** GLACIER
(Mile 102, Glenn Hwy; 7am-9pm; P) Some 18,000 years ago this glacier covered the entire area where the city of Palmer sits today. It must have appeared a supernatural force back then, whereas these days it's *merely* a grand spectacle and open geological classroom. From a distance, the wall of ice looks like it should be patrolled by guys in black furry capes with funny Northern English accents.

Weirdly enough, the glacier – or at least the part you can visit – sits on private land. The entrepreneurial guy who claimed this natural wonder for himself tightly controls access to the glacier. Entry is via Glacier Park Resort (Mile 102), which charges $25 to follow its private road to a parking lot at the terminal moraine. From there, a self-guided trail will take you a couple of hundred yards onto the gravel-laced ice, carved and braided with translucent blue streams and pitted with deep ponds.

To go further, duck into the office of MICA Guides, which leads a ton of adventurous treks out onto the ice. You *can* go hiking on your own out onto the glacier, but come prepared with hiking shoes, cold-weather gear, and a sense of perspective. Clueless, giggling tourists wearing T-shirts and flat-soled shoes walk out on the ice all the time, and inevitably, they get stuck and saved by trained rescue crews. Seriously, be careful out here. There are gaps in the ice that can literally swallow a human body, and they appear out of nowhere. There's a reason they make you sign a consent form and waiver before you hit the frozen ground.

Activities

MICA Guides ADVENTURE
(907-351-7587; www.micaguides.com; Mile 102.5, Glenn Hwy; 9am-5pm;) This excellent guide service will outfit you with a helmet, crampons and trekking poles, and lead you on a three-hour ice trek ($79) or a six-hour ice-climbing excursion ($164). It also manages a zip-line course ($79).

It also operates – wait for it – the AK Metal Rodeo, where you can seriously operate a bunch of heavy machinery and junk some cars ($149). Alaska!

Purinton Creek Trail HIKING
The trail starts at Mile 91 (look for the signpost) and continues 12 miles to the foot of Boulder Creek. Most of the final 7 miles run along the river's gravel bars. The accompanying Chugach Mountains scenery is excellent, and you'll find good camping spots along Boulder Creek.

Tours

Nova ADVENTURE
(800-746-5753; www.novalaska.com; 38100 W Glenn Hwy, Chickaloon; 8am-6pm;) Almost across the highway (at Mile 76.5) from the King Mountain State Recreation Site sits the headquarters of one of Alaska's pioneering rafting companies. Nova offers daily floats ($85) on the Matanuska River. Wilder half-day trips feature Class IV rapids around Lion's Head (from $105).

Nova can also guide you on glacier hikes (from $85) and multiday river trips on the Matanuska, Talkeetna, Copper, Chickaloon and Tana Rivers for anywhere between $950 and $2900.

Sleeping & Eating

★**Alpenglow** CAMPGROUND $$
(907-351-7587; https://micaguides.com/activities/luxury-camping; 31090 Glenn Hwy; tents from $116; P) Come to Alpenglow, at Mile 102.5, to get your glamping on. That's 'glamorous camping' if you're lucky enough to not spend too much time on the internet, and in this case means wall tents on raised platforms with fluffy beds and a view that looks straight out onto the glacier, which looks like it's going to kiss you good morning.

It has an on-site kitchen where you'll get an included breakfast, a wooden hot tub, and an Edenic location on the sort of alpine meadow that Julie Andrews likes to spin around on while singing. The one drawback is shared bathroom facilities. Managed by the folks at MICA (p323).

Matanuska Lodge LODGE $$
(907-746-0378; www.matanuskalodge.com; 34301 West Glenn Hwy; r $150-200; P) The four rooms at the Matanuska, between Miles 99 and 100, are a hybrid of cabin chic and overstuffed comfort, all lovely soft beds and explosions of color. The most expensive room (the Matanuska) has a two-person shower, a king-sized bed and a fireplace. Bow chicka bow wow. On the walls are crafty lantern-style light fixtures and plenty of art.

Tundra Rose Guest Cottages CABIN $$
(907-745-5865; www.tundrarosebnb.com; 22518 West Glenn Hwy; 2-/4-person cottages $155/165; P) In a glacier-view setting that's as pretty as the name implies, this family-run place at Mile 109.5 has a cozy and personal atmosphere. The owners also run the Grand View Cafe (p324) just down the road.

Grand View Cafe CAFE $
(907-746-4480; www.grandviewrv.com; 22518 West Glenn Hwy; sandwiches $8-11; 8am-10pm;) At Mile 109.5, find this home-spun purveyor of American road-trip favorites. You can't go wrong with the Reuben sandwich with some free (slow) wi-fi on the side. It also starts baking pizzas around 3pm every day.

Getting There & Away

Glacier View (where you can, hey, see the glacier) is near the center of the Glenn Hwy, located 60 miles east of Palmer and about 75 miles west of Glennallen. Cars are by far the easiest way around, but Interior Alaska Bus Line (p179) runs buses from Anchorage to Tok (departs 5:55am Monday, Wednesday and Friday) and can drop you off in Palmer (6:45am, $20). Buses from Tok leave at 1:45pm on the same days and arrive in Palmer at 8pm.

RICHARDSON HIGHWAY

Can we just ctrl+v and paste the word 'wow' over and over again? No? Let's earn our pay, then: the Richardson is…*beautiful.* In good light, wildflowers shimmer in the wind, while off in the distance the sheltering shoulders of the Alaska and Chugach Mountains stand guard. In the mist, the road cuts through a grey, severe series of tundra valleys, dark forests and rushing rivers. Every step of the way there are chances to hike, cycle (many cyclists go ahead and do the entire route) and stop for photos.

Alaska's first highway, the Richardson runs 366 miles from Fairbanks to Valdez, although the 98-mile stretch between Fairbanks and Delta Junction is popularly considered part of the Alcan. At mile marker 265, you'll reach Delta Junction; from here the Alcan branches away to the east while the Richardson heads south. Mile Marker 0 is in Valdez.

Delta Junction to Paxson

After departing Delta Junction's 'Triangle,' where the Alcan merges with Richardson Hwy at Mile 266, the highway passes Fort Greely (Mile 261) and, a few minutes later, the Alaska Pipeline's Pump Station No 9.

A turnoff at Mile 243.5 offers one of the best views you'll get of the pipeline, as it plunges beneath the highway. Interpretive signage provides an overview of the pipeline's history and engineering, including a fascinating explanation of how 'thermal siphons' protect the permafrost by sucking heat from areas where the pipeline is buried. There are also spectacular panoramas to the southwest of three of the highest peaks in the Alaska Range. From south to west, you can see Mt Deborah (12,339ft), Hess Mountain (11,940ft) and Mt Hayes (13,832ft).

Another interesting turnoff, at Mile 241.3, overlooks the calving grounds of the Delta buffalo herd to the west. In 1928, 23 bison were relocated here from Montana for the pleasure of hunters and today they number more than 400. The animals have established a migratory pattern that includes summering and calving along the Delta River. If you have binoculars you may be able to spot dozens of the beasts.

The first public campground between Delta Junction and Glennallen is just after Mile 238, where a short loop road leads west to Donnelly Creek State Recreation Site, which has 12 sites. This is a great place to camp, as it's seldom crowded and is extremely scenic, with good views of the towering Alaska Range. Occasionally the Delta bison herd can be seen from the campground.

At Mile 225.4 you'll find a viewpoint with picnic tables and a historical marker pointing out what little ice remains of Black Rapids Glacier to the west. Once known as the 'Galloping Glacier,' this ice river advanced 3 miles in the winter of 1936 to almost engulf the highway.

From here, the highway ascends into alpine country and the scenery turns gonzo, with the road snaking under sweeping, scree-sided peaks. At Mile 200.5, a gravel spur leads 2 miles west to Fielding Lake State Recreation Site, where a willow-riddled 17-site campground sits in a lovely area above the treeline at 2973ft.

In another 3 miles the highway crests its highest point, Isabel Pass (3000ft). The pass is marked by a sign dedicated to Captain Wilds Richardson, an early 20th century Alaska explorer, after whom the highway is named. From this point you can view Gulkana Glacier to the northeast and the Isabel Pass pipeline camp below it.

For much of the next 12 miles the highway parallels the frothing headwaters of the Gulkana River as it pours toward Paxson.

Paxson

907 / POP 40

At Mile 185.5 of the Richardson Hwy, the junction with the Denali Hwy, you'll find the small service center of Paxson. This is a blink-and-you'll-miss-it kind of town, but it's a useful frame of reference for the beginning of an absolutely enchanting stretch of road. Over the next 20 miles, the Richardson descends from the Alaska Range, presenting sweeping views of the Wrangell Mountains to the southeast and the Chugach Mountains to the southwest. Carry on along this route and you'll pass through several jaw-dropping iterations of mountain scenery before reaching Gulkana River Bridge.

Activities

Sourdough to Gulkana Bridge Float CANOEING

From Sourdough Creek Campground, you can take a placid, 35-mile river float to the highway bridge at Gulkana (Mile 126.8), making for a pleasant one- or two-day paddle.

All the land from Sourdough Creek Campground south belongs to the Ahtna Native Corporation, which charges boaters to camp. The exceptions – three single-acre sites – are signposted along the riverbanks and have short trails leading back to the highway.

Raft rentals and shuttle services for many of the area's rivers, including the Gulkana, can be arranged through River Wrangellers (p326).

Paxson to Sourdough Float CANOEING

(www.blm.gov/ak) Experienced paddlers can travel the main branch of the Gulkana River, which roughly parallels the Richardson Hwy from Paxson Lake BLM Campground to Sourdough Creek Campground. This is a 45-mile, three- to four-day journey involving several challenging rapids, including the class IV Canyon Rapids.

Although there's a short portage around these rapids, rough class III waters follow. If you're interested in the route, the BLM offers the super-informative 17-page *Gulkana River Users Guide for Paxson to Sourdough Float* for download from its website (www.blm.gov).

Sleeping

Paxson Lake BLM Campground CAMPGROUND $

(☎907-822-3217; Mile 175.5, Richardson Hwy; tent sites $6-12; P) With 50 sites peppered around a misty lakeshore, this is one of the most dramatic public campsites along the Richardson.

Getting There & Away

Paxson is about 80 miles south of Delta Junction. If you follow the Richardson Hwy south from here, you'll eventually reach the Gulkana River Bridge; from here, you are 3 miles south of Gakona Junction, where Tok Cutoff heads northeast to Tok (and eventually, Canada), and 11 miles north of Glennallen, where the Richardson Hwy intersects with the Glenn Hwy.

DON'T MISS

LODGE AT BLACK RAPIDS

As physical settings go, it's hard to beat the **Lodge at Black Rapids** (☎907-388-8391; www.lodgeatblackrapids.com; Mile 227.4, Richardson Hwy; r/ste from $125/275; P), which is situated on a particularly dramatic stretch of the Richardson Hwy. But this historic roadhouse doesn't trade on location alone. Rooms are a tasteful blend of minimalism and cabin aesthetics, featuring unique decor and natural light.

The owners can hook you up with a full slate of activities throughout the year, from flightseeing to dog mushing.

Copper Center

☎907 / POP 328

The diminutive, typically Alaskan settlement of Copper Center, 14 miles south of Glennallen, sits just off the Richardson Hwy beside the iconic, fast-flowing Copper River.

The 'town' first took root in 1898 as a waystation on the disastrous Valdez Glacier trail to the Klondike goldfields. For the 4000 or so would-be prospectors who made it over the Valdez Glacier, utilizing the so-called 'All-American route,' this was about as far as they got. Exhaustion and a calamitous scurvy outbreak at Copper Center prevented them from getting much further.

Once the prospectors had passed on (or away), Copper Center settled down to become just another gnarled Alaskan settlement on the frontier. These days it supports a small riverside community and is notable for its rafting and fishing opportunities.

Activities

Klutina Salmon Charters FISHING

(☎907-822-3991; www.klutinasalmoncharters.com; Mile 101, Old Richardson Hwy; tent/cabins $25/95) Sitting at the confluence of two legendary fishing rivers (Klutina and Copper), this professional outfit offers all kinds of customized fishing trips, as well two-hour rafting tours of the Klutina River ($99). It also runs a riverside campground with tent sites and cabins.

Tours

River Wrangellers RAFTING
(907-888-822-3967; www.riverwrangellers.com; Airport Rd, Copper Center) Offers raft rentals and shuttle services for many of the area's rivers. You can rent a self-bailing Sotar or Vanguard raft (minimum three days from $300), or take a tour down the Gulkana (from $99).

Sleeping & Eating

Copper River Princess Wilderness Lodge HOTEL $$
(907-822-4000, 800-426-0500; www.princesslodges.com; 1 Brenwick Craig Rd; r from $129; P@) More intimate than the other Princess lodges, this secluded retreat just off the Richardson Hwy, 14 miles south of Glennallen, is frequented primarily by groups of cruise-line vacationers, but can still offer an indulgence for DIYers on their way in or out of Wrangell-St Elias National Park.

There are two restaurants, country-lodge furnishings and a handy daily shuttle ($5) to the Copper Center community and national park visitor center. You can find significant discounts if you book online.

Old Town Copper Center Inn & Restaurant AMERICAN $$
(907-822-3245; www.oldtowncoppercenter.com; Mile 101, Old Richardson Hwy; mains $10-29; 6am-midnight Mon & Tue, 24hr Wed-Sun May-Sep, 9am-8pm Oct-Apr;) Guns are welcome, but keep them in your holster, explains a sign in the Copper Center Lodge. What might read as facetious anywhere else is par for the course in rural Alaska. But, fear not, the cozy restaurant is friendly to out-of-towners and the breakfasts and apple cinnamon buns are a treat. Also rents chintzy rooms (from $129).

There are vegetarian burgers, patty melts (with meat), fried chicken and all sorts of other goodness for dinner.

Getting There & Away

Copper Center is 16 miles south of Glenallen. Soaring Eagle Transit (p321) buses pass through Copper Center from Monday to Friday at 7:25am, 10am and 1:10pm on the way to Glenallen ($5).

Glennallen to Valdez

One of Alaska's most spectacular drives, the 115 miles of the Richardson Hwy between Glennallen and Valdez lead through a paradise of snowy summits, panoramic passes and stunning gorges.

Nine miles south of Glennallen is a turnoff to the Wrangell-St Elias National Park Visitor Center. Just south of the visitor center, at Mile 106, Old Richardson Hwy loops off the main highway, offering access to Copper Center. Old Richardson Hwy rejoins the Richardson at Mile 100.2.

You'll reach a lookout over **Willow Lake** (Mile 87, Richardson Hwy) FREE at Mile 87.6. The lake can be stunning on a clear day, with the water reflecting the Wrangell Mountains, a 100-mile chain that includes 11 peaks over 10,000ft. The two most prominent peaks visible from the lookout are Mt Drum (12,011ft), 28 miles to the northeast, and Mt Wrangell (14,163ft), Alaska's largest active volcano, to the east. Some days you can see a plume of steam rising from its crater.

Squirrel Creek State Campground (907-822-5932; http://dnr.alaska.gov/parks/aspunits/matsu/squircksrs.htm; Mile 79.5, Richardson Hwy; tent sites $20; P) is a scenic 25-site camping area on the banks of the creek. You can fish for grayling and rainbow trout here.

Fourteen miles further along, you'll reach what used to be the Little Tonsina River State Recreation Site. Though it's closed, a path leads down to the water, where anglers can fish for Dolly Varden most of the summer.

At Mile 28.6 the turnoff to **Worthington Glacier State Recreation Site** (907-269-8700; http://dnr.alaska.gov/parks/aspunits/kenai/worthglsrs.htm; Mile 28.7, Richardson Hwy; sunrise-sunset; P) FREE leads you to the glacier's face via a short access road. The recreation area includes outhouses, picnic tables and a large, covered viewing area. The mile-long, unmaintained **Worthington Glacier Ridge Trail** begins at the parking lot and follows the crest of the moraine. It's a scenic hike and follows the edge of the glacier, but exercise caution: never hike on the glacier itself due to its unstable crevasses.

As the highway ascends toward **Thompson Pass** (Mile 26, 2678ft), it climbs above the treeline, and the weather can be windy and foul. On the other side, several scenic turnoffs with short trails descending the ridgelines allow lucky early-summer visitors to ooh and aah at a riot of wildflowers.

Blueberry Lake State Recreation Site (http://dnr.alaska.gov/parks/aspunits/kenai/blueberrylksrs.htm; Mile 23, Richardson Hwy; tent & RV sites $14; P) offers 15 sites and several covered picnic shelters in a beautiful alpine setting surrounded by lofty peaks. There's good fishing for rainbow trout in the nearby lakes.

At Mile 14.8 you'll reach the northern end of narrow **Keystone Canyon**. Tucked away in a little bend is an abandoned hand-drilled tunnel that residents of Valdez began but never finished when they were competing with Cordova for the railroad to the Kennecott copper mines. A historical marker at the entrance briefly describes how nine companies fought to develop the short route from the coast to the mines, leading to the 'shootout in Keystone Canyon.'

For the next 2 miles you'll pass through the dark-walled canyon and, like everyone else, make a stop at two high, full-throated waterfalls: **Bridal Veil Falls** and, half a mile further, **Horsetail Falls**.

Leaving the canyon at Mile 12.8, the road begins a long, gradual descent into Valdez.

WRANGELL–ST ELIAS NATIONAL PARK

Imagine an area the size of Switzerland. Now strip away its road network, eradicate its towns and cities and take away all but 40 of its eight million people. The result would be something approximating Wrangell–St Elias National Park. Comprising 20,625 square miles of brawny ice-encrusted mountains, Wrangell–St Elias is the second-largest national park in the world after Northeast Greenland, meaning there's plenty of room for its 45,000-or-so annual visitors to get lost – very, very lost. The park's vital statistics are mind-boggling.

One more time: this park is *big*. If Wrangell–St Elias were a country it would be larger than 70 of the world's independent nations. Its biggest glacier covers an area larger than the US state of Rhode Island. Plenty of its mountain peaks have never been climbed. And that's even before you've started counting the bears, beavers, porcupines and moose.

McCarthy Road

There's only one way you can get to McCarthy by land: the bumpy, unpaved McCarthy Rd. This dirt route is a rump-shaker, but even a regular car can make it if you go slow (35mph max) and stay in the center to avoid running over old rail spikes – contact Ma Johnson's Hotel (p329) in McCarthy about car-rental companies that will let you take their vehicles on the road.

Much of the route traces the abandoned Copper River and Northwest Railroad bed that was used to transport copper from the mines to Cordova. The first few miles offer spectacular views of the Chugach Mountains, the east–west range that separates the Chitina Valley lowlands from the Gulf of Alaska. Peaks average 7000ft to 8000ft. Below is the mighty Copper River, one of the world's great waterways for king and red salmon.

Chitina

907 / POP 126

Chitina is the last taste of civilization before McCarthy. It's a riverside hamlet on the frontier where rustic house lots are littered with antediluvian vehicles and the road signs are used for target practice by locals with guns (count the bullet holes). Notwithstanding, the scenery is pretty, there's good hiking and wildlife-viewing opportunities, and Chitina is one of the few places you can easily watch **fish wheels** at work. The wheels, which look much like a paddle wheel with baskets, sit just off the banks and turn with the river's current. When a fish is caught in a basket, it's lifted up and then deposited into a trough. A slow day might see no salmon caught, while a great day could see a dozen.

Sleeping

Gilpatrick's Hotel Chitina HOTEL $$
(907-823-2244; www.hotelchitina.com; Mile 33, Edgerton Hwy; r $165) There's a reason this 100-year-old hotel/restaurant looks like a building from an old frontier town: that's essentially what it is. But this old-time relic has been renovated and redone with, if not modern luxury, at least contemporary comfort and efficiency. It has a wood-floored coziness that's endearing (if overpriced).

Drinking & Nightlife

Uncle Tom's Tavern BAR
(907-823-2253; Edgerton Hwy; 3-10pm) This friendly little dive is a nice spot to drink a beer and hear locals tell tales about shooting very dangerous animals that were apparently prowling in the area where you were just hiking. Maybe that was just our experience? In all seriousness, this is a true Alaskan Interior bar, and worth a stop if you're feeling thirsty.

Shopping

Spirit Mountain Artworks ART
(☎907-823-2222; www.spiritmountainalaska.com; Edgerton Hwy; ⏲times vary) This gallery/store, housed in a classic 'false front' store that appears in the National Register of Historic Places, sells goods created by over 100 local artists and craftspeople. Hours are fungible, as the owner lives in Homer; call ahead before visiting.

Getting There & Away

Chitina sits at the entrance to the McCarthy Rd, about 65 miles south of Glennallen, and 40 miles east of Tonsina. The **Chitina Airport** (off Edgerton Hwy) is used by Wrangell Mountain Air (p330). You can also jump on the Kennicott Shuttle (p321) here if you're heading to McCarthy; you can park your car here, in an uncovered parking lot, for free.

McCarthy

☎907 / POP 28

Alaska doesn't lack for isolated frontier towns that act as magnets for a colorful cast of folk who want to live away from everything, and nor does it suffer a paucity of tourist destinations. But it's a rare place that manages to bridge the gap between these two identities – a spot that is authentically on the edge of civilization, yet welcomes those curious folk who want to peep in on the raw, wild pulse of the Alaskan bush.

Enter McCarthy. Once the red-light district and drinking strip for bored miners bivouacked at the 'dry' mining town of Kennecott, today this is an intersection of muddy streets and a few dozen locals and seasonal workers, who work hard, play harder, and generally live life with an unvarnished gusto that's a joy to witness. It helps that they live in a valley that could give Eden a fit of jealousy.

Sights

Wrangell Mountain Center CULTURAL CENTER
(☎907-554-4464; www.wrangells.org; 👪) At the end of downtown McCarthy, check out this environmental NGO/community center with summer field courses for university students, arts and science programs for children, writing workshops and interpretative walks. The center sits in the Old Hardware Store and is always open.

McCarthy-Kennecott Historical Museum MUSEUM
(☎907-259-4550; ⏲2-7pm) This old railroad depot is worth a quick visit to view the historical photographs, mining artifacts and model of McCarthy in its heyday. The road splits at the museum, with one lane bending back 500ft to downtown (such as it is) McCarthy, and the other continuing toward Kennecott, 4.5 miles up the road.

Tours

St Elias Alpine Guides OUTDOORS
(☎907-554-4445; www.steliasguides.com) A lovable cast of outdoors enthusiasts staffs this tour outfit, which leads customers on an enormous range of trips, from mountaineering courses (from $2075) to multi-day backpacking expeditions (from $450) to rafting trips (from $95). The headquarters, the old McCarthy electrical powerhouse, is an awesome sight in and of itself.

WORTH A TRIP

LUXURY IN THE MIDDLE OF NOWHERE

For a select few with $5000 to spare, the **Ultima Thule Lodge** (☎907-854-4500; www.ultimathulelodge.com; 4-night 4-day package per person $7950) beckons like the aurora borealis. Located in the lonely backcountry of Wrangell-St Elias National Park on the Chitina River, over 100 miles from the nearest road, this fabulously luxurious lodge is the last thing you expect in such an inhospitable environment.

But far from being just another expensive resort, Ultima Thule is elegant, tasteful, unpretentious and as beautiful as the land that envelops it. For your money, you'll have one of the world's best bush pilots at your disposal, along with fully catered meals with ingredients plucked from an on-site organic garden, professional guides and equipment, accommodation in private cabins and service and comforts akin to a royal retreat. Step outside the door and there's 13.2 million uninhabited acres calling like a mythical siren. Ultima Thule's fees cover everything, including flights. Most people who've been lucky enough to go say it's worth every penny. There's a three-night minimum stay.

St Elias Alpine Guides is a partner company with **Copper Oar** (☎800-523-4453; www.copperoar.com), a popular tour company that effectively manages the rafting side of the business.

McCarthy River Tour & Outfitters RAFTING
(☎907-554-1077; www.raftthewrangells.com) This well-regarded rafting outfit takes customers on everything from four-hour SUP trips on a glacial lake ($95) to eight-day, fly-in river expeditions deep in the wilds of Wrangell-St Elias ($3150).

Wrangell Mountain Air SCENIC FLIGHTS
(☎800-478-1160, 907-554-4411; www.wrangellmountainair.com; Main St, McCarthy) Want to see Wrangell–St Elias from the air? These folks have a fantastic reputation and can do a backcountry drop or a wide range of scenic flights from $120 (35 minutes) to $270 (1½ hours) per person (two-person minimum).

McCarthy Then & Now WALKING
(tours $10) These historical walking tours of McCarthy usually kick off in the mornings from Main St. Check at Ma Johnson's Hotel for when the next one is running.

Sleeping

Glacier View Campground CAMPGROUND $
(☎907-441-5737; www.glacierviewcampground.com; tent sites $15, cabins without bath $95; P) A half-mile back from the river at the road's end, this very friendly place has stony sites with just enough scrub and space to maintain your privacy, hot showers ($10) and mountain bikes for hire (full day $25). The on-site restaurant enjoys a good local reputation for its burgers ($15), and is blessed with views of Root Glacier from the deck.

★**Ma Johnson's Hotel** HISTORIC HOTEL $$
(☎907-554-5402; www.mccarthylodge.com; Main St; d/tr $229/299) This copper-boom-era hotel has yet to make it into the second half of the 20th century – let alone the first half of the 21st. The old-fashionedness is intentional and, frankly, refreshing. Small rooms don't have electrical sockets (charge your phone in the lobby), bathrooms are shared and every floorboard creaks.

But it's comfortable and atmospheric, and you can't beat sitting on the front deck imagining you've got a walk-on role in a remake of *Butch Cassidy and the Sundance Kid*. Breakfast is included.

Currant Ridge Cabins CABIN $$
(☎907-554-4424; www.currantridgecabins.com; Mile 56.7, McCarthy Rd; cabins $225; P) On a mountainside not far from the 'end of the road' (before you reach the McCarthy bridge), these well-designed log cabins feature bathrooms (including bathtubs), full kitchens and large decks for taking in some outrageous mountain views. During the summer season, all power is provided by photo-voltaic panels.

Lancaster's Hotel HOTEL $$
(☎907-554-4402; www.mccarthylodge.com; off Main St; d/tr/q without bath $129/179/199) Run by the same guys as Ma Johnson's Hotel, the Lancaster has even fewer 'frills' and is for those who want to soak in the Main St vibe but are on a tighter budget. There's no kitchen and it has shared bathrooms, but a reading room is available and you can store your bags when you head out into the wilds.

Kennicott River Lodge & Hostel CABINS, HOSTEL $$
(☎907-554-2329, 907-554-4441; www.kennicottriverlodge.com; dm $50, cabins without bath from $130) A short walk back from the road's end is this handsome two-story log lodge with private and dorm cabins. Amenities include a great communal kitchen and common room, a bright outhouse and a Finnish sauna. Views look over to the fantastical Root Glacier in the distance.

Eating

★**Roadside Potatohead** TEX-MEX $
(The Potato; ☎907-554-4504; www.theroadsidepotatohead.com; breakfast $6-12, mains $10-18; 7am-9pm) Don't leave without popping into this food shack, where the signature burritos share a menu with overstuffed cheese steaks and delicious hummus wraps. The coffee ain't half bad either. Decor is Potatohead toys and dusty Lonely Planets, the menu is written on old pieces of cardboard, and the attitude is pure Alaskan quirkiness.

Heads up: everyone calls this place 'The Potato,' and given that nickname, you really want to try the fries.

Golden Saloon BREAKFAST $$
(☎907-554-4402; Main St; mains $11-18; 8am-midnight) Connected to McCarthy Lodge, this is the area's only true bar, with a good beer selection, pool, frequent live music and an always-intriguing cast of drinkers and beards. Food-wise, there's a menu of

first-rate bar food, including buffalo wings, loaded nachos and filling sandwiches.

McCarthy Bistro AMERICAN $$$
(☎907-554-4402; Main St; mains $26-42; ⏰7-11am & 6-11pm) One of the more pleasant absurdities of McCarthy is the way you can enjoy expertly prepared gourmet food in what, superficially, looks like Tombstone circa 1881. Wild-caught salmon, elk medallions, and a wine list that wouldn't be out of place in a major city, let alone a frontier outpost, characterize the menu.

On many evenings there's a set four-course meal with wine.

Shopping

Mountain Arts Gift Shop ARTS & CRAFTS
(www.mccarthylodge.com/mountain-arts; Main St; ⏰10am-6pm) Run by the folks at McCarthy Lodge, this little shop is stocked with local arts, clothes, jewelry, crafts and other goods that all make for a unique souvenir.

McCarthy Store & Bakery MARKET
(Main St; ⏰10am-6pm) Pop into this small shop, which makes a big effort to procure the healthy hiking essentials – including decent fruit and camping food – and treats like ice-cream and liquor.

Getting There & Away

AIR

McCarthy has a tiny gravel airport.

Copper Valley Air (☎907-822-4200; www.coppervalleyairservice.com) Has flights from Anchorage or McCarthy via Gulkana from $275 one-way.

Wrangell Mountain Air (☎907-554-4411, 800-478-1160; www.wrangellmountainair.com) Offers daily scheduled flights between McCarthy and Chitina (one-way/round-trip $129/258).

BUS

McCarthy sits at the end of McCarthy Rd (imagine that!). You can either drive this bumpy track (if your rental company allows it) or take the Kennicott Shuttle (p332). This van service leaves Glennallen daily at 7am for McCarthy (round-trip same/different day $109/149) and departs at 4:30pm for the return trip. It also stops at Chitina Airport. It's about four hours each way, with a few scenic stops and some driver commentary thrown in. Reservations are essential.

Getting Around

It's about 4½ miles heading uphill to reach Kennecott. You can walk, bike (Ma Johnson's will rent you a rig) or spend $5/10 one-way/round-trip and take the **McCarthy Kennicott Shuttle** (☎907-554-4411; www.mccarthykennicottshuttle.com; 1-way/round-trip $5/10; ⏰9am-7pm), which leaves every 30 minutes from 9am to 7pm.

Kennecott

☎907

Between 1911 and 1938, the mining outpost of Kennecott was the serious 'dry' working town to free-living, hard-drinking McCarthy. These days it is effectively an open-air museum on mining history, as well as the jump-off point for several excellent hikes.

Sights

★Concentration Mill & Leaching Plant HISTORIC SITE
(tour $28) Like a rickety fantasy hatched out of a lunatic's dream, this 14-story building once processed the copper mined out of the surrounding mountains. You can only enter via two-hour tours led by St Elias Alpine Guides (p328), but this is highly recommended for a chance to peak into a truly surreal tableau of 20th-century mining equipment.

There are three tours daily. St Elias Alpine Guides has a small kiosk at the entrance to Kennecott, where the shuttle drops off passengers.

Kennecott Mines National Historic Landmark HISTORIC SITE
(☎907-822-5234; www.nps.gov/wrst) Old mill town constitutes pretty much all of present-day Kennecott. Dozens of old wood and log buildings have been restored, stabilized or purposely left in a state of decrepitude. You're welcome to wander around the outside of the buildings at will, or you can join daily tours.

Kennicott Glacier GLACIER
'Oh no, they destroyed this valley!' If you're like 99% of visitors, that's exactly what you'll think as you reach Kennecott and look across the valley at a rolling landscape of dirt and rubble. But no, that isn't a dump of mine tailings from the copper-boom days, but the Kennicott Glacier moraine. The ice is buried underneath.

The glacier is thinning terribly and has dropped 175ft in height over the past eight decades. To put that statistic in perspective, back in the 1930s some locals didn't even

OFF THE BEATEN TRACK

NABESNA ROAD

For connoisseurs of roads less traveled, Alaska offers few lonelier motorways than the Nabesna Rd, jutting 42 miles south from the Tok Cutoff (p317) into the northern reaches of Wrangell-St Elias National Park.

Turning onto the Nabesna Rd, you'll find yourself in a place the signs call Slana (population 124). Somewhere back through the trees there's an Alaska Natives settlement on the northern banks of the Slana River, where fish wheels still scoop salmon during the summer run. Also in the area are more recent settlers: in the early 1980s this was one of the last places in the USA to be opened to homesteading.

Before continuing, stop in at the NPS's **Slana Ranger Station** (907-822-7401; Mile 0.5, Nabesna Rd, www.nps.gov/wrst; 8am-5pm Apr-Sep;), where you can get info about road conditions and hikes, purchase USGS maps, peruse displays and borrow a CD with an audio tour of the Nabesna.

In the 4 miles between the ranger station and the park entrance you'll pass a handful of accommodations. Offbeat and friendly is **Huck Hobbit's Homestead** (907-822-3196; Mile 4, Nabesna Rd; cabins per person $35; P) , a wind-and-solar-powered, 87-acre wilderness retreat. Cabins are rustic, but include a cooking area and shower block. Stay an extra day here if you can. You can rent canoes for a half-day float down the gentle Slana River ($60 per canoe, including shuttle).

Upon entering the park proper, the Nabesna Rd turns to gravel. It's manageable in a 2WD vehicle for the first 29 miles, but after that several streams flow over it, making it impassable in high water (check at the ranger station for the latest on road conditions). At mile 28.2, **Kendesnii Campground** (907-822-5234; www.nps.gov/wrst; Mile 27.8, Nabesna Rd; tent sites free; P) FREE is the only official NPS campground in Wrangell-St Elias National Park. It's nicely st up, remote and has 10 sites and vault toilets. Maintenance ends at Mile 42, though a rough track continues 4 miles to the private Nabesna Gold Mine, a national historic site.

For a comparatively easy hike, try the 3-mile **Caribou Creek Trail** (www.nps.gov/wrst; Mile 19.2, Nabesna Rd) , which ascends 800ft from the road to a dilapidated cabin with unbeatable views of the surrounding peaks. A tougher walk is the 2.5-mile **Skookum Volcano Trail** (www.nps.gov/wrst; Mile 36.2, Nabesna Rd), which climbs 1800ft through a deeply eroded volcanic system, ending at a high alpine pass frequented by Dall sheep.

realize they lived in a valley, as the ice field was so high.

Kennecott Visitor Center MUSEUM
(907-554-1105; www.nps.gov/wrst; 9am-6:30pm) The center, which sits in the town's former school, is the launching point for ranger-led activities, lectures and walks around town.

Activities

There are a few excellent hikes around town and a backcountry bonanza if you're able to fly by bush plane deeper into the national park.

Root Glacier Trail HIKING
Beginning at the far edge of town past the Concentration Mill, the Root Glacier Trail is an easy 4- or 8-mile round-trip route out to the sparkling white-and-blue ice. Signposts mark the route and the path itself is clear and well used as far as the primitive Jumbo Creek campsites.

From here you can head left to the glacier or continue straight another 2 miles along a rougher track. At the end, the Erie Mine Bunkhouse will be visible on the slopes above you. Check at the visitor center for the latest on the trail conditions. Most of this trail can also be ridden on a mountain bike.

Bonanza Mine Trail HIKING
This excellent hike from Kennecott follows an alpine trail – a round-trip of almost 9 miles. Begin on the Root Glacier Trail and turn off to the right at the clearly marked junction. This is a steep uphill walk with 3800ft of elevation gain. Once above the treeline, the view of the confluence of the Root and Kennicott Glaciers is stunning.

Expect three to five hours for this hike up if the weather is good and half that time to return. Water is available at the top, but carry at least a quart (1L) if the day is hot. Snow lingers higher up until early June.

Tours

Some of the best outfitters and guides in the state operate in Wrangell-St Elias.

Kennicott Wilderness Guides ADVENTURE
(907-554-4444, 800-664-4537; www.kennicottguides.com; Main St, Kennecott) A local guiding firm, this outfit is extremely experienced, offering activities ranging from small-group ice climbing and half-day glacier excursions (from $90) to five-day backcountry expeditions (from $1205), with a whole host of adventures offered in between.

Sleeping & Eating

Kennicott Glacier Lodge HOTEL $$$
(907-258-2350; www.kennicottlodge.com; Main St; r $195-295;) Some of Kennecott's historic mining buildings have been restored, including this grande dame, which hits the jackpot with a mix of modern comforts and old-school charm (bathrooms are shared). Rooms are cozy (those at the front have stupendous glacier views) and the hotel offers nice little extras, such as lending bear spray.

★**Meatza Wagon** FOOD TRUCK $$
(907-290-9398; mains $15; 11am-7pm;) Who'd a thunk there'd be a food truck in Kennecott? And not just a food truck, but a pretty damn delicious one that slings meatball subs, pork sandwiches, tacos and a veggie rice bowl? Eat up, then roll your stuffed butt down the mountain.

Kennicott Glacier Lodge AMERICAN $$
(907-258-2350, 800-582-5128; www.kennicottlodge.com; breakfast $10-16, lunch $9-16, dinner $33-39; 7am-10am, noon-3pm, 7pm) You'll need a reservation for the lodge's well-regarded family-style dinners, which are set three-course meals of the halibut and steak school of dining. There's only one seating: at 7pm. Otherwise, pop in for country breakfasts or Caesar salads and French dip for lunch.

Getting There & Away

The **Kennicott Shuttle** (907-822-5292; www.kennicottshuttle.com) leaves Glennallen daily at 7am for McCarthy (round-trip same/different day $109/149) and departs at 4:30pm for the return trip. It also stops at Chitina airport. It's about four hours each way, with a few scenic stops and some driver commentary thrown in. Reservations are essential.

Kodiak, Katmai & Southwest Alaska

Includes ➡

Best Places to Eat

- ➡ Monk's Rock Coffeehouse & Bookstore (p349)
- ➡ Kodiak Hana (p349)
- ➡ Amelia's (p359)
- ➡ Chart Room (p360)

Best Places to Stay

- ➡ Channel View B&B (p348)
- ➡ Brooks Camp Campground (p354)
- ➡ Best Western Kodiak Inn (p348)
- ➡ Russian River Roadhouse (p345)

Why Go?

The elongated Alaska Peninsula marks the extreme western extension of the North American continent. Tapering out into the Bering Sea like a curled crocodile's tail, it's a jumble of treeless emerald hills, precipitous cliffs and conical snow-capped peaks heavy with reminders of an erstwhile Russian culture and a still surviving Aleut one.

In the east sit Kodiak Island and Katmai National Park where you can indulge in what are, arguably, the best salmon fishing and brown-bear viewing opportunities on the planet.

Equally special are the surreal landscapes of the lower peninsula and the nebulous Aleutian Islands beyond. The Alaska Marine Highway System runs an economical ferry route, weaving its way twice monthly between Kodiak and Dutch Harbor, stopping at half a dozen pin-prick-sized, off-the-grid communities along the way. Replete with breaching whales, smoking volcanoes and poignant WWII sites, this could well be the best water-based excursion in the state.

When to Go

Kodiak

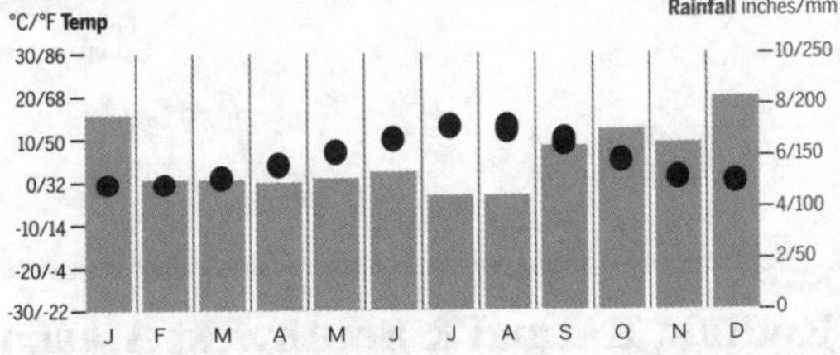

Jun Decent bear viewing and salmon fishing but with fewer crowds at the hot spots.

Jul Salmon are running, bears are fishing and humans are hoping to glimpse them both.

May–Sep The Alaska ferry runs to the Lower Alaska Peninsula and Aleutian Islands.

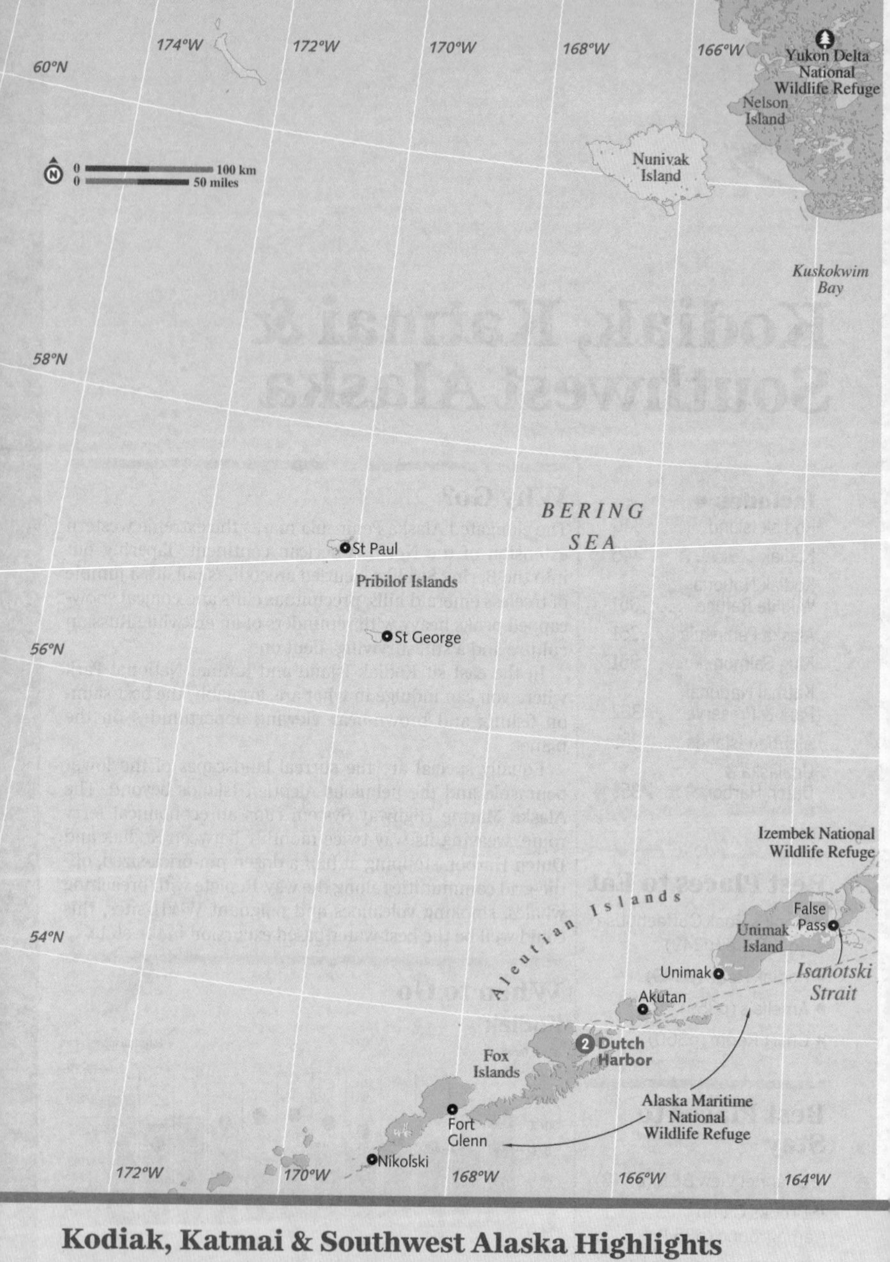

Kodiak, Katmai & Southwest Alaska Highlights

1 **Brooks Falls** (p352) Photographing brown bears as they snap salmon from a waterfall in Katmai National Park & Preserve.

2 **Dutch Harbor** (p355) Hiking to poignant WWII fortifications.

3 **MV Tustumena** (p360) Riding an Alaska Marine Highway ferry amid breaching whales and smoking volcanoes.

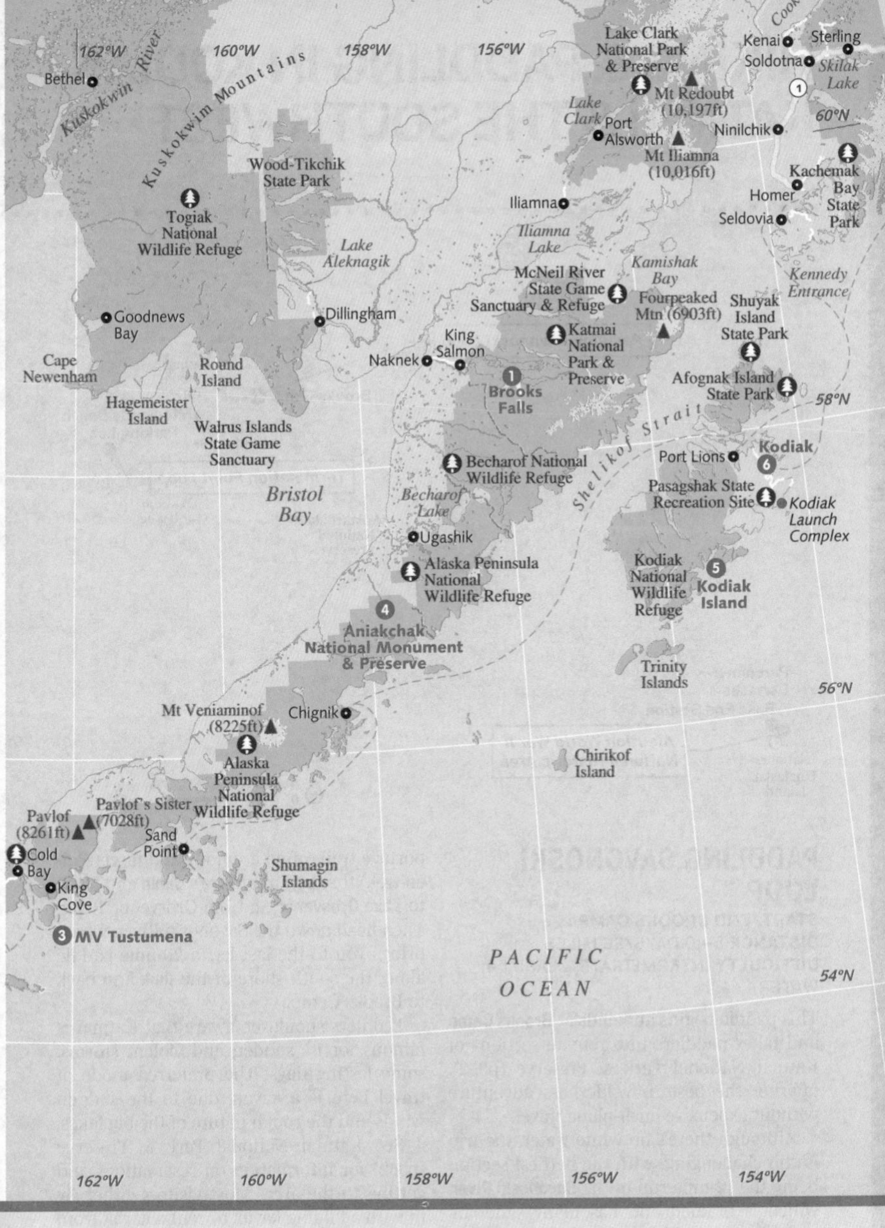

4 Remote Landscapes (p350) Treading where few feet have trodden before, such as Aniakchak National Monument.

5 Kodiak Island (p340) Renting a bicycle to tackle the small scenic road system.

6 Russian Heritage (p345) Investigating a fascinating period of regional history in Kodiak.

HIKING & PADDLING IN KODIAK, KATMAI & THE SOUTHWEST

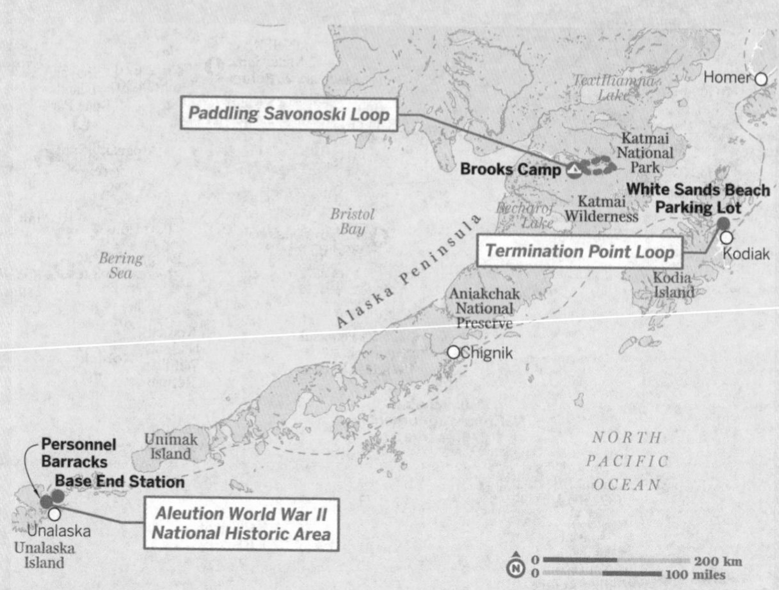

PADDLING SAVONOSKI LOOP

START/END BROOKS CAMP
DISTANCE 5–10 DAYS/86 MILES
DIFFICULTY INTERMEDIATE, CLASS I–II WATER

This paddle begins and ends at **Brooks Camp** and takes paddlers into remote sections of Katmai National Park & Preserve (p352), offering the best in wilderness adventure without expensive bush-plane travel.

Although there's no white water, the trip is still challenging, with the hardest section being the 12-mile run of the **Savonoski River**, which is braided and has many sandbars and fallen trees. The Savonoski is also prime brown-bear habitat and for this reason park rangers recommend paddling the river in a single day and not camping along it.

The first section through **Naknek Lake** is especially scenic and well protected at the end where you dip in and out of the Bay of Islands. You're then faced with a mile-long portage trail (often a muddy and insect-laden trek) that begins at **Fure's Cabin** and leads to **Lake Grosvenor** and the Grosvenor River. Then head down the Savonoski River, which brings you to the last leg, a 20-mile paddle along the south shore of the **Iliuk Arm** back to Brooks Camp.

Paddlers should be aware that Katmai is famous for its sudden and violent storms, some lasting days. The preferred mode of travel here is a kayak, due to the sudden winds and the rough nature of the big lakes.

See Katmai National Park & Preserve (p352) for information on reservations and getting to the area. Most visitors either fly in with a folding kayak or rent a kayak from Lifetime Adventures (p353) near Anchorage. Folding kayaks are $55/65 per day for a single/double or $245/280 per week. The outfitter can also arrange an unguided, week-long trip that includes airfare from Anchorage to King Salmon, floatplane charter to Brooks Camp and folding kayaks from $950 per person.

With bear-spotting paddle trips, hikes through mossy coastal forests and a stroll around one of the state's most interesting WWII sights, Southwest Alaska features trips for varied abilities and interests.

TERMINATION POINT LOOP

START/END WHITE SANDS BEACH PARKING LOT
DURATION/DISTANCE 3 HOURS/5 MILES
DIFFICULTY MODERATE

Beginning at the end of Monashka Bay Rd, on the edge of the **White Sands Beach** parking lot, this hike cuts through a wide variety of terrains, including a lush Sitka spruce forest, low meadows, bogs and one beautiful coastal stretch. It's not the easiest trail to navigate, with one section traipsing through a thick forest. If you're unsure about navigation, head out with an experienced hiker who's familiar with the trail, or skip the forest and head straight to the beach portion, taking the same route back to avoid it entirely.

The trail begins easily enough as a clear footpath, but once you're deep into the forest, the path is crisscrossed with game trails and ATV tracks, and can get confusing under the cover of the moss-laden spruces. Keep an eye on your direction (east) and eventually you'll make it to the shore.

On the coast, **Termination Point** will be to your right, jutting out into the sea. In summer, the point is blanketed in wildflowers such as purple-pink fireweed and blue lupines. Stop for lunch and gaze out into the water, keeping your eyes peeled for whales – humpbacks can often be spotted nearby.

Hang a right to follow the coast past the point to make your way back along the shore of **Monashka Bay**. Take your time here to peer into the tidepools along the beach or listen to the squawks of bald eagles in the trees. The shore turns inland back at White Sands Beach.

ALEUTIAN WORLD WAR II NATIONAL HISTORIC AREA

START PERSONNEL BARRACKS
END BASE END STATION
DURATION/DISTANCE 1 HOUR/1.2 MILES
DIFFICULTY EASY

Encompassing the former site of US Army Base Fort Schwatka, The Aleutian World War II National Historic Area makes for an easy hike, passing solemn reminders of the island's WWII history framed by excellent views of the coast. Visitors must first obtain a land-use permit (daily/weekly $6/15) from the Ounalashka Corporation (p361) .

The hike begins at the ruins of the **personnel barracks**, now just a pile of sheet metal and sun-whitened boards in a meadow, but during the war it provided housing for around 234 men. To the northeast, you'll come to the site of **Officer Country**, which were comfortable, four-person huts with their own recreational facilities, latrines and even an Officer's Club where booze was provided.

Follow the road northward and you'll reach a large, rusty metal pipe sticking out of the hill. Look closely, and you'll see a thick blast wall sticking out of the hillside. This is the **steel bunker** and **magazine war reserve**. These structures were built with heavy, corrugated steel and buried underground so they couldn't be spotted by enemy aircraft flying overhead.

Turning left and heading northwest, you'll come to the **Harbor Entrance Command Post**, from which all approaching vessels were monitored for enemy infiltrators. The structure housed radar and plotting equipment, and was entirely self-sufficient in case of attack.

Continuing along the road, you'll reach the **Battery Command Station**, a three-level bunker that served to both spot enemies and target attacks, located on the right side of the road overlooking the cliff. Firing orders were delivered next door, to **Battery 402**, a horseshoe-shaped structure that included two 8-inch guns at the end of each 'heel'. These guns were 30ft long, weighed 52 tons and could fire a 240lb shell up to 22 miles. The circular concrete platforms are all that remain of the gun mounts today.

DAY TRIPS FROM KODIAK

BEAR VIEWING IN KODIAK NATIONAL WILDLIFE REFUGE

Thousands of miles of undisturbed wilderness, brown bears the size of small cars and a sawtooth horizon of snow-dusted peaks, Kodiak National Wildlife Refuge (p345) is Alaska at its best: remote, wild and beautiful. Floatplane tours depart from Kodiak almost hourly, so your chances of snagging a ride are excellent.

☆ Best Things to See/Do/Eat

⊙Kodiak National Wildlife Refuge Visitor Center Located downtown, this visitor center is a must-see featuring interpretive displays and activities for a variety of age groups (including adults!). It's the perfect jumping-off point into the refuge. Make sure to run your hands across the sea otter pelt and take notes on the yearly habits of Kodiak bears.

Sea Hawk Air Taking a small-group tour into the refuge is one of the best ways to experience it firsthand. Bear-viewing tours via floatplane include a guided hike, lunch and plenty of bears. The scenic flight is icing on the cake.

Aquamarine Cafe & Suites Swap grizzly stories over a burger and a beer at this downtown eatery right across from the harbor.

☆ How to Get There

Air The only method of transport into these remote parts. A variety of floatplane companies operate out of Trident Basin or Lily Lake in Kodiak.

FORT ABERCROMBIE STATE PARK

Merging your average Alaskan beauty with a unique glimpse of a WWII-era outpost, Fort Abercrombie State Park (p340) makes for an excellent half- or full-day trip out of Kodiak. The park is set in an exceptional northern temperate rainforest dominated by Sitka spruce and wildflower meadows, but the real story is hidden in the abandoned military structures that dot the park.

☆ Best Things to See/Do/Eat

⊙ WWII History The pair of rusty 8-inch guns on Miller Point signal the area's strategic importance during WWII. These guns, as well as the bunkers and pillboxes that line the cliffs, are a fascinating reminder of how close the war came to American shores. The Kodiak Military History Museum also collects WWII-era communication equipment and weaponry.

Hiking Trails Easy-to-moderate trails cut through the mossy forests of Fort Abercrombie State Park, passing disused observation towers and weapons caches, wildflower meadows and scenic cliffs.

Kodiak Hana Watch fishing boats glide by over rolls of sushi sourced from local fish – you might be watching your next meal come in to port.

☆ How to Get There

Bike Rent a bike from 58 Degrees North (p347) and hit the road.

Car Just a mile down E Rezanof Dr, Fort Abercrombie is an easy drive in a rental or a taxi.

FOSSIL BEACH

At the end of a very long road, the stark, isolated beauty of Fossil Beach (p341) is a highlight of any trip to Kodiak Island. Lined with the fossilized remains of shells and other sea creatures, a visit here will have you hunting for that next specimen to add to your collection.

☆ Best Things to See/Do/Eat

Fossil Cliffs Gaze at the textures and patterns of a cliff face eons in the making, featuring bulbous cementations (mineral deposits), layers of sediment and ancient creatures embedded in the cliff.

Beachcombing and Tidepooling At low tide, the area is a scavenger hunt of sea creatures – both live and fossilized – in the tidepools and rock piles that line the shore.

Java Flats All wood surfaces and friendly faces, this small cafe in Bell's Flats is the perfect place to wrap up a day over a hot chocolate or a saucer-sized cookie. (p345)

☆ How to Get There

Car At 46 miles from town one-way, a car is the only way to get here, but the drive, winding between mountain meadows and wide bays, is excellent.

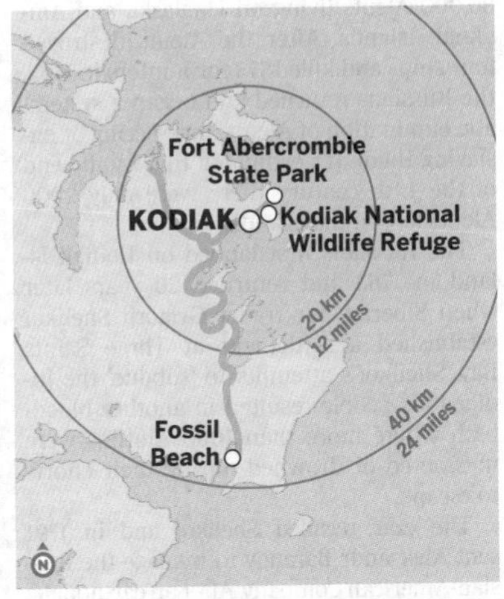

Perched on the edge of the wilderness, Kodiak is the perfect place from which to venture into the emerald beauty of the rest of the island.

History

Of all the state's regions, Southwest Alaska has had the most turbulent history, marked by massacres, violent volcanic eruptions and WWII bombings.

When Stepan Glotov and his Russian fur-trading party landed at present-day Dutch Harbor in 1759, there were more than 30,000 Aleuts living on Unalaska and Amaknak Islands. After the Aleuts destroyed four ships and killed 175 fur hunters in 1763, the Russians returned and began a systematic elimination of Aleuts, massacring or enslaving them. It's estimated that by the end of the 19th century there were only 2000 Aleuts left on the islands.

The Russians first landed on Kodiak Island in 1763 and returned 20 years later when Siberian fur trader Grigorii Shelikof established a settlement at Three Saints Bay. Shelikof's attempts to 'subdue' the indigenous people resulted in another bloodbath where more than 1000 Alutiiqs were massacred or drowned during their efforts to escape.

The czar recalled Shelikof and in 1791 sent Aleksandr Baranov to manage the Russian-American Company. After an earthquake nearly destroyed the settlement at Three Saints Bay, Baranov moved his operations to more stable ground at present-day Kodiak. It became a bustling port and was the capital of Russian America until 1804, when Baranov moved again, this time to Sitka.

Some of the past violence experienced in Southwest Alaska had natural causes. In 1912, Mt Katmai on the nearby Alaska Peninsula erupted, blotting out the sun for three days and blanketing Kodiak with 18in of ash. Kodiak's 400 residents escaped to sea on a ship but soon returned to find buildings collapsed, ash drifts several feet high and spawning salmon choking in ash-filled streams.

The town was a struggling fishing port until WWII when it became the major staging area for the North Pacific operations. At one point Kodiak's population topped 25,000, with a submarine base at Women's Bay, an army outpost at Buskin River and gun emplacements protecting Fort Abercrombie.

Kodiak was spared from attack during WWII, but the Japanese bombed Unalaska only six months after bombing Pearl Harbor, and then invaded Attu and Kiska Islands. More hardship followed: the Good Friday Earthquake of 1964 leveled downtown Kodiak and wiped out its fishing fleet; the king-crab fishery crashed in the early 1980s; and the *Exxon Valdez* oil spill soiled the coastline at the end of the decade. But this region rebounded after each disaster, and today Unalaska and Kodiak are among the top three fishing ports in the country.

Getting There & Away

Alaska Airlines (p429) services the region and provides daily flights to Kodiak, King Salmon, Unalaska, Dillingham and Bethel. Ravn Alaska (p430) also flies to Kodiak from a number of destinations throughout Alaska including Anchorage. **Grant Aviation** (☎888-359-4726; www.flygrant.com) provides air travel to remote villages in the Yukon-Kuskokwim Delta, the Aleutians and Bristol Bay.

The most affordable way to reach the region is via the Alaska Marine Highway ferry (p430), which has stops at Kodiak, Unalaska and a handful of small communities in between.

KODIAK ISLAND

Kodiak is the island of plenty. Consider its famous brown bears, the second-largest ursine creatures in the world (after the polar bear). Thanks to an unblemished ecosystem and an unlimited diet of rich salmon that spawn in Kodiak's lakes and rivers, adult male bears can weigh up to 1400lb.

Part of the wider Kodiak Archipelago and the second-largest island in the US after Hawaii's Big Island, Kodiak acts as a kind of ecological halfway house between the forested Alaskan Panhandle and the treeless Aleutian Islands. Its velvety green mountains and sheltered, ice-free bays were the site of the earliest Russian settlement in Alaska and are still home to one of the US's most important fishing fleets.

The island's main attraction – beyond its bears – is its quiet Alaskan authenticity. Only a small northeastern section of Kodiak is populated. The rest is roadless wilderness protected in the Kodiak National Wildlife Refuge.

Sights

★Fort Abercrombie State Historical Park PARK

(www.dnr.alaska.gov/parks; Abercrombie Dr; $5 per vehicle per day) This military fort, 4.5 miles northeast of Kodiak, off Monashka Bay Rd, was built by the US Army during WWII to defend against a Japanese invasion that never came. In the end, Kodiak's lousy weather kept the Japanese bombers away from the island. The fort is now a 186-acre state historical park, sitting majestically on the cliffs above scenic Monashka Bay.

Between its pair of 8in guns is Ready Ammunition Bunker, which stored 400 rounds of ammunition during the war. Today it contains the small **Kodiak Military History Museum** (☎907-486-7015; 1417 Mill Bay Road; adult/child $5/free; ⏲1-4pm Fri-Mon).

Just as interesting as the gun emplacements are the tidal pools found along the park's rocky shorelines, where an afternoon can be spent searching for sea creatures.

Afognak Island State Park STATE PARK

Afognak Island lies just north of Kodiak Island in the archipelago. Some 75,000 acres of Afognak are protected in pristine Afognak Island State Park, which has two public-use cabins: **Laura Lake Cabin** and **Pillar Lake Cabin**. The cabin at Pillar Lake is a short walk from a beautiful mile-long beach. Both cabins are accessed by floatplane, cost $45 a night, and are reserved through **Alaska Division of Parks** (☎907-486-6339; 1400 Abercrombie Dr; ⏲8am-4:30pm Mon-Fri, varies Sat & Sun). You can check cabin availability and make reservations online six months ahead.

Shuyak Island State Park STATE PARK

The northernmost island in the Kodiak Archipelago, remote and undeveloped Shuyak is 54 air miles north of Kodiak. It's only 12 miles long and 11 miles wide, but almost all the island's 47,000 acres are taken up by Shuyak Island State Park, featuring forests of virgin Sitka spruce and a rugged shoreline dotted with secluded beaches. Otters, sea lions and Dall porpoises inhabit offshore waters, while black-tailed deer and a modest population of famous Kodiak brown bears roam the interior.

Kayakers enjoy superb paddling in Shuyak's numerous sheltered inlets, coves and channels – the area boasts more protected waterways than anywhere else in the archipelago. Most of the kayaking takes place in and around Big Bay, the heart of the state park. From the bay you can paddle and portage to four public cabins and other protected bays.

The park's four cabins are on Big Bay, Neketa Bay and Carry Inlet. The cabins ($80 per night) are cedar structures with bunks for eight, woodstoves, propane lights and cooking stoves, but no running water. Shuyak Island cabins are also reserved through Alaska Division of Parks and can be reserved six months in advance online.

Fossil Beach BEACH

At the end of Pasagshak Rd, 46 miles from Kodiak, the cliffs on each side of this remote beach (p339) are lined with bowling-ball-sized concretions (where sand and silt has been cemented in minerals), the fossils of ancient shells and other protuberances from the past. Head out during low tide and you can make your way around the easternmost cliff to spot more fossils entombed in the sandstone. Keep an eye out for the herd of scraggly bison that roam the area.

For a bit of WWII history, make your way up the hillside just to the left from where the road ends. At the top, you'll see a series of bunkers and the remains of a searchlight station on Narrow Cape.

Activities

The Kodiak area has dozens of hiking trails, but few are maintained and trailheads are not always marked. Windfall and overgrowth can make following the track difficult, or even totally conceal it. Still, hiking trails are the best avenues to the natural beauty of Kodiak Island.

The best source of hiking information is the Alaska Division of Parks or the excellent *Kodiak Audubon's Hiking & Birding Guide* (sold at various places around town, including the Kodiak National Wildlife Refuge Visitor Center (p345) for $12), a large waterproof topographical map with notes on the trails and birds.

For transportation and company on the trail, the local Audubon Society offers group hikes (p348) almost every Saturday and Sunday during summer, meeting at 9:30am at the Kodiak Island Visitor Center (p350) parking lot. You can get a list of the hikes and the contact person from the visitor center or the Kodiak National Wildlife Refuge Visitor Center.

Pillar Mountain HIKING

The de rigueur hike for anyone with a couple of hours to spare, Pillar Mountain is the 1270ft summit that overlooks Kodiak town, with its sentinel wind turbines on top. If you want to get a glimpse of the island's velvety greenness and enjoy a bird's-eye view of the town, this provides instant gratification.

3

1. Aniakchak National Monument (p350)
The least visited segment of the US National Park Service's 400 protected areas offers Garden of Eden–like landscapes and a trip of a lifetime.

2. Katmai National Park & Preserve (p352)
Katmai National Park is famous for its salmon-trapping brown bears.

3. Dutch Harbor (p355)
The only natural deepwater port in the Aleutians, Dutch Harbor has over 400 vessels visit it each year; however travelers visit for the local hikes and bird-watching opportunities.

GALYNA ANDRUSHKO/SHUTTERSTOCK ©

DANIEL BRIEM/SHUTTERSTOCK ©

Pick up the bumpy dirt road to the top by walking or driving north up Thorsheim Ave and turning left on Maple Ave, which runs into Pillar Mountain Rd. You'll end up where the giant wind turbines slice through the fog. It's 2 miles one-way, but there are miles of trails along the ridge.

Pyramid Mountain HIKING

(Anton Larsen Bay Rd) The trail up Pyramid Mountain (2400ft) takes hikers up a steep, exposed shoulder of alpine tundra but rewards them with pleasant views of the valley that leads toward Anton Larsen Bay. Keep an eye out for bears while you spot wildflowers and upland birds.

Two trails, both of which start on Anton Larsen Bay Rd, lead to the top of Pyramid Mountain. Avoid the easternmost trail, accessed from the golf course, which is brush-choked and hard going. Instead, continue west to Anton Larsen Pass, where the other trail begins in the parking area on the right. It's a steep but easy-to-follow 2-mile climb to the top.

Barometer Mountain Trail HIKING

At a peak elevation of 2500ft, it might not sound high, but climbing Barometer is a tough grunt that shouldn't be taken lightly. With loose stones, several steep sections, and a couple of tear-inducing false summits, you'd better have good balance, a strong will and strong knees, especially on the way down.

The 4-mile out-and-back trail starts just past the airport runway as you head south on Chiniak Rd where there's a pullover and small sign. The path bends through trees at the start, then branches uphill through high bushes, and ultimately follows a steep open ridge. Scrambling is necessary at some sections. The views from the summit are as staggering as your gait. Take plenty of water.

Anton Larsen Pass Loop & Peak HIKING

(Anton Larsen Bay Rd) This 5-mile loop is a scenic ridge walk and an easy alpine hike. The majority of the route follows a green U-shaped valley lined with wildflowers and excellent views.

The trail begins just north of the gravel parking lot, at the pass on the left side of Anton Larsen Bay Rd. A well-defined trail leads you through meadows; at a fork, the trail heads right to cross a bridge and climbs to a broad alpine ridge. Once on top, use the rolling ridge to skirt a distinctive glacial valley before descending back to the fork in the trail.

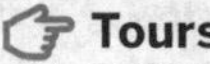

Tours

Kodiak Brown Bear Center WILDLIFE WATCHING

(☎907-433-7900; https://kodiakbearcenter.com/en; 194 Alimaq Dr) Runs bear-viewing excursions out of its remote lodge in the Kodiak Wilderness. Tours are booked as part of packages that include lodging, guided bear viewing, meals and transportation to and from Kodiak (from $4575 for four days).

Sleeping

Sleeping options on Kodiak Island are split into two groups: the inns, hotels and B&Bs found in Kodiak; or the remote lodges that populate the deep wilderness. For the latter, hiring a bush plane is almost always required (and often included in the nightly rate).

Pasagshak State Recreation Site CAMPGROUND $

(http://dnr.alaska.gov/parks/aspunits/kodiak/pasagsrs.htm; 20 Pasagshak River Rd; tent sites $15) Forty-five miles outside of town, this recreation site has six first-come, first-served tent sites on the peaceful banks of the Pasagshak River where it meets the bay of the same name.

Fort Abercrombie State Historical Park Campground CAMPGROUND $

(http://dnr.alaska.gov/parks/units/kodiak/ftaber.htm; Mile 4, E Rezanof Dr; tent & RV sites $10) Four-and-a-half miles northeast of Kodiak, this park has 13 wooded sites in a delightfully mossy forest. A few are walk-in, and feel very secluded. Trails meander around the bluffs, beach and small lake, and it's a great place to wander. Camping is first-come, first-served.

Buskin River State Recreation Site CAMPGROUND $

(http://dnr.alaska.gov/parks/aspunits/kodiak/buskinriversrs.htm; Mile 4.5, W Rezanof Dr; tent sites $15) Four miles southwest of the city, this 168-acre park includes a 15-site rustic campground, the closest to the city, along with a self-guided nature trail and good salmon fishing in the Buskin River. Camping is first-come, first-served.

Kodiak National Wildlife Refuge CABIN $

(☎907-487-2600; www.kodiak.fws.gov; per night $45) Manages nine public-use cabins on

Kodiak and Afognak Island, all of which are accessible by floatplane or boat. Transportation to and from the cabins must be organized separately. Call ahead or reserve online.

★ **Russian River Roadhouse** LODGE $$
(☎907-942-1863; www.russianriverroadhouse.com; 11322 S Russian Creek Rd; r from $150) One five-room lodge and three spacious, private cabins on the property of a former lumberyard (rusted equipment still dots the parking lot).

Eating & Drinking

★ **Java Flats** CAFE $
(☎907-487-2622; www.javaflats.com; 11206 Rezanof Dr W; breakfast $6-9, lunch $10-12; ⏰7am-3pm Wed-Sun; 📶) Saying you have the best baking within a 100-mile radius doesn't always mean much in Alaska where 100 miles is often the distance to the nearest gas station, but, take it on trust, the homemade cookies at Java are to visiting homo sapiens what salmon is to Kodiak's oversized bears. It also serves mean soups, sandwiches and salads.

Java is located at Bell's Flats, 10 miles south of Kodiak town, but it's well worth the journey – even if you're cycling.

Rendezvous BAR
(☎907-487-2233; www.facebook.com/rendezvous.kodiak/; 11652 Chiniak Hwy; ⏰11am-late; 📶) This bar and restaurant is a 15-minute drive out of town past the Coast Guard base, but its atmosphere is worth the trip. It hosts the best live music in Kodiak, with singers taking to the stage several times a month.

The clam chowder is a crowd-pleaser.

Getting There & Away

Most travelers arriving on Kodiak Island come via plane or boat through Kodiak town.

Getting Around

Roads only serve the northeast part of the island around Kodiak town – and even then they are simply miles of unpaved gravel. Renting a car (p351), which typically costs from $60 per day), is essential.

Island Air (☎907-487-4596; www.flyadq.com; 1420 Airport Way) provides daily scheduled flights to outlying villages and lodges that dot the island. Expect to pay $66 to $125 for a one-way ticket.

Kodiak

☎907 / POP 6191

Kodiak is one of outback Alaska's most pleasant towns; big enough to find uninterrupted wi-fi and a decent latte, but small enough to be laid-back and friendly. The locals are a congenial bunch who passionately love their town and aren't afraid to tell you. Glimpses of onion domes through the standard strip-mall architecture hint at an erstwhile Russian heritage, while crowds of trawlers in the harbor testify to Kodiak's modern mantle as one of Alaska's largest fishing ports, with 650 boats, including the state's largest trawl, longline and crab vessels. The fleet and the 12 shore-based processors include the *Star of Kodiak,* a WWII vessel converted into a fish plant downtown.

Despite its hardworking reputation, there's plenty for outsiders to do in Kodiak, including two excellent museums and a historical park.

Sights

★ **Alutiiq Museum & Archaeological Repository** MUSEUM
(☎844-425-8844, 907-486-7004; www.alutiiqmuseum.org; 215 Mission Rd; adult/child $7/free; ⏰10am-4pm Tue-Fri, noon-4pm Sat) The Alutiiqs (not to be confused with the Aleuts) are the subject of this brilliant Alaska Native museum. They were the original inhabitants of the Kodiak archipelago and many of them remain members of the Russian Orthodox Church. Like many native groups, their population was decimated during the 19th century, and the museum protects some precious native heritage.

There's information on the Alutiiq language (now being taught again in local schools), exhibits on harpoons and tools, masked dancing and details of some 1000-year-old petroglyphs found in the archipelago.

Kodiak National Wildlife Refuge Visitor Center WILDLIFE RESERVE
(☎907-487-2626; www.fws.gov/refuge/kodiak; 402 Center St; ⏰9am-5pm; 👪) FREE This excellent visitor center focuses on the Kodiak brown bear, the most famous resident of the refuge, with an exhibit room that's especially well suited to children, a short film on the bears and a **bookstore**. A variety of kids' programs are offered, with the schedule

Kodiak

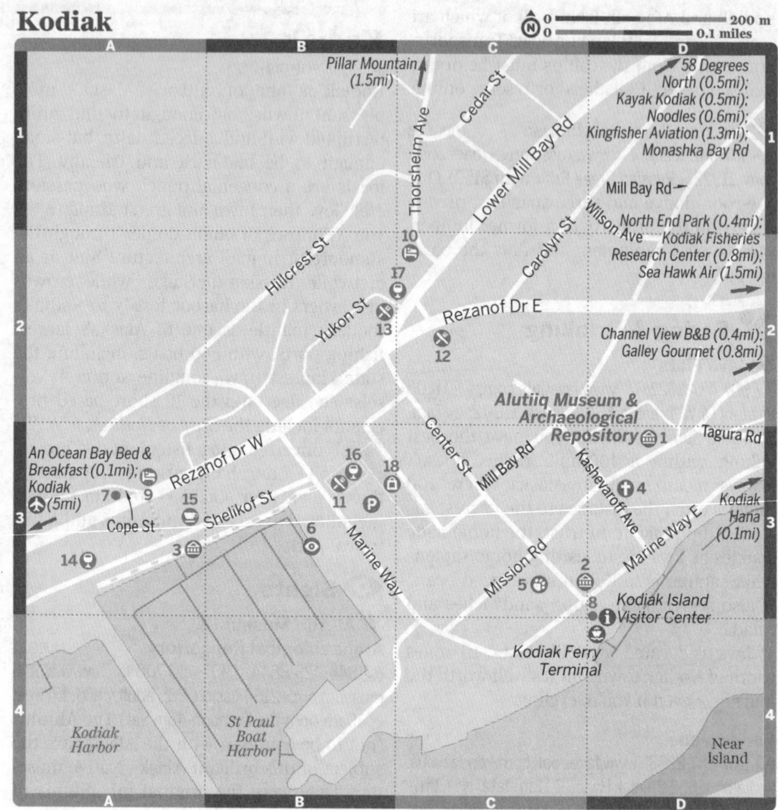

posted on the front door. Interested in seeing a big bruin? Stop here first.

St Paul Boat Harbor HARBOR

The pulse of this city can be found in its two boat harbors. St Paul Boat Harbor is downtown and the larger of the two. Begin with the **Harbor Walkway** (Shelikof St), where a series of interesting interpretive displays line the boardwalk above the docks. Then descend to the rows of vessels, where you can talk to the crews or even look for a job.

Kodiak Fisheries Research Center AQUARIUM

(907-481-1800; www.afsc.noaa.gov; Trident Way; 8am-4:30pm Mon-Sat, closed Sat in winter) FREE Opened in 1998 using funds from the Exxon-Valdez oil spill settlements, the center has an interesting lobby that includes displays about local marine life and a 19ft Cuvier's beaked whale skeleton suspended from the ceiling. Downstairs there are kid-friendly touch tanks and a large aquarium.

North End Park PARK

(Trident Way) FREE Reached as soon as you cross the bridge, this small park is laced with easy, forested trails that converge at a stairway to the shoreline. At low tide you can search the tidepools here for starfish, sea anemones and other marine life.

Baranov Museum MUSEUM

(907-486-5920; www.baranovmuseum.org; 101 Marine Way; adult/child $5/free; 10am-4pm Mon-Sat, to 3pm winter) Housed in the oldest Russian structure in Alaska, across the street from the visitor center, the Baranov Museum fills Erskine House, which the Russians built in 1808 as a storehouse for precious sea-otter pelts. Today it holds many items from the Russian period of Kodiak's history, along with fine examples of Alutiiq basketry and carvings.

Kodiak

A set of notebooks covers Katmai's historical events, including the 1964 tsunami, volcanic eruptions and both World Wars. The gift shop is particularly interesting, offering a wide selection of *matreshkas* (nesting dolls), brass samovars and other Russian crafts.

Holy Resurrection Cathedral CHURCH
(907-486-5532; 308 Kashevarof St; 8am-noon Sun, 5-7pm Thu, to 8pm Sat) Near the Alutiiq Museum on Mission Rd, Holy Resurrection Church serves the oldest Russian Orthodox parish in the New World, established in 1794. The present church, marked by its beautiful blue onion domes, was built in 1945 and is the third one to occupy this site.

Activities

Cycling

On a clear, sunny day, cycling on Kodiak's 75 miles of paved, relatively quiet roads is heaven. Traffic is only thick around the town and thins out dramatically south of the airport. A spin down to Bell's Flats (10 miles south of town) for lunch in Java Flats (p345) cafe is a must. And why stop there? The mainly unpaved, 12-mile Anton Larsen Bay Rd is popular with mountain bikers and crosses a mountain pass to the island's west side, where you will find quiet coves and shorelines to explore. With long daylight hours, a ride down to Pasagshak Bay, 46 miles south of Kodiak town, is not out of the question.

58 Degrees North CYCLING
(907-486-6249; https://58-degrees.com; 1231 Mill Bay Rd; per day $35; 11am-6pm Mon-Sat) A friendly outdoor shop that rents out mountain bikes. Rental includes helmet and lock. Ask for recommended trails to ride based on your experience and skill level.

Kayak Kodiak is run out of the same shop.

Paddling

With its many bays and protected inlets, scenic coastline and offshore rookeries, Kodiak is a kayaker's dream. **Kayak Kodiak** (907-512-5112; http://kayakingkodiak.com; 1231 Mill Bay Rd; tours from $89) rents out expedition sea kayaks (from $69 per day) to experienced kayakers, as well as providing guided tours.

Bear Viewing

Second in size only to the polar bear, Kodiak's famous 1000lb-plus brown bears are a major attraction. Various floatplane operators take bear spotters on half-day tours. Multi-day tours can be arranged through remote lodges such as the Kodiak Brown Bear Center (p344).

For day-trippers, **Frazer Lake** is Kodiak Island's most common bear-viewing destination. The lake is the second-largest salmon run on the island, and the bears know it. At peak times, up to 10 bears can be spotted. There's a 200ft fish ladder that can spoil perfect wildlife photos, but if your only goal is to see these massive ursine beasts, this is your best chance.

Several tour operators fly to the Katmai Coast to spot bears, and while these bears are certainly majestic, they aren't technically the Kodiak subspecies. When booking your tour, ask where the operator plans to go.

Kodiak weather can change at any time, so it's best to book a bear-viewing tour early in your trip – if it's canceled you have more chance of rescheduling at a later date.

Tours

★Sea Hawk Air WILDLIFE WATCHING
(907-486-8282; www.seahawkair.com; 506 Trident Way; tours $575) Flying a de Havilland Beaver floatplane that can carry up to six passengers, this operator departs out of Trident Basin and heads to either Katmai National Park & Reserve or to Kodiak Island, depending on where the bears are. Owners Jo and Rolan pack the tour with local knowledge and exceptional service.

Kodiak Audubon Hikes HIKING
(http://kodiakaudubon.blogspot.com; 100 Marine Way, Suite 200) Kodiak's Audubon Society hosts free guided hikes on most Saturdays and Sundays in summer. Groups meet in front of the Kodiak Island Visitor Center (p350) at 9:30am. Hikes are rated from 1 (easy) to 5 (difficult) and are led by knowledgeable Audubon members. Bring lunch and water.

Fish n Chip Charters FISHING
(907-539-6135; www.fishingkodiak.net; 301 Cope St; day trip $350) These guys can sort you out with what is – let's face it – the quintessential Kodiak experience: fishing. Captain Dave has decades of experience and a custom 33ft boat. Equipment is provided and you can get your catch processed afterward.

Galley Gourmet BOATING
(907-486-5079; www.galleygourmet.biz; 1223 Kouskov St; dinner cruise $175) Along with whale-watching and harbor cruises, Marty and Marion Owen offer a delightful dinner cruise aboard their 42ft yacht. Marty navigates the boat while Marion whips up meals – such as salmon Kiev with king-crab sauce, or apricots and marinated halibut wrapped in bacon – and serves them on white table linen with views of coastal scenery and wildlife.

This is about as locavore as Kodiak gets: most veggies and ingredients for Marion's meals are plucked straight from their home garden.

Kingfisher Aviation WILDLIFE WATCHING
(907-486-5155, 866-486-5155; www.kingfisheraviation.com; 1829 Mill Bay Rd; tours per person $525) Four-hour bear-viewing excursions to either Kodiak or Katmai on the mainland depending on the season. You travel on four-passenger floatplanes.

Festivals & Events

Kodiak Crab Festival CULTURAL
(www.kodiakchamber.org; Marine Way E) The town's best festival, it was first held in 1958 to celebrate the end of crabbing season. Today the week-long festival in late May features parades, a blessing of the fleet, bike and foot races, fishing-skills contests (such as a survival-suit race) and a lot of cooked king crab.

Sleeping

Lodging is expensive in Kodiak and there's a 12% sales and bed tax on top of all tariffs. The most current list of B&Bs is on the website of the visitor center (www.kodiak.org).

★Channel View B&B B&B **$$**
(907-486-2470; www.kodiakchannelview.com; 1010 Stellar Way; r/ste $145/175; wi-fi) Run by a couple of world travelers, history buffs and art collectors, Channel View offers a range of subtle delights: historic Kodiak photos, fossils collected from the island and arranged in a rainy rock garden, plus original artwork from travels abroad. Room options include a single or a queen, a studio apartment or a one-bedroom apartment.

There are views of the channel below through fir trees and from a spacious deck. Host Mary is a fifth-generation islander, and serves full gourmet breakfasts.

★Best Western Kodiak Inn HOTEL **$$**
(888-563-4254, 907-486-5712; www.kodiakinn.com; 236 W Rezanof Dr; r $210-230; wi-fi) Kodiak's largest and most upscale motel is downtown and has 81 rooms along with a fine restaurant, outdoor hot tub and airport-shuttle service. Suites run to $290 and are quite large. Also has an **Andrew Airways** desk in the lobby during the summer.

An Ocean Bay Bed & Breakfast B&B **$$**
(907-486-8315; www.oceanbaykodiak.com; 420 W Rezanof Dr; r $135) Just a few blocks from the main action downtown, this excellent, two-room property overlooking the harbor merges traditional bed & breakfast hospitality with modern, spacious rooms. There are no chintzy antiques here – both rooms are well decorated and spacious, but aim for the upstairs room with roomy vaulted ceilings. Self-serve breakfasts are provided in the form of a well-stocked pantry.

Shelikof Lodge HOTEL $$
(907-486-4141; www.shelikoflodgealaska.com; 211 Thorsheim Ave; r $135;) The Shelikof is beginning to show its age in chipped paint and carpet stains, but a good location downtown, decent rates, plus a good restaurant (breakfast all day) and a lounge make it a solid pick for an overnight in Kodiak. A bonus is the airport shuttle service, which is rare in Kodiak.

Eating

★Monk's Rock Coffeehouse & Bookstore CAFE $
(202 W Rezanof Dr; sandwiches $9-11; 8:30am-3pm Tue-Fri, to 1pm Sat) Part cafe, part library of Russian Orthodox books and icons, Monk's is an out-of-the-ordinary eating place thanks to its on-site bookshop that might have stepped straight out of Vladivostok. The dining area is comfortable, staff are friendly and the soups are recommended, especially the borscht.

Noodles THAI $
(1247 Mill Bay Rd; mains $12-15; 11:30am-2:30pm & 5-9:30pm) Cornering the market on Thai food in Kodiak, Noodles offers a nice break from the typical meals served in town. Peanut-heavy panang curry and slurp-worthy pad thai will cure those not-salmon-again hunger pangs.

Aquamarine Cafe & Suites AMERICAN $$
(907-486-2999; 508 W Marine Way; lunch $12, dinner $15-25; 10:30am-10pm) Modern and chic, the trendy decor pays a nod to Kodiak's seafaring culture while the food puts quality over quantity with tasty meat and fish dishes served with sides of rice and homemade buns, plus a menu of $15 gourmet burgers – the Lord of the Rings (a beef patty with deep-fried onion rings doused in Sriracha aioli) is highly recommended.

Kodiak Hana JAPANESE $$
(907-481-1088; 516 Marine Way; lunch special $10-13, dinner $15-25; 11:30am-2pm & 5-9pm Tue-Thu, 11:30am-2pm & 5-10pm Fri & Sat, 5-9pm Sun) The best fish in Kodiak are served in this historic power plant which has been beautifully renovated into a Japanese seafood restaurant. The waterfront location places you on an outdoor deck, or in a solarium, watching fishing boats glide right past, while feasting on almost all-local sushi and seafood, or excellent *udon, soba* and *yakisoba* noodles.

Royal Baron Pizza PIZZA $$
(907-486-4848; 113 Lower Mill Bay Rd; pizzas $15-19; 11am-10pm Mon-Sat, 2-10pm Sun) Dependable pizza has been a long time coming to Kodiak, and when Royal Baron Pizza replaced a Domino's that formerly occupied the space, the town was abuzz with the scent of oven-baked pies. Seasoned crusts, gooey cheeses and solid ingredients outshine the average service and lengthy wait times.

Drinking & Nightlife

Clustered around the city waterfront and small-boat harbor is a handful of bars that cater to Kodiak's fishing industry. If you visit these at night you'll find them interesting places, overflowing with skippers, deckhands and cannery workers drinking hard and talking lively.

★Kodiak Island Brewing Co MICROBREWERY
(907-486-2537; www.kodiakbrewery.com; 117 Lower Mill Bay Rd; noon-7pm) For proof that craft-brewing has reached the frontier, call into Kodiak's only microbrewery. It operates as a taproom rather than a pub, meaning you can bring your own food as you sample their latest ales, including the signature Liquid Sunshine. Tours of the small brewing operation are available on request.

Harborside Coffee & Goods CAFE
(907-486-5862; www.facebook.com/harborsidekodiak; 210 Shelikof St; 6am-6pm Mon-Sat, 7am-5pm Sun;) The best cuppa in town can be procured at this fount of fishing-boat gossip right on the harborside. A strong double-shot goes down well while surfing the equally strong wi-fi.

Henry's Great Alaskan PUB
(907-486-8844; www.henrysgreatalaskan.com; 512 Marine Way; 11:30am-9:30pm Mon-Thu, to 10pm Fri & Sat, to 8:30pm Sun;) Henry's is one of those bar-restaurant hybrids that you forgive poor service and average food for its drink selection. Located on the mall in front of the small-boat harbor, it's hopping with fishermen and their friends. It's not as dark or claustrophobic as other venues and the pub menu has plenty of options to soak up the booze.

B & B Bar BAR
(326 Shelikof St; noon-late) Across from the harbor, B & B claims to be Alaska's oldest bar, having served its first beer in 1899 (its original liquor license is framed on the wall). It's a fisher's bar with a giant king crab on

OFF THE BEATEN TRACK

ANIAKCHAK – A BLANK SPOT ON THE MAP

More people orbit the earth annually than set foot in **Aniakchak National Monument** (www.nps.gov/ania), the least visited segment of the US National Park Service's 400 protected areas. Here the annual visitor count routinely struggles to break two dozen. High travel costs, volatile weather, 1000lb bears (lots of 'em), and a curious lack of knowledge about the area's Garden of Eden landscapes deter the bulk of would-be adventurers. What they're missing defies written description. Imagine a kind of psychedelic cross between Crater Lake and the Ngorongoro Crater with a bit of the Colorado River thrown in for good measure. Aniakchak's centerpiece is a 6-mile-wide, 2500ft-deep caldera (a massive crater formed when a volcano collapses inward) that sits in the middle of the narrow Alaska Peninsula. The caldera has a dramatic effect on the local weather causing clouds to billow over the edges of the crater rim in what have been christened 'cloud Niagaras'.

Though known to Alaskan natives for centuries, Aniakchak lay pretty much undiscovered until 1931 when it was explored by a Jesuit priest named Bernard Hubbard who wrote about it enthusiastically in publications such as *The New York Times*. These days it sees a tiny trickle of intrepid visitors. Most fly to Port Heiden and trek up and over the crater rim carrying folding microkayaks, before descending to **Surprise Lake**, the remains of a much bigger lake that once sat in the crater. After a portage around a set of dangerous rapids called **The Gates** at a cleft in the crater rim, basic kayaking skills are required to cruise down the class II rapids of the Aniakchak River toward the Pacific Ocean where an old cannery cabin and a prearranged floatplane pick-up awaits. It's the trip of a lifetime and one not many get the opportunity to make. For more information contact the Katmai National Park Headquarters (p352) in King Salmon.

the wall, as well as the most level pool table in a town that feels an earthquake now and then. Cash only.

Shopping

Norman's Fine Gifts GIFTS & SOUVENIRS
(☎907-486-3315; www.facebook.com/Normansfinegifts; 414 W Marine Way) If a bit of Alaskan kitsch is what you're after, Norman's Fine Gifts is your spot. Peruse the bumper stickers, hooded sweatshirts and baby bibs, but keep an eye out for the odd made-in-Alaska artwork thrown in. Sister shop **Norman's Corner** (just a few doors down) is food- and homeware-focused.

Information

MEDICAL SERVICES

Kodiak Island Ambulatory Care Clinic (☎907-486-6188; 202 Center Ave, Suite 102; ⊙8am-6pm Mon-Fri, 9am-3pm Sat) For emergency and walk-in medical care.

MONEY

Wells Fargo (☎907-486-3126; 202 Marine Way; ⊙10am-5pm Mon-Fri, 10am-2pm Sat) Has a king-crab display in its ATM vestibule.

TOURIST INFORMATION

Kodiak Island Visitor Center (☎907-486-4782, 800-789-4782; www.kodiak.org; 100 Marine Way, Suite 200; ⊙8am-5pm Mon-Fri) Next to the ferry terminal, with brochures and maps of the city. During summer, the visitor center maintains extended hours to accommodate cruise traffic.

Getting There & Away

Both Alaska Airlines (p429) and its contract carrier Ravn Alaska (p430) fly to Kodiak daily. Fares are approximately one-way/return $160/330. The airport is 5 miles south of Kodiak on Chiniak Rd. Other than the offerings from a few motels, there is no shuttle service into town. **A&B Taxi** (☎907-486-4343) charges $20 for the ride.

Between May and September Alaska Marine Highway's MV *Tustumena* stops at **Kodiak Ferry Terminal** (☎907-486-3800; www.dot.state.ak.us/amhs/; 100 Marine Way) several times a week, coming from Homer (one-way $85, 9½ hours). Twice a month the 'Trusty *Tusty*' continues west to Unalaska and Dutch Harbor ($337 one-way from Kodiak, two days and 16½ hours). Several times a month the MV *Kennicott* sails to Kodiak from Homer and Whittier (one-way $85, 9 hours). The office in the ferry terminal, next to the visitor center, prints out tickets. Arrive at least two hours before sailing.

Getting Around

The settlement of Kodiak is on the east side of the island, with three main roads splintering from the city center, so a set of wheels is essential to experiencing Kodiak beyond the downtown block.

There's no public transport in Kodiak. You can procure car rental at the airport. **Budget Rent-A-Car** (907-487-2220; airport terminal; 6:30am-10:30pm), among others, has a desk, but it isn't cheap. Bank on around $60 to $90 a day. Other options are to call a taxi, walk, or – if you're heading outside town – rent a bicycle from 58 Degrees North (p347).

Kodiak National Wildlife Refuge

This 2812-sq-mile preserve, which covers the southern two-thirds of Kodiak Island, all of Ban and Uganik Islands, and a small section of Afognak Island, is the chief stronghold of the Alaska brown bear. An estimated 3500 bears reside in the refuge and the surrounding area, which is known worldwide for brown-bear viewing and hunting, and for salmon and steelhead fishing. Birdlife is plentiful: more than 200 species have been recorded, and there are 600 breeding pairs of eagles that nest within the refuge.

The refuge's diverse habitat ranges from rugged mountains and alpine meadows to wetlands, spruce forest and grassland. No roads enter the refuge, and no maintained trails lie within it.

Tours

Mid-July to mid-September is the best time to see bears, and the most common way to do it is with a bear-sighting flight. The average tour is a four-hour trip that includes two hours on the ground photographing bears, and costs $500 to $575 per person.

Kodiak Treks BEAR WATCHING
(907-487-2122; www.kodiaktreks.com; tours per person $375) Low-impact, small-group bear-watching trips from a remote lodge on an island in Uyak Bay. Noted bear biologist Harry Dodge leads guests from the lodge, by boat and boot, to various viewing spots to see up to two dozen bears. Costs cover lodging, meals and equipment but not your charter flight to Uyak Bay.

Getting There & Away

Access into the park is by charter plane or boat out of Kodiak, and most of the refuge lies at least 25 air miles away.

ALASKA PENINSULA

The Alaska Range doesn't suddenly stop at Denali. It keeps marching southwest to merge with the Aleutian Range and form the vertebrae of the Alaska Peninsula, Alaska's rugged arm that reaches out for the Aleutian Islands. This volcanic peninsula stretches some 550 miles from Cook Inlet to the tip at Isanotski Strait. It includes Alaska's largest lakes – Lake Clark, Iliamna Lake and Becharof Lake – and some of the state's most active volcanoes, with Mt Redoubt and Mt Iliamna topping more than 10,000ft in height. Wildlife abounds, communities do not.

The peninsula's most popular attraction, Katmai National Park & Preserve, has turned King Salmon into the main access point. Two other preserves – McNeil River State Game Sanctuary & Refuge and Lake Clark National Park & Preserve – also attract travelers, while the Alaska Marine Highway stops at four small communities along the peninsula on its way to the Aleutians.

King Salmon

907 / POP 316

King Salmon is the kind of place where you arrive just after breakfast and are on first-name terms with half the town by dinnertime. Almost all the people who fly in are bound for nearby Katmai National Park – the 'town' acts as both staging post and official nexus (the park HQ and visitor center are both near the airport). The oversized airport runway is testament to the erstwhile presence of the US Air Force who were stationed here until the 1990s. These days, you're more likely to bump into hunters and fishers than pilots.

Tourists bound for Katmai's Brooks Camp on floatplanes rarely linger here more than a few hours. However, if you get stuck overnight, King Salmon is a friendly enough place with a few restaurants and places to stay, as well as a river lined with floatplanes and boat docks.

Sleeping

There's a 10% room tax.

Antlers Inn INN $$
(907-246-8525, 888-735-8525; www.antlersinnak.com; 471 Alaska Peninsula Hwy; r/ste $195/270;) Antlers beckon you into the unfussy laid-back confines of the Antlers Inn, a friendly,

family-run place with shared bathrooms. Suites have kitchenettes and private baths, but – in typical 'Bush' style – are overpriced. The airport and what passes for downtown are within salmon-hooking distance.

Eating

Eddie's Fireplace Inn AMERICAN $$
(907-246-3435; 1 Main St; $14-32; 8am-8pm;) Pure outback Alaska with a grizzly yarn-spinning clientele, friendly wait staff and a straightforward no-nonsense menu that never strays too far from burgers and fried fish. Dig in like a local and you'll soon forgive them the crumby plastic tablecloths and all-pervading essence of cigarette smoke.

Information

King Salmon Visitor Center (907-246-4250; King Salmon Airport Building 1; 8am-5pm) Adjacent to the airport with topographical models, books, gifts and informed staff.

Getting There & Away

Alaska Airlines (p429) and PenAir (p340) fly up to eight times daily between Anchorage and King Salmon during summer (around $500 round-trip). Throughout the rest of the year, the flight frequency drops to twice a day for about the same price.

Katmai National Park & Preserve

'Expensive, but worth it' are perhaps the four most common words used to describe marvelous Katmai.

A national monument since 1918 and a National Park since 1980, **Katmai National Park & Preserve** (907-246-3305; www.nps.gov/katm; open year-round) FREE is famous for its salmon-trapping brown bears, epic sport-fishing potential and unusual volcanic landscapes. Unconnected to the main Alaskan road network and covering an area the size of Wales, a visit here, for most people, is a once-in-a-lifetime experience involving meticulous preplanning and a big wad of cash.

Nearly all park visitors fly in via floatplane to the main tourist area of **Brooks Camp**, 35 miles east of King Salmon. Here they will stand spine-tinglingly close to formidable 1000lb brown bears pawing giant salmon out of the river (some bears even catch the fish clean in their chops). It's the most heavily visited section of the park, equipped with a rustic lodge plus a couple of short trails.

History

The ecological diversity and abundance of Katmai National Park & Preserve has been an attraction for humans for many millennia. At its peak, the region contained some of the largest prehistoric populations in southern Alaska. Archaeological evidence dates the existence of humans in the Brooks River area to 5000 years ago. Scouring the ancient shores of Brooks and Naknek Lakes (which were at one time a single, large lake), archaeologists have found the remains of campsites, structures and tools. Today there are 20 archaeological sites in the Brooks River area.

In June 1912 the Novarupta volcano erupted violently and, with the preceding earthquakes, rocked the area now known as Katmai National Park & Preserve. The wilderness was turned into a dynamic landscape of smoking valleys, ash-covered mountains and small holes and cracks fuming with steam and gas. It was the largest volcanic eruption in the 20th century.

If the eruption had happened in New York City, people living in Chicago would have heard the explosion; the force of the eruption was 30 times greater than the 1980 eruption of Mt St Helens in the state of Washington. For two days, people in Kodiak could not see a lantern held at arm's length, and the ash, which reached half the world, lowered the average temperature in the northern hemisphere for six months after the eruption. But the most amazing aspect of this eruption is that no one was killed. Katmai is that remote.

In 1916 the National Geographic Society sent botanist Robert Griggs to explore the locality. Standing at Katmai Pass, the explorer saw for the first time the valley floor with its thousands of steam vents. He named it the Valley of Ten Thousand Smokes, and the name stuck.

Sights

Brooks Falls VIEWPOINT
Every year, hundreds of brown bears emerge from hibernation and make their way to Brooks Falls, a small but important waterfall in Katmai National Park. Around the same time, salmon begin their journey up Brooks River to spawn in Brooks Lake upstream. At

this crossroads, salmon can be seen leaping into waiting bears' jaws. Brown bear concentrations are at their highest in July, when dozens can often be spotted at or around the falls.

Valley of Ten Thousand Smokes NATURAL FEATURE

A scar in the earth left behind by the massive 1912 Novarupta volcanic eruption, the Valley of Ten Thousand Smokes is a stark landscape of deep gorges, volcanic ash and lava flows. In 1916 Robert Griggs led an expedition into the region to examine the eruption's aftermath. He found a valley of thousands of fumaroles (steam and gas vents) emitting clouds of vapor into the sky, hence the valley's name.

The post-apocalyptic spectacle served as Katmai's original raison d'être and led to the area being declared a national monument in 1918.

Visitors can access the valley by reserving a tour at Brooks Lodge (p355) or through Katmailand (p354) (from $88).

Activities

Bear Viewing

Katmai supports a healthy population of 2200 brown bears. Many of the bears arrive with instinctual punctuality at Brooks Falls on July 1 for the annual salmon spawning, which lasts until the end of the month. The bears return in September for a second showing to feed on the dead salmon carcasses.

Brooks Camp has three established bear-watching areas. From the lodge, a dirt road leads to a floating bridge over the river and the first observation deck at the lower part of the river. From here you can see the bears feeding in the mouth of the river or swimming in the bay.

Continue on the road to the Valley of Ten Thousand Smokes, and in half a mile a marked trail winds to Brooks Falls. Two more viewing platforms lie along this half-mile trail. The first sits above some shallows that occasionally draw sows trying to keep their cubs away from aggressive males at the falls.

The last deck at the falls is the prime viewing area, where you can photograph the salmon making spectacular leaps or a big brownie at the top of the cascade waiting with open jaws to catch a fish. At the peak of the salmon run, there might be eight to 12 bears here, two or three of them atop the falls themselves. The observation deck holds 40 people, and in early to mid-July it will be crammed with photographers, forcing rangers to rotate people on and off.

Brooks Camps' bear season is relatively short, but more adventurous visitors can charter floatplanes and guides to take them out to other bear-viewing areas on the coast between June and October.

Despite Katmai's dense bear population (two bears per sq mile in places) only two serious human-bear incidents have been recorded in 100 years – a testament to fine park management.

Hiking & Backpacking

Hiking and backpacking are the best ways to see the park's unusual backcountry. Like Denali National Park in Alaska's Interior, Katmai has few formal trails; backpackers follow river bars, lakeshores, gravel ridges and other natural routes. Many hiking trips begin with a ride on the park bus along the dirt road to Three Forks Overlook, in the Valley of Ten Thousand Smokes. The bus will also drop off and pick up hikers and backpackers along the road – or you can walk its full 23-mile length.

The only developed trail from Brooks Camp is a half-day trek to the top of **Dumpling Mountain** (2440ft). The trail leaves the ranger station and heads north past the campground, climbing 1.5 miles to a scenic overlook. It then continues another 2.5 miles to the mountain's summit, where there are superb views of the surrounding lakes.

Paddling

The area has some excellent paddling, including the Savonoski Loop, a five- to seven-day adventure. Other popular trips include a 30-mile paddle from Brooks Camp to the Bay of Islands and a 10-mile paddle to Margot Creek, which has good fishing and lots of bears.

Kayaks are the overwhelming choice for most paddlers due to high winds blowing across big lakes, and possible rough water. Accomplished paddlers should have no problem, but the conditions can sometimes get dicey for novices.

Lifetime Adventures KAYAKING

(907-746-4644, 800-952-8624; www.lifetimeadventure.net; single/double folding kayaks per day $55/65, folding bikes per day $30) Lifetime Adventures rents out folding kayaks and folding mountain bikes. Equipment is picked up or delivered in Anchorage.

If you have the time, this outfit offers a seven-day camping adventure that includes hiking in the Valley of Ten Thousand Smokes and kayaking near Margot River. The cost is $2300 per person and includes the flight from Anchorage, charters into the park, all equipment and guides.

Fishing

Fishing trips are popular and rainbow trout are plentiful in the park's large lakes. In fact, most park facilities were first built to accommodate anglers. Fishing populations are carefully managed by Katmai National Park & Preserve and Alaska Department of Fish and Game. Sport fishing licenses are required for nonresidents aged 16 and older and most residents 16 to 59. Further regulations exist depending on where anglers cast their reels.

Because fishers and brown bears are often attracted to the same catch, anglers must be careful when fishing in Katmai and follow safe bear country practices such as maintaining bear awareness, cutting the line if a bear approaches and safe catch storage.

 Tours

Independent Tours

The only road in Katmai is 23 miles long. It's a scenic traverse of the park that leads from the lodge, past wildlife-inhabited meadows and river valleys, and ends at **Three Forks Overlook**, which has a sweeping view of the Valley of Ten Thousand Smokes.

The peculiar landscape of this trippy valley is the result of a 1912 volcanic eruption. It covered the area in a rain of ash and opened up countless smoke vents which jetted hot steam skyward. These days, the notably less smoky valley plays second fiddle to Katmai's bear viewing, but can still be visited on a daily bus ride from Brooks Camp.

Katmailand has a daily round-trip by bus to Three Forks Overlook, leaving at 9am, with three hours at the cabin or a ranger-led hike to the valley floor, and returning at 4:30pm.

Each bus carries a ranger who talks during the bus trip and leads a short hike from the cabin into the valley below. Views from the cabin include almost 12 miles of barren, moonlike valley where the lava once oozed down, with snowcapped peaks beyond. It's an amazing sight.

The fare is a steep $88 per person (with a packed lunch $96). Sign up for the tour at the Katmailand office across from the lodge as soon as you arrive at Brooks Camp. The bus is filled most of the summer, and you often can't get a seat without making a reservation a day or two in advance.

Package Tours

Because of the logistics of getting there and the need to plan and reserve so much in advance, many visitors arrive in Katmai as part of a one-call-does-it-all package tour. A shockingly large number are part of a one-day visit, spending large sums of money for what is basically an hour or two of bear watching.

Katmailand BEAR WATCHING
(☎800-544-0551, 907-243-5448; www.katmailand.com) The concessionaire of Brooks Lodge offers packages that are geared to either anglers or bear watchers. Its one-day tour to see the bears of Brooks Falls is $778 per person from Anchorage. A three-night angler's package including all transportation, lodging and meals is $1834 per person based on double occupancy.

Hallo Bay Bear Camp BEAR WATCHING
(☎907-235-2237, 888-535-2237; www.hallobay.com; overnight tours from $1000) This ecofriendly camp is on the outside coast of Katmai National Park & Preserve and is designed exclusively for bear watching. Accommodation is rustic but authentic, complete with safari tents, cots and freeze-dried food. Packages include guides and round-trip airfare from Homer.

Sleeping

If you plan to stay at **Brooks Camp**, either at the lodge or in the campground, you must make a reservation. Otherwise, you're limited to staying in King Salmon (p351) and visiting the park on day trips.

Grosvenor Lodge, **Kulik Lodge** and Brooks Lodge are all operated by concessionaire Katmailand. Two-night stays start at $1466 per person and include round-trip flights from Anchorage.

Independent options like **Katmai Wilderness Lodge** (www.katmai-wilderness.com) and Hallo Bay Bear Camp are alternatives.

Brooks Camp Campground CAMPGROUND $
(☎907-246-3305, reservations 877-444-6777; www.recreation.gov; tent sites $12; ⊙May-Oct) Each year, reservations for the campground are accepted from the first week in January.

It might be easier to win the lottery than to get a reservation for July bear watching; often the sites are completely booked before the end of the first week. There's a seven-night maximum stay in July.

The campground holds a maximum of 60 people and reservations are made by person. If you don't provide the names of everyone in your party when you make your reservation, space will be held for just one person. The campground, for obvious reasons, is surrounded by an electrical fence.

Brooks Lodge LODGE **$$$**

(Katmailand; ☎800-544-0551, 907-243-5448; www.katmailand.com; d per person incl flight 1/2/3 nights $1096/1466/1834) The lodge has 16 rustic but comfortable rooms spread over a main lodge and several individual cabins. Each room has two twin bunk beds and a private bath with a shower. Accommodation is booked as part of a package tour that includes transportation from Anchorage. Bears often stalk the grounds.

A store at Brooks Camp sells limited supplies of freeze-dried food, white gas (for camp stoves), fishing equipment, flies, and other essentials...such as beer. You can also sign up for all-you-can-eat meals at Brooks Lodge without renting a cabin (renters pay, too): for adults, breakfasts are $17, lunches $24 and dinners $40. Also in the lodge is a lounge with a huge stone fireplace, soft chairs and bar service in the evening (including cocktails). Campers can take hot showers ($7).

Information

The visitor center (p352) is located in King Salmon.

Getting There & Away

Most visitors to Katmai fly from Anchorage into King Salmon on Alaska Airlines (p429) for between $450 and $600 round-trip. Once you're in King Salmon, a number of air-taxi companies offer the 20-minute floatplane flight out to Brooks Camp. **Katmai Air** (☎800-544-0551, 907-243-5448; www.katmaiair.com), the Katmailand-affiliated company, charges $214 for a round-trip.

Companies like Regal Air (p164) and Rust's Flying Service (p164) offer day trips straight from Anchorage, but the 2½ hour flight aboard a cramped floatplane, plus limited time with the bears, make this a less-ideal option.

ALEUTIAN ISLANDS

If Alaska is primarily characterized by both beauty and hostility, the fiery rim of volcanic islands stretching into the Pacific is the prime example of this dichotomy.

Where the Alaska Peninsula ends, the Aleutian Islands begin: a jagged 1100-mile arc that stretches across the north Pacific to within 500 miles of Russia's Kamchatka Peninsula. This is a barren, windswept and violent place, where over two dozen volcanoes are active or were active in the last 250 years.

Unalaska & Dutch Harbor

☎907 / POP 4448

Everywhere in Unalaska and Dutch Harbor, two things catch your eye: concrete pillboxes and crab pots. In a nutshell, that's the story of these twin towns on Unalaska and Amaknak Islands: the pillboxes are a reminder of the wartime past, while the crab pots acknowledge the important role of commercial fishing in the towns' future.

Located at the confluence of the Pacific Ocean and the Bering Sea, one of the world's richest fisheries, Dutch Harbor is the only natural deepwater port in the Aleutians. More than 400 vessels call here each year from as many as 14 countries, and canneries and fish-processing plants are a key feature of the industrialized port.

For travelers, it's a unique, edge-of-the-world experience. Hikes into the wildflower-laden backcountry trace the routes of ancient portages, and kayak trips around the island's bays and inlets offer some of the best birding opportunities in Alaska.

Sights

★**Museum of the Aleutians** MUSEUM

(☎907-581-5150; www.aleutians.org; 314 Salmon Way; adult/child $7/3; 11am-4pm Tue-Wed & Fri-Sat, 1-8pm Thu) This small but impressive museum is one of the best native cultural centers in Alaska. It relives the Aleutian story from prehistory through the Russian America period to WWII and the present. Exhibits are broken into sections on Russian colonization, the WWII evacuation of the Aleuts, the modern fishing industry and – most interesting – displays of the tools, boats and grass baskets that allowed these clever and creative people to live in such a harsh environment.

WORTH A TRIP

THE LOWER PENINSULA & THE ALEUTIAN ISLANDS

Most visitors to the little fishing villages on the western peninsula arrive on the Alaska Marine Highway's MV *Tustumena,* which sails from Kodiak to Unalaska and Dutch Harbor. The ferry usually stops for an hour or two: long enough to get out and walk from one end of the village to the other, and for most people, that's ample. If you decide to stay over at any village, you'll be able to find food and shelter. A one-way flight from the peninsula communities to Anchorage ranges from $450 to $525.

Chignik

The first notable settlement west of Kodiak is isolated Chignik, which harbors a couple of fish canneries and a seasonal population that fluctuates between 100 and 200. The MV *Tustumena* stops at Chignik on most, but not all, of its runs. Check ahead.

Sand Point

On the northwest coast of Popof Island, Sand Point is the largest commercial fishing base in the Aleutians, with a population of 943. It was founded in 1898 by a San Francisco fishing company as a trading post and cod-fishing station, but also bears traces of Aleut, Scandinavian and Russian heritage. The town's **St Nicholas Chapel**, a Russian Orthodox church, was built in 1936 and is now on the National Register of Historical Places. The *Tustumena* ferry only stops for an hour in Sand Point, meaning you'll have to be a very fast runner to make it the half-mile to the **Sand Point Tavern** (907-383-5050; 189 Main St, Sand Point; 3pm-2am Sun-Thu, to 3am Fri & Sat) for a beer and a game of pool.

King Cove

At the Alaska Peninsula's western end, near the entrance to Cold Bay, is King Cove, founded in 1911, when a salmon cannery was built. Today, with a population of 923, it is a commercial fishing base and home to **Peter Pan Seafoods**, whose salmon cannery is the largest operation under one roof in Alaska.

Cold Bay

Cold, treeless and very sparsely populated (population 59), Cold Bay is one of the more interesting stops on the *Tustumena* ferry route, primarily because the boat pulls in for a three-hour stopover, long enough to step ashore and get a taste of this desolate land and its off-the-grid community. If you put your name down for the wildlife-tour lottery on the *Tustumena* (and get lucky) you'll enjoy a free guided tour of nearby **Izembek National Wildlife Refuge** (907-532-2445; www.fws.gov/refuge/Izembek) FREE and possibly see a brown bear.

Cold Bay owes its existence to WWII. In 1942 a massive airstrip was built to deter a possible Japanese invasion. The airstrip remains – the fifth largest in the state – though these days it handles flights to Anchorage plus the odd emergency jumbo landing. Huge brown bears have been known to patrol the airport perimeter fence. For accommodation, look to the **Bearfoot Inn** (907-532-2327; www.bearfootinnalaska.com; 123 Bear Country Rd, Cold Bay; r $95-112), which doubles as a bar and grocery. It's conceivable to stay for two days in Cold Bay if you're arriving on the *Tustumena*, hopping back aboard as the boat makes its return trip, although this means you'll miss out on Dutch Harbor.

False Pass

This small but picturesque fishing village (population 42) on the tip of Unimak Island looks across a narrow passage at the Alaska Peninsula. False Pass sits in the shadow of the snowy Roundtop Volcano. There's a basic store at the end of the jetty and (usually) some locals selling jewelry. The *Tustumena* ferry docks for two hours.

Akutan

Founded as a fur-trading post in 1878, Akutan Island (population around 1000) is now inhabited by a stalwart group of fish-processing workers and some Aleuts. Its Russian Orthodox **Alexander Nevsky Chapel** dates from 1918. The *Tustumena* ferry reaches here at 5:30am to pick up a few fishers. Most other passengers stay in their bunks/sleeping bags.

Bunker Hill HISTORIC SITE

Part of the national historic area, this coastal battery was known to the military as Hill 400 or colloquially as Little South America (due to its shape). The hill was fortified with 155mm guns, ammunition magazines, water tanks, 22 Quonset huts and a concrete command post at the top. You can easily hike to the peak of Bunker Hill along a gravel road picked up just after crossing the bridge to Amaknak Island.

Cathedral of the Holy Ascension CHURCH

(Broadway) Unalaska is dominated by the Cathedral of the Holy Ascension, the oldest Russian-built church still standing in Alaska. It was built in 1825 and then enlarged in 1894, when its floor plan was changed to a *pekov* (the shape of a crucifix). Overlooking the bay, the church and its onion domes are Unalaska's most iconic symbol. The church contains almost 700 pieces of art, ranging from Russian Orthodox icons and books to the largest collection of 19th-century paintings in Alaska.

The best time to view the interior of the church is after services, 6:30pm on Saturday and 11am Sunday morning.

Outside the church is a small graveyard, where the largest grave marker belongs to Baron Nicholas Zass. Born in 1825 in Archangel, Russia, he eventually became bishop of the Aleutian Islands, and all of Alaska, before his death in 1882. Next door to the graveyard is the Bishop's House

Aleutian WWII Visitor Center MUSEUM

(☎907-581-9944; 2716 Airport Beach Rd; adult/child $4/free; ⏲1-6pm Wed-Sat) To learn about the 'Forgotten War,' begin at the Aleutian WWII Visitor Center, near the airport, in the original air-control tower built in 1942. Downstairs, exhibits relive the Aleutian campaign, including the bombing of Dutch Harbor by the Japanese. Upstairs is the recreated air-control tower, and in a theater you can watch documentaries about the war.

Bishop's House HISTORIC SITE

(W Broadway Ave) Commissioned by Bishop Nester, this house was first built in San Francisco in 1882, dismantled and shipped to Unalaska to be reassembled. During his return to Unalaska, the bishop fell off the deck of the ship and died, and he never had the chance to live in the house. His body was recovered and he was buried in the graveyard outside the Cathedral of the Holy Ascension.

Although it's not open for regular visitation, the house's aging red roof and wooden siding stands out amid the more modern buildings nearby.

Expedition Park PARK

(off Gilman Rd) Bald eagles are as common as crows in and around Unalaska and Dutch Harbor. There are so many birds that locals view them as scavengers, which they are by nature, rather than as the majestic symbol of the USA. One of the best places to photograph them up close and in a somewhat natural setting is Expedition Park, at the end of Bobby Storrs Boat Harbor.

Memorial Park PARK

(Summer Bay Rd) Next to a disheveled hillside graveyard overlooking the bay is Memorial Park. The park has several monuments dedicated to the Coast Guard and Navy personnel who died in WWII. Alongside pillboxes and bunkers, there are granite monuments and a peace memorial. US and Alaskan flags fly gallantly in the (usually) strong winds.

At the far end of the park, the USS *Northwest* memorial is named for a 19th-century freight ship turned floating WWII bunkhouse that was destroyed by Japanese bombs in 1942. In 1992, for the 50th anniversary of the event, the propeller was salvaged by divers and is now part of the memorial.

To get to the park, follow Bayview Ave to the southeast end of town.

Sitka Spruce Park PARK

(Biorka Dr) This national historical landmark within Dutch Harbor is where the Russians first planted Sitka spruce on the island in 1805. It's the oldest recorded afforestation project in North America. Three of the gnarly spruce trees are said to be the originals. The park also features interpretive displays and a short trail to an edge-of-the-cliff overlook.

Activities

Hiking

Because of the treeless environment, hiking is easy here. And don't worry about bears – there aren't any.

Before hiking anywhere, even Mt Ballyhoo or Bunker Hill, you must obtain a permit (per person $6 daily, $15 weekly) from the Ounalashka Corporation (p361). Also call Unalaska's Parks, Culture & Recreation Department (p361), which organizes hikes in summer for locals and visitors.

Unalaska & Dutch Harbor

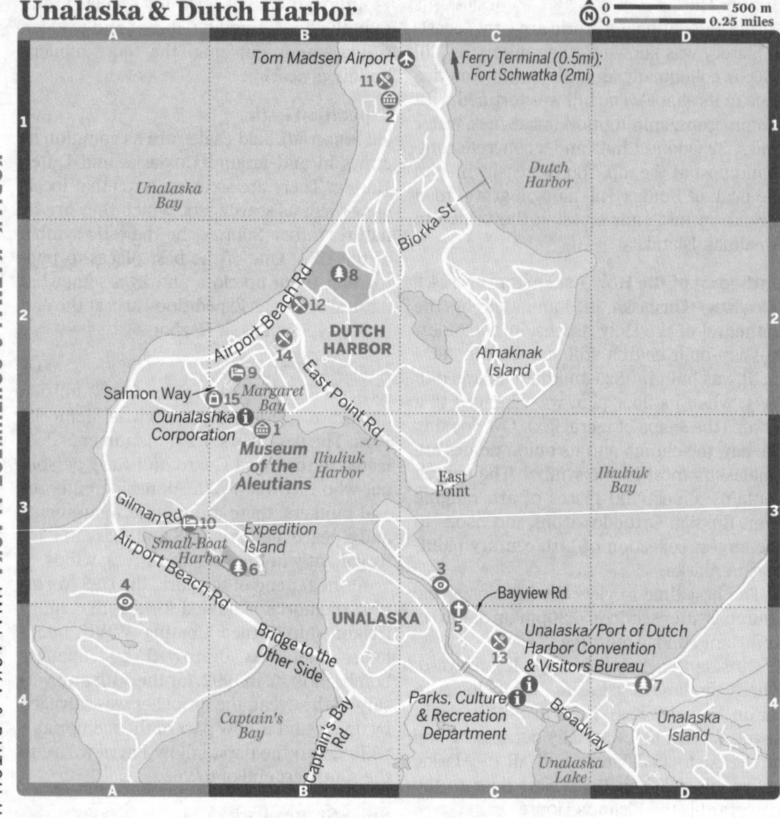

Unalaska & Dutch Harbor

★**Ugadaga Bay Trail** HIKING
(Overland Dr) On the southeast side of Unalaska, this pleasant hike is 2.2 miles one-way along an ancient portage route. More recently, the US military ran communications lines from Unalaska all the way to Seattle, and you'll see remnants of them in eroded spots. Seal hunters were using the portage as late as the 1960s.

Pyramid Trail HIKING

(Pyramid Creek Rd) Tracing an old military road, this 2.7-mile trail leads through the Pyramid Valley, a green and supremely peaceful part of the island. Although it's not far outside of town, the chirps of ground squirrels and the occasional squawk of a bald eagle are all you'll hear out here.

The trail hugs the southern flank of Mt Pyramid, and after about 1.25 miles you'll come across the remains of an old military outpost. You can turn back here or continue down the other side of the mountain to the end of the trail.

Uniktali Bay HIKING

(Captain's Bay Rd) Ending in an undeveloped bay where glass floats from Japanese fishing nets can be found, an enjoyable day can be spent hiking to Uniktali Bay, a round-trip of 8 to 10 miles.

From Captain's Bay Rd, turn south on a gravel road just before Westward Cannery. Follow the road for a mile to its end; a foot trail continues along a stream. In 2 miles, the trail runs out, and you'll reach a lake in a pass between two 2000ft peaks. Continue southeast to pick up a second stream, which empties into Uniktali Bay.

Paddling

The many protected harbors, bays and islets of Unalaska Island make for ideal sea-kayaking conditions. The scenery is stunning and the wildlife plentiful. It is possible to encounter Steller's sea lions, sea otters and harbor porpoises.

Tours

Extra Mile Tours TOURS

(907-581-1859; www.unalaskadutchharbortour.com; 2/4hr tour $50/90) Operator Bobbie Lekanoff is very knowledgeable in indigenous and WWII history, and famililar with every single flower and bird.

Sleeping

You aren't spoiled for choice here: there are two hotels in Unalaska – the Grand Aleutian and Harbor View Inn.

Campers must obtain a permit from the Ounalashka Corporation (p361). This native corporation owns most of the land out of town and allows camping.

There's an 8% hotel tax.

Harbor View Inn MOTEL $$

(907-581-3844; 88 Gilman Way; d $142; wi-fi) Affiliated with the Grand Aleutian Hotel, this basic 30-room inn is sandwiched between a shipyard and a fish-processing plant. The smell of cigarette smoke competes with the pong of fish and the bar downstairs is noisy. Grin and bear it – it's the only budget option in town.

Grand Aleutian Hotel HOTEL $$

(907-581-3844, 866-581-3844; www.grandaleutian.com; 498 Salmon Way; r/ste $189/237; wi-fi) Updated rooms with memory-foam mattresses appeal to TV crews and travelers on a loose budget. The grand views from every window help make up for the slightly utilitarian – although clean – digs. Aside from the rougher Harbor View Inn it's your only option. Book ahead!

Eating

There are 10 places to eat in Unalaska and Dutch Harbor, two in supermarkets, five affiliated to the Grand Aleutian Hotel and one at the airport. The only two truly indie places are Amelia's and Dutch Harbor Restaurant.

Dutch Harbor Restaurant ASIAN $

(907-581-5966; 3rd St & Broadway; mains $10-14; 10:30am-9:30pm Mon-Sat) An inviting, well-lit space serving great Asian staples such as chow mein, fried rice and pho. The pad thai comes in a pile the size of your face and is highly recommended. In spite of its name, this is on the Unalaska side of the island.

Safeway SUPERMARKET $

(2029 Airport Beach Rd; sandwiches $7-11; 7am-11pm) As is often the case in the remoter parts of Alaska, the local Safeway is a passable place to grab a coffee and sandwich.

★**Amelia's** MEXICAN $$

(907-581-2800; Airport Beach Rd; breakfast $11-14, dinner $15-30; 6am-10pm) This Dutch Harbor restaurant does a little of everything, from breakfast and burgers to seafood and pasta, but the majority of its menu is Mexican, including almost a dozen types of burritos. Amazingly, none of them is stuffed with crab or halibut.

Airport Restaurant ASIAN $$

(Airport Beach Rd; breakfast & lunch $11-15, dinner $16-29; 9am-11pm) A godsend of a restaurant located at an airport notorious for bad weather. Better than the usual franchise food, it does American staples along with some excellent Vietnamese dishes: try the Airport Surf – a *banh mi* (Vietnamese sandwich) in disguise. The bar is open late.

Harbor View Bar & Grill PIZZA **$$**
(☎907-581-7246; 88 Gilman Way; pizza $18-31; ⊙11:30am-1am Mon-Thu, 11:30am-2am Fri & Sat, noon-10pm Sun) At the eponymous inn, this place has pizza, salads, pasta and burgers. The rocking bar is the best place to meet a proud extra from the early seasons of *Deadliest Catch* (the reason for its local nickname, the 'Unisleaze').

Harbor Sushi JAPANESE **$$**
(88 Gilman Way; rolls $12-20; ⊙5-10:30pm Mon-Sat, to 9:30pm Sun) Directly attached to Harbor View Bar & Grill, this place serves the best sushi in a town that knows its seafood.

★**Chart Room** AMERICAN **$$$**
(☎907-581-7120; 498 Salmon Way; mains $30-50; ⊙6-11pm Mon-Sat; 10am-2pm, 6-9:30pm Sun) The swankiest restaurant in Dutch Harbor and, by definition, the Aleutian Islands, the Chart Room has more meat than seafood on its menu. It's best known for its weekend buffet brunch spread ($25) which includes king-crab legs, made-to-order omelets and chocolate-dipped strawberries. Otherwise try the local halibut, salmon, shrimp and king crab.

Drinking & Nightlife

Cape Cheerful Lounge BAR
(498 Salmon Way; ⊙3pm-midnight Mon-Sat, noon-10pm Sun) The Grand Aleutian Hotel bar is more refined than the Harbor View and in June, July and August the drinkers move to an outdoor patio for 'BBQ on the Deck' from 6-9pm. The good pub-grub menu includes sliders and barbecued meals ($12 to $18).

THE TRUSTY TUSTY

The easiest way to see 'Bush Alaska' without flying is to hop onto the **Alaska Marine Highway ferry** on its route to the eastern end of the Aleutian Islands between May and September. The MV *Tustumena*, a 290ft vessel that holds 220 passengers, is one of only two ferries in the Alaska Marine Highway fleet rated as an oceangoing ship, hence its nickname, the 'Trusty *Tusty*.' It is also one of the oldest vessels in the fleet, serving with valor since 1964. An alternative nickname, the 'Rusty Tusty,' is sometimes whispered among its passengers.

Riding the *Tusty* is truly one of the best bargains in public transportation. The scenery and wildlife are spectacular. You'll pass the perfect cones of several volcanoes, the treeless but lush green mountains of the Aleutians, and distinctive rock formations and cliffs. Whales, sea lions, otters and porpoises are commonly sighted, and birdlife abounds (more than 250 species).

Viewing wildlife and scenery depends, however, on the weather. It can be an extremely rough trip at times, deserving its title 'the cruise through the cradle of the storms.' The smoothest runs are from June to August, while in the fall 40ft waves and 80-knot winds are the norm. That's the reason for barf bags near the cabins and travel-sickness medication in the vending machines. The tiny bar – three stools, two tables – is called the Pitch and Roll Cocktail Lounge.

Cabins are available (around $700 each way) and are a worthwhile expense, but book at least three months in advance. Otherwise you can pitch a tent on deck (bring duct tape) or pitch your sleeping bag in the solarium. The *Tusty* has power outlets but no wi-fi or decent cell-phone coverage. The restaurant serves breakfast, lunch and dinner at set times and the food isn't bad. There is also a coffee machine and a vending machine. To save money stock up with your own snacks.

The *Tustumena*'s stops can vary slightly, but the most common route is (east to west): Homer, Kodiak, Chignik, Sand Point, King Cove, Cold Bay, False Pass, Akutan and Dutch Harbor.

Over half a century old, the *Tusty*'s future is in doubt. During the 2016 and 2017 summer seasons, sailings were canceled while the ship remained in dock for repairs. Communities in the Aleutians were left stranded and travelers sought alternatives. A replacement ship has been approved, but funding remains mired in the state legislature.

Shopping

Alaska Ship Supply GIFTS & SOUVENIRS
(907-581-1284; www.alaskashipsupply.com; 487 Salmon Way; 7am-10pm) This warehouse-like store is like a remote outpost of Costco with a few unique extras. The *Deadliest Catch* hoodies make a good only-in–Dutch Harbor souvenir. If you're not after fishing-trawler fashion, stock up on groceries or drop by the espresso cafe.

Information

MEDICAL SERVICES

Iliuliuk Medical Center (907-581-1202; 34 LaVelle Ct; walk-in 8:30am-6pm Mon-Fri, to 1pm Sat) Just off Airport Beach Rd near Unalaska City Hall; has walk-in and 24-hour emergency service.

MONEY

Key Bank of Alaska (907-581-1300; 487 Salmon Way) Across from the Grand Aleutian Hotel in Dutch Harbor; has a 24-hour ATM.

TOURIST INFORMATION

Ounalashka Corporation (907-581-1276; www.ounalashka.com; 400 Salmon Way; 8am-5pm Mon-Fri) Issues camping and hiking permits for daily/weekly $6/15 per person.

Parks, Culture & Recreation Department (907-581-1297; http://ci.unalaska.ak.us/parksrec/page/parks-trails; 37 S 5th St; 6am-10pm Mon-Fri, 8am-10pm Sat, noon-7pm Sun)

Unalaska/Port of Dutch Harbor Convention & Visitors Bureau (877-581-2612, 907-581-2612; www.unalaska.info; cnr 5th & Broadway, Unalaska; 9am-5pm Mon-Fri) Located in the Burma Street Russian Church, originally a military chapel built during WWII. Also opens when the ferry is in.

Getting There & Away

The MV *Tustumena* from Homer ($394) and Kodiak ($337) calls at Dutch Harbor twice monthly between May and September. The **ferry terminal** (Ballyhoo Rd) is approximately 3 miles north of Unalaska off Ballyhoo Rd. It stops in town for eight hours before returning east.

The only other way to get out of Unalaska and Dutch Harbor is by flying. There are three to four flights daily and a one-way ticket is $500 to $600. Beware: Dutch Harbor's notoriously fickle weather can delay flights. The **airport** (907-581-1254; Airport Beach Rd) is on Amaknak Island.

It's also common for checked luggage to be bumped from flights due to limited weight capacity. If this happens to you, your bags will likely be on the next flight.

Cab fare to downtown Unalaska costs $11 to $12 from the airport, or $14 to $16 from the ferry. There are a zillion cabs running all over Unalaska and Dutch Harbor, including **Aleutian Taxi** (907-581-1866). There's a long list in the airport terminal.

Getting Around

To get out and see the island by car look no further than **BC Vehicle Rental** (866-336-6659; Airport Beach Rd), which is located inside the airport and has vehicles from around $65 a day. Just outside the main terminal, **North Port Car Rental** (907-581-3880; Airport Beach Rd) has rentals starting at $79 a day.

A long list of taxis serves the community; check the visitors bureau website for an up-to-date record of companies and phone numbers.

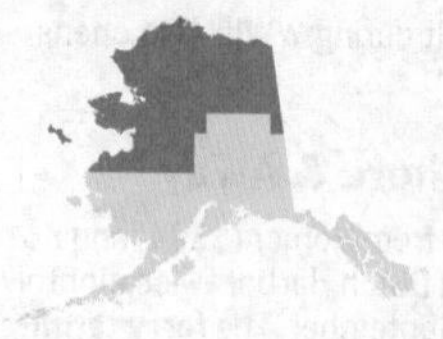

The Bush

Includes ➡

Best Places to Eat

- Pingo Bakery (p368)
- Arctic Pizza (p382)
- Sam & Lee's Chinese Restaurant (p382)
- Coldfoot Camp Restaurant (p373)
- Milano's Pizzeria (p368)

Best Places to Stay

- King Eider Inn (p382)
- Aurora Hotel (p375)
- Dredge No 7 Inn (p368)
- Top of the World Hotel (p382)
- Prudhoe Bay Hotel (p375)

Why Go?

Even the frontier has a frontier, and for Alaskans, that's the Bush. By and large, you can't come here by road; visitors must travel by air or sea or sled dog. The space is vast – larger than many countries – yet the population is smaller than many midsize cities. Still, people live here, and they embrace their place at the edge of the map, which they share with herds of musk ox, the snaking Trans-Alaska Pipeline, Iñupiat-language church services, shipping-container-chic architecture in towns like Utqiaġvik (Barrow), and the very Gates of the Arctic. Come here to embrace deep isolation, never-ending nights, endless days and true wilderness: utterly untamed landscapes that remind us humans how small we really are.

When to Go

Nome

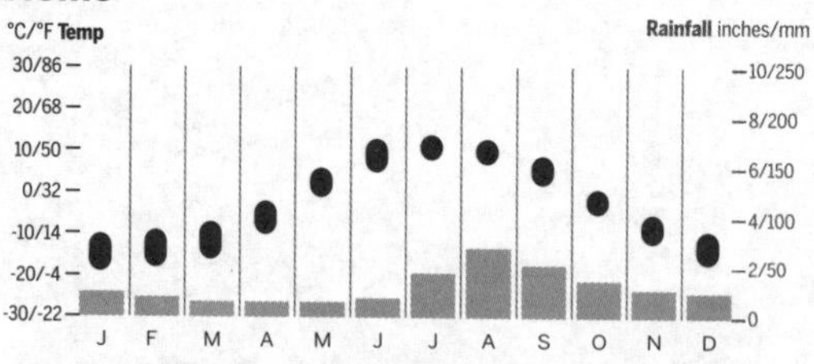

Mar The Iditarod, the world's most famous dogsled race, concludes in Nome.

Jun Utqiaġvik Iñupiat celebrate the Nalukataq festival after the spring's whale harvest.

Jun–Aug Enjoy 24-hour sunlight above the Arctic Circle.

History

The history of the Bush is largely the history of Alaska Natives. By their own accounts, they've been here since the beginning. Archaeologists say it's not been as long as that: perhaps 6000 years for the ancestors of today's Athabascans, and about 3000 years for the Iñupiat, Yupiks and Aleuts. Either way, they've displayed remarkable ingenuity and endurance, thriving as fishers, hunters and gatherers in an environment few else could even survive in.

Europeans arrived in Alaska in the 1800s, with traders and missionaries setting up shop in numerous communities along the western coast. Whalers entered the Bering

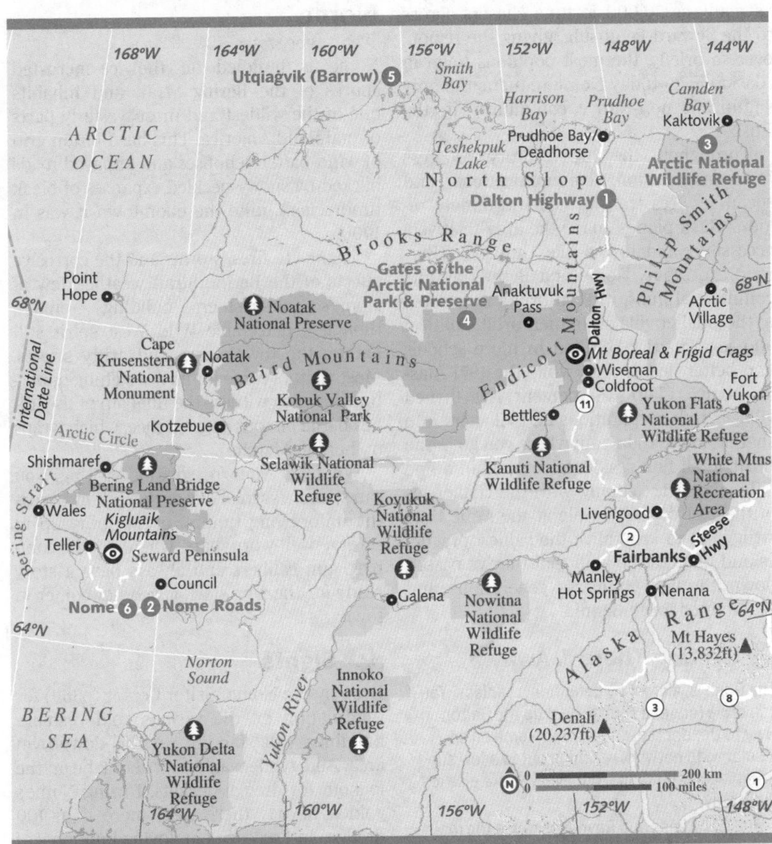

The Bush Highlights

1 Dalton Highway (p371) Driving from Interior Alaska to the shores of the Arctic Ocean on one of North America's great – and northernmost – road trips.

2 Nome Roads (p370) Exploring the roads that spread out from Nome across miles of stunning Arctic scenery.

3 Arctic National Wildlife Refuge (p372) Following caribou herds on a backcountry excursion into this remote treasure.

4 Gates of the Arctic National Park & Preserve (p378) Trekking across a slice of utter American wilderness with no other souls in sight.

5 End of the Road (p380) Heading to the surreal place where the roads end in Utqiaġvik (Barrow).

6 Nome bars (p369) Drinking with a crowd of roughneck locals in this frontier town.

Sea around the middle of the century, and soon expanded into the Arctic Ocean. By 1912 they had virtually decimated the bowhead whale population.

The most climactic event in the Bush, however, was the gold rush at Nome, triggered in 1898 (just two years after the discovery of gold in the Klondike) by the 'Three Lucky Swedes.' The stampede drew as many as 20,000 fortune chasers across to the Seward Peninsula, giving the region, ever so briefly, the most populous town in Alaska. Even today Nome remains the only significant non-Native community in the Bush.

Throughout the 20th century, progress in transportation, communications and social services transformed the remote region. 'Bush planes' made the area relatively accessible, and towns like Utqiaġvik (Barrow), Kotzebue, Nome and Bethel became commercial hubs, in turn bringing services to the smaller villages in their orbit. Political and legal battles resulted in more schools and better health care, while the 1971 Alaska Native Claims Settlement Act turned villages into corporations and villagers into shareholders. Today, anywhere you go in the Bush you'll find residents engaged in a fine balancing act – coping with the challenges of the 21st century, while at the same time struggling to keep alive the values, practices and links to the land that they've passed down through countless generations and maintained for millennia.

Getting There & Away

The Bush is, almost by definition, roadless. You can drive (or get a shuttle bus) up the Dalton Hwy to Deadhorse, and around Nome on an insular road network reaching out to a few surrounding destinations, but everywhere else it's fly-in only.

Alaska Airlines and Ravn Alaska are the main carriers, with Nome, Kotzebue and Utqiaġvik (Barrow) the main hubs. Regional airlines fly to smaller villages and provide air-taxi services into the wilderness.

WESTERN ALASKA

Severe, gorgeous and incredibly removed from civilization – even for this state – Western Alaska is home to Iñupiat, intrepid prospectors and some of the state's least-seen landscapes. Too far north (and too close to the Arctic Ocean and Bering Sea) for trees, the terrain is instead carpeted with coral-like tundra grasses and flowers, and patrolled by herds of caribou and musk ox. Highlights of the area include regional hubs like Nome, and the vast tracts of little-explored wilderness in the Noatak and Bering Land Bridge National Preserves.

Nome

907 / POP 3797

Nome is huddled on the ice-encrusted shores of the Bering Strait and inhabits one of the wildest and most westerly parts of mainland America. This hard-bitten grid of wind-battered houses and unpaved roads backed by snow-speckled expanses of bleak tundra isn't quite the boomtown it was in 1900.

Thanks to fires, storms and the corrosive effects of the Bering Strait weather, few of Nome's gold-rush-era buildings remain, though a detectable Wild West spirit still haunts the town's bars and gritty streets. Most visitors come for bird-watching opportunities or to witness the final lap of the Iditarod, the famous dogsled race, which wraps up here in March.

Whatever your reason for visiting, you can spend a surreal day or two hiking across the unforgiving tundra, or warming up in several well-worn bars where locals compare gun calibers and always have a story ready for the next slack-jawed newcomer in town.

Sights

Drop by the Nome Visitor Center (p369) for information on the various gold rush-era buildings still standing in the downtown area. And, while wandering about, be on the lookout for dredge buckets. During Nome's golden heyday there were more than 100 dredges in use, each employing hundreds of buckets to scoop up gravel and dirt. Today you'll see the buckets all over town, many used as giant flowerpots.

The Carrie McLain Museum (p366), Katirvk Cultural Center and Kegoayah Kozga Public Library (p366) are all located in the airy, ultra-contemporary Richard Foster Building (p366), located at 100 W 7th Ave.

Katirvk Cultural Center MUSEUM

(907-443-4340; www.kawerak.org/katirvik.html; 100 W 7th Ave, Richard Foster Bldg; $10; 2-6pm Thu & Fri, to 4pm Sat; P) The word 'Katirvk'

Nome

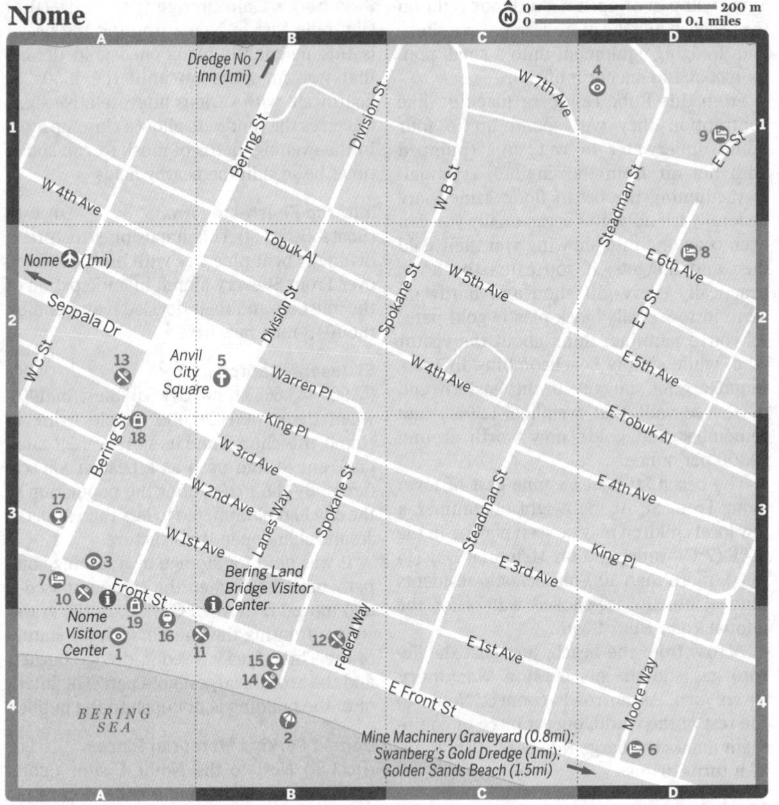

Nome

Sights

Carrie McLain Museum ....(see 4)
1 Donald Perkins Memorial Plaza A4
2 Golden Sands Beach B4
3 Iditarod Finish-Line Arch A3
Katirvk Cultural Center ....(see 4)
4 Richard Foster Building D1
5 St Joseph Church B2

Sleeping

6 Aurora Inn D4
7 Nome Nugget Inn A3
8 Nome Recreation Center D2
9 Sluicebox D1

Eating

10 Bering Sea Bar & Grill A3
11 Husky Restaurant B4
12 Milano's Pizzeria B4
13 Pingo Bakery A2
14 Polar Café B4

Drinking & Nightlife

15 Board of Trade Saloon B4
16 Breaker's Bar A4
17 Polaris Bar A3

Shopping

18 Chukotka Alaska A3
19 Maruskiya's of Nome A3

comes from the Iñupiat term for 'gathering place.' In this case, the 'place' in question is a small, modern museum that explores local indigenous culture and folkways.

Golden Sands Beach BEACH

Sand zero, so to speak, of Nome's famed gold rush, this beach is still open to recreational mining and all summer long you can watch miners set up work camps along the shore.

Some will pan or open a sluice box right on the beach, while the more serious rig a sluice and dredging equipment onto a small pontoon boat and anchor it offshore.

From this Rube Goldberg machine–like contraption they will spend up to four hours underwater in wet suits (pumped with hot air from the engine), essentially vacuuming the ocean floor. Miners are generally friendly, and occasionally you can even coax one into showing you their gold dust and nuggets. If you catch the fever, practically every gift shop and hardware store in town sells black-plastic gold pans. As you're panning, think about the visitor who, while simply beachcombing in 1984, found a 3.5in nugget at the eastern end of the seawall that weighed 1.29oz, and remember that gold's now worth around $1300 per ounce.

The beach stretches a mile east of town along Front St. At the height of summer, a few local children may be seen playing in the 45°F (7°C) water, and on Memorial Day (in May), more than 100 masochistic residents plunge into the ice-choked waters for the annual **Polar Bear Swim**.

Across from the beach, just past the Tesoro gas station, sits a **Mine Machinery Graveyard**. As no roads connect Nome to the rest of the world, once a piece of equipment makes the barge-ride here, it stays until it turns to dust.

Carrie McLain Museum MUSEUM

(☎907-443-6630; www.nomealaska.org; 100 W 7th Ave, Richard Foster Bldg; adult/child $7/6; ⊙noon-7pm Mon-Thu, to 6pm Sat; P) Once effectively an attic of Nome 'stuff,' the Carrie McLain Museum has evolved over the years into a professionally presented museum that profiles the history of Nome and Western Alaska. Many of the institution's more than 15,000 artifacts relate to gold-rush days, including racks of mining equipment, historical documents and photo albums.

Richard Foster Building LANDMARK

(100 W 7th Ave; P) The futuristic aesthetic of this municipal building stands in stark contrast to Nome's historic homes and storefronts. Inside, you'll find the Carrie McLain Museum, Katirvk Cultural Center (p364) and **Kegoayah Kozga Public Library** (☎907-443-6628; www.nomealaska.org; ⊙noon-7pm Mon-Thu, to 6pm Fri & Sat; 📶).

Swanberg's Gold Dredge LANDMARK

One mile east of Nome fronting the beach is this poignantly abandoned gold dredge that was in operation until the 1950s. A boardwalk with various interpretative signs traverses the tundra to allow a close-up look. In the evening, herds of musk ox can sometimes be seen in the nearby fields.

Iditarod Finish-Line Arch LANDMARK

(Front & Bering St) This imposing structure, a distinctly bent pine tree with burls, is raised over Front St every March in anticipation of the mushers and their dogsled teams ending the 1049-mile race here.

St Joseph Church CHURCH

(☎907-443-6663; Anvil City Sq) Built in 1901, when there were 20,000 people living in Nome, this church and its spire were located on Front St and used as a beacon for seafarers. By the 1920s, after the population of the city had plummeted to less than 900, the Jesuits abandoned the structure.

It was used for storage by a mining company until 1996 when the city purchased it and moved it to Anvil City Sq. In the grassy square fronting the church, look for statues of the Three Lucky Swedes, dredge buckets and the 'world's largest gold pan.' The interior of the building is not open to the public.

Donald Perkins Memorial Plaza PLAZA

(Front St) Next to the Nome Visitor Center is this plaza, containing a collection of old mining detritus.

Activities

If you're well prepared and the weather holds, the backcountry surrounding Nome can be hiking heaven. Though there are no marked trails in the region, the area's three highways offer perfect access into the tundra and mountains. What's more, the lack of trees and big, rolling topography make route-finding fairly simple: just pick a point and go for it. For those who'd like a little more direction, a multipage list of suggested day hikes is available from the Nome Visitor Center.

Also providing great info on local trekking is the Bering Land Bridge Visitor Center (p369). Throughout the summer the center leads very popular and free guided day hikes, as well as birding tours in May and June. Contact the center for exact times and dates.

NOME: KLONDIKE'S SEQUEL

Type the words 'Alaska' and 'gold rush' into an internet search engine and your first result will probably contain the word 'Klondike.' There's just one small problem: Klondike is in the Yukon Territory in Canada. Its erroneous listing as an Alaskan gold rush came about because of the key role Alaska played as a supply center and point of embarkation for thousands of American 'stampeders' heading north in 1897.

The first true Alaskan gold rush ignited near present-day Nome in 1898 when three Swedish prospectors (the 'Three Lucky Swedes,' as they became known), blown off course in a small boat, discovered gold deposits in a river called Anvil Creek near Cape Nome. Coming so soon after the mania in the Yukon and giving fresh wind to many of the disgruntled and semi-destitute stampeders, Nome acted as Klondike's frenzied sequel, a kind of *Godfather Part II* with an equally colorful cast of despicable characters.

Nome's rise was meteoric. By 1899 when gold was discovered on Nome's beaches, Klondike's stampeders were leaving Dawson City in their droves to descend on the region. The nascent city, which hadn't even existed two years previously, briefly morphed into the largest in Alaska with over 20,000 hardy souls squeezed into makeshift wooden buildings or saggy canvas tents on the beach. Rather like Klondike, Nome attracted an abnormally high number of unsavory characters, including US lawman and veteran of the Gunfight at the OK Corral, Wyatt Earp, who set up and ran the profitable Dexter Saloon in town, a bar that allegedly doubled as a brothel.

The beauty of Nome's gold was that it was easily extractable. As much of it lay deposited on the beach, you didn't need heavy-duty dredging equipment to retrieve it, although dredges were often used. With seasonal sea access via steamship, the region was easier to reach than Klondike and thus attracted its fair share of chancers, no-hopers and blatant criminals. Within months of the strike, the fledgling settlement, in contrast to the relatively law-abiding Dawson City (well policed by the Canadian Mounties), was filled with debauchery. Holdups, gambling, prostitution, fist fights, drunkenness and robbery became endemic.

'Drunken gamblers groveled in the dust; women, shameless scarlet women...of exceedingly grotesque character but universally décolleté, reveled as recklessly as any of their tipsy companions,' wrote prudish new arrival Sarah Fell in 1900.

The frenzy of Nome had died by about 1905 and the town quickly reinvented itself as a small but stable settlement, known since 1972 as the endpoint for the Iditarod dogsled race. It wasn't Alaska's last gold rush. Fairbanks hit the jackpot in 1902 but it never reached the heights of Nome and its brief flirtation with notoriety.

Anvil Mountain HIKING

The climb up 1062ft Anvil Mountain is the closest hike to Nome and the only one that can be easily pulled off without a car. It's about a half-mile to the summit, through wonderful wildflower patches.

At the top you'll find the giant parabolic antennae of the Cold War–era White Alice Communications System, plus great views of town and the ocean, as well as the odd passing musk ox. To start, follow Bering St out of town to where it changes to the Teller Hwy. About 2.5 miles down the Teller Hwy turn right on the Dexter Bypass and look for an obvious dirt road, about half a mile in, climbing up the hillside.

Tours

The Nome Visitor Center (p369) can hook you up with operators for fishing, hunting and dogsled rides, as well as snowcat and snowmobile tours in season.

Akau Alaska Gold & Resort TOURS

(☎760-500-1329, 760-855-2855; www.akaugold.com; Old Glacier Creek Rd) This 'resort' offers gold-panning, sluicing and metal-detecting trips (from $150) along with tours of old gold-rush-era ruins and machinery, fishing trips and ATV rentals. They can also throw in accommodations and meal packages (contact them for the latest rates) if you wish to stay in the lodge and cabins, located 7 miles outside Nome on Old Glacier Creek Rd, which branches off the Nome–Teller Rd.

Nome Discovery Tours TOURS
(907-443-2814; tours $65-185) We've met lots of tour guides, but only one who's mayor of the town he gives tours about. Richard Beneville is an old song-and-dance man who decided to hang up his tap shoes to live out in the Alaska wilds. He offers everything from two-hour evening tundra exploration drives to full-day excursions to Teller.

For what it's worth, 'mayor' is a ceremonial job in Nome, but Richard may well be busy with municipal stuff, so call ahead.

Sleeping

You can camp for free on Golden Sands Beach, but do so a bit down the beach as the street sweepers dump debris here daily. Further from town it's unofficially permissible to camp just about anywhere: avoid private property and active mining claims, and clean up after yourself.

Nome tacks on a 6% bed tax to accommodations. Book rooms well in advance in summer and up to a year before Iditarod.

Nome Recreation Center ACCOMMODATION SERVICES $
(208 E 6th Ave; showers $7; 5:30am-10pm Mon-Fri) You can take a shower here and use the sauna, a nice way to clean up if you've been camping in the area.

Dredge No 7 Inn B&B $$
(907-304-1270; www.dredge7inn.com; 1700 Teller Hwy; ste $195; P) A cozy apparition in the unashamedly basic confines of Nome, Dredge No 7 is a modern inn that strikes a nice balance between rustic charm and some fine Martha Stewart–inspired flourishes. Bright, private suites share a spacious kitchen and the common areas are decked out with leather sofas and fireplace. Breakfast items are left in your room.

The inn is about a mile north of town on a large lot with open views across the tundra from the back deck. It also has an annex, the Sluicebox, in town. The Dredge can arrange vehicle rentals.

Sluicebox HOTEL $$
(907-304-1270; www.dredge7inn.com/suites.htm; 608 D St; ste $195;) This is the downtown annex for the Dredge No 7 Inn. Rooms are a little more modern, but no less charming, than accommodations at the 'main' Dredge No 7 out on the Teller Hwy.

Nome Nugget Inn HOTEL $$
(907-443-2323; www.nuggetinnhotel.com; 315 Front St; r $130-150;) In the thick of what passes for downtown, the slightly disheveled Nugget has 45 smallish rooms, about half with ocean views. The clapboard front and memorabilia-laden lobby promise much, but the rooms are compact and characterless – think cheap motel.

Aurora Inn HOTEL $$$
(907-443-3838; www.aurorainnome.com; 302 Front St; r $185-275;) Nome's most hotel-like accommodations are at the far edge of town, and just a short walk to Golden Sands Beach. The neat and tidy Aurora offers generic-style comfort in simple no-surprises rooms, some with full kitchenettes.

Eating

There are almost a dozen places to eat in Nome, mostly sit-down restaurants offering that odd Arctic mix of pizza, Chinese and US-style grub.

Opening hours are sometimes casual, with businesses displaying cryptic signs like 'open most days about 9am or 10am, occasionally as early as 7am; some days we aren't here at all.' You have been warned.

Pingo Bakery CAFE $
(907-387-0654; 308 Bering St; mains $10-16; 11:30am-3pm & 5:30-8pm Wed-Fri, 8:30am-3pm & 5:30-8pm Sat, 8:30am-5pm Sun) For Pingo shout 'bingo!,' especially if you arrive on a day when this precious little cafe is open. Best way to find out? Follow your nose. You'll catch the heady aroma of freshly baked cinnamon buns long before you see the flashing neon sign. Snack-seekers grab the croissants, cookies and big buns. Those with larger appetites tackle the roasted halibut pizza.

Milano's Pizzeria AMERICAN $$
(907-443-2924; cnr Front St & Federal Way, Old Federal Bldg; $11-34; 11am-11pm) Despite the name, Milano's serves way more than pizza. This local favorite slings subs, cheesesteaks, tempura, terikyaki, spaghetti, sushi, ramen and (why not?) a lobster dinner. The pizza itself is also pretty damn good.

Bering Sea Bar & Grill JAPANESE $$
(907-443-4900; www.beringsearestaurant.com; 305 Front St; mains $13-34; 6am-2am Sun-Thu, til 3am Fri & Sat) Is this the best sushi we've ever had? No, but it's the only sushi we've

had overlooking the icy Bering Sea, and that's something. You can also grub on not-so-Japanese but very Alaskan favorites like chili cheese fries, mushroom burgers and nachos.

Husky Restaurant JAPANESE **$$**

(907-443-1300; 235 Front St; mains $12-28; 11am-11pm) This cheap (by Nome standards) and cheerful diner does up platters of gyoza, chicken katsu, teriyaki and the usual Arctic slate of burgers and sandwiches.

Polar Café AMERICAN **$$**

(907-443-5191; 204 Front St; mains $19-28; 6am-10pm;) This popular waterfront eatery serves straightforward food that hits the spot – at least in Nome. As a bonus it has open views of the Bering Sea, friendly service and a $10 salad bar.

Drinking & Nightlife

Even by Alaskan standards, drinking in Nome is legendary. There are more saloons here than in the rest of Bush Alaska combined, which unfortunately means drunks wandering the streets, sometimes from morning till night. Most bars are clustered around Front St and can be classified as 'dives.'

Breaker's Bar BAR

(243 Front St; 10am-midnight) Dive in with the beards and the baseball caps and listen to Nomers discuss gun preferences and tussles with local grizzly bears. The decor's retro without even realizing it and the floor smells like 1973. Pool shooters play 'winner stays on' out back.

Board of Trade Saloon BAR

(907-443-2611; 212 Front St; 10am-2am Sun-Thu, to 3am Fri & Sat) Dating back to the callow years of the gold rush, this saloon claims to be the oldest on the Bering Sea and was (is?) certainly the most notorious. It's raucous, dingy, and full of professional drinkers in a state of eternal pickling, which is all to say – this spot has a ton of character.

Shopping

Maruskiya's of Nome ARTS & CRAFTS

(907-443-2955; 247 Front St; hrs vary) Sells a nice selection of indigenous arts and crafts, and is also *the* place to go for your 'There's No Place Like Nome' T-shirt.

Their hours are, and we quote: 'Open most days about 9 or 10. Occasionally as early as 7, but some days as late as 12 or 1. We close about 6:30 or 7. Occasionally about 5 or 6, but sometimes as late as 11 or 12.'

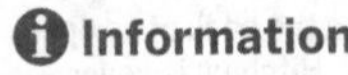

Information

MONEY

Wells Fargo (907-443-2223; 109a Front St; 10am-5pm Mon-Thu, til 6pm Fri) In the historic Miner's and Merchant's Bank building (dating from 1904); has a 24-hour ATM.

TOURIST INFORMATION

Bering Land Bridge Visitor Center (800-471-2352; www.nps.gov/bela; 179 Front St; 8am-5pm Mon-Fri, 9am-3pm Sat) In the Sitnasuak Native Corporation building, this National Park Service (NPS) center represents the Bering Land Bridge National Preserve near Nome. Inside are displays on mammoths, early Alaska Native culture and reindeer herding, plus info on the preserve.

Nome Visitor Center (907-443-6555; www.visitnomealaska.com; 301 Front St; 8am-7pm Mon-Fri, 10am-6pm Sat & Sun summer, 9am-5pm Mon-Fri winter;) Make this your first stop in Nome: the extremely helpful staff will load you with brochures, advice and coffee.

Getting There & Away

Disconnected from the main Alaskan road grid, Nome has three insular roads, all of which dead-end in the icy tundra just below the Arctic Circle. Anchorage lies 537 crow-flying miles to the southeast, while Siberian Russia bristles a mere 160 miles across the Bering Strait. You can almost taste the vodka.

Tiny **Nome Airport** (Airport Rd) is a little more than a mile from town. Nome is well served by Alaska Airlines (p429), which offers at least two daily flights to Anchorage for $500 to $600 round-trip (book well in advance). Most flights take roughly 90 minutes, but some via Kotzebue can take literally half a day with waits and transfers. You can also try Ravn Alaska (p430).

Bering Air (907-443-5464; www.beringair.com; Nome Airport) offers flights to numerous small settlements and Native villages across the length and breadth of the Bush.

Getting Around

From the airport to Nome it's an easy walk – or catch a cab for $6 per person (they always congregate at the airport).

If renting a vehicle, book well ahead of time. **Stampede Rent-A-Car** (907-443-3838; 302 Front St; hrs vary) is at the Aurora Inn and offers SUVs, vans and pickups. Dredge No 7 Inn also rents out trucks and SUVs. Both offer unlimited miles. When budgeting for a rental, keep in mind that gas in Nome is expensive and your vehicle likely won't get good mileage.

Hitchhiking is possible and locals are really good about picking people up. But you must be patient – and willing to sit in the back of an open pickup on very dusty roads. Hitching is never entirely safe, and we don't recommend it. Travelers who hitch should understand that they are taking a small but potentially serious risk.

Nome–Council Road

This 73-mile route, which heads northeast to the old mining village of Council, offers the most landscape diversity out of all Nome's road trips. For the first 30 miles it hugs the glimmering Bering Sea coastline and passes a motley, but very photogenic, array of shacks, cabins, tipis and Quonset huts used by Nome residents as summer cottages and fishing and hunting camps. Alaska Natives have hunted and fished in this area for millennia, and the many depressions dotting the landscape are the sites of former camps. On sunny days, the miles of beaches outside Nome beckon – but note how far inland autumn storms have tossed driftwood.

At Mile 22 the road passes Safety Roadhouse, a dollar-bill-bedecked dive of a watering hole, and then crosses the birders' wonderland of Safety Sound, which once formed the eastern edge of the Bering Land Bridge. A further 10 miles along is Bonanza Crossing, on the far side of which is the Last Train to Nowhere, a series of abandoned locomotives. Just to the north is the ghost town of Solomon, which was originally established in 1900 and once boasted a population of 1000 and seven saloons. The town was destroyed by a storm in 1913, relocated to higher ground and then further decimated by the 1918 flu epidemic.

Near Mile 40 you pass the first of two gold dredges within a couple of miles of each other. By 1912 almost 40 dredges worked the Seward Peninsula, and many are still visible from the Nome road system. The two on this road are in the best shape and are the most picturesque. Nome–Council Rd begins climbing after the second dredge and reaches Stookum Pass at Mile 53. There's a parking area at the pass, so you can pull off and admire the views or take a hike on the nearby ridges.

The road ends at Mile 73 at Council. Actually, the road ends at the banks of the Niukluk River, and Council is on the other side. Most of the houses here are weekend getaways for people living in Nome, and there are no year-round residents. Locals drive across the river – with the water often reaching their running boards. Tourists with rental vehicles should stay put. There are no services or shops in Council, but the Niukluk is an excellent place to fish for grayling.

Kougarok Road

Also known as Nome–Taylor Rd, Kougarok Rd leads 86 miles north from Nome through the heart of the Kigluaik Mountains. Along the way are a few artifacts from the gold-rush days and the best mountain scenery and hiking in the Nome area. Take this drive, which is an all-day affair heading there and back again, if you want a taste of the wintry, severe mountain landscape of the high tundra.

The Kigluaiks spring up almost immediately, flanking the road until around Mile 40, where the free, BLM-operated **Salmon Lake Campground** (Mile 40, Kougarok Rd; free; P) is located. The outlet for the Pilgrim

LAST TRAIN TO NOWHERE

In all of Bush Alaska, it's almost certainly the most-photographed landmark: a set of steam locomotives, utterly out of place and out of time, moldering on the Arctic tundra off the Nome–Council Rd, hundreds of miles from the nearest functioning railway. Dubbed the 'Last Train to Nowhere,' the three engines first plied the elevated lines of New York City in the 1880s, until Manhattan switched from steam to electric-driven trains. In 1903 the upstart Council City & Solomon River Railroad purchased the locomotives and transported them north, hoping to profit by servicing inland mines from the coast. Though the company surveyed some 50 miles of potential track, only half of that was built. By 1907 the operation went belly-up. Six years later a powerful storm sealed the Last Train's fate by destroying the Solomon River railroad bridge and stranding the engines on the tundra forever. Truly, it was the end of the line.

River, where you can watch sockeye salmon spawn in August, is close by.

Just before Mile 54 is Pilgrim River Rd, a rocky lane that heads northwest. The road climbs a pass where there's great ridge walking, then descends into a valley dotted with small tundra lakes. Less than 8 miles from Kougarok Rd, Pilgrim River Rd ends at the gate of Pilgrim Hot Springs. A roadhouse and saloon were located here during the gold rush, but they burned down in 1908. Later there was an orphanage for children who lost their parents in the 1918 influenza epidemic. If you want to enter the hot-spring area, first check in at the Nome Visitor Center (p369) as you'll need to fill out a form.

Kougarok Rd crosses Pilgrim River at Mile 60, the Kuzitrin River at Mile 68 and the Kougarok Bridge at Mile 86. This is one of the best areas to look for herds of musk ox. At all three bridges you can fish for grayling, Dolly Varden trout and salmon, among other species.

Beyond the Kougarok Bridge the road becomes a rough track impassable for cars. The extremely determined, however, can shoulder a pack and continue overland for a very challenging, boggy, unmarked 30-plus miles to Serpentine Hot Springs, inside the Bering Land Bridge National Preserve. A free, first-come, first-served bunkhouse-style cabin here sleeps 15 to 20, and there's a bathhouse for slipping into the 140°F to 170°F (60°C to 76.7°C) waters. Almost no one hikes both ways; consider chartering a plane in or out. Check at the Bering Land Bridge Visitor Center (p369) in Nome for flight operators and also to pick up its informative brochure on the springs.

Nome–Teller Road

The Nome–Teller Rd leads 73 miles (a one-way drive of at least two hours) from Nome to Teller, a year-round, subsistence Iñupiat village of 256 people. The landscape en route is vast and undulating, with steep climbs across spectacular rolling tundra. Hiking opportunities are numerous, as are chances to view musk ox and a portion of the reindeer herd communally owned by families in Teller. The huge Alaska Gold Company dredge, which operated until the mid-1990s, lies just north of Nome.

Teller lies at the westernmost end of the westernmost road in North America. This wind-wracked community overlooks the slate waters of the Bering Sea and stretches along a tapering gravel spit near the mouth of Grantley Harbor. Roald Amundsen, one of the greatest figures in polar exploration, returned to earth here after his legendary 70-hour airship flight over the North Pole on May 14, 1926. In 1985 Teller again made the headlines when Libby Riddles, then a Teller resident, became the first woman to win the Iditarod dogsled race.

With rising sea levels and melting permafrost, there are plans to move Teller, but the move, if it happens, will take several years.

ARCTIC ALASKA

OK traveler, you made it – this is as far out as you can get in a state that's already pretty damn isolated. Not many people make it to the Alaskan Arctic, because doing so takes a lot of time and money, but the rewards – utter wilderness, lonely isolation and the gray sea pounding a gravel beach on the north shore of America – are pretty sweet.

The towns out here are windswept and seemingly assembled from the cast-off junk of a science-fiction movie, but they're also extremely, appealingly weird. Of course, there's also plenty of outdoor stuff to do: paddling the numerous rivers, backpacking in little-visited national parks and preserves or driving the precarious and prodigious Dalton Hwy.

Dalton Highway

When you look at a map of Alaska, the north coast of the state feels truly remote, a faraway place that seems only reachable by air. But there is a road to the top of the world, and it's one of North America's great drives. The Dalton Hwy, also known as the Haul Rd, is a *long,* winding truck route that cuts 414 miles from Alaska's Interior to the North Slope, paralleling the Trans-Alaska Pipeline to its source at the Prudhoe Bay Oil Field. Along the way it passes evergreen quilts of taiga, the Gothic majesty of the Brooks Range and the chilling flatness of the Arctic tundra.

The road is open year-round, but you should only tackle it between late May and early September, when there's virtually endless light and little snow and ice. Expect

OFF THE BEATEN TRACK

ARCTIC NATIONAL WILDLIFE REFUGE

The **Arctic National Wildlife Refuge** (ANWR; ☎907-456-0250; www.fws.gov/refuge/arctic) is a 30,625-sq-mile wilderness in Alaska's northeast corner, straddling the eastern Brooks Range from the treeless Arctic Coast to the taiga of the Porcupine River Valley. For years, the refuge has been the subject of a debate over whether to drill beneath its coastal plain, which is thought to contain vast reserves of crude oil and natural gas.

Beyond the bragging rights it brings from visiting one of the most remote regions of the world, ANWR (an-wahr) attracts with its boundless wilderness and surprisingly diverse wildlife. This 'Serengeti of the north' is home to dozens of land mammals, including grizzlies, musk ox, Dall sheep and the second-largest herd of caribou in North America. Over 20 rivers cut through the region, several suitable for multiday paddles, as well as the four highest peaks in the Brooks Range. For adventurers, photographers and lovers of all things untamed and untrammeled, there are few more appealing destinations.

But visiting here is a challenge as well. There are no facilities of any sort. Literally millions of mosquitoes will decide you are an acceptable source of protein. The area is an Arctic desert, and giardia is present in the few water sources. You need to be comfortable camping around bears, and you must camp in such a way that bears won't come near you. ANWR is incredible, but only seasoned outdoors explorers should apply.

Even getting to ANWR is easier said than done. There's only one place it can be accessed by car: just north of Atigun Pass on the Dalton Hwy, where the road and the refuge briefly touch. To get deep into the refuge, you will need to fly. For a list of charter companies, consult the refuge's website or visit the Public Lands desk at the Morris Thompson Cultural & Visitors Center (p299) in Fairbanks. **Wilderness Alaska** (☎907-345-3567; www.wildernessalaska.com; 1wk trips $3400-5000) offers over 20 different ANWR trips, from rafting to following the caribou herds.

One of the gateways to the refuge is **Kaktovik**, an Iñupiat village on the northern shore of Barter Island in the Beaufort Sea, 160 miles east of Deadhorse. Kaktovik is the place to see polar bears in the wild, especially in September when they feed close to the town. For more information (and accommodations), contact the village's **Waldo Arms Hotel** (☎866-469-7590; www.waldoarmshotel.com; 2011 Lake Rd; r from $200; 📶).

a 40mph average and two hard days to reach Deadhorse, at the edge of everything.

ℹ Information

For more information on the Dalton Hwy, visit the Alaska Public Lands Information Center in the Morris Thompson Cultural & Visitors Center (p299) in Fairbanks and pick up a copy of the 24-page leaflet *Dalton Highway Visitor Guide*, which can also be downloaded from www.blm.gov. The guide covers history, safety, services, accommodations, points of interest and wildlife, and also includes mileage charts and maps.

The **BLM Central Yukon Field Office** (☎907-474-2200; www.blm.gov/office/central-yukon-field-office) maintains the highway's campgrounds, rest areas and visitor center.

ℹ Getting There & Away

Amazing, but true: you can catch a bus to the Arctic Ocean. The vans of **Dalton Highway Express** (Map p300; ☎907-474-3555; www.daltonhighwayexpress.com; 3820 University Ave S; one way/return to Deadhorse $250/500) head north twice a week between Fairbanks and Prudhoe Bay from early June to late August, but only if they have bookings. Vans stop overnight at Deadhorse and give you time to take an early morning oilfield tour before returning the next day. As it's a 16-hour journey one way, you may wish to fly back. Warning: spending more than a day in Deadhorse can invoke serious cabin fever. The one-way fare to the Arctic Circle is $84, Coldfoot $106, Wiseman $125 and Deadhorse $250.

Trucks and SUVs can be rented in Fairbanks from Arctic Outfitters (p309).

Mile 0 to 175

Mile 0 of the Dalton is at the junction with the Elliott Hwy, 84 miles from Fairbanks. Immediately, the Haul Rd announces itself: the pavement ends and loose gravel and blind curves begin. A road sign informs you that the speed limit is 50mph – for the next 414 miles!

This first section of highway carries you through scraggy boreal (taiga) forest. At Mile 56 the highway crosses the 2290ft-long, wooden-decked **Yukon River Bridge** – the only place where the legendary waterway is spanned in Alaska. On the far bank is the tiny BLM-run **Yukon Crossing Visitor Contact Station** (www.blm.gov/ak/st/en/prog/recreation/dalton_hwy.html; ⏱9am-6pm Jun-Aug), small on exhibits, but big on friendly advice.

On the opposite side of the highway is the **Yukon River Camp** (☎907-474-3557; www.yukonrivercamp.com; Dalton Hwy; r with shared bath $219; P), a utilitarian truck stop with work-camp-style rooms, showers, costly gas, a gift shop and a **restaurant** (☎907-474-3557; www.yukonrivercamp.com; mains $14-22; ⏱6am-10pm mid-May–mid-Sep).

The road then clambers back out of the river valley, across burned-over patches of forest (the remains of Interior-wide fires in 2004 and 2005), and into an alpine area with the 40ft-high granite tor of Finger Mountain beckoning to the east. You pass the imaginary line of the **Arctic Circle** at Mile 115, and for good 24-7 views of the sun, continue to **Gobblers Knob**, a hilltop lookout at Mile 132. From Gobblers Knob northward, the pyramids of the Brooks Range begin to dominate the scene. In the next 50 miles you'll cross several grayling-rich streams, including Prospect Creek, which, in January 1971, experienced America's lowest-ever temperature: -80°F (-62°C).

Coldfoot

☎907 / POP 5

At Mile 175, in a mountain-rimmed hollow, you'll arrive in the 'village' of Coldfoot. It basically feels like and acts as a parking rest stop. Originally Slate Creek, the settlement was renamed when the first settlers, a group of greenhorn miners, got 'cold feet' at the thought of spending the 1898 winter in the district and headed south. Coldfoot was a ghost town by 1912, but nowadays there is an airstrip, post office and trooper detachment.

Sights

Arctic Interagency Visitor Center VISITOR CENTER
(☎907-678-5209; CentralYukon@blm.gov; ⏱11am-10pm Jun-Aug) This impressive $5-million structure was opened in 2004 and features museum-quality displays about the Arctic and its denizens. There's a small series of paths on the outskirts that lead to a decidedly unnatural wonder – a chunk of the Trans-Alaska Pipeline. Ranger-led activities and talks regularly occur in the evening.

Sleeping

Marion Creek Campground CAMPGROUND $
(Mile 180, Dalton Hwy; tent & RV sites $8; P) The area's best lodging is down the highway 5 miles from Coldfoot at Marion Creek Campground. This 27-site place almost always has space and is in an open spruce forest with stunning views of the Brooks Range.

Eating

Coldfoot Camp Restaurant AMERICAN $$
(☎907-474-3500; Mile 175, Dalton Hwy; mains $10-20; ⏱5am-10pm) Within the Coldfoot Camp complex, this restaurant serves an all-you-can-eat buffet that doles out rib-sticking meat-and-potatoes-style food. It's simple, solid stuff, more than enough calorific energy to get you to Deadhorse.

Getting There & Away

While it's not the Dalton's exact halfway point, most drivers on the highway treat Coldfoot as such, and spend the night here before moving on to Deadhorse (240 miles) or Fairbanks (254 miles).

Wiseman

☎907 / POP 14

This century-old log-cabin village, the only authentic 'town' on the Dalton Hwy, occupies an enviable spot, overhung by peaks and fronting the Middle Fork of the Koyukuk River. Its heyday was 1910, when it replaced the original Coldfoot as a hub for area gold miners. Today, this pretty settlement is the genuine frontier deal – a scattering of cabins, many with 'No Trespassing' signs, and decorated with antlers and deer skulls.

Sights

Wiseman Historical Museum MUSEUM
(⏱hrs vary) FREE Located near the entrance to town, this museum is only open to tour-bus groups, but individual travelers might try to see if Wiseman's wise man, Jack Reakoff, is around. This engaging, urbane trapper will discourse at length about local history and wildlife

Sleeping

Arctic Getaway Alaska Cabin Rentals CABIN $$
(☎907-678-4456; www.arcticgetaway.com; cabins incl breakfast $135-295; P) Offers a sunny two-person cabin and antique-laden four-person cabins. All come with breakfast and have kitchenettes available for making other meals.

Boreal Lodge CABIN $$
(☎907-678-4556; www.boreallodge.com; s/d without bath $150; P) This comfortable option boasts fairly institutional rooms and a full kitchen that guests can use.

Eating

You'll need to bring your own food out here, as there are no dedicated eating options.

Getting There & Away

Wiseman is about 14 miles north of Coldfoot and 230 miles south of Deadhorse, and is accessible via a short dirt spur road at Mile 189.

Mile 190 to 414

North from Wiseman the Dalton skirts the eastern edge of Gates of the Arctic National Park. Dall sheep are often visible on the mountain slopes, and by Mile 194 the first views appear of the massive wall of **Sukakpak Mountain** (4459ft) looming dead ahead. At Mile 235 you kiss the woods goodbye: the famed **Last Spruce** (now dead) stands near a turnout on the highway's east side.

Atigun Pass (Mile 242), at an elevation of 4739ft, is the highest highway pass in Alaska and marks the Continental Divide. The view from the top – with the Philip Smith Mountains to the east and the Endicotts to the west – will steal your breath away.

Once you reach the turnoff for the undeveloped Galbraith Lake Campground at Mile 275, the Brooks Range is largely behind you. From here on down it's all rolling tundra. In this terrain, hiking and camping options are limitless, wildflowers and berries grow in profusion, and wildlife is rather easy to spot, not least because from May 10 to August 2 the sun never sets.

At the beginning and end of summer, watch for migrating waterbirds thronging roadside ponds, and caribou – members of the 22,000-head Central Arctic herd – grazing nearby. Also, keep an eye out for weird polar phenomena such as pingos – protuberant hills with a frozen center – and ice-wedge polygons, which shape the tundra into bizarre geometric patterns.

After a few bazillion hours (kidding…sort of), you'll reach the Arctic Coastal Plain, a sure sign that you're almost at Deadhorse. This is what the wrapper says: an utterly flat expanse of tundra grass broken by the odd pingo and countless small, shallow lakes, formed from permafrost melts. These lakes are pretty, and often have good fishing, but fair warning: each one is home to veritable clouds of mosquitoes, who are all eager to dine on your sweet, sweet blood.

Deadhorse

☎907 / POP 50

Sprawling, industrial Deadhorse supports the humongous Prudhoe Bay Oil Field at the north end of the Dalton Hwy. It's a gray, windswept and pebble-strewn dystopia, with a skyline of oil rigs and warehouses. Throw in expensive gas, wandering bears and lots of mosquitoes, 54 days of consecutive darkness in winter, a permanent population of less than 50, and an architectural style best described as Stalinist Siberian meets *Mad Max 2*.

No right-minded traveler would come here if it wasn't the end point of a truly epic journey. That said, a night in the military-camp-like confines of the Prudhoe Bay Hotel, with its industrial carpets and nail-biting, calendar-checking oil workers, makes for the conclusion of an exhausting road trip you probably won't forget in a hurry.

Tours

Having come this far, most travelers venture to dip their toe in the Arctic Ocean on a brief organized excursion with the **Arctic Ocean Shuttle** (☎907-474-3565; www.arcticoceanshuttle.com; Deadhorse Camp; tours per person $69; ⏲tours 8:30am & 3:30pm). But you can skip this tour if you love the Arctic and are intending to travel to Utqiaġvik – you can see and swim in the ocean there for free.

Sleeping

There's a limited number of (expensive) hotels in Deadhorse, and if you want to stay at them, you'll need to book in advance. Camping is technically not allowed due to wildlife concerns, but in practice, some people camp south of town off the highway. We can't recommend this practice, as bears are not uncommon in the area.

Prudhoe Bay Hotel HOTEL $$

(☎907-659-2449; www.prudhoebayhotel.com; Airport Way; dm with shared bath $125, r with private bath $160; P 📶) 'Take your boots off at the door!' proclaims the sign. The Prudhoe Bay is that kind of hotel. Long corridors with industrial carpets are full of weather-beaten oil workers wandering around in their hole-y socks. But, after the long haul up the Dalton Hwy, it's – weirdly – just what you need: a truly Alaskan experience.

Rooms are surprisingly cozy (with TVs), but the best deal is the cafeteria. Grab as much food as you can stuff in your rucksack – it's all included. Nonguests can also eat here (breakfast/lunch/dinner $12/15/20).

Aurora Hotel HOTEL $$$

(☎907-670-0600; www.theaurorahotel.net; 123 E Lake Colleen Dr; s $150-170, d $270; P 📶) The Aurora overlooks Colleen Lake and is located almost a mile from the airport. It's newer and larger than the Prudhoe Bay Hotel and comes with some handy extras. The fitness room will save you jogging around outside with the grizzly and polar bears.

Deadhorse Camp HOTEL $$$

(☎907-474-3565; www.deadhorsecamp.com; Mile 413.6, Dalton Hwy; s/d with shared bath $219/259; 📶) On the edge of 'town,' this accommodation option is not as conveniently situated as others. It's a more downbeat version of the Prudhoe Bay Hotel. Bathrooms are shared.

THE ALASKA PIPELINE

Love it or loathe it, if you're driving Alaska's Richardson or Dalton Hwys, the Trans-Alaska Pipeline will be your traveling companion. The steely tube, 4ft wide and 800 miles long, parallels the highways from Prudhoe Bay on the Arctic Ocean down to Valdez, Alaska's northernmost ice-free port. En route, it spans 500-odd waterways and three mountain ranges, transporting about 600,000 barrels of crude oil per day – 12% of US domestic production – to tankers waiting in Prince William Sound. Back in its heyday, the pipeline was carrying around 2 million barrels per day. With dwindling reserves, however, they've cut down the flow and expect to continue to reduce it unless new sources, such as those in the Arctic National Wildlife Refuge, are opened up for drilling.

Before construction began in 1974, the debate over the pipeline was among America's hardest-fought conservation battles. Both sides viewed themselves as defenders of the Last Frontier; boosters viewed the project as a grand act of Alaskan pioneering, and opponents called it an affront to all that's wild and wonderful about the 49th state. After the pipeline's completion – three years and $8 billion later – the late University of Alaska president William R Wood likened it to 'a silken thread, half-hidden across the palace carpet.' Many have had less kind words for it, especially in light of the numerous spills that have occurred over the years.

For about 380 of its miles, the Trans-Alaska Pipeline – like most pipelines – runs underground. Elsewhere it can't, because the 110°F to 55.6°F (43.3°C to 13.1°C) oil it carries would melt the permafrost. It's in those places – particularly where it crosses the highway – that you'll get your best look at the line. Especially good views can be had at Mile 243.5 of the Richardson Hwy south of Delta Junction, on the Dalton Hwy at the Yukon River crossing, and at the spur road to Wiseman. Just north of Fairbanks you can walk right up to the pipeline, stand under it, and even move in for a kiss if you are so inclined (as some are).

Be forewarned, however: elsewhere it's a bad move to get too close to the pipeline. After September 11, 2001, officials identified the pipe as Alaska's number-one terrorist target, ramping up security and for a while even operating a checkpoint on the Dalton Hwy. Their fears weren't entirely unfounded: in 1999 Canadian Alfred Reumayr was arrested for plotting to blow up the pipeline (apparently to make big profits on oil futures). In 2001 a drunken hunter shot it with a .338-caliber rifle and 285,000 gallons spewed out. Officials say the pipeline has been shot – with no spillage caused – dozens of other times.

1

2

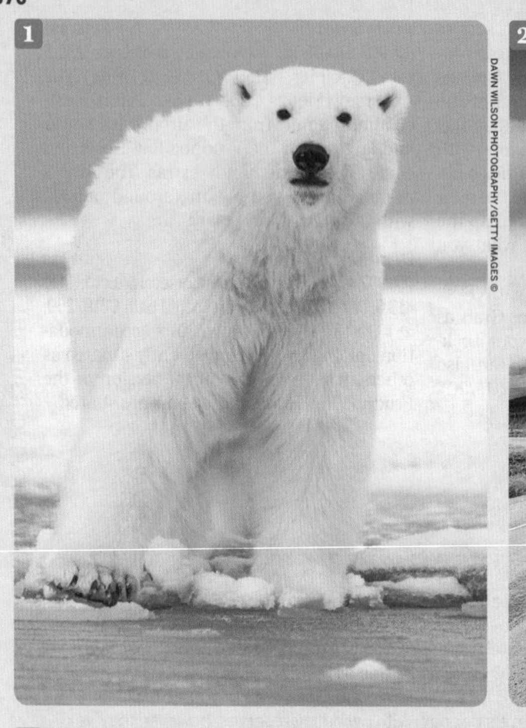

DAWN WILSON PHOTOGRAPHY/GETTY IMAGES ©

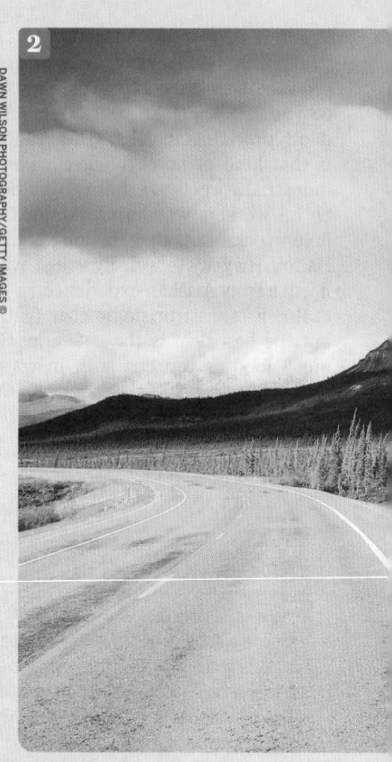

4

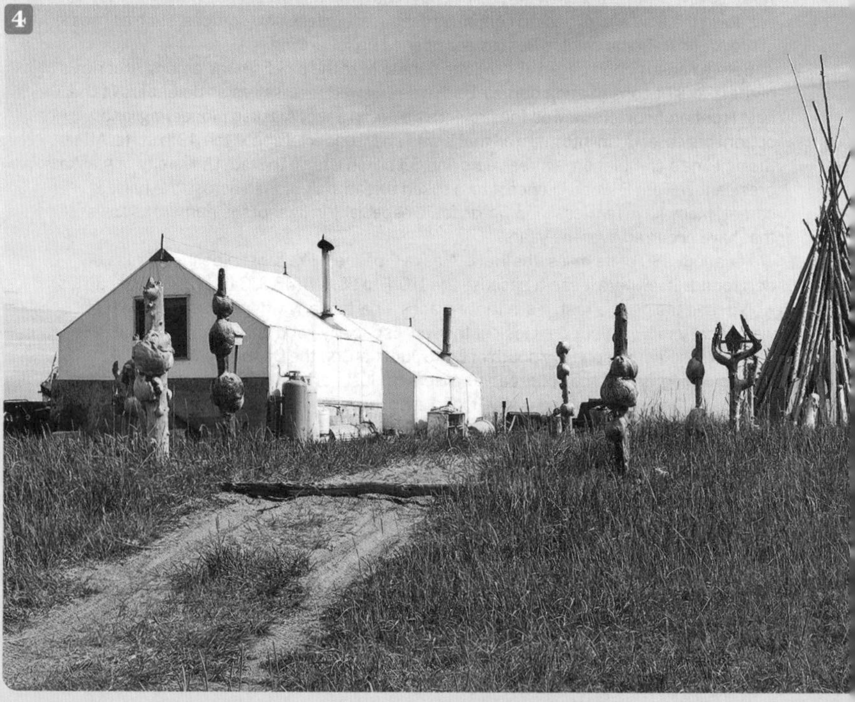

MENNO SCHAEFER/SHUTTERSTOCK ©

JOHN ELK III/GETTY IMAGES ©

JOHN ELK III/GETTY IMAGES ©

1. Arctic National Wildlife Refuge (p372)
Polar bears are among the wide array of wildlife that live within the ANWR.

2. Dalton Highway (p371)
Sukakpak Mountain (p374) is visible from Mile 194 on the Dalton Highway, one of North America's great drives.

3. Kougarok Road (p371)
Also known as Nome–Taylor Rd, Kougarok Rd leads 86 miles north from Nome through the center of the Kigluaik Mountains.

4. Nome–Council Road (p370) Coastal houses on the Nome–Council Rd.

Eating

As there are no restaurants in Deadhorse, each hotel runs its own cafeteria where you can eat as much as you like (included in the room price). It's good chow, too.

Getting There & Away

The only road connection is via the Dalton Hwy. Dalton Highway Express heads south at 8am on Sundays and Wednesdays (June to August). The 16-hour journey to Fairbanks costs $250 one-way.

From **Deadhorse Airport** (907-659-2553) there are daily flights to Anchorage, plus connections to Utqiaġvik. The ultra-friendly airport is opposite the Prudhoe Bay Hotel.

Gas in Deadhorse is as expensive as you'll ever find in the USA, which, given all the oil around, is kind of ironic.

Gates of the Arctic National Park & Preserve

Unchanged in four millennia, this massive preserved space protects a contiguous wilderness that stretches for over 27,000 sq miles – the equivalent of nearly two Switzerlands – harboring no roads, no cellphone coverage and a population of precisely zero.

Not surprisingly, you don't come here to stroll along interpretive boardwalks, or even follow something as rudimentary as a trail (there aren't any). Tackled alone, this is a land for brave travelers with advanced outdoor experience, plenty of time on their hands and a flexible budget (read: it's costly). Alternatively, you can sign up with one of a handful of agencies and go on a guided backcountry or flightseeing tour.

Sights

Kobuk Valley National Park NATIONAL PARK
(907-442-3890; www.nps.gov/kova) This park has a desolate, severe beauty, and is best known for its Arctic sand dunes – like a Saharan desert in the midst of the tundra – and migrating caribou.

Noatak National Preserve NATIONAL PARK
(907-442-3890; www.nps.gov/noat) This enormous tundra river basin is home to some of the most pristine, intact Arctic ecosystems in the USA.

Activities

Hiking

Most backpackers enter the park by way of charter air-taxis, which can land on lakes, rivers or river bars. Once on the ground they often follow the long, open valleys for extended treks or work their way to higher elevations where open tundra provides good hiking terrain.

While this appears to make planning an impossibly vague task, the landscape limits the areas that aircraft can land or pick you up, as well as where you can hike. Park staff suggest consulting flight and guide companies, as well as topographic maps, for possible routes and then running it by them to make sure the area is not overused. If it is, they can suggest alternatives.

The only treks that don't require chartering a plane are those beginning from the Dalton Hwy (near Wiseman), or from the village of Anaktuvuk Pass. For hikes from the highway, which lead into several different areas along the eastern border of the park, stop at the Arctic Interagency Visitor Center (p373) in Coldfoot for assistance and advice on trip planning. Several well-known routes in this area are showing too much wear and are even beginning to affect the livelihood of subsistence hunters.

Hiking into the park from Anaktuvuk Pass is surprisingly one of the more economical options, as you only need to pay for a regular scheduled flight to the village from Fairbanks. From the airstrip it's just a few miles' hike into the northern edge of the park. You can camp for free by the airstrip if needed, but elsewhere get permission until you enter the park.

Paddling

Floatable rivers in the park include the John, Alatna, Noatak, Kobuk, Koyukuk and Tinayguk. The waterways range in difficulty from Class I to III, and you should consult the park or guide companies about possible routes.

Canoes can be rented in Bettles at the Bettles Lodge for around $270 per week.

Tours

Brooks Range Aviation SCENIC FLIGHTS
(800-692-5443; http://brooksrange.com; Bettles Field; per 2- or 3-person plane $2035, per 6-person plane $3120) These guys run four- to 4½-hour flightseeing tours of Gates of the Arctic

LOCAL KNOWLEDGE

ACCESSING THE PARK

Gates of the Arctic National Park & Preserve is more accessible than Kobuk Valley National Park and Noatak National Preserve in that it starts just 5 miles west of the Dalton Hwy, meaning you can technically hike in, although charter flights out of Coldfoot and Bettles are more common. Kobuk Valley and Noatak are both reached via charters out of the small settlement of Kotzebue.

Bettles (population 12) is the main gateway to Gates of the Arctic, offering meals, lodging and air transport into the backcountry. Other visitors fly in from Coldfoot on the Dalton Hwy, or hike in directly from Wiseman, just north of Coldfoot. To the north, the remote Alaska Native village of Anaktuvuk Pass is another access point if traveling by foot, though you'll need to fly here first. Contact the Anaktuvuk Ranger Station for more information on visiting the park from here.

and Kobuk Valley National Parks, with a brief landing in each. You are encouraged to overnight in Bettles. Note that rates are by plane (either a two- or three-seater Cessna 185 or a six-seater de Havilland Beaver), not per person.

Arctic Wild ADVENTURE
(907-479-8203; www.arcticwild.com) Arrange a fantastic eight-day guided backpacking trip in the Gates of the Arctic National Park for $4300 per person, a four-day journey into Kobuk Valley National Park for $5700, or a 10-day canoeing/hiking trip on the Noatak River from $5600. Trips run in August.

Sleeping

Bettles Lodge LODGE $$$
(907-692-5111; www.bettleslodge.com; tour packages incl accommodation per person s/d $890/1020, plus $250/275 each additional night) This 1952-vintage six-room lodge (now a National Historic Site) provides accommodations in the tiny settlement of Bettles. There's a common area with books and games, and decent meals are provided. Even better, the lodge organizes multiple trips and tours in Gates of the Arctic National Park. It's not posh but it's peaceful.

Lodging here is arranged by package tours, which take in some of the most fantastic scenery in the Arctic. The list of package options is enormous; visit the website or call for details.

Information

For more information, check out the park's website (www.nps.gov/gaar). If the 'Plan Your Visit' section doesn't answer all your questions, contact the park directly.

Anaktuvuk Ranger Station (907-661-3520; www.nps.gov/gaar; 8am-5pm Jun-Sep) Can help you plan your trip from Anaktuvuk.

Bettles Ranger Station & Visitor Center (907-692-5495; www.nps.gov/gaar; 8am-5pm Jun-Sep) In a log building less than a quarter mile from the airstrip.

Getting There & Away

Wright Air Service (907-474-0502; www.wrightairservice.com) flies into Gates of the Arctic daily from Fairbanks to Bettles ($340 round-trip) and Anaktuvuk Pass ($380 round-trip).

From Bettles it's necessary to charter an air-taxi to your destination within the park. Most areas can be reached in under two hours. Check with Brooks Range Aviation or **Coyote Air Service** (907-678-3993; www.flycoyote.com) for air charters.

A changing list of concessionaires flies into Noatak and Kobuk. Check the park websites for a complete list of air services that are authorized to fly into these parks.

Utqiaġvik (Barrow)

907 / POPULATION 4335

The northernmost settlement in the USA, and the largest Iñupiat community in Alaska, Utqiaġvik – still most commonly referred to as Barrow – is a flat, bleak, fogbound and strangely evocative place situated 330 miles above the Arctic Circle. It's a town of surprising contradictions, the greatest being that the weather is perpetual winter, yet the people are some of the warmest in Alaska.

The paradoxes don't end there. Utqiaġvik's wealth is famous: due to the spoils of North Slope petroleum it boasts excellent modern facilities, such as its Iñupiat Heritage Center and North Slope Borough offices,

OFF THE BEATEN TRACK

ST LAWRENCE ISLAND

Way out in the Bering Sea only 40 miles from mainland Russia and 125 miles southwest of Nome, St Lawrence Island isn't the kind of place you pop into on your way to somewhere else. Inhabited primarily by Alaskan and Siberian Yupik, it provides a good opportunity to watch birds and sea mammals. There are basic hotels in its two main settlements **Gambell** and **Savoonga**, and a new road system allows for easier access to birding areas. If you want to make an independent visit out here contact Sivuqaq, Inc at ☎907-985-5826; they'll help arrange lodging and can direct you to the supply store in Gambell.

Ravn Alaska (p430) and Bering Air (p370) fly to Gambell from Nome daily for around $530 to $540 round-trip. Birders are probably better off hitching onto an organized trip with **Wilderness Birding Adventures** (☎907-299-3937; www.wildernessbirding.com). Trips, which start at $3700, are run to coincide with the spring and fall migrations (ie early June and early September).

that are unusual in a town this size. On the flip side, it's an Arctic slum packed with ramshackle structures wallowing in frozen mud. It's expensive, the weather is hostile and the wind howls, yet a visit here is utterly unforgettable, a chance to witness life at the true edge of the world.

Sights

End of the Road — LANDMARK

(Point Barrow) FREE The northernmost extremity of the US (though not, as locals sometimes claim, North America) is **Point Barrow**, but it's tough to get to this narrow strip of land. Tours drive *almost* all the way, but the last two to three miles is a beach full of soft, sandy sinkholes. Rather, drive to the end of the road and enjoy the surreal scenery.

For what it's worth, getting to the end of the road still feels like driving to the end of the world. You roll up a cold, windswept, lonely road, flanked by the occasional shack and 'palm trees' fashioned from whale baleen. To the north, you'll see the Arctic Ocean, shaded from slate gray to icy black and breaking on the pebbly shore – assuming the water isn't filled with ice pack. Occasionally, you'll see a walrus carcass swelling on the beach. Point Barrow is roughly 12 miles north of Utqiaġvik proper.

We can't stress this enough: *do not attempt to drive all the way to Point Barrow.* Once the road ends, driving conditions become extremely hazardous. Locals know their way through the area, but we saw tourists sink their rented SUVs into the sand; they had to be towed out, and at no small expense. Your best way out to the point is to make friends with a local who will give you a ride. We can't recommend hiking from the end of the road because of frequent polar bear activity in the area.

Iñupiat Heritage Center — CULTURAL CENTER

(☎907-852-0422; www.nps.gov/inup; Ahkovak St; $10; ⌚8:30am-5pm Mon-Fri year-round, plus 1-5pm Sat & Sun mid May–mid-Sep; P) This 24,000-sq-ft facility houses a museum, gift shop and a large multipurpose room where short traditional dancing-and-drumming performances take place each afternoon. Local craftspeople work in a studio in the back of the facility, and are happy to talk about their art. They also set up kiosks for their goods from 2pm to 4pm in the foyer.

In the center's galleries, displays include everything from poster-sized, black-and-white portraits of local elders to a 35ft-long replica of a bowhead skeleton to a detailed (and artifact-rich) breakdown of traditional whaling culture and hunting practices. You can also try on an Iñupiat parka, undoubtedly the warmest article of clothing you'll ever have the privilege of donning.

Ilisagvik College — COLLEGE

(☎907-852-3333; www.ilisagvik.edu; 100 Stevenson St; P) Ilisagvik is the only tribal-controlled college in Alaska, and the northernmost community college in the country. The campus consists of a main building where you can find most classrooms and faculty offices, surrounded by the usual lunar-landing-style Utqiaġvik facilities. In the main building, you'll find friendly local students and teachers who are usually happy to tell you about their community.

The college hosts permanent and visiting academics who are some of the world's foremost experts on Arctic ecosystems, cultures and folkways; for obvious reasons, scientists studying the impact of climate change are also working here on an increasing basis. Call ahead to find out about free lecture series that are open to visitors and the community. There are no official hours for visiting the college, although obviously students aren't likely to be around later in the evening. Free wi-fi is available in the main building.

North Slope Borough Offices NOTABLE BUILDING

(907-852-2611; www.north-slope.org; 1274 Agvik St; P) FREE Encompassing some 88,695 sq miles of land area, the Alaskan borough of North Slope is larger than all but 10 American states, but with a population of just under 10,000, lower than that of many American small towns. This is the administrative office for this vast, sparsely populated land division; the lobby is filled with indigenous artifacts.

There's usually a security guard on duty; if you're asked why you're here (you usually won't be), just say you'd like to see the local arts and crafts on display. There are no set hours for visiting as security is on hand 24 hours a day, but the doors are locked after the last office workers head home (usually around 6pm; folks arrive for work around 9am).

Utqiaġvik Presbyterian Church CHURCH

(907-852-6566; 1265 Agvik St; Sun service in English/Iñupiat 11am/7:30pm) This old church stands humble but strong, battered by the unceasing sea salt and snow winds of the far north. The church welcomes visitors to its services, one of which is conducted in the Iñupiat language on Sunday evenings, but please be respectful, and don't be surprised when they offer you communion.

Ukpiagvik ARCHAEOLOGICAL SITE

(Apayauk & Ogrook Sts) FREE In the southwest corner of town, you'll see – well, you may or may not see, but you'll be on top of – the remains of the ancient village of Ukpiagvik. The site is marked by the remains of semi-subterranean sod huts, which appear as little rises upon the flat landscape.

Activities

The main thing to do at the 'top of the world' is bundle up, stand on the shore of the Arctic Ocean, dip something of yourself in the water and gaze toward the North Pole.

Hiking

You can stroll the gravel roads, or gray-sand beaches, that parallel the sea to view *umiaks* (traditional kayaks), giant jawbones of bowhead whales, fish-drying racks and the jumbled Arctic pack ice that even in July spans the horizon.

On the waterfront opposite Apayauk St at the southwest end of town (turn left as you exit the airport) is Ukpiagvik, the site of an ancient Iñupiat village. From that site, continue southwest out of town and when the road splits go left toward Freshwater Lake. After about 3 miles you'll come to a row of satellite dishes that face directly out and not up. It's an odd sight, making for an interesting photo, and drives home just how far north you are.

Birding & Wildlife-Watching

Not many people would describe Utqiaġvik as 'paradise,' except, perhaps, for dedicated birders. At least 185 avian species make a stop here during the summer months. Most serious twitchers are on organized tours, but anyone with a pair of binoculars will find a few hours out of town a rewarding experience. In the absence of trees, birds nest on the ground and are easy to spot. Snowy owls are common.

If you want to see a polar bear, it's best to take a tour. But don't get your hopes up too high: they're tough to spot, especially in the summer months.

Tours

Tundra Tours TOURS

(907-852-3900; www.tundratoursinc.com; 3060 Eben Hopson St; tours per person $160) Taking a three- to four-hour summer tour (mid May to mid-September) with Tundra Tours, run out of the Top of the World Hotel (p382), is one of the better ways to piece together Utqiaġvik's essential sights and spot wildlife. Trips includes a tundra walk to Iñupiat sod huts and a look around the Iñupiat Heritage Center.

At other times of the year, Tundra Tours offers a condensed, two-hour version of the above for $75, on weekdays only.

Wilderness Birding Adventures BIRDWATCHING

(907-299-3937; www.wildernessbirding.com; tours $1600-5950) Run by a band of passionate avian wildlife enthusiasts, this outfit leads small-group birding tours to the Arctic region. Their Utqiaġvik trip is a quest to spot the elusive, pink Ross's Gull; a three-day tour with all meals and lodging included runs $2600 and departs in early October.

Festivals & Events

Nalukataq CULTURAL

(Whaling Festival; Jun) The Nalukataq festival is held in late June, when the spring whaling hunt has been completed. Depending on how successful the whaling captains have been, the festival lasts anywhere from a few days to more than a week. It's a rare cultural experience and one of the best reasons to visit Utqiaġvik.

The main event of the festival is the **blanket toss**, in which locals use a sealskin tarp to toss people into the air – the effect is much like bouncing on a trampoline. For the jumper, the object is to reach the biggest heights (this supposedly replicates ancient efforts to spot game in the distance) and inevitably there are a number of sprains and fractures.

One Iñupiat tradition calls for whaling crews to share their bounty with the village, and during the festival you'll see families carrying off platters and plastic bags full of raw whale meat. Dishes served include *muktuk*, the pink blubbery part of the whale, which is boiled, pickled or even eaten raw with hot mustard, seasoning salt or soy sauce .

While we recognize the importance of whaling in Native Alaskan communities, the practice is condemned by conservationists and the sale of whale meat is illegal in the US. Customary and traditional use of whale meat is regulated by Alaskan state law.

Sleeping

Camping is ill-advised around Utqiaġvik due to extreme weather and the potential for up-close encounters with curious, carnivorous polar bears.

Given Utqiaġvik's compact size, it's possible to catch a morning flight in and a late evening flight out and still see just about everything you're likely to see.

Book well in advance if you do plan to spend the night, and note that there's a 5% bed tax.

King Eider Inn INN $$

(907-852-4700; www.kingeider.net; 1752 Ahkovak St; r/ste from $189/239;) With a snug log-cabin feel, wood-post beds and an inviting fireplace in the lobby, the Eider is a pleasant antidote to the dystopia outside. It's almost directly across from the airport exit.

Barrow Airport Inn HOTEL $$

(907-852-2525; airportinn@barrow.com; 1815 Momegana St; r winter/summer $168/195;) This place is a few minutes' walk from the airport, and has rooms that are simply furnished but do the trick for a night's stay. Some have kitchenettes, but these are usually booked far in advance by research teams.

Top of the World Hotel HOTEL $$$

(907-852-3900; www.tundratoursinc.com; 3060 Eben Hopson St; s/d $304/338; @) The Top of the World lives up to its name (it's the northernmost hotel in North America), and is also surprisingly plush, with large airy communal spaces, topical Arctic mosaics, boutique-style rooms and a pretty decent restaurant.

The catch? Like most things in Utqiaġvik, it's mega-expensive.

Eating

Utqiaġvik has a handful of places to eat, though none of them look much like restaurants from the outside. Pizza, Japanese, Chinese, Mexican and Korean are all on offer.

Osaka JAPANESE $$

(907-852-4100; 980 Stevenson St; mains $14-30; 6am-midnight) We're partial to any place that has reindeer sausage *and* a BLT *and* teriyaki platters, bento boxes and sushi rolls. You can even get Hawaiian *loco moco* (two burger patties served on rice with an egg and gravy – yum).

Arctic Pizza INTERNATIONAL, PIZZA $$

(907-852-4222; 125 Apayauq St; mains $17-37; 11:30am-11:30pm) Pizza's just half of it. This Arctic Ocean–abutting restaurant's multifarious menu also includes pasta, Chinese food, burgers, salads, soups, sandwiches and nachos. The decor (unkempt-diner chic) promises little, but the food, spurred on by the vicious winds outside and the very friendly owner, warms you up nicely.

Sam & Lee's Chinese Restaurant AMERICAN, CHINESE $$

(907-852-5555; 1052 Kiogak St; mains $15-38; 6am-2am) Don't be fooled by the name – yes, there's Chinese food dishes like cashew chicken, but this joint also has good American-style breakfasts and a cheeseburger that is roughly the size of a small child. In

Signpost in Utqiaġvik

addition to the food, the bright diner atmosphere and lively staff make this a popular local hangout.

Niggivikut Restaurant AMERICAN $$
(☎907-852-3900; 3060 Eben Hopson St; mains $15-33; ⊙6am-10pm Mon-Sat, 8am-10pm Sun) You can get pancakes pretty much anywhere in the US, but only in the Niggivikut can you enjoy them while gazing in wonder at the iceberg-choked Arctic Ocean. This restaurant in the Top of the World Hotel has booths in front of large Arctic-facing windows and a no-surprises American menu.

Cruz's Mexican Grill MEXICAN $$
(☎907-852-2253; off Brower St; mains $20-35; ⊙11am-6pm Mon-Thu, to 8pm Fri & Sat) We've never seen simple Mexican fare sold at this price, but then again, we've never had it north of the Arctic Circle either, so that's a decent trade-off. All of the usual Tex-Mex favorites – tacos, enchiladas, burritos and chimichangas – are available, and honestly, pretty damn good. It has a bakery selling scones and cheesecake too, because why not?

Located across from the Top of the World Hotel.

AC Store SUPERMARKET $$
(☎907-852-6711; www.alaskacommercial.com; Ahkovak & North Star St; ⊙7am-10pm Mon-Sat, 9am-9pm Sun) Over in Browerville across from the Iñupiat Heritage Center, this supermarket has quick eats and groceries at diet-inducing prices. Many visitors come by just to take pictures of the $10-plus gallons of milk. It also has a small selection of Iñupiat art, handicrafts and parkas.

ℹ Information

INTERNET ACCESS

The airport has strong and free wi-fi, as do hotels.

MONEY

Wells Fargo (☎907-852-6200; cnr Agvik & Kiogak Sts; ⊙10am-5pm Mon-Thu, to 6pm Fri) Has a 24-hour ATM.

TOURIST INFORMATION

You can pick up a map and information guide at the airport and most restaurants and hotels.

ℹ Getting There & Away

While you can get to Utqiaġvik in the winter by ice road, it's best to fly. **Wiley Post–Will Rogers Memorial Airport** (☎907-852-6199; 1747 Ahkovak St) is served by Alaska Airlines (p429) and Ravn Alaska (p430), with daily flights to Fairbanks, Anchorage and Deadhorse.

ℹ Getting Around

The airport is an easy stroll from all three of Utqiaġvik's hotels, and most other points of interest can also be reached by walking. However, cabs are available for a flat fee of $6.

You can rent cars through local hotels, or call **UIC Car Rental** (☎907-852-2700; cnr Ahkovak & Tapak Sts; ⊙hrs vary), but be ready for sticker shock – car rentals here are expensive.

Child wearing Tlingit mask

Understand Alaska

History

The Aleuts called it Alaxsxag – where the sea breaks its back. The Russians christened it Bolshaya Zemlya, or the Great Land. Today, it's simply known as Alaska. The history of this subcontinent – the largest of the US' 50 states – has all the trappings of an epic: massive migrations, cultural annihilation, oil and gold rushes. From European settlement on, the history of this state is largely linked to the acquisition of the vast natural resources of this great frontier.

Early Alaskans

Many parts of Alaska's early history are still under debate; at the heart of this is how North America was first populated. Some say the first Alaskans migrated from Asia to America between 15,000 and 30,000 years ago, during an ice age that lowered the sea level and created a 900-mile land bridge linking Siberia and Alaska. The nomadic groups who crossed the bridge were not bent on exploration but on following the animal herds that provided them with food and clothing. Others posit that there was more continued contact between the Old and New Worlds, with continual migrations and commerce by boat.

The first major migration, which came across the land bridge from Asia, was by the Tlingits and the Haidas, who settled throughout the Southeast and British Columbia, and the Athabascans, a nomadic tribe that settled in the Interior. The other two major groups were the Iñupiat, who settled the north coast of Alaska and Canada (where they are known as Inuit), and the Yupik, who settled Southwest Alaska. The smallest group of Alaska Natives to arrive was the Aleuts of the Aleutian Islands. The Iñupiat, Yupik and Aleuts are believed to have migrated 3000 years ago and were well established by the time the Europeans arrived.

The complete skeleton of a thalattosaur, a marine reptile that lived 200 million years ago, was found in Southeast Alaska, near Kake, in 2011.

The matrilineal Tlingit and Haida cultures were quite advanced. The tribes had permanent settlements and a class system that included chiefs, nobles, commoners and slaves – though upward (and downward) mobility were still possible. These tribes were noted for their excellent wood carving, especially carved poles, called totems, which can still be seen in Ketchikan, Sitka and many other places in the Southeast. The

TIMELINE

28,000–13,000 BCE

The first Alaskans arrive, migrating across a 900-mile land bridge from Asia to North America – or perhaps by boat. They settle throughout the state and establish unique civilizations.

2000–1500 BCE

Permanent settlements in high Arctic areas start to form, first in Siberia, then spreading across Alaska and Canada and into Greenland.

1741 CE

Danish explorer Vitus Bering, becomes the first European to set foot in Alaska. His lieutenant returns to Europe with pelts that trigger a rush across the Aleutian chain.

Tlingits were spread across the Southeast in large numbers and occasionally went as far south as Seattle in their huge dugout canoes. Both groups had few problems gathering food, as fish and game were plentiful in the Southeast.

Many tribes of the Pacific Northwest, including the Tlingit and Haida, celebrated 'potlatches.' These unique gatherings were in many ways designed to redistribute goods. Nobles would host the feasts, give gifts, free (or sometimes kill) slaves, and occasionally throw large copper shield-like objects into the ocean as a sign of their wealth. The practice was suppressed by Western interests (and even made illegal for a time) but remains today in some forms. Recent evidence indicates that Athabascan tribes also celebrated a version of the potlatch, possibly indicating a continual exchange of ideas and technologies between the numerous tribes.

Life was not so easy for the Aleuts, Iñupiat and Yupik. With much colder winters and cooler summers, these people had to develop a highly effective sea-hunting culture to sustain life in the harsh regions of Alaska. This was especially true for the Iñupiat, who could not have survived the winters without their skilled ice-hunting techniques. In spring, armed only with jade-tipped harpoons, the Iñupiat, in skin-covered kayaks called *bidarkas* and *umiaks,* stalked and killed 60-ton bowhead whales. Though motorized boats replaced the kayaks and modern harpoons the jade-tipped spears, the whaling tradition lives on in places such as Utqiaġvik (Barrow).

There are over 2700 identified archaeological sites in Alaska. With extremely difficult field conditions, only a few of them have been thoroughly investigated. The limited evidence indicates these date back just 12,000 years – less than other parts of the Americas.

Age of Exploration

Due to the cold and stormy North Pacific, Alaska was one of the last places in the world to be mapped by Europeans.

Spanish Admiral Bartholomé de Fonte is credited by many with making the first European trip into Alaskan waters in 1640, but the first written record of the area was made by Vitus Bering, a Danish navigator sailing for the Russian tsar. In 1728 Bering's explorations demonstrated that America and Asia were two separate continents. Thirteen years later, Bering became the first European to set foot in Alaska, near Cordova. Bering and many of his crew died from scurvy during that journey, but his lieutenant returned to Europe with fur pelts and tales of fabulous seal and otter colonies, and Alaska's first boom was underway. The Aleutian Islands were quickly overtaken, with settlements at Unalaska and Kodiak Island. Chaos followed, as bands of Russian hunters robbed and murdered each other for furs, while the Aleuts, living near the hunting grounds, were almost annihilated through massacres, disease and forced labor. By the 1790s Russia had organized the Russian-American Company to regulate the fur trade and ease the violent competition.

1778

British explorer Captain James Cook looks for the Northwest Passage, but is eventually turned back by 12ft ice walls. British and American fur traders rush north, competing with Russian interests.

1784

Russian Grigorii Shelikhov establishes the first permanent European settlement at Kodiak Island. Eight years later he is granted a monopoly on furs as head of the Russian-American Company.

1784

With the introduction of European diseases, thousands of Alaska Natives perish.

1804

With four warships, Aleksandr Baranov defeats the Tlingit at Sitka and then establishes New Archangel (Sitka's former name) as the new capital of the Russian-American Company.

FUR TRADERS & WHALERS ARRIVE

While Alaska lacks the great wars between indigenous peoples and settlers that occurred in other parts of the US, the settlement by Russian fur traders, whalers and other outside forces had a lasting impact on Alaska Native tribes. Before European contact, there were an estimated 80,000 people living in Alaska – a figure the state would not reach again until WWII.

Diseases introduced by Europeans were the biggest killers, but there were also limited violent clashes, especially between Russian fur traders and the Aleut. Slavery and the introduction of alcohol were other primary factors in the reduction of Alaska Native populations; some estimates indicate that during the Russian-American period the Aleut lost 80% of its tribe, and the Chugach, Tlingit, Haida and Dena'ina each lost 50%. The whalers that arrived at Iñupiat villages in the mid-19th century were similarly destructive, introducing alcohol, which devastated the lifestyles of entire villages. When the 50th anniversary of the Alaska Hwy was celebrated in 1992, many Alaska Natives and Canadians called the event a 'commemoration' not a 'celebration,' due to the destructive forces that the link to Canada and the rest of the USA brought.

The British arrived when Captain James Cook began searching the area for the Northwest Passage. On his third and final voyage, Cook sailed north from Vancouver Island to Southcentral Alaska in 1778, anchoring at what is now Cook Inlet before continuing on to the Aleutian Islands, Bering Sea and Arctic Ocean. The French sent Jean-François de Galaup, comte de La Pérouse, who in 1786 made it as far as Lituya Bay, now part of Glacier Bay National Park. The wicked tides within the long, narrow bay caught the exploration party off guard, killing 21 sailors and discouraging the French from colonizing the area.

Having depleted the fur colonies in the Aleutians, Aleksandr Baranov, who headed the Russian-American Company, moved his territorial capital from Kodiak to Sitka, where he built a stunning city, dubbed 'an American Paris in Alaska.' But Russian control of Alaska remained limited, and at the height of their residency, only 800 full-time Russian inhabitants lived here.

Seward's Folly

By the 1860s the Russians found themselves badly overextended: their involvement in Napoleon's European wars, a declining fur industry and the long lines of shipping between Sitka and the heartland of Russia were draining their national treasury. The country made several overtures to the USA to purchase Alaska, but it wasn't until 1867 that Secre-

1857

Coal mining begins at Coal Harbor and a new chapter in mineral extraction starts.

1867

Secretary of State William H Seward negotiates the US purchase of Alaska from Russia for $7.2 million. It takes six months for Congress to approve the treaty.

1878

Ten years after a salmon saltery is opened in Klawock on Prince of Wales Island, a San Francisco company builds the first salmon cannery in Alaska.

1880

Led by Tlingit Chief Kowee, Richard Harris and Joe Juneau discover gold in Silver Bow Basin. The next year miners change their tent city's name from Harrisburg to Juneau.

tary of State William H Seward signed a treaty to purchase the state for $7.2 million – less than 2¢ an acre.

By then the US public was in an uproar over the purchase of 'Seward's Ice Box' or 'Walrussia,' and on the Senate floor, the battle to ratify the treaty lasted six months. On October 18, 1867, the formal transfer of Alaska to the Americans took place in Sitka. In post–Civil War America, Alaska remained a lawless, unorganized territory for another 20 years.

This great land, remote and inaccessible to all but a few hardy settlers, stayed a dark, frozen mystery to most people, but eventually its riches were uncovered. First it was through whaling, then the phenomenal salmon runs, with the first canneries built in 1878 on Prince of Wales Island.

The Alaskan Gold Rush

What truly brought Alaska to the world's attention was gold. The promise of quick riches and frontier adventures was the most effective lure Alaska has ever had and, to some degree, still has today. Gold was discovered in the Gastineau Channel in the 1880s, and the towns of Juneau and Douglas sprang up overnight. In 1896 one of the world's most colorful gold rushes took place in the Klondike region of Canada's Yukon Territory, just across the border.

Often called 'the last grand adventure,' the Klondike gold rush occurred when the country and much of the world was suffering a severe recession. When the banner headline of the *Seattle Post-Intelligencer* bellowed 'GOLD! GOLD! GOLD! GOLD!' on July 17, 1897, thousands of people quit their jobs and sold their homes to finance a trip to the newly created boomtown of Skagway. From this tent city almost 30,000 prospectors tackled the steep Chilkoot Trail to Lake Bennett, where they built crude rafts to float the rest of the way to the goldfields. Nearly as many people returned home along the same route, broke and disillusioned.

The number of miners who made fortunes was small, but the tales and legends that emerged were endless. The Klondike stampede, though it only lasted from 1896 to the early 1900s, was Alaska's most colorful era and earned the state the reputation of being the country's last frontier.

Within three years of the Klondike stampede Alaska's population doubled to 63,592, including more than 30,000 non-Native people. Nome, another gold boomtown, was the largest city in the territory, with 12,000 residents, while gold prompted the capital to be moved from Sitka to Juneau. Politically, this was also the beginning of true Alaskan 'state building' – railroads were built, governing bodies were created, support industries were established, and a non-voting Alaskan delegate was sent to Congress in 1906. Nevertheless, it was still largely a transient state, with men outnumbering women five to one, and few people building their life-long homes here.

The last shot of the Civil War was fired in the Bering Sea by the CSS *Shenandoah* on June 22, 1865, 74 days after the Battle of Appomattox.

1882

A US Navy cutter shells Angoon in retaliation for an uprising and then sends a landing party to loot and burn what remains of the Alaska Native village.

1884

Local governing begins. Alaska is named the District of Alaska, the first step toward statehood.

1896

Oil is discovered in Cook Inlet, but there is no major extraction from Alaska for another seven decades.

1898

Klondike gold rush turns Skagway into Alaska's largest city, with a population of 10,000. Canadian Mounties describe the lawless town as 'little better than a hell on earth.'

World War II

In June 1942, only six months after their attack on Pearl Harbor, the Japanese opened their Aleutian Islands campaign by bombing Dutch Harbor for two days and then taking Attu and Kiska Islands. Other than Guam, it was the only foreign invasion of US soil during WWII and is often dubbed 'the Forgotten War' because most Americans are unaware of what happened in Alaska. The battle to retake Attu Island was a bloody one. After 19 days and landing more than 15,000 troops, US forces recaptured the plot of barren land, but only after suffering 3929 casualties, including 549 deaths. Of the more than 2300 Japanese on Attu, fewer than 30 surrendered, with many taking their own lives.

The Alcan & Statehood

Following the Japanese attack on the Aleutian Islands in 1942, Congress panicked and rushed to protect the rest of Alaska. Large army and air-force bases were set up at Anchorage, Fairbanks, Sitka and Whittier, and thousands of military personnel were stationed in Alaska. But it was the famous Alcan (also known as the Alaska Hwy) that was the single most important project of the military expansion. The road was built by the military, but Alaska's residents benefited, as the Alcan helped them access and make use of Alaska's natural resources.

In 1916 Alaska's territorial legislature submitted its first statehood bill. The effort was first quashed by the Seattle-based canned-salmon industry, which wanted to prevent local control of Alaska's resources; then the stock market crash of 1929 and WWII kept Congress occupied with more-demanding issues. But the growth that came with the Alcan, and to a lesser degree the new military bases, pushed Alaska firmly into the American culture and renewed its drive for statehood. When the US Senate passed the Alaska statehood bill on June 30, 1958, Alaska had made it into the Union and was officially proclaimed the country's 49th state by President Dwight Eisenhower the following January.

Alaska entered the 1960s full of promise, but then disaster struck: the most powerful earthquake ever recorded in North America (registering 9.2 on the Richter scale) hit Southcentral Alaska on Good Friday morning in 1964. More than 100 lives were lost, and damage was estimated at $500 million. In Anchorage, office buildings sank 10ft into the ground, and houses slid more than 1200ft off a bluff into Knik Arm. A tidal wave virtually obliterated the community of Valdez. In Kodiak and Seward, 32ft of the coastline slipped into the Gulf of Alaska, and Cordova lost its entire harbor as the sea rose 16ft.

To enter Canada on the Chilkoot Trail, miners were required to carry a year's supply of food, including 400lb of flour and 200lb of bacon.

1900

The capital is moved from Sitka to Juneau, but as yet there are no roads to the capital.

1913

Walter Harper, an Alaska Native, becomes the first person to summit Mt McKinley (Denali). He is joined by Harry Karstens, who later becomes the first superintendent of Denali National Park.

1915

Anchorage is founded when Ship Creek is chosen as a survey camp to build the Alaska Railroad and after a year is a tent city of 2000.

1935

The first of 200 Depression-era families from Minnesota, Wisconsin and Michigan arrive in the Matanuska Valley to begin farming as part of Franklin Roosevelt's New Deal experiment and Palmer is established.

The Alaskan Black-Gold Rush

The devastating 1964 earthquake left the newborn state in a shambles, but a more pleasant gift from nature soon rushed Alaska to recovery and beyond. In 1968 Atlantic Richfield discovered massive oil deposits underneath Prudhoe Bay in the Arctic Ocean. The value of the oil doubled after the Arab oil embargo of 1973. However, it couldn't be tapped until there was a pipeline to transport it to the warm-water port of Valdez. And the pipeline couldn't be built until the US Congress, which still administered most of the land, settled the intense controversy among industry, environmentalists and Alaska Natives over historical claims to the land.

The *Alaska Native Claims Settlement Act* of 1971 was an unprecedented piece of legislation that opened the way for a consortium of oil companies to undertake the construction of the 789-mile pipeline. The act allocated $962.5 million and 44 million acres (including mineral rights) to Alaska Natives. Half of the money went directly to the Alaska Native villages, while the other half funded the creation of 12 Native corporations. There are now 13 Alaska Native corporations in Alaska; they manage land, invest in diverse endeavors and provide dividends to Alaska Native peoples.

The Trans-Alaska Pipeline took three years to build, cost more than $8 billion – in 1977 dollars – and, at the time, was the most expensive private construction project ever undertaken.

BUILDING THE ALCAN

A land link between Alaska and the rest of the USA was envisioned as early as 1930, but it took WWII to turn the nation's attention north to embark on one of the greatest engineering feats of the 20th century: constructing a 1390-mile road through remote wilderness.

Deemed a military necessity and authorized by President Franklin Roosevelt only two months after the attack on Pearl Harbor, the Alcan was designed to be an overland route far enough inland to be out of range of airplanes transported on Japanese aircraft carriers. The exact route followed old winter roads, trap lines and pack trails, and by March 9, 1942, construction had begun. Within three months, more than 10,000 troops, most of them from the US Army Corps of Engineers, were in the Canadian wilderness. They endured temperatures of -30°F (-34.4°C) in April, snowfalls in June and swarms of mosquitoes and gnats for most of the summer.

When a final link was completed near Kluane Lake in late October, the Alcan was open, having been built in only eight months and 12 days.

1942

Japan bombs Dutch Harbor for two days during WWII and then invades the remote Aleutian Islands of Attu and Kiska. Americans build the Alcan (Alaska Hwy).

1959

Alaska officially becomes the 49th state when President Dwight Eisenhower signs the statehood declaration on January 3. The state's population swells.

1964

North America's worst earthquake, 9.2 on the Richter scale, takes place on Good Friday, devastating Anchorage and Southcentral Alaska, with 131 people losing their lives.

1968

Oil and natural gas are discovered at Prudhoe Bay on the North Slope. The next year the state of Alaska stages a $900 million North Slope oil-lease sale.

UNCLE TED

Ted Stevens was already a decorated WWII pilot and Harvard Law School graduate when in 1953, after accepting a position in Fairbanks, he moved to Alaska with his wife by driving the Alaska Hwy in the dead of winter. A mere six months later, Stevens was appointed the US Attorney for Fairbanks and was eventually elected as a state representative. In 1968 Stevens was appointed US senator for Alaska and held that position until 2009, never receiving less than 66% of the vote after his first election in 1970.

Such longevity allowed Stevens to break Strom Thurmond's record as the longest-serving Republican senator in 2007, with 38 years and three months of continual service. For the majority of Alaskans, Stevens had always been their senator – the reason many dubbed him 'senator for life.'

The senator was duly noted for his ability to bring home the 'pork': in 2008 the Feds returned \$295 per Alaskan citizen in local projects (other states average only \$34 per person). In 2005 Stevens was ridiculed by the national media when, in a speech from the Senate floor, he angrily opposed diverting the Bridge to Nowhere funds to help New Orleans recover from Hurricane Katrina. Congress dropped the specific allocation for the bridge, but Alaska still received the money and simply spent it elsewhere.

Stevens' legendary Senate tenure came to an end in 2009. The previous year, a jury found him guilty of federal corruption – failing to report tens of thousands of dollars in gifts and services he had received from friends – and convicted him of seven felony charges. Stevens vowed to appeal the decision, but in November Alaskans had had enough and narrowly voted him out of office in his bid for an eighth term. The indictment was dismissed after a federal probe found evidence of prosecutorial misconduct.

In 2010 Stevens was killed in a not-unusual Alaskan accident: a small-plane crash (outside Dillingham in Southwest Alaska).

The oil began to flow on June 20, 1977, and for a decade oil gave Alaska an economic base that was the envy of every other state, accounting for as much as 90% of state-government revenue. With oil proceeds, the state created the Alaska Permanent Fund – which has grown from just \$700,000 to over \$44 billion today. Full-time residents still receive annual dividend checks, although due to ongoing budget crises, the returns on those checks have been drastically slashed in recent years.

From Pump Station No 1 to Valdez, the Trans-Alaska Pipeline crosses three mountain ranges, 34 major rivers and 500 streams.

In the explosive growth period of the mid-1980s, Alaskans enjoyed the highest per-capita income in the country. The state's budget was in the billions. Legislators in Juneau transformed Anchorage into a stunning city, with sports arenas, libraries and performing-arts centers, and provided virtually every bush town with a million-dollar school. From 1980 to 1986 this state of only half a million residents generated revenue of \$26 billion.

1971

President Richard Nixon signs the *Alaska Native Claims Settlement Act* to pave the way for the Trans-Alaska Pipeline. Alaska Natives give up claims in return for nearly \$1 billion and 44 million acres.

1973

The first Iditarod Trail Sled Dog Race is held on an old dog-team mail route blazed in 1910. The winner covers the 1049-mile race between Wasilla and Nome in 20 days.

1980

President Jimmy Carter signs the *Alaska National Interests Lands Conservation Act* (ANILCA), preserving 79.54 million acres of wilderness and creating or enlarging 15 national parks.

1985

Libby Riddles of Teller gambles by departing in a blizzard when no other musher would and becomes the first woman to win the Iditarod Trail Sled Dog Race.

Disaster at Valdez

For most Alaskans, the abundant oil made it hard to see beyond the gleam of the oil dollar. Reality hit hard in 1989, when the *Exxon Valdez*, a 987ft Exxon oil supertanker, rammed Bligh Reef a few hours out of the port of Valdez. The ship spilled almost 11 million gallons of North Slope crude oil into the bountiful waters of Prince William Sound. Alaskans and the rest of the world watched in horror as the oil spill quickly became too large for booms to contain, spreading 600 miles from the grounding site. State residents were shocked as oil began to appear elsewhere, from the glacier-carved cliffs of Kenai Fjords to the bird rookeries of Katmai National Park. The spill eventually contaminated 1567 miles of shoreline and killed an estimated 100,000 to 250,000 birds and 2800 sea otters, also decimating fish populations. The fisheries are just now recovering from the spill, as are animal populations, though you can still find oil just below the sand on many beaches.

Out of the Channel: the Exxon Valdez Oil Spill in Prince William Sound (1999), by John Keeble, is an in-depth account of Exxon's response and cover-up, which the author contends did more damage than the original spill.

Today the oil, like other resources exploited in the past, is simply running out. That pot of gold called Prudhoe Bay began its decline in 1988 and now produces less than half of its 1987 peak of two million barrels a day. The end of the Cold War and the subsequent downsizing of the US military in the early 1990s was more bad economic news for Alaska. Alaskan state revenues, once the envy of every other state governor in the country, went tumbling along with the declining oil royalties. With some 90% of its state budget derived from oil revenue, Alaska was awash in red ink from the early 1990s until 2004, managing a balanced budget only twice.

To Drill or Not to Drill

Drilling for oil in the Arctic National Wildlife Refuge (ANWR), the vast tract of tundra and mountains on Alaska's North Slope, has been a hot topic since the 1970s. It was temporarily reignited in 2019 when the Trump administration expressed interest in opening the entire coastal plain for oil and gas exploration. Despite public outcry stoked by fears that drilling would exacerbate climate change and interfere with important polar bear and caribou habitats, the administration pressed ahead, announcing an oil and gas leasing program in August 2020.

While an auction on leases was held in January 2021, the roll-out never really got out of the starting blocks. In July of the same year, the newly inaugurated President Biden issued an executive order suspending all drilling leases in the ANWR for the foreseeable future. Environmental campaigners heaved a sigh of relief.

1989

The *Exxon Valdez* runs aground on Bligh Reef and spills almost 11 million gallons of oil into Prince William Sound; it's the US' biggest human-made environmental disaster until the 2010 *Deepwater Horizon* oil spill.

2006

Sarah Palin, former mayor of Wasilla, stuns the political world by beating the incumbent governor to become Alaska's first female governor. She later unsuccessfully runs for US Vice President.

2015

Alaska becomes the third state in the country to legalize marijuana use.

2020

In the first year of the COVID-19 pandemic, Alaska's cruise-passenger traffic falls 100%, from 1.33 million in 2019 to zero in 2020.

Living in Alaska

Cut off from the rest of the United States, this great northern oasis has been attracting renegades, free thinkers, roughneck profiteers and nature-lovers from the very beginning. Alaska is about independence, individualism and taking care of business. It's a state of transient workers, rugged frontiersmen and women, and down-home sensibilities, and a place that attracts the eccentric in all of us. And that's what makes the Alaskan way of life so fascinating.

Regional Identity

Most of Alaska may be rural, roadless areas collectively known as the Bush, but most Alaskans are urban. Almost 70% of the residents live in the three largest cities: Anchorage, Fairbanks and Juneau.

The vast majority of households in rural Alaska participate in subsistence living. Studies show that 86% use game and 95% use fish. There are also Alaskans who gather and hunt the majority of their food and live in small villages that can only be reached by boat, plane or, in the winter, snowmobile. But the majority live in urban neighborhoods, work a nine-to-five job and shop at the supermarket.

And most Alaskans are newcomers. Only about a third of the state's population was born in Alaska; the rest moved there. Such a transient population creates a melting pot of ideas, philosophies and priorities. What they usually have in common is an interest in the great outdoors: they were lured here to either exploit it or enjoy it, and many residents do a little of both.

At the turn of the 20th century, numerous Sami people, from northern Scandinavia and Russia, were brought to Alaska to teach reindeer husbandry to the Iñupiat. Domesticated reindeer aren't native to these lands, though their wild cousins, the caribou, are. Franklin Roosevelt's *Reindeer Act* prohibited the ownership of reindeer herds by non-Natives in Alaska.

Thus debates in Alaska usually center on access to land, resources, and, in particular, the wilderness. There are some liberal bastions of environmentalism, Juneau and Homer being the best known, but over the years Alaskans have moved to the right, voting for Republican presidents, fighting tax increases and becoming one of the first states to pass a constitutional amendment banning same-sex marriages (which was later struck down within the court system). Alaska also became the third state in the USA to legalize cannabis use, in 2015.

Alaska is a firearms-friendly state, and travelers should know that opinions that favor gun control will likely not be appreciated, especially in rural areas. To be fair, many Alaskans live in places where the nearest law enforcement is hundreds of miles away, while the nearest bear is sometimes right outside their door. Even the most hardcore environmentalist may keep a rifle on hand for protection from wildlife if they live in an isolated enough area. Drive past any street sign in rural Alaska, and you'll likely notice it's been used as target practice.

Travelers come to visit and marvel at the grand scenery. But Alaskans are here to stay, so they need to make a living in their chosen home, a land where there is little industry or farming. They regard trees, oil and fish as an opportunity to do that.

Lifestyle

In Anchorage, residents can shop at enclosed malls, spend an afternoon at one of 162 parks, go in-line skating along paved bike paths, or get in their car and drive to another town. By contrast, in Nunapitchuk, 400 miles west of Anchorage on the swampy tundra of the Yukon–Kuskokwim Delta, the population is 526, there are no roads to or within town, homes and buildings are connected by a network of boardwalks, and there is just one store and a health clinic.

Rural or urban, Alaskans tend to be individualistic, following few outside trends and, instead, adhering to what their harsh environment dictates. Mother Nature and those -30°F (-34.4°C) winter days are responsible for the Alaskan dress code, even in Anchorage's finest restaurants. Alaskans also like to take care of things on their own, and many seek out spartan and tough living conditions. In the Bush, most homes feature a pile of old airplane parts, broken-down cars and construction materials in the front yard – you never know when a hard-to-find part may come in handy.

With that said, American visitors will find that most of the locals they meet in towns and cities have lifestyles similar to their own. They work, they love their weekends, they live in a variety of homes big and small, and they participate in double-coupon days at supermarkets. They may well have a hunting or fishing camp set up in an isolated area, but this is a place of retreat, as opposed to a place of residence.

Still, it is difficult to overstate the gap between urban and rural Alaska. In the deep Bush and Interior, communities are often entirely cut off from overland infrastructure, including groceries, and have limited (if any) access to law enforcement, medical care and public education. In indigenous communities, English may be a second language. The logistics of governing and managing a state of both concentrated urban areas and such extreme far-flung localities are akin to the challenges facing developing world economies.

Even in remote villages, satellite-TV dishes and internet access provide connections to the rest of the world, which can both reduce or exacerbate a feeling of isolation. Internet access can make it easier to take online classes or remotely fill out employment or college applications, but it can also yield tragic consequences. In 2017, for example, a 16-year-old indigenous hunter from Gambell Island brought down a bowhead whale – a source of enormous respect and honor in a village where a whale is often the main source of winter protein in a sustenance diet. The hunter posted pictures of his kill online and was then inundated with social-media hate messages from animal-rights activists, including death threats. He suffered through subsequent depression, although the local indigenous community rallied around him.

Alaska has social ills, exacerbated in large measure by the environment. The isolation of small towns and the darkness of winter have contributed to Alaska being one of the top 10 states for binge and heavy drinking, and depending on the year, fifth or sixth overall for the amount of alcohol sold per capita. Since the 1980s, Alaska has seen some of the highest per-capita use of controlled drugs in the country, and its suicide rate is twice the national average. Alcohol abuse and suicide rates are higher for Alaska Natives than other populations. In rural areas, methamphetamine abuse is becoming widespread.

To survive this climate and to avoid such demons, you have to possess a passion for the land and an individualistic approach to a lifestyle that few, other than Alaskans, would choose.

According to a marketing research firm, Anchorage has three coffee shops per 10,000 residents, beating out even Seattle, and making it, per capita, the country's mocha mecca.

Alaska in the Popular Imagination

Alaska has a role in the collective imagination as a mysterious, often frozen, dramatically scenic land. Not surprisingly, the state's portrayal in popular media often reflects this idea.

Literature

Two of the best-known writers identified with Alaska were not native to the land nor did they spend much time there, but Jack London and Robert Service turned their Alaskan adventures into literary careers.

The first print run of Jack London's *Call of the Wild* – 10,000 books – sold out in 24 hours. London, an American, departed for the Klondike Gold Rush in 1897, hoping to get rich panning gold. Instead he produced 50 books of fiction and nonfiction in just 17 years, and became the country's highest-paid writer of the day.

Service, a Canadian bank teller, was transferred to Dawson City in 1902 and then wrote his first book of verse, *The Spell of the Yukon*. The work was an immediate success and contained his best-known ballads, 'The Shooting of Dan McGrew' and 'The Cremation of Sam McGee.' Both portray the hardship and violence of life during the gold rush.

Alaska's contemporary luminaries of literature are no less elegant in capturing the spirit of the Far North. Kotzebue author Seth Kantner followed his critically acclaimed first novel, *Ordinary Wolves,* with the equally intriguing *Shopping for Porcupine,* a series of short stories about

THE IDITAROD

The Iditarod is one of the most iconic races in the world, and dog mushing is one of Alaska's most beloved pastimes. Supporters say sled dogs are born and bred to run, and if you've ever been tethered to a team flying across the frozen tundra, you'd probably agree. But a growing number of opponents say races like the Iditarod are cruel. Numerous reports of underfed, beaten and culled sled dogs at operations in Canada, Colorado and Alaska beg the question: should you support a race that has seen the death of 140-plus dogs since 1973? Should you even take a tourist trip on a dogsled?

Pros & Cons

People for the Ethical Treatment of Animals (PETA) is opposed to dogsledding, while other groups like the Sled Dog Action Coalition and US Humane Society support recreational mushing as long as cruel practices (like beating dogs) do not occur. One issue is that winning times are dropping – from 20 days in 1973 to around 10 today – putting greater stress on the dogs, who suffer from ulcers, bruised and lacerated paws, and damaged lungs. On the Iditarod, about one or two dogs die each year (four died in 2017, but none died from 2010 to 2012), and around one third end up dropping out of the race.

There's also the questionable practice of culling, where hundreds of substandard dogs are either given away or euthanized by their owners to ensure faster pedigrees. Race supporters cite new standards put in place to ensure the safety of dogs, including veterinarian checkups, mandatory breaks and drug tests.

Defenders of the Iditarod point out that as animal-abuse issues go, dog mushing is high profile and low impact, and even allowing for a per-capita comparison, far more dogs die in shelters than in the race. They argue that sled dogs have been bred to run, and are happiest running, and depressed when not allowed to pull a sled. It is said that the cold of the race is an environment the dogs desire; dog teams from the far northern Arctic can actually have issues racing because the route to Nome is too *warm* for them.

It is difficult to overstate the cultural impact of the race. As a test of animal-human companionship, individual endurance, and human will against the harsh environment, the Iditarod represents and exalts a set of values that are held sacred by many Alaskans. In some ways, the question of *if* these values should be honored – or if they can be honored in another fashion – is at the heart of the heated debate over the race.

growing up in the Alaska wilderness. *The Raven's Gift* by Don Rearden is a harrowing tale of village isolation and tundra survival, while *The Snow Child* is a standout debut from Pulitzer Prize–finalist Eowyn Ivey. One of the best Alaska Native novels is *Two Old Women* by Velma Wallis, an Athabascan born in Fort Yukon. This moving tale covers the saga of two elderly women abandoned by their migrating tribe during a harsh winter.

Other Alaskans who have captured the soul of the Far North include Nick Jans, whose *The Last Light Breaking* is considered a classic on life among the Iñupiat, and Sherry Simpson, who chronicles living in Fairbanks in the series of wonderful stories, *The Way Winter Comes*. For entertaining fiction using Alaska's commercial fishing as a stage, there's Bill McCloskey, whose three novels have characters ranging from the greenhorn fisherman to the hard-nosed cannery manager, with the plotline leaping from one to the next. His first, *Highliners,* is still his best.

The War Journal of Lila Ann Smith (2007), by Irving Warner, is a moving historical novel, based on the invasion of Attu by the Japanese in WWII, and the Aleuts who became prisoners of war.

Small cabins and long winter nights filled with sinister thoughts have also given rise to Alaska's share of mystery writers. Dean of the Alaskan whodunit is *New York Times* best-seller Dana Stabenow, whose ex-DA investigator Kate Shugak has appeared in around 20 novels, some of which are free as e-books. Sue Henry is equally prolific, with musher-turned-crime-solver Jessie Arnold in novels such as *Murder on the Iditarod Trail* and *Cold Company.*

Alaska is also popular ground for nonfiction. Jon Krakauer's *Into the Wild* explores the lost journeyer Christopher McCandless and humanity's desire to seek isolation and connection with the earth. John McPhee's 1991 classic *Coming into the Country* explores the explosive personalities of Alaska's fringe.

Cinema & TV

Hollywood and Alaska occasionally mix, especially in Hyder. This tiny, isolated town (population 83) has been the setting for numerous films, such as *Insomnia* (2002), in which Al Pacino plays a cop sent to a small Alaskan town to investigate a killer played by Robin Williams. There's also *Bear Island* (1978), loaded with stars, and *Ice Man* (1984), about scientists who find a frozen prehistoric man and bring him back to life. The 2007 movie *Into the Wild* featured many Alaska locations, including Anchorage, Healy, Denali National Park, Cantwell and the Copper River. Recent Hollywood tax breaks have also led to more films being shot in the 49th state.

A state with an entire season of nighttime has no shortage of noir and horror, and *30 Days of Night* (2007), about vampires devouring a town during the sunless winter, is an excellent example of the genre.

Alaska has also been the backdrop for TV, including the Emmy Award–winning series *Northern Exposure,* but reality TV is where it's hit the mother lode. The Discovery Channel has basically staked its lineup on Alaska, with shows like *Alaskan Bush People* and the ever-popular crab-fight-fest, *Deadliest Catch.* Everywhere in-between you have spin-offs about gold mining, ice-trucking, survival and logging.

Music

Alaskan composer John Luther Adams won a Pulitzer Prize for Music in 2014 for his Become Ocean composition, which is inspired by the waterways and rhythms of Alaska. Singer-songwriter Jewel was raised in Homer and got her start playing local bars with her father. Hip-hop has become the preferred sonic expression for many Alaska Natives; if you get a chance, check out Samuel Johns, an Athabascan rapper who hails from Anchorage.

Alaska Natives

Alaska Natives play an integral part in the Great Land's modern-day politics, culture and commerce. While their cultural imprint stretches back 10,000 years, present-day traditions and practices are evolving, dying off and transforming as the tide of Western influences sweeps through the state. Economically and politically, much of the work of the tribes happens on a village level, while the 13 Native corporations established by the *Alaska Native Claims Settlement Act* manage vast land and financial assets.

Village Life

Before 1940, Alaska Natives were in the majority. They now represent roughly 15% of the population. With 36,000 Alaska Natives, Anchorage is sometimes called the state's 'largest Native village.' Tribes once inhabited separate regions: the Aleuts and Alutiiqs lived from Prince William Sound to the Aleutian Islands; the Iñupiat, Yupik and Cupik occupied

Above Iñupiat clan house

Alaska's northern and western coasts; the Athabascan populated the Interior; and the Tlingit, Haida, Eyak and Tsimshian lived along the southeast coasts. Urban migration has blurred lines.

Two thirds of Alaska Natives live in villages within their ancestral lands. Though outwardly modern, the heart of village life is still the practice of subsistence hunting, fishing and gathering – depending on the community, 50% or more of village diets still comes from subsistence food gathering. The situation is exacerbated in remote communities where outside foodstuffs are prohibitively marked-up due to the cost of transportation.

Though critical to rural economies, the customs and traditions associated with subsistence are also the basis of Native culture. Subsistence activities are cooperative, helping maintain community bonds, preserve traditional festivities and oral histories, facilitate a spiritual connection to the land, and provide inspiration and material for artists.

Samuel Johns, who also goes by the stage name AK REBEL, is an Anchorage-based rapper and hip-hop MC who regularly pens songs about issues impacting the Alaska Native community. Give him a listen if you want to hear a passionate, contemporary indigenous voice.

Language

Alaska has at least 20 distinct Native languages. Native language use varies: the last Eyak speaker died in 2008, Haida has only a handful of speakers remaining, but Yupik is still spoken by about half the population. Even so, few children are currently learning any Native language as their mother tongue, though there is a mounting interest to ensure Native-language preservation and instruction.

Many of the Native tribes have specialized vocabularies. For instance, modern linguists say the Iñupiat have about 70 terms for ice and the Yupik language has 50 words for snow.

Arts & Crafts

Alaska Natives produce much of the state's most creative work. Not content to rest on tradition, contemporary indigenous artists push boundaries and reinterpret old forms.

Traditionally, Native artisans gathered their materials in the fall and began work in December, when cold weather forced them to remain inside. Materials varied according to what the local environment or trade routes could supply, and included wood, ivory, bone, antler, birch bark and grasses.

Production of Native crafts for a Western market began in the 18th century with Iñupiat ivory carvers and, later, Aleut basket weavers, adapting traditional forms for collectors. Today, the sale of Native art comprises a large slice of the economy in many Bush communities.

Carving

Ivory carving is practically synonymous with the Iñupiat, though they will also use wood, bone and antler. In addition to sculptures depicting hunting scenes or wild animals, scrimshaw (known as 'engraved ivory') is also produced. These incredibly detailed etchings often present a vignette of daily life on a whale bone or walrus tusk.

Yupik carvings tend to have more intricate surface detailing, and feature stylized designs. Red clay paint is sometimes used for coloring.

Natives of the Southeast, such as the Haida and Tlingit, have a lively woodcarving tradition that's heavy on abstractions based on clan symbols. Their totem poles are known worldwide but they are also masters at wood masks and bentwood boxes.

Purchasing ivory and bone crafts made from at-risk species is a personal decision for visitors to Alaska. Across the globe, it's a frowned-upon practice, particularly where ivory poaching poses serious risks to wildlife populations. In Alaska, it's a bit different. Alaska Natives are permitted to hunt endangered species – and most experts say that

A northwest coast wooden mask

Alaska Native harvests have no impact on populations of species like whales. They also use every part of the animal, rely on the meat for their subsistence lifestyle and make a little extra spending money by creating some amazing crafts from bone and ivory.

Dolls & Masks

All Native groups share a love of dolls, and traditionally used them in ceremonies, as fertility symbols, for play and for teaching young girls about motherhood. Modern doll-making is said to have begun in the 1940s in Kotzebue with the work of Ethel Washington, and continues today as one of the most vibrant Native art forms. Dolls can look realistic or be deliberate caricatures, such as the Chevak area 'ugly-faced' dolls with their wrinkled leather faces and humorous expressions.

Masks were traditionally used by Yupik and Iñupiat peoples for midwinter hunting festivals. Today you can find wonderful examples carved in wood and sewn from caribou.

Basketry

Perhaps no single form represents indigenous art better than basketry. Decorative patterns are geometric or reflect the region's animals, insects or plants. Athabascans weave baskets from alder, willow roots and birch bark; the Tlingit use cedar bark and spruce root; Yupik often decorate their baskets with sea-lion whiskers and feathers, and a few dye them with seal guts. Iñupiat are famous for using whale baleen, but this is in fact a 20th-century invention.

The Aleuts are perhaps the most renowned basket weavers. Using rye grass, which is tough but pliable, artists create tiny, intricately woven pieces that are highly valued.

Ceremonial Yupik mask

Embroidery & Clothing

Athabascan women traditionally decorated clothing with dyed quills, but after Europeans introduced beads and embroidery techniques they quickly became masters of this decorative art. Their long, hanging baby belts are often purchased as wall hangings.

Both Haida and Yupik are renowned for *mukluks* (knee-high boots) and decorative parkas.

Challenges

There are 229 federally recognized tribes in Alaska, but no reservation system. In 1971 Alaska Natives renounced claims to aboriginal lands in return for 44 million acres of land, $962.5 million and 100 shares per person in regional, urban and village corporations. While the settlement was a cause of pride, it has done little for employment and household income.

There are many other social challenges. Few issues are as serious as alcohol abuse, which has led to a high rate of fetal alcohol syndrome, domestic violence, crime and suicide. Since 1980 the state has allowed local control of alcohol and dozens of villages have voted on some form of prohibition, with varying results. Needless to say, you shouldn't introduce alcohol to Native dry villages. Other challenges include recruiting sufficient teachers, police officers and medical professionals to the Bush, and improving the diet of Native people. One study in the *American Journal of Public Health* concluded there were lower risks of suicide in Alaska Native villages with more prominent traditional elders, job access, higher incomes and married couples.

Top Places to See Native Art

- *University of Alaska Museum of the North*
- *Alaska Native Medical Center*
- *Iñupiat Heritage Center*
- *Totem Heritage Center*
- *Sitka National Historical Park*
- *Alaska Native Heritage Center*

Landscapes

It's one thing to be told Denali is the tallest mountain in North America; it's another to see it crowning the sky in Denali National Park. It's a mountain so tall, so massive and so overwhelming it has visitors stumbling off the park buses. As a state, Alaska is the same, a place so huge, so wild and so unpopulated it's incomprehensible to most people until they arrive.

The Land

Dramatic mountain ranges arch across the landmass of Alaska. The Pacific Mountain System, which includes the Alaska, Aleutian and St Elias Ranges, as well as the Chugach and Kenai Mountains, sweeps along the south before dipping into the sea southwest of Kodiak Island. Further north looms the imposing and little-visited Brooks Range, skirting the Arctic Circle.

In between the Alaska and Brooks Ranges is Interior Alaska, an immense plateau rippled by foothills, low mountains and magnificent rivers, among them the third-longest in the USA, the mighty Yukon River, which runs for 2300 miles. North of the Brooks Range is the North Slope, a coastal plain of scrubby tundra that gently descends to the Arctic Ocean.

In geological terms Alaska is relatively young and still very active. The state represents the northern boundary of the chain of Pacific Ocean volcanoes known as the 'Ring of Fire' and is the most seismically active region of North America. In fact, Alaska claims 52% of the earthquakes that occur in the country and averages more than 13 each day. Most are mild shakes, but some are deadly. Three of the six largest earthquakes in the world – and seven of the 10 largest in the USA – have occurred in Alaska.

Most of the state's volcanoes lie in a 1550-mile arc from the Alaska Peninsula to the tip of the Aleutian Islands. This area contains more than 65 volcanoes, 46 of which have been active in the last 200 years. Even in the past four decades Alaska has averaged more than two eruptions per year. If you spend any time in this state, or read about its history, you will quickly recognize that belching volcanoes and trembling earthquakes (as much as glaciers and towering peaks) are defining characteristics of the last frontier.

The Alaska Volcano Observatory website (www.avo.alaska.edu) has webcams and a 'volcano alert' map so you can see what's shaking and where.

Southeast Alaska

Southeast Alaska is a 500-mile coastal strip extending from north of Prince Rupert right across to the Gulf of Alaska. In between are the hundreds of islands of the Alexander Archipelago, and a narrow strip of coast, separated from Canada's mainland by the glacier-filled Coast Mountains. Winding through the middle of the region is the Inside Passage waterway; it's the lifeline for isolated communities, as the rugged terrain prohibits road-building. High annual rainfall and mild temperatures have turned the Southeast into rainforest, broken up by majestic mountain ranges, glaciers and fjords.

Wrangell-St Elias National Park (p327)

Prince William Sound & Kenai Peninsula

Like the Southeast, much of this region (also known as Southcentral Alaska) is a jumble of rugged mountains, glaciers, steep fjords and lush forests. This mix of terrain makes Kenai Peninsula a superb recreational area for backpacking, fishing and boating, while Prince William Sound, home of Columbia Glacier, is a mecca for kayakers and other adventurers.

Geographically, the Kenai Peninsula is a grab-bag. The Chugach Range receives the most attention, but in fact mountains only cover around two thirds of the peninsula. On the east side of the peninsula is glorious Kenai Fjords National Park, encompassing tidewater glaciers that pour down from one of the continent's largest ice fields, as well as the steep-sided fjords those glaciers have carved. Abutting the park in places, and taking in much of the most southerly part of the Kenai Peninsula, is Kachemak Bay State Park, a wondrous land of mountains, forests and fjords.

Want to see if Denali is clouded over before you visit? Check out Denali National Park's webcam for the latest conditions (www.nps.gov/dena/learn/photosmultimedia/webcams.htm).

Covering much of the interior of the peninsula, the Kenai National Wildlife Refuge offers excellent canoeing and hiking routes, plus some of the world's best salmon fishing. On the west side, the land flattens out into a marshy, lake-pocked region excellent for canoeing and trout fishing.

Prince William Sound is completely enveloped by the vast Chugach National Forest, the second-largest national forest in the US.

Southwest Alaska

Stretching 1500 miles from Kodiak Island to the International Date Line, the Southwest is spread out over four areas: the Kodiak Archipelago including Kodiak Island, the Alaska Peninsula, the Aleutian Islands and Bristol Bay. For the most part it is an island-studded region with stormy

ALASKA'S GLACIERS

Alaska is one of the few places in the world where active glaciation occurs on a grand scale. There are an estimated 100,000 glaciers in Alaska, covering 28,000 sq miles, or 3% of the state, and containing three-quarters of all Alaska's fresh water. The effects of glaciation, both from current and ice age glaciers, are visible everywhere and include wide U-shaped valleys, kettle ponds, fjords and heavily silted rivers.

Glaciers are formed when the snowfall exceeds the rate of melting and the solid cap of ice that forms begins to flow like a frozen river. The rate of flow, or retreat, can be anything but 'glacial,' and sometimes reaches tens of yards per day. While most of Alaska's glaciers are in rapid retreat, roughly 2% of them are advancing – actually growing in size. With that said, climate change is exacerbating the melt rates of some glaciers; guides working at the Matanuska Glacier, for example, report that local ice is retreating at unprecedented levels.

Glaciers are impressive-looking formations, and because ice absorbs all the colors of the spectrum except blue, they often give off a distinct blue tinge. The more overcast the day, the bluer glacial ice appears. The exceptions are glaciers that are covered with layers of rock and silt (the glacier's moraine) and appear more like mounds of dirt. For example, the Kennicott Glacier in Wrangell-St Elias National Park is often mistaken for a vast dump of old mine tailings. Wrangell-St Elias is one of the best places in the world to see rock glaciers. Rather than an ice glacier covered with rock, a rock glacier reverses the composition ratio; they're 90% moving rock and silt held together by ice, and advance more slowly than normal ice glaciers.

The largest glacier in Alaska is the Malaspina, which sits at the southern base of Mt St Elias and blankets 850 sq miles.

One of the most spectacular sights is watching – and hearing – tidewater glaciers 'calve' icebergs (the act of releasing small to massive chunks of glacier). Tidewater glaciers extend from a land base into the sea (or a lake) and calve icebergs in massive explosions of water. Active tidewater glaciers can be viewed from tour boats in Glacier Bay National Park, Kenai Fjords National Park and Prince William Sound, which has the largest collection in Alaska.

weather and violent volcanoes. This is the northern rim of the Ring of Fire, and along the Alaska Peninsula and the Aleutian Islands is the greatest concentration of volcanoes in North America.

Southwest Alaska is home to some of the state's largest and most intriguing national parks and refuges. Katmai National Park & Preserve, on the Alaska Peninsula, and Kodiak National Wildlife Refuge are renowned for bear-watching. Lake Clark National Park & Preserve, across Cook Inlet from Anchorage, is a wilderness playground for rafters, anglers and hikers.

Most of the Aleutian Islands and part of the Alaska Peninsula form the huge Alaska Maritime National Wildlife Refuge, headquartered in Homer. The refuge encompasses 3.5 million acres and more than 2500 islands, and is home to 80% of the 50 million seabirds that nest in Alaska.

Denali & the Interior

With the Alaska Range to the north, the Wrangell and Chugach Mountains to the south and the Talkeetna Mountains cutting through the middle, the Interior has a rugged appearance matching that of either Southeast or Southcentral Alaska.

Mountains are everywhere. The formidable Alaska Range creates a jagged spine through the Interior's midsection, while the smaller ranges – the Chugach, Talkeetna and Wrangell to the south and the White Mountains to the north – sit on the flanks. From each of these mountain ranges run major river systems. Spruce and birch predominate in the lowland valleys with their tidy lakes. Higher up on the broad tundra

Glacier Bay National Park & Preserve (p125)

meadows, spectacular wildflowers show their colors during summer months. Wildfire also plays its role here, wiping out vast swaths of forest nearly every summer.

The big name here, of course, is Denali National Park, blessed with the continent's mightiest mountain and abundant wildlife. Wrangell–St Elias National Park, located in the region's southeast corner, is the largest national park in the US and a treasure house of glaciers and untouched wilderness. Up in the Interior's northeast is Yukon-Charley Rivers National Preserve, located at the nexus of two of the state's legendary waterways.

The Bush

This is the largest slice of Alaska and includes the Brooks Range, Arctic Alaska and western Alaska on the Bering Sea. The remote, hard-to-reach Bush is separated from the rest of the state by mountains, rivers and vast roadless distances.

The mighty Brooks Range slices this region in two. To the north, a vast plain of tundra sweeps down to the frozen wasteland of the Arctic Ocean. In the western reaches, near towns such as Nome and Kotzebue, you'll find more tundra, as well as a flat landscape of lakes and slow-moving rivers closer to the Bering Sea, and rolling coastal hills and larger mountains heading toward the interior. In the far north, the Arctic Coastal Plain is a flat series of wetlands, lakes, rivers and tundra that extends all the way to the Arctic Ocean.

The Bush has several national parks and preserves. Gates of the Arctic National Park & Preserve spans the spires of the Brooks Range and offers spectacular hiking and paddling. Near Kotzebue is Kobuk Valley National Park, known for the Great Kobuk Sand Dunes and the oft-paddled Kobuk River, with the mountain-ringed Noatak National Preserve just to the north.

The heaviest recorded annual snowfall in Alaska was 974.5in at Thompson Pass, north of Valdez, in the winter of 1952–53.

Major Vegetation Zones of Alaska

With its vast territory extending from the frigid Arctic Ocean to the temperate Gulf of Alaska, and encompassing mountain ranges, river valleys, sweeping plains, island chains and a range of climatic conditions, Alaska harbors a diversity of ecosystems. Most of the state, however, can be categorized into three large zones: tundra, taiga and temperate forest.

Tundra

Tundra comes from the Finnish word for barren or treeless land. Of course, tundra isn't completely barren but often a bewitching landscape of grasses, herbs, mosses, lichens and, during the short summer, wildflowers. Nevertheless, tundra soil is generally poor, the diversity of plants is low and the growing season extremely short: sometimes plants have as little as 1½ months a year to sprout.

Lowland tundra extends along the coastal regions of the Arctic, and the deltas of western Alaska around Nome. What's referred to as upland tundra covers the land at higher elevations above the treeline throughout the Alaska Range, as well as across the Brooks Range and all along the Aleutians.

Taiga

Taiga, also called boreal forest, runs from Interior Alaska through Canada and down past the Great Lakes. Taiga forests are low and damp, often broken up with lakes and bogs. The most common species of trees are white spruce, black spruce, birch and aspen. Trees tend to be short and scraggly, and grow in thickets.

Most of Interior Alaska (at lower elevations) is covered in taiga. It's great moose habitat, so keep your eyes peeled in such areas.

Between the taiga and tundra is a transitional area in which species from either zone may be found. On the ride up the Dalton Hwy, a famous 'Last Spruce' is a curious testament to the fact that while transitions rarely have exact boundaries, they do have to end somewhere.

Coastal Temperate Forest

Alaska's temperate forests are found, no surprise, in southeastern Alaska, along the Gulf of Alaska, as well as the eastern edge of the Kenai Peninsula. They form part of the system of coastal rainforests that runs north from the Pacific Northwest and are dominated by Sitka spruce and other softwoods. Precipitation is high in this region and the winters mild; as a result trees can grow to be giants over 230ft tall. It's no surprise that Alaska Natives from this region are masters at woodcarving, and created the splendid totem-pole culture that is now famous around the world.

The Southwest's vast and volcanic Aniakchak National Monument & Preserve is exceedingly difficult to access, and consistently the country's least visited national park site – in 2016 it only hosted 100 visitors.

Climate

Oceans surround 75% of Alaska, the terrain is mountainous and the sun shines at a low angle. All this gives the state an extremely variable climate, and daily weather that is infamous for its unpredictability.

For visitors, the most spectacular part of Alaska's climate is its long days. At Point Barrow, Alaska's northernmost point, the sun doesn't set for 2½ months from May to August. In other Alaskan regions, the longest day is on June 21 (the summer solstice), when the sun sets for only two hours in Fairbanks and for five hours in the Southeast. Even after sunset in late June, however, there is still no real darkness, just a long twilight.

Southeast Alaska

The Southeast has a temperate maritime climate; like Seattle, but wetter. Juneau averages 57in of precipitation (rain or snow) annually, and Ketchikan gets 154in, most of which is rain as winter temperatures are mild.

CLIMATE CHANGE & ALASKA

Alaska's temperatures are rising, causing permafrost to melt, coastlines to erode, forests to die (or push north into new territory), and Arctic sea ice and glaciers to melt at alarming rates (90% of Southeast glaciers are retreating rapidly). Some scientists now predict the Arctic Ocean will be entirely ice-free in summer by 2040, or even sooner. Meanwhile, Portage Glacier can no longer be viewed from its visitor center, and Mendenhall Glacier is expected to retreat totally onto land and cease being a tidewater glacier within a few years.

Northern Alaska is ground zero when it comes to global warming, and with the vast majority of the land sitting on permafrost – and aboriginal traditions and whole ecosystems inextricably tied to the frozen earth and sea – the very balance of nature has been thrown into disaccord. At Shishmaref, a barrier island village on the Seward Peninsula, residents have watched with horror as homes have literally slipped into the Bering Sea due to the loss of protective sea ice that buffers them against storms. And Shishmaref is just one of 160 rural communities the US Army Corps of Engineers has identified as being threatened by erosion. Relocation plans have already begun for several of these.

Paradoxically, in Juneau sea levels are dropping as billions of tons of ice have melted away, literally springing the land to new heights. In some areas the land is rising three inches a year, the highest rate in North America. As a result, water tables are dropping, wetlands are drying up and property lines are having to be redrawn.

Beyond the disaster for humans, the changes to the Alaskan landscape and climate will have dramatic effects on the highly adapted organisms that call this place home. In Juneau, the rising land has already caused channels that once facilitated salmon runs to silt up and grass over. In the Far North, melting summer sea ice is expected to put such pressure on the polar bear that it has been listed as a 'threatened' species.

Prince William Sound & Kenai Peninsula

Precipitation is the norm in Prince William Sound. In summer, Valdez is the driest of the towns; Whittier is by far the wettest. In all communities, average July daytime temperatures are barely above 60°F (15.6°C). So no matter what your travel plans are, pack your fleece and some bombproof wet-weather gear.

Weather-wise, the Kenai Peninsula is a compromise: drier than Prince William Sound, warmer than the Bush, wetter and cooler (in summer) than the Interior. Especially on the coast, extremes of heat and cold are unusual. Seward's normal daily high in July is 62°F (16.7°C). Rainfall is quite high on the eastern coasts of the peninsula around Seward and Kenai Fjords National Park; moderate in the south near Homer and Seldovia; and somewhat less frequent on the west coast and inland around Soldotna and Cooper Landing.

Anchorage

Shielded from the dark fury of Southcentral Alaska's worst weather by the Kenai Mountains, the Anchorage Bowl receives only 14in of rain annually and enjoys a relatively mild climate: January averages 13°F (-10.6°C) and July about 58°F (14.4°C). Technically a sub-Arctic desert, Anchorage does have more than its fair share of overcast days, however, especially in early and late summer.

Southwest Alaska

With little to protect it from the high winds and storms that sweep across the North Pacific, the Southwest is home to the very worst weather in Alaska. Kodiak is greatly affected by the turbulent Gulf of Alaska and receives 80in of rain per year, along with regular blankets of pea-soup fog and occasional blustery winds. On the northern edge of the Pacific,

MAJOR PARKS OF ALASKA

PARK	FEATURES	ACTIVITIES
Admiralty Island National Monument (p124)	wilderness island, chain of lakes, brown bears, marine wildlife	bear-watching, kayaking, canoeing, cabin rentals
Chena River State Recreation Area (p310)	Chena River, alpine areas, granite tors, campgrounds, cabin rentals	backpacking, canoeing, hiking
Chugach State Park (p152)	Chugach Mountains, alpine trails, Eklutna Lake	backpacking, mountain biking, paddling, hiking, campgrounds
Denali National Park (p272)	Denali, brown bears, caribou, Wonder Lake, campground	wildlife-viewing, backpacking, hiking, park bus tours
Denali State Park (p294)	alpine scenery, trails, views of Denali, campgrounds	backpacking, hiking, camping
Gates of the Arctic National Park & Preserve (p378)	Brooks Range, Noatak River, treeless tundra, caribou	rafting, canoeing, backpacking, fishing
Glacier Bay National Park & Preserve (p125)	tidewater glaciers, whales, Fairweather Mountains	kayaking, camping, whale-watching, lodge, boat cruises
Independence Mine State Historical Park (p189)	Talkeetna Mountains, alpine scenery, gold-mine ruins, visitor center	mine tours, hiking
Kachemak Bay State Park (p262)	glaciers, protected coves, alpine areas, cabin rentals	kayaking, backpacking, boat cruises
Katmai National Park & Preserve (p352)	Valley of Ten Thousand Smokes, volcanoes, brown bears, lodge	fishing, bear-watching, backpacking, kayaking
Kenai Fjords National Park (p236)	tidewater glaciers, whales, marine wildlife, steep fjords, cabin rental	boat cruises, kayaking, hiking
Kenai National Wildlife Refuge (p240)	chain of lakes, Russian River, moose, campgrounds	fishing, canoeing, wildlife-watching, hiking
Kodiak National Wildlife Refuge (p351)	giant bears, rich salmon runs, wilderness lodges, cabin rentals	bear-watching, flightseeing, cabin rentals
Misty Fiords National Monument (p83)	steep fjords, 3000ft sea cliffs, lush rainforest	boat cruises, kayaking, cabin rentals, flightseeing
Tracy Arm-Fords Terror Wilderness Area (p108)	glaciers, steep fjords, parade of icebergs, marine wildlife	boat cruises, kayaking, wildlife-watching
Wrangell–St Elias National Park (p327)	mountainous terrain, Kennecott mine ruins, glaciers	backpacking, flightseeing, rafting, biking, mine tours

Unalaska and the Alaskan Peninsula receive less rain (annual precipitation ranges from 60in to 70in), but are renowned for unpredictable and stormy bouts of weather. Southwest summer temperatures range from 45°F to 65°F (7°C to 18°C). For the clearest weather, try visiting in early summer or fall.

Denali & the Interior

In this region of mountains and spacious valleys, the climate varies greatly and the weather can change on a dime. In January temperatures can sink to -60°F (-51°C) for days at a time, while in July they often soar to above 90°F (32°C). The norm for the summer is long days with temperatures of 60°F to 70°F (15.6°C to 21.1°C). However, it is common for Denali National Park to experience at least one dump of snowfall in the lowlands between June and August.

Here, more than anywhere else in the state, it's important to have warm clothes while still being able to strip down to a T-shirt and hiking shorts. Most of the area's 10in to 15in of annual precipitation comes in the form of summer showers, with cloudy conditions common, especially north of Denali. The Denali mountain, in the eponymous National Park, tends to be hidden by clouds more often than not.

In the Interior and up around Fairbanks, precipitation is light, but temperatures can fluctuate by more than 100°F during the year. Fort Yukon holds the record for the state's highest temperature, at 100°F (37.8°C) in June 1915, yet it once recorded a temperature of -78°F (-61.1°C) in winter. Fairbanks has the odd summer's day that hits 90°F (32°C) and always has nights during winter that drop below -60°F (-51.1°C).

The Bush

Due to its geographical diversity, the Bush is a land of many climates. In inland areas, winter holds sway from mid-September to early May, with ceaseless weeks of clear skies, negligible humidity and temperatures colder than anywhere else in America. Alaska's all-time low, -80°F (-62°C), was recorded at Prospect Creek Camp, just off the Dalton Hwy. Closer to the ocean winter lingers even longer than inland, but it is incrementally less chilly.

During the brief summer, visitors to the Bush should be prepared for anything. Utqiaġvik and Prudhoe Bay may demand a parka: July highs there often don't hit 40°F (4.5°C). Along the Dalton Hwy and around Nome, the weather is famously variable. Intense heat (stoked by the unsetting sun) can be as much of a concern as cold.

National, State & Regional Parks

One of the main attractions of Alaska is public land, where you can play and roam freely over an area of 348,000 sq miles, more than twice the size of California. The agency in charge of the most territory is the Bureau of Land Management (BLM; www.blm.gov), followed by the US Fish & Wildlife Service (USFWS; www.fws.gov) and the National Park Service (www.nps.gov).

Alaska's national parks are the crown jewels as far as most travelers are concerned, and attract more than two million visitors a year. The most popular units are Klondike Gold Rush National Historical Park, which draws 860,000 visitors a year, and Denali National Park, home of Denali, which sees around half that number. Other busy units are Glacier Bay National Park, a highlight of every cruise-ship itinerary in the Southeast, and Kenai Fjords National Park in Seward.

Alaska State Parks (www.alaskastateparks.org) oversees 123 units that are not nearly as renowned as most national parks, and thus far less crowded at trailheads and in campgrounds. The largest is the 2500-sq-mile Wood-Tikchik State Park, a roadless wilderness north of Dillingham that's bigger than the state of Delaware. The most popular is Chugach State Park, the 773-sq-mile unit that is Anchorage's after-work playground.

Both the BLM and the USFWS oversee many refuges and preserves that are remote, hard to reach and not set up with visitor facilities such as campgrounds and trails. The major exception is the Kenai National Wildlife Refuge, an easy drive from Anchorage and a popular weekend destination for locals and tourists alike.

For more pre-trip information, contact the Alaska Public Lands Information Centers (www.alaskacenters.gov).

Roadside Geology of Alaska (1988), by Cathy Connor and Daniel O'Haire, explores the geology you see from the road, covering everything from earthquakes to why there's gold on the beaches of Nome – not dull reading by any means.

Lake Clark National Park & Preserve (p351)

Environmental Issues

Alaska's vast tracts of pristine land and beloved status as the USA's last wild frontier mean that its environmental issues are, more often than not, national debates. These days the focus of those debates (and a fair amount of action) centers on the effects of global warming and resource management, especially the push for mining and drilling in reserve lands.

Village Voices (www.alaskavillagevoices.org) is an informative magazine focusing on the issues facing rural Alaska Natives, including the high costs of energy, homelessness, the legacy of Head Start, an early childhood health program, and poor nutrition.

Land

The proposed Pebble Mine development in Bristol Bay has been one of the most contentious environmental issues this century. The stakes are huge for all sides. Pebble is potentially the second-largest ore deposit of its type in the world, with copper and gold deposits estimated to be worth a staggering $500 billion. But the minerals would be extracted from near the headwaters of Bristol Bay and require a 2-mile-wide open pit that could pollute streams that support the world's largest run of wild salmon.

That issue saw an unlikely alliance of environmentalists, commercial fishers and Alaska Natives up in arms, and in 2013 the mine project was put on hold as investors pulled out. But under the Trump administration the Environmental Protection Agency (EPA) has allowed the Pebble Partnership to apply for a federal permit to begin work on the mine development. In September 2017, after meeting with Pebble Partnership CEO Tom Collier, EPA Administrator Scott Pruitt directed the agency to withdraw an Obama-era proposal to protect the Bristol Bay watershed from certain mining activities.

Oil exploration in the Arctic National Wildlife Refuge (ANWR) is another unresolved issue, despite a political battle that has raged in the lower 48 since the earliest days of the Reagan presidency. The refuge is often labeled by environmentalists as America's Serengeti, an unspoiled wilderness inhabited by 45 species of mammals, including grizzly bears, polar bears and wolves. Millions of migratory birds use the refuge to nest, and every spring the country's second-largest caribou herd, 150,000 strong, gives birth to 40,000 calves there. Though estimates of the amount of recoverable oil have dropped considerably in recent years, industry is still eager to jump in, and politicians continue to argue that ANWR can help the country achieve energy independence.

Fisheries

The problems of resource exploitation are not restricted to oil, gas and minerals. After the king-crab fishery collapsed in 1982, the commercial fishing industry was rebuilt on pollock (also known as whiting), whose mild flavor made it the choice for imitation crab, frozen fish sticks, and fish sandwiches served at fast-food restaurants. Pollock are groundfish – fish that live on, in, or near the sea floor – and are a crucial species in the Bering Sea ecosystem. The Alaskan pollock catch constitutes the largest fishery in the country, and accounts for almost one third of all US seafood landings by weight. The Marine Stewardship Council rates pollock caught from the eastern Bering Sea, Aleutian Islands and the Gulf of Alaska as a sustainable fishery.

Salmon is an incredibly important fishery to Alaskans on both a commercial and recreational level. The future of the species remains in question. During 2017, Bristol Bay, which produces 40% of the world's harvested sockeye salmon, experienced a record-breaking salmon run. On the flip side, the Kuskokwim River, an important source of king salmon, experienced one of the worst runs in history. The reasons for local fishery collapses remain a mystery, though theories about climate change and its many effects as well as overfishing have the most traction. Native communities along the Arctic Alaska coast participate in sustenance-level hunting of bowhead whales, an activity with deep cultural roots. A complex social hierarchy determines who is allowed to captain and crew whaling boats, as well as the order of whale meat distribution. Whaling in Alaska is regulated at the state and federal level, with quotas set by the International Whaling Commission (IWC); from 2013 to 2018, indigenous Arctic communities in Alaska and Chukotka (Russia) were allowed to take 336 whales in total.

Rural Issues

Waste management is a hot issue in Alaska's rural communities, many of which are not connected to the rest of the state by convenient transportation routes. Though burning garbage is still a common way of reducing trash, as is dumping, more and more communities have begun to build recycling centers, practice composting and haul back to Anchorage whatever they can. A free program called Flying Cans takes bundled aluminum cans from rural communities to recycling plants in Anchorage via scheduled cargo flights. Energy-saving education programs are also making their way across the state, as are greenhouses. The latter are expected to have a positive impact on both nutrition and the amount of fuel used to supply rural villages with fresh produce.

For more information on environmental issues, contact these conservation organizations:

- Alaska Sierra Club (www.alaska.sierraclub.org)
- No Dirty Gold (www.nodirtygold.org) A campaign opposing ecologically destructive gold mining around the world.
- Southeast Alaska Conservation Council (www.seacc.org)
- Wilderness Society (www.wilderness.org)

Top Humpback whale, Glacier Bay (p125)

Bottom Dall sheep, Polychrome Pass Overlook, Denali National Park & Preserve (p274)

Wildlife

Alaska's vast landscape and waters allow the space for wild creatures to roam, and wildlife-watching is a major draw for visitors to the state. Spotting wildlife can be as dramatic as a flight over feeding grizzlies or as simple as a walk to see moose in an Anchorage park.

Land Mammals

Alaska boasts one of the earth's great concentrations of wildlife, and some species that are threatened or endangered elsewhere – brown bears, for example – thrive in the 49th state.

Bears

There are three species of bear in Alaska: brown, black and polar. Of these, you're most likely to see brown bears, as they have the greatest range.

Above Polar bear in the Arctic National Wildlife Refuge (p372)

Brown and grizzly bears are now listed as the same species *(Ursus arctos)* but there are differences. Browns live along the coast, where abundant salmon runs help them reach weights exceeding 800lb, or 1500lb in the case of the famed Kodiak. Grizzlies are browns found inland and subsist largely on grass. Normally a male weighs from 500lb to 700lb, and females half that. The most common way to identify any brown bear is by the prominent shoulder hump, easily seen behind the neck when the animal is on all fours.

Alaska has an estimated 30,000 brown bears, or more than 98% of the US population. In July and August you can see the bears fishing alongside rivers. In early fall they move into tundra regions and open meadows to feed on berries.

Though black bears *(Ursus americanus),* which may also be colored brown or cinnamon, are the USA's most widely distributed bruin, their range is limited in Alaska. They live in most forested areas of the state, but not north of the Brooks Range, on the Seward Peninsula, or on many large islands, such as Kodiak and Admiralty. The average male black weighs from 180lb to 250lb.

Polar bears *(Ursus maritimus)* dwell only in the far north and their adaptation to a life on sea ice has given them a white, water-repellent coat, dense underfur, specialized teeth for a carnivorous diet (primarily seals), and hair that almost completely covers the bottom of their feet. A male polar bear weighs between 600lb and 1200lb. Plan on stopping at the zoo in Anchorage, or taking a lengthy side trip to Utqiaġvik (Barrow) or Kaktovik, if you want to see one.

Moose

Moose are long-legged in the extreme, but short-bodied despite sporting huge racks of antlers. They're the world's largest members of the deer family, and the Alaskan species is the largest of all. A newborn weighs 35lb and can grow to more than 300lb in five months; cows weigh 800lb to 1200lb; and bulls 1000lb to more than 1600lb, with antlers up to 70in wide.

The moose population stands at around 175,000, and historically the animal has been the most important game species in Alaska. Some 20,000 are officially hunted each year.

Caribou

Although roughly 750,000 caribou live in Alaska across 32 herds, they are relatively difficult to view as they inhabit the Interior north up to the Arctic Sea. This is a shame as the migration of the Western Arctic herd, the largest in North America with almost 325,000 animals, is one of the great wildlife events left on earth. The herd uses the North Slope for its calving area, and in late August many of the animals cross the Noatak River and journey southward.

There is only one indigenous amphibian in Alaska: the hardy little wood frog; they spend seven months of the year quite literally frozen, before thawing out and hopping on with their lives, no doubt wondering, 'Why did we move here?'

There have been steep declines in the state's caribou population recently; the Central Arctic herd's numbers have dropped by over 50%, for example. The reason for this remains a mystery, although wildlife biologists seem to agree that changing environmental conditions, partly attributable to climate change, are a factor.

Caribou range in weight from 150lb to more than 400lb. The animals are crucial to the Iñupiat and other Alaska Natives, who hunt them to support their subsistence lifestyle.

The best place to see caribou is Denali National Park.

Wolves

While gray wolves are struggling throughout most of the USA, in Alaska their numbers are strong despite predator control programs. In total, about 7000 to 10,000 wolves live in Alaska, spread throughout almost every region of the state. Adult males average 85lb to 115lb, and their pelts can be gray, black, off-white, brown or yellow, with some tinges approaching red. Wolves travel, hunt, feed and operate in the social unit of a pack. In the Southeast their principal food is deer, in the Interior it's moose and in Arctic Alaska it's caribou.

Mountain Goats & Dall Sheep

Often confused with Dall sheep, mountain goats have longer hair, short black horns and deep chests. They range throughout the Southeast, fanning out north and west into the coastal mountains of Cook Inlet, as well as the Chugach and Wrangell Mountains. Good locations to see them include Glacier Bay and Wrangell-St Elias National Park.

Dall Sheep are more numerous and widespread, numbering close to 80,000, and live in the Alaska, Wrangell, Chugach and Kenai mountain ranges. They are often seen at Windy Corner, on the Seward Hwy, and in Denali National Park. Another good spot is on the Harding Ice Field trail in Seward.

The best time to catch rams in a horn-clashing battle for social dominance is right before the mating period, which begins in November.

Lynx

This intriguing-looking feline has unusually large paws to help it move swiftly over snowpack as it hunts snowshoe hare, its primary food source. Lynx inhabit most forested areas of Alaska, but your chances of seeing one depend on the hare population, which fluctuates over an eight- to 11-year cycle.

Beavers & River Otters

Around lakes and rivers you stand a good chance of seeing river otters and beavers or, at the very least, beaver lodges and dams. Both animals live throughout the state, with the exception of the North Slope. Otters range from 15lb to 35lb, while beavers weigh between 40lb and 70lb, although 100lb beavers have been recorded in Alaska.

Fish & Marine Mammals

Whales

The three most common whales seen in coastal waters are the 50ft-long humpback, the smaller bowhead whale and the gray whale. The humpback is the most frequently seen on cruise ships and ferries, as they often lift their flukes (tails) out of the water to begin a dive, or blow every few seconds when resting.

Tour boats head out of almost every Southeast Alaska port loaded with whale-watching passengers. You can also join such trips in Kenai Fjords National Park and in Kodiak.

In northern Alaska, a different sort of whaling boat heads out for a different whaling season. Eleven indigenous communities on the Arctic

TOP PLACES TO SEE...

Brown bears Katmai National Park & Preserve (p352), Anan Creek Wildlife Observatory (p88)

Moose Kenai National Wildlife Refuge (p240), Denali National Park (p272)

Seals Tracy Arm (p108), Prince William Sound (p192)

Humpback whales Glacier Bay National Park & Preserve (p125), Sitka (p99)

Puffins St Lazaria Island National Wildlife Refuge (p104)

Walrus

Alaskan coast are allowed to take a certain number of bowhead whales per year (usually around 75 in total, out of a bowhead population of 10,000). These hunts are considered seminal to local traditional culture, and for basic food needs in subsistence communities.

At the Sitka WhaleFest (www.sitkawhalefest.org) in early November, visitors and locals gather to listen to world-renowned biologists talk about whales, and then hop on boats to go look for them.

Everyone knows the *real* state bird of Alaska is the mosquito. There are 35 blood-sucking species here, and they are relentless, especially on the North Slope, where they will swarm you the second you leave your car. Only ocean winds and DEET spray are preventative.

Dolphins & Porpoises

Dolphins and harbor porpoises are commonly seen in Alaskan waters, even from the decks of public ferries. Occasionally, passengers will also spot a pod of orcas (killer whales), and sometimes belugas, both large members of the dolphin family. Orcas, which can be more than 20ft long, are easily identified by their high black-and-white dorsal fins.

The white-colored beluga ranges in length from 11ft to 16ft and weighs more than 3000lb.There are two populations of belugas in Alaska: the endangered Cook Inlet area population, and the Bering Sea area population. In the spring and fall, roughly May and September, pods of the Cook Inlet belugas feed in Turnagain Arm, right outside Anchorage. Lines of cars pull to the side of the Seward Hwy to watch these mammals surface; the best pullout is aptly named Beluga Point. The 74,500 belugas that live off Alaskan shores travel in herds of 10 to several hundred.

Salmon

Five kinds of wild salmon can be found in Alaska: sockeye (also referred to as red salmon), king (or chinook), pink (or humpy), coho (or silver) and chum. For sheer wonders of nature it's hard to beat a run of thousands of salmon swimming upstream to spawn. From late July to mid-September, many coastal streams are so choked with the fish that at times individual fish have to wait their turn to swim through narrow gaps of shallow water.

In the heart of Anchorage, Ship Creek supports runs of king, coho and pink. From a viewing platform you can watch the fish spawning upriver and also the locals trying to catch one for dinner. In downtown Ketchikan, you can watch salmon in Ketchikan Creek.

Mind of the Raven: Investigations and Adventures with Wolf-Birds, by Bernd Heinrich, is a fascinating deep dive into the mental acuity of the raven, the most intelligent bird in the world, and a constant, *quork*-ing presence on many an Alaskan camping trip.

Seals

The most commonly seen marine mammal, seals are often found basking in the sun on ice floes. Six species exist in Alaska, but most visitors will encounter the harbor seal, whose range includes the Southeast, Prince William Sound and the entire Gulf of Alaska. The average male weighs 200lb, reached by a diet of herring, flounder, salmon, squid and small crabs.

The ringed and bearded seals inhabit the northern Bering, Chukchi and Beaufort Seas, where sea ice forms during winter.

Steller sea lions, the largest member of the 'eared seals' family, range from Japan to California, but are divided from the Gulf of Alaska into two stocks: the endangered Western stock and the threatened Eastern stock. Females can weigh close to 800lb, while males can reach 2500lb. A day trip in Kenai Fjords National Park will take you to sea-lion haul-outs, where you can view a crowd of them resting on rocks.

Walruses

Like the seal, the Pacific walrus is a pinniped (fin-footed animal) but this much larger creature is less commonly spotted. Walruses summer in the far northern Chukchi Sea and though they may number over 200,000, most visitors are likely only to encounter the tusks of these creatures in the carving of a Native artist.

Birds

Alaska's vast open spaces and diversity of habitat make it unusually rich in birdlife. Over 445 species have been identified statewide.

Bald Eagles

While elsewhere in America the bald eagle (a magnificent bird with a wingspan of over 8ft) is on the endangered species list, in Alaska it's commonly sighted in the Southeast, Prince William Sound and Dutch Harbor in the Aleutian Islands.

Ptarmigan

The state bird is a cousin of the prairie grouse. Three species can be found throughout Alaska in high, treeless country.

Seabirds & Waterfowl

Alaskan seabirds include the crowd-pleasing horned and tufted puffins, six species of auklet and three species of albatross (which boast a wingspan of up to 7ft). The optimum way to see these is on a wildlife cruise to coastal breeding islands such as St Lazaria Island, home to 1500 pairs of breeding tufted puffins.

An amazing variety of waterfowl migrate to Alaska each summer, including trumpeter swans, Canada geese, eider, the colorful harlequin duck and five species of loon.

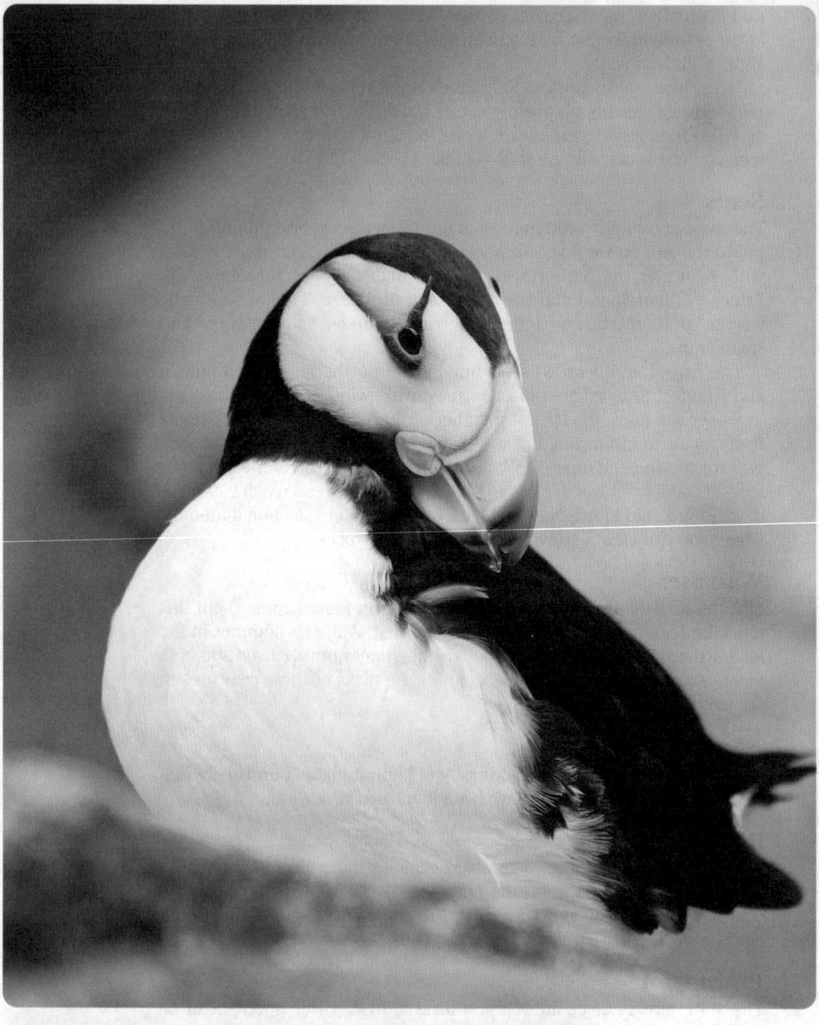

JACOBLOYACANO/SHUTTERSTOCK ©

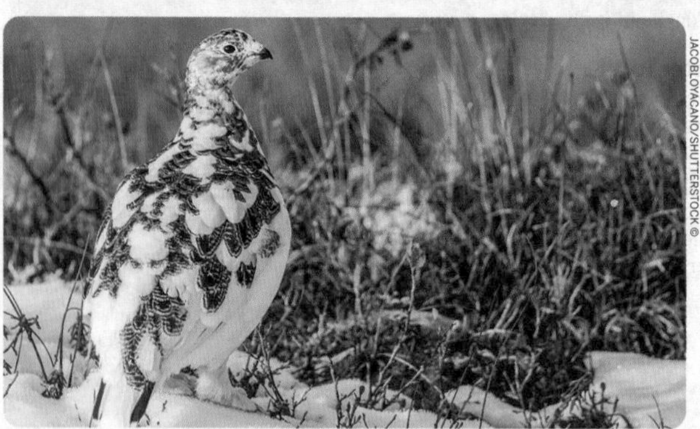

Top Alaskan puffin

Bottom Ptarmigan (p417), Denali National Park & Preserve

Watching grizzly bears, Denali National Park & Preserve (p272)

RON SANFORD/GETTY IMAGES ©

Survival Guide

Directory A–Z

Accessible Travel

Thanks to the American Disabilities Act, many state and federal parks have installed wheelchair-accessible sites and restrooms in their campgrounds. You can call the **Alaska Public Lands Information Center** (Map p304; ☎907-456-0527; www.alaskacenters.gov; 101 Dunkel St, Fairbanks; ⏰8am-6pm) to receive a map and campground guide to such facilities. The Alaska Marine Highway ferries, the Alaska Railroad and many bus services and cruise ships are also equipped with wheelchair lifts and ramps to make their facilities easier to access. Chain motels and large hotels in cities and towns often have rooms set up for guests with disabilities, while some wilderness guiding companies are experienced in handling wheelchair-bound clients on rafting and kayaking expeditions.

Access Alaska (www.accessalaska.org) Includes statewide tourist information on accessible services and sites.

Challenge Alaska (☎907-344-7399; www.challengealaska.org) A nonprofit organization dedicated to providing recreation opportunities for those with disabilities.

Flying Wheels Travel (☎877-451-5006; www.flyingwheelstravel.com) A full-service travel agency specializing in disabled travel.

Society for Accessible Travel & Hospitality (☎212-447-7284; www.sath.org) Lobbies for better facilities and publishes *Open World* online magazine.

Download Lonely Planet's free Accessible Travel guides from https://shop.lonelyplanet.com/categories/accessible-travel.com.

PRACTICALITIES

Media

Newspapers Alaska has more than 30 daily, weekly and trade newspapers, with the *Anchorage Daily News* being the largest and the closest thing to a statewide newspaper.

TV and radio The largest cities have local TV stations, while radio stations are found all over Alaska. NTSC is the standard video system (not compatible with PAL or SECAM).

Laundry

Almost every town in Alaska has a laundromat, the place to go to clean your clothes (usually $3 per load) or take a shower ($3 to $5).

Weights & Measures

US distances are in feet, yards and miles. Dry weights are in ounces (oz), pounds (lb) and tons, and liquids are in pints, quarts and gallons. The US gallon is about 20% less than the imperial gallon.

Accommodations

B&Bs

For travelers who want nothing to do with a tent, B&Bs can be an acceptable compromise between sleeping on the ground and sleeping in high-priced lodges.

Some B&Bs are bargains, and most are cheaper than major hotels, but plan on spending $90 to $130 per night for a double room.

Many visitor centers have sections devoted to the B&Bs in their area, and courtesy booking phones. You can contact B&B reservation services to book rooms before your trip.

Camping & Caravan Parks

Camping is king in Alaska and with a tent you'll always have cheap accommodations in the Far North. There are state, federal and private campgrounds from Ketchikan to Fairbanks. Nightly fees range from free to $15 for rustic public campgrounds and from $30 to $45 to park your RV in a deluxe private campground with full hookup and heated restrooms with showers. Many towns that cater to tourists operate a municipal campground. For commercial campgrounds there's the **Alaska Campground Owner's Association** (☎866-339-9082; www.alaskacampgrounds.net).

Increasingly popular these days is 'glamping' – glamorous camping done in wall tents that are often raised on platforms or otherwise placed on hard floors. These 'glamp' tents are often as well appointed as a nice hotel room, although you have to go outside to use the bathroom. Expect to pay anywhere from $65 to $120 for glamping accommodations, which can also often be found at state hostels.

Hostels

Thanks to an influx of backpackers and foreign travelers each summer, the number of hostels offering budget accommodations in Alaska increases almost annually.

Alaska's hostels offer budget bunkrooms and kitchen facilities for nightly fees that range from $10 (which usually just covers camping) to $35. The Alaska Hostel Association (www.alaskahostelassociation.org) is a good source of information.

Hotels & Motels

Hotels and motels are often the most expensive lodgings you can book, and they tend to be full during summer. Without being part of a tour or having advance reservations, you may have trouble finding a bed available in some towns.

Tribal companies and the cruise-ship industry (for the land portions of their tours) are also responsible for a growing number of luxury hotels popping up across the state.

Resorts

Resorts – upscale hotels that have rooms, restaurants, pools and on-site activities – are not as common in Alaska as elsewhere in the USA, but are increasing in number due to the patronage of large companies, such as Princess Tours. A unique Alaskan take on the resort phenomenon are remote, sometimes plane-accessible-only lodges like **Ultima Thule Lodge** (☎907-854-4500; www.ultimathulelodge.com; 4-night 4-day package per person $7950). You pay top dollar at such destinations, but all meals are covered and the natural setting is something sliced out of Eden.

Customs Regulations

For a complete list of US customs regulations, visit the official portal for US Customs & Border Protection (www.cbp.gov). Click on 'Travel' to find out the basics.

Travelers are allowed to bring personal goods (including camping and hiking equipment) into the USA and Canada free of duty, along with food for two days and up to 100 cigars, 200 cigarettes and 1L of liquor or wine.

There are no forms to fill out if you are a foreign visitor bringing a vehicle into Alaska, whether it is a bicycle, motorcycle or car, nor are there forms for hunting rifles or fishing gear. Hunting rifles – handguns and automatic weapons are prohibited – must be registered in your own country, and you should bring proof of registration. There is no limit to the amount of money you can bring into Alaska, but anything over $10,000 must be registered with customs officials.

Keep in mind endangered-species laws prohibit transporting products made of bone, skin, fur, ivory, etc, through Canada without a permit. Importing and exporting such items into the USA is also prohibited. If you have any doubt about a gift or item you want to purchase, call the **US Fish & Wildlife Service** (USFWS; ☎907-271-6198; www.fws.gov) in Anchorage or check the website.

Hunters and anglers who want to ship home their salmon, halibut or rack of caribou can do so easily. Most outfitters and guides will make the arrangements for you, including properly packaging the game. In the case of fish, most towns have a storage company that will hold your salmon or halibut in a freezer until you are ready to leave Alaska. When frozen, seafood can usually make the trip to any city in the lower 48 without thawing.

SLEEPING PRICE RANGES

The following price ranges refer to a double room in high season, not including local taxes.

$ less than $100

$$ $100–250

$$$ more than $250

Discount Cards

Most museums, parks and major attractions will offer reduced rates to seniors and students, but most accommodations, restaurants and small tour companies will not.

➡ Best seniors card for US travelers to carry is issued by the American Association of Retired Persons (www.aarp.org).

- For students, an International Student Identity Card (www.isic.org) will often result in discounts for attractions in cities and major towns.
- There are no Hostelling International chapters in Alaska so the HI card is of little use in the Far North.

Electricity

Embassies & Consulates

International travelers needing to locate the US embassy in their home country should visit the website of the US Department of State (http://usembassy.state.gov), which has links to all of them.

There are no embassies in Alaska, but there is a handful of foreign consulates in Anchorage to assist overseas travelers with unusual problems.

Food

The Alaskan eating scene gets better and more sophisticated by the day, but it's also stridently casual, and while you may experience the occasional wait, reservations are rarely needed.

Restaurants You'll encounter Pacific Rim cuisines, fresh game, local produce and the occasional sticker shock, but pretension and white-table-cloth attitude are foreign concepts here.

Bars Many bars double as restaurants, serving big portions of protein to soak up the booze on those long Alaskan nights.

Roadhouses In the Alaskan hinterlands, roadhouses are lodging, food and drinking spots all rolled into one.

Cafes

The mainstay of Alaskan restaurants, particularly in small towns, is the main-street cafe.

It opens early in the morning serving eggs, bacon, pancakes and oatmeal, and continues with hamburgers, fries and grilled sandwiches for lunch.

There is almost always halibut and salmon on the dinner menu.

Most small towns also have a hamburger hut – a small shack or trailer with picnic tables outside – serving burgers, hot dogs, wraps or fried fish.

Vegetarians & Vegans

While places catering to vegans are rare throughout Alaska, you will find at least one health-food store in most midsize towns and cities, as well as a number of restaurants advertising 'vegetarian options.' Alternatively, search out Chinese and other Asian restaurants for the best selection of meatless dishes. Also keep in mind that Carrs, Safeway and other large supermarkets often have well-stocked salad bars, self-serve affairs at $8 per pound.

Health

There is a high level of hygiene found in Alaska, so most common infectious diseases will not be a significant concern for travelers. Superb medical care and rapid evacuation to major hospitals are both available.

Availability & Cost of Healthcare

The US has an excellent health system, and healthcare availability in Alaska is widespread in the main population centers. However, the cost of health care in Alaska, as in the rest of the USA, is extremely high.

COVID-19 Travel

In a state heavily reliant on tourism, Alaska avoided imposing overly stringent travel restrictions during the pandemic. You can check recent updates at: www.covid19.alaska.gov/travelers. Be aware that some communities in Alaska have their own separate COVID-19 rules.

COVID-19 restrictions are subject to change at short notice. It is wise to keep checking right up until your day of departure. It is also prudent to take out a good insurance policy that covers you for illness, hospitalization, trip cancellation and potential hotel bills if you are forced to quarantine.

Environmental Hazards

The most dangerous health threat outdoors is hypothermia. Dress in layers topped with a well-made, waterproof outer layer and always pack wool mittens and a hat.

Due to Alaska's long summer days, sunburn and windburn are a primary concern for anyone trekking or paddling. Use a good sunscreen on exposed skin, even on cloudy days, and a hat and sunglasses for additional protection.

Alaska is notorious for its biting insects, including mosquitoes, black flies, no-see-ums and deer flies. Wear long-sleeved shirts, pants that can be tucked into socks and a snug cap. Use a high-potency insect repellent and head nets in areas where there are excessive insects.

In recent years, paralytic shellfish poisoning (PSP) from eating mussels and clams has become a problem in Alaska. For a list of beaches safe to clam, check with the Alaska Division of Environmental Health (www.dec.alaska.gov/eh).

Altitude sickness is also a danger when climbing mountains such as Denali. See the national park website (www.nps.gov/dena/planyourvisit/part2medicalissues.htm) for more information.

Tap Water

Tap water in Alaska is safe to drink, but you should purify surface water taken from lakes and streams that is to be used for cooking and drinking. The simplest ways to purify water are to boil it thoroughly or use a high-quality filter.

Insurance

A travel insurance policy to cover theft, loss and medical problems is a smart investment.

Coverage depends on your insurance and type of ticket but should cover delays by striking employees or company actions, or a cancellation of a trip.

Such coverage may seem expensive but it's nowhere near the price of a trip to Alaska or the cost of a medical emergency in the USA.

Some policies offer lower and higher medical-expense options; the higher ones are chiefly for countries such as the USA, which have extremely high medical costs. There is a wide variety of medical and emergency repatriation policies and it's important to talk to your health-care provider for recommendations.

Internet Access

It's easy to surf the net, make online reservations or retrieve email in Alaska. Most towns, even the smallest ones, have free internet access at libraries.

If you have a laptop or phone, free wi-fi is common in Alaska at bookstores, hotels, coffee shops, airport terminals and bars, although reception may be patchier than it is in the lower 48.

If you're not from the US, remember you will need an AC adapter and a plug adapter for US sockets.

Legal Matters

The use of drugs (except marijuana) is against the law and results in severe penalties, especially for cocaine, which is heavily abused in Alaska.

The minimum drinking age in Alaska is 21 and a government-issued photo ID (passport or driver's license) will be needed if a bartender questions your age. Alcohol abuse is also a problem in Alaska, and it's a serious offense if you are caught driving under the influence of alcohol (DUI).

The blood alcohol limit in Alaska is 0.08% and the penalty for DUI is a three-month driver's license revocation. You may also be given a fine and jail time.

If you are stopped by the police for any reason while driving, remember there is no system of paying on-the-spot fines and bribery is not something that works in Alaska.

For traffic violations, the officer will explain your options to you and many violations can often be handled through the mail with a credit card.

EATING PRICE RANGES

The following price ranges refer to a main course at dinner.

$ less than $15

$$ $15–25

$$$ more than $25

LGBTIQ+ Travelers

The LGBT community in Alaska is far smaller and much less open than in major US cities, and Alaskans in general are not as tolerant of diversity.

In 1998 Alaska passed a constitutional amendment banning same-sex marriages. However, attitudes are slowly changing. A 2014 poll found 47% of Alaskan voters in favor of same-sex marriage.

In Anchorage, the only city in Alaska of any real size, there is **Identity Inc** (☎907-929-4528; www.identityinc.org), which has a gay and lesbian helpline, a handful of openly gay clubs and bars, and a weeklong PrideFest (http://alaskapride.org) in mid-June.

The **Southeast Alaska Gay & Lesbian Alliance** (www.seagla.org) is based in Juneau and offers links and travel lists geared to gay visitors. The list is short, however, because most towns do not have an openly active gay community.

In rural Alaska, same-sex couples should exercise discretion.

Maps

Unlike many places in the world, Alaska has no shortage of accurate maps. There are detailed US Geological Survey (USGS) topographical maps for almost every corner of the state, even though most of it is still wilderness, while every visitor center has free city and road maps that are more than adequate to get from one town to the next. For free downloadable maps and driving directions there's Google Maps (http://maps.google.com).

For trekking in the backcountry and in wilderness areas, the USGS topographical maps are worth the small cost. The maps come in a variety of scales, but hikers prefer the smallest scale of 1:63,360, with each inch equal to a mile. Canoeists and other river runners can get away with the 1:250,000 map.

You can order maps in advance directly from **USGS** (☎888-275-8747; www.usgs.gov) or you can view and order custom topo maps from cartography websites such as **Mytopo** (☎877-587-9004; www.mytopo.com). GPS units and accompanying mapping software that includes Alaska are available from Garmin (www.garmin.com).

Money

Prices quoted are in US dollars unless otherwise stated. Keep in mind that the Canadian system is also dollars and cents but is a separate currency.

ATMs

In Alaska ATMs are everywhere: at banks, gas stations, supermarkets, airports and even some visitor centers.

At most ATMs you can use a credit card (Visa, MasterCard, etc), a debit card or an ATM card that is linked to the Plus or Cirrus ATM networks.

There is generally a fee ($1 to $3) for withdrawing cash from an ATM, but the exchange rate on transactions is usually as good if not better than what you'll get anywhere else.

Cash

Hard cash still works. It may not be the safest way to carry funds, but nobody will hassle you when you purchase something with US dollars. Most businesses along the Alcan in Canada will also take US dollars.

US coins come in denominations of 1¢ (penny), 5¢ (nickel), 10¢ (dime), 25¢ (quarter) and the seldom seen 50¢ (half-dollar).

Quarters are the most commonly used coins in vending machines and parking meters, so it's handy to have a stash of them.

Notes, commonly called bills, come in $1, $2, $5, $10, $20, $50 and $100 denominations.

Credit Cards

Like in the rest of the USA, Alaskan merchants are ready and willing to accept just about all major credit cards.

Visa and MasterCard are the most widely accepted cards, but American Express and Discovery are also widely used.

Places that accept Visa and MasterCard are also likely to accept debit cards. If you are an overseas visitor, check with your bank at home to confirm that your debit card will be accepted in the USA.

Moneychangers

Banks are the best place to exchange foreign currencies as the exchange counters at the airports typically have poorer rates.

Wells Fargo (☎800-956-4442; www.wellsfargo.com), the nation's sixth-largest bank, is the dominant player in Alaska with more than 400 branches, eight in Anchorage alone. Wells Fargo can meet the needs of most visitors, including changing currency and offering 24-hour ATMs.

Tipping

Tipping in Alaska, like in the rest of the USA, is expected.

Bars If you order food at the table and it's brought to you, tip 15%, the same as at restaurants; 10% if you're having a drink or appetizer at the bar.

Restaurants From 15% for cafes/chain eateries to 20% for upscale restaurants.

Taxis 15%.

Tour guides 10% for bus tour guides, 15% to 20% for wilderness guides on glacier treks or white-water-rafting trips.

Opening Hours

Banks 9am to 4pm/5pm Monday to Friday; 9am to 1pm Saturday (main branches)

Bars and clubs City bars until 2am or later, especially on weekends; clubs to 2am or beyond

Post offices 9am to 5pm Monday to Friday; noon to 3pm Saturday (main branches open longer)

Restaurants and cafes Breakfast at cafes/coffee shops from 7am or earlier; some restaurants open only for lunch (noon to 3pm) or dinner (4 to 10pm, later in cities); Asian restaurants often have split hours: 11am to 2pm and from 4pm.

Shops 10am to 8pm/6pm (larger/smaller stores) Monday to Friday; 9am to 5pm Saturday; 10am to 5pm Sunday (larger stores)

Post

The **US Postal Service** (www.usps.com) is one of the world's busiest and most reliable, but even it needs another day or two to get

BEARS IN ALASKA

Too often travelers decide to skip a wilderness trip because they hear too many bear stories. Your own equipment and outdoor experience should determine whether you take a trek into the woods, not the possibility of meeting a bear on the trail. The **Alaska Department of Fish & Game** (licensing 907-465-2376, main office 907-465-4100; www.adfg.alaska.gov) emphasizes that the probability of being injured by a bear is one-fiftieth the chance of being injured in a car accident on any Alaskan highway.

The best way to avoid bears is to follow a few commonsense rules. Bears charge only when they feel trapped, when a hiker comes between a sow and her cubs, or when enticed by food. Sing or clap when traveling through thick bush, and don't camp near bear food sources or in the middle of an obvious bear path. Stay away from thick berry patches, streams choked with salmon or beaches littered with bear droppings.

Set up the spot where you will cook and eat at least 30yd to 50yd away from your tent. In coastal areas, many backpackers eat in the tidal zone, knowing that when the high tide comes in, all evidence of food will be washed away.

At night try to place your food sacks 10ft or more off the ground by hanging them in a tree. Or consider investing in a lightweight bear-resistant container. A bear usually finds a food bag using its great sense of smell. Avoid odorous foods, such as bacon or sardines, in areas with high concentrations of bears, and don't take food, cosmetics or deodorant into the tent at night.

letters and postcards to and from Alaska. With an abundance of internet cafes and the availability of internet at libraries, hostels and hotels, think email for quick notes to friends and family. For packages, especially heavy ones, it's faster to use private carriers in Alaska such as **United Parcel Service** (800-742-5877; www.ups.com) or **Federal Express** (www.fedex.com).

Public Holidays

Public holidays for Alaskan residents may involve state and federal offices being closed, bus services curtailed, and store hours reduced.

New Year's Day January 1

Martin Luther King Day Third Monday in January

Presidents' Day Third Monday in February

Seward's Day Last Monday in March

Easter Sunday Late March or early April

Memorial Day Last Monday in May

Independence Day (Fourth of July) July 4

Labor Day First Monday in September

Columbus Day Second Monday in October

Alaska Day October 18

Veterans' Day November 11

Thanksgiving Day Fourth Thursday in November

Christmas Day December 25

Responsible Travel

You can avoid carbon-heavy internal flights in Alaska if you stick to the main train, road and ferry network.

Remote places that can be reached without a private car or plane include Prudhoe Bay, Wrangell–St Elias National Park, Dutch Harbor, Tok and Chicken.

For those with more time on their hands, it's possible to get a public ferry from Bellingham, WA, in the Lower 48 up to Ketchikan, Juneau and beyond.

Camping is a good low-carbon accommodation option and remains a strong part of the culture in Alaska. There's also an abundance of backcountry cabins for rent.

Safe Travel

Alaska is a relatively safe place. The main dangers lurk in its extensive wilderness areas. These can be largely avoided by taking a few basic precautions.

- Alaska has an abundance of wild animals, even in urban areas. Carry pepper spray and avoid direct animal encounters.
- Beware of glacier crevasses and calving icebergs.
- In these northern climes fickle weather can change on a dime. Come prepared for the worst, even in high summer.
- Roads are rough and there is a lack of services, so if driving long distances ensure your vehicle is kept stocked with emergency supplies.

Telephone

Cell Phones

Cell (mobile) phones work in Alaska and Alaskans love them as much as anywhere else in the USA. When calling home or locally in cities and towns, reception is excellent but overall, in a state this large, cell-phone coverage can be unpredictable and sporadic at times. The culprits in most cases are mountains.

Most travelers still find their cell phones to be very useful. Before you head north, however, check your cell-phone provider's roaming agreements and blackout areas. It may be possible for international travelers to purchase a prepaid SIM card that can be used in their phones for local calls and voicemail. You can also purchase inexpensive cell phones from AT&T along with prepaid cards for calls.

Better still, with a wi-fi connection you can call using Skype or WhatsApp for free.

Phone Codes

Telephone area codes are simple in Alaska: the entire state shares 907, except Hyder, which uses 250. Phone numbers that begin with 800, 877 and 866 are toll-free numbers and there is no charge for using one to call a hotel or tour operator. If you're calling from abroad, the country code for the USA is 1.

Time

With the exception of several Aleutian Island communities and Hyder, a small community on the Alaska–British Columbia border, the entire state shares the same time zone, Alaska Time, which is one hour earlier than Pacific Standard Time – the zone in which Seattle, WA, falls. When it is noon in Anchorage, it is 4pm in New York, 9pm in London and 7am the following day in Melbourne, Australia. Although there is a movement to abolish it, Alaska still has Daylight Saving Time when, like most of the country, the state sets clocks back one hour in November and forward one hour in March.

Toilets

Toilets in Alaska, as in the rest of the US, are modern and generally clean – when you can find them. Many campgrounds and wilderness areas have non-flushable latrines, which may (or may not) have toilet paper and hand disinfectant available. As a precaution, it's a good idea to carry both when traveling outside cities.

Tourist Information

The first place to contact when planning your adventure is the **Alaska Travel Industry Association** (☎907-929-2842; www.alaskatia.org), the state's tourism marketing arm. From the ATIA you can request a copy of the *Alaska Vacation Planner*, an annually updated magazine, as well as a state highway map and schedules for the Alaska Marine Highway ferry service.

Almost every city, town and village has a tourist contact center, whether it is a visitor center, a chamber of commerce or a hut near the ferry dock. These places are good sources of free maps, information on local accommodations and directions to the nearest campground or hiking trail. The **National Recreation Reservation System** (☎877-444-6777; www.recreation.gov) is the national camping booking system.

Most trips to Alaska pass through one of the state's three largest cities. All have large visitors bureaus that will send out city guides in advance.

For other tourist information:

Admiralty Island National Monument (☎907-586-8800; www.fs.fed.us/visit/destination/admiralty-island-national-monument)

Mountaineering Club of Alaska (http://mtnclubak.org)

National Park Service (☎907-983-2921; www.nps.gov/state/ak)

Tourism Yukon (☎800-661-0494; www.travelyukon.com)

USFS Glacier Ranger District (☎907-783-3242; www.fs.fed.us/r10/chugach)

Visas

Since September 11, the US has continually fine-tuned its national security guidelines and entry requirements. Double-check current visa and passport regulations before arriving in the USA, and apply for visas early to avoid delays. Overseas travelers may need one visa, possibly two. For citizens of many countries a US visa is required, while if you're taking the Alcan or the Alaska Marine Highway ferry from Prince Rupert in British Columbia, you may also need a Canadian visa. The Alcan begins in Canada, requiring travelers to pass from the USA into Canada and back into the USA again.

Canadians entering the USA must have proof of Canadian citizenship, such as a passport; visitors from countries in the Visa Waiver Program may not need a visa. Visitors from all other countries need to have a US visa and a valid passport. Check the website of the **US State Department** (www.travel.state.gov) for full details.

Note that overseas travelers should be aware of the process to re-enter the USA. Sometimes visitors get stuck in Canada due to their single-entry visa into the USA, used up when passing through the lower 48. Canadian immigration officers often caution people whom they feel might have difficulty returning to the USA. More information about visa and other requirements for entering Canada is available on the website of the **Canada**

Border Services Agency (www.cbsa-asfc.gc.ca).

Visa Application

Apart from Canadians and those entering under the Visa Waiver Program, foreign visitors need to obtain a visa from a US consulate or embassy. Most applicants must now schedule a personal interview, to which you need to bring all your documentation and proof of fee payment. Wait times for interviews vary, but afterward, barring problems, visa issuance takes from a few days to a few weeks. If concerned about a delay, check the websites of the **US State Department** (www.travel.state.gov), which provides a list of wait times calculated by country.

Your passport must be valid for at least six months longer than your intended stay in the USA. You'll need a recent photo (2in by 2in) and you must pay a $160 processing fee, plus in a few cases an additional visa-issuance fee (check the State Department website for details). In addition to the main nonimmigration visa application form (DS-156), all men aged 16 to 45 must complete an additional form (DS-157) that details their travel plans.

Visa applicants are required to show documentation of financial stability, a round-trip or onward ticket and 'binding obligations' that will ensure their return home, such as family ties, a home or a job.

Visa Waiver Program

The Visa Waiver Program (VWP) lets citizens of some countries enter the USA for tourism purposes for up to 90 days without having a US visa. Currently there are 40 participating countries in the VWP, including Austria, Australia, Belgium, Denmark, Finland, France, Germany, Iceland, Ireland, Italy, Japan, the Netherlands, New Zealand, Norway, Spain, Sweden, Switzerland and the UK.

Under the program you must have a round-trip or onward ticket that is nonrefundable in the USA, a machine-readable passport (with two lines of letters, numbers and '<<<' along the bottom of the passport information page) and be able to show evidence of financial solvency.

Citizens of VWP countries must register online prior to their trip with the **Electronic System for Travel Authorization** (ESTA; https://esta.cbp.dhs.gov/esta), an automated system used to determine the eligibility of visitors traveling to the US. There is a $14 fee. Beware, there are several bogus ESTA websites.

The VWP also applies to passengers transiting the US. Once obtained the visa waiver is valid for two years. You can check your current status online.

Volunteering

For many travelers the only way to enjoy Alaska is to volunteer. You won't get paid, but you're often given room, board and work in a spectacular setting. Most volunteer roles are with federal or state agencies and range from trail crew workers and campground hosts to volunteering at the **Arctic Interagency Visitor Center** (907-678-5209; CentralYukon@blm.gov; 11am-10pm Jun-Aug) in Coldfoot and collecting botanical inventories.

The following organizations offer a range of volunteering opportunities.

Alaska Division of Parks & Outdoor Recreation (907-269-8400; http://dnr.alaska.gov/parks)

Bureau of Land Management (BLM; 907-271-5960; www.blm.gov)

Chugach National Forest (907-743-9500; www.fs.usda.gov/chugach)

Student Conservation Association (907-771-8493; www.thesca.org)

Tongass National Forest (907-586-8800; www.fs.usda.gov/tongass)

Women Travelers

While most violent crime rates are lower here than elsewhere in the USA, women should be careful at night in unfamiliar neighborhoods in cities like Anchorage and Fairbanks or when hitching alone. Use common sense; don't be afraid to say no to lifts. If camping alone, have pepper spray and know how to use it.

Alaska Women's Network (www.alaskawomensnetwork.org) Has listings of women-owned B&Bs and travel agencies across the state.

Women's Flyfishing (www.womensflyfishing.net) Alaska's premier outfitter for women-only fly-fishing trips and a great web resource for women arriving in Alaska with a fly rod.

Transportation

GETTING THERE & AWAY

Whether you're from the US or overseas, traveling to Alaska is like traveling to a foreign country. By sea it takes almost a week on the Alaska Marine Highway ferry to reach Whittier in Prince William Sound from the lower 48. By land a motorist in the Midwest needs 10 days to drive straight to Fairbanks.

If you're coming from the US mainland, the quickest and least expensive way to reach Alaska is to fly nonstop from a number of cities. If you're coming from Asia or Europe, it's almost impossible to fly directly to Alaska as few international airlines maintain a direct service to Anchorage, except for seasonal flights from Frankfurt on **Condor Airlines** (☎800-524-6975; www.condor.com). Most international travelers come through the gateway cities of Seattle, Portland, Minneapolis or Denver.

Entering the Country/Region

Since the September 11 terrorist attacks, air travel in the USA has permanently changed and you can now expect vigilant baggage-screening procedures and personal searches. In short, you're going to have to take your shoes off. Non-US citizens should be prepared for an exhaustive questioning process at Immigration.

Crossing the border into Alaska from Canada used to be a relaxed process – US citizens often passed across with just a driver's license. Now this process has also become more complicated, and all travelers should have a passport and expect more substantial questioning and possible vehicle searches.

Passport

If you are traveling to Alaska from overseas, you need a passport. If you are a US resident passing through Canada, you will need a passport to re-enter the USA. Make sure your passport does not expire during the trip, and if you are entering the USA through the Visa Waiver Program (VWP) you *must* have a machine-readable passport. If you are traveling with children, it's best to bring a photocopy of their birth certificates. If one parent is traveling with children alone, they will likely be asked for a letter of agreement from the other parent.

Air

Airports & Airlines

The vast majority of visitors to Alaska, and almost all international services, fly into **Ted Stevens Anchorage International Airport** (ANC;

CLIMATE CHANGE & TRAVEL

Every form of transport that relies on carbon-based fuel generates CO_2, the main cause of human-induced climate change. Modern travel is dependent on airplanes, which might use less fuel per kilometer per person than most cars but travel much greater distances. The altitude at which aircraft emit gases (including CO_2) and particles also contributes to their climate change impact. Many websites offer 'carbon calculators' that allow people to estimate the carbon emissions generated by their journey and, for those who wish to do so, to offset the impact of the greenhouse gases emitted with contributions to portfolios of climate-friendly initiatives throughout the world. Lonely Planet offsets the carbon footprint of all staff and author travel.

DEPARTURE TAX

Departure tax is included in the price of a ticket.

Map p158; www.dot.state.ak.us/anc; ; 7). International flights arrive at the north terminal; domestic flights arrive at the south terminal and a complimentary shuttle service runs between the two every 15 minutes. You'll find bus services, taxis and car-rental companies at both terminals. The airport has the usual services, including baggage storage, ATMs, currency exchange, free wi-fi, and courtesy phones to various Anchorage hotels.

Alaska's only other (very limited) international airport is **Fairbanks International Airport** (Map p300; 907-474-2500; www.dot.state.ak.us/faiiap), with seasonal flights to Frankfurt in Germany.

Airlines serving Alaska include:

Alaska Airlines (800-426-0333; www.alaskaair.com)

American Airlines (800-443-7300; www.aa.com)

Condor Airlines (800-524-6975; www.condor.com)

Delta Air Lines (800-221-1212; www.delta.com)

JetBlue (800-538-2583; www.jetblue.com)

Sun Country Airlines (800-359-6786; www.suncountry.com)

United Airlines (800-863-8331; www.united.com)

Tickets

Due to its lack of direct and international flights, Anchorage, and thus Alaska, is not the most competitive place for airfares. Begin any online ticket search by first checking travel websites and then compare the prices against the websites of airlines that service Alaska, particularly Alaska Airlines, as it often has internet specials offered nowhere else. For a good overview of online ticket agencies and lists of travel agents worldwide, visit **Airinfo** (www.airinfo.aero).

Seattle serves as the major hub for flights into Alaska. Alaska Airlines owns the lion's share of the market, with 20 flights per day to Anchorage as well as direct flights to Ketchikan, Juneau and Fairbanks.

You can also book a nonstop flight to Anchorage from a number of other US cities. Delta flies in from Minneapolis, Atlanta and Salt Lake City. American Airlines arrives in Anchorage from Dallas, LA and Phoenix; JetBlue from Portland;. Alaska Airlines, naturally, flies nonstop from numerous cities including Los Angeles, Denver, Chicago and Portland.

Condor has direct seasonal flights to Frankfurt in Germany from both Anchorage and Fairbanks.

Land

What began as the Alaska-Canada Military Hwy is today the Alcan (the Alaska Hwy). This amazing 1390-mile road starts at Dawson Creek in British Columbia, ends at Delta Junction and in between winds through the vast wilderness of northwest Canada and Alaska. For those with the time, the Alcan is a unique journey north. There are basically two options on the Alcan: car or bus.

Bus

A combination of buses will take you from Seattle via the Alcan to Alaska, but service is limited and the ride is a very long. From Seattle, **Greyhound** (800-661-8747; www.greyhound.com) goes to Whitehorse, a 60-hour-plus ride. A one-way ticket is around $200 if you purchase in advance online. From Whitehorse, **Alaska/Yukon Trails** (Map p300; 907-479-2277; www.alaskashuttle.com) leaves Sunday, Tuesday and Friday for Fairbanks for $385. This journey, via Dawson City, takes two days.

Car & Motorcycle

Without a doubt, driving your own car to Alaska allows you the most freedom. You can leave when you want, stop where you feel like it and plan your itinerary as you go along. It's not cheap driving to Alaska, and that's not even considering the wear and tear from the thousands of miles you'll put on your vehicle.

The Alcan is now entirely paved and, although sections of jarring potholes, frost heaves (the rippling effect of the pavement caused by freezing and thawing) and loose gravel still exist, the infamous rough conditions of a few decades ago no longer prevail. Food, gas and lodging can be found almost every 20 to 50 miles along the highway, with 100 miles being the longest stretch between fuel stops.

On the Canadian side, you'll find kilometer posts (as opposed to the mileposts found in Alaska), which are placed every 5km after the zero point in Dawson Creek. Most Alcan veterans say 300 miles a day is a good pace – one that will allow for plenty of stops to see the scenery or wildlife.

Along the way, **Tourism Yukon** (800-661-0494; www.travelyukon.com) operates a number of visitor centers stocked with brochures and maps.

Hitching

Hitchhiking is probably more common in Alaska than it is in the rest of the USA, and even more so on rural dirt roads such as the McCarthy Rd and the Denali Hwy than it is on the major paved routes.

Hitching is never entirely safe, and we don't recommend it. Travellers who hitch should understand that they are taking a small but potentially serious risk.

That said, if you're properly prepared and have sufficient time, thumbing your way along the Alcan can be an easy way to see the country while meeting local people and saving money.

The Alcan seems to inspire the pioneer spirit in travelers who drive along it. Drivers are good about picking up hitchhikers, much better than those across the lower 48; the only problem is that there aren't really enough of them.

Any part of the Alcan can be slow, but some sections are notoriously bad. The worst is probably Haines Junction, the crossroads in the Yukon where southbound hitch-hikers often get stranded trying to thumb a ride to Haines in Southeast Alaska.

If you'd rather not hitchhike the entire Alcan, take the Alaska Marine Highway ferry from Bellingham, WA, to Haines, stick your thumb out and start hitchhiking from there; you'll cut the journey in half but still travel along the highway's most spectacular parts.

Sea

As an alternative to the Alcan, you can travel the Southeast's Inside Passage from the lower 48. The comprehensive **Alaska Marine Highway** (AMHS; ☎800-642-0066; www.dot.state.ak.us/amhs) runs regular car ferries up from Bellingham, WA, linking all of the main cities in the Panhandle as well as communities in Prince William Sound and the Kenai Peninsula.

Alternatively there are cruise ships. Indeed, the bulk of Alaska's tourists (around one million per year) arrive on pre-arranged cruise-ship packages, which generally start out from Vancouver, Seattle or San Francisco.

Tours

Package tours can often be the most affordable way to see a large chunk of Alaska, if your needs include the better hotels in each town and a full breakfast every morning. But they move quickly, leaving little time for an all-day hike or other activities.

Companies offering Alaska packages:

Alaska Collection (☎888-602-3323; www.alaskacollection.com)

Alaska Wildland Adventures (☎800-334-8730; www.alaskawildland.com; tours $3000-8100)

Gray Line (Map p166; ☎888-425-1737; www.graylineofalaska.com; Hilton Anchorage, 500 W 3rd Ave, Anchorage)

Green Tortoise Alternative Travel (☎800-867-8647, 415-956-7500; www.greentortoise.com; tours $789-1089)

GETTING AROUND

Air

Scheduled flights are cheaper than charter flights.

Airlines in Alaska

Alaska Airlines (☎800-426-0333; www.alaskaair.com) serves a surprisingly comprehensive list of destinations. The rest is picked up by several smaller airlines:

Alaska Seaplanes (☎907-789-3331; www.flyalaskaseaplanes.com) Juneau, Haines and Northern Panhandle

Ravn Alaska (☎907-266-8394, 800-866-8394; www.ravnalaska.com) Fairbanks, Nome, Barrow, Deadhorse, Valdez and Kodiak

Taquan Air (☎800-770-8800; www.taquanair.com) Ketchikan, Prince of Wales Island and Southern Panhandle

Bush Planes

With 75% of the state inaccessible by road, small, single-engine planes known as 'bush planes' are the backbone of intrastate transport. They carry residents and supplies to desolate areas of the Bush, take anglers to some of the best fishing spots in the country and drop off backpackers in the middle of untouched wilderness.

In the larger cities of Anchorage, Fairbanks, Juneau and Ketchikan, it pays to compare prices before chartering a plane. In most small towns and villages you'll be lucky if there's a choice.

Bush aircraft include floatplanes, which land and take off on water, and beachlanders with oversized tires that can use rough gravel shorelines as air strips. Fares vary with the type of plane, its size, the number of passengers and the amount of flying time. On average, chartering a Cessna 185 that can carry three passengers and a limited amount of gear will cost up to $500 for an hour of flying time. A Cessna 206, a slightly larger plane that will hold four passengers, costs up to $550, while a Beaver, capable of hauling five passengers with gear, costs in the vicinity of $600 an hour. When chartering a plane to drop you off in the wilderness, you must pay for both the air time to your drop-off point and for the return to the departure point.

Double-check all pickup times and places when flying to a wilderness area. Bush pilots fly over the pickup point and if you're not there, they usually return to base, call the authorities and still charge you for the flight.

Always schedule extra days around a charter flight. It's not uncommon to be 'socked in' by weather for a day or two until a plane can fly in. Don't panic: they know you're there.

Bicycle

For those who want to bike it, Alaska offers a variety of cycling adventures on paved roads under the Arctic sun that allows you to peddle until midnight if you want. A bicycle can be carried on Alaska Marine Highway ferries for an additional fee and is a great way to explore small towns without renting a car.

Most road cyclists avoid gravel, but cycling the Alcan (an increasingly popular trip) does involve riding over some gravel breaks in the paved asphalt. Mountain bikers, on the other hand, are in heaven on gravel roads such as the Denali Hwy in the Interior.

If you arrive in Alaska without a bicycle, some towns have rentals; expect to pay $30 to $50 a day. You can take your bicycle on the airlines for an excess luggage fee. Alaska Airlines charges $75.

Anchorage's **Arctic Bicycle Club** (907-566-0177; www.arcticbicycleclub.org) is Alaska's largest bicycle club and sponsors a wide variety of road-bike and mountain-bike tours during the summer. Its website includes a list of Alaska cycle shops.

Other bicycle groups:

Bike Anchorage (907-891-8906; www.bikeanchorage.org) The main bicycle advocacy organization in Anchorage.

Fairbanks Cycle Club (www.fairbankscycleclub.org) Has info on cycling in the Fairbanks region.

Juneau Rides (https://juneaurides.org) Advocates for cycling in Juneau; the website has plenty of local cycling information.

Boat

The **Alaska Marine Highway ferry** (AMHS; 800-642-0066; www.dot.state.ak.us/amhs) calls at 35 ports across 3500 miles of coastline from Bellingham, WA, to Dutch Harbor in the Aleutians. There are nine regular vessels serving four main regions: the southeast (Ketchikan up to Skagway), the Cross-Gulf Route (Juneau to Whittier), Southcentral Alaska (Prince William Sound, the Kenai Peninsula and Kodiak) and the Southwest (the Alaska Peninsula and the Aleutian Islands).

In some cities – namely Juneau, Sitka and Haines – the ferry terminal is located several miles outside town, necessitating a bus/taxi transfer.

The Southeast is also served by the **Inter-Island Ferry Authority** (866-308-4848; www.interislandferry.com), which connects Ketchikan with Prince of Wales Island; and **Haines-Skagway Fast Ferry** (Map p140; 888-766-2103; www.hainesskagwayfastferry.com; one way adult/child $36/18), linking Skagway and Haines.

Bus

While there is no statewide bus network, and no Greyhound, various shuttle buses (usually 12-seater vans) cover most of Alaska's main highways in the summer, though they don't always run daily. Check online for schedules and prices and book in advance.

Car & Motorcycle

Not a lot of roads reach a lot of Alaska but what asphalt there is leads to some seriously spectacular scenery. That's the best reason to tour the state in a car or motorcycle, whether you arrive with your own or rent one. With personal wheels you can stop and go at will and sneak away from the RVers and tour buses.

Automobile Associations

AAA (800-332-6119; www.aaa.com), the most widespread automobile association in the USA, has one office in Alaska, **Anchorage Service Center** (907-344-4310; 3565 Arctic Blvd, Anchorage), which offers the usual, including maps, discounts and emergency road service.

Fuel & Spare Parts

Gas is widely available on all the main highways and tourist routes in Alaska. In Anchorage and Fairbanks the cost of gas will only be 10¢ to 15¢ per gallon higher than in the rest of the country. Along the Alcan, in Bush communities such as Nome, and at lone gas stations on remote roads, prices will be shockingly high.

Along heavily traveled roads, most towns will have a car mechanic, though you might have to wait a day for a part to come up from Anchorage. In some small towns, you might be out of luck. For anybody driving to and around Alaska, a full-size spare tire and replacement belts are a must.

Insurance

Liability insurance – which covers damage you may cause to another vehicle in the event of an accident – is required when driving in Alaska but not always offered by rental agencies because most Americans are already covered by their regular car insurance. This is particularly true with many of the discount rental places. Major car agencies offer Collision Damage Waiver (CDW) to cover damage to the rental car in case of an accident. This can up the rental fee by $15 a day or more and many have deductibles as high as $1000. It's better, and far cheaper, to arrive with rental-car insurance obtained through your insurance company, as a member of AAA, or as a perk of many credit cards, including American Express.

Rental & Purchase

For two or more people, car rental is an affordable way to travel, far less expensive than taking a bus or a train. At most rental agencies, you'll need a valid driver's license, a major credit card and you'll also need to be at least 21 years old (sometimes 25). It is almost always cheaper to rent in town rather than at the airport because of extra taxes levied on airport rentals.

Read any rental contract carefully, especially details on driving on gravel or dirt roads. Many agencies, particularly those in the Fairbanks area, will not allow their compacts on dirt roads. If you violate the contract and have an accident, insurance will not cover repairs. Also be conscious of the per-mile rate of a rental. Add up the mileage you aim to cover and then choose between the 100 free miles per day or the more expensive unlimited mileage plan.

Vehicles from affordable car-rental places are always heavily booked during the summer. Try to reserve at least a month in advance.

MOTORHOMES

RVers flock to the land of the midnight sun in astounding numbers. This is the reason why more than a dozen companies, almost all of them based in Anchorage, will rent you a motorhome. Renting a recreational vehicle is so popular you have to reserve them four to five months in advance.

ABC Motorhomes (☎800-421-7456; www.abcmotorhome.com)

Clippership Motorhome Rentals (☎800-421-3456; www.clippershiprv.com)

Great Alaskan Holidays (☎888-225-2752, 907-248-7777; www.greatalaskanholidays.com; rental per day from $105)

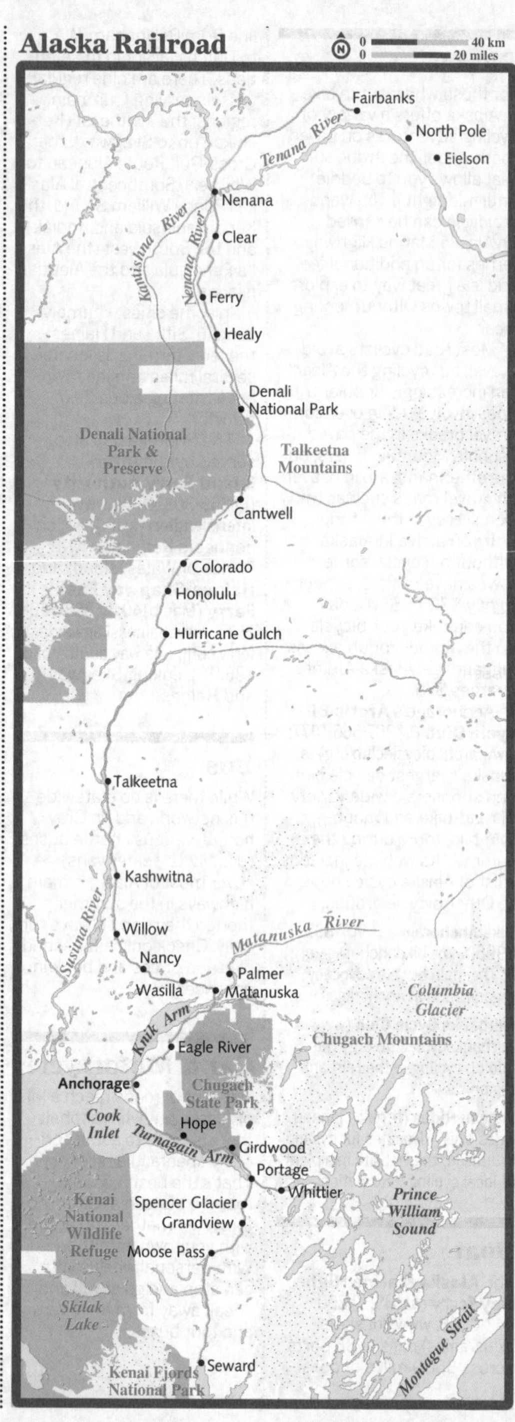

Road Conditions & Hazards

For road conditions, closures and other travel advisories for the Alaska highway system, even while you're driving, contact the state's **Alaska511** (☎511, outside Alaska 866-282-7577; http://511.alaska.gov).

Local Transportation

In cities and most mid-size towns there will be taxi service. On occasion, the Alaska Marine Highway ferry port is located outside town. Sometimes a shuttle service is available, otherwise a combination of taxi and local bus must be used. There are also limited local bus services in some cities, with the most extensive systems in Anchorage, Fairbanks, Juneau and Ketchikan.

Train

Alaska Railroad

It took eight years to build it, but today the **Alaska Railroad** (☎800-544-0552; www.akrr.com) stretches 470 miles from Seward to Fairbanks through spectacular scenery. You'll save more money traveling by bus down the George Parks Hwy, but few travelers regret booking the Alaska Railroad and viewing the pristine wilderness from its comfortable cars.

SERVICES

The Alaska Railroad operates a year-round service between Fairbanks and Anchorage, as well as summer services (from late May to mid-September) from Anchorage to Whittier and from Anchorage to Seward.

The most popular run is the 336-mile trip from Anchorage to Fairbanks, stopping at Denali National Park. Northbound, at Mile 279, the train passes within 46 miles of Denali, a stunning sight from the viewing domes on a clear day. It then slows down to cross the 918ft bridge over Hurricane Gulch.

The ride between Anchorage and Seward may be one of the most spectacular train trips in the world. From Anchorage, the 114-mile trip begins by skirting the 60-mile-long Turnagain Arm on Cook Inlet and then swings south, climbs over mountain passes, spans deep river gorges and comes within half a mile of three glaciers.

The Anchorage–Whittier service, which includes a stop in Girdwood and passes through two long tunnels, turns Whittier into a fun day trip. So does riding Alaska Railroad's *Hurricane Turn*, one of America's last flagstop trains, which departs from Talkeetna.

RESERVATIONS

You can reserve a seat and purchase tickets online through the website of **Alaska Railroad** (☎800-544-0552; www.akrr.com); this is highly recommended for the Anchorage–Denali service in July and early August.

White Pass & Yukon Route

The White Pass & Yukon Railroad was built during the height of the Klondike Gold Rush, and it's still possible to travel it from Skagway to Carcross in the Yukon and complete the journey to Whitehorse by bus. One-way train-bus combo tickets cost $129/64.50 per adult/child. The trip is classed as a 'tour,' with a guide giving interesting commentary.

Reservations are highly recommended at any time during the summer. Contact **White Pass & Yukon Route** (☎800-343-7373; www.whitepassrailroad.com) for information.

Glossary

Alcan or **Alaska Hwy** – the main overland route into Alaska. Although the highway is almost entirely paved now, completing a journey along this legendary road is still a special accomplishment. The Alcan begins at the Mile 0 milepost in Dawson Creek (northeastern British Columbia, Canada), heads northwest through Whitehorse, the capital of the Yukon Territory (Canada), and officially ends at Delta Junction (Mile 1390), 101 miles southeast of Fairbanks.

AMS – acute mountain sickness; occurs at high altitudes and can be fatal

ANWR – Arctic National Wildlife Refuge; the 1.5-million-acre wilderness area that oil-company officials and Alaskans have been pushing hard to open up for oil and gas drilling.

ATV – all-terrain vehicle

aurora borealis or **northern lights** – the mystical snakes of light that weave across the sky from the northern horizon. It's a spectacular show on clear nights and can occur at almost any time of the year. The lights are the result of gas particles colliding with solar electrons and are best viewed from the Interior, away from city lights, between late summer and winter.

bidarka – a skin-covered sea kayak used by the Aleuts

BLM – Bureau of Land Management; the federal agency that maintains much of the wilderness around and north of Fairbanks, including cabins and campgrounds

blue cloud – what Southeasterners call a break in the clouds.

breakup – when the ice on rivers suddenly begins to melt, breaks up and flows downstream; many residents also use this term to describe spring in Alaska, when the rain begins, the snow melts and everything turns to mud and slush.

bunny boots – large, oversized and usually white plastic boots used extensively in subzero weather to prevent the feet from freezing.

Bush, the – any area in the state that is not connected by road to Anchorage or is not part of the Alaska Marine Highway.

cabin fever – a winter condition in which Alaskans go stir-crazy in their one-room cabins because of too little sunlight and too much time spent indoors.

cache – a small hut or storage room built high off the ground to keep supplies and spare food away from roaming bears and wolves; the term, however, has found its way on to the neon signs of everything from liquor stores to pizza parlors in the cities.

calve – (of an ice mass) to separate or break so a part of the ice becomes detached.

capital move – the political issue that raged in the early 1980s, concerning moving the state capital from Juneau closer to Anchorage; although residents rejected funding the move north in a 1982 state election, the issue continues to divide Alaska.

cheechako – tenderfoot, greenhorn or somebody trying to survive their first year in Alaska.

chum – not your mate or good buddy, but a nickname for dog salmon.

clear-cut – an area where loggers have cut every tree.

d-2 – the lands issue of the late 1970s, which pitted environmentalists against developers over the federal government's preservation of 156,250 sq miles of Alaskan wilderness as wildlife reserves, forests and national parks.

dividend days – the period in October when residents receive their Permanent Fund checks and Alaska goes on a spending spree.

Eskimo ice cream – an Iñupiat food made of whipped animal fat, berries, seal oil and sometimes shredded caribou meat.

fish wheel – a wooden trap powered by a river's current

that scoops salmon or other large fish out of a river into a holding tank

freeze-up – the point in November or December when most rivers and lakes ice over, signaling to Alaskans that their long winter has started in earnest

humpie – a nickname for the humpback or pink salmon, the mainstay of the fishing industry in the Southeast.

ice worm – a small, thin black worm that thrives in glacial ice and was made famous by a Robert Service poem.

Iditarod – the 1049-mile sled-dog race run every March from Anchorage to Nome. The winner usually completes the course in less than 14 days and takes home $50,000.

Lower 48 – an Alaskan term for continental USA.

moose nuggets – hard, smooth droppings; some enterprising resident in Homer has capitalized on them by baking, varnishing and trimming them with evergreen leaves to sell during Christmas as Moostletoe.

mukluks – lightweight boots of sealskin trimmed with fur, made by the Iñupiat.

muktuk – whale skin and blubber; also known as *maktak*, it is a delicacy among Iñupiat and is eaten in a variety of ways, including raw, pickled and boiled.

muskeg – the bogs in Alaska, where layers of matted plant life float on top of stagnant water; these are bad areas in which to hike.

North Slope – the gentle plain that extends from the Brooks Range north to the Arctic Ocean.

no-see-um – nickname for the tiny gnats found throughout much of the Alaskan wilderness, especially in the Interior and parts of the Brooks Range.

NPS – National Park Service; administers 82,656 sq miles in Alaska and its 15 national parks include such popular units as Denali, Glacier Bay, Kenai Fjords and Klondike Gold Rush National Historical Park.

Outside – to residents, any place that isn't Alaska.

Outsider – to residents, anyone who isn't an Alaskan.

permafrost – permanently frozen subsoil that covers two-thirds of the state but is disappearing due to global warming.

petroglyphs – ancient rock carvings.

portage – an area of land between waterways over which paddlers carry their boats.

potlatch – a traditional gathering of indigenous people held to commemorate any memorable occasion.

qiviut – the wool of the musk ox, often woven into garments.

RVers – those folks who opt to travel in a motorhome.

scat – animal droppings; however, the term is usually used to describe bear droppings. If the scat is dark brown or bluish and somewhat square in shape, a bear has passed by; if it is steaming, the bear is eating blueberries around the next bend.

scrimshaw – hand-carved ivory from walrus tusks or whale bones.

sourdough – any old-timer in the state who, it is said, is 'sour on the country but without enough dough to get out;' newer residents believe the term applies to anybody who has survived an Alaskan winter; the term also applies to a 'yeasty' mixture used to make bread or pancakes.

Southeast sneakers – the tall, reddish-brown rubber boots that Southeast residents wear when it rains, and often when it doesn't; also known as 'Ketchikan tennis shoes,' 'Sitka slippers' and 'Petersburg pumps' among other names.

squaw candy – salmon that has been dried or smoked into jerky.

stinkhead – an Iñupiat 'treat' made by burying a salmon head in the sand; leave the head to ferment for up to 10 days then dig it up, wash off the sand and enjoy.

taku wind – Juneau's sudden gusts of wind, which may exceed 100mph in the spring and fall; often the winds cause horizontal rain, which, as the name indicates, comes straight at you instead of falling on you; in Anchorage and throughout the Interior, these sudden rushes of air over or through mountain gaps are called 'williwaws'.

tundra – vast, treeless plains.

UA – University of Alaska

ulu – a fan-shaped knife that Alaska Natives traditionally use to chop and scrape meat; now used by gift shops to lure tourists.

umiaks – leather boats made by the Iñupiat people.

USFS – US Forest Service; oversees the Tongass and Chugach National Forests, and the 190 cabins, hiking trails, kayak routes and campgrounds within them.

USFWS – US Fish & Wildlife Service; administers 16 federal wildlife refuges in Alaska, more than 120,312 sq miles.

USGS – US Geological Society; makes topographic maps, including those covering almost every corner of Alaska.

Behind the Scenes

SEND US YOUR FEEDBACK

We love to hear from travelers – your comments keep us on our toes and help make our books better. Our well-traveled team reads every word on what you loved or loathed about this book. Although we cannot reply individually to your submissions, we always guarantee that your feedback goes straight to the appropriate authors, in time for the next edition. Each person who sends us information is thanked in the next edition – the most useful submissions are rewarded with a selection of digital PDF chapters.

Visit **lonelyplanet.com/contact** to submit your updates and suggestions or to ask for help. Our award-winning website also features inspirational travel stories, news and discussions.

Note: We may edit, reproduce and incorporate your comments in Lonely Planet products such as guidebooks, websites and digital products, so let us know if you don't want your comments reproduced or your name acknowledged. For a copy of our privacy policy visit lonelyplanet.com/legal.

OUR READERS

Many thanks to the travelers who used the last edition and wrote to us with helpful hints, useful advice and interesting anecdotes:

Amy Moser, Ben Had, Curt Johnson, Haya Kaspi, John Davis, Mike Von der Porten, Nicole Emanuel, Stephen Martin

WRITER THANKS

Brendan Sainsbury

Thanks to all the pilots, ferry captains, chefs, travel guides, hoteliers, National Park rangers and innocent bystanders who helped me – unwittingly or otherwise – during this research. Special thanks to my nephew, Matt, and my son, Kieran, for their company on the road in Juneau and Sitka.

Catherine Bodry

Guidebook projects are never solo, and I'm grateful for the help and support of many. Thanks to Steph Johnson, Emily Mechtenberg, Jenny Miller and Josh Kelly for friendship and companionship. Thanks to Michael and Micheley for the Homer homestead cabin and Seward retreat. To the Lonely Planet staff: thanks for always being responsive and patient with my luddite questions. Finally, thanks to the authors before me who've paved the way; LP was my first guide to Alaska back in 1999.

Alexander Howard

A huge thanks to the barkeeps, B&B owners, restaurant staff and all the Alaskans that kept me out of trouble in bear country. Thanks also to my co-writers Catherine Bodry, Adam Karlin and Brendan Sainsbury for the advice, input and hard work that they put into this book. Huge thanks to Evan Godt, for pulling strings. Thanks to my parents – their support and adventurousness – and to Danielle for forever making the road a lot less lonely.

Adam Karlin

Thanks to: Alexander Howard, Evan Godt, Catherine Bodry, Brendan Sainsbury, Ernest in Barrow, the crazy wolf lady outside of Fairbanks, Ben Spatz for pushing me to visit his state, mom and dad for support, Sanda for waiting for me, and Rachel for joining me on an absolutely wonderful adventure across the Bush.

ACKNOWLEDGEMENTS

Climate map data adapted from Peel MC, Finlayson BL & McMahon TA (2007) 'Updated World Map of the Köppen-Geiger Climate Classification', Hydrology and Earth System Sciences, 11, 163344.

Cover photograph: Matanuska Glacier, DCrane/Shutterstock ©

THIS BOOK

This 13th edition of Lonely Planet's *Alaska* guidebook was researched and written by Brendan Sainsbury, Catherine Bodry, Alexander Howard and Adam Karlin, all of whom also researched and wrote the previous edition. This guidebook was produced by the following:

Commissioning Editor Angela Tinson

Product Editors Kirsten Rawlings, Kate Kiely, Kate Mathews

Cartographers Julie Sheridan, Alison Lyall

Book Designers Catalina Aragón, Mazzy Prinsep

Assisting Editors James Bainbridge, Imogen Bannister, Michelle Coxall, Charlotte Orr, Simon Williamson

Cover Researcher Naomi Parker

Thanks to Andrea Dobbin, Grace Dobell, Sasha Drew, Evan Godt, Shona Gray, Paul Harding, Sonia Kapoor, Monique Perrin, Kathryn Rowan, Amanda Williamson

Index

Map Pages **000**
Photo Pages **000**

I

J

K

Map Pages **000**
Photo Pages **000**

Map Legend

Sights
- Beach
- Bird Sanctuary
- Buddhist
- Castle/Palace
- Christian
- Confucian
- Hindu
- Islamic
- Jain
- Jewish
- Monument
- Museum/Gallery/Historic Building
- Ruin
- Shinto
- Sikh
- Taoist
- Winery/Vineyard
- Zoo/Wildlife Sanctuary
- Other Sight

Activities, Courses & Tours
- Bodysurfing
- Diving
- Canoeing/Kayaking
- Course/Tour
- Sento Hot Baths/Onsen
- Skiing
- Snorkeling
- Surfing
- Swimming/Pool
- Walking
- Windsurfing
- Other Activity

Sleeping
- Sleeping
- Camping

Eating
- Eating

Drinking & Nightlife
- Drinking & Nightlife
- Cafe

Entertainment
- Entertainment

Shopping
- Shopping

Information
- Bank
- Embassy/Consulate
- Hospital/Medical
- Internet
- Police
- Post Office
- Telephone
- Toilet
- Tourist Information
- Other Information

Geographic
- Beach
- Gate
- Hut/Shelter
- Lighthouse
- Lookout
- Mountain/Volcano
- Oasis
- Park
- Pass
- Picnic Area
- Waterfall

Population
- Capital (National)
- Capital (State/Province)
- City/Large Town
- Town/Village

Transport
- Airport
- BART station
- Border crossing
- Boston T station
- Bus
- Cable car/Funicular
- Cycling
- Ferry
- Metro/Muni station
- Monorail
- Parking
- Petrol station
- Subway/SkyTrain station
- Taxi
- Train station/Railway
- Tram
- Underground station
- Other Transport

Note: Not all symbols displayed above appear on the maps in this book

Routes
- Tollway
- Freeway
- Primary
- Secondary
- Tertiary
- Lane
- Unsealed road
- Road under construction
- Plaza/Mall
- Steps
- Tunnel
- Pedestrian overpass
- Walking Tour
- Walking Tour detour
- Path/Walking Trail

Boundaries
- International
- State/Province
- Disputed
- Regional/Suburb
- Marine Park
- Cliff
- Wall

Hydrography
- River, Creek
- Intermittent River
- Canal
- Water
- Dry/Salt/Intermittent Lake
- Reef

Areas
- Airport/Runway
- Beach/Desert
- Cemetery (Christian)
- Cemetery (Other)
- Glacier
- Mudflat
- Park/Forest
- Sight (Building)
- Sportsground
- Swamp/Mangrove

OUR STORY

A beat-up old car, a few dollars in the pocket and a sense of adventure. In 1972 that's all Tony and Maureen Wheeler needed for the trip of a lifetime – across Europe and Asia overland to Australia. It took several months, and at the end – broke but inspired – they sat at their kitchen table writing and stapling together their first travel guide, *Across Asia on the Cheap*. Within a week they'd sold 1500 copies. Lonely Planet was born.

Today, Lonely Planet has offices in the US, Ireland and China, with a network of more than 2000 contributors in every corner of the globe. We share Tony's belief that 'a great guidebook should do three things: inform, educate and amuse'.

OUR WRITERS

Brendan Sainsbury

Curator, Juneau & the Southeast, Prince William Sound Originally from Hampshire, England, Brendan has traveled all over Alaska from Ketchikan in the south to Deadhorse in the north by bus, train, kayak, bicycle, ferry, airplane and his own two feet. Memorable moments have included taking a bus up the Dalton Highway from Fairbanks to the Arctic Ocean, catching a ferry through the off-the-grid Alaskan peninsula to the Aleutian Islands, and running the Chilkoot trail in the footsteps of the Klondike 'stampeders' in a day. Now based in Vancouver, Canada, Brendan has contributed to more than 50 Lonely Planet guides including six editions of LP *Cuba*. Brendan also wrote the Plan Your Trips chapters (with the exception of Outdoor Activities & Adventures) and Survival Guide.

Catherine Bodry

Anchorage & Around, Kenai Peninsula Catherine is based in Anchorage, Alaska, but spends much of her time in Southeast Asia. As a writer, she's covered Alaska, Thailand and China, among other destinations. A lover of mountains, she spends as much time as possible in or near hills, whether it's running, hiking, camping, berry picking, rafting or just gazing at them. For Lonely Planet, she's contributed to about a dozen guide and trade books including several editions of *Alaska*, as well as *Canada*, *Thailand* and *Pacific Northwest Trips*.

Alexander Howard

Kodiak, Katmai & Southwest Alaska Alex is a Nashville-based editor, writer and photographer for Lonely Planet. Since joining Lonely Planet in 2014, he has commissioned, edited and managed 34 guidebooks covering Canada and the Western United States. His work frequently takes him into the field, including trekking into the lava fields of Hawai'i and scuba diving in Bali.

Adam Karlin

Denali & the Interior, The Bush Adam has contributed to dozens of Lonely Planet guidebooks, covering an alphabetical spread that ranges from the Andaman Islands to the Zimbabwe border. As a journalist, he has written on travel, crime, politics, archaeology and the Sri Lankan Civil War, among other topics. He has sent dispatches from every continent barring Antarctica (one day!) and his essays and articles have featured in the BBC, NPR, and multiple non-fiction anthologies. Adam is based out of New Orleans, which explains his love of wetlands, food and good music. Learn more at http://walkonfine.com or Instagram @adamwalkonfine. Adam also wrote the Outdoor Activities & Adventures chapter plus the Understand Alaska chapters.

Published by Lonely Planet Global Limited
CRN 554153
13th edition – Aug 2022
ISBN 978 1 78701 518 0

10 9 8 7 6 5 4 3 2 1
Printed in China

Although the authors and Lonely Planet have taken all reasonable care in preparing this book, we make no warranty about the accuracy or completeness of its content and, to the maximum extent permitted, disclaim all liability arising from its use.